WITHDRAWN

GEORGE ROCHBERG

A BIO-BIBLIOGRAPHIC GUIDE TO HIS LIFE AND WORKS

by

Joan DeVee Dixon

PENDRAGON PRESS

STUYVESANT, NY

MUSICOLOGICAL SERIES FROM PENDRAGON PRESS

AESTHETICS IN MUSIC SERIES
AMERICAN LISZT SOCIETY SERIES
ANNOTATED REFERENCE TOOLS IN MUSIC
SERIES
DANCE AND MUSIC
FESTSCHRIFT SERIES
FRENCH OPERA IN THE 17th AND 18th
CENTURIES
HARMONOLOGIA: STUDIES IN MUSIC THEORY
THE HISTORICAL HARPSICHORD SERIES
THE JUILLIARD PERFORMANCE GUIDES
MONOGRAPHS IN MUSICOLOGY SERIES
MUSICAL LIFE IN 19TH-CENTURY FRANCE
THE COMPLETE WORKS OF G. B. PERGOLESI
PERGOLESI STUDIES/STUDI PERGOLESIANI
RILM RETROSPECTIVES SERIES
THE SOCIOLOGY OF MUSIC SERIES
STUDIES IN CENTRAL AND EASTERN
EUROPEAN MUSIC
STUDIES IN THE MUSIC OF CZECHOSLOVAKIA
THEMATIC CATALOGUE SERIES

The Library of Congress Cataloging-in-Publication Data
Dixon, Joan DeVee.
    George Rochberg : a bibliographic guide to his life and works / by Joan DeVee
Dixon
      p. cm.
    ISBN 0-945193-12-2 :
    1.Rochberg, George--Bibliography. I. Title
    ML 134.R575D6 1992
    016.78'092--dc20
                                       92-3452
                                         CIP
                                         MN

To George Rochberg
in honor of his seventieth birthday
(05 July 1988)

Plate 2: Dmitri Mitropoulos and George Rochberg after the world première of *Night Music* (23 April 1953)

CONTENTS

LIST OF ILLUSTRATIONS

ACKNOWLEDGMENTS

My deepest gratitude to Mr. and Mrs. George Rochberg and those listed below.

For the freedom to "blaze my own trails", I express my grateful appreciation to Pendragon Press and my editor, Robert Kessler.

My sincere thanks to the following persons for encouraging me, supporting me, and/or "putting up with me" during this project: Donald Adams, Alderson-Broaddus College, Bryan Anton, Shelley Davis, Timothy DeWitt, Fritz & Juanita Ehren, Julius Erlenbach, Michael & Nancy Farrell, First Baptist Church of Clarksville [AR], Elizabeth & Jim Fleming, Bradford Gowen, David Herman, Virginia Houghton, Milan Kaderavek, George Katz, Igor Kipnis, Nolan Long, Anne & Eldon Miller, Holly Mitchell, Peter Peters, John Shipp, Joan Smalley, Stuart Steltzer, Gene Stephenson, Melvin Strauss, Clyde Thompson, Nelita True, University of the Ozarks, Billy & Gwen Usery, WAMSO (Women's Association of the Minnesota Orchestra), John Wannamaker, Waldo Widell, Judy Williams, and my family and friends.

CONTRIBUTORS

THEODORE PRESSER COMPANY: Arnold Broido, Larry Sandberg, Thomas Broido, Martha Cox.

GALAXY MUSIC CORPORATION.

MCA MUSIC.

ORIGINAL MANUSCRIPTS AND DOCUMENTS: Library of Congress, Music Division; New York Public Library, Music

Division; Houghton Library (Harvard University), Hans Moldenhauer Collection; Theodore Presser Company.

LIBRARIAN: Stuart Steltzer of the University of the Ozarks.

GERMAN TRANSLATIONS: Dr. Holly Mitchell of the University of the Ozarks.

SPANISH TRANSLATIONS: Sandra Reyes of the University of the Ozarks.

HEBREW TRANSLATIONS: Rabbi Matthew Friedman and Rabbi David Shoneveld of Hebrew Union College.

PROOFREADING: Clyde Thompson of Alderson Broaddus College, and Gwen Usery of Clarksville [AR] High School English Department.

WORD PROCESSING: Kevin Dean Dixon, Douglas "Dusty" Fisher, Vicki Holder, and numerous other students from Alderson Broaddus College and the University of the Ozarks.

OTHER CONTRIBUTORS: William Albright, William Bolcom, George Boziwick, David Burge, Curt Cacioppo, George Crumb, Shelley Davis, Norman Fischer, Bradford Gowen, Janice Harsanyi, David Herman, Karel Husa, Milan Kaderavek, Igor Kipnis, Jerome Kohl, Mike Linton, Jerome Lowenthal, Alan Mandel, Bert Margolis, Kenneth Moore, Ward Moore, Vivian Perlis, Neva Pilgrim, Wendy Richards, John Robilette, Paul Satre, Susan Scea, David Shapiro, Vilem Sokol, Vladimir Sokoloff, Isaac Stern, Melvin Strauss, Joseph Schwantner, Christopher Wilkinson, Carol Wincenc, Zvi Zeitlin.

OTHER CONTRIBUTORS: Chicago Symphony Orchestra, Cleveland Orchestra, Concert Artists Guild, John F. Kennedy Center for the Performing Arts, Minnesota Orchestra, New York Philharmonic, Philadelphia Orchestra, Pittsburgh New Music Ensemble, Pittsburgh Symphony Orchestra, San Francisco Symphony Orchestra, Santa Fe Chamber Music Festival, Seattle Youth Orchestra, St. Louis Symphony Orchestra.

OTHER CONTRIBUTORS: Alderson Broaddus College Catholic University of America, Curtis Institute of Music, Drake University, Eastman School of Music, Harvard University, The Juilliard School, Settlement Music School [Philadelphia], United States Information Agency-Artistic Ambassador Program, University of Delaware, University of Maryland, University of Northern Iowa, University of the Ozarks, West Virginia University, Yale University.

OTHER CONTRIBUTORS: American Choral Foundation, *American Record Guide*, American String Teachers Association, *Baltimore Sun, Buffalo News, Chicago Tribune, The Christian Science Monitor, ClariNetwork, Clavier, Instrumentalist*, Composers Recordings Incorporated (CRI), Contemporary Record Society, Crystal Records, *Detroit News, Ear Magazine, In Theory Only*, International Society of Performing Arts Administrators (ISPAA), Francis Antony Limited, *Journal of the American Musicological Society (JAMS), The Juilliard Journal, Kansas City Star, Kansas City Times, Lake Charles [LA] American Press, Lansing [MI] State Journal, Music Article Guide, Music Educators Journal*, Music Teachers National Association (MTNA), Music Educators National Conference (MENC), *Musical America*, Musical Heritage Society, *The New Yorker, Newsweek*, Nonesuch Records, *Notes, Opera Journal, Opera News*, Oral History: American Music, Owl Records, *Pacific Monthly/Prelude, Pan Pipes, Perspectives of New Music, Philadelphia Inquirer, Piano Quarterly, San Francisco Chronicle*, Sonneck Society, *Spectator Magazine, St. Louis Post-Dispatch, St. Paul Pioneer Press Dispatch, Stereo Review, Syracuse Newspapers (Herald-Journal, Post-Standard, Herald-American), Time Magazine*, WQXR Radio [New York City], *Yale Review*.

Plate 3: George Rochberg points out his name on a billboard advertising the Pittsburgh Symphony Orchestra's performance of his *Sixth Symphony* in Leningrad (07 October 1989).

INTRODUCTION

My incentives for writing/researching this guide were severalfold. First, George Rochberg is such a well-known composer that it was surprising to find so little written about his music, save an occasional thesis or review. Second, while researching Rochberg's life and works, I found a great many discrepencies among published sources. In short, I soon realized that there are a great many inaccuracies in prior publications on Rochberg and his music. The intent of this book, therefore, is to provide the scholar, performer, and critic with a thorough and accurate guide to Rochberg's life and works.

The Seventieth Birthday

Much of this book was compiled during Rochberg's seventieth year. It, therefore, seemed appropriate not only to dedicate the volume to him in honor of this grand occasion, but also to invite several of his colleagues, associates, and friends to join in this celebration of his seventieth year. Several of these "open letters" in honor of Rochberg's seventieth have been included here.

HAPPY BIRTHDAY GEORGE!

I number George Rochberg among my most important teachers. Not that the eight weeks at Tanglewood–when I was twenty-one years old–was adequate to assess his brilliance as a person and artist. No, that took some time and reflection, indeed whatever wisdom that comes from the passage of time.

He represented much more that a young composer could value: integrity, joy, a sense of exploration, professionalism. And the thing that I remember most clearly was his thoughtfulness. Widely read and deeply cultured, he impressed then as now as an artist versed in many fields.

George is justly famed for the words and music that punctured contemporary musical conceits, namely, stylistic uniformity and linear history. In the mid-sixties, his inquiries confirmed the feelings of several young composers that a new music could be pursued, free of then-current orthodoxies.

Over the years since then, I have valued the counsel and friendship of both George and Gene (his perfect partner). Though my music offerings–and my dedications thereon–may say it much better, I still wish to extend my heartfelt greetings on his seventieth birthday!

William Albright

George Rochberg became one of my heroes around 1965, when his use of past styles, quotations, etc. was a healthy reaction to a doctrinaire modernism that had most composers in a strangle-hold. He still is extremely high in my estimation, especially for the music that contains an emotional intensity and an openness of approach. He is also the rare composer with a very broad general culture, and this has brought forth beautiful music. I have learned much from him and hold him in the greatest respect.

William Bolcom

I made a trip to Penn to meet George in 1976, having listened to the recording of his *Third Quartet*, and having studied his liner notes for it many times. In George I found a soulmate who deeply believed in the enduring relevance of the achievements of our musical past, in the past as the soil from which new harvests would be born. His impatience with arrogant and immature notions of "originality" attracted definition and affirmation of high values that the act of his composing proclaimed. In 1985 I had the honor to première George's *Four Short Sonatas* in New York, and received their dedication. The second of these, *Molto rubato*, which echoes in George's *Fifth Symphony*, speaks with a prophetic urgency. Today George's voice–a precious, lone voice–rings as ever with the message and encouragement that humankind can still be capable of making and drawing needed sustenance from great art. *Cent' anni, Giorgio!*

Curt Cacioppo

My warmest greetings to George on the occasion of your seventieth birthday! As a longtime admirer of your music, I look forward to all those (as yet) unwritten works. And I would be very much surprised if your future essays didn't (mysteriously) weave together all the varied strands of your many musics!

George Crumb

To be involved in a première is one of the supreme joys of being a musician. It is filled with a unique kind of creative evergy; the performer's actively bonding with the composer's intention to "give birth" to a new work for the first time. When the composer is George Rochberg, and the string quartet is the Concord, the experience is magnified enormously. And to have that experience repeated six times with *String Quartets Nos. 3–7*, the *Piano Quintet*, and *Cello Quintet* (or ten if you include the *First and Second Quartets*, *Duo Concertante*, and *Ricordanza* we recorded in addition to the premières) is certainly overwhelming. We started our relationship together with the commission of the *Third String Quartet* (as a result of our Naumburg Chamber Music Award), a work that turned the music world upside down. (I have still never experienced an ovation like that one. After the performance, the clamour of cheers, screams, boos and applause was deafening. We had no idea that the work would be so highly controversial.) George is an exacting master, and engaged our imagination on a highly conceptual level and scrupulously focused our attention on every detail of color, balance, and character. The bonding experience between George and the Concords was so intense and begged to be repeated again and again. In the history of the string quartet, there have been several examples of this kind of relationship (Schuppanzigh/Beethoven, Joachim/Brahms, and Kolisch/Schönberg) that have significantly enriched our musical culture. I am honored to have been a part of that contribution and to be able to count George and Gene Rochberg among my most intense personal friends. From an even more personal perspective, I especially treasure the many performances and the recording of *Ricordanza* that George and I played. Above all, George's passion is a model for all musicians; teaching us that there is no reason to engage in our art unless we are committed to the fullest extent of our being.

Norman Fischer

Any time spent in talking with, or about, George Rochberg is an "occasion" for me. But it is an extra delight to congratulate him on his seventieth birthday! I have felt very close to George, and to his music, ever since I premièred his *Second String Quartet* in 1962. I am deeply grateful to him for the many beautiful songs he has written, which I continue to sing with much joy. My warmest greetings to you, George, and please continue to write songs!

Janice Harsanyi

I have been always impressed by the strength, poetry, construction, and message in George Rochberg's music. Every work he has written has a fresh formal shape and interesting new ideas, both musically satisfying and marked by a great American composer.

Also impressive to me is the man; his courageous break from the strict serialism has been an inspiration to many composers.

My sincere wishes for many new works from George Rochberg!

Karel Husa

Meeting George at Tanglewood over twenty years ago was surely one of the most memorable and significant events of my career, not only because of *Nach Bach*, which resulted from that first encounter, but because of the warm friendship that transpired. Because he lives some four hours away from my home in Connecticut and we all lead such hectic musical existences, we seldom have an opportunity to get together—which I greatly regret—but when we speak, that friendship is always instantly and palpably rekindled. Perhaps my bias is showing, but George for me is also without question one of the great composers of our time; I loved his music before I ever met him and am full of admiration and fascination for every one of his new works as they appear.

Igor Kipnis

If George Rochberg did not exist, it would be necessary not merely to invent him, but to name him George Rochberg: George, because he tills the most fertile artistic soil, and Rochberg, because he dwells amongst eagles.

When an artist of extraordinary gifts follows single-mindedly his soul's own premise, the results must be illuminating–so have they been with George.

Jerome Lowenthal

I have the greatest respect for George Rochberg as a continually vibrant, interesting and very gifted composer and a sensitive, sophisticated, loveable man.

Kenneth Moore

George Rochberg's *Viola Sonata* is a major addition to the viola and piano repertoire and it deserves many, many performances by other artists.

Joseph de Pasquale

Like all master composers, Rochberg's music has a distinctive sound. He has the honor, as Stravinsky did in the first half of the twentieth century, of being the pivotal composer stylistically in the second half of the century. His wide-ranging curiosity and his interest in art as transcendent are reflected in his music. Also important have been his integrity and the desire to communicate with his audience. I have been fortunate to have known and worked with George Rochberg and am grateful to him, not only for the beauty he has given the world, but for his friendship as well. So here's wishing

George Rochberg a happy seventieth birthday!! I hope he has many, many more.

Neva Pilgrim

It is my pleasure to salute George Rochberg, one of our country's most important and distinguished composers. His seminal work during the sixties was of special significance to me and to many composers of my generation. His strong and direct music provided new and reinvigorated musical pathways for many of us to consider. The legacy of his unswerving artistic vision remains a potent force shaping the framework of our contemporary musical thought.

Joseph Schwantner

To my dear friend George: With boundless gratitude for the privilege of having been allowed to share in your creative spirit. Congratulations on a youthful "seventy." Now sit down and COMPOSE!

Vilem Sokol

Dear George,

As always, you are a step ahead of me. My seventieth comes eighteen months hence, in 1990–but while I will never catch up with you chronologically, we can continue to be together musically and personally for many decades to come.

It seems only yesterday that when the Pittsburgh Symphony decided to commission a new *Violin Concerto* in memory of Donald Steinfirst, William Steinberg and I concluded that you were the only one who should do it. And you agreed. It was a labor of love, your own unashamed passion for music, a budding companionship between our two families and, as I learned later, a memorial to a lost loved one that comes out so clearly in the haunting moments as the last movement ends.

You are a seminal force in American composition. Your deep knowledge of and affection for the history of music, the evolution of today from yesterday as the path leading to tomorrow is a refreshing beacon in today's creativity. And thank heavens, you believe more strongly in the necessity of the human being in music than the power of machines to reproduce our true sounds.

So happy birthday, George. It is just another marker on your voyage of search and discovery. Bravo for the past, the present and a continuingly beautiful musical future.

With much love, Isaac.

Isaac Stern

It was in the sixties that I knew and collaborated with George Rochberg. That was a time when many things seemed to be boiling in the musical pot, not the least of which was a troublesome and youthful fantasy that we had no artistic connection with or responsibility for the past. History, they said, was for the historian, evolution for the scientist and continuum for the keyboard player.

Rochberg objected and, for many of us, thus became the leader of an undeclared counter-revolution. He was attracted to the "...many layered density of human existence and the contradictory nature of all human experience." He perceived that the "...past and present are [always] juxtaposed," thus: sound-collage. [Quotes from Rochberg's *Music for the Magic Theater* program notes.]

Thank you George, for your inspiring mentorship, your unswerving colleagueship, your profound humanity and, above all, your music. May you please live another thousand years. Happy Birthday and all other days.

Melvin Strauss

George Rochberg composed his *Slow Fires of Autumn* for me on the occasion of my winning the first Naumburg Solo Flute competition in 1978. The world première was given in April 1978 at Alice Tully Hall, Lincoln Center, NY by myself, Carol Wincenc, flutist and Nancy Allen, harpist.

This was the first experience I'd had to receive a work written especially for me by a renown composer under such auspicious circumstances! Little did I know then that this collaboration would ignite a crucial and treasured element of my career as a solo flutist.

What I remember so vividly in those meetings with George in my upper-west-side apartment was not only the rich exchange of musical ideas–he would ask, "How do you do 'that' on the flute?", "Is 'this' sonority possible?", "This passage must be played in a burst and flurry of ff,"–but the intensity of feelings, as this work had deep personal significance for George which he shared with me. Years later I was to take my first tour to Japan which brought home for me many of these feelings, a uniquely creative spirit generated by that culture and George's experience of it.

I knew I had ventured into a most special place–performer with composer, together, bonded, and committed to a process of inquiry and discovery. It couldn't have begun in a more timely and dramatic fashion.

Slow Fires to me is a work of great beauty and a great challenge to perform. It is one I shall grow with beyond its first ten years and into the decades to come.

And now to the man who brought this work into being and made an invitation to me, may I return the gift manifold through my admiration and performances of the work. Happiest of birthdays, George!

Carol Wincenc

A commonplace thing happened to me on my way to my studio one day in 1974: receipt of a newly published musical composition in the mail. But a cursory glance at the lengthy piece aroused in me a tinge of excitement for the ideas it conveyed and the way they were treated appealed strongly to my imagination.

A set of fifty unaccompanied *Variations* on the theme of Paganini's *24th Caprice* ranging in style from the seventeenth century into the future is certainly an original idea, despite the fact that the Paganini theme has provoked and inspired composers for nearly 150 years. Liszt, Brahms, Szymanowsky, Rachmaninoff, Blacher, Ginastera–these are but a few of the composers who were inspired by it.

I immediately called George Rochberg and the result was an ensuing close friendship, a public première of the work in

New York City, San Francisco, Boston, and eventually many other centers around the world.

Rochberg came to the recording session which took place on June 1, 1976, at the Eastman Theatre in Rochester. He was uncompromisingly demanding for as close as possible a realization of his imagined conception of the piece. While it resulted in hard work for me, I nevertheless felt that I could also give free rein to my own imagination in a work that is perhaps one of the most spectacular written for violin in many years.

Audience reactions are interesting. Young composers are often either deeply disturbed by it or highly exhilarated. Those disturbed feel somehow that it betrays their century. Those exhilarated feel that is releases music from the *cul-de-sac* of serialism and atonality.

When I first tried the piece out on a group of students and teachers at the Eastman School in the presence of the composer, there were some sharp questions regarding the "propriety" and even "moral rightness" of some of the purely tonal heart-on-sleeve *Variations*, as well as those *Variations* which include direct quotes from Beethoven, Schubert, Brahms, Mahler, and Webern. Both Mr. Rochberg and I explained that quotes as well as outright lifts were perfectly common in olden days and no one criticizes Berg or Brahms anymore for their allusions to Wagner and Beethoven although at one time there was considerable criticism. Concerning the simple, tonal outpourings in some *Variations*, the young composer is disturbed by the notion that it is a cheap trick to please the public. I counter that it is extremely difficult to write a tasteful, simple tune in A minor and call attention to the inescapable fact that even those *Variations* written in styles reminiscent of Vivaldi, Schumann, and Haydn bear the unmistakable imprint of Rochberg's twentieth century American personality. The composers I have discussed this with have no quarrel with the "modern" and "far-out" *Variations* since these are in keeping with accepted twentieth century compositional styles. Their disturbance emanates from the seeming stylistic inconsistency between the *Variations*. In other words, I have encountered among young and older composers an orthodoxy regarding sources of innovation and inspiration. These must be in the

present and in the future, but not in the past. Anyone drawing from our old roots is accused of leaning on them and of a
certain parasitism. When I asked a young composer to tell me
honestly whether his musical mind, when unconsciously
"noodling," does so atonaly or tonaly, I was told I was being
"unfair."

I have touched upon the above polemic to demonstrate that
Rochberg's music provokes and does not leave the listener in-
different. In playing the *Variations* publicly I felt invariably
that they are definitely an audience piece. Audiences are
spellbound by the treatment of the instrument, by the sonori-
ties, and by the fascination of recognizable snatches. The
non-professional music lover is not puzzled by the multiplicity
of styles. He is engaged and entertained by them, as well as
relieved, for the work has many elements of fun of a highly
sophisticated nature.

I feel that George Rochberg has contributed greatly
towards the breaking of the barriers between contemporary
music and its old roots. Many composers are beginning to go
to the great old masters for guidance and inspiration. That in
the process a genuinely creative mind will reflect its own age
is inevitable, no matter how evident the ancestral influences.

This is December, 1988. I am happy to see that fourteen
years after the appearance of George Rochberg's *Caprice Variations* more and more violinists are playing it. I am proud to
have been the first to record it in its entirety.

My warmest wishes to George Rochberg on the occasion of
his seventieth birthday.

Zvi Zeitlin

The Thinking of George Rochberg

The following quotations by Rochberg are taken from several sources. They are jewels among jewels–a summation, if you will, of Rochberg's. thought and style. I came across many of these statements while writing my book and am including them here, (1) because they were too precious to leave out, and (2) so that the reader might more fully appreciate the true artistry, integrity, and thought behind Rochberg's music.

The most profound influence on my early career was Johannes Brahms. By the time I was fifteen or sixteen, I had really discovered Brahms. His music took over my entire consciousness until I was about nineteen or twenty.

13 November 1982

I had begun to study Schönberg with considerable intensity [ca. 1947] and it was from the very beginning a love-hate relationship (very ambivalent). But I realized that his was a powerful mind and an enormous musical brain, and it didn't matter to me whether I liked it or not, I had to find out what was there, why it was there, [and] how it was made.

13 November 1982

The essential difference between my twelve-tone music and everyone else's is that mine is melodic.

1982

After Paul died, that absolutely made it necessary for me to wash my hands of the whole thing [serialism].

1982

I'm not interested in the continued use of serial ideas. In my *Fourth, Fifth, and Sixth String Quartets,* there are a number of movements that are heavily atonal; that is to say, they're freely chromatic. I suppose, if one cared to look very closely, one might find collections of twelve notes, or significant collections of partial twelve-note rows. But I wouldn't make a conscious effort to employ such devices which are, quite frankly, played out for me.

16 March 1980

It dawned on me that a piece of music by Boulez was not a hell of a lot different from a piece of music by Ives or a piece of music by Berio or a piece of music by me or a piece of music by anyone else. And, in a curious way, I set out to prove that to myself [in the *Contra Mortem et Tempus*].

1982

I think borrowing is one of the essential traditions of music, an ancient one. And if you're a borrower, as I am, then I see nothing to prevent borrowing from oneself. I was looking for a theme for a variation movement I wanted to include in the *Piano Quintet*, and I'd always loved that particular section that serves as a *Coda* for the slow movement of *Electrikaleidoscope*. It's seven bars long, and something in me said, "It's perfect. It's just right for what I want," so I simply lifted it out of context and gave it another kind of shape and function. That's not at all uncommon for me, and I know that its not uncommon for a number of other composers living today. Either consciously or unconsciously, we borrow from ourselves. I prefer to do it consciously.

16 March 1980

Jacob Druckman was at the first performance of *Electrikaleidoscope*; afterwards, we went to a party. The players were there, along with other composers–and Jake said, "Here we are, knocking our brains out, trying to be shocking and controversial, and George does it without even trying."

16 March 1980

It has taken me all these years to recognize and embrace the fact that at root I am a complete romantic and especially now that the question arises on all sides: After abstraction, what next? The answer rings out clearly: The "New Romanticism".

1963

I used to think it was pure nostalgia, a longing for a past Golden Age which always brought me back to the supremely wrought clarities and identities of the old music. Now I realize it was not nostalgia at all but a deep, abiding, personal need for clear ideas, for vitality and power expressed without impediments, for grace and beauty of line, for convincing harmonic motion, for transcendent feeling.

1972

At no time in my life have I ever let go of very profound feelings for the old music and for the traditions that both created that music and have come out of that music.

13 November 1982

That [tonality] was the world from which I never really escaped, the world that reclaimed me.

1982

I love Bartók, and believe he is truly a master and a major figure, yet I find it hard to put him beside Beethoven or Haydn–whose range of conception and realization is so enormous. Much of this has to do with the climate of the times. In earlier centuries artists' psyches were steeped in convictions about the nobility of man. When you hear Mozart or Brahms, you hear a certainty and conviction about the "rightness" of things. Modern thought and psychology have made that impossible. There is a lack of belief now, and it is reflected in music.

September 1985

The real trouble with electronic music is that it is incapable of expressing passion on any level. There is no love in it. Utterly, this is what music must be, a form of love conveyed through sound–shaped by the human need to say, to utter, to project its painful knowledge of life through an expressive medium.

20 April 1963

They [the perennial avant-gardists] really should stop tormenting themselves, each other, the musicians, and the audience.

19 February 1979

Modernism ended up allowing us only a postage-stamp-sized space to stand on.

29 May 1983

I think we've made too much of the fact that this is the 20th century. I don't think it matters when something happens, it only matters that something is good. This is why we still play and listen to Beethoven. Beethoven still interests us.

13 November 1982

I have always clung fast to these fundamentals: that music was given man so he could express the best he was capable of; that the best he was capable of had to do with his deepest feelings; that his deepest feelings are rooted in what I believe to be a moral order in the universe which underlies all real existence.

ca. 1963

Music is the sound of the human heart, shaped and guided by the mind. It is the sounding of the human consciousness in all of its possible states of being.

16 November 1980

Brahms, for me, still remains as a kind of exemplar of what a real composer must be; which is to say, someone who possesses a powerful intellect and is able to use that intellect to shape and guide an equally powerful emotional nature. If you [only] have one or the other, you're not going to have a complete composer.

ca. 1976

I love the purity of the string quartet. First of all as a sound medium. I love the challenge of the purely technical craft, the challenge of making the parts both independent and at the same time related. That is a very hard thing to do.

12 October 1983

There are those wonderful moments, those times when you really, literally, feel as though something is being given to you. And those are perhaps the happiest moments. At that time, it's as though you don't have to think, you just simply have to listen to what is happening inside your head and get it down on paper just as fast as you know how.

16 November 1980

From the moment I can remember, all I have heard [is] nothing but talk of war and problems and troubles of every conceivable kind. And it goes on. You cannot escape this. And I suppose that you can ignore it, but I have always found myself involved. Perhaps this is what some people mean when they call me a Romantic, because struggle, tension of a certain kind, *Sturm und Drang*, is all part of a Romantic aesthetic.

ca. 1976

I think that my music is largely a gestural music. And it is very emotional. I like to think of my music as a passionate music (not always, but at it's most intense, absolutely). It's also a strongly rhythmic music, which is not to be overlooked because it's out of the metric force that the energy can be released.

1982

I fundamentally believe that music grows out of the need to say certain things in certain ways. The only point for me is not whether I have produced a jumble of styles, but [whether or not] I have said what I wanted to.

13 November 1982

I would like to be able to look back on these things [my compositions] later and say, "Yes, I made my contribution. I still believe in these works; I think that they're valid. I think that they're good as music. They have nothing to do with all of the politics and aesthetics battles; they have outlasted that whole business." I think that's the way it has to be. That's the way all real works turn out: They rise above the time from which they emerged.

16 March 1980

It is my sincere hope that the materils included in this introduction and the volume which follows will prove engaging enough so as to attract the reader toward a greater survey of Rochberg and his music. For if, as a result of this text, Rochberg's music gains more performances, a larger audience, a better understanding and a greater appreciation, then indeed my work will have been well worth the effort.

I would like to once again state that every attempt has been made to summarize George Rochberg's life and work as faithfully and accurately as possible. However, I would welcome copies of any materials which may have escaped me prior to the publication of this text.

Joan DeVee Dixon
13613 Kober Road
La Porte City, IA
50651
01 June 1990

PRIMARY WORKS CITED IN THIS GUIDE

Alphabetical Listing

Apocalyptica [I] for Large Wind Ensemble.

Arioso for Piano Solo.

Bartokiana for Piano Solo.

Behold, My Servant (Everything That Lives Is Holy) for a cappella Mixed Chorus.

Between Two Worlds (Ukiyo-e III), Five Images for Flute and Piano.

Black Sounds (Apocalyptica II) for Seventeen Winds.

Blake Songs for Soprano and Chamber Ensemble.

La Bocca della Verità, Music for Oboe and Piano.

La Bocca della Verità, Music for Violin and Piano.

Book of Contrapuntal Pieces for Keyboard Instruments.

Book of Songs for Voice and Piano.

Cantes Flamencos for High Baritone.

Cantio Sacra for Chamber Orchestra.

Caprice Variations for Unaccompanied Violin.

Carnival Music, Suite for Piano Solo.

Chamber Symphony for Nine Instruments.

Cheltenham Concerto for Small Orchestra.

Concerto for Oboe and Orchestra.

Concerto for Violin and Orchestra.

The Confidence Man, An Opera in Two Parts.

Contra Mortem et Tempus for Flute, Clarinet, Violin, and Piano.

David, the Psalmist for Tenor Solo and Orchestra.

Dialogues for Clarinet and Piano.

Duo for Oboe and Bassoon.

Duo Concertante for Violin and Cello.

Electrikaleidoscope for Amplified Flute, Clarinet, Violin, Cello, Piano, and Electric Piano.

Eleven Songs for Mezzo-Soprano and Piano.

Fanfares for Massed Trumpets, Horns, and Trombones.

Fantasies for Voice and Piano.

Four Short Sonatas for Piano Solo.

Four Songs of Solomon for Voice and Piano.

Imago Mundi (Image of the World) for Large Orchestra.

Muse of Fire for Flute and Guitar.

Music for "The Alchemist" for Soprano and Eleven Players.

Music for the Magic Theater for a Chamber Ensemble of Fifteen Players [original version].

Music for the Magic Theater for Small Orchestra [orchestral version].

Nach Bach, Fantasy for Harpsichord or Piano.

Night Music for Orchestra.

Octet, A Grand Fantasia for Flute, Clarinet, Horn, Violin, Viola, Cello, Bass, and Piano.

Ora Pro Nobis for Flute and Guitar.

Partita-Variations for Piano Solo.

Passions [According to the Twentieth Century] for Actors, Dancers, Singers, Choruses, Speakers, and Instrumentalists.

Phaedra, Monodrama for Mezzo-Soprano and Orchestra.

Prelude on "Happy Birthday" for Almost Two Pianos.

Quartet for Piano, Violin, Viola, and Cello.

Quintet for Piano and String Quartet.

Quintet for String Quintet [double cello].

Rhapsody and Prayer for Violin and Piano.

Ricordanza (Soliloquy) for Cello and Piano.

Sacred Song of Reconciliation (Mizmur l'Piyus) for Bass-Baritone and Small Orchestra.

Serenata d'estate for Flute, Harp, Guitar, Violin, Viola, and Cello.

Slow Fires of Autumn (Ukiyo-e II) for Flute and Harp.

Sonata for Viola and Piano.

Sonata for Violin and Piano.

Sonata-Fantasia for Piano Solo.

Songs in Praise of Krishna for Soprano and Piano.

Songs of Inanna and Dumuzi for Contralto and Piano.

String Quartet No. 1.

String Quartet No. 2 with Soprano.

Instrumental Listing

ALTO (Voice)
See VOICE, CHORUS, and OPERA.

BAND
See WIND ENSEMBLE.

BARITONE (Voice)
See VOICE, CHORUS, and OPERA.

BASS (String)
See STRING BASS.

BASS (Voice)
See VOICE, CHORUS, and OPERA.

BASSOON (Chamber)
Chamber Symphony for Nine Instruments.
Duo for Oboe and Bassoon.
*Music for the Magic Theater for a Chamber Ensemble of Fifteen Players
    [original version].*
To the Dark Wood, Music for Woodwind Quintet.

BRASS
Fanfares for Massed Trumpets, Horns, and Trombones.

CELESTA (Chamber)
Blake Songs for Soprano and Chamber Ensemble.
See KEYBOARD (Celesta, Harpsichord, Piano).

CELLO
See VIOLONCELLO.

CHAMBER MUSIC
Blake Songs for Soprano and Chamber Ensemble.
Chamber Symphony for Nine Instruments.
Contra Mortem et Tempus for Flute, Clarinet, Violin, and Piano.
Duo Concertante for Violin and Cello.
*Electrikaleidoscope for Amplified Flute, Clarinet, Violin, Cello, Piano, and
    Electric Piano.*
Music for "The Alchemist" for Soprano and Eleven Players.
*Music for the Magic Theater for a Chamber Ensemble of Fifteen Players
    [original version].*

Octet, A Grand Fantasia for Flute, Clarinet, Horn, Violin, Viola, Cello, Bass, and Piano.

Quartet for Piano, Violin, Viola, and Cello.

Quintet for Piano and String Quartet.

Quintet for String Quintet [double cello].

Serenata d'Estate for Flute, Harp, Guitar, Violin, Viola, and Cello.

Slow Fires of Autumn (Ukiyo-e II) for Flute and Harp.

String Quartet No. 1.

String Quartet No. 2 with Soprano.

String Quartet No. 3.

String Quartet No. 4, "The Concord Quartets".

String Quartet No. 5, "The Concord Quartets".

String Quartet No. 6, "The Concord Quartets".

String Quartet No. 7 with Baritone.

Tableaux (Sound Pictures from the "Silver Talons of Piero Kostrov," by Paul Rochberg) for Soprano, Two Actors' Voices, Small Men's Chorus, and Twelve Players.

To the Dark Wood, Music for Woodwind Quintet.

Trio for Clarinet, Horn, and Piano.

Trio [No. 1] for Violin, Cello, and Piano.

Trio [No. 2] for Violin, Cello, and Piano.

CHORUS
See VOICE, CHORUS, and OPERA.

CLARINET (Solo)
Dialogues for Clarinet and Piano.

CLARINET (Chamber)
Blake Songs for Soprano and Chamber Ensemble.

Chamber Symphony for Nine Instruments.

Contra Mortem et Tempus for Flute, Clarinet, Violin, and Piano.

Electrikaleidoscope for Amplified Flute, Clarinet, Violin, Cello, Piano, and Electric Piano.

Music for "The Alchemist" for Soprano and Eleven Players.

Music for the Magic Theater for a Chamber Ensemble of Fifteen Players [original version].

Octet, A Grand Fantasia for Flute, Clarinet, Horn, Violin, Viola, Cello, Bass, and Piano.

Tableaux (Sound Pictures from the "Silver Talons of Piero Kostrov," by Paul Rochberg) for Soprano, Two Actors' Voices, Small Men's Chorus, and Twelve Players.

To the Dark Wood, Music for Woodwind Quintet.

Trio for Clarinet, Horn, and Piano.

FLUTE (Solo)

Between Two Worlds (Ukiyo-e III), Five Images for Flute and Piano.

Slow Fires of Autumn (Ukiyo-e II) for Flute and Harp.

FLUTE (Chamber)

Blake Songs for Soprano and Chamber Ensemble.

Contra Mortem et Tempus for Flute, Clarinet, Violin, and Piano.

Electrikaleidoscope for Amplified Flute, Clarinet, Violin, Cello, Piano, and Electric Piano.

Muse of Fire for Flute and Guitar.

Music for "The Alchemist" for Soprano and Eleven Players.

Music for the Magic Theater for a Chamber Ensemble of Fifteen Players [original version].

Octet, A Grand Fantasia for Flute, Clarinet, Horn, Violin, Viola, Cello, Bass, and Piano.

Ora Pro Nobis for Flute and Guitar.

Tableaux (Sound Pictures from the "Silver Talons of Piero Kostrov," by Paul Rochberg) for Soprano, Two Actors' Voices, Small Men's Chorus, and Twelve Players.

To the Dark Wood, Music for Woodwind Quintet.

GUITAR (Chamber)

Muse of Fire for Flute and Guitar.

Ora Pro Nobis for Flute and Guitar.

Serenata d'estate for Flute, Harp, Guitar, Violin, Viola, and Cello.

HARP (Solo)

Ukiyo-e (Pictures of the Floating World) for Solo Harp.

HARP (Chamber)

Blake Songs for Soprano and Chamber Ensemble.

Serenata d'estate for Flute, Harp, Guitar, Violin, Viola, and Cello.

Slow Fires of Autumn (Ukiyo-e II) for Flute and Harp.

HARPSICHORD

Nach Bach, Fantasy for Harpsichord or Piano.

See KEYBOARD (Celesta, Harpsichord, Piano).

KEYBOARD (Celesta, Harpsichord, Piano)

Music for "The Alchemist" for Soprano and Eleven Players.

Tableaux (Sound Pictures from the "Silver Talons of Piero Kostrov," by Paul Rochberg) for Soprano, Two Actors' Voices, Small Men's Chorus, and Twelve Players.

HORN (Chamber)

Chamber Symphony for Nine Instruments.

Music for the Magic Theater for a Chamber Ensemble of Fifteen Players [original version].

Octet, A Grand Fantasia for Flute, Clarinet, Horn, Violin, Viola, Cello, Bass, and Piano.

Tableaux (Sound Pictures from the "Silver Talons of Piero Kostrov," by Paul Rochberg) for Soprano, Two Actors' Voices, Small Men's Chorus, and Twelve Players.

To the Dark Wood, Music for Woodwind Quintet.

Trio for Clarinet, Horn, and Piano.

MEZZO-SOPRANO (Voice)

See **VOICE, CHORUS, and OPERA.**

MISCELLANEOUS

Passions [According to the Twentieth Century] for Actors, Dancers, Singers, Choruses, Speakers, and Instrumentalists.

Tableaux (Sound Pictures from the "Silver Talons of Piero Kostrov," by Paul Rochberg) for Soprano, Two Actors' Voices, Small Men's Chorus, and Twelve Players.

OBOE (Solo)

La Bocca della Verità, Music for Oboe and Piano.

Concerto for Oboe and Orchestra.

Three Cadenzas for Mozart's Concerto for Oboe, K. 314.

OBOE (Chamber)

Chamber Symphony for Nine Instruments.

Duo for Oboe and Bassoon.

Music for the Magic Theater for a Chamber Ensemble of Fifteen Players [original version].

To the Dark Wood, Music for Woodwind Quintet.

OPERA

See **VOICE, CHORUS, and OPERA.**

ORCHESTRAL WORKS

Cantio Sacra for Small Orchestra.

Cheltenham Concerto for Small Orchestra.

Concerto for Oboe and Orchestra.

Concerto for Violin and Orchestra.

David, the Psalmist for Tenor Solo and Orchestra.

Imago Mundi (Image of the World) for Large Orchestra.

Music for the Magic Theater for Small Orchestra [orchestral version].

Night Music for Orchestra.

Phaedra, a Monodrama for Mezzo-Soprano and Orchestra.

Sacred Song of Reconciliation (Mizmur l'Piyus) for Bass-Baritone and Small Orchestra.

Suite No. 1 (Based on the Opera "The Confidence Man") for Large Orchestra.

Suite No. 2 (Based on the Opera "The Confidence Man") for Solo Voices, Chorus, and Orchestra.

Symphony No. 1 for Orchestra [three-movement version].

Symphony No. 1 for Orchestra [five-movement version].

Symphony No. 2 for Orchestra.

Symphony No. 3 for Vocal Soloists, Chamber Chorus, Double Chorus, and Large Orchestra.

Symphony No. 4 for Large Orchestra.

Symphony No. 5 for Orchestra.

Symphony No. 6 for Orchestra.

Time-Span I for Orchestra.

Time-Span II for Orchestra.

Transcendental Variations for String Orchestra.

Zodiac for Orchestra.

PERCUSSION (Chamber)

Music for "The Alchemist" for Soprano and Eleven Players.

Tableaux (Sound Pictures from the "Silver Talons of Piero Kostrov," by Paul Rochberg) for Soprano, Two Actors' Voices, Small Men's Chorus, and Twelve Players.

PIANO (Solo)

Arioso for Piano Solo.

Bartokiana for Piano Solo.

Book of Contrapuntal Pieces for Keyboard Instruments.

Carnival Music, Suite for Piano Solo.

Four Short Sonatas for Piano Solo.

Nach Bach, Fantasy for Harpsichord or Piano.

Partita-Variations for Piano Solo.

Prelude on "Happy Birthday" for Almost Two Pianos.

Sonata-Fantasia for Piano Solo.

Twelve Bagatelles for Piano Solo.

Two Preludes and Fughettas from the Book of Contrapuntal Pieces for Keyboard Instruments.

PIANO (Accompanying)

Between Two Worlds (Ukiyo-e III), Five Images for Flute and Piano.

La Bocca della Verità, Music for Oboe and Piano.

La Bocca della Verità, Music for Violin and Piano.

Book of Songs for Voice and Piano.

Dialogues for Clarinet and Piano.

Eleven Songs for Mezzo-Soprano and Piano.

Fantasies for Voice and Piano.

Four Songs of Solomon for Voice and Piano.

Rhapsody and Prayer for Violin and Piano.

Ricordanza (Soliloquy) for Cello and Piano.

Sonata for Viola and Piano.

Sonata for Violin and Piano.

Songs in Praise of Krishna for Soprano and Piano.

Songs of Inanna and Dumuzi for Contralto and Piano.

Two Songs from "Tableaux" [for Soprano and Piano].

PIANO (Chamber)

Contra Mortem et Tempus for Flute, Clarinet, Violin, and Piano.

Electrikaleidoscope for Amplified Flute, Clarinet, Violin, Cello, Piano, and Electric Piano.

Music for the Magic Theater for a Chamber Ensemble of Fifteen Players [original version].

Octet, A Grand Fantasia for Flute, Clarinet, Horn, Violin, Viola, Cello, Bass, and Piano.

Quartet for Piano, Violin, Viola, and Cello.

Quintet for Piano and String Quartet.

Trio for Clarinet, Horn, and Piano.

Trio [No. 1] for Violin, Cello, and Piano.

Trio [No. 2] for Violin, Cello, and Piano.

See KEYBOARD (Celesta, Harpsichord, Piano).

SOPRANO (Voice)
See *VOICE, CHORUS, and OPERA.*

STRING BASS (Chamber)
Music for "The Alchemist" for Soprano and Eleven Players.
*Music for the Magic Theater for a Chamber Ensemble of Fifteen Players
[original version].*
*Octet, A Grand Fantasia for Flute, Clarinet, Horn, Violin, Viola, Cello,
Bass, and Piano.*
*Tableaux (Sound Pictures from the "Silver Talons of Piero Kostrov," by
Paul Rochberg) for Soprano, Two Actors' Voices, Small Men's
Chorus, and Twelve Players.*

STRING QUARTET
Quintet for Piano and String Quartet.
Quintet for String Quintet [double cello].
String Quartet No. 1.
String Quartet No. 2 with Soprano.
String Quartet No. 3.
String Quartet No. 4, "The Concord Quartets."
String Quartet No. 5, "The Concord Quartets."
String Quartet No. 6, "The Concord Quartets."
String Quartet No. 7 with Baritone.

SYMPHONY
See *ORCHESTRAL WORKS.*

TENOR (Voice)
See *VOICE, CHORUS, and OPERA.*

TROMBONE (Chamber)
Chamber Symphony for Nine Instruments.
*Music for the Magic Theater for a Chamber Ensemble of Fifteen Players
[original version].*
*Tableaux (Sound Pictures from the "Silver Talons of Piero Kostrov," by
Paul Rochberg) for Soprano, Two Actors' Voices, Small Men's
Chorus, and Twelve Players.*

TRUMPET (Chamber)
Chamber Symphony for Nine Instruments.
Music for "The Alchemist" for Soprano and Eleven Players.
*Music for the Magic Theater for a Chamber Ensemble of Fifteen Players
[original version].*

Tableaux (Sound Pictures from the "Silver Talons of Piero Kostrov," by Paul Rochberg) for Soprano, Two Actors' Voices, Small Men's Chorus, and Twelve Players.

TUBA (Chamber)
Music for the Magic Theater [original version].

VIOLA (Solo)
Sonata for Viola and Piano.

VIOLA (Chamber)
Blake Songs for Soprano and Chamber Ensemble.
Chamber Symphony for Nine Instruments.
Music for "The Alchemist" for Soprano and Eleven Players.
Music for the Magic Theater for a Chamber Ensemble of Fifteen Players [original version].
Octet, A Grand Fantasia for Flute, Clarinet, Horn, Violin, Viola, Cello, Bass, and Piano.
Quartet for Piano, Violin, Viola, and Cello.
Quintet for Piano and String Quartet.
Quintet for String Quintet [double cello].
Serenata d'estate for Flute, Harp, Guitar, Violin, Viola, and Cello.
String Quartet No. 1.
String Quartet No. 2 with Soprano.
String Quartet No. 3.
String Quartet No. 4, "The Concord Quartets."
String Quartet No. 5, "The Concord Quartets."
String Quartet No. 6, "The Concord Quartets."
String Quartet No. 7 with Baritone.
Tableaux (Sound Pictures from the "Silver Talons of Piero Kostrov," by Paul Rochberg) for Soprano, Two Actors' Voices, Small Men's Chorus, and Twelve Players.

VIOLIN (Solo)
La Bocca della Verità, Music for Violin and Piano.
Caprice Variations for Unaccompanied Violin.
Concerto for Violin and Orchestra.
Rhapsody and Prayer for Violin and Piano.
Sonata for Violin and Piano.

VIOLIN (Chamber)

Blake Songs for Soprano and Chamber Ensemble.

Chamber Symphony for Nine Instruments.

Contra Mortem et Tempus for Flute, Clarinet, Violin, and Piano.

Duo Concertante for Violin and Cello.

Electrikaleidoscope for Amplified Flute, Clarinet, Violin, Cello, Piano, and Electric Piano.

Music for "The Alchemist" for Soprano and Eleven Players.

Music for the Magic Theater for a Chamber Ensemble of Fifteen Players [original version].

Octet, A Grand Fantasia for Flute, Clarinet, Horn, Violin, Viola, Cello, Bass, and Piano.

Quartet for Piano, Violin, Viola, and Cello.

Quintet for Piano and String Quartet.

Quintet for String Quintet [double cello].

Serenata d'estate for Flute, Harp, Guitar, Violin, Viola, and Cello.

String Quartet No. 1.

String Quartet No. 2 with Soprano.

String Quartet No. 3.

String Quartet No. 4, "The Concord Quartets."

String Quartet No. 5, "The Concord Quartets."

String Quartet No. 6, "The Concord Quartets."

String Quartet No. 7 with Baritone.

(Violin, Chamber, cont.)

Tableaux (Sound Pictures from the "Silver Talons of Piero Kostrov," by Paul Rochberg) for Soprano, Two Actors' Voices, Small Men's Chorus, and Twelve Players.

Trio [No. 1] for Violin, Cello, and Piano.

Trio [No. 2] for Violin, Cello, and Piano.

VIOLONCELLO (Solo)

Night Music for Orchestra.

Ricordanza (Soliloquy) for Cello and Piano.

VIOLONCELLO (Chamber)

Blake Songs for Soprano and Chamber Ensemble.

Chamber Symphony for Nine Instruments.

Duo Concertante for Violin and Cello.

Electrikaleidoscope for Amplified Flute, Clarinet, Violin, Cello, Piano, and Electric Piano.

Music for "The Alchemist" for Soprano and Eleven Players.

Music for the Magic Theater for a Chamber Ensemble of Fifteen Players [original version].

Octet, A Grand Fantasia for Flute, Clarinet, Horn, Violin, Viola, Cello, Bass, and Piano.

Quartet for Piano, Violin, Viola, and Cello.

Quintet for Piano and String Quartet.

Quintet for String Quintet [double cello].

Serenata d'estate for Flute, Harp, Guitar, Violin, Viola, and Cello.

String Quartet No. 1.

String Quartet No. 2 with Soprano.

String Quartet No. 3.

String Quartet No. 4, "The Concord Quartets."

String Quartet No. 5, "The Concord Quartets."

String Quartet No. 6, "The Concord Quartets."

String Quartet No. 7 with Baritone.

Tableaux (Sound Pictures from the "Silver Talons of Piero Kostrov," by Paul Rochberg) for Soprano, Two Actors' Voices, Small Men's Chorus, and Twelve Players.

Trio [No. 1] for Violin, Cello, and Piano.

Trio [No. 2] for Violin, Cello, and Piano.

VOICE, CHORUS, and OPERA

Behold, My Servant (Everything That Lives Is Holy) for a cappella Mixed Chorus.

Blake Songs for Soprano and Chamber Ensemble.

Book of Songs for Voice and Piano.

Cantes Flamencos for High Baritone.

The Confidence Man, An Opera in Two Parts.

David, the Psalmist for Tenor Solo and Orchestra.

Eleven Songs for Mezzo-Soprano and Piano.

Fantasies for Voice and Piano.

Four Songs of Solomon for Voice and Piano.

Music for "The Alchemist" for Soprano and Eleven Players.

Passions [According to the Twentieth Century] for Actors, Dancers, Singers, Choruses, Speakers, and Instrumentalists.

Phaedra, a Monodrama for Mezzo-Soprano and Orchestra.

Sacred Song of Reconciliation (Mizmur l'Piyus) for Bass-Baritone and Small Orchestra.

Songs in Praise of Krishna for Soprano and Piano.

Songs of Inanna and Dumuzi for Contralto and Piano.

Suite No. 2 (Based on the Opera "The Confidence Man") for Solo Voices, Chorus, and Orchestra.

String Quartet No. 2 with Soprano.

String Quartet No. 7 with Baritone.

Symphony No. 3 for Vocal Soloists, Chamber Chorus, Double Chorus, and Large Orchestra.

Tableaux (Sound Pictures from the "Silver Talons of Piero Kostrov," by Paul Rochberg) for Soprano, Two Actors' Voices, Small Men's Chorus, and Twelve Players.

Three Psalms for a cappella Mixed Chorus.

Two Songs from "Tableaux" [for Soprano and Piano].

WIND ENSEMBLE

Apocalyptica [I] for Large Wind Ensemble.

Black Sounds (Apocalyptica II) for Seventeen Winds.

WOODWIND QUINTET

To the Dark Wood, Music for Woodwind Quintet.

LIST OF ABBREVIATIONS

TP	Theodore Presser Company
MCA	MCA Music
Galaxy	Galaxy Music Corporation
MS	Manuscript
Parts on Rental	Parts available only on rental from the publisher
Rental	Full-score available only on rental from the publisher
N/A	Not available
ca.	circa
n.d.	No date available
n.a.	No authors attributed
n.t.	No title given

INSTRUMENTATION

Woodwinds:

Pc	Piccolo
Fl	Flute
AFl	Alto Flute
Ob	Oboe
EH	English Horn
Cl (E)	E-flat Clarinet
Cl	B-flat Clarinet
Cl (A)	A Clarinet
BCl	Bass clarinet

CBCl	Contra Bass clarinet
Bsn	Bassoon
CBsn	Contra Bassoon
ASax	Alto Saxophone
TSax	Tenor Saxophone
BSax	Baritone Saxophone

Brass:

Hn	F Horn
PcTpt	Piccolo Trumpet
Crnt	Cornet
Tpt	B-flat Trumpet
Tpt (C)	C Trumpet
Euph	Euphonium
Tbn	Tenor Trombone
BTbn	Bass Trombone
CTbn	Contra Trombone
Tba	Tuba
CTba	Contra Tuba

Percussion:

Perc	Percussion
Timp	Timpani
Glock	Glockenspiel
Xyl	Xylophone
Vib	Vibraphone
Tri	Triangle
Tamb	Tambourine
TBel	Tubular bells
SnDr	Snare drum
TnDr	Tenor drum
TT	Tam-tams
LgBsDr	Large bass drum

SmBsDr	Small bass drum
ACy	Antique cymbals
Cy	Cymbal
CrCy	Crash cymbals
LgSusCy	Large suspended cymbal

Other:

Pn	Piano
ElPn	Electric Piano
ElHpsch	Electric Harpsichord
Hp	Harp
Cel	Celesta
Kybd	Keyboard
(H)	High
(M)	Medium
(L)	Low
(H-M-L)	High - Medium - Low
(H-L)	High - Low
Lg	Large
Sm	Small
(L-M-S)	Large - Medium - Small
(L-S)	Large - Small

Strings:

Str	Full strings
Vln	Violin
Vla	Viola
Vlc	Violoncello
StrB	String bass

Voice:

Sop	Soprano
Mz	Mezzo Soprano
Alto	Alto

Ten	Tenor
Bar	Baritone
Bs	Bass
SATB	Soprano, Alto, Tenor, Bass

Combinations:

3 Fl (Pc)	3 Flutes, one doubling on Piccolo
3 Perc	Requires three percussionists

PART ONE:
THE COMPOSITIONS

Plate 4: George Rochberg, Loren Maazel, and the Pittsburgh Symphony Orchestra following a performance of the *Sixth Symphony* (Leningrad, 07 October 1989).

I. CHRONOLOGY OF ROCHBERG'S LIFE AND WORKS

1912
George's mother Anna and father Morris immigrate to the United States from the Ukraine.

1918
Aaron George Rochberg is born in Paterson, NJ (05 July 1918).

1919
The Rochberg family moves to Passaic, NJ.

1927
Rochberg family moves to Passaic Park, NJ.

1928 or 1929
Family purchases a piano. George begins piano lessons with Kathleen Hall.

1930 or 1931
George continues piano lessons with Julius Koehl.

1933–1934
George gives several duo piano performances with Julius Koehl on WOR (Mutual Broadcasting Co.) NY.

1933–1941
George plays regularly in dance bands and combos.

COMPOSITIONS

I Can't Forget (Copyright 12 September 1933). Words and music by A. George Rochberg.

1935

George graduates from Passaic [NJ] High School. Yearbook lists activities as follows: Freshman debating team, Debating club, Junior class treasurer, Junior prom committee, and Orchestra.

COMPOSITIONS

Class Song (June 1935). Words and music by George Rochberg.

Fall 1935 to Spring 1939

George attends Montclair [NJ] State Teachers College (1935–1939). Sings in the college choir (bass section) all four years. From his sophomore to his senior year, George works as the pianist/ composer for the Montclair State College Dance Club.

1937

George studies voice privately in Passaic with Mildred Ippolito.

COMPOSITIONS

Book of Songs for Voice and Piano (1937–1969) [Unpublished]: 1. *There was an Aged King* (11 December 1937, Revised 27 April 1969); 26. *The Blind Man at the Fair* (First version ca. 1937, Second version 10 October 1947, Revised 20 May 1969).

1938

COMPOSITIONS

Book of Songs for Voice and Piano (1937–1969) [Unpublished]: 2. *With Rue My Heart Is Laden* (22 June 1938, Revised 16 May 1969); 3. *Warum sind denn die Rosen so blass?* (10 July 1938, Revised 21 April 1969), 4. *When I am Dead, My Dearest* (16 October 1938, Revised 21 April 1969).

1939

Spring, BA from Montclair State College.

Fall, attends the Mannes School of Music. Studies composition with Hans Weisse (1939), Leopold Mannes (1940), and George Szell (1941–1942).

COMPOSITIONS

Ballade for Piano Solo (January 1939).

Book of Songs for Voice and Piano (1937–1939) [Unpublished]: 5. *Minnelied* (23 November 1939, Revised 19 April 1969)

1940

COMPOSITIONS

Book of Contrapuntal Pieces for Keyboard Instruments (1940–1979, Collection compiled 15 January–04 February 1979) [Unpublished]: 1. *Invention: Con spirito* (29 April 1940); 2. *Capriccio: Allegro ma non troppo* (15 January–27 February 1940); 3. *Fugue: Molto andante espressivo* (Fall 1940).

Book of Songs for Voice and Piano (1937–1939) [Unpublished]: 6. *Du bist wie eine Blume* (10 September 1940).

1941

George marries Gene Rosenfeld [Rochberg], 18 August 1941 in Minneapolis.

George and Gene move to New York City and live there from September 1941 to November 1942.

COMPOSITIONS

Variations on an Original Theme for Piano Solo (1941, Revision completed 18 April 1969) [Unpublished].

Book of Songs for Voice and Piano (1937–1939) [Unpublished]: 7. *Dirge* (18 June 1941, Revised 24 May 1969); 8. *There Be None of Beauty's Daughters [A]* (17 July 1941, Revised 24 April 1969).

1942

George is drafted by the Army in November.

PREMIÈRES

Variations on an Original Theme; George Rochberg, piano; Mannes School, New York City; 1942.

1943

COMPOSITIONS

261st Infantry Song (19 November 1943). Words by T. G. Keegan and Aaron G. Rochberg, Music by Aaron G. Rochberg.

March of the Halberds (Copyright 03 December 1943).

1944

George is wounded on 23 September 1944 in Mons, France.

Rochbergs' son Paul is born 28 September 1944.

COMPOSITIONS

Song of the Doughboy (11 April 1944, Camp Shelby, MS). Words and music by Aaron George Rochberg.

Little Suite [Unpublished]: *I. Prelude* (23 November 1944), England; *II. Humoresque* (27 January 1945), Belgium; *III. Fantasy* (13 December 1944), Fontainbleau; *IV. Prelude* (16 December 1944), Fontainbleau; *V. Fughetta* (25 January 1945), Belgium; *VI. Invention* (25 January 1945), Belgium; *VII. Toccata* (15 December 1944), Fontainbleau.

Music for Gene and Paul (1944) [Unpublished].

Book of Songs for Voice and Piano (1937–1939) [Unpublished]: *10. Lullaby (Vocalise)* (First version, piano sketch, October 1944, Second version 23 August 1945, Revised 22 May 1969).

1945

George is discharged from the Army [Purple Heart and Oak Leaf Cluster] in July 1945.

George and Gene move to Philadelphia in the Fall.

George attends the Curtis Institute of Music. Studies with Rosario Scalero (1945–1946) and Gian Carlo Menotti (1946–1947 or 1948).

COMPOSITIONS
Book of Songs for Voice and Piano (1937–1939) [Unpublished]:
10. *Lullaby (Vocalise)* (First version, piano sketch October 1944, Second version 23 August 1945, Revised 22 May 1969).

1946

COMPOSITIONS
Duo for Oboe and Bassoon (1946, Revised 1969 for publication).
Four Songs of Solomon for Voice and Piano (1946).
Fantasia and Fugue for Orchestra (1946) [Unpublished].
Book of Contrapuntal Pieces for Keyboard Instruments (1940–1979, Collection compiled 15 January–04 February 1979) [Unpublished]: *4. Prelude and Fughetta No. 1* (P: 28 August 1946; F: 16 September 1946) [Published 1980]; *5. Prelude and Fughetta No. 2* (P: 17 September 1946; F: 29 August 1946) [Published 1980]; *6. Four Inventions* (1946): *I. Non troppo Allegro, II. Non troppo Allegro, III. Brisk, IV. Brisk; 7. Canon in Song Form: Slow and Tranquil* (1946); *8. Fugue: Largamente; serioso ed espressivo* (March 1946); *9. Ten Two-Part Canons* (1946): *I. Moderato, cantabile, II. Con moto ed espressivo, III. Allegretto grazioso, IV. Adagio ma non troppo, V. Andante, VI. Broadly, VII. Moderato con spirito, VIII. Adagio sostenuto, IX. Allegro Con moto (after Beethoven), X. Molto espressivo, 10. Canon on a Ground Bass by Purcell* (1946); *11. Four-part Canon: Grave* (21 March 1946); *12. Seven [Four-part] Chorales Treated Canonically: I. Ach wie nichtig, ach wie fluchtig* (22 June 1946), *II. Jesus Christe, Unser Heiland* (22 June 1946), *III. Strat mich nicht in deinem Zorn* (22 June 1946), *IV. Wie bist du, Seele?* (24 June 1946), *V. Nun sich der Tag (with contrary motion canon)* (June 1946), *VI. Kommt Seelen dieser Tag: Allegretto* (1946), *VII. In Dulce Jubilo* (23 June 1946); *13. Five Two-part Canons in Contrary Motion* (1946): *I. Allegro vivace, II. No. 1 in Double Counterpoint, III. Alla marcia, IV. Allegro vivace, V. No. 4 in Double Counterpoint; 14. Eight-part Infinite Canon on a subject of J.S. Bach: Presto* (1946); *15. Fugue: Adagio espressivo* (March 1946); *16. Double Fugue for Two*

Pianos: Allegro moderato ed energico (1946); *17. Fugue for
Two Pianos: Allegro ma non troppo e risoluto* (March 1946);
*18. Eight three-part Canons for Organ: I. Unison (with free
bass voice): Adagio* (30 June 1946), *II. At the Second (with free
bass voice): Molto adagio* (30 June 1946), *III. At the Third
(with free bass voice): Allegretto* (30 June 1946), *IV. At the
Fourth (with free bass voice): Allegro giocoso* (31 July 1946),
V. At the Fifth (with free bass voice): Adagio (31 July 1946),
VI. At the Sixth (with free bass voice): Allegro moderato (01
August 1946), *VII. At the Seventh (with two voices in bass
and alto): Adagio espressivo* (02 August 1946), *VIII. At the
Octave (with free bass voice): Allegro ma non troppo* (02
August 1946).

Book of Songs for Voice and Piano (1937–1939) [Unpublished]:
11. February Spring (February 1946); *12. Ophelia's Song* (04
April 1946, Revised 29 April 1969); *13. Night Song at Amalfi*
(08 April 1946, Revised 29 April 1969); *14. Song of Shadows*
(09 April 1946, Revised 04 May 1969); *15. No Fall of Tears*
(22 April 1946, Revised 17 May 1969); *16. Song of Day* (24
April 1946, Revised 28 April 1969); Numbers 17–20 from
Four Songs of Solomon: *17. Rise Up, My Love* (Summer or
Fall, 1946); *18. Come, My Beloved* (Summer or Fall, 1946);
19. Set Me as a Seal (Summer or Fall, 1946); *20. Behold,
Thou Art Fair* (13 August 1946); *21. Du meine heilige Eein-
samkeit [A]* (14 August 1946, Revised 27 April 1969);
24. Sweetest Love (First version 12 April 1946, Second version 20 August 1947, Revised 02 May 1969).

1947

COMPOSITIONS

Orchestral Suite in Four Movements (1947) [Unpublished].
Sonata No. 1 for Piano (1947) [Unpublished].
Book of Songs for Voice and Piano (1937–1939) [Unpublished]:
23. Who Has Seen the Wind? (1947); *24. Sweetest Love* (First
version 12 April 1946, Second version 20 August 1947, Revised 02 May 1969); *25. Bright Cap and Streamers* (16 September 1947, Revised 01 May 1969); *26. The Blind Man at
the Fair* (First version ca. 1937, Second version 10 October

1947, Revised 20 May 1969); *27. Du meine heilige Einsamkeit [B]* (25 September 1947).

PREMIÈRES

Four Songs of Solomon for Voice and Piano; David Lloyd, tenor and George Rochberg, piano; Philadelphia, PA; 1947.

1948

Spring, BM from the Curtis Institute of Music.

Fall 1948–Spring 1949, attends the University of Pennsylvania, Philadelphia, PA.

Fall, Full-time member of the faculty at the Curtis Institute of Music.

COMPOSITIONS

Begins *Symphony No. 1 for Orchestra [three-movement version]* (Fall 1948–Spring 1949, Revised 1957–Summer 1977].

Night Music for Orchestra (Fall 1948–Spring 1949, Revised 1957–1977) [Originally *Symphony No. 1, II. Night Music*].

Capriccio for Orchestra (Fall 1948–Spring 1949, Revised 1957–1977) [Originally *Symphony No. 1, III. Capriccio*].

Sonata No. 2 for Piano (27 July–28 October 1948, Revised September 1949) [Unpublished].

Trio for Clarinet, Horn, and Piano (1948, Revised 1980 for publication).

Book of Contrapuntal Pieces for Keyboard Instruments (1940–1979, Collection compiled 15 January–04 February 1979) [Unpublished]: 20. *Fugue: Allegro ma non troppo* (1948–1949).

Book of Songs for Voice and Piano (1937–1939) [Unpublished]: 22. *Lira-la-la* (22 October 1948).

PREMIÈRES

Fantasia and Fugue for Orchestra; Eastman Orchestra, Howard Hanson conducting; Eastman School of Music, Rochester, NY; 1948.

1949

Spring, MA from the University of Pennsylvania, Philadelphia, PA.

COMPOSITIONS

Finishes *Symphony No. 1 for Orchestra [three-movement version]* (Fall 1948–Spring 1949, Revised 1957–Summer 1977].

Five Smooth Stones for Soloists, Chorus, and Large Orchestra (1949) [Unpublished].

Capriccio for Two Pianos (1949) [Unpublished].

Book of Songs for Voice and Piano (1937–1939) [Unpublished]: *28. There Be None of Beauty's Daughters [B]* (05 December 1949); *30. Ecce Puer* (First version 21 December 1949, Second version 26 August 1951, Revised 25 May 1969).

1950

COMPOSITIONS

Begins *String Quartet No. 1* (1950–May 1952). Begun in Rome.

Concert Piece for Two Pianos and Orchestra (1950–1951) [Unpublished].

AWARDS

Fulbright Fellowship, 1950–1951. American Academy in Rome Fellowship, 1950–1951. Summer of 1950 to the summer 1951, George, Gene, and Paul live in Rome and George has a studio at the Academy.

1951

In the summer of 1951, George and Gene move back to Philadelphia.

1951–1954 George works full-time as a Music Editor for Theodore Presser and part-time (one day a week) as a member of the faculty at the Curtis Institute of Music.

COMPOSITIONS

Continues to work on *String Quartet No. 1* (1950–May 1952).

Book of Songs for Voice and Piano (1937–1939) [Unpublished]: *29. Piping Down the Valley's Wild* (13 February 1951, Revised 24 May 1969); *30. Ecce Puer* (First version 21 December 1949, Second version 26 August 1951, Revised 25 May 1969).

1952

Rochbergs' daughter Francesca is born 08 May 1952.

COMPOSITIONS

Finishes *String Quartet No. 1* (1950–May 1952).

Twelve Bagatelles for Piano Solo (07 June–19 September 1952).

AWARDS

George Gershwin Memorial Award for *Night Music for Orchestra*.

1953

COMPOSITIONS

Cantio Sacra: Warum betrubst du dich, mein Herz by Samuel Scheidt. Transcribed for Chamber Orchestra (06–19 April 1953).

Chamber Symphony for Nine Instruments (1953).

PREMIÈRES

Night Music for Orchestra; New York Philharmonic, Dmitri Mitropoulos conducting; Carnegie Hall, New York City; 23 April 1953.

String Quartet No. 1; Galimir String Quartet; Composers' Forum, MacMillan Theater, Columbia University, New York City; January 1953.

Twelve Bagatelles for Piano Solo; George Rochberg, piano; Composers' Forum, MacMillan Theater, Columbia University, New York City; January 1953.

1954

George becomes Director of Publications at Theodore Presser and leaves the Curtis Institute of Music faculty.

COMPOSITIONS

Three Psalms for a cappella Mixed Chorus (1954).

David, the Psalmist for Tenor Solo and Orchestra (1954, Revised February 1967).

1955

COMPOSITIONS

Begins *Symphony No. 2 for Orchestra* (Winter 1955–Spring 1956).

Serenate d'estate for Flute, Harp, Guitar, Violin, Viola, and Cello (1955).

Duo Concertante for Violin and Cello (1955, Revised 1959 for publication).

Fantasia for Violin and Piano (1955) [Unpublished].

PREMIÈRES

Chamber Symphony for Nine Instruments; Baltimore Chamber Society, Hugo Weisgall conducting; Baltimore, MD; 1955.

1956

COMPOSITIONS

Finishes *Symphony No. 2 for Orchestra* (Winter 1955–Spring 1956).

Sonata-Fantasia for Piano Solo (19 July–30 October 1956).

Arioso for Piano Solo (*Little Suite, Prelude* composed 23 November 1944, Revised ca. 1956).

Bartokiana for Piano Solo (ca. 1956).

PREMIÈRES

Duo Concertante for Violin and Cello; Irwin Eisenberg, violin and Charles Brennand, cello; private performance, Philadelphia, PA; 1956.

AWARDS

Guggenheim Fellowship, 1956–1957.

Society for the Publication of American Music Award for *String Quartet No. 1.*

1957

April 1957 to August 1957, George, Gene, Paul, and Francesca live in Mexico under a Guggenheim Fellowship.

COMPOSITIONS

Begins revisions *Symphony No. 1 for Orchestra [five-movement version]* (Fall 1948–Spring 1949, Revised 1957–1971–June 1972, May–June 1977].

La Bocca della Verità for Oboe and Piano (1957).

Dialogues for Clarinet and Piano (1957–1958). Commissioned by the Koussevitsky Foundation in the Library of Congress.

Waltzes for String Orchestra (1957) [Unpublished].

Waltz Serenade for Orchestra (1957) [Unpublished].

Blake Songs for Soprano and Chamber Ensemble (1957, Revised 1961–1962 for publication). Written in Mexico City.

Book of Songs for Voice and Piano (1937–1939) [Unpublished]: Numbers 31–32 from *Blake Songs: 31. Ah! Sunflower* (First version 1957, Second version 1962, Transcribed 28 May 1969); *32. Nurse's Song* (First version 1957, Second version 1962, Transcribed 30 May 1969); Number 35 originally from *Blake Songs: 35. Tyger! Tyger!* (First version 22 June–19 July 1957, Second version 23 June–02 July 1969).

1958

COMPOSITIONS

Cheltenham Concerto for Small Orchestra (1958). Commissioned by the Cheltenham Art Center, Philadelphia, PA.

PREMIÈRES

Waltz Serenade for Orchestra; Cincinnati Symphony Orchestra, Thor Johnson conducting; 14, 15 February 1958.

Symphony No. 1 for Orchestra [three-movement version]; Philadephia Orchestra, Eugene Ormandy conducting; 28, 29 March 1958.

Dialogues for Clarinet and Piano; Eric Simon, clarinet and Alicia Schachter, piano; Carl Fischer Concert Hall, New York City; 29 April 1958.

Cheltenham Concerto for Small Orchestra; The Philadelphia Chamber Music Society, Herbert Fiss conducting; Philadelphia, PA; 18 May 1958.

Sonata-Fantasia for Piano Solo; Howard Liebow, piano; Juilliard School of Music, New York City; 03 March 1958.

Waltzes for String Orchestra; Philadelphia Chamber Music Society, Herbert Fiss conducting; Temple University; 1958.

Serenata d'estate for Flute, Harp, Guitar, Violin, Viola, and Cello; "Music in Our Time," Arthur Winograd conducting; New York City; 04 May 1958.

1959

COMPOSITIONS

Begins *String Quartet No. 2 with Soprano* (1959–27 August 1961).

Duo Concertante for Violin and Cello (1955, Revised 1959 for publication).

PREMIÈRES

Symphony No. 2 for Orchestra; Cleveland Orchestra, George Szell conducting; Severance Hall, Cleveland, OH; 26, 28 February 1959.

AWARDS

First Prize, Italian International Society for Contemporary Music [ISCM] International Music Competition for the *Cheltenham Concerto for Small Orchestra.*

1960

George leaves Theodore Presser and assumes the position of Acting Chair of the Music Department at the University of Pennsylvania, Philadelphia, PA.

COMPOSITIONS

Continues to work on *String Quartet No. 2 with Soprano* (1959–27 August 1961).

Time Span I for Orchestra (1960). Commissioned by the St. Louis Symphony [Unpublished].

PREMIÈRES

Time-Span I for Orchestra; St. Louis Symphony Orchestra; St. Louis, MO; 22 October 1960.

La Bocca della Verità for Oboe and Piano; Joseph Marx, oboe and David Tudor, piano; Philadelphia, PA; 21 January 1960.

1961

Rochbergs' son Paul has his first operation for cancer (a brain tumor) on 17 October 1961.

Fall, George becomes Chair of the Music Department at the University of Pennsylvania, Philadephia, PA.

COMPOSITIONS

Finishes *String Quartet No. 2 with Soprano* (1959–27 August 1961).

Revises *Blake Songs for Soprano and Chamber Ensemble* (1957, Revised 1961–1962 for publication).

PREMIÈRES

Blake Songs for Soprano and Chamber Ensemble; Shirley Sudock, soprano, Hartt Chamber Players, Ralph Shapey conducting; International Society for Contemporary Music [ISCM], New School, New York City; 06 October 1961.

AWARDS

Naumburg Recording Award for *Symphony No. 2 for Orchestra*, by The New York Philharmonic, Werner Torkanowsky conducting.

1962

COMPOSITIONS

Time-Span II for Orchestra (1960, Revised January–March 1962).

Book of Songs for Voice and Piano (1937–1939) [Unpublished]: Numbers 31–32 from *Blake Songs*: *31. Ah! Sunflower* (First version 1957, Second version 1962, Transcribed 28 May 1969); *32. Nurse's Song* (First version 1957, Second version 1962, Transcribed 30 May 1969).

Begins *Trio [No. 1] for Violin, Cello, and Piano* (November 1962–July 1963).

PREMIÈRES

String Quartet No. 2 with Soprano; Janice Harsanyi, soprano and the Philadelphia String Quartet; Contemporary Chamber Music Society of Philadelphia; 23 March 1962 (private performance).

String Quartet No. 2 with Soprano; Janice Harsanyi, soprano and the Philadelphia String Quartet; University of Pennsylvania, Philadelphia, PA; 30 March 1962 (first public performance).

AWARDS

Honorary Doctorate in Music, Montclair State University, New Jersey.

National Institute of Arts and Letters Grant [for the recording of *String Quartet No. 2 with Soprano*, by Janice Harsanyi, soprano and the Philadelphia String Quartet].

1963

COMPOSITIONS

Finishes *Trio [No. 1] for Violin, Cello, and Piano* (November 1962–July 1963).

1964

George's father dies in the Spring.

Rochbergs' son Paul dies 22 November 1964.

COMPOSITIONS

Zodiac for Orchestra (*Twelve Bagatelles for Piano Solo* composed: 07 June–19 September 1952; Transcribed for orchestra: August 1964).

Apocalyptica [I] for Wind Ensemble (1964). Commissioned by the Montclair State College [NJ] Development Fund.

Begins *Passions [According to the Twentieth Century] for Singers, Jazz Quintet, Brass Ensemble, Percussion, Piano, and Tape* (1964–1967) [Unpublished].

PREMIÈRES

Time-Span II for Orchestra; Buffalo Philharmonic Orchestra, George Rochberg conducting; Buffalo, NY; 19 January 1964.

Trio [No. 1] for Violin, Cello, and Piano; Nieuw Amsterdam Trio; Buffalo, NY; 1964.

AWARDS

Honorary Doctorate in Music, Musical Academy of Philadephia (now the College of the Performing Arts).

RESIDENCIES

Spring Semester 1964: Slee Professor of Music, State University of New York [SUNY] at Buffalo.

1965

COMPOSITIONS

Contra Mortem et Tempus for Flute, Clarinet, Violin, and Piano (1965). Commissioned by the Bowdoin Contemporary Music Festival for the Aeolian Chamber Players.

La Bocca della Verità for Violin and Piano (1957, Transcribed 1965).

Black Sounds (Apocalyptica II) for Seventeen Winds (1965). Commissioned by Lincoln Center for a dance called *The Act*, choreographed by Anna Sokolow for inclusion in a special television composite project Lincoln Center developed in cooperation with WNET television of New York City.

Music for "The Alchemist" (A Play by Ben Jonson) for Soprano and Eleven Players (1965). Commissioned by the Vivian Beaumont Theater, Lincoln Center, New York City.

Music for the Magic Theater for a Chamber Ensemble of Fifteen Players [original version] (1965). Commissioned by the Fromm Foundation for the 75th Anniversary of the University of Chicago.

Continues to work on *Passions [According to the Twentieth Century] for Singers, Jazz Quintet, Brass Ensemble, Percussion, Piano, and Tape* (1964–1967) [Unpublished].

PREMIÈRES

Zodiac for Orchestra; Cincinnati Symphony, Max Rudolph conducting; Cincinnati, OH; 08 May 1965.

Apocalyptica [I] for Large Wind Ensemble; Montclair State College [NJ] Band, Ward Moore conducting; Memorial Auditorium, Montclair State College; 19 May 1965.

Contra Mortem et Tempus for Flute, Clarinet, Violin, and Piano; Aeolian Chamber Players (Lewis Kaplan, violin, Thomas Nyfenger, flute, Lloyd Greenberg, clarinet, Gilbert Kalish, piano); Summer Music Festival, Bowdoin College; 18 August 1965.

Black Sounds (Apocalyptica II) for Seventeen Winds; premièred with a dance called *The Act*, choreographed by Anna Sokolow, and included in a special television composite project Lincoln Center developed in cooperation with WNET television of New York City; 24 September 1965.

1966

COMPOSITIONS

Begins *Symphony No. 3 for Vocal Soloists, Chamber Chorus, Double Chorus, and Large Orchestra* (1966–21 March 1969). Commissioned by the Juilliard School of Music.

Nach Bach, Fantasy for Harpsichord or Piano (10–26 July 1966). Written at Tanglewood for Harpsichordist Igor Kipnis.

Begins *Music for "The Alchemist" for Soprano and Eleven Players [concert version]* (August–September 1966, August–October–02 November 1968).

Continues to work on *Passions [According to the Twentieth Century] for Singers, Jazz Quintet, Brass Ensemble, Percussion, Piano, and Tape* (1964–1967) [Unpublished].

PREMIÈRES

Music for "The Alchemist" (A Play by Ben Jonson) for Soprano and Eleven Players; Vivian Beaumont Theater; Lincoln Center, New York City; 13 October 1966.

David, the Psalmist for Tenor Solo and Orchestra; University of Pennsylvania Orchestra, Melvin Strauss conducting; University of Pennsylvania, Philadelphia, PA; 08 December 1966.

AWARDS

Guggenheim Fellowship, 1966–1967.

RESIDENCIES

Summer, Composer-In-Residence at Tanglewood (The Berkshire Music Center), Lenox, MA.

1967

COMPOSITIONS

Continues to work on *Symphony No. 3 for Vocal Soloists, Chamber Chorus, Double Chorus, and Large Orchestra* (1966–21 March 1969).

Finishes *Passions [According to the Twentieth Century] for Singers, Jazz Quintet, Brass Ensemble, Percussion, Piano, and Tape* (1964–1967) [Unpublished].

Revises *David, the Psalmist for Tenor Solo and Orchestra* (1954, Revised February 1967).

PREMIÈRES

Music for the Magic Theater for a Chamber Ensemble of Fifteen Players [original version]; University of Chicago Contemporary Chamber Players, Ralph Shapey conducting; University of Chicago, Chicago, IL; 24 January 1967.

Nach Bach, Fantasy for Harpsichord or Piano; Igor Kipnis, harpsichord; Annenberg Auditorium, University of Pennsylvania, Philadelphia, PA; 27 January 1967.

1968

George steps down from the Music Department Chair at the University of Pennsylvania, Philadelphia, PA. Remains on the music faculty teaching composition and advanced theory.

COMPOSITIONS

Continues to work on *Symphony No. 3 for Vocal Soloists, Chamber Chorus, Double Chorus, and Large Orchestra* (1966–21 March 1969).

Finishes *Music for "The Alchemist" for Soprano and Eleven Players [concert version]* (August–September 1966, August–October–02 November 1968).

Fanfares for Massed Trumpets, Horns, and Trombones (Finished 22 January 1968). Commissioned by the Settlement School in Philadelphia for their Sixtieth Anniversary.

Tableaux (Sound Pictures from "The Silver Talons of Piero Kostrov" by Paul Rochberg) for Soprano, Two Actors' Voices, Small Men's Chorus, and Twelve Players (August–September 1968).

PREMIÈRES

Fanfares for Massed Trumpets, Horns, and Trombones; Settlement Music School, Sigmund Hering conducting; Settlement Music School, Philadelphia, PA; 17 March 1968.

Piano Trio [No. 1] for Violin, Cello, and Piano; Nieuw Amsterdam Trio; Buffalo, NY; 1968.

1969

COMPOSITIONS

Finishes *Symphony No. 3 for Vocal Soloists, Chamber Chorus, Double Chorus, and Large Orchestra* (1966–21 March 1969).

Prelude on "Happy Birthday" for Almost Two Pianos (Finished July 1969). Commissioned by the Philadelphia Orchestral Association for Ormandy's and the Orchestra's collective seventieth birthdays.

Revises *Duo for Oboe and Bassoon* (1946, Revised 1969 for publication).

Cantes Flamencos for High Baritone (July–September 1969) [Unpublished].

Eleven Songs for Mezzo-Soprano and Piano (13 September–28 November 1969).

Two Songs from "Tableaux" [for Soprano and Piano] (August–September 1968, Transcribed 31 May–01 June 1969).

Music for the Magic Theater for Small Orchestra [orchestral version] (1969).

Revises *Variations on an Original Theme for Piano Solo* (1941, Revision completed 18 April 1969) [Unpublished].

Revises *Duo for Oboe and Bassoon* (1946, Revised 1969 for publication).

Book of Songs for Voice and Piano (1937–1939) [Unpublished]: 1. *There was an Aged King* (11 December 1937, Revised 27 April 1969); 2. *With Rue My Heart Is Laden* (22 June 1938, Revised 16 May 1969); 3. *Warum sind denn die Rosen so blass?* (10 July 1938, Revised 21 April 1969); 4. *When I am Dead, My Dearest* (16 October 1938, Revised 21 April 1969); 5. *Minnelied* (23 November 1939, Revised 19 April 1969); 6. *Du bist wie eine Blume* (10 September 1940); 7. *Dirge* (18 June 1941, Revised 24 May 1969); 8. *There Be None of Beauty's Daughters [A]* (17 July 1941, Revised 24 April 1969); 9. *Oh, My Love's Like a Red, Red Rose* (17–18 August 1945, Revised 19 May 1969); 10. *Lullaby (Vocalise)* (First version, piano sketch October 1944, Second version 23

August 1945, Revised 22 May 1969); *11. February Spring* (February 1946); *12. Ophelia's Song* (04 April 1946, Revised 29 April 1969); *13. Night Song at Amalfi* (08 April 1946, Revised 29 April 1969); *14. Song of Shadows* (09 April 1946, Revised 04 May 1969); *15. No Fall of Tears* (22 April 1946, Revised 17 May 1969); *16. Song of Day* (24 April 1946, Revised 28 April 1969); Numbers 17–20 from *Four Songs of Solomon: 17. Rise Up, My Love* (Summer or Fall, 1946); *18. Come, My Beloved* (Summer or Fall, 1946); *19. Set Me as a Seal* (Summer or Fall, 1946); *20. Behold, Thou Art Fair* (13 August 1946); *21. Du meine heilige Einsamkeit [A]* (14 August 1946, Revised 27 April 1969); *22. Lira-la-la* (22 October 1948); *23. Who Has Seen the Wind?* (1947); *24. Sweetest Love* (First version 12 April 1946, Second version 20 August 1947, Revised 02 May 1969); *25. Bright Cap and Streamers* (16 September 1947, Revised 01 May 1969); *26. The Blind Man at the Fair* (First version ca. 1937, Second version 10 October 1947, Revised 20 May 1969); *27. Du meine heilige Einsamkeit [B]* (25 September 1947); *28. There Be None of Beauty's Daughters [B]* (05 December 1949); *29. Piping Down the Valley's Wild* (13 February 1951, Revised 24 May 1969); *30. Ecce Puer* (First version 21 December 1949, Second version 26 August 1951, Revised 25 May 1969); Numbers 31–32 from *Blake Songs: 31. Ah! Sunflower* (First version 1957, Second version 1962, Transcribed 28 May 1969), *32. Nurse's Song* (First version 1957, Second version 1962, Transcribed 30 May 1969); Numbers 33–34 from *Tableaux: 33. Night Piece* (August–September 1968, Transcribed 01 June 1969), *34. Ballade* (August–September 1968, Transcribed 31 May 1969); Number 35 originally from *Blake Songs: 35. Tyger! Tyger!* (First version 22 June–19 July 1957, Second version 23 June–02 July 1969).

PREMIÈRES

Music for the Magic Theater for Small Orchestra [orchestral version]; Buffalo Philharmonic, Melvin Strauss conducting; 19, 21 January 1969.

Music for "The Alchemist" for Soprano and Eleven Players [concert version]; University of Washington Contemporary

Group, Robert Suderberg conducting; University of Washington, Seattle, WA; 31 October 1969.

Tableaux (Sound Pictures from "The Silver Talons of Piero Kostrov" by Paul Rochberg) for Soprano, Two Actors' Voices, Small Men's Chorus, and Twelve Players; Elizabeth Suderberg, soprano and the University of Washington Contemporary Group, Robert Suderberg conducting; University of Washington, Seattle, WA; 31 October 1969.

1970

COMPOSITIONS

Caprice Variations for Unaccompanied Violin (January–February 1970).

Sacred Song of Reconciliation (Mizmor l'Piyus) for Bass-Baritone and Small Orchestra (1970). Commissioned by Testimonium in celebration of the city of Jerusalem.

Songs in Praise of Krishna for Soprano and Piano (Summer 1970). Written for Neva Pilgrim.

PREMIÈRES

Eleven Songs for Mezzo-Soprano and Piano; Neva Pilgrim, soprano and George Rochberg, piano; St. Mary's Church, Philadelphia, PA; 01 April 1970.

Caprice Variations for Unaccompanied Vioin; Lewis Kaplan, violin; WBAI (New York City) "Free Music Store" Live Broadcast; 02 April 1970.

Symphony No. 3 for Vocal Soloists, Chamber Chorus, Double Chorus, and Large Orchestra; Juilliard Orchestra, Juilliard Chorus, and the Collegiate Chorale, Abraham Kaplan conducting, Joyce Mathis, soprano, Joy Blackett, alto, John Russell, tenor, Robert Shiesley, bass; Juilliard Theater, Lincoln Center, New York City; 24 November 1970.

1971

COMPOSITIONS

Fantasies for Voice and Piano (1971).

Carnival Music, Suite for Piano Solo (1971). Written for Jerome Lowenthal.

Begins *String Quartet No. 3* (December 1971–February 1972). Commissioned by the Concord String Quartet.

PREMIÈRES

Sacred Song of Reconciliation (Mizmur l'Piyus) for Bass-Baritone and Small Orchestra; Testimonium, Gary Bertini conducting; Jerusalem, Israel; 05 January 1971.

Songs in Praise of Krishna for Soprano and Piano; Neva Pilgrim, soprano and George Rochberg, piano; University of Illinois, Champaign-Urbana, IL; 16 March 1971.

1972

COMPOSITIONS

Finishes *String Quartet No. 3* (December 1971–February 1972).

Electrikaleidoscope for Amplified Flute, Clarinet, Violin, Cello, Piano, and Electric Piano (August 1972, Revised December 1972). Commissioned by the Aeolian Chamber Players.

Ricordanza (Soliloquy) for Cello and Piano (1972).

PREMIÈRES

Carnival Music, Suite for Piano Solo; Jerome Lowenthal, piano; Academy of Music, Philadephia, PA; 04 May 1972.

String Quartet No. 3; Concord String Quartet (Mark Sokol, violin, Andrew Jennings, violin, John Kochanowski, viola, Norman Fisher, cello); Alice Tully Hall, New York City; 15 May 1972.

Electrikaleleidoscope for Amplified Flute, Clarinet, Violin, Cello, Piano, and Electric Piano; Aeolian Chamber Players (Lewis Kaplan, violin, Jerry Grossman, cello, Erich Graf, flute, Richard Wasley, clarinet, Walter Ponce, piano); Town Hall, New York City; 19 December 1972.

AWARDS

National Endowment for the Arts [NEA] Grant.

Naumburg Chamber Composition Award for *String Quartet No. 3*.

RESIDENCIES

Summer, Aspen Music Festival, Composer-In-Residence.

1973

COMPOSITIONS

Imago Mundi (Image of the World) for Large Orchestra (1973).
Commissioned by the Baltimore Symphony Orchestra.

Ukiyo-e (Pictures of the Floating World) for Harp (1973). Commissioned by Harpist Marcella de Cray.

Behold, My Servant (Everything that Lives Is Holy) for a cappella Mixed Chorus (1973). Commissioned by the Jewish Theological Seminary.

Begins *Phaedra, a Monodrama in Seven Scenes for Mezzo-Soprano and Orchestra* (1973–24 March 1974). Libretto by Gene Rochberg. Commissioned by the New Music Ensemble of Syracuse, NY with assistance from the New York State Council on the Arts.

PREMIÈRES

Behold, My Servant for a cappella Mixed Chorus; Jewish Theological Seminary, New York City; 23 October 1973.

Ricordanza (Soliloquy) for Cello and Piano; Micheal Rudiakov, cello, and Evelyn Crochet, piano; Gardner Museum, Boston; 1973.

AWARDS

National Endowment for the Arts [NEA] Grant (1973–1974).

1974

COMPOSITIONS

Finishes *Phaedra, a Monodrama in Seven Scenes for Mezzo-Soprano and Orchestra* (1973–24 March 1974). Libretto by Gene Rochberg.

Concerto for Violin and Orchestra (Spring–Summer 1974). Commissioned by the Pittsburgh Symphony Orchestra for Violinist Isaac Stern, with assistance from the National Endowment for the Arts and the *Pittsburgh Post-Gazette*.

PREMIÈRES

Imago Mundi (Image of the World) for Large Orchestra; Baltimore Symphony Orchestra, Sergiu Commissiona conducting; Lyric Theater, Baltimore, MD; 08, 09 May 1974.

Imago Mundi (Image of the World) for Large Orchestra; Baltimore Symphony Orchestra, Sergiu Commissiona conducting; Carnegie Hall, New York City; 10 May 1974.

1975

COMPOSITIONS

Transcendental Variations for String Orchestra (String Quartet No. 3, III. Variations composed 1971–1972; Transcribed for string orchestra 1975).

Quintet for Piano and String Quartet (July–December 1975). Written for Jerome Lowenthal and the Concord String Quartet.

Begins *Partita Variations for Piano Solo* (31 December 1975–04 February 1976). Commissioned by Etsuko Tazaki on a grant from the Edyth Bush Charitable Foundation, Inc., for the Bicentennial Series of the Washington Performing Arts Society [WAPS] of Washington, D.C.

PREMIÈRES

Concerto for Violin and Orchestra; Isaac Stern, violin and the Pittsburgh Symphony Orchestra, Donald Johanes conducting; Heinz Hall, Pittsburgh, PA; 04, 05, 06 April 1975.

Ukiyo-e (Pictures of the Floating World) for Solo Harp; Marcella De Cray, harp; San Francisco Contemporary Music Players Concert, Grape Stake Art Gallery, San Francisco, CA; 28 April 1975.

1976

COMPOSITIONS

Finishes *Partita Variations for Piano Solo* (31 December 1975–04 February 1976).

Symphony No. 4 for Large Orchestra (1976). Commissioned by the Seattle Youth Orchestra, Vilem Sokol, Musical Director, in celebration of the Bicentennial of the United States of America. Grateful acknowledgements to Mrs. Louis Brechemin and to the Washington State American Bicentennial Committee and the Washington State Arts Commission which provided additional funds.

PREMIÈRES

Symphony No. 4 for Large Orchestra; Seattle Youth Orchestra, Vilem Sokol conducting; Seattle, WA; 15 November 1976.

Phaedra, a Monodrama in Seven Scenes for Mezzo-Soprano and Orchestra; Neva Pilgrim, soprano and the Syracuse Symphony, David Loebel conducting; Lincoln Auditorium, Syracuse, NY; 09 January 1976.

Quintet for Piano and String Quartet; Jerome Lowenthal, piano and the Concord String Quartet; Alice Tully Hall, New York City; 15 March 1976.

Partita-Variations for Piano Solo; Etsuko Tazaki, piano; Kennedy Center, Washington, D.C.; 04 December 1976.

1977

COMPOSITIONS

Finishes revision of *Symphony No. 1 for Orchestra [five-movement version]* (Fall 1948–Spring 1949, Revised 1957–Summer 1977).

Songs of Inanna and Dumuzi for Contralto and Piano (1977). Commissioned by Morton Newman for his wife Barbara.

Book of Contrapuntal Pieces for Keyboard Instruments (1940–1979, Collection compiled 15 January–04 February 1979) [Unpublished]: 20. *Fugue for One Piano, Four-hands: Adagio religioso, serioso* [A transcription of *String Quartet No. 4, II. Fuga* (1977)].

"The Concord Quartets": String Quartet No. 4 (Finished 18 December 1977). Commissioned by the Concord String Quartet.

1978

COMPOSITIONS

"The Concord Quartets": String Quartet No. 5 (Finished 25 March 1978). Commissioned by the Concord String Quartet.

"The Concord Quartets": String Quartet No. 6 (Finished 14 August 1978). Commissioned by the Concord String Quartet.

Begins *Slow Fires of Autumn (Ukiyo-e II) for Flute and Harp* (November 1978–January 1979). Commissioned by the Walter H. Naumburg Foundation for the New York Debut of flutist Carol Wincenc.

PREMIÈRES

Songs of Inanna and Dumuzi for Contralto and Piano; Katherine Cienzinski, alto and George Reeves, piano; Van Pelt Auditorium, Philadelphia Museum of Art, Philadelphia, PA; 29 January 1978.

1979

COMPOSITIONS

Finishes *Slow Fires of Autumn (Ukiyo-e II) for Flute and Harp* (November 1978–January 1979).

Sonata for Viola and Piano (1979). Commissioned by Brigham Young University and the American Viola Society for William Primrose's seventy-fifth birthday celebration, Seventh International Viola Congress.

String Quartet No. 7 with Baritone (08 June–20 September 1979). Commissioned in honor of the School of Music of the University of Michigan from funds supplied by the Horace H. Rackham School of Graduate Studies of the University of Michigan and the Oliver Ditson Fund of the School of Music (1880–1980), for Leslie Guinn and the Concord String Quartet.

Book of Contrapuntal Pieces for Keyboard Instruments (1940–1979, Collection compiled 15 January–04 February 1979) [Unpublished]: 4. *Prelude and Fughetta No. 1* (P: 28 August 1946; F: 16 September 1946) [Published 1980]; 5. *Prelude and Fughetta No. 2* (P: 17 September 1946; F: 29 August 1946) [Published 1980]; 6. *Four Inventions* (1946): *I. Non troppo Allegro, II. Non troppo Allegro, III. Brisk, IV. Brisk*; 7. *Canon in Song Form: Slow and Tranquil* (1946); 8. *Fugue: Largamente; serioso ed espressivo* (March 1946); 9. *Ten Two-Part Canons* (1946): *I. Moderato; cantabile, II. Con moto ed espressivo, III. Allegretto grazioso, IV. Adagio ma non troppo, V. Andante, VI. Broadly, VII. Moderato con spirito, VIII. Adagio sostenuto, IX. Allegro Con moto (after*

Beethoven), X. *Molto espressivo;* 10. *Canon on a Ground Bass by Purcell* (1946); 11. *Four-part Canon: Grave* (21 March 1946); 12. *Seven [Four-part] Chorales Treated Canonically: I. Ach wie nichtig, ach wie fluchtig* (22 June 1946), *II. Jesus Christe, Unser Heiland* (22 June 1946), *III. Strat mich nicht in deinem Zorn* (22 June 1946), *IV. Wie bist du, Seele?* (24 June 1946), *V. Nun sich der Tag (with contrary motion canon)* (June 1946), *VI. Kommt Seelen dieser Tag: Allegretto* (1946), *VII. In Dulce Jubilo* (23 June 1946); 13. *Five Two-part Canons in Contrary Motion* (1946): *I. Allegro vivace, II. No. 1 in Double Counterpoint, III. Alla marcia, IV. Allegro vivace, V. No. 4 in Double Counterpoint;* 14. *Eight-part Infinite Canon on a subject of J.S. Bach: Presto* (1946); 15. *Fugue: Adagio espressivo* (March 1946); 16. *Double Fugue for Two Pianos: Allegro moderato ed energico* (1946); 17. *Fugue for Two Pianos: Allegro ma non troppo e risoluto* (March 1946); 18. *Eight three-part Canons for Organ: I. Unison (with free bass voice): Adagio* (30 June 1946), *II. At the Second (with free bass voice): Molto adagio* (30 June 1946), *III. At the Third (with free bass voice): Allegretto* (30 June 1946), *IV. At the Fourth (with free bass voice): Allegro giocoso* (31 July 1946), *V. At the Fifth (with free bass voice): Adagio* (31 July 1946), *VI. At the Sixth (with free bass voice): Allegro moderato* (01 August 1946), *VII. At the Seventh (with two voices in bass and alto): Adagio espressivo* (02 August 1946), *VIII. At the Octave (with free bass voice): Allegro ma non troppo* (02 August 1946); 19. *Fugue: Allegro ma non troppo* (1948–1949); 20. *Fugue for One Piano, Four-hands: Adagio religioso; serioso* [A transcription of *String Quartet No. 4, II. Fuga* (1977)].

Begins *Octet, A Grand Fantasia for Flute, Clarinet, Horn, Violin, Viola, Cello, Bass, and Piano* (23 November 1979–12 January 1980). Commissioned by the Chamber Music Society of Lincoln Center, New York City, made possible by a generous gift from Marvin Sloves.

PREMIÈRES

String Quartet No. 4, String Quartet No. 5, and *String Quartet No. 6, "The Concord Quartets";* Concord String Quartet

(Mark Sokol, violin, Andrew Jennings, violin, John Kochanowski, viola, Norman Fisher, cello); University of Pennsylvania, Philadelphia, PA; 20 January 1979.

Slow Fires of Autumn (Ukiyo-e II) of Flute and Harp; Carol Wincenc, flute and Nancy Allen, harp; Alice Tully Hall, New York City; 23 April 1979.

Sonata for Viola and Piano; Joseph de Pasquale, violin and Vladimir Sokoloff, piano; Seventh International Violin Congress, Provo, Utah; 14 July 1979.

AWARDS

First Prize, Kennedy Center Friedheim Awards for *String Quartet No. 4, "The Concord Quartets"*.

Named Walter H. Annenberg Professor of the Humanities at the University of Pennsylvania, Philadelphia, PA.

1980

COMPOSITIONS

Finishes *Octet, A Grand Fantasia for Flute, Clarinet, Horn, Violin, Viola, Cello, Bass, and Piano* (23 November 1979–12 January 1980).

Revises *Trio for Piano, Clarinet, and Horn* (1948, Revised 1980 for publication).

Begins *The Confidence Man, An Opera in Two Parts* (1980–1982). Libretto by Gene Rochberg. Commissioned by the Santa Fe Opera.

PREMIÈRES

String Quartet No. 7 with Baritone; Leslie Guinn, baritone and the Concord String Quartet (Mark Sokol, violin, Andrew Jennings, violin, John Kochanowski, viola, Norman Fisher, cello); University of Michigan, Ann Arbor, MI; 27 January 1980.

Octet, A Grand Fantasia for Flute, Clarinet, Horn, Violin, Viola, Cello, Bass, and Piano; Chamber Music Society of Lincoln Center (Renee Siebert, flute, Gervase DePeyer, clarinet, Robert Routch, horn, Ani Kavafian, violin, Marcus Thompson, viola, Leslie Parnas, cello, Alvin Brehm, bass,

John Browning, piano); Alice Tully Hall, New York City;
25, 27 April 1980.

*Octet, A Grand Fantasia for Flute, Clarinet, Horn, Violin, Viola,
Cello, Bass, and Piano*; Chamber Music Society of Lincoln
Center (Renee Siebert, flute, Gervase DePeyer, clarinet,
Robert Routch, horn, Ani Kavafian, violin, Marcus
Thompson, viola, Leslie Parnas, cello, Alvin Brehm, bass,
John Browning, piano); Concert Hall, Kennedy Center,
Washington, D.C.; 26 April 1980.

AWARDS

Honorary Doctorate of Music, University of Michigan, Ann
Arbor, MI.

1981

COMPOSITIONS

Continues to work on *The Confidence Man, An Opera in Two
Parts* (1980–1982). Libretto by Gene Rochberg.

Quintet for String Quintet [double cello] (1981). Commissioned
by the Concord String Quartet for their Tenth Anniversary.

AWARDS

Distinguished Pennsylvanian.

1982

Fall semester 1982: on leave from the University of Pennsylvania, Philadelphia, PA.

COMPOSITIONS

Finishes *The Confidence Man, An Opera in Two Parts* (1980–
1982). Libretto by Gene Rochberg.

Between Two Worlds (Ukiyo-e III), Five Images for Flute and Piano
(Fall 1982). Commissioned by Lennie and Marvin Wolfgang for their daughter Karen.

PREMIÈRES

Quintet for String Quintet [double cello]; Concord String Quartet, and Bonnie Thron, cello; Curtis Institute of Music,
Philadelphia, PA; 06 January 1982.

The Confidence Man, An Opera in Two Parts. Libretto by Gene Rochberg; Santa Fe Opera; 31 July 1982.

1983

Spring semester, on leave from the University of Pennsylvania, Philadelphia, PA. Retires from the University of Pennsylvania at the end of the spring term.

COMPOSITIONS

Concerto for Oboe and Orchestra (1983). Commissioned by the New York Philharmonic for Oboist Joseph Robinson.

Quartet for Piano, Violin, Viola, and Cello (1983). Commissioned by Frank Taplin.

PREMIÈRES

Between Two Worlds (Ukiyo-e III), Five Images for Flute and Piano; Sue Ann Kahn, flute and Vladimir Sokoloff, piano; National Flute Association Convention, Philadephia, PA; 19 August 1983.

1984

COMPOSITIONS

Four Short Sonatas for Piano Solo (1984). Commissioned by the United States Information Agency [USIA] for its Artistic Ambassador Program.

Symphony No. 5 for Orchestra (Spring–28 November 1984). Commissioned by the Chicago Symphony Orchestra for the Sesquicentennial celebration of the city of Chicago.

PREMIÈRES

Four Short Sonatas for Piano Solo; Michael Caldwell, piano; Palermos Santissimo Salvatore, Palmero, Italy; 07 June 1984.

Concerto for Oboe and Orchestra; Joseph Robinson, oboe, and the New York Philharmonic, Zubin Mehta conducting; Avery Fischer Hall, New York City; 13–18 December 1984.

1985

COMPOSITIONS

Trio [No. 2] for Violin, Cello, and Piano (1985). Commissioned by the Elizabeth Sprague Coolidge Foundation in the Library of Congress for the Beaux Arts Trio.

To the Dark Wood, Music for Woodwind Quintet (1985). Commissioned by the Earle Page Foundation of the University of New England, Armidale, Australia, for the Promotion of Contemporary Classical Music, on behalf of the Canberra Wind Soloists.

PREMIÈRES

Quartet for Violin, Viola, Cello, and Piano; Christopher O'Riley, piano, Alexis Galpherine, violin, Miles Hoffman, viola, and Peter Wiley, cello; Library of Congress Summer Festival, Washington, D.C.; 18 June 1985.

AWARDS

Brandeis Creative Arts Award, Gold Medal in Music.

Inducted into membership, American Academy and Institute of Arts and Letters.

Honorary Doctorate in Music, University of Pennsylvania, Philadelphia, PA.

1986

COMPOSITIONS

Begins *Symphony No. 6 for Orchestra* (Spring 1986–January 1987). Commissioned by the Pittsburgh Symphony Orchestra and the Pennsylvania Council on the Arts.

PREMIÈRES

Symphony No. 5 for Orchestra; Chicago Symphony Orchestra, Sir Georg Solti conducting; Orchestra Hall, Chicago, IL; 30 January 1986.

Piano Trio [No. 2] for Violin, Cello, and Piano; Beaux Arts Trio (Menahem Pressler, piano, Isadore Cohen, violin, Bernard Greenhouse, cello); Library of Congress, Washington, D.C.; 27, 28 February 1986.

To the Dark Wood, Music for Woodwind Quintet; Canberra Wind Soloists (Vernon Hill, flute, Alan Vivian, clarinet, Hector

McDonald, horn, Richard McIntyre, bassoon, David Nutall, oboe); University Hall, University of New England, Armidale, Australia; 03 October 1986.

AWARDS

Lancaster Symphony Composers Award.

Elected Fellow of the American Academy of Arts and Sciences.

1987

COMPOSITIONS

Finishes *Symphony No. 6 for Orchestra* (Spring 1986–January 1987).

Three Cadenzas for the Mozart Concerto for Oboe, in C Major, K. 314 (27–31 May 1987). Commissioned by Joseph Robinson.

Begins *Suite No. 1 (Based on the Opera "The Confidence Man") for Large Orchestra* (1987–1988).

Begins *Suite No. 2 (Based on the Opera "The Confidence Man") for Solo Voices, Chorus, and Orchestra* (1987–1988).

PREMIÈRES

Three Cadenzas for the Mozart Concerto for Oboe, in C Major, K. 314; Joseph Robinson, oboe, with the New York Philharmonic, Zubin Mehta conducting; Garden State Arts Center, New Jersey; 21 July 1987.

Symphony No. 6 for Orchestra; Pittsburgh Symphony Orchestra, Lorin Maazel conducting; Heinz Hall, Pittsburgh, PA; 16, 17, 18 October 1987.

AWARDS

Andre and Clara Mertens Contemporary Composer Award; University of Bridgeport, Bridgeport, CT.

Alfred I. DuPont Award for Outstanding Conductors and Composers; Delaware Symphony, Wilmington, DE.

1988

COMPOSITIONS

Finishes *Suite No. 1 (Based on the Opera" The Confidence Man") for Large Orchestra* (1987–1988).

Finishes *Suite No. 2 (Based on the Opera "The Confidence Man")
for Solo Voices, Chorus, and Orchestra* (1987–1988).

Sonata for Violin and Piano (1988). Commissioned by the McKim
Fund in the Music Division of the Library of Congress
and Concert Artists Guild for Maria Bachmann.

AWARDS

Honorary Doctorate in Music, Curtis Institute of Music.

Second Prize, Kennedy Center Friedheim Awards for *Symphony No. 6 for Orchestra.*

1989

COMPOSITIONS

Rhapsody and Prayer for Violin and Piano (26 January–27 February 1989). Commissioned by the 1990 International Violin
Competition of Indianapolis as a required work for all
contestants.

Begins *Ora Pro Nobis for Flute and Guitar* (1989–February 1990).
Written for Eliot Fisk and Paula Robison.

PREMIÈRES

Sonata for Violin and Piano; Maria Bachmann, violin and John
Klibinoff, piano; Ambassador Auditorium, Los Angeles;
10 April 1989.

Symphony No. 6 for Orchestra [European premières]. Pittsburgh
Symphony Orchestra 1989 European Tour, Lorin Maazel
conducting; Leningrad (07 October 1989), Moscow (09
October 1989), Warsaw (12 October 1989).

*Suite No. 1 (Based on the Opera "The Confidence Man") for Large
Orchestra*; Nashville Symphony Orchestra, Kenneth
Schermerhorn, conducting; 27, 28 October 1989.

1990

COMPOSITIONS

Finishes *Ora Pro Nobis for Flute and Guitar* (1989–February
1990). Written for Eliot Fisk and Paula Robison.

Muse of Fire for Flute and Guitar (Finished April 1990). Commissioned by Carnegie Hall as part of their centennial celebration (1991). Written for Eliot Fisk and Paula Robison.

PREMIÈRES

Rhapsody and Prayer for Violin and Piano; 1990 International Violin Competition of Indianapolis; required of all contestants; September 1990.

RESIDENCIES

The Bellagio Study and Conference Center, Rockefeller Foundation, Bellagio, Italy; 07 April–03 May 1990.

1991

PREMIÈRES

Muse of Fire for Flute and Guitar; Eliot Fisk, guitar and Paula Robison, flute; Weill Hall (Carnegie Recital Hall), New York City; 01 February 1991.

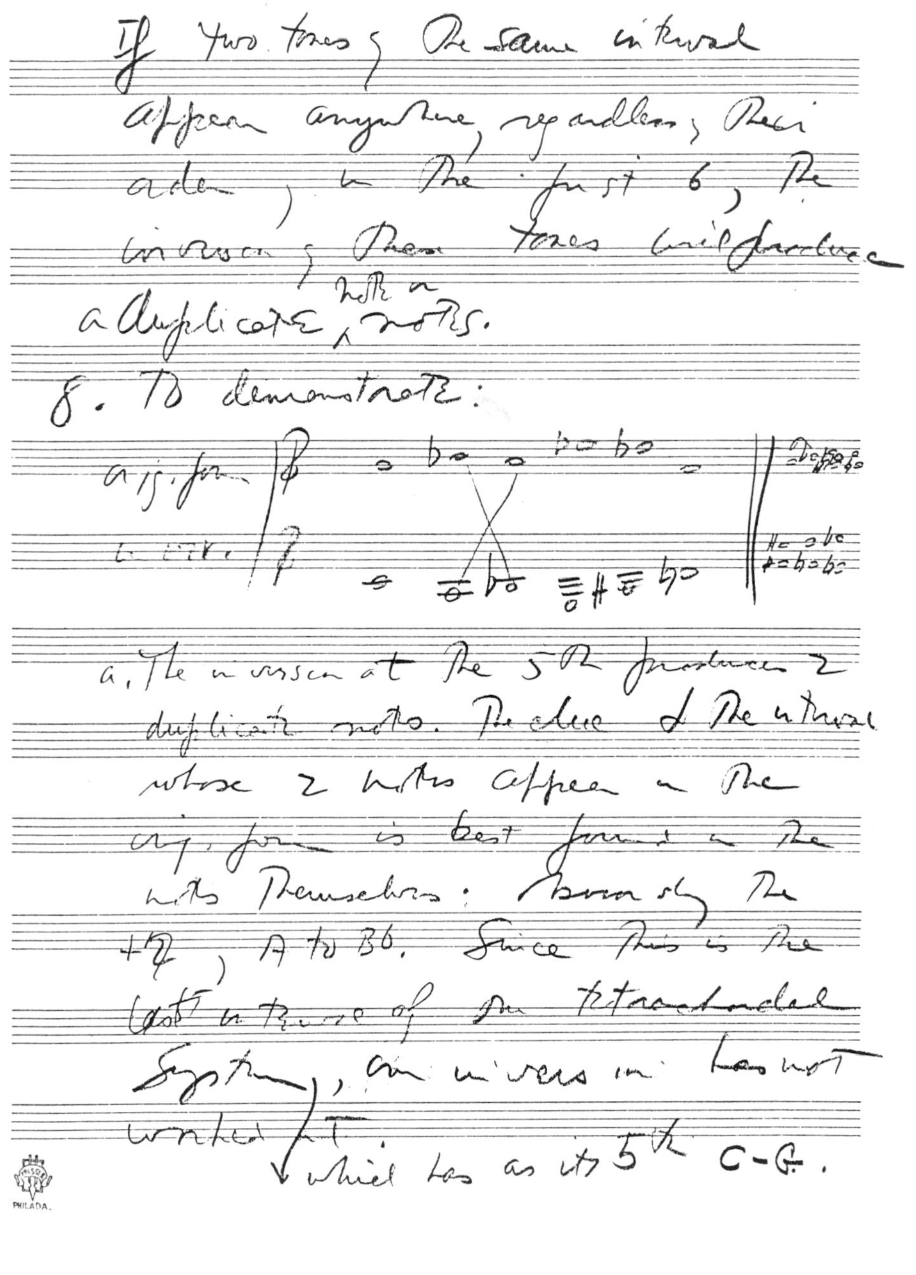

Plate 5: Autograph of page from *The Hexachord and Its Relation to the Twelve-tone Row* (First draft, 1954). Used by permission of George Rochberg.

II. THIRTEEN PIANO PIECES*

in celebration of Rochberg's Seventieth Birthday (July 5, 1988)

INTRODUCTION

To honor George Rochberg on his seventieth birthday, it was my idea to commission a series of piano pieces based on themes from his work. Choosing from among the many gifted young men and women who had studied with George was extremely difficult, and I will always regret that this volume had to be limited for obvious practical reasons.

The pieces assembled here constitute wide variety and imagination and serve as hommage to a composer as teacher and friend whose own work, though it spans a long lifetime, is happily not yet finished.

When music appeared to falter as styles and fads arose to choke off its very essence, it was George Rochberg who broke through in powerful works of his own to reconnect with the grand traditions of music which were all but lost. This volume, written so generously and movingly by a younger generation than his own, echoes in its special way the effect Rochberg and his values have had. When in 1985, Brandeis University awarded George Rochberg the Gold Medal for Creative Achievement, the citation spoke of his having melted "the ice in contemporary music." The work of the young composers in this volume attests to this recognition and, clearly, they have made music with the freedom to express themselves in musical ideas of character, quality, and beauty—without which no art can remain viable.

*Commissioned by Gene Rochberg.

George Rochberg's seventieth birthday is only days away from our fourty-seventh wedding anniversary so, I consider these piano pieces a grand and glorious gift for both occasions and thank those who made it possible with all my heart.

Gene Rochberg

Newtown Square, PA

05 July 1988

William Albright
Stoptime for George Rochberg

Ingrid Arauco
Triptych

William Bolcom
Variations on a Theme by George Rochberg

Cart Cacioppo
Tre brani da Variationi caratteristiche sul nome d'un Maestro

Robert Carl
From Him to Me

Daniel Dorf
Romanza on a Theme by Rochberg

Stephen Hartke
Sonatina Fantasia

Yinam Leef
How Far East, How Further West?

Jay Riese
Tableau fugitif

Stephen Jaffe
Impromptu (Variations on a Theme of George Rochberg)

Robert Kyr
Images of Reminiscence

Paul Reale
Sonata Rochbergiana

Michael Rose
Fantasia Marcia

III. WORKS

Apocalyptica [I] for Large Wind Ensemble

DATE OF COMPOSITION: 1964.

PUBLISHED: TP. 1966.

PAGES: 52.

TIMING: ca. 20'00".

COMMISSION: Montclair State College Development Fund.

PREMIÈRE: Montclair State College Band, Ward Moore conducting; Montclair [NJ] State College, Memorial Auditorium; 19 May 1965.

DEDICATION: to Bernard and Florence Siegel.

RECORDING: N/A.

INSTRUMENTATION: 3 Fl (Pc), Ob, Cl (E), 3 Cl (ACl), BCl, CBCl, 2
ASax, TSax, BSax, 2 Crnt, 2 Tpt, 4 Hn, 3 Tbn, Euph, Tba,
StrB; 12 Perc: Perc 1: Piano, Perc 2: Chimes (TBel), Glock,
Perc 3: Vib, Tri, Perc 4: 2 SusCy, Slapstick, Anvil or Iron
Pipe (at 80 release Anvil to Perc 7), Perc 5: 2 Gongs (L-S), 2
Cowbells (H-L) (at 75 release Cowbells to Perc 10), Perc 6:
SmSnDr, Field Drum (at 75 take Sleigh Bells from Perc 11),
Perc 7: 3 TT (H-M-L) (at 80 take Anvil from Perc 4), Perc 8:
TnDr, SmBsDr-laid flat, LgBsDr-laid flat (at 80 take CrCy
from Perc 12; at 127 release CrCy to Perc 12), Perc 9: 2
Maracas (L-S), Steel Plate, Wind Chimes (Bamboo), Perc
10: Guiro, Tamb (at 75 take Cowbells from Perc 5), Perc 11:
Large Ratchet, Wood Block (H-M-L), Temple Blocks
(H-M-L), Sleig Bells (at 75 release Sleigh Bells to Perc 6),
Perc 12: String Drum (lion's roar), CrCy (at 80 release CrCy
to to Perc 8; at 127 take CrCy from Perc 8).

QUOTED AT THE BEGINNING OF THE SCORE:

> Blow, winds, and crack your cheeks! rage! blow!
> You cataracts and hurricanes, spout
> Till you have drench'd our steeples, drown'd the cocks!
> You sulphorous and thought-executing fires,
> Vaunt-couriers of oak-cleaving thunderbolts,
> Singe my white head! And thou, all-shaking thunder.
> Strike flat the thick rotundity o' the world,
> Crack nature's molds, all germens spill at once
> That make ingrateful man!
>
>

William Shakespeare
King Lear, Act III, Scene II

Arioso for Piano Solo

DATE OF COMPOSITION: *Little Suite: Prelude* (1944), Revised ca. 1956.

PUBLISHED: TP. 1957.

PAGES: 2.

TIMING: 2'20".

COMMISSION: Part of Theodore Presser's Contemporary Piano Music by Distinguished American Composers Series, Isadore Freed editor.

PREMIÈRE: N/A.

DEDICATION: None.

RECORDING: N/A.

Bartokiana for Piano Solo

DATE OF COMPOSITION: ca. 1956.

PUBLISHED: TP. 1957.

PAGES: 4.

TIMING: ca. 1'45".

COMMISSION: Part of Theodore Presser's Contemporary Piano Music by Distinguished American Composers Series, Isadore Freed editor.

PREMIÈRE: N/A.

DEDICATION: None.

RECORDING: N/A.

Behold, My Servant (Everything That Lives Is Holy), for a cappella Mixed Chorus

DATE OF COMPOSITION: 1973.

PUBLISHED: TP. 1974.

PAGES: 23.

TIMING: ca. 8'00".

COMMISSION: Jewish Theological Seminary, New York City.

PREMIÈRE: Jewish Theological Seminary, New York City; 23 October 1973.

DEDICATION: None.

RECORDING: N/A.

INSTRUMENTATION: SATB, *divisi, a cappella.*

Between Two Worlds (Ukiyo-e III), Five Images for Flute and Piano

I. Fantasia

II. Scherzoso (Fast dance)

III. Night Scene (A)

IV. Sarabande (Slow dance)

V. Night Scene (B)

DATE OF COMPOSITION: Fall 1982.

PUBLISHED: 1983.

PAGES: 18 (piano score), 6 (flute part).

TIMING: ca. 10'00".

COMMISSION: Lennie and Marvin Wolfgang for their daughter Karen.

PREMIÈRE: Sue Ann Kahn, flute and Vladimir Sokoloff, piano; National Flute Association Convention Philadelphia; 19 August 1983.

DEDICATION: to Karen Wolfgang.

RECORDING: Sue Ann Kahn, flute and Andrew Willis, piano, CRI 531.

NOTES BY THE COMPOSER:

Between Two Worlds was written in Jerusalem during the late fall of 1982 for family friend Karen Wolfgang, a flutist.

Ukiyo-e (Pictures of a Floating World) refers to a style of Japanese painting whose masters did not draw from nature but stored images in the mind until the mood was upon them to paint.

My imagistic music rarely refers to external events of impressions but more often to a deep-seated sense of fluctuating internal feelings and perceptions difficult to sustain or structure but which, nevertheless, eventually become the source of musical ideas.

The title *Between Two Worlds* suggests not only the realms of nature and culture between which we find ourselves tenuously situated but also the strong feelings (that I experienced while living briefly in the strife-torn Middle East).

Used by permission of George Rochberg.

Black Sounds (Apocalyptica II) for Seventeen Winds

DATE OF COMPOSITION: 1965.

PUBLISHED: TP. MS. Rental. 1977.

PAGES: 86.

TIMING: ca. 12'00".

COMMISSION: Lincoln Center for a dance called *The Act*, choreographed by Anna Sokolow, for inclusion in a special television composite project Lincoln Center developed in cooperation with WNET television of New York City.

ORIGINAL VERSION PREMIÈRE: Premièred with a dance called *The Act*, choreographed by Anna Sokolow, for inclusion in a special television composite project Lincoln Center developed in cooperation with WNET television of New York City; 24 September 1965.

CONCERT VERSION PREMIÈRE: Tanglewood, Gunther Schuller conducting.

DEDICATION: to Anna Sokolow.

RECORDING: Oberlin Wind Ensemble, Kenneth Moore conducting, Grenadilla 1019 (1977).

AWARDS: The Lincoln Center, WNET television show received the *Prix d'Italia*, 1965.

INSTRUMENTATION: 2 Fl (Pc), Ob, Cl (E), Cl (BCl), 2 Hn, 2 Tpt (C), Tbn, BTbn, Tba, Pn (Cel); 4 Perc: Perc 1: Timp, LgBsDr, SmSnDr, CrCy, Slapstick, Temple blocks, SmTri, Tamb, Steel plate, Anvil (or Iron Pipe), Windchimes (Bamboo); Perc 2: Chimes (TBel), Glock, Sleigh bells, LgTri, Guiro, Claves, Large ratchet, LgGong; Perc 3: LgSusCy, SmSusCy, Gongs (L-M-S), Vib, Claves, Woodblocks; Perc 4: SmSnDr, Field Drum, SmBsDr, Vib, Claves, Slapstick, Cowbells (H-M-L), LgSusCy.

NOTES BY THE COMPOSER:

In 1964, I wrote a large wind ensemble work entitled *Apocalyptica*. From this work I drew the material for a seventeen-player wind piece called *Black Sounds*. This new work was done in 1965 on commission from Lincoln Center for a dance called *The Act*, choreographed by Anna Sokolow for inclusion in a special television composite project Lincoln Center developed in cooperation with WNET television of New York City. Later that show was awarded the *Prix d'Italia*. Since the dance concerned itself with the "act of murder", the music, to be appropriately "black" had to be unrelenting it its intensity, dark in its gesture. The result was a totally chromaticized texture, though not necessarily atonal. In a through-composed, single movement *Black Sounds* is stylistically consistent from beginning to end. At the time I wrote it, I also thought of it as an "homage" to Varèse whom I admired greatly for his directness and power of expression.

Blake Songs for Soprano and Chamber Ensemble

I. Ah! Sunflower

II. Nurse's Song

III. The Fly

IV. The Sick Rose

DATE OF COMPOSITION: 1957, Revised 1961–1962 for publication.

PUBLISHED: MCA. 1963.

PAGES: 30.

TIMING: ca. 12'00".

COMMISSION: None.

PREMIÈRE: Shirley Sudock, soprano and the Hartt Chamber Players, Ralph Shapey conducting; International Society for Contemporary Music [ISCM] Concert, New York City; 06 October 1961.

DEDICATION: to my son, Paul.

RECORDING: Jan DeGaetani, soprano and the Contemporary Chamber Ensemble, Arthur Weisberg conducting, Nonesuch 71302.

INSTRUMENTATION: Fl, Cl, BCl, Cel, Hp, Vln, Vla, Vlc, Soprano solo.

NOTES BY THE COMPOSER:

The *Blake Songs* attempt to reveal through voice and instrumental color the hidden, below-the-surface aspects and resonances evoked in me by Blake's poetry. The deceptive naivete of Blake's verbal art is only a thin coating overlaying the dark and potent images he creates–images that appeal directly to the heart.

Each song derives its essential form from its text. The point at which the surface of the form of the music meets the surface of the form of the texts is in the use of "strophe" and "refrain." These songs constitute only a fragment of a larger group of settings of *Blake Songs* planned by the composer.

Ah! Sunflower, whose vocal line is more florid than that of the other songs, expresses the mystery of time and the world-weariness of human existence.

Nurse's Song is almost somnambulistic, attempting to capture the tenderness of love for children and its accompanying fear and anxiety, while at the same time looking back down the corridor of time and youth.

The Fly capsulizes the whole existence of man with incisive whimsical insight and satiric bite.

The Sick Rose is the dramatic core of the four songs, projecting the corruption of life and the presence of evil in the midst of what is potentially good and even beautiful.

The first performance of the Blake Songs took place in the fall of 1961 in New York City under the auspices of the International Society for Contemporary Music [ISCM], Ralph Shapey conducting the Hartt Chamber Players with Shirley Sudock, soprano.

Copyright 1963 MCA.

Used by permission of the publisher.

La Bocca della Veritá, Music for Oboe and Piano

DATE OF COMPOSITION: 1957.

PUBLISHED: TP (Impero-Verlag). 1964.

PAGES: 23 (piano score), 8 (oboe part).

TIMING: ca. 12'00".

COMMISSION: None.

PREMIÈRE: Josef Marx, oboe and David Tudor, piano; Philadelphia, PA; 21 January 1960.

DEDICATION: for Josef Marx.

RECORDINGS: (1) James Ostryniec, oboe and Charles Wuorinen, piano, CRI 432; (2) Ronald Roseman, oboe and Gilbert Kalish, piano, Ars Nova/Ars Antigua, AN 1008.

NOTES BY THE COMPOSER:

I wrote *La Bocca della Verità* in 1958 for Josef Marx, the oboist. The first performances were given by him and David Tudor, the pianist, in Philadelphia on January 21, 1960, and in New York on February 12, 1960.

La Bocca della Verità is a fantasy in which the oboe and piano confront each other on different levels of affirmation and contradiction. The shape of the music is the eventual result of the projection of successive phrases of varying lengths and proportions. It is up to the performers to decide whether a phrase is a continuation of, or a reaction to the preceding phrase.

The title was given the work after it was written. I wanted to characterize the music in terms other than formal or technical. One of the legends connected with the title is that in Neolithic times a tribal seer or priest stood behind a huge, open-mouthed stone mask and prophesied or delivered oracular sayings. Paraphrasing Loren Eiseley's remark, "Man is an oracular animal," the oboe has always been, for me, an "oracular" instrument.

Used by permission of George Rochberg.

NOTES BY THE COMPOSER:

If any principle of structure was observed at the time I wrote *La Bocca della Verità*, it would have to be described in psychological terms, *i.e.*, each phrase stimulates a response which confirms or contradicts the gesture of the activating phrase.

Used by permission of George Rochberg.

PREFACE BY THE COMPOSER:

The first performance of this work was given by Josef Marx, oboist and David Tudor, pianist in Philadelphia on January 21, 1960. The same performers gave it in New York February 12, 1960. The title was given the work after it was written in an attempt to characterize it in terms other than formal or technical and therefore in no way suggests a program; although the composer is well aware that, having given the work such a title, he has invited the danger of all sorts of speculation as to the "meaning" of the music. One of the legends connected with the title is that in Neolithic times a tribal seer or priest stood behind a huge stone mask with an open mouth and prophesied or delivered oracular sayings.

Copyright 1964 Theodore Presser Company.

Used by permission of the publisher.

La Bocca della Verità, Music for Violin and Piano

DATE OF COMPOSITION: 1965.

PUBLISHED: TP (Impero-Verlag). 1965.

PAGES: 23 (piano score), 8 (violin part).

TIMING: ca. 12'00".

COMMISSION: None.

PREMIÈRE: Lewis Kaplan, violin and Gilbert Kalish, piano; New York City; n.d.

DEDICATION: None.

RECORDING: N/A.

PREFACE BY THE COMPOSER:

This transcription for violin and piano was made by the composer in 1965. The first performance of this work was given by Josef Marx, oboist and David Tudor, pianist in Philadelphia on January 21, 1960. The title was given the work after it was written in an attempt to characterize it in terms other than formal or technical and therefore in no way suggests a program; although the composer is well aware that, having given the work such a title, he has invited the danger of all sorts of speculation as to the "meaning" of the music. One of the legends connected with the title is that in Neolithic times a tribal seer or priest stood behind a huge stone mask with an open mouth and prophesied or delivered oracular sayings.

Copyright 1965 Theodore Presser Company.

Used by permission of the publisher.

Book of Contrapuntal Pieces for Keyboard Instruments

1. Invention: Con spirito [2 parts]

DATE OF COMPOSITION: 29 April 1940.

2. Capriccio: Allegro ma non troppo [3 parts]

DATE OF COMPOSITION: 15 January–27 February 1940.

3. Fugue: Molto andante espressivo [3 parts]

DATE OF COMPOSITION: Fall 1940.

4. Prelude and Fughetta No. 1 [3 parts]

DATE OF COMPOSITION: P: 28 August 1946; F: 16 September 1946.

5. Prelude and Fughetta No. 2 [3 parts]

DATE OF COMPOSITION: P: 17 September 1946; F: 29 August 1946.

6. Four Inventions

I. Non troppo allegro [2 parts]

DATE OF COMPOSITION: 1946.

II. Non troppo allegro [2 parts]

DATE OF COMPOSITION: 1946.

III. Brisk [2 parts]

DATE OF COMPOSITION: n.d.

IV. Brisk [2 parts]

DATE OF COMPOSITION: 1946.

7. Canon in Song Form: Slow and Tranquil [3 parts]

DATE OF COMPOSITION: 1946.

8. Fugue: Largamente; Serioso ed espressivo [3 parts]

DATE OF COMPOSITION: March 1946.

9. Ten Two-Part Canons

DATE OF COMPOSITION: 1946.

I. Moderato, cantabile

II. Con moto ed espressivo

III. Allegretto grazioso

IV. Adagio ma non troppo

V. Andante

VI. Broadly

VII. Moderato con spirito

VIII. Adagio sostenuto

IX. Allegro con moto (after Beethoven)

X. Molto espressivo

10. Canon on a Ground Bass by Purcell [3 parts]

DATE OF COMPOSITION: 1946.

11.Four-partCanon:Grave

DATE OF COMPOSITION: 21 March 1946.

12.Seven[Four-part]ChoralesTreatedCanonically

I. Ach wie nichtig, ach wie fluchtig [Tune in Bass]

DATE OF COMPOSITION: 22 June 1946.

II. Jesus Christe, Unser Heiland [Tune in Tenor]

DATE OF COMPOSITION: 22 June 1946.

III. Strat mich nicht in deinem Zor [Tune in Alto]

DATE OF COMPOSITION: 22 June 1946.

IV. Wie bist du, Seele? [Tune in Tenor]

DATE OF COMPOSITION: 24 June 1946.

V. Nun sich der Tag (with contrary motion canon) [Tune in Tenor]

DATE OF COMPOSTION: June 1946.

VI. Kommt Seelen dieser Tag: Allegretto

DATE OF COMPOSITION: 1946.

VII. In Dulce Jubilo [Tune in Bass]

DATE OF COMPOSITION: 23 June 1946.

13.FiveTwo-partCanonsinContraryMotion

DATE OF COMPOSITION: 1946.

I. Allegro vivace

II. No. 1 in Double Counterpoint

III. Alla marcia

IV. Allegro vivace

V. No. 4 in Double Counterpoint

14. Eight-part Infinite Canon on a Subject of J.S. Bach: Presto

DATE OF COMPOSITION: 1946.

15. Fugue: Adagio espressivo [3 parts]

DATE OF COMPOSITION: March 1946.

16. Double Fugue for Two Pianos: Allegro moderato ed energico [4 parts]

DATE OF COMPOSITION: 1946.

17. Fugue for Two Pianos: Allegro ma non troppo e risoluto [4 parts]

DATE OF COMPOSITION: March 1946.

18. Eight Three-part Canons for Organ

I. Unison (with free bass voice): Adagio

DATE OF COMPOSITION: 30 June 1946.

II. At the Second (with free bass voice): Molto adagio

DATE OF COMPOSTION: 30 June 1946.

III. At the Third (with free bass voice): Allegretto

DATE OF COMPOSITION: 30 June 1946.

IV. At the Fourth (with free bass voice): Allegro giocoso

DATE OF COMPOSITION: 31 June 1946.

V. At the Fifth (with free bass voice): Adagio

DATE OF COMPOSITION: 31 June 1946.

VI. At the Sixth (with free bass voice): Allegro moderato

DATE OF COMPOSITION: 01 August 1946.

VII. At the Seventh (with two voices in bass and alto): Adagio espressivo

DATE OF COMPOSITION: 02 August 1946.

VIII. At the Octave (with free bass voice): Allegro ma non troppo

DATE OF COMPOSITION: 02 August 1946.

19. Fugue: Allegro ma non troppo

DATE OF COMPOSITION: 1948–1949.

20. Fugue for One Piano, Four-hands: Adagio religioso, serioso

DATE OF COMPOSITION: 1977.

DATE OF COMPOSITION OF VARIOUS PIECES: 1940–1979.

COLLECTION OF PIECES COMPILED: 15 January–04 February 1979.

PUBLISHED: TP. MS. 1979.

PAGES: 103.

COMMISSION: None.

PREMIÈRE: N/A.

DEDICATION: to the memory of Rose Horowitz.

RECORDING: N/A.

PREFACE BY THE COMPOSER:

All but one of the pieces in this book were written in the fourties. Only the *Fugue*, transcribed for one piano, four-hands, from the *Adagio* movement of my *Fourth String Quartet* is a recent composition (1977).

While all the pieces, with the exception of the *Eight Canons for Organ*, are intended to be played on the piano, even the *Canons for Organ* may be played at one piano by two players using three hands. (The same is true in the case of the *Canon on a Ground Bass by Purcell*.) Possibly, some of the two and three part pieces for solo piano could be rendered on the harpsichord if one is available and the taste of the player leads him to prefer the older instrument to the more modern piano.

The reason for gathering these studies in the art of counterpoint embracing the canon, invertible counterpoint and the fugue is not complicated; I wanted to make available in one volume the bulk of my early efforts in this ancient and demanding craft so that (1) they could be performed by amateur or professional musicians for their own delectation (whether in private or in public); and (2) they could be used as stimulation and encouragement to my own students and other young, aspiring composers.

This volume, written out between January 15 and February 4, 1979, is dedicated to the memory of Rose Horowitz–a selfless, remarkable woman who by her help and encouragement in my early years as a student in New York City before the Second World War taught me the living importance and beauty of generosity of heart and spirit.

Copyright 1979 Theodore Presser Company.

Used by permission of the publisher.

Book of Songs for Voice and Piano

1. There was an Aged King

DATE OF COMPOSITION: 11 December 1937, Revised 27 April 1969.

2. With Rue My Heart Is Laden

DATE OF COMPOSITION: 22 June 1938, Revised 16 May 1969.

3. Warum sind denn die Rosen so blass?

DATE OF COMPOSITION: 10 July 1938, Revised 21 April 1969.

4. When I am Dead, My Dearest

DATE OF COMPOSITION: 16 October 1938, Revised 21 April 1969.

5. Minnelied

DATE OF COMPOSITION: 23 November 1939, Revised 19 April 1969.

6. Du bist wie eine Blume

DATE OF COMPOSITION: 10 September 1940.

7. Dirge

DATE OF COMPOSITION: 18 June 1941, Revised 24 May 1969.

8. There Be None of Beauty's Daughters [A]

DATE OF COMPOSITION: 17 July 1941, Revised 24 April 1969.

9. Oh, My Love's Like a Red, Red Rose

DATE OF COMPOSITION: 17–18 August 1945, Revised 19 May 1969.

10. Lullaby (Vocalise)

DATE OF COMPOSITION: First version, piano sketch October 1944, Second version 23 August 1945, Revised 22 May 1969.

11. February Spring

DATE OF COMPOSITION: February 1946.

12. Ophelia's Song

DATE OF COMPOSITION: 04 April 1946, Revised 29 April 1969.

13. Night Song at Amalfi

DATE OF COMPOSITION: 08 April 1946, Revised 29 April 1969.

14. Song of Shadows

DATE OF COMPOSITION: 09 April 1946, Revised 04 May 1969.

15. No Fall of Tears

DATE OF COMPOSITION: 22 April 1946, Revised 17 May 1969.

16. Song of Day

DATE OF COMPOSITION: 24 April 1946, Revised 28 April 1969.

Numbers 17–20 from *Four Songs of Solomon*:

17. Rise Up, My Love

DATE OF COMPOSITION: Summer or Fall, 1946.

18. Come, My Beloved

DATE OF COMPOSITION: Summer or Fall, 1946.

19. Set Me as a Seal

DATE OF COMPOSITION: Summer or Fall, 1946.

20. Behold, Thou Art Fair

DATE OF COMPOSITION: August 1946.

21. Du meine heilige Einsamkeit [A]

DATE OF COMPOSITION : 14 August 1946, Revised 27 April 1969.

22. Lira-la-la

DATE OF COMPOSITION: 22 October 1948.

23. Who Has Seen the Wind?

DATE OF COMPOSITION: 1947.

24. Sweetest Love

DATE OF COMPOSITION: First version 02 May 1969.

25. Bright Cap and Streamers

DATE OF COMPOSITION: 16 September 1947, Revised 01 May 1969.

26. The Blind Man at the Fair

DATE OF COMPOSITION: First version ca. 1937, Second version 10 October 1947, Revised 20 May 1969.

27. Du meine heilige Einsamkeit [B]

DATE OF COMPOSITION: 25 September 1947.

28. There Be None of Beauty's Daughters [B]

DATE OF COMPOSITION: 05 December 1949.

29. Piping Down the Valley's Wild

DATE OF COMPOSITION: 13 February 1951, Revised 24 May 1969.

30. Ecce Puer

DATE OF COMPOSITION: First version 21 December 1949, Second version 26 August 1951, Revised 25 May 1969.

Numbers 31–32 from *Blake Songs*:

31. Ah! Sunflower

DATE OF COMPOSITION: First version 1957, Second version 1962, Transcribed 28 May 1969.

32. Nurse's Song

DATE OF COMPOSITION: First version 1957, Second version 1962, Transcribed 30 May 1969.

Numbers 33–34 from *Tableaux*:

33. Night Piece

DATE OF COMPOSITION: August–September 1968, Transcribed 01 June 1969.

34. Ballade

DATE OF COMPOSITION: August–September 1968, Transcribed 31 May 1969.

Number 35 originally from *Blake Songs*:

35. Tyger! Tyger!

DATE OF COMPOSITION: First version 22 June–19 July 1957, Second version 23 June–02 July 1969.

DATE OF COMPOSITION OF VARIOUS PIECES: 1937–1969.

COLLECTION OF PIECES COMPILED: April–July 1969.

PUBLISHED: TP. MS. 1969.

PAGES: 164.

COMMISSION: None.

PREMIÈRE: N/A.

DEDICATION: None.

RECORDING: N/A.

Cantes Flamencos for High Baritone

I. *Ven aca, mujer del mundo*

II. *¡Ay, Deblica Bari!*

III. *Dale Limosna, mujer*

DATE OF COMPOSITION: July–September 1969.

UNPUBLISHED: TP. MS. n.d.

TIMING: N/A.

PAGES: ca. 27.

COMMISSION: None.

PREMIÈRE: N/A.

DEDICATION: None.

RECORDINGS: N/A.

PREFACE BY THE COMPOSER:

Cante flamenco is a style of singing. To the best of my knowledge it is not composed as we understand "composition" in the formal sense. Yet when one hears authentic *flamenco* singing one soon comes to realize that it is much more than a passionately exotic style of folk expression or a very special attitude toward and method of vocal production. It is also a unique way of dealing with certain types of melodic motives and shapes; of working around and through melodic motives and tropes; of developing the vocal line through rich embellishments and great melismatic unfoldings which ride on the open vowels of the Spanish language.

Cante flamenco is invariably intense, high-pitched emotionally and seems to emerge at the very threshold of human pain or ecstasy. There is no preparation for it. It simply bursts forth.

I am well aware that it is virtually impossible for someone not brought up in a tradition as unique as *cante flamenco* to compose in it. I have not composed in it but from it, basing these songs on the style as I have heard it and understand it. I hope I have not gone too far afield and have even captured, by some minor miracle, its accent and passion.

While most flamenco singing is done with guitar accompaniment, some–as I learned from the *Antologia del Cante Flamenco*, a series of recordings issued by *Hispavox, S.A., Madrid*–is performed unaccompanied. This is the style I have chosen to follow–to allow myself maximum freedom in pursuit of a monodic ideal.

The first and second songs are free transcriptions of two songs from the group which the editors of the *Antologia* called *Cantes sin Guitarra*. I have tried to capture on paper the essence and the spirit of both the style of singing and the shape of the phrases. *Dale Limosna, mujer* the third song (composed first), is my own work.

There are two general points about performance: (1) The *flamenco* singers I have heard, live and recorded, always sing in the throat, using the mask for the most intense moments. They tend to push the voice very hard at the top of their emotional range, sometimes developing a grating harshness which matches the passion of their utterance. They have a way of covering the voice which gives it a special poignance, a plangent penetration. It is their way of singing–wholly appropriate to what they are singing about. Since it is not likely singers brought up and trained in the formal attitudes of either lied or opera can enter into the flamenco singer's world readily, I would like to recommend that those who do attempt to sing these songs use their voices as freely as possible, moving from chest to throat to mask like the best "pop" singers are able to do. Also where the tessitura puts too much of a strain on the vocal cords, switch to falsetto, *i.e.*, head tones unsupported by either chest or throat. This may require practice to be sure but will serve the style of hese songs better than straining the throat.

(2) It is possible to amplify the effect of these songs by singing into an open grand piano (preferably lid off) while another person depresses the damper pedal (*tre corde*). The especially intense notes of the singer will set the matching strings vibrating sympathetically and the damper pedal will catch them and gather them up, providing a kind of reverberating wash of sound. The singer and pianist may wish to "phrase" these reverberations by releasing the pedal at preselected points, etc. The use of the piano in the manner described is, of course, optional.

Used by permission of George Rochberg.

Cantio Sacra for Chamber Orchestra

A transcription of *Warum betrubst du dich, mein Herz* by Samuel Scheidt.

I. *Versus. Choralis in Cantu.*

II. *Versus. Choralis in Cantu.*

III. *Versus. Choralis in Tenore.*

IV. *Versus. Choralis in Cantu.*

V. *Versus. Choralis in Cantu.*

VI. *Versus. Bicinium contrapuncto duplici.*

VII. *Choralis in Cantu.*

VIII. *Versus. Choralis in Tenore.*

IX. *Versus. Choralis in Basso.*

X. *Versus. Choralis in Basso.*

XI. *Versus. Choralis in Cantu.*

XII. *Versus. Choralis in Cantu Colorato.*

DATE OF COMPOSITION: 06–19 April 1953.

UNPUBLISHED: MS. 1954.

PAGES: 38.

TIMING: ca. 12'00".

COMMISSION: None.

PREMIÈRE: New School of Music Orchestra, Arthur Cohn conducting; ca. 1955–1956.

DEDICATION: to Alexander Ringer.

RECORDING: N/A.

INSTRUMENTATION: 2 Ob (EH), 2 Tpt (C), Tbn, Str.

PREFACE BY THE COMPOSER:

This transcription is designed primarily for chamber orchestra. However, it may be performed without detriment to the music or the integrity of the transcription by a larger-than-chamber-size string section, even one approaching proportions of the symphony orchestra.

The tempo of each section, marked *Versus* is left to the discretion of the conductor. However, one suggestion is offered: that in those sections which are taken slowly *(I, II, V, VI, VIII, & IX)* the quarter note be equal to about 72, metronome mark; in those taken more quickly *(III, IV, VII, X, XI, & XII)* the quarter be equal to the eighth note of slower sections (or about 100 to 132). In this way the conductor will find his way to the most suitable tempo for each *Versus*.

Dynamic marks (p, f, etc.), *crescendi*, and *decrescendi* are suggestions and not to be taken literally.

In general the performance of this music should be straight-forward without the usual blandishments of individual "interpretation." However, there is no question that a *ritard* is called for the last half or the penultimate measure, although care should be taken to keep within just proportions. This set of chorale variations (originally for organ) may be found in the *Tabulatura Nova* of Samuel Scheidt, Volume I.

Copyright 1954 George Rochberg.

Used by permission of George Rochberg.

Caprice Variations for Unaccompanied Violin

1. Allegro energico
2. Presto
3. Allegro molto e con fuoco
4. Poco allegro ma quasi recitando
5. Poco agitato ma con molto rubato
6. Poco allegretto ma con rubato
7. Presto, after Beethoven, *Op. 74, Scherzo*
8. Languido, after Schubert, *Waltz, Op. 9, No. 22*
9. Non troppo presto, after Brahms, *Op. 35, Bk I, No. 2*
10. Vivace, after Brahms, *Op. 35, Bk. I, No. 3*
11. Andante, after Brahms, *Op. 35, Bk. I, No. 11*
12. Andante con moto, after Brahms, *Op. 35, Bk. I, No. 12*
13. Feroce, energico, after Brahms, *Op. 35, Bk. II, No. 10*
14. Alla guitarra; allegretto con molto rubato
15. Con grazia; un poco agitato
16. Andante amoroso
17. Poco adagio
18. Allegro fantastico
19. Vivace, Exact rhythm throughout
20. Quasi cadenza; andante con molto espressivo
21. Allegro con brio, after Beethoven, *Symphony No. 7, Finale*
22. Molto espressivo e cantando
23. Andante grazioso e tranquillo
24. Allegretto
25. Scherzo
26. Con brio
27. Aria
28. Molto agitato
29. Lento ma non troppo
30. Poco allegretto e leggiero

31. Molto adagio

32. Allegro assai; burlesco

33. Moderato; con amore

34. Molto adagio

35. Allegro molto; fantastico

36. Largo; sereno

37. Barcarolle

38. Can-can tempo: presto

39. Elegiac; fantastico

40. Robust: do not rush

41. Allegro molto, after Webern, *Passacaglia, Op. 1*

42. Nocturnal; slow

43. Andantino

44. Scherzo, after Mahler, *Symphony No. 5, Scherzo*

45. Presto

46. Bravura; sempre recitando; in the "grand manner"

47. Arabesque; fantastico

48. Moderately fast: fantastico

49. Feroce

50. Fantasy

51. Quasi Presto; robusto, Paganini's Theme, *Caprice XXIV, Book 2*

DATE OF COMPOSITION: January–February 1970.

PUBLISHED: Galaxy. 1973.

TIMING: ca. 62'00".

PAGES: 52.

COMMISSION: None.

PREMIÈRE: Lewis Kaplan, violin; WBAI "Free Music Store" live broadcast; New York City; 02 April 1970.

DEDICATION: for Daniel Kobialka.

RECORDINGS: (1) Gidon Kremer, violin, DG 415484; (2) Zvi Zeitlin, violin, MHS 3719 (1977).

NOTES BY THE COMPOSER:

It is understood that both the form and performance style of Paganini's theme, the concluding music of the *Caprice Variations*, have been altered somewhat in order to provide a fitting envoi for this work.

Considering the number of *Caprice-Variations* which comprise this work, the performer, if he so chooses, may want to omit some of the repeats in order to reduce the duration of performance time to manageable length, especially when the entire work is being performed. It is suggested, however, that the performer observe all or most repeats in the faster *Variations* in order to establish clearly their style and gestural character. In slower *Variations* let artistic discretion be the judge of which repeats to drop.

If the player chooses not to perform the entire set, he is at liberty to select those sections which will add up to a satisfying whole in musical terms and still represent the intentions of the work. In a shortened performance version, it is strongly urged, though, that the performer include as many of *Variations 5, 18, 19, 33, 34, 35, 39, 41, 42, 45, 47, 48, 49,* and *50* as possible, so as to preserve a balance in the stylistic spread which is a fundamental premise of this work.

NOTES BY THE COMPOSER:

This set of *Fifty Variations* for solo violin was written in early 1970 and given its first performance (in entirety) in New York on April 2, 1970. These *Variations*–some of them only seconds long–cover a wide range of "styles" (Baroque to twentieth century) and "languages" (tonal to atonal).

Since a complete performance of the *Variations* takes well over an hour, for this evening's performance Jerry Wigler and I have made a selection of approximately half the number of the complete set. Ordinarily, cutting down on the size of a complete work is justifiably frowned upon; but in this case, given the exigencies of performance time, I have no objections, particularly since the spirit and attitude of the work are in no way lost and the representation of styles and languages is maintained.

The theme of the work is the famous *Caprice* by Paganini on which any number of sets of variations have been composed–notably the two books Brahms did for piano solo and the Rachmaninoff *Rhapsody for Piano and Orchestra*.

The impetus for composing this work came from a request from a young violinist which happened to coincide in time with my interest in the variation theme in general and the Brahms double set in particular. I have paid homage to Brahms by including some of his *Variations* in transcription form; where it seemed musically possible I have also paid homage to Beethoven, Schubert, Bartók, Webern, Stravinsky–all great masters of the art of variation–by quoting them as well as commenting on them.

Used by permission of George Rochberg.

Carnival Music, Suite for Piano Solo

I. Fanfares and March

II. Blues

III. Largo doloroso

IV. Sfumato

V. Toccata-Rag

DATE OF COMPOSITION: 1971.

PUBLISHED: TP. 1975.

PAGES: 39.

TIMING: 21'35".

WRITTEN FOR: Jerome Lowenthal.

PREMIÈRE: Jerome Lowenthal, piano; Academy of Music, Philadephia, PA; 04 May 1972.

DEDICATION: to Jerome Lowenthal.

RECORDINGS: (1) Alan Mandel, piano, Grenadilla 1019 (1977); (2) Alan Mandel, piano, Grenadilla GSC-1069 (1977).

NOTES BY THE COMPOSER:

The three works recorded here [*Carnival Music, Nach Bach,* and *Black Sounds*] are of such a diverse nature that I can point to no common principle or attitude that connects them–unless it be my strong penchant for producing works which range over the spectrum of everything that interests me in music and which I am capable of bringing to artistic realization. In contradistinction to the obsession with the single-gesture which seems to be a primary motivation for some, I prefer the freer, more open psychology of the multiple-gesture. In this way, individual sections or movements of a work or entire works themselves sometimes act as catalysts for opposite tendencies or directions to emerge–and even complement each other. Tension for me exists precisely in juxtaposing opposites; and resolution is achieved by bringing these opposites into a balance of complementarity.

While it is not necessary to make too much of nature's principles of positive/negative, male/female, yin/yang, etc., it is worth mentioning briefly that wholeness derives not so much from the logic of inner consistency as from establishing a balanced relationship and interplay between diverse forces and functions.

Perhaps the clearest example contained in this recording of the ideas I have just sketched is the five-movement *Carnival Music* which I wrote for the pianist, Jerome Lowenthal, in 1970. Each of the individual movements titled (1) *Fanfares and March,* (2) *Blues,* (3) *Sfumato,* (4) *Largo doloroso,* and (5) *Toccata-Rag,* basically pursues its own characteristic tendencies with only brief references in V to materials first presented in I and II. However, the work as a whole "hangs together" largely through contrasting intensities of opposities: different musics which refer either to "popular" sources (march, blues, ragtime) or to more "serious" musical traditions; musics which are by turn diatonic and/or chromatic or mixtures of both. *Largo doloroso* is the only consistently chromatic piece in the work and bears a distant relation to the old baroque "aria" or "air."

The *sfumato* movement ("sfumato," a painting term, referring to figures emerging from veiled or smoky backgrounds) combines both the chromatic and the diatonic by first establishing a chromatic accompaniment (or background) of veiled, repetitive shapes against which, as the piece goes on, appear transformed references to Brahms and Bach keyboard pieces. The form of this movement is the result of the on-again, off-again appearance of these altered quotes interwoven into the material of the background.

I chose the over-all title *Carnival Music* to suggest the side-by-side presence in both living reality and cultural reality of the "lighter" and the "heavier," the "popular" and the "serious." It is, oddly enough, a sign of the times that such a simultaneity has to be commented on at all when we consider that both sets of conditions co-existed quite compatibly and unselfconciously in the music of the eighteenth and nineteenth centuries–even into the early twentieth century. Of course, carnivals of the real sort–which I loved in my childhood for their color, life and magic, later revealed their sleazy side; and so, with no intent to deprecate, I wrote into the work a "blues" movement. All "blues"–usually improvised; rarely "composed"–belong to an old and honorable theme and variations tradition.

Perhaps the contradiction for me exists in a real love for the very source of jazz improvisation combined with unpleasant memories of depressing circumstances in which I played this music during my teens–taverns, "roadside rests," joints, etc. The *Toccata-Rag* movement contains many-sided references to a mixed keyboard tradition which includes, among other things, a piano-roll parody of *Farmer Grey* music of children's film cartoons fame. One of the reviewers of the first performance of *Carnival Music* suggested it was an "autobiographical work." Perhaps he was right–even though a composer should be careful how much he concedes to a reviewer.

Harrington Park, NJ 07640
Used by permission of Grenadilla Productions.

Chamber Symphony for Nine Instruments

I. Allegro tempo giusto

II. Adagio

III. Marcia

IV. Allegro assai

DATE OF COMPOSITION: 1953.

PUBLISHED: TP. Parts on Rental. 1978.

PAGES: 52.

TIMING: ca. 18'00".

COMMISSION: None.

PREMIÈRE: Baltimore Chamber Society, Hugo Weisgall conducting; 1955.

DEDICATION: to my dear wife, Gene.

RECORDING: Oberlin Chamber Orchestra, Kenneth Moore conducting, Desto 6444.

INSTRUMENTATION: Ob, Cl, Bsn, Hn, Tpt (C), Tbn, Vln, Vla, Vlc.

NOTES BY THE COMPOSER:

The Chamber Symphony received its first performance in 1955 by the Baltimore Chamber Society conducted by Hugo Weisgall. Its four movements include two classically-oriented sonata-forms which open and close the work; a second movement, *Adagio*, which is largely canonic and a third movement which is a *March*. Instrumentally, the three woodwinds (oboe, clarinet, and bassoon), three brass (horn, trumpet, and trombone) and three strings (violin, viola, and cello) comprise more of a small orchestra than they do a chamber ensemble. Although, from time to time, the "chamber" character clearly takes over. The work is completely thematic. While each movement has its own center of thematic gravity, the center of the work itself, its structural source, so to speak, is a row. Because the beginning of one of the forms of the row evoked a constant undercurrent of association with the *Fratello motif* from Luigi Dallapiccola's *Il Prigionero*, I wove into the fabric of the *Adagio* a quotation from that work. This was the first time I used the device consciously.

Copyright 1975 CMS/Desto Records.

Used by permission of CMS/Desto Records.

NOTES BY THE COMPOSER:

I wrote my *Chamber Symphony for Nine Instruments* in 1953. It received its first performance shortly after it was completed by the Baltimore Chamber Society with Hugo Weisgall conducting.

The *Chamber Symphony* is the first large-scale instrumental work I attempted using a twelve-tone row to organize the melodic/harmonic levels and interrelationships. Beyond this, the music unfolds in each of the four movements as structural gestures which proceed on their own level of activity.

Preoccupied as I am now with various ways of dealing with tonality, it is ironic, if not surprising, to discover that underlying my use of the twelve-tones in the *Chamber Symphony* are strong tonal tendencies.

Used by permission of George Rochberg.

Cheltenham Concerto for Small Orchestra

I. Ricercare–(Strings)

II. Scherzo (A)–(Woodwind Quintet)

Interjection (1)–(Strings)

III. Scherzo (B)–(Strings)

Interjection (2)–(Strings)

IV. Trio–(Brass)

Interjection (3)–(Strings)

V. Scherzo (B)–(Brass, Strings)

Interjection (4)–(Strings)

VI. Scherzo (A)–(woodwind and Brass)

VII. Ricercare (Tutti)

DATE OF COMPOSITION: 1958.

PUBLISHED: TP (Edition Suvini). 1960.

PAGES: 40.

TIMING: ca. 15'00".

COMMISSION: Cheltenham Art Center, Cheltenham [Philadephia], PA.

PREMIÈRE: The Philadelphia Chamber Music Society, Herbert Fiss, conducting; Cheltenham Art Center, Philadelphia, PA; 18 May 1958.

DEDICATION: None.

RECORDING: N/A.

AWARDS: First Prize, Italian International Society for Contemporary Music [ISCM], International Music Competition; 1959.

INSTRUMENTATION: Fl, Ob, Cl, Bsn, Hn, Tpt (C), Tbn, Str.

NOTES BY THE COMPOSER:

This work was composed in the early months of 1958 on a commission from the Cheltenham Art Center, Philadelphia. The first performance took place on May 18, 1958. Although played without pause, its architecture is conceived as a kind of mirror form of seven main sections, as follows:

I. Ricercare–(Strings)

II. Scherzo (A)–(Woodwind Quintet)

III. Scherzo (B)–(Strings)

IV. Trio–(Brass)

V. Scherzo (B)–(Brass, Strings)

VI. Scherzo (A)–(Woodwind and Brass)

VII. Ricercare (Tutti)

The single *Trio* stands for both *Scherzo A* and *Scherzo B*. A minor, though still functionally important part of the architecture of the work is the use of what I call *"Interjections"*. These are brief, independent sections given only to the strings which dramatically interrupt the course of the music. Based on the serial technique, this work represents my personal application of Webern's device of working with simultaneous transpositions. I have also attempted to discover means by which fragmentized intervallic relationships may be linked in ever-growing chains of melody. In this way, although no single instrument ever plays more than motivic fragments, the total is conceived as a constantly evolving melodic line whose ultimate comprehension depends entirely on the most intimate coordination of the brief motifs. Not only have I been concerned to insure the melodic life of my music; the harmonic problem has absorbed me intensely too. Here, as in my efforts to produce melody, I have relied entirely on my acoustical intuitions (my inner ear) as a composer, striving to achieve a particular harmonic quality which flowed from the character of the row. The essential aspects of the over-all timbre of the work are related to the architectural structure while the details of timbre are the result of harmonic-melodic necessity as they occur within the sections themselves.

Used by permission of George Rochberg.

Concerto for Oboe and Orchestra

DATE OF COMPOSITION: 1983.

PUBLISHED: TP. MS. Rental. 1983.

PAGES: 83.

PIANO REDUCTION PUBLISHED: TP. 1985.

PAGES: 28 (piano score), 11 (oboe part).

TIMING: 18'00".

COMMISSION: New York Philharmonic.

PREMIÈRE: Joseph Robinson, oboe and the New York Philharmonic Orchestra, Zubin Mehta conducting; 13–18 December 1984.

DEDICATION: to Joseph Robinson.

RECORDING: Joseph Robinson, oboe and the New York Philharmonic, Zubin Mehta conducting, New World 335.

INSTRUMENTATION: 2 Fl (Pc), 2 Cl, 2 Bsn, 4 Hn, 2 Tpt, 3 Trb, Tba, Timp, Perc. (Xyl, Tamb, TBel, SmBsDr, Deep gong, LgSusCy), Cel, Hp, Str, Solo oboe.

NOTES BY THE COMPOSER:

In this *Concerto*, I have made no effort to exploit the extremes of the oboe because, as I see it, the main reason for writing a piece is to say something, not to concentrate on the purely technical characteristics of an instrument. Except for a few tuttis, the oboe is prominent throughout, although the writing for the solo is not virtuosic in the usual sense; rather, the work demands an expressive virtuosity from the soloist.

To my ear, the oboe has a special voice in its purely expressive, plangent quality, its probing kind of singing. Of all the woodwinds, I think the oboe is the most full of personality. This *Concerto* was designed for Joseph Robinson, and while writing it I had very much in mind his approach to the instrument, which is lyric and involves wonderful phrasing and marvelous tone.

Formally, the *Concerto* is rhapsodic, cast in four parts played without pause. The first and last sections present the essential pool of ideas out of which the expressive aspects of the work derive; however, neither has only one characteristic or quality throughout, because each divides into smaller units of gesture. The first section, a poco andante with two middle parts, is mostly slow music–poetic, lyric, singing– while the word scherzo conveys the character of the second: lively, ironic, with constantly shifting meters. The *Concerto's* third section, a march, is again a kind of ironic music, but for the most part in regular meter. In the second and third parts I have tried to reveal aspects of the oboe that are opposed to the plangent–satiric, comic, slightly acerbic; nevertheless, great seriousness is involved in both.

There are two oboe cadenzas, occurring between the first and second and the third and fourth sections. They are entirely different in character, the first being a kind of expansive arioso, the second taking its cue from the atmosphere of the march. The work's final part, primarily slow and reflective, contains references to ideas from the first section, although none of the material returns in exactly the same way. My feeling is that this music deepens the expressive world of the opening. The final twenty bars are a kind of coda with quiet, delicate tone-clusters, and the piece ends softly, fading away.

I think of my *Oboe Concerto* as being the most poetic of my recent efforts, and I have no hesitation in terming it a romantic work. Although the writing tends to be highly chromatic, there is, overall, a strong sense of tonal direction in line and harmony.

> Copyright 1984 Philharmonic-Symphony Society of New York, Inc.
>
> Used by permission of the New York Philharmonic.
>
> Used by permission of George Rochberg.

Concerto for Violin and Orchestra

PART I:

I. Introduction (pause)

II. Intermezzo (A) (segue to)

III. Fantasia (pause)

PART II:

IV. Intermezzo (B) (pause)

V. Epilogue

DATE OF COMPOSITION: Spring–Summer 1974.

PUBLISHED: TP. MS. Rental. 1975.

PAGES: 199.

PIANO REDUCTION PUBLISHED: TP. 1977.

PAGES: 52 (piano score), 22 (violin part).

TIMING: 40′00″.

COMMISSION: Pittsburgh Symphony Orchestra for Violinist Isaac Stern with assistance from the National Endowment for the Arts and the *Pittsburgh Post-Gazette*.

PREMIÈRE: Isaac Stern, violin with the Pittsburgh Symphony, Donald Johanos conducting; 04, 05, 06 April 1975.

DEDICATION: to the memory of Donald Steinfirst.

RECORDING: Isaac Stern, violin and the Pittsburgh Symphony Orchestra, Andre Previn conducting, CBS M-35149.

INSTRUMENTATION: 3 Fl (Pc), 3 Ob (EH), 3 Cl (BCl), 2 Bsn, CBsn, 4 Hn, 3 Tpt (C), 2 Tbn, BTbn, Tba, Timp, 2 Hp, Cel, Str, Solo Violin.

NOTES BY THE COMPOSER:

The bulk of the writing of my *Violin Concerto* took place in the spring and summer of 1974. It is an elegiac work–even romantic in spirit. From the first ideas that came to me through their eventual realization, I was conscious of one thing: to work out of the tradition of the violin concerto which began with Mozart and continued through Bartók and Schönberg. It was this tradition which established the *Concerto* in symphonic terms so that the orchestra plays an important role, variously supporting the soloist, commenting on what he does, sharing musical ideas with him, asserting its independence from him when the flow of the design demands it. I have adapted this tradition to my own needs and interests.

Basically my *Concerto* is a tonal work with occasional excursions into atonal chromaticism. The predominant key centers of the work are D and B-flat.

The movements of the *Concerto* are as follows:

Part I: I. Introduction (pause)

II. Intermezzo (A) (segue to)

III. Fantasia (pause)

Part II: IV. Intermezzo (B) (pause)

V. Epilogue

Movements *I, III* and *V* share ideas in common although each has its own emotional and structural character. Movements *II* and *IV* are essentially different from each other despite their common designation as *Intermezzi. II* is a kind of *burletta; IV* a kind of *berceuse* (or lullaby) combined with scherzando-like material which bears close relation to some ideas in *II*. A march tune which is treated fully in *IV* is alluded to in *II* but in an incomplete state.

While every movement but *V* has passages for the violin alone which approach the bravura, released attitude of the traditional cadenza, it is only in *IV* that an extended cadenza occurs.

Used by permission of George Rochberg.

The Confidence Man (A Comic Fable), Opera in Two Parts, Based on the Novel by Herman Melville, Libretto by Gene Rochberg

PROLOGUE

ACT I:

SCENE 1:   Main square, Crystal City on the Mississippi

SCENE 2:   Early Morning, April 1

SCENE 3:   Same

SCENE 4:   Same

SCENE 5:   Town Square

SCENE 6:   In front of the Candle Shop

SCENE 7:   Same

ACT II:

SCENE 1:   Inside the Barber Shop

SCENE 2:   Same

SCENE 3:   In front of China Aster's Shop

SCENE 4:   Within a Magic Circle

SCENE 5:   The Candle Shop

SCENE 6:   Town Square

SCENE 7:   Same

EPILOGUE: Town Cemetery, early morning, not long afterwards

DATE OF COMPOSITION: 1980–1982.

PUBLISHED: TP. MS. Rental. 1982.

PAGES: 847.

LIBRETTO PUBLISHED: TP. 1982.

PAGES: 32.

TIMING: ca. 2 hours, 20 minutes.

COMMISSION: Santa Fe Opera.

PREMIÈRE: Santa Fe Opera, William Harwood conductor, Richard Pearlma staging, John Scheffler scenery and costumes, Craig Miller lighting, Peter Anastos choreography, Brent Ellis (The Confidence Man), Neil Rosenshein (China Aster), Sunny Joy Langton (Annabella), Richard Best (Old Plain Talk), Robert Osborne (Old Prudence), Deborah Cook (The Angel of Bright Future), Michael Fiacco (Orchis), Carolyn James (Mrs. Orchis), Joseph Frank (The Barber); 31 July 1982.

DEDICATION: None.

RECORDING: N/A.

INSTRUMENTATION: 3 Fl (Pc), 3 Ob (EH), 3 Cl (BCl), 3 Bsn (CBsn), 4 Hn, 3 Tpt (C), 2 Tbn, BTbn, Tba, Timp, Hp, Perc (Xyl, Glock), Vocal Soloists, Choir.

SYNOPSIS BY THE COMPOSER:

The *Prologue* opens with the sudden and magical appearance of The Confidence Man who immediately begins to work his wiles and confidence games. With each new game he changes his costume, and with each change, another man appears dressed in the clothes he has just discarded. In this fashion three men appear, Avatars of The Confidence Man, to form a *tableau vivant*–a visual metaphor for his multi-faced nature. To make the point that man lives or dies by trust and faith in his fellow man, this "protean charmer" invites the audience to come with him to Crystal City on the Mississippi where the story of China Aster will unfold and prove his thesis.

At the beginning of *Act I*, the townspeople go about their business while a young peddler hawks his wares. The Confidence Man and his Avatars stroll about arousing considerable interest. The Missourian engages The Confidence Man in an acrimonious dialogue and the "great hoaxer" illustrates his point of view by acting out a story with one of his

Avatars. In the next scene, China Aster, a candlemaker, appears with his wife, Annabella. They are a struggling, loving young couple. Orchis, China's friend, who has won a lottery prize, offers China a check for one thousand dollars to improve his business. Annabella refuses to take Orchis seriously and leaves. Orchis then inveigles China into taking the check and giving him a four-year note. When China thinks better of it and tries to retrieve his note, Orchis departs, leaving China distressed and conflicted. China attempts to return the check once more, but Orchis, together with The Confidence Man, encourages him to cash it. China is further enticed by a dream of The Angel of Bright Future who showers him with gold and virtually seduces him into believing that cashing the check will completely change his life. Later, when he tells Annabella, Old Plain Talk, and Old Prudence of his vision and his determination to follow his dream, they ridicule Orchis and dreams of riches. A heated argument ensues which sends the old men off in a huff. Annabella gently tries to warn China against his dream–but to no avail.

Act II occurs a year later and begins in the Barber Shop where Old Prudence is examining a $3.00 bill with a counterfeit bill detector to the amusement and annoyance of the Barber. The Confidence Man enters, followed closely by Old Plain Talk, from whom we learn that China has fallen on exceedingly hard times as a result of the loan, and that Orchis, dramatically changed, has returned to get his money back. Not only is he married, but he has joined a religious sect. The two old men rush out to find China and tell him the bad news, leaving the wily Barber and The Confidence Man to play out still another version of the con-game.

When Orchis and his wife appear at the Candle Shop, they find China and Annabella also drastically changed. Orchis is determined to get his money no matter what and leaves demanding that it be ready for him in three days. China, already despairing, loses all hope after another visitation from The Angel of Bright Future, who, this time, shows her harsh and cruel nature. She blames China for his troubles, castigating him for losing his faith and confidence. Meanwhile the long-awaited Minstrel Show has come to town. At the climax of the minstrel production, China rushes onstage, pursued by angry creditors. The real and unreal dramas collide; China falls to the ground. Annabella accuses the townspeople of bringing about China's death, lashing out at them for their vileness, yet asking for their help and sympathy. Old Plain Talk and Old Prudence each take her by the hand when The Confidence Man directs the men to take down the door of the Candle Shop so that China can be carried home. The procession files out singing a hymn which concludes offstage.

In the *Epilogue* Old Prudence reads China's epitaph. China has attributed his troubles to putting his faith in a "bright view" of life rather than heeding "the sober view," but Old Prudence believes otherwise. According to him, the "root of it all was a friendly loan." The people disperse; last to go are The Confidence Man and his Avatars. Their final words are: "Something yet may follow from this masquerade."

The lights go down. When they come up again, the entire cast is assembled onstage, giving voice to the sentiment that no matter what happens, life can go on only if we place the trust of "perfect confidence" in each other.

Contra Mortem et Tempus for Flute, Clarinet, Violin, and Piano

DATE OF COMPOSITION: 1965.

PUBLISHED: TP. 1967.

PAGES: 38 (no separate parts).

TIMING: ca. 12'00".

COMMISSION: Bowdoin Contemporary Music Festival for the Aeolian Chamber Players.

PREMIÈRE: Aeolian Chamber Players (Lewis Kaplan, violin, Thomas Nyfenger, flute, Lloyd Greenberg, clarinet, Gilbert Kalish, piano); Summer Music Festival, Bowdoin College; 18 August 1965.

DEDICATION: to Lewis Kaplan and the Aeolian Chamber Players.

RECORDING: Aeolian Chamber Players, CRI 231.

INSTRUMENTATION: Fl, Cl, Vln, Pn.

NOTES BY THE COMPOSER:

After the death of my son Paul in 1964, it became crystal clear to me that I could not continue writing so-called "serial" music... It was finished...hollow...meaningless. It also became clearer than ever before that the only justification for claiming one was engaged in the artistic act was to open one's art completely to life and its entire gamut of terrors and joys (real and imagined); and to find, if one could, new ways to transmute these into whatever magic one was capable of. I rediscovered and reaffirmed with an intensity I had never known before the basic impulse which had led me to want to compose music in the first place a long time ago.

With the loss of my son I was overwhelmed by the realization that death–and time which, as we humans reckon it, brings an end to all living things–could only be overcome by life itself; and to me this meant through art, by practicing my art as a living thing (in my marrow bone), free of the posturing cant and foolishness abroad these days which wants to seal art off from life.

Life and art. Human experience and the "iconography of imagination." Chaos refracted through human sensitivities, through the human spirit. I am only too painfully aware of the paradox inherent in the idea that art cannot die. But if there is such a thing as spirit, then human life is surely its expression here on earth; and art is just as surely one of the great doors or one of the tiny apertures (which ever way it appears to us–and it can be both at different times) through which we can pass or peer into the world of the infinite. Hence the title of my work; *Against Death and Time*.

As for the procedures I employed in composing this work, it is much too complex to describe in simple words. Besides it would shed little light, if any, on the musical results. In the most general terms, it is a "collage" or "assemblage" of scraps and bits from the music of other composers (as well as an earlier work of my own) composed for one or more of the same instruments, singly or in combination, performed by the players of the Aeolian Chamber Ensemble for whom the work was intended. All of this odd assortment of restructured "found forms" was put together in two weeks time. The resulting work became the first in a series of compositions of varying intentions and dimensions which include my *Music for the Magic Theater* (1965), *Music for "The Alchemist"* (1966), *Nach Bach* (1966), and *Passions [According to the Twentieth Century]* (1967). At present, I am working on my *Third Symphony*, the most ambitious project in this series (for multiple choruses, soloists, large orchestra) which shares with the other works my urge to bring together in simultaneous/successive combinations everything germane to my musical purpose: not only raw and refracted quotations from the music of other composers (regardless of when they composed it; or how) but also multi-lingual levels of musical speech ranging through history and the present. One of the side affects of this inner adventure is a new-found joy in the infinitude of music and the unending capacity of man to produce convincing and valid musical images and gestures regardless of the time and cultural conditions under which these projections emerge. I have learned that there is no greater provincialism than that which denies the past, that there is no greater danger to the human spirit than to proclaim value only for its narrow slice of contemporaneity.

The only way I can describe the internal sensation of working this way is to compare it to a high-wire act: it is equally liberating and dangerous. But pursuit of real art, like life itself, has nothing to do with the spurious comforts of security, safety and society. If it is going to count at all, it has to take place up there....

Used by permission of George Rochberg.

David, the Psalmist for Tenor Solo and Orchestra

I. *Shema Yisroel* (Prelude)

II. Psalm 6 (*Lamnatzeach binginos al hashminis mizmor l'dovid*)

III. Interlude

IV. Psalm 29 (*Mizmor l'dovid*)

V. Interlude

VI. Psalm 57 (*Lamnatzeach al tasches l'dovid michtom b'vorcho mipne shoul bam'oro*)

VII. *Shema Yisroel* (Postlude)

DATE OF COMPOSITION: 1954, Revised February 1967.

PUBLISHED: TP. MS. Rental. 1967.

PAGES: 85.

PIANO REDUCTION PUBLISHED: MS. Copyright 1954 George Rochberg.

PAGES: 47.

TIMING: ca. 25'00".

COMMISSION: None.

PREMIÈRE: University of Pennsylvania Orchestra, Melvin Strauss conducting; University of Pennsylvania, Philadelphia, PA; 08 December 1966.

DEDICATION: None.

RECORDING: N/A.

INSTRUMENTATION: Pc, 2 Fl, 2 Ob, EH, 2 Cl, BCl, 2 Bsn, CBsn, 4 Hn, 3 Tpt (C), 3 Tbn, Tba, Timp, Perc (Cy, TT, SnDr, BsDr), Str, Tenor Solo.

Dialogues for Clarinet and Piano

I. ♪= 168

II. ♪= 144–152

III. ♩ = ca. 66

IV. Burlesca

DATE OF COMPOSITION: 1957–1958.

PUBLISHED: TP. 1959.

PAGES: 30 (piano score), 12 (A clarinet part), 12 (B-flat clarinet part).

TIMING: ca. 17'00".

COMMISSION: Serge Koussevitsky Foundation in the Library of Congress.

PREMIÈRE: Eric Simon, clarinet and Alicia Schacter, piano; Carl Fischer Concert Hall, New York City; 29 April 1958.

DEDICATION: to the memory of Serge and Natalie Koussevitsky.

RECORDING: John Russo, clarinet and Lydia Russo, piano, Capra 1204.

NOTES BY THE COMPOSER:

I composed my *Dialogues for Clarinet and Piano* in 1957 on commission from the Koussevitsky Foundation. During the mid-fifties, I was particularly intent on mastering the gestural and harmonic possibilities which seemed to me inherent in twelve-tone chromaticism. In that period, each successive work offered a fresh opportunity to explore further things I had already made my own, to try things I hadn't tried yet, to work out new or different solutions to what was still the essential problem: to compose convincing music in a completely systematized chromatic palette without sacrificing clarity of structure, rhythmic vitality, or clear-cut melodic and motivic ideas. The *Dialogues* emerged as perhaps the loosest, most flexible, gesturally speaking work of that time.

Each of the four movements develops its own sharply defined characteristics, while at the same time preserving binding consistencies which apply to melodic, motivic, and harmonic levels and maintaining an essential "duo" (or equal partner) relationship between the clarinet and piano. The first movement, basically whimsical in spirit, constantly fluctuates around a fast beat *via rubato*. The second movement drives hard and steadily; relaxes in its *trio* into rubato again, then drives relentlessly to the end. There is no better way to describe the third movement than to call it "romantic," if indeed the word can be applied to any music whose expressive qualities are deeply subjective, reflective, warm, and lyric regardless of the language through which that music speaks. In the last movement, the whimsy and energy of the first two movements return, but in a new way, and the work ends on a clear note of finality.

The first performance of *Dialogues* was given in New York in 1958 by the clarinetist, Eric Simon.

Used by permission of George Rochberg.

Duo for Oboe and Bassoon

I. Allegro giocoso

II. Andante tranquillo ed un poco rubato

III. Marziale

IV. Allegro con umore

DATE OF COMPOSITION: 1946, Revised 1979 for publication.

PUBLISHED: TP. 1980.

PAGES: 20 (no separate parts).

TIMING: ca. 11'00".

COMMISSION: None.

PREMIÈRE: N/A.

DEDICATION: to my friend, Sol Schoenbach.

RECORDING: N/A.

Duo Concertante for Violin and Cello

DATE OF COMPOSITION: 1955, Revised 1959 for publication.

PUBLISHED: TP. 1960.

PAGES: 16 (no separate parts).

TIMING: 12'30".

COMMISSION: None.

PREMIÈRE: Irwin Eisenberg, violin and Charles Brennand, cello; private performance, Philadelphia, PA; 1956.

DEDICATION: in memory of Richard Bernheimer.

RECORDINGS: (1) Mark Sokol, violin and Norman Fischer, cello, CRI 337; (2) Daniel Kobialka, violin, and Jan Kobialka, cello, Advance Records, S-6.

NOTES BY THE COMPOSER:

Duo Concertante is composed in a series of continuous gestures which seemingly oppose and contradict each other; its form is essentially in two parts with a clearly stated recapitulation in the second part. If the *First Quartet* can be described as a romantic work, then the *Duo* should be described as an expressionistic one.

Used by permission of George Rochberg.

NOTES BY THE COMPOSER:

The *Duo Concertante* was written in 1955 and later given its first performance privately in Philadelphia by Irving Eisenberg and the late Charles Brennand, both, at the time, members of the Philadelphia Orchestra and the Philadelphia String Quartet. During this period of the middle fifties I was completely preoccupied with unlocking the musical possibilities of the hexachord (a specific structure inherent in the twelve-tone method) in a thoroughly expressive fashion. The result was a passionately emotional work–one I look back on not without a certain fondness. It is composed in a series of continuous gestures which seemingly oppose and contradict each other, yet which complement each other as true opposites tend to do. Its form is essentially in two parts with a clearly stated recapitulation in the second part.

Used by permission of George Rochberg.

NOTES BY THE COMPOSER:

The *Duo Concertante for Violin and Cello* was composed in 1955 and revised for publication in 1959. Its first performance took place in Philadelphia in 1956.

Formally the work is made up of two parts. Part one presents a variety of ideas, gestures and harmonic explorations of the hexachords on which the work is based. Part two either reiterates or varies the material of part one.

In this *Duo*, I hoped for an observable, perceptual simplicity of utterance. This is why the phrases of this work often seem to be entities unto themselves, rarely extended through a process of development, also why sudden shifts in character, direction, and mood work without the usual interference.

If there was one obsession I had in the writing of the work, it was to provide the players a vehicle for true dialogue. I wanted them to be able to "talk" to each other as equals; and, if occasion warranted, even to "talk back." I wanted also to make the instruments to sound as rich as possible. In the case of strings their capacity for lyricism of varying degrees of intensity, gradation of dynamics, and volume, and their very considerable range of every variety of attack also engaged my interest. Most important of all, however, was my feeling that I was writing ensemble music. At the same time there was also the self-imposed problem of creating an impression of a free unfolding, yet one which would reveal, on closer inspection, a formal control which precluded any arbitrary action. In this sense, then, the work is a *fantasia*, which could be defined as a "composed improvisation."

Used by permission of George Rochberg.

Electrikaleidoscope for Amplified Flute, Clarinet, Violin, Cello, Piano, and Electric Piano

I. Double Canon Overture

II. Blues Rock (A)

III. Adagio–March–Adagio

IV. Blues Rock (B)

V. Tag Finale

DATE OF COMPOSITION: August 1972, Revised December 1972.

PUBLISHED: TP. MS. Rental. 1977.

PAGES: 96.

TIMING: ca. 25'00"

COMMISSION: Aeolian Chamber Players.

PREMIÈRE: Aeolian Chamber Players (Lewis Kaplan, violin, Jerry Grossman, cello, Erich Graf, flute, Richard Wasley, clarinet, Walter Ponce, piano); Town Hall, New York City; 19 December 1972.

DEDICATION: for the Aeolian Chamber Players; the following dedication is included in the score after the third movement: to the memory of the eleven Israeli athletes who fell victim to the world's madness September 5–6, 1972 at the Olympic Games in Munich, Germany.

RECORDING: The Twentieth Century Consort, Smithsonian collection (NO22A) #1022, CONSORT I.

INSTRUMENTATION: Amplified Fl, Cl, Vln, Vlc, Pn, and ElPn.

Eleven Songs for Mezzo-Soprano and Piano

I. Sunrise, a Morning Sound

II. We Are Like the Mayflies

III. I am Baffled by This Wall

IV. Spectral Butterfly

V. All My Life

VI. *Le Sacre du Printemps*

VII. Black Tulips

VIII. Nightbird Berates

IX. So Late!

X. Angel's Wings (Ballad)

XI. How to Explain (Ballad)

DATE OF COMPOSITION: 13 September–28 November 1969.

PUBLISHED: TP. 1973.

PAGES: 36.

TIMING: 20'50".

COMMISSION: None.

PREMIÈRE: Neva Pilgrim, soprano and George Rochberg, piano; St. Mary's Church, Philadelphia, PA; 01 April 1970.

DEDICATIONS: to the memory of my son, Paul.

RECORDING: Sharon Mabry, mezzo-soprano and Patsy Wade, piano, Owl-28.

NOTES BY THE COMPOSER:

These songs were written between September 13 and November 28, 1969, in groups of three, four, and five successively–though not the in order in which they appear here–and were given their first performance on April 1, 1970, by Neva Pilgrim with the composer at the piano. The first of the three groups–*We are like the Mayflies, All My Life*, and *I Am Baffled by This Wall*–was dedicated to my wife on her birthday.

When he died in November 1964, my son left about 150 poems, the majority of them having been written before 1961. Even while he was still writing, I often thought of setting them; but it was not until the late summer of 1968 when I wrote the *Tableaux* based on fragments and images from his story *The Silver Talons of Piero Kostrov*, that I was able to find a way to approach his uniquely individual language. From the beginning (he was fourteen when he began to write poetry), Paul's poems and stories had a surface spareness which belied the richness and density of his images and emotional range. There is only one other poet in the English language whose early work has the same general characteristic: William Blake. But it was more likely Japanese and Chinese poetry which influenced his attitude toward language, its texture and its capacity to imply more than it actually said. The surreal, fantasist worlds of Rimbaud and Redon also worked their special magic on his inner life.

These are "songs" then in the most traditional sense; and I have attempted to reveal through each setting the particular world of each poem however brief some of them might be. The piano "accompanies" the voice at times; but it also behaves in other ways—commenting as the need arises or creating an environment in which the singer can project the verbal phrase and its imagery on her own. As always when dealing directly with someone else's work, one hopes that he has not interfered with or obscured the essence of it, but rather projected it in a new and clear light where its integrity remains intact.

NOTES BY THE COMPOSER:

When he died in November 1964 at the age of twenty, my son Paul left about 150 poems, most of them written in the years between the time he was fourteen and nineteen. From the very beginning Paul's poems and stories had a surface spareness which belied the richness and density of his images and emotional range. For me there is only one other poet in the English language whose early work has the same general characteristic: William Blake. In *Chelsea Magazine*, Christopher Davis wrote:

> They speak in his voice about things and feelings he perfectly understood, rarely about ideas for ideas' sake. They are direct and unobscure, since he was not uncertain about them, and modest in the best sense of the word; he did not say more than he knew and did not paint over the bad places with talent. Above all they are poetic—that is, they are sung, not spoken.

These are "songs" then in the most traditional sense; and I have attempted to reveal through each setting the particular world of each poem, however brief some of them may be. The piano "accompanies" the voice at all times, and in one instance the pianist very briefly sings with the mezzo-soprano. The piano also behaves in other ways—commenting as the need arises or creating an environment in which the singer can project the verbal phrase and its imagery on her own. As always when dealing directly with someone else's work, one hopes that he has not interfered with or obscured the essence of it, but rather projected it in a new and clear light where its integrity remains intact.

Fanfares for Massed Trumpets, Horns, and Trombones

DATE OF COMPOSITION: Finished 22 January 1968.

PUBLISHED: TP. MS. Rental. 1977.

PAGES: 25.

TIMING: ca. 6'00".

COMMISSION: Settlement School (Philadelphia) for their sixtieth anniversary.

PREMIÈRE: Settlement School Brass Ensemble, Sigmund Hering conducting; Settlement School; 17 March 1968.

DEDICATION: None.

RECORDING: N/A.

INSTRUMENTATION: Tpt, Hn, Trb.

Fantasies for Voice and Piano

I. The Toadstools in a Fairy Ring

II. There Were Frog Prints in the Rime

III. The Frogs Hold Court

IV. Five Chessmen on a Board

DATE OF COMPOSITION: 1971.

PUBLISHED: TP. 1975.

PAGES: 10.

TIMING: ca. 5'00".

COMMISSION: None.

PREMIÈRE: N/A.

DEDICATION: for my dear wife on our thirtieth anniversary.

RECORDING: N/A.

Four Short Sonatas for Piano Solo

Sonata No. 1: Poco allegro piacevole

Sonata No. 2: Molto rubato

Sonata No. 3: Allegro assai

Sonata No. 4: Presto

DATE OF COMPOSITION: 1984.

PUBLISHED: TP. 1986.

PAGES: 20.

TIMING: 12'00".

COMMISSION: United States Information Agency [USIA] for its Artistic Ambassador Program.

PREMIÈRE: Michael Caldwell, piano; Palermos Santissimo Salvatore, Palermo, Italy; 07 June 1984.

DEDICATION: to Curt Cacioppo.

RECORDING: N/A.

Four Songs of Solomon for Voice and Piano

I. Rise up, My Love

II. Come, My Beloved

III. Set Me as a Seal

IV. Behold! Thou Art Fair

DATE OF COMPOSITION: 1946.

PUBLISHED: TP. 1949.

PAGES: 15.

TIMING: ca. 7'00".

COMMISSION: None.

PREMIÈRE: David Lloyd, tenor and George Rochberg, piano; Philadelphia, PA; 1947.

DEDICATION: to my wife.

RECORDING: N/A.

Imago Mundi *(Image of the World) for Large Orchestra*

I. Adagio

II. Alla marcia; grotesque; a touch of macabre

III. Fantasia

IV. Fanfares; molto allegro

DATE OF COMPOSITION: 1973.

PUBLISHED: TP. MS. Rental. 1977.

PAGES: 120.

TIMING: ca. 20'00".

COMMISSION: Baltimore Symphony Orchestra.

PREMIÈRE: Baltimore   Symphony   Orchestra,   Sergiu
Commissiona conducting; Lyric Theater, Baltimore, MD;
08, 09 May 1974.

DEDICATION: None.

RECORDING: N/A.

INSTRUMENTATION: 3 Fl (Pc), 2 Ob, EH, 3 Cl (BCl), 2 Bsn, CBsn,
4 Hn, 3 Tpt (C), 2 Tbn, Tba, Timp, Hp, Cel, Str; 3 Perc: Perc
1: Glock, ACy, Guiro, Deep TT, Perc 2: Tamb, LgSusCy,
Log drum (tenor range), Perc 3: Guiro, BsDr.

NOTES BY THE COMPOSER:

Composers today are faced with the confusion of too
many choices–a veritable supermarket of aesthetic/theoreti-
cal ideas, notions, ways, and means–and no commonly accepted standards, no commonly held language, no
commonly held set of beliefs about music itself. In such an
environment the composer is at liberty to proceed at his
own peril. More recently, my personal solution to this com-
munal dilemma has been to compose by gesture and image
rather than device or method. In the process I have tried to
find every conceivable way that interests me to combine
and recombine music, ways which work in musical rather
than theoretical dimensions.

The hope of contemporary music lies, it seems to me, in
learning how to reconcile all manner of opposites, contra-

dictions, paradoxes: the past with the present; tonality with atonality; the impulses of Western musical traditions with those of the Orient; pulse-oriented rhythmic patterns with non-pulse patterns; and so on. That is why, in my most recent music, I have preferred the unalloyed purities of tonal music combined with the oppressive chromaticism of atonality–which belongs to an entirely different realm of expressive possibilities. And that is why, in this present work, *Imago Mundi*, I have combined elements of traditional Japanese *Gagaku* music which is primarily melodic (and elegantly so) with Western melodic/harmonic rhythmic tendencies which embrace the simplicities of marching tunes and fanfares and the complexities of chromatic (or atonal) harmony and simultaneous musics (two or more distinct patterns of speed/texture/color occurring together).

I have, regardless of the specific elements deployed, tried to stay with those things which can be sung or danced to or marched to without in any sense inhibiting my fancy about how they can be presented. If it is logical, as it appears to me, to marry contradictory elements, it is just as logical, I feel, to try to marry those elements or aspects of Western and Eastern musical cultures which resonate in my ears and spirit and find an echo in my thoughts. In the case of *Gagaku*, I find a remarkably basic melodic attitude which bears curious resemblances to Western musical phraseology and implied harmony; and it is these resemblances (and associations or correspondences) which I have tried to emphasize and make my own.

Since I like simple ideas to appear in complex settings and complex ideas to give the appearance of simplicity, *Imago Mundi*, despite all its inner contradictions in terms of gesture, image, sources, etc., is built on large, clear lines of structural articulation and has no "program" as such, regardless of the larger circumference of reference and intention suggested by the title. The first and last sections are intimately related largely through their use of *Gagaku* and other gestures. The second section subdivides into *Alla Marcia*, *Fantasia*, and *Fanfares*. In the last section all the ideas presented previously are summed up and brought together in new combinations, some of them developments or extensions of things stated more directly and simply earlier.

Imago Mundi was written in 1973, following a trip to Japan in the summer of that year, on commission from the Baltimore Symphony. The first performance on May 8, 1974, is dedicated to my daughter, Chessie on her twenty-second birthday.

Used by permission of George Rochberg.

Muse of Fire for Flute and Guitar

DATE OF COMPOSITION: Finished April 1990.

PUBLISHED: TP. 1991.

PAGES: MS. 88.

TIMING: ca. 18'00".

COMMISSION: Carnegie Hall as part of their centennial celebration, 1991.

WRITTEN FOR: Eliot Fisk and Paula Robison.

PREMIÈRE: 01 February 1991; Weill Hall (Carnegie Recital Hall), New York City; Eliot Fisk, guitar and Paula Robison, flute.

DEDICATION: to Eliot Fisk and Paula Robison.

RECORDING: N/A.

Music for "The Alchemist" (a play by Ben Jonson), for Soprano and Eleven Players

I. Opening Music/Bell-chime Music/Bell-Chime Music with Four Interjections

II. Dol as "Lady" Music

III. Scena (Dol's "Mad" Music), in "buffa" style, for Soprano and Ensemble

IV. Kastnil's Angry Music/Tribulation Wholesome and Ananias' Angry Music

V. Pantomime Music

VI. Bell-Chime Music/Queen of Fairy Music

VII. Mammon's March

VIII. Fight Music/Mammon's March/Bell-Chime Music

IX. Anabaptists' Music (Quasi religioso)

X. The Spanish Don's Music

XI. The Spanish Don's Love Music/Tribulation Whole- some and Ananias' Angry Music/Kastnil's Angry Music

XII. Love Wit's Return/Bim-Bim (Neighbor's Brouha)

XIII. Pantomime Music

XIV. Ending Music

DATE OF COMPOSITION: 1965. Concert version: August–September 1966, August–October–02 November 1968.

PUBLISHED: TP. MS. Rental. 1989.

PAGES: 168.

TIMING: ca. 20'00".

COMMISSION: Vivian Beaumont Theater, Lincoln Center.

ORIGINAL VERSION PREMIÈRE: Vivian Beaumont Theater, Lincoln Center; 13 October 1966. Repertoire Theater of Lincoln Center (Herbert Blau, Jules Irving, directors; Robert Symonds, associate director). Staged by Jules Irving; setting and costumes, James Hart Stearns; lighting, John Gleason; musical director and general manager, Stanley Gilkey. Managing director, Alan Mandell; technical director, Jose Sevilla; stage managers, James Kershaw, Timothy Ward, and David Sullivan. Cast: Subtle: Michael O'Sullivan; Jeremy Common: Robert Symmonds; Dol Common: Nancy Marchand; Dapper: Lee Goodman; Abel Drugger: Ray Fry; Sir Epicure Mammon: George Voskovec; Pertinax Surly: Michael Granger; Ananias: Earl Montgomery; Tribulation Wolesome: Aline MacMahon; Kastril: Robert Phalen; Dame Pliant: Elizabeth Huddle; Lovewit: Philip Bosco; Parson: Glenn Mazen; Officers: Robert Haswekk, and Peter Nyberg; Neighbors: Frank Bayer, Marketa Kinbrell, Beatrice Manley, Glenn Mazen, Peter Nyberg, Priscilla Pointer, Judith Propper, Tom Rosqui, Shirley Jac Wagner, Ronald Weygand, and Erica Yohn.

CONCERT VERSION PREMIÈRE: Elizabeth Suderberg, soprano and the University of Washington Contemporary Group, Robert Suderberg conducting; University of Washington, Seattle, WA; 31 October 1969.

DEDICATION: to my dear friends Wharton Esherick and Mima Philips.

RECORDING: N/A.

INSTRUMENTATION: ENSEMBLE A: Fl (Pc), Cl (A; B; E), Tpt (C), Vln, StrB; Pn, Hrpsch, Cel; Perc: Timbales, SmBsDr, LgBsDr, Timp, 2 SusCy (L-S), Glock, ACy, Vib, TBel, Tamb, Castenets; "Small stuff" for improvised passages ("bursts"): Tri, Cowbells, Woodblocks, Timbales (or other small flat drums); ENSEMBLE B: Fl (Pc), Cl (A, B-flat, E-flat), Tpt (C); Perc: Vib, Glock, 2 TnDr; Bell-Chime Music: Fl takes Glass wind chimes and Large temple bells, Cl takes Small temple bells, Tpt takes Cel.

NOTES BY THE COMPOSER:

It was my original intention, after deciding to do something about the music composed for the stage presentation– to give it a more integrated shape for "live" concert performance, to arrange the order of the separate pieces in such a way as to allow for narration and dancers through which (and whom) the wonderful and wild wit of Ben Jonson would take wing in the concert hall and, hopefully, give those usually staid precincts of artistic performance an edge, an environment, an atmosphere rarely, if ever, experienced in them. While I still may carry this first idea out some day, what I am offering here is different–but no less in its planned freight of deviltry and ironic projections, all in the name of a good, loud, and hearty laugh at the spectacle of Man and Woman in their pursuit of Life's Goals, "putting each other on" and "putting each other down."

For those who cherish the nineteenth century notion that a twentieth century artist must be "original", I can provide no comfort at all. Besides going back to Renaissance sources for some of the music I have incorporated here, I have also composed my own "diatonic" music where it seemed absolutely appropriate and therefore necessary to my purpose. Where the dramatic situation required it, I have composed a more "contemporary"-sounding music–when the circumstances were either wholly "fanciful" or "noisy." The various combinations of these "musics" has resulted in an unfolding assemblage.

Copyright 1977 Theodore Presser Company.

Used by permission of the publisher.

Music for the Magic Theater for a Chamber Ensemble of Fifteen Players [original version]

DATE OF COMPOSITION: 1965.

PUBLISHED: TP. MS. Parts on rental. 1972.

PAGES: 112.

TIMING: ca. 30'00".

COMMISSION: Fromm Foundation for the University of Chicago's Seventy-fifth Anniversary.

PREMIÈRE: University of Chicago Contemporary Chamber Players, Ralph Shapey conducting; 24 January 1967.

DEDICATION: None.

RECORDING: N/A.

INSTRUMENTATION: Fl (Pc), Ob, Cl (B; E), Bsn, 2 Hn, Tpt (C), Tbn, Tba, Pn, 2 Vln, Vlc, Vla, StrB.

Music for the Magic Theater for Small Orchestra [orchestral version]

DATE OF COMPOSITION: 1969.

PUBLISHED: TP. MS. Parts on rental. 1972.

PAGES: 112.

TIMING: ca. 30'00"

COMMISSION: Fromm Foundation for the University of Chicago's Seventy-fifth Anniversary; 24 January 1967.

PREMIÈRE: Buffalo Philharmonic, Melvin Strauss conducting; 19, 21 January 1969.

DEDICATION: None.

RECORDING: Oberlin Orchestra, Kenneth Moore conducting, Desto 6444.

INSTRUMENTATION: Fl (Pc), Ob, Cl (B; E), Bsn, 4 Hn, Tpt (C), Tbn, Tba, Pn, Str.

QUOTED AT THE BEGINNING OF THE SCORE:

I understood it all. I understood Pablo. I understood Mozart, and somewhere behind me I heard his ghastly laughter.

I knew that all the hundred thousand pieces of life's game were in my pocket. A glimpse of its meaning had stirred my reason and I was determined to begin afresh. I would sample its tortures once more and shudder again at its senselessness. I would traverse not once more, but often, the hell of my inner being.

One day I would be a better hand at the game. One day I would learn to laugh. Pablo was waiting for me, and Mozart too.

Hermann Hesse
Steppenwolf

NOTES BY THE COMPOSER:

Despite its title, *Music for the Magic Theater*, this is not a "musical theater" piece. The impulse to compose the work in the way I did and my decision to call it what I did stem from entirely different sources than the ones which, as I understand them, motivate today's "musical theater" pieces.

If anything, the musical urge which produced *The Magic Theater* had its roots long ago in my obsession with the many-layered density of human existence and the contradictory nature of all human experience. That plus my increasing disbelief in the value of all unitary systems or methods of composing "contemporary" music. The result, impossible for me to define technically, is a kind of sound-collage in which the past and present are quite literally juxtaposed. To do this, I have quoted Mozart, Beethoven, Mahler, Varèse in various ways–sometimes pure, other times not-so-pure; but always with love and respect–and, I hope, also understanding. The technical problem I posed for myself was how to move from one epoch to another, how to "modulate" from one musical syntax to another without creating a pastiche of "styles." Part of the solution was to pit these different levels against each other, successively and simultaneously. This in turn raised problems having to do with handling different times, different speeds. I have worked close to the edge of disorder and chaos to create "perceptual dissonance" in order that passages or sections not made up of contradictory elements may them emerge with utmost aural clarity, *i.e.*, "perceptual consonance."

The title is drawn from Hermann Hesse's novel *Steppenwolf* where the "magic theater" stands as the symbol of each man's inner life and in which, if he is allowed to enter, he may perhaps discover himself for the first time. The question always is: what does he discover? Hesse's answer seems to me to be: the whole world of human possibilities from which one must choose oneself. Applying this to music, specifically this music, the answer for me is: the whole world of musical possibilities from which I choose myself as composer.

Used by permission of George Rochberg.

NOTES BY THE COMPOSER:

The musical urge which produced *The Magic Theater* had its roots long ago in my obsession with the many-layered density of human existence and the contradictory nature of all human experience. The result, impossible for me to describe technically, is a sound-collage in which the past and present are juxtaposed. I have quoted Mozart, Beethoven, Mahler, Varèse in various ways–sometimes pure, other times not-so-pure; but always with love and respect–and, I hope, also understanding. The essential technical problem I posed for myself was how to "modulate" from one musical "dialect" to another. Part of the solution was to pit different dialects against each other, successively and simultaneously. This in turn raised problems having to do with handling different gestures, different speeds. I have worked close to the edge of disorder to create "perceptual dissonance" in order that passages or sections not made up of contradictory elements may then emerge with utmost aural clarity, *i.e.,* "perceptual consonance."

Used by permission of George Rochberg.

NOTES BY THE COMPOSER:

Act I: in which the present and the past are all mixed up...and it is difficult to decide or to know where reality is.

Act II: in which the past haunts us with its nostalgic beauty...and calls to us from the depths of inner spaces of heart and mind...but the past is all shadow and dream–insubstantial...and we can't hold on to it because the present is too pressing...

Act III: in which we realize that only the present is really real...because it is all we have...but in the end it too is shadow and dream...and disappears...into what?

The *Music for the Magic Theater* was commissioned by the Fromm Foundation for the seventy-fifth anniversary of the University of Chicago and was given its first performance on January 24, 1967, by the University of Chicago Contemporary Players, conducted by Ralph Shapey. In its original version it was composed for fifteen players. The orchestral version recorded here was first played by the Buffalo Philharmonic on January 19 and 21, 1969, Melvin Strauss conducting. The essential divergence between the original "chamber" version and the "orchestral" one lies in the enlargement of strings from five soloists to a full complement of the orchesral string quintet plus doubling the original two horn parts in tutti passages. The work falls into three parts or "acts," the first and third enclosing a reworking of the *Adagio* from Mozart's *Divertimento, K. 287* in the manner of a concerto in which the piano and the solo violin share the major roles, the piano predominating. Even though other composers (Varèse, Webern, Mahler, Beethoven) are quoted, my primary interest was not in a raw or literal presentation of a variety of sources, but rather in the projection of an almost cinematic series of shifting ideas and levels which, nevertheless, combine in an inevitable fashion, despite sharp contradictions and paradoxes, to produce totality, a unity. In its combinations of the past and present, of seemingly accidental, unrelated images whose placement in the stream of time obeys no apparent logic, the work partakes of the state of dreaming–whether asleep or awake; and like all dreams, it becomes a fantasy, a fiction of the mind nonetheless real.

The title came after the work was completed and was taken from Hermann Hesse's novel *Steppenwolf*, in which, as in this work, the "magic theater" functions as that mental domain where reality and fantasy, where past and future, where real history and imagined history confront each other to create new configurations and new openings for living existence. In this way the title became a metaphor for the internal character of the music and the music became a metaphor for the contradictory levels of the contemporary state of mind which in Mircea Eliade's phrase is the "coincidentia oppositorum" of all true existence.

Used by permission of George Rochberg.

NOTES BY THE COMPOSER:

Three matters deserve special comment: first, the notation of the music; second, the use of quotation and the stylistic shifts they produce; and third, the transcription of the *Adagio* from Mozart's *Divertimento K. 287*, which comprises the bulk of *Act II*.

With reference to the notation: metered passages, whether of my own composition or quoted from other composers need no special comment since they observe the conventions of pulse and metric articulation, rhythmically speaking. However, the open, unmetered passages which employ proportional (or visual) notation are another matter entirely; for in these passages, not only must the conductor discover the overall gesture and shape in the indicated speed–usually verbal rather than metronomic–but the individual players must discover and project the gestural shapes of their own parts. I am aware of certain dangers inherent in such a style of notation. Nonetheless, I have sufficient faith in the musical instincts and experience of performers today to feel that I can trust them to respond with intelligence and sensitivity to what is being asked of them. The essential neutrality of the notation indicates variability in inventing phrase shapes and rhythmic groupings. In a sense, each player becomes an actor who is given lines to speak which do not tell him precisely how to project them. His decisions are as much dependent on the specific context he is dealing with at any given moment as they are on cooperating with the conductor who now assumes the additional role of stage director. Which leads me to the second point about stylistic shifts occasioned by the use of quotations from various periods of history.

Together the conductor and players must make "sense" out of what is given. Since he cannot "beat time" in much of the score, the conductor-director must convey by whatever means at his disposal–signs, gestures, looks, attitude–the life and pace of the music. His directorial role becomes particularly sensitive when it comes to establishing the juxtapositions of and movement to and from style to style. Each style characteristic must be projected as though it existed by itself, regardless of what lies on either side. No attempt should be made to relate these different styles which exist on separate levels or planes of musical action. Some of these planes occur simultaneously, others successively. The "collage" or "montage" formulations which result in sudden changes in attitude, gesture, speed, and dynamics as well as frequent interruption in the flow of events comprise the essential articulation of the musical structure, *i.e.*, the way in happens. It may prove helpful to approach the work as "cinematic," its discontinuous, non-narrative aural images combined in ways not unlike the handling of visual images in films by Fellini, Antonioni, Resnais, and others. I am not commenting on similarities of context but rather on the relationships of compositional attitudes which tend toward the art of combination and the disruption of "normal" expectations of continuity and temporal relations. Neither my work nor the films I have in mind (*Marienbad, Hiroshima mon amour, Morgan, Juliette of the Spirits*) relate to the old logic of cause and effect or of linear movement. On the contrary, they deal in contradictions and paradoxes.

Act II begins with a transcription of the *Adagio* from Mozart's *Divertimento, K. 287.* The conductor will discover that in order to make it really work he must play it as though it were coming from a great distance; and must, therefore, avoid a literal rendition which, while appropriate to a performance of a work by Mozart himself under the usual concert conditions, would prove entirely out of place here–in fact, fatal. The transcription must stand in relation to *Acts I* and *III* as a middle panel, in the background, while *Acts I* and *II* occupy the foreground. If *Act II* is "cool" then *Acts I* and *III* are "hot." Since this is being written after the initial performances have already taken place, I can attest to the peculiar strength of response, both positive and negative, to the presence in the work of the transcription of a Mozart movement virtually in toto: it seems to test the perceptual courage of listeners (musicians and laymen alike) by putting in question the whole concept of what is "contemporary," how far that concept may be stretched today and what it can include. The presence of the transcription abrogates the nineteenth to early twentieth century notion of "originality," puts the paraphernalia of its aesthetic completely aside; but precisely because of this it creates responses which have little, if anything, to do with musical values *per se* but rather with vested interests challenged whether in art, religion, or politics. For all these reasons (and many more besides), it is not necessary to overstate the performance of the transcription but rather to go in the opposite direction–understate, underplay. It will make its presence felt even more if it is projected in a detached manner–floating out ever so gently, almost whispered at times.

The world of this music is surreal more than it is abstract. In its combinations of the past and present, seemingly accidental, unrelated aural images whose placement in time obeys no conventional logic, it attempts to create a musical soundscape which is strangely and oddly familiar. In this it partakes of the state of dreaming–whether asleep or awake–in which the familiar objects, places, and people of our lives often transform themselves in unexpected ways; and in which, often enough, the completely "unknown" intrudes on our mental world. Dreams are "fantasies." So are art works–fictions of the mind which assume reality–painful or pleasureable depending on how their contents affect us–but nevertheless a reality which transcends the chaotic and the mundane.

The title of my work is taken from the last part of Hermann Hesse's novel *Steppenwolf.* After being "condemned" to learn to live and to laugh, Harry Haller, lover of the Immortals (among whom he gives a special place to Goethe and to Mozart), says:

> I knew that all the hundred thousand pieces of life's game were in my pocket. A glimpse of its meaning had stirred my reason and I was determined to begin afresh. I would sample its tortures once more and shudder again at its senselessness. I would traverse not once more, but often, the hell of my inner being.

Nach Bach, Fantasy for Harpsichord or Piano

DATE OF COMPOSITION: Summer 1966. Tanglewood.

PUBLISHED: TP. 1967.

PAGES: 16.

TIMING: ca. 8'00".

COMMISSION: Igor Kipnis.

PREMIÈRE: Igor Kipnis, harpsichord; Annenberg Auditorium, University of Pennsylvania, Philadelphia, PA; 27 January 1967.

DEDICATION: Igor Kipnis.

RECORDING: Igor Kipnis, harpsichord, Grenadilla 1019.

PREFACE BY THE COMPOSER:

I wrote *Nach Bach* in July 1966, while at Tanglewood, for Igor Kipnis. Before getting to work we had a long session together discussing the technical problems of the harpsichord (about which I literally knew nothing), Kipnis de-

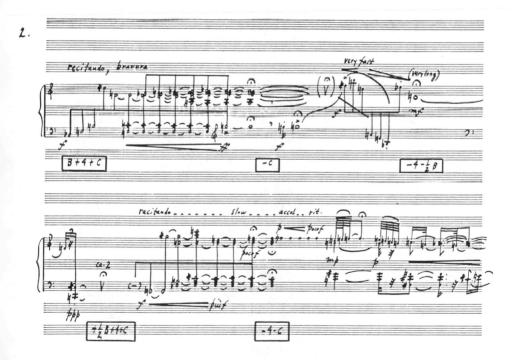

Plate 6: Autograph of page 1 of *Nach Bach* (1966). Copyright 1967 Theodore Presser Company. Used by permission of the publisher.

monstrating the use of pedals in connection with registration, attack, and timbral characteristics, etc. What came out finally without any conscious effort on my part was a piece which built into its musical structure just about every color combination possible on the instrument Kipnis plays. The work uses the Bach *Partita No. 6 in e minor* as "source" and becomes a commentary on it, so to speak: quoting, splicing, transforming Bach mixed with "free" passages which simulate the harmonic world and manner of the *Partita*, or not as the case may be. In a solo piece there was little opportunity for simultaneous collage passages. Consequently, shifts in gesture and language (tonal/atonal) occur successively rather than in parallel streams. My chief interest, besides discovering the instrument *qua* instrument, was to "take off" from the harmonic dialect (as I like to call differences in harmony viewed over long periods) of Bach; and even to show—but not didactically—that the dialects of harmony are really, after all, only that and not different languages.

Used by permission of George Rochberg.

NOTES BY THE COMPOSER:

In 1966 Igor Kipnis asked me to write a harpsichord piece for him. We were both at Tanglewood that summer and he was good enough to put his own custom-built harpsichord at my disposal. *Nach Bach* was the result. The "nach" (or "after," *i.e.*, based on, derived from) in the title refers to my choosing J.S. Bach's *Partita in e minor* as a basic text on which to "comment" musically. Inevitably there are both raw "quotes" and transformed "quotes"—favorite passages which I loved and felt were stamped indelibly with the best qualities of Bach. While I would not place my idea of musical "commentary" necessarily in the same category as variants or variations on another composer's theme or development sections of sonatas or chorale preludes, etc., it relates to these earlier attitudes and practices, at least in the sense that something pre-existing, or "given," is worked on, extended in new and possibly unexpected directions.

Most of the commentary in *Nach Bach* on basically tonal/diatonic music is couched in chromatic/atonal terms. The form of the work, like the *sfumato* movement of the *Carnival Music,* is open, asymmetrical and progressive, *i.e.,* non-repetitive, and so akin, in spirit at least, to the old "fantasia" idea of Bach and Mozart.

Night Music for Orchestra

DATE OF COMPOSITION: 1948–1949, Revised 1957–1977.

PUBLISHED: TP. 1956.

PAGES: 57.

TIMING: ca. 12'00".

COMMISSION: None.

PREMIÈRE: New York Philharmonic, Dimitri Mitropoulos conducting; Carnegie Hall, New York City; 23 April 1953.

DEDICATION: None.

RECORDING: Louisville Orchestra, Robert Whitney conducting, LOU 623.

AWARDS: 1952 George Gershwin Memorial Award.

INSTRUMENTATION: Pc, 2 Fl, 3 Ob, (EH), 3 Cl (BCl), 2 Bsn, CBsn, Hn, 3 Tpt (C), 3 Tbn, Tba, Timp, Perc (BsDr, Cy), Hp, Str.

NOTES BY THE COMPOSER:

It is difficult for me to say anything new about a work I wrote twelve years ago, in 1949. Looking back at a time when I was trying to find myself, it seems that the distance I've covered in the intervening years may only be illusory. What I mean is that I am still interested in the same basic problems that absorbed me then. I still want to achieve in the music I'm writing the same degree of uninhibited, passionate expression that typifies my *Night Music.* This doesn't mean, however, that I'm writing the same piece over and over again. On the contrary, I'm doing what every serious artist tries to do: to find my way to the center of existence, to the meaning of things, and to record that search in works which reflect the many different routes taken to find that center and meaning.

The title should not be taken too literally since it was an afterthought and owes its existence to the music rather than the other way around... Even the word "night" must be approached as a symbol of whatever is dark, unknown, awesome, mysterious, or daemonic.

Used by permission of George Rochberg.

NOTES BY THE COMPOSER:

In the fall of 1948, I began the composition of my *First Symphony* which I planned in five movements. In the spring of 1949, I had completed it. After showing the work to several of my friends and colleagues, I realized that one of the movements would have to be taken out in order to make the *Symphony* tighter and less "monumental" in size. The movement I extracted was the second–the first of two slow movements– because it seemed most capable of standing on its own. This movement I decided to call *Night Music for Orchestra* because of its essentially poetic quality. The title should not be taken literally since it is an afterthought and owes its existence to the music rather than the other way around. Even the word "night" must be approached as a symbol of whatever is dark, unknown, awesome, mysterious, or daemonic. This then is the genesis of my piece.

In form, the piece is a large "A B A" structure. However the material of "B" projected by a solo cello against a background of muted strings, harp, and one flute (the solo cello being interrupted by two statements of muted brass and woodwinds) is based on the ideas stated in "A." The general character of the music is chromatic but it is not atonal. However, this piece and the *Symphony* directly preceded my first efforts in the technique of twelve-tone composition which resulted in my *First String Quartet* and *Twelve Bagatelles for Piano Solo* written in 1952.

Used by permission of George Rochberg.

Octet, A Grand Fantasia for Flute, Clarinet, Horn, Violin, Viola, Cello, Bass, and Piano

DATE OF COMPOSITION: 23 November 1979–12 January 1980.

PUBLISHED: TP. MS. Rental. 1980.

PAGES: 65.

TIMING: ca. 23'00".

COMMISSION: Chamber Music Society of Lincoln Center, New York City, made possible by a generous gift from Marvin Sloves.

PREMIÈRE: Chamber Music Society of Lincoln Center (Renee Siebert, flute, Gervase de Peyer, clarinet, Robert Routch, horn, Ani Kavafian, violin, Marcus Thompson, viola, Leslie Parnas, cello, Alvin Brehm, bass, and John Browning, piano); Alice Tully Hall, New York City; 25, 27 April 1980.

DEDICATION: to my dear friends Edith and Paul Mocsanyi.

RECORDING: N/A.

INSTRUMENTATION: Fl, Cl, Hn, Pn, Vln, Vla, Vlc, StrB.

NOTES BY THE COMPOSER:

This work was written between November 23, 1979, and January 12, 1980, on commission from the Chamber Music Society of Lincoln Center. It is dedicated to my dear friends Edith and Paul Mocsanyi.

I call it *A Grand Fantasia* to identify its character which is essentially a continuous series of unfolding, connecting gestures whose coherence derives more from the use and transformation of a basic set of motives–melodic, harmonic, and textural–than from the formal design of exterior structure. It is the last in a long series of varied chamber works which have occupied me over the last decade, works in which I explore the possibilities of a larger palette of expressive means than allowed by modernism *per se*.

Music is much more than a product of sheer rationality and intellect–that side of ourselves on which modernism has placed such a high premium. Nor is music a descent into inchoate subjectivity, reflecting in mirror fashion–as some would have it–the turbulent conditions of our times. Music is a direct utterance of the human soul, the release of the human heart in sound in as many of its forms of sensibilities as we are capable of imagining and realizing. These forms or modes of sensibility, therefore, can include even the narrow limits of modernism which can now be used selectively (each according to his own vision and imaginative needs) as part of the total spectrum giving expression to what lies in the human heart. It is only when the modernist insists too much that he goes wrong; because life is not only the tendency toward the intelligent invention of patterns of logical relationships; or the tendency toward producing chaos and noise and senseless gestures; or a piling up of meaningless "events." It is also the warming smile, the agonized cry, the tender glance, the firmness of friendship, power of love and a million other simple and complex states, all happening simultaneously to millions of human beings everywhere. We transform the modern experience (mostly of pain, disaffection, anger, frustration) into the darker colors of an expanded palette which still includes the gold of joy, the blue of love, and the red of vitality. We identify ourselves and our art by the breadth of what it includes, not by the narrow space of what it excludes.

My *Octet* makes no pretense to being totally inclusive. No piece of music can be that and retain its own special quality and form of coherence. If the *Octet* leans more heavily on the darker colors of atonal chromaticism than on the brighter ones of tonal diatonicism, that is entirely purposeful. What I have tried to accomplish in this work is a fusion of atonal harmonic means with the directionality of tonal principles derived from the major-minor system. My experience with atonality and, more recently, with tonality, has led me to the point where I felt it was possible to fuse the two by establishing the peculiar bite and pungency of atonal means on the solid ground of tonal direction. In that way, they interpenetrate each other and new kinds of relationships emerge. There is no theory attached to this. It is simply using one's ears in a different, possibly a new way to arrive at levels of organization which pure diatonicism and pure chromaticism do not allow. Such fusion, if it can be made to work, opens out on a still further enlargement of the possible means of musical expression. The *Octet* is my first conscious effort to realize this further enlargement.

Used by permission of George Rochberg.

Ora Pro Nobis for Flute and Guitar

DATE OF COMPOSITION: 1989–1990. Completed February 1990.
PUBLISHED: TP. 1991.
PAGES: 16.
TIMING: ca. 12'00".
WRITTEN FOR: Eliot Fisk and Paula Robison.
PREMIÈRE: N/A.
DEDICATION: to Eliot Fisk.
RECORDING: N/A.

Partita Variations for Piano Solo

I. Preludium
II. Intermezzo
III. Burlesca
IV. Cortege
V. Impromptu
VI. The Deepest Carillon
Tema: Ballade
VII. Capriccio
VIII. Minuetto
IX. Canon
X. Nocturne
XI. Arabesque
XII. Fuga a tre voce

DATE OF COMPOSITION: 31 December 1975–04 February 1976.
PUBLISHED: TP. 1977.
PAGES: 40.
TIMING: ca. 28'00".

COMMISSION: Etsuko Tazaki on a grant from the Edyth Bush Charitable Foundation Inc., for the Bicentennial Series of the Washington Performing Arts Society.

PREMIÈRE: Esuko Tazaki, piano; Kennedy Center, Washington, D.C.; 04 December 1976.

DEDICATION: to the memory of Edyth Bush.

RECORDING: N/A.

NOTES BY THE COMPOSER:

"Tradition," T.S. Eliot says, "cannot be inherited, and if you want it, you must obtain it by great labour." No statement I know (or could devise myself) sums up better my own view of the present task facing the serious composer. To regain through conscious and intense effort a meaningfully personal connection with the traditions of the past and integrate that variegated past with an equally variegated present into a large, as inclusive as possible, spectrum of seeming opposites is, I believe, to re-establish the inner tension a composer needs today in order to make the richest possible musical statements of which he is capable. Without this he remains caught in the narrow passes of the exclusive "modern."

The *Partita Variations for Piano Solo* is a direct outgrowth of this belief. It comprises thirteen sections—a "bakers dozen"—built around a tonal theme (lying between *VI* and *VII*, but itself unnumbered) which is varied directly in some instances (*II*, *VII*, and *X* for example); indirectly in others (*I* and *IV* for example); and not at all in still others (*VI* and *XI* for example). Hence the combination of terms in the title which simply provides a general indication of the mixture of "suite" and "variations."

The variety of form or genre-types is, of course, basic to the plan of the work. I have purposefully juxtaposed contrapuntal sections (*Capriccio*, a tonal piece in double counterpoint; *Canon*, a twelve-tone rhythmic canon; a tonal *Fugue* in three voices) with tonal or atonal melodic pieces (*Intermezzo*, *Impromptu*, *Nocturne*, *Minuetto*, etc.) and with atonal pieces which are largely gestural or textural.

The work was composed between December 31, 1975, and February 4, 1976.

Used by permission of George Rochberg.

Passions [According to the Twentieth Century] for Actors, Dancers, Singers, Choruses, Speakers, and Instrumentalists

Scene A

Passion I

  Scene B

  Passion II

  Scene C

  Passion III

  Scene D

DATE OF COMPOSITION: 1964–1967.

PUBLISHED: TP. MS. 1967.

PAGES: 78.

TIMING: ca. 60'00".

COMMISSION: None.

PREMIÈRE: Never performed.

DEDICATION: None.

RECORDING: N/A.

PERFORMERS:

  SCENE A:

      Herod the Great (Actor)

      Two Counsellors (Actors)

      Two Mixed Choruses (used in Passions)

      Jazz Quintet (Tpt, Tn Sax, Piano, Bass, Drums)

  PASSION I:

      Alto Solo (Singer)

      Cantor (Baritone) (Singer)

      Small Chorus of Six Men (Singers)

      Three Male Speakers (Baritone, Bass, Basso profundo) (Actors)

      Two Mixed Choruses

      Brass Ensemble (3 Tpt, 4 Hn, 3 Trb), Perc.

SCENE B:
> Herod (Actor)
> Soldiers (small group of 4 to 8) (Actors)
> Two Mixed Choruses
> Men's Chorus (drawn from larger Choruses) (Singers)
> Brass Ensemble (3 Tpt, 4 Hn, 3 Trb), Perc.

PASSION II:
> Soprano Solo (Singer)
> Alto Solo (Singer)
> Two Mixed Choruses
> Brass Ensemble (3 Tpt, 4 Hn, 3 Trb), Piano, Perc.

SCENE C:
> Actors/Dancers (for 3 Dumb Shows)
> Soprano Voice (Andromache) (Actress)
> Tenor Voice (Cain) (Actor)
> Baritone-Bass Voice (Oedipus) (Actor)

PASSION III:
> Soprano Solo (Singer)
> Alto Solo (Singer)
> Cantor (Baritone) (Singer)
> Two Mixed Choruses
> Six Men's Voices (Singers)
> Three Male Speakers (Baritone, Bass, Basso profundo) (Actors)
> Brass Ensemble (3 Tpt, 4 Hn, 3 Trb), Piano, Tape, Perc.

SCENE D:
> Herod (Actor)
> Soldiers (Actors)
> Two Mixed Choruses
> Small Men's Chorus
> Brass Ensemble (3 Tpt, 4 Hn, 3 Trb), Perc.
> Jazz Quintet

NOTES BY THE COMPOSER:

This combination of play, spectacle and music, speaking and singing, dance, and tableau is a work intended for theatrical production rather than concert performance. In fact, it is not likely that, considering the technical requirements of the work, a concert hall would be adequate to the demands or that a musical director could begin to approach them.

In the juxtaposition of *Scenes* and *Passions*, I have tried to achieve the greatest possible variety and tension between the vocabulary of the contemporary theater and some of the traditions of opera and oratorio–although in this connection there is no overt use of such traditions. The theatrical aspects are obvious enough in the *Scenes* drawn from the medieval mystery play *Herod the Great*. The traditions, somewhat distilled and abstracted, of opera and oratorio–which tend to magnetize themselves around the projection of individual and collective feelings respectively (though not always)–are developed in the *Passions*.

Since the subject matter (or content) of the *Scenes* and *Passions* is essentially the same, projecting in a multiplicity of ways the unrestrained and perpetual violence of man which in this part of the cycle of his history is a staggering record of murder in all forms–suicide, fraticide, patricide– and in the twentieth century has reached peaks of incredible intensity and horror (and still goes on), I felt free to develop a form of presentation in which juxtaposition, sudden shifts of level and extensive collage effects would, in fact, make even clearer the dramatic impulses behind the work, by underlining them and sharpening their focus through fresh combinations of seemingly unrelated things. I also felt free, therefore, to move back and forth (without transitions, bridges, connections, etc.) in human history and consciousness, bringing together myth and fact, the Trojan War and the Vietnam War, Herod and Hitler, the slaughter of The Innocents and the death camps, Beethoven's "millions" and our "millions." With few exceptions (which circumstances required I write myself), the texts I have used were all drawn from sources ancient and modern; and, wherever possible, are offered in the original language. Hence the use of Latin, Greek, Hebrew, Medieval mystery play English, contemporary English, Spanish, German, Italian. For me, this reinforces the universality of the treatment of the subject which cuts across the entire range of human history, culture, and experience.

The structural differences between the *Scenes* and *Passions*, though clear enough from certain points of view, deserve additional comment. Structurally, the *Scenes* provide the frame within which the *Passions* take place–and without which they would lack an anchor. The *Scenes* are *convex*. They are narrative, to be watched the way any unfolding story is or can be whether in the theater or cinema. They are to be thrust at the audience, leaving it no option for "interpretation." They are essentially simple, concrete, and direct. Even (or especially) the inclusion of jazz, the *Horst Wessel Song*, and the Nazi arm salute should make what is going on perfectly plain despite the Biblical source of the story itself. The *Passions*, on the other hand, are *concave*. They are collages of music and speech–old and new in terms of human consciousness an action, history, real or imagined events. The density of their internal structure removes them from narration (although occasionally there are "narrative" elements) proper and strives to engage the audience at its most intense levels of private and collective response. While in a sense spectacles themselves, the *Passions* are essentially internalized, contrasting sharply with the *Scenes* which are externalized projections (with the possible exception of *Scene C*). Therefore, it is in the alternating movement between *Scenes* and *Passions* that I hope also to achieve the effect of "push and pull," of large-scale movements which oscillate from outside to inside, never letting-up on the tension and emotional force of what is being projected.

Since we who live in the twentieth century have inherited all of history, culturally and neurologically, not only does the combination of texts from everywhere and everytime, so to speak, seem right and plausible to me but also the use of musical quotation, whether of a generalized stylistic type or an actual work. Hence the use of jazz improvisation and the *Horst Wessel Song* in the *Scenes*, the extensive quotation from the Choral movement of Beethoven's *Ninth Symphony* in *Passion III*, and the use of pseudo-Gregorian chant in the same *Passion*. In the case of the Beethoven, the quotation becomes intrinsic to the structure itself; in fact, for me, constitutes the particular dramatic core of *Passion III* because of the text Beethoven used. The incorporation of his music became inevitable. In this cultural "folding-over" (as Teilhard de Chardin puts it) we cannot escape any longer the peculiar and powerful sense that all things and all times, however worthy or unworthy, belong to us. At least, we have not been able to escape their consequences, humanly and artistically. That is why this work records in its own way my own obsessive sense of this strange outcome of what is euphemistically called the "evolution of man."

The production of this work should involve, ideally, the use of slides, television cameras and, if possible, film as well. I have purposely left "open" the visual aspect of the work in this version because I know that only in actual production can the right solutions be discovered. Nevertheless, a few hints and suggestions (aside from any in the score) as to where and how I envision the structural use of television and film. *Scenes A, B,* and *D* are, strictly speaking, "live." However, while I have called for three *dumb shows* in *Scene C*, it is conceivable that only one of them (*Herod's Soldiers / Women of Bethlehem*) be acted/danced "live" while the others (*The Murder at the Crossroads [Oedipus and Laius] and the Murder in the Fields [Cain and Abel]*) could be filmed in advance and projected on screens in the theater. I envision the use of television cameras in the *Passions*–enlarging the faces and/or figures of singers, speakers, and dancers/actors to intensify the live aspects of performance: the small chorus of six men wearing cowls and face masks (*Passion I*); the figure of Hecuba whenever she appears (alto solo); the soprano's scream (*Passion II*); the dancers pantomiming the self-immolation of the Buddhist monk (*Passion II*); etc. In general, whenever a structural use of television can be devised, enlarging and intensifying the impact of what is happening on stage, this seems to me to be valid and called for. I have indicated the specific use of slides in one place only (*Passion I*). This does not limit the use of this device, however. In this connection (and including the use of film), I want to make very plain one categorical restriction: no photographic scenes of concentration camps; no film clips of Hitler and company; of S.S. troops, of actual physical brutality; etc. I do not impose this because of personal squeamishness but because for artistic purposes I feel they simply do not work. They are too raw, too factual, too literal. They remain brute, undigested facts. My purpose is not to horrify and deaden sensibility or to repeat what has been said over and over again in films and works of a purely "documentary" nature through devices necessary to that genre of projection but to try to bring that portion of human consciousness I can reach through this work to a pitch where whatever moral sense an audience and its individual members are capable of can be invoked. ("A tear is an intellectual thing." –Blake)

Among the implacable forces of life and the cosmos which man has to contend with is his own implacable nature. He has finally been brought face to face with Medusa– without benefit of Theseus' shield. Man has discovered he is Medusa; and whether he likes it or not he must now and at last look upon his own image, however unnerving it may be. That is what my *Passions [According to the Twentieth Century]* are about.

George Rochberg, 13 April 1967.

Phaedra, Monodrama for Mezzo-Soprano and Orchestra

Text freely adapted by Gene Rochberg from Robert Lowell's verse translation of Racine's Phèdre.

I. Aria: "In May, in Brilliant Athens"

II. Orchestral Interlude: Black Sails

III. Aria: "You Monster"

IV. Orchestral Interlude: Theseus Homecoming

V. Supplication: "Theseus, I Heard the Deluge of Your Voice"

VI. Cabaletta: "My Last Calamity Has Come"

VII. Orchestral Postlude: The Death of Hippolytus

DATE OF COMPOSITION: 1973–March 1974.

PUBLISHED: TP. MS. Rental. 1977.

PAGES: 272.

PIANO REDUCTION PUBLISHED: TP. MS. n.d.

PAGES: 77.

TIMING: ca. 35'00".

COMMISSION: New Music Ensemble of Syracuse, NY, with assistance from the New York State Council on the Arts.

PREMIÈRE: Neva Pilgrim, soprano and the Syracuse Symphony, David Loebel conducting; 09 January 1976.

DEDICATION: for Jan DeGaetani.

RECORDING: N/A.

INSTRUMENTATION: 2 Fl (Pc), 2 Ob (EH), 2 Cl (BCl), 2 Bsn (CBsn), 4 Hn, 3 Tpt, 2 Tbn, BTbn, Timp, 2 Perc, Str.

SYNOPSIS BY THE COMPOSER:

The story of Phaedra is briefly told. After Theseus kills the minotaur in the labyrinth of Minos, King of Crete, Theseus leaves for Greece with Ariadne and Phaedra, her younger sister. Theseus abandons Ariadne on the island of Naxos and takes Phaedra to Athens to become his bride. On her wedding day she sees Hippolytus, Theseus' son, for the first time and falls madly, insanely in love with him. From that point on, the tragic web of circumstances (created by the gods according to the Greeks) gradually enfolds them all. Phaedra, hearing that Theseus has died at sea, confesses her all-consuming passion to Hippolytus who rejects her because he loves Aricia, an Athenian princess whose father and brothers, political rivals of Theseus, have been put to death by the King of Athens. The report of Theseus' death is false, however, and when he returns home, Phaedra accuses Hippolytus of trying to seduce her. Theseus, enraged, calls on Poseidon, The Sea-God, to kill his son. Full of remorse, Phaedra pleads with Theseus to spare Hippolytus. When Phaedra learns, however, that Hippolytus loves Aricia, she falls into an uncontrollable rage. The news of Hippolytus' death reaches the court. Before she dies, having taken poison, Phaedra confesses to Theseus that it was she who loved Hippolytus and that he was innocent of her false accusations.

NOTES BY THE COMPOSER:

I have chosen only the high points, the peaks of Phaedra's tragedy in the belief that only through her agony the essence of the ancient and terrible but all-too-human drama will emerge and that only that essence truly lends itself to musical setting. The instrumental portions of this work supply a kind of musical metaphor for those key narrative aspects which, had they been treated vocally, would have required composing an opera. This would have, in my view, diluted the power of the single-minded concentration of the monumental figure of Phaedra, the pawn and victim of Venus, the goddess of love, and the radiant splendor of her barbaric ferocity.

Prelude on "Happy Birthday" for Almost Two Pianos

DATE OF COMPOSITION: Finished July 1969.

PUBLISHED: TP. 1971.

PAGES: 3.

TIMING: ca. 3'00".

COMMISSION: Philadelphia Orchestra Assocation for the collective seventieth birthdays of the Orchestra and Eugene Ormandy.

PREMIERE: N/A.

DEDICATION: None.

RECORDING: N/A.

Quartet for Violin, Viola, Cello, and Piano

DATE OF COMPOSITION: 1983.

PUBLISHED: TP. Parts available on special order from the publisher. 1985.

PAGES: 42.

TIMING: ca. 20'00".

COMMISSION: Frank Taplin.

PREMIÈRE: Christopher O'Riley, piano, Alexis Galperine, violin, Miles Hoffman, viola, and Peter Wiley, cello; Library of Congress Summer Festival, Washington, D.C.; 18 June 1985.

DEDICATION: None.

RECORDING: Forthcoming.

Quintet for Piano and String Quartet

I. Introduction

II. Fantasia

III. Fugue: Scherzo

IV. Sfumato

V. Little Variations

VI. Molto Allegro con Spirito

VII. Epilogue

DATE OF COMPOSITION: July–December 1975.

PUBLISHED:

TP. Parts available on special order from the publisher. 1984.

PAGES: 128.

TIMING: ca. 48'00".

WRITTEN FOR: Jerome Lowenthal and the Concord String Quartet.

PREMIÈRE: Jerome Lowenthal and the Concord String Quartet; Alice Tully Hall, Lincoln Center, New York City; 15 March 1976.

DEDICATION: to my wife.

RECORDING: Alan Marks, piano and the Concord String Quartet, Nonesuch 78011.

NOTES BY THE COMPOSER:

My *Piano Quintet* had its inception during a live broadcast on Robert Sherman's WQXR program in 1973, when Jerome Lowenthal played my *Carnival Music* for piano and the Concord String Quartet performed part of my *Third String Quartet*. Even though I advanced the idea of writing a *Piano Quintet* for them more casually than seriously, the idea eventually took hold and the work began to form itself, starting from something I had begun to hear at the time—the second movement opening piano flourish which found its way, transformed, into one of the ideas for the sixth movement. I sketched the work between July and late October of 1975 and wrote out the score by early December.

The plan for the *Quintet* develops as an over-all emotional scenario in which movements are either tonal, atonal, or mixed, depending on what I wanted to say in a progression from dark to light, to dark again—mournful, troubled, and haunted states which alternate with serene and exuberant ones.

It is important to point out the thematic weave, so to speak, which ties various movements together. *I* and *VII*, serving as *Introduction* and *Epilogue* respectively, are different versions of the same material. *II* shares strong but different thematic connection with *IV* and *VI*. *III* and *V* are linked by a single transitional passage which occurs in *III* and is echoed, as it were, in *V*.

The forms of the various movements move from free, unconventional shapes (the atonal sections: *I, IV, VII*) to highly controlled structures (the tonal sections: *III, V*). The "mixed" sections which play back and forth between near-atonality and tonality also have "mixed" forms, *i.e., II* is a *Fantasia* and, while *V* is a *Sonata-form* (but not in the strictly classical sense), it has moments of *Fantasy* which break into the tight, periodic nature of the movement and loosen it up. The "center piece," *IV*, is a piano solo lying between two ensemble sections of which *III* is a *Fugue* interrupted by a *Scherzo*, and *V* is a set of *Variations* on a seven-bar theme.

In composing the work, I had very much in mind the special qualities I associate with both Lowenthal and the Concord–their high seriousness, virtuosic power and intense lyricism. At least on one level the *Piano Quintet* owes its particular characteristics to how I linked them together in my mind.

The work is dedicated to my wife.

I am happy to acknowledge here assistance in the form of a grant from the National Endowment for the Arts [NEA] which made work on the *Quintet* possible.

Used by permission of George Rochberg.

Quintet for String Quintet [double cello]

I. Overtura

II. Aria

III. Scherzo

IV. Notturno

V. Burletta

DATE OF COMPOSITION: 1981.

PUBLISHED: TP. Parts available on special order from the publisher. 1983.

PAGES: 92.

TIMING: ca. 27'00".

COMMISSION: Concord String Quartet for their Tenth Anniversary.

PREMIÈRE: Concord String Quartet, and Bonnie Thron, cello; Curtis Institute of Music, Philadelphia; 06 January 1982.

DEDICATION: to my dear friends, Clare and Vartan Gregorian.

RECORDING: N/A.

Rhapsody and Prayer for Violin and Piano

DATE OF COMPOSITION: 26 January 1989–27 February 1989.

PUBLISHED: TP. 1989.

PAGES: N/A.

TIMING: ca. 9'00".

COMMISSION: 1990 International Violin Competition of Indianapolis, as a required piece for all contestants.

PREMIÈRE: 1990 International Violin Competition of Indianapolis; September 1990.

DEDICATION: to Chessi, Geno, and Jacob [Rochberg-Halton].

RECORDING: N/A.

Ricordanza (Soliloquy) for Cello and Piano

DATE OF COMPOSITION: 1972.

PUBLISHED: TP. 1974.

PAGES: 8 (piano score), 3 (cello part).

TIMING: ca. 12'00".

COMMISSION: None.

PREMIÈRE: Michael Rudiakov, cello and Evelyn Crochet, piano; Gardner Museum, Boston, MA; 1973.

DEDICATION: to the memory of my nephew Robert Rochberg.

RECORDING: Norman Fischer, cello and George Rochberg, piano, CRI 337.

NOTES BY THE COMPOSER:

Ricordanza, which is dedicated to the memory of my nephew, Robert Rochberg, is a commentary on the opening solo cello statement of Beethoven's *C Major Cello Sonata, Opus 102, No. 1*. The form of the *Ricordanza* is a simple ABA, the first section in A Major, the second in F, the third beginning in D-flat and completing itself in A Major. The opening and closing portions belong primarily to the cello cantilena (although the piano part has its own clearly made melodic design), while the middle section develops a close dialogue between the cello and piano. The character of this work, too, is romantic.

Used by permission of George Rochberg.

NOTES BY THE COMPOSER:

Ricordanza, composed in 1972 and given its first performance in Boston by Michael Rudiakov in 1973, is a "commentary" on the opening cello statement of Beethoven's *Cello Sonata, Opus 102, No. 1*. A tonal piece in every sense, it is the outgrowth of my conscious decision to re-embrace tonality without concessions to modernism. The form of the work is a simple ABA, the first section in A major, the second in F, the third beginning in D-flat and completing itself in A major. The opening and closing portions belong primarily to the cello cantilena (although the piano part has its own clearly made melodic design), while the middle section develops a close dialogue between the cello and piano.

Like my other tonal music of recent years, *Ricordanza* seems to have stirred considerable controversy and consternation in certain circles. This is more a comment, I believe, on the structures and limits of contemporary tastes than on the music itself, which will still, in the nature of things, have to make its way (or not) in the world simply as music, not as an "argument" for or against aesthetic positions.

Used by permission of George Rochberg.

Sacred Song of Reconciliation (Mizmur l'Piyus) for Bass-Baritone and Small Orchestra

I. *Hu taraf*

II. *Ki hineni vore*

III. *V'hay'ta*

IV. *Mi im ssi-ssu*

V. *Hu taraf*

DATE OF COMPOSITION: 1970.

PUBLISHED: TP. MS. Rental. 1971.

PAGES: 56.

TIMING: ca. 10'00".

COMMISSION: Testimonium in celebration of the city of Jerusalem.

PREMIÈRE: Testimonium, Gary Bertini conducting; Jerusalem, Israel; 05 January 1971.

DEDICATION: None.

RECORDING: N/A.

INSTRUMENTATION: Fl (Pc), Ob, Cl (B; E), Bsn, Hn, BTbn, Str, 2 Pn (lids off), Perc: Marimba, Vib, Glock, 2 Timbales (H-L), 2 TnDr (H-L), Flexitone, LgSusCy, LgBsDr, TBel, Deep TT, Japanese Kabuki blocks.

Serenata d'estate for Flute, Harp, Guitar, Violin, Viola, and Cello

DATE OF COMPOSITION: 1955.

PUBLISHED: MCA. 1963.

PAGES: 23.

TIMING: 11'00".

COMMISSION: None.

PREMIÈRE: "Music in our Time," Arthur Winograd conducting; New York City; 04 May 1958.

DEDICATION: to my daughter, Frances.

RECORDING: Contemporary Chamber Ensemble, Arthur Weisberg conducting, Nonesuch 71220.

INSTRUMENTATION: Fl, Hp, Guitar, Vln, Vla, Vlc.

NOTES BY THE COMPOSER:

Serenata d'estate, as the title suggests, belongs to that genre of "program music" which expresses a spontaneous feeling response to nature in terms of musical ideas alone. Its pitch structure is based on serial techniques; its form is a freely evolved "fantasia" made up of a number of short, interconnecting sections in which measured music alternates with unmeasured music.

While there are no themes in the usual sense, melodic motives and characteristic figures bind the sections together to create a sense of unity of expression and structure. The composer employs "recall" of ideas for its structural as well as psychological values.

The relative coolness of the flute, harp, and guitar are off-set by the greater warmth of the strings to provide subtle balances and contrasts in a constantly shifting surface of timbre.

Serenata d'estate was first performed during the 1958–1959 season in New York City under the auspices of "Music in Our Time," Arthur Winograd, conducting.

Copyright 1963 MCA.

Used by permission of the publisher.

Slow Fires of Autumn (Ukiyo-e II) for Flute and Harp

DATE OF COMPOSITION: November 1978–January 1979.

PUBLISHED: TP. 1980.

PAGES: 23 (harp score), 11 (flute part)

TIMING: ca. 18'00".

COMMISSION: Walter W. Naumburg Foundation for the New York debut of flutist Carol Wincenc.

PREMIERE: Carol Wincenc, flute and Nancy Allen, harp; Alice Tully Hall, New York City; 23 April 1979.

DEDICATION: None.

RECORDING: Carol Winenc, flute and Nancy Allen, harp, CRI 436.

NOTES BY THE COMPOSER:

I wrote *Slow Fires of Autumn for Flute and Harp* between November 1978 and January 1979, on commission from the Naumburg Foundation for Carol Wincenc's New York debut. Since it borrows some material from an earlier work for harp solo which I called *Ukiyo-e,* I decided to sub-title the new work *Ukiyo-e II.*

The term ukiyo-e (oo-key-oh-ay) refers to a traditional school of Japanese painting whose great beauty and often piercing charm lies in its power to image the world not as static, fixed forms of "reality" but as floating pictures of radiant qualities which range from states of forlorness and emptiness to quiet or ecstatic joy. While writing, I happened to be reading an obscure work of D.H. Lawrence, published in 1931, called *Apocalypse*. One passage which caught my attention was virtually a description of the necessary mental condition for composing *Ukiyo-e* whether in sound, word or color:

> Allow the mind to move in cycles, or to flit here and there over a cluster of images...one cycle finished...drop or rise to another level and be in a new world at once.
>
> *Laurence Block*

The main title of my work is a way of suggesting the purely subjective sources of the music, at the same time suggesting the more impersonal world of nature in which we move, observe and share in the cosmic process of the fires of autumn slowly, inexorably burning themselves out to make way for new life after the long sleep of winter.

This work, coming directly on the heels of my *Concord Quartets*, has nothing in common with them. Where they are concentrated, formalized and structured articulations, this music is completely imagistic. Structured, yes; but not formal. It inhabits a totally different world–one which balances for me the more strenuous world of western traditions with other ways of thinking and making music which sometimes appeal to me. The Japanese flavor of the music of *Slow Fires Of Autumn* derives principally from my use of an old Japanese folk-tune which appears in its simplest form in the last section of the work.

Used by permission of George Rochberg.

Sonata for Viola and Piano

I. Allegro moderato

II. Adagio lamentoso

III. Fantasia: Epilogue

DATE OF COMPOSITION: 1979.

PUBLISHED: TP. 1979.

PAGES: 30 (piano score), 10 (viola part)

TIMING: ca. 20'00".

COMMISSION: Brigham Young University and the American Viola Society for William Primrose's seventy-fifth birthday celebration, Seventh International Viola Congress.

PREMIÈRE: Joseph de Pasquale, viola and Vladimir Sokoloff, piano (by request of Mr. Primrose); Seventh International Viola Congress, Provo, Utah; 14 July 1979.

DEDICATION: None.

RECORDING: N/A.

Sonata for Violin and Piano

I. Sarabande

II. Scherzo: Capriccioso

III. Ardentemente

IV. Finale

DATE OF COMPOSITION: 1988.

PUBLISHED: TP. MS. 1988.

PAGES: N/A.

TIMING: ca. 28'00"

COMMISSION: Concert Artists Guild and the McKim Fund in the Music Division of the Library of Congress for Maria Bachmann, First Prize Winner of the 1986 Concert Artist Guild International New York Competition, with public funds from the New York State Arts Council.

PREMIÈRE: Maria Bachmann, violin and John Klibinoff, piano; Los Angeles, CA; 10 April 1989.

DEDICATION: None.

RECORDING: Forthcoming.

NOTES BY THE COMPOSER:

I wrote my *Violin and Piano Sonata* in the spring and summer of 1988 for Maria Bachmann on a joint commission from the Concert Artists Guild and the Library of Congress. Maria's unlimited expressive powers–matched and supported by her remarkable technical command–served as both challenge and inspiration in conceiving and carrying out my plans for a large-scale, multi-movement work which would encompass a wide range of musical ideas and emotional states. Within this "theater of the soul," a drama of extremes takes place which allows the violin and its duo-partner the piano to give voice to their fullest possible expressive-technical range.

For the New York première, I was asked to suggest a repertoire work as a complementary balance to my own. I chose the Brahms *G Major Sonata* because it seemed to me a perfect foil for my own work written probably one hundred years later–yet both belonging to and sharing the spirit of romanticism, the Brahms almost classically contained, mine, straining at the limits of what is musically possible today.

Used by permission of George Rochberg.

Sonata-Fantasia for Piano Solo

Prologue: Con intensita

Movement I: Quasi tempo I, ma con molto rubato

Interlude A (Tempo I)

Movement II: Allegro scherzoso

Interlude B (Tempo I)

Movement III: Molto lento, contemplativo, quasi parlando

Epilogue (Tempo I)

DATE OF COMPOSITION: 19 July–30 October 1956.

PUBLISHED: TP. 1958.

PAGES: 32.

TIMING: 23'00".

COMMISSION: None.

PREMIÈRE: Howard Lebow, piano; Juilliard School of Music, New York City; 03 March 1958.

DEDICATION: for Gene [Rochberg].

Songs in Praise of Krishna for Soprano and Piano

I. Hymn to Krishna (I): It Was in Bitter Maytime

II. Hymn to Krishna (II): After Long Sorrow

III. Her Slender Body

IV. As the Mirror to My Hand

V. O Madhava, How Shall I Tell You of My Terror?

VI. Lord of My Heart

VII. I Brought Honey

VIII. My Mind Is Not on Housework

IX. I Place Beauty Spots

X. Shining One

XI. My Moon-Faced One

XII. Beloved, What More Shall I Say to You?

XIII. Let the Earth of My Body

XIV. O My Friend, My Sorrow Is Unending

DATE OF COMPOSITION: Summer, 1970.

PUBLISHED: TP. 1981.

PAGES: 63.

TIMING: ca. 35'00".

WRITTEN FOR: Neva Pilgrim.

PREMIÈRE: Neva Pilgrim, soprano and George Rochberg, piano; the University of Illinois; 16 March 1971.

DEDICATION: for Neva Pilgrim.

NOTES BY THE COMPOSER:

I wrote the cycle *Songs in Praise of Krishna* during the summer of 1970 for Neva Pilgrim, who gave the first performance with me at the University of Illinois on March 16, 1971.

The texts for this cycle of fourteen songs are drawn from a small volume called *In Praise of Krishna*, beautifully translated from the *Bengali* by Denise Delertov and Edward C. Dimock, Jr. These lyrics celebrate the classical Indian legend of Radha, a beautiful girl, and Krishna, the god, or more symbolically, the longing of flesh for spirit and spirit for flesh. Nowhere in poetry have I found a more beautiful union of purity and sensuality or a more immediate projection of the ecstasy and joys, anguish and pain, of human love, longing, and loss than expressed in these lyrics.

Although I wrote what appears to be a traditional song cycle, my inner intention was to set the poems as though they were a libretto for an opera—which, in a very real sense, they are since they center on the passions of human and divine love. Three characters "speak": Radha, Krishna, and an old woman—Krishna's messenger to Radha. Each character has his or her own "music," at least in the psychological sense. Since Radha is at the center of the poems, she sings ten of the fourteen songs, and running through her songs are connective musical threads of related motives, thematic ideas, and harmonic progressions.

When the cycle begins, we are literally at the end of the story: in *Hymn I*, Radha is describing how Krishna has left her. She is full of the pain of loss. The events of *Hymn II*, though appearing as the second song of the cycle, occur somewhere halfway through the story; Krishna has returned and Radha alternates between the pain of remembering his absence and the joy of having him back. From *III* to *XIV*, the final song of farewell, each song capsulizes a different shade of the progression of Radha's passion. Krishna's songs, *III* and *XI*, are interpolations of a kind to show the character of Krishna whose love for Radha is curiously remote–cool and detached–yet full of sweetness and desire. In her two songs, *IX* and *X*, the old woman messenger pleads with Radha and flatters her, all with the intention of softening her anger against the newly returned Krishna. Here the songs attempt to express the psychology of a person who, though old, is still full of pride and vanity and is grieving over the passing of youth.

This leaves the songs which express Radha's deepest, most personal feelings; the joys of her first awareness of love, *IV*; the terrors and fears accompanying the knowledge that she will give herself to Krishna, *V*; her sense of deep fulfillment after being with Krishna, *VI*; the bitterness and jealousy over his faithlessness, *VII*; her distractedness and painful uncertainty, *VIII*; her absolute ecstasy and complete submission to love, *XII*. In the last song, *XIV*, the transcendent, shining Radha of *XIII* is transformed into the suffering woman who must learn to live with loss–the loss of her lover and dearest friend.

Used by permission of George Rochberg.

PREFACE BY THE COMPOSER:

I have drawn the texts for this cycle from *In Praise of Krishna*, a small volume of poetry itself drawn from a much vaster body of lyrics by Vaishnava poets of Bengal–lyrics which were produced between the fourteenth and seventeenth centuries by a "great bhakti (enthusiastic and devotional) movement which swept across northern and eastern India." These poems celebrate the legend of the love of Radha, the Gopi, and Krishna, the god. As Edward Dimock, Jr., says in his introduction:

The burning of human love and longing comes, in poetry at least, from a spark of the divine; man's "yearning for a twin of flesh," as one of the Vaishnava poets says, is a reflection of some primordial, long-forgotten lust, and pain of separation.

Three characters "speak" in the cycle: Radha, Krishna, and an old woman whom Krishna sends as a messenger to Radha to plead with her to return to him. The cycle was written for the soprano, Neva Pilgrim.

Copyright 1981 Theodore Presser Company.

Used by permission of the publisher.

Songs of Inanna and Dumuzi for Contralto and Piano

I. *ša lam-lam-ma*1 (Luxuriant Heart)

II. He Blossoms, He Abounds (*ba-lam ba-lam-lam*)

III. She Calls for the Bed of Joy (Invocation I)

IV. *he-tum-tum* (May He Bring)

V. *lu-bi-mu lu-bi-mu* (My Lubi, My Lubi)

VI. May the Tigris and the Euphrates (Invocation II)

VII. Luxuriant Heart (*ša lam-lam-ma*)

DATE OF COMPOSITION: 1977.

PUBLISHED: TP. 1983.

PAGES: 63.

TIMING: ca. 25'00".

COMMISSION: Morton Newman for his wife Barbara.

PREMIÈRE: Katherine Cienzinski, alto, and George Reeves, piano; Van Pelt Auditorium, Philadelphia Museum of Art, Philadelphia, PA; 29 January 1978.

DEDICATION: None.

RECORDING: N/A.

NOTES BY THE COMPOSER:

Songs of Inanna and Dumuzi, commissioned by Morton Newman through the Philadelphia Chapter of Young Audiences, Inc., and dedicated to Barbara Newman, were completed May 9, 1977. Some of the songs are settings of the original Sumerian texts, others are in English translation, and still others are written in a mixture of different settings of the same texts, the former in Sumerian and the latter in English.

The texts of the *Songs of Inanna and Dumuzi* are translated by my daughter, Francesca Rochberg-Halton, who supplied the following note:

> The literary compositions expressing the love between the young shepherd god Dumuzi and the goddess Inanna are written in cuneiform on clay tablets from ancient Mesopotamia, and belong to the genre of Sumerian Liturgical texts. First written down during the Third Dynasty of Ur, approximately 2000 B.C., the texts have come down to us in copies made by scribes living several centuries later, long after Sumerian had died out as a spoken language. Sumerian literary and cultic texts, such as the Inanna-Dumuzi poems, were regarded as *belles lettres* and were carefully preserved by the Babylonians as symbols of the Sumerian culture they so highly revered.
>
> Many of the Inanna-Dumuzi compositions were recited or sung in the *hieros gamos*, the sacred marriage ceremony. The Sumerian king, in his role as Dumuzi-Amausumgalanna, ritually wed the goddess Inanna, and in so doing, ensured fecundity and prosperity in his land and for his people. Our incomplete knowledge of the origins and development of the sacred marriage rite and its relationship to the Inanna-Dumuzi texts hampers our understanding of the precise religious or cultic meaning and function of these texts. Yet we recognize in them a celebration of the richness of life, the fertility of the earth, the joy of love; and we respond to their great freedom of expression.

When I began to consider the possibility of making settings of the Inanna-Dumuzi cycle, I discussed my plan with the artist Fritz Janschka. Janschka's enthusiam for the visual imagery of these ancient texts was immediate and we agreed that we would collaborate in the project. By the time I had completed the last song, he was already at work and shortly afterwards had produced his set of seven "illustrations" in water color whose luminous colors and imagery capture the qualities of the Sumerian sacred marriage cycle in unbelievably brilliant and rich fashion.

Used by permission of George Rochberg.

NOTE TO THE PERFORMER BY FRANCESCA ROCHBERG-HALTON:

The literary compositions expressing the love between the young shepherd god Dumuzi and the goddess Inanna are written in cuneiform on clay tablets from ancient Mesopotamia, and belong to the genre of Sumerian liturgical texts. First written down during the Third Dynasty of Ur, approximately 2000 B.C., the texts have come down to us in copies made by scribes living several centuries later, long after Sumerian had died out as a spoken language. Sumerian literary and cultic texts, such as the Inanna-Dumuzi poems, were regarded as *belles lettres* and were preserved by for centuries by the Babylonians as an integral part of the scribal tradition that had originated with Sumerian culture.

Inanna, called "queen of heaven," is the Sumerian goddess of love and a central figure in the Sumerian pantheon. She is later known as Ishtar in Akkadian mythology, and becomes perhaps most famous as the West-Semitic Astarte, or 'Anat. She is the sister both of the sun god Utu (Akkadian Šamaš), and the goddess of death, queen of the Nether World, Ereskigal. In Sumerian mythology, Inanna is a complex character, sometimes appearing as an innocent young girl, sometimes as a queen full of wrath and trickery. Several mythological accounts of the relationship of Inanna to the god Dumuzi (the Biblical Tammuz) are extant. In one, Dumuzi, the shepherd-god vies with Enkimdu, the farmer-god, over who will be chosen as the maid Inanna's spouse. Inanna's brother Utu advises her to marry Dumuzi, but she is unwilling and prefers Enkimdu. The myth takes the form of a dispute between Dumuzi and Enkimdu, a symbolic cultural comparison of the relative virtues and merits of shepherding and farming. In another myth, which relates to the death of Dumuzi, Dumuzi is already the lover and husband of Inanna, but Inanna's ambition to rule even the Nether World brings about Dumuzi's destruction, as he is sent to dwell forever in the realm of death as a substitute for Inanna. The Inanna-Dumuzi mythology provides the background for the poetic composition known as *Songs of Inanna (bal.bal.e Inanna.kam)*.

Many of the Inanna-Dumuzi compositions were recited or sung in the *hieros gamos*, the sacred marriage ceremony. The Sumerian king, in his role as Dumuzi-Amausum-galanna, ritually wed the goddess Inanna, and in so doing, ensured fecundity and prosperity in his land and for his people. Our incomplete knowledge of the origins and development of the sacred marriage rite and its relationship to the Inanna-Dumuzi texts hampers our understanding of the precise religious or cultic meaning and function of these texts. Apart from the meaning within their original context, however, the celebration of the richness of life, the fertility of the earth, the joy of love, and their great freedom of expression, are levels of appreciation not dependent upon cultural context, to which even we moderns can immediately respond.

> *Francesca*
> *Rochberg-Halton*
> *June 1982*

String Quartet No. 1

I. Molto Adagio

II. Vivace

III. Molto Tranquillo

IV. Allegro energico

DATE OF COMPOSITION: 1950–May 1952.

PUBLISHED: Carl Fischer [TP]. Parts available on special order from the publisher. 1957.

PAGES: 42.

TIMING: 20'00".

COMMISSION: None.

PREMIÈRE: Galimir String Quartet; Composers' Forum, MacMillian Theater, Columbia University, New York City; January 1953.

DEDICATION: to Gene and 'Cesca [Rochberg].

RECORDING: the Concord String Quartet, CRI 337.

AWARDS: Society for the Publication of American Music Award, 1956.

NOTES BY THE COMPOSER:

> The opening *Adagio* of the *Quartet* forms a kind of spacious, lyric-dramatic introduction to the work; the *Scherzo* which follows owes a good deal to Bartók and Berg; the third movement is intensely lyric throughout with canons and canonic imitations binding texture together; the final movement is a not-too-conventional sonata-form, the kind of structure which used to open, rather than close, large-scale chamber works.

> Used by permission of George Rochberg.

NOTES BY THE COMPOSER:

> The *First String Quartet* was begun at the American Academy in Rome in 1950 and completed in Philadelphia in May 1952. It was while in Rome that the possibilities of a more intense chromatic music, which had begun to take shape in my mind in 1948, came to fruition. In composing this *Quartet* I came closer than ever before to grappling with the rigors of the twelve-tone method without committing myself to it completely as I did in the works which followed in the years after.

> The opening *Molto adagio* forms a kind of spacious, lyric-dramatic introduction to the work. The *Scherzo* which follows, marked *Vivace*, is a driving, propulsive piece–more daemonic than playful. The third movement, which takes the normal position of the traditional slow movement and is marked *Molto tranquillo*, is intensely lyrical throughout. One of the principal devices I used in binding the texture together is canonic imitation. The final movement, *Allergro energico*, is a not-too-conventional sonata form, the kind of

structure which used to open, rather than close, large-scale chamber works.

The first performance of this *Quartet* was given by the Galimir String Quartet in January 1953 at the MacMillan Theater of Columbia University, New York City.

Used by permission of George Rochberg.

String Quartet No. 2 with Soprano

DATE OF COMPOSITION: 1959–27 August 1961.

PUBLISHED: TP. 1971.

PAGES: 48 (no separate parts).

TIMING: ca. 25'00".

COMMISSION: Contemporary Chamber Music Society of Philadelphia.

PREMIÈRES: (1) Janice Harsanyi, soprano and the Philadelphia String Quartet; Contemporary Chamber Music Society of Philadelphia, PA; 23 March 1962 (private performance); (2) Janice Harsanyi, soprano and the Philadelphia String Quartet; University of Pennsylvania, Philadelphia, PA; 30 March 1962 (public performance).

DEDICATION: None.

RECORDINGS: (1) Philadelphia String Quartet with Janice Harsanyi, soprano, CRI 164; (2) Concord String Quartet with Phyllis Bryn-Julson, soprano, Turnabout, TV-S 34524.

AWARDS: National Institute of Arts and Letters Grant, for the recording of *String Quartet No. 2.*

NOTES BY THE COMPOSER:

The *Second String Quartet, with Soprano* was completed in late August 1961. Commissioned by the Contemporary Chamber Music Society of Philadelphia, it was first performed privately on March 23, 1962; then exactly one week later it was given its first public performance at the University of Pennsylvania by the Philadelphia String Quartet (then the Stringart Quartet) with Janice Harsanyi, soprano.

Originally I planned to call the work something like "Fantasies and Arabesques for String Quartet" because two terms, "fantasia" and "arabesque," describe best the main gestural characteristics of the music. They also suggest, in a general way, the free (but never arbitrary) manner in which the structural pattern, moving between the two, evolves, resulting in the final shape of the music.

The work as a whole is in two large parts: first, purely instrumental; second, vocal-instrumental with two *Ariosi* for the soprano separated by a *Quasi cadenza* for the string quartet. This *Quasi cadenza* emerges from the end of the first *Arioso* and leads directly into the second *Arioso*. The text is drawn from the opening and closing stanzas of Rainer Maria Rilke's *Ninth Duino Elegy* in an English version translated by Harry Behn.

There are two purely technical features which are necessary to mention: (1) the use of tempo simultaneity, and (2) the relation of the voice to the quartet. I say "necessary" because it is impossible to separate the "what" of a work from its "how." If composers speak too much these days about the "how" of their music it may be either because there is no "what" to discuss, however generally and vaguely, or because the "what" is so hard to pin down in words that it eludes one completely. Whatever the case may be, one of the fundamental conceptions of my *Second Quartet*, affecting its "what" profoundly, is the notion of tempo simultaneity, first introduced into contemporary music by Charles Ives. Two basic speeds (associated with either a "fantasia" or "arabesque" quality) plus their doubles– ♩ = 108 / ♩ = 54; ♩ = 72 / ♩ = 144–are employed throughout the work. Combinations of these speeds, for example 108 and 72, 54 and 144, result in the intensification of the expressive structure, creating at the same time a play with the possibilities of order-disorder; but a play which, I want to stress, is wholly within my control and not left to hazard or chance–or the performers. Since I believe that tempo is an expressive gesture like any of the other, though different, possibilities of expressive gesture which exist in music, there is for me no separation between the technical solution of tempo simultaneity and its expressive intent. The intent creates the problem; the solution of the problem achieves the intent. In the *Quasi cadenza* section lying between the two *Ariosi*, the four tempi are presented together for a time, finally giving way to the fastest speed, which continues to all but the very last vocal statement (*Immeasurable being wells in my heart*) with which the work ends. As to the relation of the voice to the *Quartet*, I hope I have achieved a kind of free rendering in which there is no interference of formal design with the emotional curve of the text. To accomplish this I made the voice a partner, not the leader, in the musical proceedings. Though the soprano's lines are newly conceived, the *Quartet* first draws on the early part of the work and later on the vocal part as well for its share in the vocal-instrumental partnership. Thus I attempted a structure in which the voice is independent of the *Quartet* and *vice versa*. This made it possible to write instrumental passages in their own terms without sacrificing them to the voice. Also it made possible an open situation in which voice and instruments could go together; or one could drop out while the other continued; or one entered freely after the other had begun, thus dispensing entirely with the paraphernalia of introduction, interludes, bridges, transitions, and the like.

Finally, it is possible to suggest that the work exists on two levels, the one abstract, the other concrete. The first part of the *Quartet*, purely instrumental, surely tends towards the abstract; and intentionally so. So far as "subject matter" goes–definable themes, rhythms, etc.–there is none in the usual sense. What takes place is, instead, a purposeful play with order-disorder, a movement between fantasia and arabesque, and tempo combinations which are deeply involved in both. With the entry of the voice, the music moves into the realm of the concrete. There is "subject matter" both in terms of words and music. The voice reclaims the music from the abstract and indeterminate, brings it back fully within the sphere of what is most deeply and in-

tensely human–a concern with the questions of existence itself.

Used by permission of George Rochberg.

NOTES BY THE COMPOSER:

The composition of my *Second Quartet* occupied me over a two-
year period, from 1959 to 1961. The first part of the work was
completed in the summer of 1959, the second in the summer of
1961. Between those two summers, I was completely caught up
by the transition from the publishing world in which I had
worked for a living since 1951, to the academic world where I
have been ever since. The demands of the changeover inevitably slowed me down–although I did produce an orchestral
work in the spring of 1961. When I got back to the *Quartet,* my
whole concept of the work had undergone a fundamental
change: from a purely instrumental conception to one which
involved the voice. It seemed absolutely necessary to balance
the abstract nature of the first part with the concreteness
which only the human voice, singing a personally meaningful
and expressive text, could lend to the second part. I chose to set
the opening and closing sections of the *Ninth Duino Elegy* by
Rilke, one of my favorite poems by one of my favorite poets.
The particular appeal of the poem (and Rilke's general appeal
to me) was rooted in its existential attitude toward the human
condition, an attitude which not only expresses the absurdity
of the act of living itself but which can transform that potential
sense of cosmic or individual despair into the positive energies
of affirmation and acceptance. Rilke states our condition and
the progression of his own beliefs from the lines, *"Once for
everything / Once, no more,"* to, *"And we are needed by all this here
and now,"* to, *"Earth, my adored / I obey / You need no other springs
to win me,"* and finally to, *"Immeasureable being dwells in my
heart."* Each of the stanzas forms the basis for an *Arioso,* a vocal
attitude lying somewhere between heightened recitative and
aria. Despite the borrowing of this style from the traditions of
opera, the *Ariosi* do not alter the chamber style of the *Quartet.*
Between the *Ariosi* there occurs a quartet *Cadenza* whose com-
pactness and emotionalism are generated by the existential atmosphere inherent in the text.

The relation of the voice to the quartet is unlike the usual or conventional relation that links voice and instrumental textures–whether piano, quartet, chamber ensemble, or orchestra. My effort was to give the soprano the role of partner rather than leader in the context. In this way, I avoided the subordination of the quartet's role to that of mere accompaniment, at the same time releasing the voice and the quartet from each other for greater independence of movement. The result is an interplay between voice and quartet which allows each to move along the line of its emotional curve without inhibiting the other, retaining at the same time coordination of their mutually interdependent functions.

The *Quartet* is a serialist work, *i.e.*, based on a row of twelve tones. It shares with my other works of the same period an essential preoccupation with deriving all gestures, thematic and harmonic content from the possibilities of the particular pitch configuration which comprises the row or series of the work. While I was never an adherent of "total" serialism, which meant the application of the same single-mindedness to the parameters or dimensions of timbre, dynamics, and rhythm, I did carry out in the *Quartet* an idea which I took from Charles Ives: simultaneity of different speeds. The idea itself was really not "new" in the sense of having been invented by Ives. He simply developed the combination of slow moving music against faster music, common to Bach, Beethoven, Berlioz, Wagner, and others to a significant level of differentiation in which the two musics lost their metric common denominator and proceeded on their own–though still in tandem. The specific use I made in the *Quartet* of this idea of speed differentiation arranged itself around two basic tempos: ♩ = 108, and ♩ = 72, each of which had its partner either by halving the value of the beat (♩ = 108 / ♪ = 54) or doubling its value (♩ = 72 / ♪ = 144). Given four speeds which, when combined with each other, produced different conditions of internal intensity appropriate to the emotional plan of the work, I was able to maintain overall rhythmic relatedness and invent at the same time, a sufficient range of means to keep the continuity of the *Quartet* open and flexible as well as to overcome the problem of a continuously evolving stream of music without resorting to the stopping and starting of movement structure or too obvious section separation.

The *Second Quartet* was commissioned by the Contemporary Chamber Music Society (now defunct) of Philadelphia and was first performed privately on March 23, 1962. One week later its first public performance took place at the University of Pennsylvania with the Philadelphia String Quartet and Janice Harsanyi, soprano. It is worth noting here that what in those days seemed horrendously difficult to prepare for performance (more than 100 hours of rehearsal time preceded the first performance) now seems reasonably approachable, though still difficult given the nature of the work and its combination of quartet and voice rarely having the visual security and comfort of synchronous metric organization. It is surely a measure of the distance we've come in approximately a decade of experience with contemporary music and the incredible skill which the best performers of the day bring to its performance.

Used by permission of George Rochberg.

String Quartet No. 3

Part A:

I. Introduction: Fantasia

II. March

Part B:

III. Variation

Part C:

IV. March

V. Finale: Scherzos and Serenades

DATE OF COMPOSITION: December 1971–February 1972.

PUBLISHED: Galaxy. 1973.

PAGES: 80.

TIMING: ca. 47'00".

COMMISSION: Concord String Quartet.

PREMIÈRE: Concord String Quartet (Mark Sokol, violin, Andrew Jennings, violin, John Kochanowski, viola, Norman Fischer, cello); Alice Tully Hall, New York City; 15 May 1972.

DEDICATION: None.

RECORDING: Concord String Quartet, Nonesuch 71283.

AWARDS: Naumburg Chamber Composition Award, 1972.

NOTES BY THE COMPOSER:

My *Third String Quartet*, composed for the Concord String Quartet, comes at the end of almost twenty-five years of a ceaseless search for the most potent and effective way to translate my musical energies into the clearest and most direct patterns of feeling and thought. At the beginning of this search, I entered the world of atonality and serialism and came to terms with the musical esperanto that Arnold Schönberg had conceived, seeking not only mastery of the syntax and craft of this special language but also its expressive possibilities. In those early years I felt a new liberation; it seemed I had found the means to say what I wanted or had to. I was convinced of the historical inevitability of the twelve-tone language–I felt I was living at the very edge of the musical frontier, of history itself.

Webern's personal style began to have its impact on my work about 1957, and the result was an even more concentrated and refined use of serialism. In what I regard as my best work of that period, the *String Quartet No. 2* (1959–1961), I attempted for the first time to incorporate Charles Ives's device of simultaneous musics or tempos. In the *Second Quartet*, I restricted myself to the simultaneity of different tempos; this was because serialism, with its total-chromatic foundation, is not "divisible"–it does not allow for the juxtaposition of perceptibly different musics. I suspect that the fascination with the possibilities Ives opened was one of the factors that led me to recognize the severe, binding limitations in serialism. By the beginning of the sixties, I had become completely dissatisfied with its inherently narrow terms. I found the palette of constant chromaticism increasingly constricting, nor could I accept any longer the limited range of gestures that always seemed to channel the music into some form or other of expressionism. The over-intense manner of serialism and its tendency to inhibit physical pulse and rhythm led me to express serenity, tranquility, grace, wit, and energy. It became necessary to move on.

My last serial work was a *Trio for Violin, Cello, and Piano* (1963). From then on I have been engaged in an effort to rediscover the larger and more sweeping gestures of the past, to reconcile my love for that past and its traditions with my relation to the present and its often destructive pressures. This has been an almost impossible task; it has taken many forms; all of them have led me back to the world of tonal music.

Most recently, my search has led me to an ongoing reconsideration of what the "past" (musical or otherwise) means. Current biological research corroborates Darwin: we bear the past in us. We do not, cannot, begin all over again in each generation, because the past is indelibly printed on our central nervous systems. Each of us is part of a vast physical-mental-spiritual web of previous lives, existences, modes of thought, behavior, and perception; of actions and feelings reaching much further back than what we call "history." We are filaments of a universal mind; we dream each other's dreams and those of our ancestors. Time, thus, is not linear, but radial. The idea of the renewal, the rediscovery of music began to haunt me in the early sixties. I came to realize that the music of the "old masters" was a living presence, that its spiritual values had not been displaced or destroyed by the new music. The shock wave of this enlargement of vision was to alter my whole attitude toward what was musically possible today.

Not yet ready to re-embrace "tonality" without reserve, I began to approach it first by quoting tonal music of the past, in assemblages or collages of different musics (*Contra*

Mortem et Tempus and *Music for the Magic Theater*, both 1965), and later in commentaries on works of the past (*Nach Bach*, 1966); later, I would compose sections of movements or whole movements in the language of tonality (*Symphony No. 3*, 1966–1969). By 1972 I had arrived at the possibility not only of a real and personal rapprochement with the past (which had become of primary importance), but also of the combination of different gestures and languages within the frame of a single work.

My *Third Quartet*, composed between December 1971 and February 1972, is the first major work to emerge from what I have come to think of as "the time of turning." Every artist needs a way of viewing his situation in terms of where he's been, where he is now, and where he must go. The pursuit of art is much more than achieving technical mastery of means or even a personal style; it is a spiritual journey toward the transcendence of art and of the artist's ego. In my "time of turning," I have had to abandon the notion of "originality," in which the personal style of the artist and his ego are the supreme values; the pursuit of the one-idea, uni-dimensional work and gesture which seems to have dominated the esthetics of art in the twentieth century; and the received idea that it is necessary to divorce oneself from the past, to eschew the taint of association with those great masters who not only preceded us but (let it not be forgotten) created the art of music itself. In these ways I am turning away from what I consider the cultural pathology of my own time toward what can only be called a possibility: that music can be renewed by regaining contact with the tradition and means of the past, to re-emerge as a spiritual force with reactivated powers of melodic thought, rhythmic pulse, and large-scale structure.

As I see it, these things are only possible with tonality; the inclusion of tonality in a multi-gestured music such as the *Third Quartet* makes possible the combination and juxtaposition of a variety of means which denies neither the past nor the present. In this *Quartet*, I draw heavily on the melodic-harmonic language of the nineteenth century (even more specifically on the "styles" of Beethoven and Mahler), but in this open ambience tonal and atonal can live side by side–the decision of which to use depends entirely on the character and essence of the musical gesture. In this way, the inner spectrum of the music is enlarged and expanded; many musical languages are spoken in order to make the larger statement convincing.

The fantasia-like introduction contains both atonal and tonal ideas, violent and tranquil gestures, directly juxtaposed to each other without apparent connection. While each of the two *Marches* is a unit by itself, they share common ideas–tunes, accompaniments, gestural attitudes. The second *March* takes off, after its own introduction, from a tune barely suggested at the end of the first *March* and proceeds on its way to finally working back to common ground. The *Variations* (on a theme of my own) are clearly and unambiguously tonal (in A Major) and embrace the harmonic/polyphonic palette of the Classical and Romantic traditions. The *Finale* develops out of the alternation of *Scherzos* and *Serenades*: the first *Scherzo*, highly chromatic and rhythmic, is followed by the first *Serenade* which is tonal (in D Major); the center *Scherzo* (in B-flat) is a *fugato* whose motivic ideas are derived from the initial *Scherzo-Serenade* confrontation; the *Serenade* is repeated with minor alterations and expanded somewhat; out of its last open-ended phrase comes the final *Scherzo* which extends and amplifies the first one, carrying the *Quartet* to its conclusion.

It would be impossible for me to end these notes without speaking of the important role of the Concord String Quartet. Not only was their invitation to compose a new work for them welcome, but it has led to one of those remarkable and happy associations that a composer dreams of having with performers who miraculously understand what he is trying to say in his music. The emotional and intellectual fervor, the musical sense of phrase and rhythm, the uncanny sense of ensemble which characterize the Concord would be remarkable at any time; and in the case of this recording it insures the perfect realization of my work down to the last detail.

NOTES BY THE COMPOSER:

Between my *Second Quartet,* written in 1959–1961, and this new *Quartet,* written between December 1971, and February 1972, for the Concord String Quartet, lies a decade and more of change so fundamental in my development that not only is the serialism of the *Second Quartet* and the period in which I wrote it finished for me, but so also is the time of quoting and making collages and assemblages which literally led me back into the tonal world during the late sixties and into a reconsideration of the most serious and basic questions that confront the composer.

Whatever other emotional or expressive content my new *Quartet* conveys, it is primarily ironic in tone and in spirit. While irony may be intellectual in its exercise, I see it as a mask for wounded sensibilities–in fact, a curious kind of objectification of them, and, in particular, as a kind of defense, however partial and imperfect, against the "slings and arrows of outrageous fortune."

When I accepted the Concord's welcome invitation to write a new *Quartet* for them, it seemed to me time to say a kind of music I had begun to feel very strongly–in fact, irresistibly–the summer before when I wrote my *Carnival Music for Piano Solo* (for Jerome Lowenthal)–a music which left behind obvious modernisms, a music which relied almost entirely on basic, simple genres and structures, on direct and uncomplicated gestures. This explains, in part at least, why the *Quartet* is first cousin to the piano work in spirit but not in fact, except perhaps for the presence in both of marches, melodies and accompaniments, repetitions, clearly defined characters and form dependent on nothing more mysterious than direct succession of ideas or their juxtapositions. The kinship is intensified even more, perhaps, by the daemonic, gargoyle-like impulses which kept pushing through, in the *Quartet* especially. To give these impulses their head I found it absolutely essential to reinstate pulse; and in order to reinstate pulse it became necessary to work with metric forces and the disposition of their energies which would allow the music to proceed unimpeded, without strain or inhibition.

The five movements of the *Quartet* are arranged in three parts. The first movement serves to set the essential gargoyle-like character of the *Quartet*, but is mixed with music of an opposite character. The two *Marches* contain some of the same tunes. However, the second *March* takes off (after its own introduction) from a tune barely suggested near the end of the first *March*, and works its way back to common ground. The *Variations* on a theme of my own are unambiguously in A Major and cover a harmonic range which embraces the Classical and Romantic traditions. The *Finale* alternates *Scherzos* and *Serenades*: the opening *Scherzo* is followed by a *Serenade* (in D); the center *Scherzo* (in B-flat) is in reality a *fugato* which draws its motivic ideas from the first *Scherzo-Serenade* confrontation; the *Serenade* returns somewhat, but not greatly, altered, and out of its open-ended last phrase comes the final *Scherzo*, which is an extension and amplification of the first one.

Used by permission of George Rochberg.

String Quartet No. 4, "The Concord Quartets"

I. Fantasia (Ironica)

II. Fuga

III. Serenade

IV. Fantasia (Serioso)

DATE OF COMPOSITION: 1977.

PUBLISHED: TP. MS. Parts available on special order from the publisher. 1979.

PAGES: 57.

TIMING: ca. 25'00".

COMMISSION: Concord String Quartet.

PREMIÈRE: Concord String Quartet (Mark Sokol, violin, Andrew Jennings, violin, John Kochanowski, viola, Norman Fischer, cello); University of Pennsylvania, Philadelphia, PA; 20 January 1979.

DEDICATION: for Mark Sokol, Andrew Jennings, John Kochanowski, and Norman Fischer (the Concord String Quartet.)

RECORDING: Concord String Quartet, RCA ARL2-4198.

AWARDS: First Prize, Kennedy Center Friedheim Awards, 1979.

NOTES BY THE COMPOSER:

I can't be sure when the idea of writing a set of three *Quartets* came to me. Perhaps it had something to do with writing what I used to think of, about ten years ago, as a "concert of music," a whole evening of stylistically varied, interconnected chamber works. Certainly, in part, it stemmed from the awe and wonderment I have always felt when contemplating the multiple opuses of a Haydn or a Beethoven.

By April 1977 I had gathered together as many principal ideas–sometimes just scraps, sometimes fairly complete–as I thought I would need to compose a set of three works, each with at least four movements, and began to plan various orders, keeping in mind always several criteria which were important to me: among these were the desire to ensure maximum variety of gesture and texture and the broadest spectrum I could command, from the purest diatonicism to the most complex chromaticism. The strongest impulse guiding me was the desire to make each *Quartet* an artistic unit in itself and therefore as tight in emotional projection and construction as possible. Whatever else entered into the writing of these works, the classical ideal was constantly before me as a goal and model to try to achieve–and certainly to emulate in spirit.

Quartet No. 4 was completed on December 18, 1977, *No. 5* on March 25, 1978, and *No. 6* on August 14, 1978. *No. 4* is the most concentrated of the three *Quartets*, although its *Ser-*

enade is, if taken by itself, a "rubato" piece, loose-jointed and rhythmically elastic. *No. 5* is more open emotionally than *No. 4*–and less chromatic–despite the fact that its second and third movements (*Mesto* and *Scherzo*) are heavily contrapuntal, with canons and fugal treatment serving as the main devices. *No. 6* is probably the most open of the three, with the widest range of gestures. It is certainly the longest.

Each *Quartet* has in common a *Serenade*–which, for me, has become a kind of personal genre or type, allowing me the opportunity to express lightness, fancy, a sense of play. These *Serenades* range from the tonally oriented chromaticism of *No. 4* to the atonal chromaticism of *No. 5* and *No. 6*. The *Fantasias* of *No. 4* and *No. 6* are highly gestural and dramatic, free, atonal forms which follow the particular emotional curves I felt their positions in their respective works required. All of the other movements express various degrees of the tonal palette, from the classically diatonic *Fuga* of *No. 4* to the romantic *Rondo-Finale* of *No. 5*.

I have stated many times, in various ways, my conviction that the composer of today must re-establish a deep and firm connection with music again through a rapprochement with the past and its traditions. This is the only way he can break out of the bind of a narrowly modernist aesthetic and its minimalist tendencies. These *Quartets* are, simply, my way of continuing to be a practicing composer who believes that music remains what it has always been: a sign that man is capable of transcending the limits and constraints of his material existence.

I have named this set *The Concord Quartets* in honor of my friends who comprise the Concord String Quartet. Many of the ideas and gestures in these works are musical crystalizations of feelings I have about them individually and collectively. It was, among other things, their incomparable qualities as musicians and human beings that I had in mind during the gestation and writing of these *Quartets*.

I want to express here my profound thanks and gratitiude to my friends and colleagues in the Music Department of the University of Pennsylvania, as well as to

The Philadelphia Saving Fund Society, for making this series of concerts of my music possible and, particularly, for the honor they do me in celebrating, in this fashion, my sixtieth birthday.

Used by permission of George Rochberg.

String Quartet No. 5, "The Concord Quartets"

I. Molto allegro marziale

II. Mesto

III. Scherzo

IV. Serenade

V. Rondo-Finale

DATE OF COMPOSITION: 1978.

PUBLISHED: TP. MS. Parts available on special order from the publisher. 1979.

PAGES: 65.

TIMING: ca. 30'00".

COMMISSION: Concord String Quartet.

PREMIÈRE: Concord String Quartet (Mark Sokol, violin, Andrew Jennings, violin, John Kochanowski, viola, Norman Fischer, cello); University of Pennsylvania, Philadelphia, PA; 20 January 1979.

DEDICATION: for Morton Newman.

RECORDING: Concord String Quartet, RCA ARL2-4198.

NOTES BY THE COMPOSER: See *String Quartet No. 4.*

String Quartet No. 6, "The Concord Quartets"

I. Fantasia

II. Scherzo-Humoresque

III. Variations (on Pachelbel Canon)

IV. Serenade

V. Introduction and Finale

DATE OF COMPOSITION: 1978.

PUBLISHED: TP. MS. Parts available on special order from the publisher. 1979.

PAGES: 83.

TIMING: ca. 35'00".

COMMISSION: Concord String Quartet.

PREMIÈRE: Concord String Quartet (Mark Sokol, violin, Andrew Jennings, violin, John Kochanowski, viola, Norman Fischer, cello); University of Pennsylvania, Philadelphia, PA; 20 January 1979.

DEDICATION: for Isaac Stern.

RECORDING: Concord String Quartet, RCA ARL2-4198.

NOTES BY THE COMPOSER: See *String Quartet No. 4.*

String Quartet No. 7 with Baritone

I. The Beast of Night

II. Floating in a Dream

III. Cavalry

IV. And When the Dream Had Faded

DATE OF COMPOSITION: 08 June–20 September 1979.

PUBLISHED: TP. MS. Rental. 1979.

PAGES: 80.

TIMING: ca. 23'00".

COMMISSION: In honor of the Centennial of the School of Music of the University of Michigan from funds supplied by the Horace H. Rackham School of Graduate Studies of the University of Michigan and the Oliver Ditson Fund of the School of Music (1880–1980), for Leslie Guinn and the Concord String Quartet.

PREMIÈRE: Leslie Guinn, baritone, and the Concord String Quartet (Mark Sokol, violin, Andrew Jennings, violin, John Kochanowski, viola, Norman Fischer, cello); University of Michigan, Ann Arbor, MI; 27 January 1980.

DEDICATION: to Leslie Guinn.

RECORDING: Leslie Guinn and the Concord String Quartet, Nonesuch 78017.

NOTES BY THE COMPOSER:

I wrote my *Seventh String Quartet* between June 8 and September 20, 1979, for Leslie Guinn, baritone, and the Concord String Quartet on commission from the University of Michigan to honor the centennial of its School of Music.

The texts I chose for this work are from poems by my son Paul, who died at the age of twenty in 1964. These particular poems have long been among my favorites because of their dark beauty and sharply chiseled images. I carried certain lines with me for years–not because my son had written them, but because they were powerful verbal icons that had struck off the sparks of truth about existence. I knew they were as true for Paul's experience as for my own and other's who have walked the strange borderlands between waking and sleeping, life and death. They are, each in its own way, strange word-dreams full of the knowledge of love–but also full of fear and terror; yet everything resolves in understanding and pain is washed away.

I have tried to treat the voice and the quartet as integral parts of an ensemble, giving the voice and the instruments an equal share in the projection of musical and dramatic ideas. The quartet frequently accompanies the voice (*colla voce*) but just as frequently acts independently of the voice or establishes the texture within which the voice is heard as a common bond.

Used by permission of George Rochberg.

Suite No. 1 (Based on the Opera "The Confidence Man") for Large Orchestra

I. Presto

II. Allegro moderato

III. Allegro con spirito

IV. Un poco moto, soave e misterioso

V. Molto sereno

VI. Estatico

DATE OF COMPOSITION: 1987–1988.

PUBLISHED: TP. MS. Rental. 1988.

PAGES: 200.

TIMING: ca. 30'00"

COMMISSION: None.

PREMIÈRE: Nashville Symphony Orchestra, Kenneth Schermerhorn conducting; 27, 28 October 1989.

DEDICATION: to our dear friends, Stella and Matthew Moore.

RECORDING: N/A.

INSTRUMENTATION: Pc (Fl, AFl), 2 Fl, 2 Ob, EH, Cl (E), Cl, BCl,
2 Bsn, CBsn, 4 Hn, 3 Tpt (C), 2 Tbn, BTbn, Tba, Cel, Hp,
Glock, Xyl, Vib, ACy, TBel, Timp, Perc (Tri, CrCy, LgSusCy,
TT (L-M), SnDr, LgBsDr), Str.

Suite No. 2 (Based on the Opera "The Confidence Man") for Solo Voices, Chorus, and Orchestra

I. Choral Pastoral

II. Scene

III. Aria

IV. Trio

V. Aria

VI. Arioso

VII. Hymn and Finale

DATE OF COMPOSITION: 1987–1988.

PUBLISHED: TP. MS. Rental. 1988.

PAGES: 150.

TIMING: ca. 30'00"

COMMISSION: None.

PREMIÈRE: N/A.

DEDICATION: to our dear friends Porter Aichele and Fritz
Janaschka.

RECORDING: N/A.

INSTRUMENTATION: Sop (Annabella), Ten (China Aster), Bar
(The Confidence Man), 2 Bs (Old Plain Talk, Old Prudence),
Mixed Chorus [All soloists in movements II and VII should

be drawn from the chorus]; 3 Fl (Pc), 3 Ob (EH), 2 Cl (B, A), Cl (BCl), 2 Bsn, CBsn, 4 Hn, 3 Tpt (C), 2 Tbn, BTbn, Tba, Timp, Cel, Hp, TBel, Perc (CrCy, LgSusCy, TT, LgBsDr, SmBsDr, 2 Military Drums), Strings.

Symphony No. 1 for Orchestra [three-movement version]

I. Allegro risoluto

II. Tema e variazioni: Adagio

III. Finale: Adagio–Allegro giocoso

DATE OF COMPOSITION: Fall 1948–Spring 1949.

PUBLISHED: TP. Parts on Rental. 1957.

PAGES: 152.

TIMING: 23'55".

COMMISSION: None.

PREMIÈRE: Philadelphia Orchestra, Eugene Ormandy conducting; 28 March 1958.

DEDICATION: to my mother, in memoriam.

RECORDING: Louisville Symphony Orchestra, Robert Whitney conducting, LOU 634 (ca. 1963).

INSTRUMENTATION: 3 Fl (Pc), 3 Ob (EH), 3 Cl (BCl), 2 Bsn, CBsn, 4 Hn, 3 Tpt (C), 2 Tbn, BTbn, Tba, Timp, Hp, Pn, Perc (Side drum, BsDr, LgSusCy, CrCy, Tamb, Tri, Gong (H-M), Bongos (H-L), TBel), Str.

NOTES BY THE COMPOSER:

In retrospect, I see this work (on which I lavished much love and energy) as the culmination of my first efforts to absorb and make my own the language of the twentieth century.   As in the case of every composer who began his serious work after the Second World War, the influence of composers like Stravinsky, Bartók, Berg, and Schönberg were bound to have their effect; although it will be observed that I did not in this work reach as far as the total chromaticism of Schönberg despite leanings in that direction which were more fully realized in later works. At the same time, certain elements in the initial conception were untouched by any revision and remained within what I felt to be the eighteenth-nineteenth century classical tradition, an insistence on formal design whose internal logic is essentially that of statement–development–restatement. As a result, the end movements are sonata forms; the middle one, *Variations*, is on a theme of my own construction. The work therefore is grounded in a strong tonal feeling despite the restless external aspects of chromaticism which may suggest what is often and erroneously called "atonality". The most primitive kind of twelve-tone row is used in the first movement, second theme; but it functions only melodically and motivically rather than harmonically and contrapuntally and in no way actually affects the general tonal orientation of the music.

There is no program in the usual sense but there is, if you will, an emotional life expressed in and through the music whose character is undeniably affirmative. More than that, I remember quite distinctly being moved by the desire to produce a work whose structure and manner of projection would convey intense energy, not physical energy alone but the kind of which William Blake has said: "Energy is eternal delight."

Used by permission of George Rochberg.

NOTES BY THE COMPOSER:

It [*Symphony No. 1*] is not what I would write now; but it is what I wrote when I was thirty years old. It is an act of youth, full of conviction and assertive belief; I believe in what it is musically and emotionally. I still like its raw power and dark passion, its rhythmic force and its cutting edge, its tender moments and reflective qualities. I can say this because it is—and has been for a long time—completely outside of me and I can look at it that way.

Used by permission of George Rochberg.

Symphony No. 1 for Orchestra [five-movement version]

I. Allegro risoluto

II. Night Music

III. Capriccio

IV. Tema e variazioni: Adagio

V. Finale: Adagio–Allegro giocoso

DATE OF COMPOSITION: Fall 1948–Spring 1949, Revised 1957, 1971–June 1972, May–June 1977.

PUBLISHED: TP. MS. Rental. 1977.

PAGES: N/A.

TIMING: ca. 60'00".

COMMISSION: None.

PREMIÈRE: N/A.

DEDICATION: to my mother, in memoriam.

RECORDING: N/A.

INSTRUMENTATION: 3 Fl (Pc), 3 Ob (EH), 3 Cl (BCl), 2 Bsn, CBsn, 4 Hn, 3 Tpt (C), 2 Tbn, BTbn, Tba, Timp, Hp, Pn, Perc (Side drum, BsDr, LgSusCy, CrCy, Tamb, Tri, Gong (H-M), Bongos (H-L), TBel), Str.

NOTES BY THE COMPOSER:

Although a published version (in three movements) of my *First Symphony* has existed since 1957, the work was conceived and composed in 1948–1949 as a five-movement *Symphony*. This score restores the *Symphony* to its original form.

At the time it was first written, it seemed to many of my friends and colleagues much too long and, therefore, impractical for the then current performance tastes and practices–which do not seem to have changed very much in thirty years, with the sole exception that Mahler has achieved his rightful place in the orchestral repertoire. Who would play an hour or more long *Symphony* by an unknown, young composer?   Not yet tough enough or resistant enough to expedient–and therefore bad, though well-meaning–advice, I began the painful process of paring down the work. As a first, firm step I took out two movements: The second movement, an *Adagio*, which was performed in 1953 as a separate work under the title *Night Music* and was later published by itself in 1957; and the third movement, a *Capriccio*, which was often performed in the fifties in a two-piano version (but later withdrawn) but never as an orchestral piece. These two movements are now restored to their original positions in the order of the five movements. The second major step toward a more "practical" version involved severe cuts in all three remaining movements, some of which I never regretted–for purely structural reasons, some of which are now restored in this final version.

It was inevitable that surgery so severe would leave me with more than the usual, normal dissatisfactions a composer feels once a work is completed, even when no changes of such major proportions as I have just described take place. As the years went on, I felt increasingly that I had mistreated my own work badly even if, at the time, the reasons for having done so seemed "right." My discontent with the state of the *Symphony* grew to the point where finally in 1971 I began to work at the job of restoration. By June 1972, I completed the score of the first three movements. New works occupied my attention in the ensuing years and made further work on the restoration impossible. Finally, in May/June 1977 I took it up again, completing the last two movements. The gestural character and musical style of the *Symphony* remain unchanged. What has changed, however, are details of orchestraion. In brief, the essential spirit of the work is identical with what I composed in 1948/1949 but it is projected through a richer, more varied physical voice.

Whatever its fate may be and whatever imperfections still remain, I am content; the work exists again in the form in which I originally conceived it.

Symphony No. 2 for Orchestra

I. Declamando

II. Allegro Scherzando

III. Adagio

IV. Tempo primo, ma incalzando

DATE OF COMPOSITION: Winter 1955–Spring 1956.

PUBLISHED: TP. Parts on Rental. 1961.

PAGES: 163.

TIMING: ca. 26'00".

COMMISSION: None.

PREMIÈRE: Cleveland Symphony Orchestra, George Szell conducting; 26, 28 February 1959.

DEDICATION: to George Szell and the Cleveland Orchestra.

RECORDINGS: (1) New York Philharmonic, Werner Torkanowsky conducting, CRI 492; (2) New York Philharmonic, Werner Torkanowsky conducting, Columbia ML 5779 and Columbia MS 6379.

AWARDS: Naumburg Recording Award, 1961.

INSTRUMENTATION: Pc, 2 Fl, 2 Ob, EH, 2 Cl, BCl, 2 Bsn, CBsn, 4 Hn, 3 Tpt (C), 3 Tbn, Tba, Timp, Xyl, Perc (SnDr, TnDr, BsDr, Cy, Gong, Tri, Tamb), Hp, Str.

NOTES BY THE COMPOSER:

This work was composed between the winter of 1955 and the spring of 1956, although the ideas for it were sketched as early as 1952–1954.   There are four sections played without interruption and linked by brief *Interludes*. The first, marked *Declamando*, is a sonata-form structure while the second is a *Scherzo* with a contrasting *Trio*. In the third section, *Molto tranquillo*, chamber ensemble rather than the full orchestra predominates, the music speaking through solo instruments. The final section, returning to the use of orchestral forces, restates materials first heard in the opening section, the characteristic gestures of the music being freer, more fantasia-like than before.

Everything in the work is drawn from a single twelve-tone row. The problem was to find a way to employ a total chromatic palette, melodic and harmonic, on a large scale true to what the term "symphony" has come to mean after Beethoven, without losing a sense of proportion, continuity, growth. The language is contemporary but the adherence to concepts of logic of musical discourse is traditional.

The emotional tone of the work is dark, intense. It ends on a note of resignation which, despite the generally assertive character of the music, seems quite appropriate.

Used by permission of George Rochberg.

NOTES BY THE COMPOSER:

The *Second Symphony* is based on a single twelve-tone row which is symmetrical; for example, the row is divided into two groups of six (or hexachords), the second group being a rearrangement of the mirror inversion of the first group. Because of the particular organization of the row, there are three self-generated mirror inversions of the row, each mirror starting on a different pitch. While the notes in any half-group of six remain the same, they rotate position retaining their identity as a group.

This provides ample opportunity for continually new melodic formations as well as a harmonic structure which is organically derived from the relations existing between row and mirror (or mirrors). This also means that it is not always necessary to use the entire twelve-note row in its original form. It is also possible to achieve all the twelve notes by combining, for example, the first group of six of the original with the corresponding group of one of the mirrors; or the second group of the original with the corresponding group of the mirror. Although the basic pitch material is completely determined in advance, in no way does this hinder the free activity of the imagination.

The work itself is in four movements played without interruption. The first, marked *Declamando*, begins with winds, brasses, and percussion announcing in unison the basic theme broken up into three short phrases immediately followed by the same theme played by the strings and horns in a sustained, longer-breathed, impassioned tone with harmonic punctuations by low brass and winds.

Without bridge, a counter-theme, more lyric, is stated by the winds, accompanied now by strings, and combined with the first theme as upper and lower parts respectively (and *vice versa* later). After this opening group of melodies played by the sections of the orchestra, there follows a more lightly scored group of ideas which starts with an oboe solo, harp, and strings. This section is extended through various contrapuntal combinations of the material stated by the oboe. There is a brief, purely harmonic interlude (based on harmonies deriving from combinations of the row and mirror) leading abruptly into a development section based on motives deriving from the longer themes presented in the exposition. The recapitulation begins triple forte with the theme and counter-theme combined as described earlier. The first movement closes with a brief *Adagio Interlude* linking it to the *Allegro Scherzoso* which follows. This is playful, brusque, motivically fragmented. Constructed like the classical *Scherzo* movement, it contains a *Trio* in which the syncopations offer the merest hint of jazz, like a touch of spice. The *Allegro Scherzoso* returns, the material distributed somewhat differently in the orchestra than before. Ending in a rush, this movement links directly to an *Interlude* which precedes the third movement, *Molto Tranquillo*. The *Interlude* is made up entirely of combinations of intervals of fourths and fifths. In the *Molto Tranquillo* orchestral textures are suspended in favor of soloistic chamber ensembles. Oboe solo and muted violas begin, followed by groups of winds and horns, clarinets and solo strings, etc.

The sustained quality of this movement is interrupted by brief *animando* passages whose restlessness refers back to the first and second movements. A theme of the first movement played by solo oboe is briefly brought back, this time played by solo clarinet. After a searing climax in which a six-note motive is harmonized successively by each of its three mirrors, the coolness of the *Molto Tranquillo* returns, ending on triple piano. Immediately there follows an *Interlude* drawing on material from the *Allegro Scherzoso* which links the third movement to the *Finale*; the closing movement is in part a re-statement of the ideas presented in the first movement and a new idea which, as it combines with motives drawn from the first theme, gradually develops to an enormous climax.

Flowing out of this passage of maximum intensity the *Declamando* themes are heightened still further, breaking into a rushing cadenza-like passage for strings, then joined by winds. The movement ends with the simplest music of all, played *Adagio sostenuto e calmo*, in an attitude of complete resignation.   It begins with celli and basses doubled by bassoon and contrabassoon harmonized by horn chords.

Two gong strokes, played "pp," bring the work to an end.

Copyright 1959 Theodore Presser Company.

Used by permission of the publisher.

Symphony No. 3 for Vocal Soloists, Chamber Chorus, Double Chorus, and Large Orchestra

DATE OF COMPOSITION: 1966–21 March 1969.

PUBLISHED: TP. MS. Rental. 1977.

PAGES: 163.

TIMING: ca. 40'00".

COMMISSION: Juilliard School of Music, New York City.

PREMIÈRE: Juilliard Orchestra and Chorus, Collegiate Chorale, Abraham Kaplan conducting, Joyce Mathis, so-prano, Joy Blakett, alto, John Russill, tenor, Robert Shiesley, bass; Juilliard Theater, Lincoln Center, New York City; 24 November 1970

DEDICATION: None.

RECORDING: N/A.

INSTRUMENTATION: 6 Fl (2 Pc), 6 Ob (EH), 2 Cl (E; B), 3 Cl, BCl, CBCl, 5 Bsn, CBsn, 6 Hn, 8 Tpt, 4 Tbn, 2 BTbn, CTbn, 3 Tba (CTba), 2 Timp, LgBsDr, 3 TT or Gongs (H-M-L), TBel, Steel bell plates (L), LgBsDr, ACy, SmTri, Pn, Pipe organ,

ElOrgan (L), Glock, Cel, Vib; Vocal soloists: Sop, Alto, Ten, and Bs; Chamber chorus: S I & II, A I & II, T I & II, B I & II; preferred 4 per part (total: 16–32); Double chorus: Chorus I (SATB), Chorus II (SATB); at least 80 per chorus (total: 160 minimum).

NOTES BY THE COMPOSER:

The texts are derived from several sources. Although I call this work a *Symphony*, I think of it as a *Passion [According to the Twentieth Century]*. It is, in fact, an offshoot of a larger idea which I conceived in 1959–only a few parts of which have been brought to completion to date, the *Third Symphony* among them. The texts–each of which has its associated "music" drawn from a specific work of another composer–bear their load of awesome religious-theological meaning and unify themselves around my idea of twentieth century man's "passion"–the terrible drama of his struggle with his own nature.

One essential line of text dominates the entire work: "*Was verfolgst du mich? (Why do you persecute me?)*." These are the words which Jesus spoke to Saul of Tarsus, who, while on the road to Damascus, saw in a vision the man whose doctrines and followers he held as anathema. After his vision, Saul became Paul and travelled the length and breadth of the known civilized world to spread and establish the belief in the divinity of the man he had formerly despised.

The phrase "*Why do you persecute me?*" has another profound association for me. In it I hear echoed the words of David, feared and hunted down relentlessly by that other Saul, the first King of Israel annointed by the Prophet Samuel: "*Wherefore doth my Lord thus pursue after his servant? for what have I done? or what evil is in my hands?*"

A second line dominates my work and associates itself directly with the phrase, "*Was verfolgst du mich?*": "*Durch Adam's Fall ist ganz verderbt (Through Adam's Fall All Is Lost).*" These words from the Lutheran chorale repertory call to mind the whole range of theological and philosophical speculations whose story form was given us in Genesis:

the expulsion of Adam and Eve from the Garden of Eden. Whether historical reality or myth, man's greatest metaphysical hunger and nostalgia centers around the idea of a "paradise lost", a time of innocence, a golden epoch when he lived at peace with himself and the other creatures of this world.

It was inevitable that the texts I have used be conveyed through the "musics" in which they received their greatest projections. Since I do not wish to enter into polemics, aesthetics or theory here, I will simply by-pass the questions of why I feel it possible to use other composers' music or how I make use of such music.

Suffice it to say I have little faith in explanations *per se* of music, and certainly none in the kind, when speaking of the species of work that this is, which resort to journalistic cliche phrases like "found forms," "assemblage," "collage," "quotes," etc. The Schütz Cantata *Saul, Saul, Saul, Was verfolgst du mich?* is incorporated in its entirety–although its appearance is considerably altered from its first form.

I have also employed elements from J.S. Bach's two *Chorale Preludes* for organ based on *Durch Adam's Fall ist ganz verderbt*. The *Agnus Dei* music from Beethoven's *Missa Solemnis* is also incorporated in the body of my work. Besides these textually derived and associated "musics", I have set to words quite literally the fugue from Beethoven's *Eroica, March Funebre*. In this case I have made a *double fugue* by adding to Beethoven's music the *fugue* subject from the earlier *fugue* set to: "*Was verfolgst du mich?*"

There are other references of a specifically instrumental kind: (1) to Beethoven's *Fifth* and *Ninth Symphonies* (also treated vocally), (2) *Fanfares* from the Mahler *First* and *Second Symphonies*, and (3) to the "question" and one of the "answers" of Ives *Unanswered Question*.

Whether my *Third Symphony* is viewed as "contemporary" does not matter. I attach no special importance to the attribution of "contemporary." To put it plainly, I have tried to write a piece of music whose *raison d'etre* lies precisely in the impulse to speak to my fellow-man in the language I know best of the things closest to my heart. It is my confession of need and hope that our kind will indeed "prevail", and in prevailing, rediscover that lost Garden of Eden in which life is precious and has its own divinity.

Used by permission of George Rochberg.

Symphony No. 4 for Orchestra

I. Adagio–Andante con moto

II. Serenade–Scherzo

III. Introduction and Finale

DATE OF COMPOSITION: 1976.

PUBLISHED: TP. MS. Rental. 1977.

PAGES: 189.

TIMING: ca. 45'00".

COMMISSION: Seattle Youth orchestra, Vilem Sokol, Musical Director in celebration of the Bicentennial of the United States of America. Grateful acknowledgements to Mrs. Louis Brechemin and to the Washington State American Revolution Bicentennial Committee and the Washington State Arts Commission which provided additional funds.

PREMIÈRE: Seattle Youth Orchestra, Vilem Sokol conducting; Opera House, Seattle, WA; 15 November 1976.

DEDICATION: to Vilem Sokol.

RECORDING: N/A.

INSTRUMENTATION: 3 Fl (Pc), 3 Ob (EH), 2 Cl, BCl, 2 Bsn, CBsn, 4Hn, 3 Tpt (C), 3 Tbn, Tba, Cel, Hp, Timp, 3 Perc (Glock, Tamb, Tri, Side drum, BsDr, SmSusCy, LgSusCy), Hp, Str.

NOTES BY THE COMPOSER:

I wrote my *Fourth Symphony* on commission for the Seattle Youth Symphony in 1976. Its first performance took place in Seattle on November 15, 1976, with the Seattle Youth Orchestra, Vilem Sokol conducting.

The essential style of the language is tonal–a tonality which is broad-ranging enough to include not only the diatonic and the chromatic but the atonal as well.

The first movement alternates between two tempi, an *Adagio* and an *Andante con moto*. The harmonic spectrum of these tempi moves between a purely diatonic and a considerably enlarged chromatic palette.

While it may seem odd to say that "atonality" is capable of yielding clearly tonal results, that is precisely the case with the second movement which I call *Serenade-Scherzo*.

The third and last movement, *Introduction and Finale*, uses the frame of the old classical sonata-form but interrupts it twice with ideas drawn from both the *Introduction* and the first movement. The principal tempo of the *Finale* is presto.

Used by permission of George Rochberg.

Symphony No. 5 for Orchestra

I. Opening Statement

II. Episode 1

II. Development 1

IV. Episode 2

V. Developement 2

VI. Episode 3

VII. Finale

DATE OF COMPOSITION: Spring–28 November 1984.

PUBLISHED: TP. MS. Rental. 1986.

PAGES: 147.

TIMING: ca. 25'00".

COMMISSION: Chicago Symphony Orchestra for the Sesquicentennial celebration of the city of Chicago.

PREMIÈRE: Chicago Symphony Orchestra, Sir Georg Solti conducting; 30 January 1986.

DEDICATION: None.

RECORDING: N/A.

INSTRUMENTATION: Pc, 2 Fl, 2 Ob, EH, 2 Cl, BCl, 2 Bsn, CBsn,
4 Hn, 4 Tpt, 3 Tbn, Tba, Timp, Cel, Pn, Vib, Hp, Perc (Xyl,
TBel, Roto-toms, SnDr, TnDr, BsDr, LgSusCy, CrCy), Str.

NOTES BY THE COMPOSER:

My *Fifth Symphony* is an intense, passionate work of an
emotional scale which I hope wholly befits the city, the occasion, the conductor, and the orchestra for which it was
written. It was John Edwards, long-time executive director
and manager of the Chicago Symphony Orchestra, who
originally approached me with the idea of writing such a
work and I am truly sorry he is not here any longer to share
these first performances with me and his colleagues.

The character of this work is mainly chromatic with virtually no overt references to the tonal palette which most
people have come to associate with my music. Its form,
which derives from its general content, is unique for me,
not so much because it is cast in seven sections comprising
one large-scale, uninterrupted movement, but because I
have tried to mix formal procedures with imagistic ones in a
process of organic growth stemming from a core.

The sections take the following order:

I. Opening Statement

II. Episode 1

III. Development 1

IV. Episode 2

V. Development 2

VI. Episode 3

VII. Finale

One has to imagine a kind of constantly evolving and
spiralling funnel, starting from the opening statement–the
core of the work–which, as it spirals upward and outward
in increasingly widening turns with each new section,
gathers up ideas and materials already stated until at the *Finale* everything which has been previously expressed is
brought together and unified.

Organic growth as such–where everything is related to everything else–has always fascinated me, both in nature and in art, and still constitutes for me the great challenge in writing music. While organic growth itself would seem to suggest a kind of monolithic process of sameness, it is more difficult, I believe, to achieve when seemingly different characters and qualities are brought together–and this is the route I have taken.

The listener should, therefore, not be surprised at the sudden differences which emerge in the three episodes, which I think of as imagistic rather than formal. The *first episode* is the most dramatically explosive of the three, the *second* centers on the horns of the orchestra which are constantly "calling" to each other, perhaps evoking a sense of distance and even longing, while the *third* is the most tranquil and coloristic. Perhaps the sectional aspect of the structure of the work and the individual nature of the various sections suggest an anti-traditional approach to large-scale form, but it is in the more formal development sections and the *Finale* where I have attempted to reconcile what I like most about tradition with a more personal attitude.

The work was sketched in the spring and summer of 1984 and the orchestration completed November 28, 1984.

Used by permission of George Rochberg.

Symphony No. 6 for Orchestra

I. Fantasia: Allegro

II. Marcia

DATE OF COMPOSITION: Spring 1986–January 1987.

PUBLISHED: TP. MS. Rental. 1987.

PAGES: 203.

TIMING: ca. 33'00".

COMMISSION: Pittsburgh Symphony Orchestra and the Pennsylvania Council on the Arts.

PREMIÈRE: the Pittsburgh Symphony Orchestra, Lorin Maazel conducting; Heinz Hall, Pittsburgh; 16, 17, 18 October 1987.

DEDICATION: None.

RECORDING: N/A.

INSTRUMENTATION: Pc, 3 Fl, 3 Ob, EH, Cl (E), 2 Cl (B), BCl, 3 Bsn, CBsn, 4 Hn, 4 Tpt (C), 2 Tbn, BTbn, Tba, Cel, 2 Hp, 2 Timp, Xyl, Vib, TBel, Perc (Tri, SmSusCy, LgSuSCy, CrCy, TT, Whip (Slapstick), Guiro, SnDr, TnDr, BsDr), Str.

AWARDS: Second prize, Kennedy Center Friedhiem Awards, 1988.

NOTES BY THE COMPOSER:

I don't recollect exactly when I decided that my *Sixth Symphony* would be the second of a trilogy, starting with my *Fifth Symphony* written for Sir Georg Solti and the Chicago Symphony in 1984, and to be completed by a seventh in the next few years. The only reason for conceiving such an idea was to draw together within a large conceptual frame musical ideas, structural forms, emotional substances and gestures which, while clearly different from each other from work to work, nevertheless share an all-embracing unity of attitudes I hold toward the present-day orchestra as a compelling medium of expression in particular and the gamut of musical thinking that has interested me in recent years in general. Where the *Fifth Symphony* is compact, emotionally intense and driven, structurally concentrated and condensed, the *Sixth Symphony* is–though still intense, especially in its first part–more open, structurally freer, and in a way, more public in its projection, particularly in its second part. Since the *Seventh* does not yet exist, it would be premature to attempt to describe what I have in mind.

The *Sixth* is in two parts designated *Fantasia* and *Marcia* respectively. Central to the *Fantasia* are various kinds of *fanfares*, evoking not only the ancient association with what we now know to be the false glories of war but also the hidden, underlying tragic implications of mankind's perennial passion for making war and its inability to rid itself of a sophisticated barbarism rationalized as the military side of national defense. I find nothing glorious in death and destructuion regardless of the rhetorics overtly or covertly advanced in their cause. These fanfares come in unexpected ways and in unexpected places during the course of the *Fantasia*, emerging out of or interrupting or taking over other kinds of musical ideas. The core of this ensemble of other ideas is a *Lento* which goes below the surface of things into dark and probing regions and provides the basis for deriving different yet related motifs and melodic ideas.

Part Two is comprised of a series of three different *Marches* of which the first is the over-all frame for the second and third. In the old classical tradition of character pieces such as the scherzo, march, and dance forms, contrasting parts were called "trios." In that sense, each of these two other *Marches* can be thought of as an extended "trio." *Fanfares* again occur in these "trios"–some of them variants of fanfares from the *Fantasia*, others brand new. The main tune of the third *March*–all three *Marches* have clearly defined tunes of different character and attitude–was the principal tune of a parade march I wrote in 1943 or 1944 for the 65th Infantry Division Band when I was briefly attached as a Special Service officer to one of the companies of that division while it was in training in Camp Shelby, Mississippi. The march itself is "lost"– *i.e.*, I possess no copy of it; but the tune I use in this work haunted me during all the ensuing time after WWII, and I knew someday I would make use of it. The figures in the woodwinds accompanying this tune are drawn from the material of the second *March*, thus making a kind of polyphonic joining of the two. What perhaps can be called the *Epilogue*–really an extended *Coda*–of *Part II* pulls the *Marches* back into the world of the *Fantasia*.

The several tonalities of the work act more like magnetic poles than the tonalities of more traditional music. E-flat serves as the *Fantasia's* essential tonal pole. The *Marches* are magnetized around g minor, A-flat major, and G–B-flat–D major respectively. The *Epilogue* (or *Coda*) is drawn back into the orbit of the E-flat pole.

I have not attempted to convert the orchestra into a huge, multi-voiced chamber ensemble but rather to take advantage of the massed families (and their possible mixtures in color and texture) of the winds, brasses, percussion, harps, and strings. The canvas of the work is large and, in a sense, designed to allow for maximum clarity through projection in orchestral sound.

The work was sketched in the spring and summer of 1986 and orchestrated in the fall and winter of 1986–1987. It was completed in January 1987. Commissioned by the Pittsburgh Symphony Society for Lorin Maazel, it is the second work I have written for the Pittsburgh Symphony–the first being my *Violin Concerto* introduced by Isaac Stern. I believe very strongly that music should be, whenever possible, written for specific performers or performing organizations. It makes the act of writing the music more real, more immediately human, and completely concrete.

Used by permission of George Rochberg.

Tableaux (Sound Pictures from the "Silver Talons of Piero Kostrov," by Paul Rochberg) for Soprano, Two Actors' Voices, Small Men's Chorus, and Twelve Players

PART I:

1. Night Piece: "I Heard a Woman Singing . . ."
2. Morning Bells Music
3. The Cathedral
4. Night Piece: "Night. Again night . . ."

PART II:

5. Silver Talons Music
6. Echo Night Piece: "Night. Again night . . ."
7. The Chant
8. The Light

PART III:

9. Ballad: "If I Were Sure . . ."

10. Night Piece: "We Sleep . . ."

11. The Eagle

12. "And Yet You Are . . ."

DATE OF COMPOSITION: August–September 1968.

PUBLISHED: TP. MS. Parts on Rental. 1972.

PAGES: 51.

TIMING: ca. 21'30".

COMMISSION: None.

PREMIÈRE: Elizabeth Suderburg, soprano and the University of Washington Contemporary Group, Robert Suderburg conducting; University of Washington, Seattle, WA; 31 October 1969.

DEDICATION: for Elizabeth and Robert Suderburg.

RECORDING: Jan DeGaetani, soprano and the Penn Contemporary Players, Richard Wernick conducting, Turnabout TV-S 34492.

INSTRUMENTATION: Fl (AFl; Pc), Cl (A; E), Tpt (C) & (Pc Tpt C), Hn, Tbn, Pn, Cel, ElHrpsch or ElPn), Perc, Vln, Vla, Vlc, StrB.

NOTES BY THE COMPOSER:

Tableaux, Sound Pictures, written for Elizabeth and Robert Suderberg and based on my son Paul's story, *The Silver Talons of Piero Kostrov*, was composed for soprano, a small ensemble of singing/speaking voices and eleven players in August and September 1968. The instrumental ensemble consists of: Flute (Alto Flute; Piccolo), Clarinet (A; E-flat), Trumpet in C (Piccolo Trumpet in C), Horn, Trombone, Keyboard (Piano, Celesta, Baldwin Electric Harpsichord or R M I Electra Piano), Percussion, Violin, Viola, Cello, and Bass.

The Silver Talons of Piero Kostrov (published in the magazine *Chelsea Seventeen*, August 1965 issue) is a surreal tale of terror and love. Its atmosphere and actions are dominated by Kostrov's real or imagined fears, the "silver talons" of the human psyche which rend and tear and eventually destroy love and life. Kostrov, their maker, becomes their victim.

I selected from the story those images which characterized it for me in musical terms and made each one the basis of a section of the work, conceiving each section as a fixed static projection in sound–hence the title. It is through accumulation and movement around a core of emotional states rather than through development or growth that the work builds itself into a whole. The juxtaposition of violently contrasting moods which mirror the passions of the story is the primary means determining the order of musical events.

In a sense, then, I set a story to music. This turns out to be a completely different problem from that of the usual one of setting poetry. The emotional, therefore structural, curve of *Tableaux* was in no way dictated by the text of the story but rather by a free disposition of the psychological content and substance of its selected images. Conceivably, I could have arrived at a different disposition or chosen another set of images. Theoretically, I suppose, the possibilities are infinite. But one could not escape the iron demands of capturing in sound the dark fantasy of the story and its particular world of time and space. The use of voices serves to project the recurring motifs of the story; the instrumental ensemble establishes a parallel sound-world to the sound-world built into the story itself through the style of writing.

There are twelve sections divided into three parts:

Part I: 1. Night Piece: "I Heard a Woman Singing..."

2. Morning Bells Music

3. The Cathedral

4. Night Piece: "Night. Again night..."

Part II: 5. Silver Talons Music

6. Echo Night Piece: "Night. Again night..."

7. The Chant

8. The Light

Part III: 9. Ballad: "If I Were Sure . . ."

10. Night Piece: "We Sleep . . ."

11. The Eagle

12. "And Yet You Are . . ."

For the soprano I chose verbal phrases. Still other vocal passages, whispered or spoken or sung, are assigned to a three-part male chorus, two speaking voices (male and female) and members of the ensemble. *Numbers 2, 3, 5, 7, and 11* are primarily instrumental, though not exclusively so. The four *Night Pieces* are all for soprano with instrumental setting–as are *Numbers 9* and *12*. In writing for soprano I have tried to take a direct and simple attitude towards the related problems of prosody and vocal style. Emotional clarity was my only aim. Because I consider melismatic writing for the voice to be either rhetorical, florid, or purely decorative, and any one of these emotional stances would be antithetic to the world of Piero Kostrov, I virtually eschewed melisma. The sole exception occurs in *Number 2*–unless one is willing to consider the vocalise of *Number 1* "melismatic".

Equally important to me is the matter of the quality of vocal production itself. In *Tableaux* I began to move in a direction–recently realized more fully in a cycle of *Eleven Songs for Voice and Piano* to poems of my son–which abandons the view of the female voice as an essentially "falsetto" voice, *i.e.*, from the head, in favor of expanding its range into the chest and throat. Singing in the mask and head is a comparatively recent (since opera and *bel canto*) Western preference although it was not always so. It is not used at all by non-western singers, for example, *cante jondo flamenco* singers of Spain, or South Indian singers who, like American "pop" singers, sing only from the chest and throat. (It is more than interesting to observe that among male rock singers the "falsetto" range has become part and parcel of their vocal style though certainly not to the exclusion of the natural voice produced in the chest.)

The *Echo Night Piece*, in contrast to the piece it echoes which calls for head tones, requires the singer to use her natural voice in order to project in an easy, relaxed yet full style somewhat analogous in delivery to "pop" singing.

In conclusion, a word about the treatment of the instrumental music. The structural elements, if one can even call them that, range from close, half-step chromatic reiterative patterns to fourth/fifth drone ostinati; from "bending" individual pitches (horn, vibraphone, and electric harpsichord) to wide intervallic glissandi; from coupling whistling with string harmonics to violent cluster formation attacks.

Harmony exists, but not counterpoint. And it might even be possible, by stretching a point, to speak not of "harmony" but of extended and layered heterophony. There is controlled aleatory in the form of "circle music" as well as other devices which provide limited choices of time of attacks, group patterning of pitches given, etc. Finally, while I myself would not call *Tableaux* "musical theater" (I am still not sure there is more to the term than a certain aura of glamour bordering on pretention), it seems to have called up that association for some people. For me, it remains an attempt to create a very particular and special musical world, true to the story of *The Silver Talons of Piero Kostrov* and the spirit behind that story.

Used by permission of George Rochberg.

Three Cadenzas for Mozart's Concerto for Oboe, K. 314

I. Liberamente

II. Adagio ma non troppo

III. Rondo: Allegretto

DATE OF COMPOSITION: 27–31 May 1987.

PUBLISHED: TP. 1988.

PAGES: 8.

TIMING: total duration of ca. 6'00".

COMMISSION: Joseph Robinson.

PREMIÈRE: Joseph Robinson, oboe, with the New York Philharmonic, Zubin Mehta conducting; Garden State Arts
Center, New Jersey; 21 July 1987.

DEDICATION: to my friend Joseph Robinson.

RECORDING: N/A.

INSTRUMENTATION: Oboe solo.

Three Commentaries

1. on B–A–C–H
2. on Pachelbel Canon (and ground bass)
3. on Passacaglia (diatonic and chromatic)

DATE OF COMPOSITION: 1968–1978.

PAGES: 21.

NOTES BY THE COMPOSER:

These *Commentaries* are not music for performance,
rather music for a unique kind of reflection and study, cen-
tering on and drawing attention to the *collective* rather than
individual nature of musical ideas. What I hope they will
show is that behind the scrim of shifting appearances can
be discerned the form or shape of a fundamental image or
idea that remains constant, that is common to all the different manifestations of that particular idea–regardless of the
issues of historical style or of individual usage of the conventions of any given historical style. What they cannot
show is how this phenomenon works, *i.e.*, how it happens
that collective ideas come about in the first place, how they
are already imprinted, as I believe they are, on the minds
and ears of composers of successive generations. For now
this must remain a mystery closed to us–not unlike the
mystery of human language itself which seems to have
emerged from the race of man collectively while its use,
spoken and written, necessarily always tends to be individual yet remains subject to the vagaries and conditions
of social custom and habit as well as of geographic locale
and historical epoch. In this phenomenon of changing sur-
faces and multifarious appearances we witness the process
of transformation of a basic musical idea which cannot be

said (or demonstrated) to have originated with any single composer or perhaps, even, in any single period; and may, therefore, be viewed as a metaphor of evolution, in this case the evolution of the musical mind. It is even possible, with this curious situation before us, to speculate that what we call the "history of music"–at least on the level of the ideas composers employed as melodic and/or harmonic material– can be viewed not as the old straight-line, linear process of stylistic evolution, each style superseding the previous one either by a process of absorption and extension or by out and out refection in favor of seemingly new "possibilities" but rather as a form of radially spiralling mental "arms" moving our from a central core or central cache of fundamental images so that these arms can be read back and forth from sources in the collective musical consciousness to their transformations effected by individual imagination and formulation.

The central "texts" and their surrounding commentaries are related not so much by conscious emulation and modelling or direct influence and appropriation (although in some instances that could certainly be the case) as by the arresting phenomenon of composers of widely differing styles and times referring to or drawing upon (undoubtedly unconsciously) some anterior, unrevealed mental source(s) which remains constant and invariant and is in no way altered or affected by the changes which occur on the historical plane or through the process of evolving styles. It is even possible to suggest that the musical ideas embedded in the central texts I have chosen may themselves be transformed appearances of yet deeper ideas which are even more basic but are not yet susceptible to detection.

It is my purpose to attempt to trace out the interconnections, as I have found them, in various works by various composers, perhaps none of them necessarily aware either of the source ideas they were drawing on or their other appearances in works by composers contemporaneous with them or by their very nature, belong to no one in particular because they tend to be more generally archetypal than specific personal ideas. They run like a discernible red thread, one discovered, from the works of one composer to another, taking on different colorations of style and personality and same primal stuff. As archetypes of musical thinking they alter only their surface with each new appearance, disguising themselves in the outer dress of diatonic or chromatic, or tonal and non-tonal pitch structure–thus proving that their underlying power to enter (or emerge from) a composer's mind and take on renewed life in his individual style or personality, yet belonging to him alone.

In preparing these *Commentaries* I have not attempted to be complete, *i.e.*, to show all possible manifestations that may exist. I don't believe it necessary. On the other hand, there is no question in my mind that innumerable additional instances could be readily discovered by further investigation and study of the literature. I have restricted myself to three basic archetypal ideas; but these are, I am also convinced, no the only ones which exist. Again further research would serve to widen the possible range of source ideas mysteriously locked into the ears lof musicians.

The idea for the physical format I have used is derived from the Hebrew *Tractate Kiddushin* in which each page contains a central, traditional Talmudic text which is surrounded above and below and on both sides by commentary gathered over the centuries. This ancient format developed by the Talmudic commentators was also used in later times by the Church fathers when commenting on texts from Scripture. Its application and value to the purposes I have in mind are self-evident and should make comparison of examples by different composers from different periods readily possible, all the while having before one the musical idea of which they are all near or far variants variations or transformations.

Used by permission of George Rochberg.

Three Psalms for a cappella Mixed Chorus

Psalm 23

Psalm 43

Psalm 150

DATE OF COMPOSITION: 1954.

PUBLISHED: TP. 1956.

TIMING: ca. 12'00".

COMMISSION: None.

PREMIERE: N/A.

RECORDING: *Psalm 23*: Trinity Church, New York City. *Psalm 150*: Oberlin Choir, recorded at Town Hall, New York City.

Psalm 23:

PAGES: 9.

DEDICATION: to my Mother and Father.

INSTRUMENTATION: SATB, *a cappella*.

Psalm 43:

PAGES: 12.

DEDICATION: to Hugo Weisgall.

INSTRUMENTATION: SSATBB, *a cappella*.

Psalm 150:

PAGES: 19.

DEDICATION: to my Brother.

INSTRUMENTATION: SATB, *divisi, a cappella*.

Time-Span I for Orchestra

DATE OF COMPOSITION: 1960.

UNPUBLISHED: Withdrawn by the composer.

PAGES: N/A.

TIMING: ca. 10'00".

COMMISSION: St. Louis Symphony Orchestra.

PREMIÈRE: St. Louis Symphony Orchestra; St. Louis, MO; 22 October 1960.

DEDICATION: None.

RECORDING: N/A.

INSTRUMENTATION: 3 Fl, 2 Ob, EH, 2 Cl, BCl, 2 Bsn, 4 Hn, 3 Tpt, 3Tbn, Tba, Cel, Pn, Perc (TBells, Deep gong, Vib), Str.

Time-Span II for Orchestra

DATE OF COMPOSITION: January–March 1962.

PUBLISHED: MCA. Parts on Rental. 1965.

PAGES: 44.

TIMING: ca. 10'00".

COMMISSION: None.

PREMIÈRE: Buffalo Philharmonic Orchestra, George Rochberg conducting; Buffalo, New York; 19 January 1964.

DEDICATION: to the memory of my son Paul whose time-span was so brief.

RECORDING: N/A.

INSTRUMENTATION: 3 Fl, 2 Ob, EH, 2 Cl, BCl, 2 Bsn, 4 Hn, 3 Tpt, 3 Tbn, Tba, Cel, Pn, Perc (TBells, Deep gong, Vib), Str.

NOTES BY THE COMPOSER:

Time-Span II is a total reshaping of Time-Span I, composed in 1960 and withdrawn by the composer from performance after the completion of the new version between January and March 1962. The overall musical gesture is implied in the title of the work: an essentially slow, continuously evolving arc of phrases through a duration which, though measured by the clock as ten minutes, lies outside of time measurement. The continuously spunout phrases develop intensity through melodic inflection and a radiant orchestral timbre internally and externally.

It is a music of presence. It defines, as only music can, a state of being. There is no climax in the usual sense. The generating chain of melodic phrases leads inevitably to a sense of expanding duration, larger than clocktime, which lifts the music out of the realm of physical rhythm and meter. The composer has used the language of his time but has transformed it into music which is once again human.

The first performance of *Time-Span II* took place January 19, 1964, in Buffalo, New York, the composer conducting the Buffalo Philharmonic Orchestra.

Copyright 1965 MCA.

Used by permission of the publisher.

To the Dark Wood, Music for Woodwind Quintet

DATE OF COMPOSITION: 1985.

PUBLISHED: TP. 1986.

PAGES: 38 (full score), 9 (flute part), 9 (oboe part), 9 (clarinet part), 9 (horn part), 10 (bassoon part).

TIMING: ca. 15'30".

COMMISSION: Earle Page College Foundation of the University of New England, Armidale, Australia, for the Promotion of Contemporary Classical Music, on behalf of the Canberra Wind Soloists.

PREMIÈRE: Canberra Wind Soloists (Vernon Hill, flute, Alan Vivian, clarinet, Hector McDonald, horn, Richard McIntyre, bassoon, David Nutall, oboe); University Hall, University of New England, Armidale, Australia; 03 October 1986.

DEDICATION: None.

RECORDING: N/A.

INSTRUMENTATION: Fl, Ob, Cl, Hn, Bsn.

NOTES BY THE COMPOSER:

The title of this work is metaphoric and is intended to indicate the nature of the music in the most general sense. There is no "program" as such; but there is an expressive tone which pervades and characterizes the atmosphere, the world within which the music takes place: the world of nature and the old mythology which still haunts the mind of man. Even though the great religious orthodoxies have tried to separate man from nature and nature from man, the great god Pan still roams the woods with his entourage of satyrs and nymphs and occasionally, in those states of awareness increasingly open to human beings, reveals himself–but never completely. The "calling" which is characteristic of this music is warrant of man's longing for a life which transcends rationalism with its arid, barren effects as well as of nature's longing for man's poetic healing symphathies. Both need each other to reach fulfillment; but in the frustration of that fulfillment there is a quality of sadness and darkness which is more than and different from the sadness we associate with the unfulfilled desires of an individual human ego in a purely human world. All these were the feeling and thoughts which went through me as I wrote the music; and, in assigning a central role to the horn, I did so because it seems to me that it is the horn which is the wind instrument which best conveys not only the longing, sadness, and darkness I wanted to express, but also the nobility possible to these qualities. If the other instruments in the wind quintet sometimes suggest and echo the vocabulary of bird calls, that is by conscious design; and, if they sometimes utter phrases which suggest purely human feelings, that too is by conscious design.

To the Dark Wood consists of a single movement constructed around three main characterizations of music: *Molto Adagio, Andante*, and *Allegro*. These are further subdivided into eight tempo/thematic groupings.

The work was commissioned by the Earle Page College Foundation for the pormotion of contemporary classical music.

Copyright 1986 Theodore Presser Company.

Used by permission of the publisher.

Transcendental Variations for String Orchestra

DATE OF COMPOSITION: *String Quartet No. 3, III.   Variations* (1971–1972); Transcribed for Orchestra (1975).

PUBLISHED: Galaxy. 1977.

PAGES: 16.

TIMING: ca. 16'00".

COMMISSION: None.

PREMIÈRE: N/A.

DEDICATION: to Adolf and Isolde Klarmann.

RECORDING: N/A.

INSTRUMENTATION: Str.

Trio for Clarinet, Horn, and Piano

I. Liberamente e molto espressivo–Allegro con molto

II. Adagio

III. Adagio–Allegro–Allegro giocosamente

DATE OF COMPOSITION: 1948, Revised for publication 1980.

PUBLISHED: TP. 1981.

PAGES: 80 (piano score), 9 (horn part), 11 (clarinet part).

TIMING: ca. 23'00".

COMMISSION: None.

PREMIÈRE: N/A.

DEDICATION: None.

RECORDING: Larry Combs, clarinet, Gail Williams, horn, and Mary Ann Covert, piano, Crystal Records 731.

Trio [No. 1] for Violin, Cello, and Piano

DATE OF COMPOSITION: November 1962–July 1963.

PUBLISHED: TP. 1967.

PAGES: 28 (no separate parts).

TIMING: 18'37".

COMMISSION: Nieuw Amsterdam Trio.

PREMIÈRE: Nieuw Amsterdam Trio; Buffalo, NY; 1964.

DEDICATION: None.

RECORDING: Kees Kooper, violin, Fred Sherry, cello, and Mary Louise Boehm, piano, Turnabout TV-S 34520.

NOTES BY THE COMPOSER:

The first performance of the *Trio for Violin, Cello, and Piano* was given in Buffalo, NY (while I was Slee Professor at the State University of New York at Buffalo), in the spring of 1964 by the Nieuw Amsterdam Trio for whom it was written. It was my last work in the twelve-tone method and still bears, for me, the marks of my struggles to transform the abstract palette of ordered chromaticism into something more than mere pattern and design.

It is one continuous movement which is articulated structurally by an essential soloistic/ensemble dichotomy. Each instrument, therefore, has its own level of solo activity. Beyond that there are "duos" and "trios"; so in a sense the "conversation" between the three instruments is open and dynamic. Only at the very end of the work do they combine to produce one single gesture.

As in all my music—and my twelve-tone works in particular—I tried in the *Trio* to discover a "harmony" special to the conditions of that work which would unify the sounds around a basic aural concept—whether that concept is analyzable or not—and produce, as a result, an identifiable, definable musical substance.

Used by permission of George Rochberg.

Trio [No. 2] for Violin, Cello, and Piano

I. Amabile

II. Largo

III. Allegro con spirito

DATE OF COMPOSITION: 1985.

PUBLISHED: TP. Parts available on special order from the publisher. 1986.

PAGES: 74.

TIMING: ca. 23'00".

COMMISSION: Elizabeth Sprague Coolidge Foundation in the Library of Congress.

PREMIÈRE: Beaux Arts Trio (Menahem Pressler, piano, Isadore Cohen, violin, Bernard Greenhouse, cello); Library of Congress Auditorium, Washington, D.C.; 27, 28 February 1986.

DEDICATION: to the Beaux Arts Trio.

RECORDING: N/A.

NOTES BY THE COMPOSER:

My *Trio for Piano, Violin, and Cello* was composed in 1985 for the Beaux Arts Trio under a commission from the Elizabeth Sprague Coolidge Foundation in the Library of Congress. Its first performances took place February 27 and 28, 1986, at the Library.

It is actually my second *Piano Trio*, the first having been written in 1963 and given its première in Buffalo in 1964 by the Nieuw Amsterdam Trio. It is not only the distance in time between the writing of the two *Trios* that differentiates them; it is also the distance in language and style. The first *Trio* was the last work I wrote in serial style. After 1963, I gradually found my way back to writing my own tonal music. The new *Trio* is thoroughly tonal in language, with an extended vocabulary of chromatic intensities. The first and third movements are in E Major and explore in different ways the traditional sonata form of statement, development, and recapitulation. The second movement is in B-flat Major–a very restless B-flat Major, which moves slowly and inexorably through many subtonalities until it leads directly back to the E Major of the third movement.

The music is frankly melodic–the only way, I believe, to write genuinely tonal music. Since a piano trio is an ensemble of equals, I have tried to treat each instrument as partners in a common musical discourse.

Used by permission of George Rochberg.

Twelve Bagatelles for Piano

I. Drammaticamente e con un tempo libero

II. Scherzo e tempo giusto

III. Con brio

IV. Tempo di marcia

V. Quasi parlando

VI. Satirico

VII. Teneramente e liricamente

VIII. Giocoso

IX. Intenso, con un setimento di destino

X. $\downarrow$. = 88   [dotted quarter]

XI. Con moto, passionatamente

XII. Burlesca

DATE OF COMPOSITION: 07 June–19 September 1952.

PUBLISHED: TP. 1955.

PAGES: 15.

TIMING: 11'00".

COMMISSION: None.

PREMIÈRE: George Rochberg, piano; Composers' Forum, Mac-Millan Theater, Columbia University, New York City; January 1953.

DEDICATION: to Luigi Dallapiccola.

RECORDING: David Burge, piano, Advance FGR-3.

NOTES BY THE COMPOSER:

The *Bagatelles* were my first twelve-tone music, composed between June and August 1952. The first eight came in one burst–within the space of a week. I broke off work to take a trip to Tanglewood, where I played what I had just written for Luigi Dallapiccola, teaching there that summer. His enthusiastic response confirmed my own feelings about what I was doing, so much so that when I returned home I was able to complete the remaining four pieces in fairly short order. In January 1953, I gave the *Bagatelles* their first public performance at the MacMillan Theater, Columbia University.

The pieces seem to have survived both changes in my own way of working over the years as well as changes in the musical atmosphere of the fifties and sixties. This being the case, the fact of their survival could hardly be attributed, it seems to me, to their being twelve-tone *per se*. While it is surely not a composer's business to concern himself with such matters, I can only guess that whatever value the *Bagatelles* have is a purely musical one, perhaps most of all because the spontaneity of their emergence gave them a sense of entirety–despite their individual brevity.

Used by permission of George Rochberg.

Two Preludes and Fughettas from The Book of Contrapuntal Pieces for Keyboard Instruments (1940–1979)

Prelude and Fughetta No. 1 (in triple counterpoint)

Prelude and Fughetta No. 2 (in triple counterpoint)

DATE OF COMPOSITION: *Prelude No. 1:* 28 August 1946; *Fugue No. 1:* 16 September 1946; *Prelude No. 2:* 17 September 1946; *Fugue No. 2:* 29 August 1946

PUBLISHED: TP. 1980.

PAGES: 5 each (10 pages total).

TIMING: ca. 5'00" each.

COMMISSION: None.

PREMIÈRE: N/A.

DEDICATION: to the memory of Hans Weisse.

RECORDING: Bradford Gowen, piano (exerpts), record included in *Piano Quarterly* CXXII (Summer 1983).

Two Songs from "Tableaux" [for Voice and Piano]

I. Ballade

II. Night Piece

DATE OF COMPOSITION: Composed August–September 1968, Transcribed 31 May–01 June 1969.

PUBLISHED: TP. 1971.

PAGES: 7.

TIMING: ca. 2'30".

COMMISSION: None.

PREMIÈRE: N/A.

DEDICATION: None.

RECORDING: N/A.

Ukiyo-e (Pictures of the Floating World) for Solo Harp

DATE OF COMPOSITION: 1973.

PUBLISHED: TP. 1976.

PAGES: 14.

TIMING: ca. 10'00".

COMMISSION: Marcella De Cray.

PREMIÈRE: Marcella De Cray, harp; San Francisco Contemporary Music Players Concert, Grape Stake Art Gallery, San Francisco, CA; 28 April 1975.

DEDICATION: for Marcella De Cray.

RECORDING: Marcella De Cray, harp, Grenadilla 1063.

NOTES BY THE COMPOSER:

The term *ukiyo-e* refers to a traditional school of Japanese painting whose great beauty and often piercing charm lies in its power to image the world not as static, fixed forms of "reality," but as floating pictures of radiant qualities which range from states of forlorness and emptiness to quiet or ecstatic joy.

Used by permission of George Rochberg.

Zodiac for Orchestra

Group A

I. Drammaticamente e con un tempo libero

II. Scherzo e tempo giusto

III. Con brio

Pause ca. 8" before proceeding to IV

Group B

IV. Tempo di marcia

V. Quasi parlando

VI. Satirico

Pause ca. 5" before proceeding to VII.

Group C

VII. Teneramente e liricamente

VIII. Giocoso

IX. Intenso, con un setimento di destino

Pause ca. 3"–4" before proceeding to X.

Group D

X. $\dot{\quad}$.= 72   [dotted quarter]

XI. Con moto, passionatamente

Pause ca. 3" before proceeding to XII.

Group E

XII. Burlesca

DATE OF COMPOSITION: *Twelve Bagatelles* (07 June–19 September 1952); Transcribed for Orchestra (August 1964).

PUBLISHED: TP. Parts on Rental. 1974.

PAGES: 63.

TIMING: ca. 13'15".

COMMISSION: None.

PREMIÈRE: Cincinnati Symphony, Max Rudolph conducting; Cincinnati, OH; 08 May 1965.

DEDICATION: in memory of Paul (Rochberg).

RECORDING: N/A.

INSTRUMENTATION: Pc, 2 Fl, 2 Ob, EH, Cl (E), 2 Cl, BCl, Bsn, CBsn, 4 Hn, 3 Tpt (C), 2 Tbn, BTbn, Tba, Str, Pn, Hp, Cel, Timp, 4 Perc: Perc 1: Field drum, TnDr, SmBsDr (laid flat), LgBsDr (laid flat), Tamb; Perc 2: 2 Temple blocks (H-L), take TnDr in VI, take Tri in XII; Perc 3: ACy, SusCy (L-S), Large Gong, Xyl; Perc 4: 3 Untuned TT (H-M-L), 2 Bongos (H-L).

NOTES BY THE COMPOSER:

Zodiac is a version for large orchestra of the *Twelve Bagatelles for Piano Solo*, written in 1952.

I was interested primarily in the instrumental timbral possibilities which I had always felt were implicit in the original work. In some cases, no rewriting or recomposing was necessary, while in others I found it better to change things in order to take full advantage of orchestral color.

The title of the work has no astrological significance that I am aware of. *Zodiac* also implies a circle completed; and it was this connotation which made me feel the term was appropriate. For the work is a twelve-tone composition–and inherent in the idea of the row (or series) of twelve notes is the concept of rotation, pitches orbiting around a common order which holds them in relationship to each other. One may or may not hear this in the music itself. What is important is that this principle of the constant rotation of pitches is a guide to the composer while he is working. The twelve related sections of the work also, of course, have their association with the title.

The *Bagatelles* were my first pieces in twelve-tone; the *Zodiac* my last.

Used by permission of George Rochberg.

IV. ROCHBERG COMPOSITIONS THAT USE MATERIALS FROM WORKS BY OTHER COMPOSERS

LISTED BY WORK

Carnival Music, Suite for Piano Solo

Bach, J. S. *Das Well-Tempierte Klavier, Tiel I, Prelude XXII* transformation of material used in *Carnival Music, Suite for Piano Solo, III. Largo.*

Bach, J.S. *Sinfonia No. 9* quotations and transformations used in *Carnival Music, Suite for Piano Solo, IV. Sfumato.*

Brahms, Johannes. *Capriccio, Op. 76, No. 8* transformation used in *Carnival Music, Suite for Piano Solo, IV. Sfumato.*

Cantio Sacra for Chamber Orchestra

Scheidt, Samuel. *Warum betrubst Du Dich mein Herz* transcription used in *Cantio Sacra for Chamber Orchestra.*

Caprice Variations for Unaccompanied Violin

Beethoven, Ludwig van. *String Quartet, Op. 74, III. Scherzo* used in the *Caprice Variations for Unaccompanied Violin, VII. Presto.*

Beethoven, Ludwig van. *Symphony No. 7, IV. Finale* used in the *Caprice Variations for Unaccompanied Violin, XXI. Allegro con brio.*

Brahms, Johannes. *Paganini Variations, Op. 35, Book II, No. 2* transcription used in the *Caprice Variations for Unaccompanied Violin, IX. Non troppo presto.*

Brahms, Johannes. *Paganini Variations, Op. 35, Book II, No. 3* transcription used in the *Caprice Variations for Unaccompanied Violin, X. Vivace.*

Brahms, Johannes. *Paganini Variations, Op. 35, Book II, No. 11* transcription used in the *Caprice Variations for Unaccompanied Violin, XI. Andante.*

Brahms, Johannes. *Paganini Variations, Op. 35, Book II, No. 12* transcription used in the *Caprice Variations for Unaccompanied Violin, XII. Andante con moto.*

Brahms, Johannes. *Paganini Variations, Op. 35, Book II, No. 10* used in the *Caprice Variations for Unaccompanied Violin, XIII. Feroce, energico.*

Mahler, Gustav. *Symphony No. 5, III. Scherzo* transformation used in the *Caprice Variations for Unaccompanied Violin, XLIV. Scherzo.*

Paganini, Niccolò. *Caprice, Book II, Op. 1, No. 24* used in the *Caprice Variations for Unaccompanied Violin, LI. Quasi presto.*

Schubert, Franz. *Waltz, Op. 9, No. 22* transformation used in the *Caprice Variations for Unaccompanied Violin, VIII. Languido.*

Webern, Anton. *Passacaglia, Op. 1* transformation used in the *Caprice Variations for Unaccompanied Violin, XLI. Allegro molto.*

Chamber Symphony for Nine Instruments

Dallapiccola, Luigi. *Il Prigioniero, Fratello Motif* quoted in the *Chamber Symphony for Nine Instruments, II. Adagio.*

Contra Mortem et Tempus for Flute, Clarinet, Violin, and Piano

Berg, Alban. *Vier Stücke für Klarinette und Klavier, Op. 5* transformation used in *Contra Mortem et Tempus for Flute, Clarinet, Violin, and Piano.*

Berio, Luciano. *Sequenza I per Flauto Solo* transformation used in *Contra Mortem et Tempus for Flute, Clarinet, Violin, and Piano.*

Boulez, Pierre. *Sonatine pour Flûte et Piano* transformation used in *Contra Mortem et Tempus for Flute, Clarinet, Violin, and Piano.*

Ives, Charles. *Piano Trio* transformation used in *Contra Mortem et Tempus for Flute, Clarinet, Violin, and Piano.*

Varèse, Edgard. *Density 21,5 pour Solo Flûte* transformation used in *Contra Mortem et Tempus for Flute, Clarinet, Violin, and Piano.*

Webern, Anton. *Vier Stücke für Geige und Klavier, Op. 7* transformation used in *Contra Mortem et Tempus for Flute, Clarinet, Violin, and Piano.*

Electrikaleidoscope for Amplified Flute, Clarinet, Violin, Cello, Piano, and Electric Piano

Stravinsky, Igor. *Agon* quoted in *Electrikaleidoscope for Amplified Flute, Clarinet, Violin, Cello, Piano, and Electric Piano.*

Susato, Tylman [attributed]. Tune used in *Electrikaleidoscope for Amplified Flute, Clarinet, Violin, Cello, Piano, and Electric Piano.*

Thomas, David C. *Spinning Wheel [American "Pop" Song]* referred to in *Electrikaleidoscope for Amplified Flute, Clarinet, Violin, Cello, Piano, and Electric Piano.*

Imago Mundi (Image of the World) for Large Orchestra

Uses transformation of traditional Japanese *Gaguku.*

Music for "The Alchemist" for Soprano and Eleven Players

Susato, Tylman [attributed]. Tune used in *Music for "The Alchemist" for Soprano and Eleven Players*.

Music for the Magic Theater for Chamber Ensemble or Small Orchestra

Beethoven, Ludwig van. *String Quartet, Op. 130* quoted in *Music for the Magic Theater for Chamber Ensemble or Small Orchestra*.

Davis, Miles. *Stella by Starlight [Recording]* transformation used in *Music for the Magic Theater for Chamber Ensemble or Small Orchestra*.

Mahler, Gustav. *Symphony No. 9, IV. Adagio* quoted in *Music for the Magic Theater for Chamber Ensemble or Small Orchestra*.

Mozart, Wolfgang Amadeus. *Divertimento, K. 287, II. Adagio*, quoted in *Music for the Magic Theater for Chamber Ensemble or Small Orchestra*.

Stockhausen, Karlheinz. *Nr. 5 Zeitmasse für fünf Holzbläser* quoted in *Music for the Magic Theater for Chamber Ensemble or Small Orchestra*.

Varèse, Edgard. *Déserts* quotations used in *Music for the Magic Theater for Chamber Ensemble or Small Orchestra*.

Webern, Anton. *Concerto for Nine Instruments, Op. 24*, transformation used in *Music for the Magic Theater for Chamber Ensemble or Small Orchestra*.

Nach Bach, Fantasy for Harpsichord or Piano

Bach, J. S. *Partita No. 6, Toccata, Allemande, Air*, and *Sarabande* quotations plus commentary used in *Nach Bach, A Fantasy for Harpsichord or Piano*.

Brahms, Johannes. *Intermezzo, Op. 117, No. 3* quoted in *Nach Bach, A Fantasy for Harpsichord or Piano*.

Chopin, Frédéric. *Etude, Op. 10, No. 6* referred to in *Nach Bach, A Fantasy for Harpsichord or Piano*.

Schumann, Robert. *Papillons, Op. 2, XII. Finale* referred to in *Nach Bach, A Fantasy for Harpsichord or Piano.*

Prelude on "Happy Birthday" for Almost Two Pianos

Beethoven, Ludwig van. Optional quote (to be chosen by the performer) may be used in *Prelude on "Happy Birthday" for Almost Two Pianos.*

Brahms, Johannes. Optional quote (to be chosen by the performer) may be used in *Prelude on "Happy Birthday" for Almost Two Pianos.*

Hill, Mildred J. and Patty [Smith] Hill. Traditional "Happy Birthday" tune is the material on which Prelude on *"Happy Birthday" for Almost Two Pianos* is based.

Radio Station Broadcast. Optional "live broadcast" (to be chosen by the performer) may used at one point in *Prelude on "Happy Birthday" for Almost Two Pianos.*

Sousa, John Philip. Optional quote (to be chosen by the performer) may be used in *Prelude on "Happy Birthday" for Almost Two Pianos.*

Ricordanza (Soliloquy) for Cello and Piano

Beethoven, Ludwig van. *Sonata for Cello, Op. 102, No. 1* commentary used in *Ricordanza (Soliloquy), for Cello and Piano.*

Slow Fires of Autumn for Flute and Harp

Japanese folk tune appears in the last section of the work.

Sonata-Fantasia for Piano Solo

Schönberg, Arnold. *Fünf Klavierstücke Op. 23, No. 1* quotations used in the *Sonata-Fantasia for Piano Solo.*

String Quartet No. 4

Mahler, Gustav. *Waltz* materials used in *String Quartet No. 4, III. Serenade.*

String Quartet No. 5

Schubert, Franz. *String Quartet in G Major* materials used in *String Quartet No. 5, III. Scherzo.*

String Quartet No. 6

Beethoven, Ludwig van. *String Quartet, Op. 18, No. 2* quoted in *String Quartet No. 6, V. Introduction and Finale.*

Pachelbel, Johann. *Canon [Bass]* used in *String Quartet No. 6, III. Variations (on the Pachelbel Canon).*

Symphony No. 3 for Vocal Soloists, Chamber Chorus, Double Chorus, and Large Orchestra

Bach, J. S. *Two Chorale Preludes* on *Durch Adams Fall ist ganz verderbt,* used in *Symphony No. 3 for Vocal Soloists, Chamber Chorus, Double Chorus, and Large Orchestra.*

Beethoven, Ludwig van. *Missa Solemnis, Agnus Dei* used in *Symphony No. 3 for Vocal Soloists, Chamber Chorus, Double Chorus, and Large Orchestra.*

Beethoven, Ludwig van. *Symphony No. 3, III. Marcia funebre* transformation used in *Symphony No. 3 for Vocal Soloists, Chamber Chorus, Double Chorus, and Large Orchestra.*

Beethoven, Ludwig van. *Symphony No. 5* transformation used in *Symphony No. 3 for Vocal Soloists, Chamber Chorus, Double Chorus, and Large Orchestra.*

Beethoven, Ludwig van. *Symphony No. 9* transformation used in *Symphony No. 3 for Vocal Soloists, Chamber Chorus, Double Chorus, and Large Orchestra.*

Mahler, Gustav. *Symphony No. 1* quoted in *Symphony No. 3 for Vocal Soloists, Chamber Chorus, Double Chorus, and Large Orchestra.*

Mahler, Gustav. *Symphony No. 2* quoted in *Symphony No. 3 for Vocal Soloists, Chamber Chorus, Double Chorus, and Large Orchestra.*

Schütz, Heinrich. *Symphonica Sacra: Saul, Saul, Saul, was verfolgst Du Mich?* transformation used in *Symphony No. 3 for*

Vocal Soloists, Chamber Chorus, Double Chorus, and Large Orchestra.

Ukiyo-e (Pictures of the Floating World) for Solo Harp

Mahler, Gustav. *Das Lied von der Erde* quoted in *Ukiyo-e (Pictures of the Floating World) for Solo Harp.*

LISTED BY COMPOSER

Johann Sebastian Bach

Das Well-Tempierte Klavier, Tiel I, Prelude XXII transformation of material used in *Carnival Music, Suite for Piano Solo, III. Largo.*

Sinfonia No. 9 quotations and transformations used in *Carnival Music, Suite for Piano Solo, IV. Sfumato.*

Partita No. 6, Toccata, Allemande, Air, and *Sarabande* quotations plus commentary used in *Nach Bach, A Fantasy for Harpsichord or Piano.*

Two Chorale Preludes on *Durch Adams Fall ist ganz verderbt,* used in *Symphony No. 3 for Vocal Soloists, Chamber Chorus, Double Chorus, and Large Orchestra.*

Ludwig van Beethoven

Missa Solemnis, Agnus Dei used in *Symphony No. 3 for Vocal Soloists, Chamber Chorus, Double Chorus, and Large Orchestra.*

Sonata for Cello, Op. 102, No. 1 commentary used in *Ricordanza (Soliloquy) for Cello and Piano.*

String Quartet Op. 18, No. 2, materials used in *String Quartet No. 6, V. Introduction and Finale.*

String Quartet, Op. 74, III. Scherzo used in the *Caprice Variations for Unaccompanied Violin, VII. Presto.*

String Quartet, Op. 130 quoted in *Music for the Magic Theater for Chamber Ensemble or Small Orchestra.*

Symphony No. 3, III. Marcia funebre transformation used in *Symphony No. 3 for Vocal Soloists, Chamber Chorus, Double Chorus, and Large Orchestra.*

Symphony No. 5, transformation used in *Symphony No. 3 for Vocal Soloists, Chamber Chorus, Double Chorus, and Large Orchestra.*

Symphony No. 7, IV. Finale used in the *Caprice Variations for Unaccompanied Violin, XXI. Allegro con brio.*

Symphony No. 9, transformation used in *Symphony No. 3 for Vocal Soloists, Chamber Chorus, Double Chorus, and Large Orchestra.*

Optional quote (to be chosen by the performer) may be used in *Prelude on "Happy Birthday" for Almost Two Pianos.*

Alban Berg

Vier Stücke für Klarinette und Klavier, Op. 5 transformation used in *Contra Mortem et Tempus for Flute, Clarinet, Violin, and Piano.*

Luciano Berio

Sequenza I per Flauto Solo transformation used in *Contra Mortem et Tempus for Flute, Clarinet, Violin, and Piano.*

Pierre Boulez

Sonatine pour Flûte et Piano transformation used in *Contra Mortem et Tempus for Flute, Clarinet, Violin, and Piano.*

Johannes Brahms

Capriccio, Op. 76, No. 8 transformation used in *Carnival Music, Suite for Piano Solo, IV. Sfumato.*

Intermezzo, Op. 117, No. 3 quoted in *Nach Bach, A Fantasy for Harpsichord or Piano.*

Paganini Variations, Op. 35, Book II, No. 2 transcription used in the *Caprice Variations for Unaccompanied Violin, IX. Non troppo presto.*

Paganini Variations, Op. 35, Book II, No. 3 transcription used in the *Caprice Variations for Unaccompanied Violin, X. Vivace.*

Paganini Variations, Op. 35, Book II, No. 11 transcription used in the *Caprice Variations for Unaccompanied Violin, XI. Andante.*

Paganini Variations, Op. 35, Book II, No. 12 transcription used in the *Caprice Variations for Unaccompanied Violin, XII. Andante con moto.*

Paganini Variations, Op. 35, Book II, No. 10 used in the *Caprice Variations for Unaccompanied Violin, XIII. Feroce, energico.*

Optional quote (to be chosen by the performer) may be used in *Prelude on "Happy Birthday" for Almost Two Pianos.*

Frédéric Chopin
Etude, Op. 10, No. 6 referred to in *Nach Bach, A Fantasy for Harpsichord or Piano.*

Luigi Dallapiccola
Il Prigioniero, Fratello Motif quoted in the *Chamber Symphony for Nine Instruments, II. Adagio.*

Miles Davis
Stella by Starlight [recording] transformation used in *Music for the Magic Theater for Chamber Ensemble or Small Orchestra.*

Mildred J. Hill and Patty [Smith] Hill
Traditional "Happy Birthday" tune quoted in the *Prelude on "Happy Birthday" for Almost Two Pianos.*

Charles Ives
Piano Trio transformation used in *Contra Mortem et Tempus for Flute, Clarinet, Violin, and Piano.*

Unanswered Question used in *Symphony No. 3 for Vocal Soloists, Chamber Chorus, Double Chorus, and Large Orchestra.*

Gustav Mahler

Das Lied von der Erde quoted in *Ukiyo-e (Pictures of the Floating World) for Solo Harp.*

Symphony No. 1 transformation used in the *Symphony No. 3 for Vocal Soloists, Chamber Chorus, Double Chorus, and Large Orchestra.*

Symphony No. 2 transformation used in the *Symphony No. 3 for Vocal Soloists, Chamber Chorus, Double Chorus, and Large Orchestra.*

Symphony No. 5, III. Scherzo transformation used in the *Caprice Variations for Unaccompanied Violin, XLIV. Scherzo.*

Symphony No. 9, IV. Adagio quoted in *Music for the Magic Theater for Chamber Ensemble or Small Orchestra.*

Waltz material used in *String Quartet No. 4, III. Serenade.*

Wolfgang Amadeus Mozart

Divertimento, K. 287, II. Adagio, quoted in *Music for the Magic Theater for Chamber Ensemble or Small Orchestra.*

Johann Pachelbel

Canon [Bass] used in *String Quartet No. 6, III. Variations (on the Pachelbel Canon).*

Niccolò Paganini

Caprice, Book II, Op. 1, No. 24 used in the *Caprice Variations for Unaccompanied Violin, LI. Quasi presto.*

Samuel Scheidt

Warum betrubst Du Dich mein Herz transcription used in *Cantio Sacra for Chamber Orchestra.*

Arnold Schönberg

Fünf Klavierstücke Op. 23, No. 1 quotations used in the *Sonata-Fantasia for Piano Solo.*

Franz Schubert

Waltz, Op. 9, No. 22 transformation used in the *Caprice Variations for Unaccompanied Violin, VIII. Languido.*

String Quartet in G Major, materials used in *String Quartet No. 5, III. Scherzo.*

Robert Schumann

Papillons, Op. 2, XII. Finale referred to in *Nach Bach, A Fantasy for Harpsichord or Piano.*

Heinrich Schütz

Symphonica Sacra: Saul, Saul, Saul, was verfolgst Du Mich? transformation used in *Symphony No. 3 for Vocal Soloists, Chamber Chorus, Double Chorus, and Large Orchestra.*

John Philip Sousa

Optional quote (to be chosen by the performer) may be used in *Prelude on "Happy Birthday" for Almost Two Pianos.*

Karlheinz Stockhausen

Nr. 5 Zeitmasse für fünf Holzbläser quoted in *Music for the Magic Theater for Chamber Ensemble or Small Orchestra.*

Igor Stravinsky

Agon quoted in *Electrikaleidoscope for Amplified Flute, Clarinet, Violin, Cello, Piano, and Electric Piano.*

Tylman Susato [attributed]

Tune used in *Music for "The Alchemist" for Soprano and Eleven Players.*

Tune used in *Electrikaleidoscope for Amplified Flute, Clarinet, Violin, Cello, Piano, and Electric Piano.*

David C. Thomas

Spinning Wheel [American "Pop" song] referred to in *Electrikaleidoscope for Amplified Flute, Clarinet, Violin, Cello, Piano, and Electric Piano.*

Edgard Varèse

Density 21,5 pour Solo Flûte transformation used in *Contra Mortem et Tempus for Flute, Clarinet, Violin, and Piano.*

Déserts quotations used in *Music for the Magic Theater for Chamber Ensemble or Small Orchestra.*

Anton Webern

Concerto for Nine Instruments, Op. 24, transformation used in *Music for the Magic Theater for Chamber Ensemble or Small Orchestra.*

Passacaglia, Op. 1 transformation used in the *Caprice Variations for Unaccompanied Violin, XLI. Allegro molto.*

Vier Stücke für Geige und Klavier, Op. 7 transformation used in *Contra Mortem et Tempus for Flute, Violin, Clarinet, and Piano.*

Other

Japanese folk tune appears in the last section of *Slow Fires of Autumn for Flute and Harp.*

Japanese *Gagaku* tansformations used in *Imago Mundi (Image of the World) for Large Orchestra.*

Optional "live" radio station broadcast may be used in *Prelude on "Happy Birthday" for Almost Two Pianos.*

V. ROCHBERG COMPOSITIONS THAT USE MATERIALS FROM OTHER WORKS BY ROCHBERG

Apocalyptica [I] for Large Wind Ensemble (1964)

Materials used in *Black Sounds (Apocalyptica II) for Seventeen Winds* (1965).

Arioso for Piano Solo (1956)

A reworked version of *Little Suite, IV. Prelude* (16 December 1944, Fontainbleau, France) [Unpublished].

Ballade for Piano Solo [Unpublished] (1939)

Reworked and used in the *Partita Variations for Piano Solo, Tema: Ballade* (1976).

Black Sounds (Apocalyptica II) for Seventeen Winds (1965)

Materials drawn from *Apocalyptica [I] for Large Wind Ensemble* (1964).

Book of Contrapuntal Pieces for Keyboard Instruments (1940–1979)

Includes *Canons, Inventions,* and *Fugues* (1940–1946); *Sonata No. 2 for Piano Solo, Fugue* (1948); a transcription [piano four-hand] of *String Quartet No. 4, II. Fuga* (1977).

Book of Songs for Voice and Piano (1937–1969)

30. *Ecce Puer* (First version 21 December 1949, Second version 26 August 1951, Revised 25 May 1969), used in the *Quintet for Piano and String Quartet, II. Fantasia* (1976).

Capriccio for Orchestra (1948–1949)

Originally *Symphony No. 1 for Orchestra, III. Capriccio*; lifted from its position in *Symphony No. 1 for Orchestra [three-movement version]* (1948–1949); later restored to its original position in *Symphony No. 1 for Orchestra [five movement version]* (1948–1949, Revised 1957–1977).

Transcribed and titled *Capriccio for Two Pianos* [Unpublished] (1950).

Capriccio for Two Pianos [Unpublished] (1950)

A transcription of *Symphony No. 1 for Orchestra, III. Capriccio* (1948–1949, Revised 1957–1977).

Caprice Variations for Unaccompanied Violin (1971)

18. *Allegro fantastico* theme used in *String Quartet No. 3, I. Introduction–Fantasia* (1972–1973).

Carnival Music, Suite for Piano Solo (1971)

A transcription of *I. Fanfares and March* is quoted in *Symphony No. 6 for Orchestra, II. Marches* (1986).

Chamber Symphony for Nine Instruments (1953)

Uses the same twelve-tone row as the *Serenata d'estate for Flute, Harp, Guitar, Violin, Viola, and Cello* (1955).

The Confidence Man, An Opera in Two Parts (1980–1982)

Materials used in *Suite No. 1 (Based on the Opera "The Confidence Man") for Large Orchestra* (1987–1988).

Materials used in *Suite No. 2 (Based on the Opera "The Confidence Man") for Solo Voices, Chorus, and Orchestra* (1987–1988).

Transformations used in the *Quintet for String Quintet [double cello]* (1975).

Contra Mortem et Tempus for Flute, Clarinet, Violin, and Piano (1965)

Uses transformations of the *Dialogues for Clarinet and Piano* (1957).

Materials reworked and included in *Sonata for Violin and Piano* (1988).

Dialogues for Clarinet and Piano (1957)

Transformations used in the *Contra Mortem et Tempus for Flute, Clarinet, Violin, and Piano* (1965).

Electrikaleidoscope for Amplified Flute, Clarinet, Violin, Cello, Piano, and Electric Piano (1972)

Uses materials from *Music for "The Alchemist" for Soprano and Eleven Players, Double Canon and Fight Music* (1965).

Coda becomes the *Theme* of *Quintet for Piano and String Quartet, V. Little Variations* (1975).

Fantasies for Voice and Piano (1971)

Materials reused in *String Quartet No. 3*.

Four Short Sonatas for Piano Solo (1984)

Sonata No. 2 is used in *Symphony No. 5 for Orchestra* (1984).

A complete reworking of *Sonata No. 3* is used in the *Trio [No. 2] for Violin, Cello, and Piano, III. Allegro con spirito* (1985).

Sonata No. 4 is an adaption of the accompaniment from *Songs of Inanna and Dumuzi, IV. he-tum-tum (May He Bring)* (1984).

March of the Halberds [Unpublished] (1943).

Used in *Symphony No. 6 for Orchestra, II. Marches* (1986).

Music for "The Alchemist," for Soprano and Eleven Players (1965)

Materials from the *Double Canon* and *Fight Music* are used in *Electrikaleidoscope for Amplified Flute, Clarinet, Violin, Cello, Piano, and Electric Piano* (1972).

Music for the Magic Theater for Chamber Ensemble or Small Orchestra (1965)

Includes quotations from *String Quartet No. 2 with Soprano* (1959–1961).

Referred to in the *Sonata-Fantasia for Piano Solo* (1956).

Nach Bach, Fantasy for Harpsichord or Piano (1966)

A revised version of the middle section is used in the *Partita Variations, XI. Arabesque* (1976).

Night Music for Orchestra (1948–1949)

Originally *Symphony No. 1 for Orchestra, II. Night Music*; cut from its position in *Symphony No. 1 for Orchestra [three-movement version]* (1948–1949); later restored to its original position in *Symphony No. 1 for Orchestra [five-movement version]* (1948–1949, Revised 1957–1977).

Partita Variations for Piano Solo (1976)

Tema: Ballade is a reworked version of the *Ballade for Piano Solo* [Unpublished] (1939).

IV. Cortege includes materials, transformed and expanded from the *Quintet for Piano and String Quartet, I. Introduction and VII. Epilogue* (1975).

VI. The Deepest Carillon uses much of the same pitch material as the *Quintet for Piano and String Quartet, IV. Sfumato* (1975).

XI. Arabesque is a revision of the middle section of *Nach Bach, Fantasy for Harpsichord or Piano* (1966).

Quintet for Piano and String Quartet (1975)

I. Introduction and VII. Epilogue transformed and expanded materials used in the Partita Variations, IV. Cortege (1976).

II. Fantasia uses material from Book of Songs for Voice and Piano (1937–1969), 30. Ecce Puer (First version 21 December 1949, Second version 26 August 1951, Revised 25 May 1969).

IV. Sfumato uses much of the same material as the Partita Variations, VI. The Deepest Carillon (1976).

V. Little Variations [Theme] taken from Electrikaleidoscope for Amplified Flute, Clarinet, Violin, Cello, Piano, and Electric Piano, Coda (1972).

Quintet for String Quintet [double cello] (1975)

Includes transformations of materials from The Confidence Man, An Opera in Two Parts.

Serenata d'estate for Flute, Harp, Guitar, Violin, Viola, and Cello (1955)

Uses the same twelve-tone row as the Chamber Symphony for Nine Instruments (1953).

Sonata for Violin and Piano (1988)

Includes reworked materials from Contra Mortem et Tempus for Flute, Violin, Clarinet, and Piano (1965).

Sonata No. 2 for Piano Solo (1948)

Fugue, included in the Book of Contrapuntal Pieces for Keyboard Instruments, 19. Fugue: Allegro ma non troppo (1979).

Sonata-Fantasia for Piano Solo (1956)

Referred to in the Music for the Magic Theater for Chamber Ensemble or Small Orchestra (1965).

Songs of Innana & Dumuzi for Contralto and Piano (1977)

The accompaniment of *IV. he-tum-tum (May He Bring)* is adapted and used in the *Four Short Sonatas, Sonata No. 4* (1984).

String Quartet No. 2 with Soprano (1961)

Quoted in the *Music for the Magic Theater for Chamber Ensemble or Small Orchestra* (1965).

String Quartet No. 3 (1972–1973)

Includes materials from the *Fantasies for Voice and Piano* (1971).

I. *Introduction–Fantasia [Theme]* taken from *Caprice Variations for Unaccompanied Violin, 18. Allegro fantastico* (1971).

III. *Variations* transcribed for string orchestra and titled *Transcendental Variations for String Orchestra* (1975).

String Quartet No. 4 (1977)

Fugue, transcribed [piano four-hand] and included in the *Book of Contrapuntal Pieces for Keyboard Instruments, 20. Fugue for One Piano, Four-hands: Adagio religioso, serioso* (1979).

Suite No. 1 for Orchestra (1987–1988)

Based on materials from *The Confidence Man, An Opera in Two Parts* (1980–1982).

Suite No. 2 for Solo Voices, Chorus, and Orchestra (1987–1988)

Based on materials from *The Confidence Man, An Opera in Two Parts* (1980–1982).

Symphony No. 1 for Orchestra (1948–1949, Revised 1957–1977)

II. *Night Music for Orchestra* (1948–1949) cut from its original place in *Symphony No. 1 for Orchestra [three-movement version]* (1948–1949) and published separately as *Night Music for Orchestra* (1948–1949); later restored to its original place in *Symphony No. 1 for Orchestra [five-movement version]* (1948–1949, Revised 1957–1977).

III. *Capriccio for Orchestra* (1948–1949) cut from its original place in *Symphony No. 1 for Orchestra [three-movement version]* (1948–1949); published separately as *Capriccio for Orchestra* (1948–1949); later restored to its original place in *Symphony No. 1 for Orchestra [five-movement version]* (1948–1949, Revised 1957–1977).

Symphony No. 4 for Large Orchestra (1976)

II. *Serenade–Scherzo* is a reworked version of the *Waltz Serenade for Orchestra* (1957).

Symphony No. 5 for Orchestra (1984)

Uses materials from *Four Short Sonatas, Sonata No. 2* (1984).

Symphony No. 6 for Orchestra (1986)

II. *Marches* includes a transcribed quotation from *Carnival Music, I. Fanfares and March* (1971).

II. *Marches* includes the *March of the Halberds* [Unpublished] (1943).

Transcendental Variations for String Orchestra (1975)

A transcription of *String Quartet No. 3, III. Variations* (1971–1972).

Trio [No. 2] for Violin, Cello, and Piano (1985)

III. *Allegro con spirito* is a complete reworking of the *Four Short Sonatas, Sonata No. 3* (1984).

Twelve Bagatelles for Piano Solo (1952)

Transcribed for orchestra (with some slight revisions) and titled *Zodiac for Orchestra* (1964).

Waltz Serenade for Orchestra (1957)

A transcription of the *Waltzes for String Orchestra* (1957).

Waltzes for String Orchestra (1957)

Transcribed and titled *Waltz Serenade for Orchestra* (1957).

Reworked and used in *Symphony No. 4 for Large Orchestra, II. Serenade–Scherzo* (1976).

Zodiac for Orchestra (1964)

A slightly revised transcription of the *Twelve Bagatelles for Piano Solo* (1952).

VI: AN INTRODUCTION TO THE POEMS AND STORIES OF PAUL ROCHBERG

Many of the texts which George Rochberg has used in his compositions for voice are taken from the poems and stories written by his son Paul Rochberg (1944–1964). Because the next chapter includes all of the texts by Paul which George has set to music, George and Gene Rochberg and I all felt it would be appropriate to also include George's introduction to Paul's work as a part of this volume. Our primary reason for including this introductory note was to provide the reader of this volume with a greater understanding and appreciation of Paul and his work.

The complete works of Paul Rochberg have been published by Muse of Fire (Newtown Square, PA, 1990). The following note was written in 1988 by George Rochberg to serve as an introduction to that publication.

Note by George Rochberg

One day in 1958, when Paul was fourteen, he came downstairs from his room with a batch of poems and asked us read them and tell him what we thought of them. That was the first we knew of his desire to be a poet. It was also cause for quiet celebration for my wife and me because we believed then (and still believe) that making or performing art is among the highest callings to which a human being can aspire. As a young woman, my wife was an actress; and our daughter,

Francesca, had a career as a ballet dancer before she became a scholar in the field of Assyriology.

I don't remember whether any of the poems Paul showed us that first time found their way into what he later came to call his Black Book. These were the poems he worked on and polished until they were as perfect as he knew how to make them. By the time he died on November 22, 1964, he had collected one hundred and two poems in a black binder, hence *The Black Book*. Some of these were gathered into sets or groups. For example, a set of three called *Africans*, a set of three numbered poems but untitled, a group of nine called *Dandelion Seed*, a group of six *Fantasies*, a larger group of eleven brief *Haiku Faux*, and the largest of all: fifteen satirical poems Paul entitled *The Confusin' Odes* as "translated by Zera Pund" which are irreverently salty and pungent parodies of Ezra Pound's "versions" of Confucian odes.

It's not surprising that Paul began to write—first, poetry, and a little later, fiction. From his very earliest years he had been fed a rich diet of Mother goose rhymes, A.A. Milne, and every kind of folk and fairy tale and story. Words and verbal images became the most natural things in the world for him, as they were to become for his younger sister Francesca. From the time he was a year old and able to talk, Paul took an absolute delight in words which, as he grew into adolescence, developed into fanciful word-play and sometimes wild forms of punning. This tendency showed itself even in the way he treated Italian (which he spoke at the age of six when the family spent a year in Italy) and Spanish (which came when the four of us lived in Mexico City for five months in the spring and summer of 1957). He loved French which he learned in school, perhaps because it was the language of Rimbaud who was, for Paul, one of his most favorite poets. His love of word-play and punning gave him a rare appreciation and insight into James Joyce. And his intense interest in the experiments with parallel story-line structure in the dark work of the Canadian novelist, Malcom Lowry influenced his handling of his most accomplished story, *The Silver Talons* of Piero Kostrov. The few French poems in this volume are undoubtedly a florenscence of his love of language generally, and perhaps, Rimbaud particularly. His native bent for wit and humor, the bizarre and grotesque, and satiric and ironic are clearly reflected in his *Confusin' Odes* and the long, surrealistic anti-war poem, *Calvalry*.

But there was another side to Paul's nature: a marked sensitivity to and fineness of feeling for the nuance both in the world of nature and in human beings. This brought a strength and refinement of image and expression to his work, especially his shorter poems. Daniel Hoffman, the poet and critic, made special note of this in the citation given Paul's work posthumously by the Philadelphia Art Alliance on April 28, 1966:

> We have chosen to give special citation to the poems of Paul Rochberg, late of Newtown Square, Pennsylvania, not because these were among the last he wrote but because his poems are a genuine achievement and give lasting pleasure. His was the gift to catch a moment of feeling or perception in a evanescent image, a fine rhythm, a caught reality that lives with strength and delicacy of outline. There is an oriental feeling in these little poems, which brim with spare delight.

This sense of Paul's qualities was voiced by Arthur Darack, then editor of the magazine, *Dimension Cincinnati*. In the May, 1965 issue he published nine poems and added this note:

> Paul Rochberg died at the age of 20, and with him ended rich hopes. He was an enchanting youth, full of intellectual and physical grace. But he was also on the the most talented members of his generation. "Of his generation"—how terrible to say this of one whose last two years were spent in agony, undergoing a fruitless series of desperate operations for an illness that he must have known would tolerate no recovery. Despite it all, he went on writing poetry, of beauty, of an almost painful insight, and of an astonishing verbal resource. He wrote prose too, and he had a skill in parody and wit that would have distinguished him in any mature company. Grillparzer's epitaph for Franz Schubert surely applies: "...here entombed a rich treasure but still fairer hopes."

From the time he began to write, Paul sought out more experienced poets and writers for guidance and criticism. He worked for a period with Ronald Goodman, a then young Philadelphia poet. He met with Ted Solateroff, the New York critic and editor, who gave him the kind of solid encouragement a young writer needs in order to pursue his work. Surely the most important of these mentors was Christopher Davis, the playwright and novelist, now teaching at Bryn Mawr College. Paul and "Kit" Davis, became good friends and met frequently to discuss Paul's work in progress. While I'm certain Paul already had a deeply instinctive capacity for self-critical appraisal where his work was concerned, it was Davis's own sense of the intense demands of craftsmanship one must make upon oneself if one is to produce anything approaching art in writing that helped sharpen and increase Paul's developing powers of craft, structure, choice of words and images. Davis was instrumental in helping to bring to publication in the New York magazine, *Chelsea Seventeen*, *The Silver Talons of Piero Kostrov* and three poems, among them, *Calvary*. These were Paul's first works to appear in a national "little magazine." Unfortunately he did not live to savor the joy of first publication and the beginning of public recognition by his peers: the issue came out in the spring of 1965, some six months too late.

Davis understood Paul's work better than anyone. In his note in *Chelsea Seventeen* he said, "It is writing that stands for itself and does not need to derive special value from the fact that Paul was a prodigy." He went on to say that,

> Upon everything connected with art, as well as with artists Paul turned clear eyes...Paul was raised among artists; he had no romantic idea either of them or of their ambitions. He was never dazzled by reputation; what is more to the point he was not dazzled by skill. Remarkably, his judgements were good—that is, they opened one's eyes to possibilities one had never considered. He had the gift of primary vision—an ironic, often humorous view unclouded by others' opinions;

and he went for the truth like a terrier for its quarry. He could be rude about the truth. It is certain that he had not time for nonsense, for flattery, and knew it...Paul wrote over a hundred poems and never quit reworking them. They speak in his own voice about things and feelings he perfectly understood, rarely about ideas for ideas' sake. They are direct and unobscure, since he was not uncertain about them and modest in the best sense of the word: he did not say more then he knew and did not paint over the bad places with talent. Above all they are poetic—that is, they are sung, not spoken.

At the end of his note Davis turned to Paul's stories and said of *The Silver Talons*:

It is, I believe, a triumph of the technique of expressing emotion and thought by means of the manipulation of the senses. We see. We hear through muffled dreaming layers. We touch things. We are sensible to two, three, four things simultaneously visions are superimposed upon each other; the objects we feel change, slide away. It is a near-perfectly functioning prose medium for a poet's thought. One sees where it comes from. Paul liked the *nouvelle vague* in films; he admired Robbe-Grillet, Malcom Lowry, Rimbaud, and Joyce. But it is Paul's voice we hear.

Paralleling Paul's obsession with writing ran an almost equally obsessive love of music, in particular, the "Bebop" style of 1950's jazz, that burst of incredible musical vitality in improvisation that came with the appearance on the scene of musicians like Thelonious Monk, Jerry Mulligan, Charlie "Bird" Parker, Miles Davis, John Coltrane and others. By the time he was fifteen, Paul had gone from the clarinet (which he played in the school band) to, first the tenor saxophone and, then, what became his great love, the baritone saxophone—a physically enormous instrument fully capable of shaking the house to it foundations if blown at maximum power. He learned to improvise in the "Bebop" style with skill and invention because he had a good ear. He went to New York as often as he could to hear the best jazz performers of the time—he was especially impressed with Maynard Ferguson—built up an important collection of jazz recordings, and also played as often as he could locally for parties and school dances.

Paul used to love to tell the story of how he met his favorite "Bebop" pianist, Thelonious Monk. Growing impatient for Monk to appear at a jazz concert in progress at the Philadelphia Civic Center, Paul and some friends went backstage hoping to find him and, if possible, to speak to him. There was Monk, moving about restlessly. The boys approached and tried to strike up a conversation with Monk who was known for being withdrawn and laconic. Trying to catch his interest, Paul said, "You know, my father is a composer." Monk stopped dead in his tracks and asked, "What kind of music does he write?" "Twelve-tone music," Paul replied. At which point Monk's face suddenly took on a deeply puzzled look and he muttered almost as much to himself as to Paul, "I always thought there was *thirteen* tones."

Paul's natural feel for jazz—its rhythms and ethos—spilled over into his poetry on more than one occasion. "Hip-cat sung 'pare dat frown / Don't put dat drummer down," No. 76 of the *Cunfusin' Odes* and "Yeller bard, let mah pone alone / Yeller bard, let mah tone atone," No. 187 of the same group, are both prime instances where Paul used the released style and rhythm and ripe language of "hip" and "jive" talk which became part of the 60's scene taken over from black culture and jazz. In the uncollected (undated) poems *Pierce the air* is a celebration of the burning energy of jazz played on Paul's favorite instrument, the baritone sax. Paul's energy and love of literature combined, while still a student in high school, to seek out those who, like himself, were fledgling writers and poets. With them he founded Marple-Newtown High School's first literary magazine which he named, *Dinos*. The first issue appeared in the spring of 1961. Since Paul was a junior and the school insisted that the editor be a senior, Paul swallowed his disappointment; but, in fact, it was he who shaped and guided the destiny of the magazine. In 1969, still a flourishing active part of its school's life, the spring issue of *Dinos* was dedicated "to the magazine's founder—Paul Rochberg." In the editor's note the dedication reads:

> "Why *Dinos*? The word is Greek and means vortex: a metaphor for the spinning whirlpool of human experience which, having gone round and round, is finally drawn to a center...*Dinos* is the realization of only one of his (Paul's) many dreams..."

In the years immediately following Paul's death my own music began to change radically. The need to include Paul's work in mine, to extend his mental, spiritual life through my own as far as that was possible led me to write a series of song cycles and other kinds of musical settings of his poetry. I chose those poems of his which I loved for the imagery, flavor and emotional texture—poems I felt were intrinsically musical. The first of five such works was a large chamber ensemble with soprano, small male chorus, and two speaking voices. I called it *Tableaux* and it drew its texts from *The Silver Talons*. That was in 1968. A year later I set, for mezzo-soprano and piano, eleven poems—those whose remarkable spareness still managed to convey unmistakeable beauty of atmosphere and feeling tone. Among these *Eleven Songs*, to name only a few, are *We are like the Mayflies / that live only hours, I am baffled by this wall, How to explain, Are the wings of a bird / not angel's wings*? That same year, 1969, I transcribed for voice and piano, two songs from *Tableaux*. In 1971, I chose four of the six *Fantasies* and set them for baritone and piano. The fifth of the works in which I set Paul's poems came in 1979 when I wrote for the baritone, Leslie Guinn, and the Concord String Quartet, my *Seventh String Quartet*. I chose four longer poems of Paul's and devoted a substantial movement to each in order to give them the size and range of emotional expression and power locked into their images and lines. These poems in order of their appearance are: *The beast of night, Floating in a dream, Calvary2, and And when the dream had faded.*

The present volume [*Paul Rochberg: Poems and Stories*] has been arranged in four parts. The first is devoted to *The Black Book* poems—those Paul considered truly finished; parts two and three, to the uncollected poems—those dated in the original manuscripts and those undated; and part four to the four stories. My wife and I have preserved as many of the dates as we could find in Paul's drafts and manuscripts with an eye to indicating precisely when, in the range of the six years he wrote poetry, from 1958 to 1964, they were produced. Had he lived it is quite possible he might have rejected many or perhaps only some of the "uncollected" verses; but there are those like the *Pieces of the Sea* which is a late poem (1964) and which exists in two dated versions here, I believe Paul might have reworked until it met his standards. Because we felt we could not make such decisions and because we wanted to include everything regardless of their state of polish, my wife and I decided the better course was to bring out all of Paul's work in one volume. Only for reasons of clarity in presentation did we decide on devoting a separate part each to the dated uncollected poems and the undated uncollected ones.

The four stories included cover almost Paul's entire writing career. *Distances* was the first story he wrote; and if I remember correctly, it was a piece he did for a writing class when he became a student at The Haverford School for Boys in the fall of 1961. *The Seer* was later incorporated, certainly large parts of it, if not its entirety, in *The Silver Talons* where, following the clues he found for himself in Malcom Lowry, he developed its parallel structures in such a way that it becomes difficult to decide where prose leaves off and poetry takes over and vice versa. Clearly, *The Silver Talons* is his most ambitious fiction and indicates what might have followed if he had had the chance to pursue this way of working. *The Song of the Deepest Carillon* is basically a worked-over draft. It was the last story Paul attempted, a story which dealt with his hospital experience, and would undoubtedly have gone through many more drafts and re-workings before he considered it a completed, finished piece of work.

Paul loved the world more than himself. From early on he disdained the view that many people in our culture, and especially young poets and writers hold fast: that the part—their individuality, their ego—is greater than the whole. He knew that he could not master his art and his craft unless he simultaneously mastered himself, that trying to do the one without the other would lead only to the confusions of frustration, failure, futility. In the many conversations we had, I came to realize that these were not things he had learned but rather were deeply embedded in his nataure. This is, I believe, what accounts for his profound and searching honesty, his clear sense that behind the scrim of all physical materiality lies a shimmering reality more fantastic than the merely rational or empirical view of things will allow. It accounts too for his power to compress worlds into a few words or images, to show subtle and complex orders of life simply and directly—without self-consciousness or arbitrary artifice. He was as poet and person, generous and warm, never stingy of feeling or merely clever. His mind—and therefore his work—was centripetal; he sought the core of things. His perspective on himself, other human beings and the world of nature was the larger on the organic wholeness in which he saw life and death as two sides of the same reality, the same inalterable necessity which everything in the universe must undergo. Blatant egotism and sentimentality were anathema to him—and his work shows it. That is why, I believe, his work rings true and shines with a purity which can only be called spiritual.

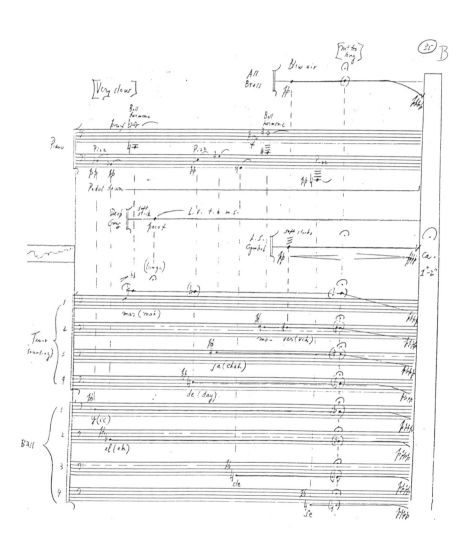

Plate 7: Autograph of page *Passions [According to the Twentieth Century]* (1964-1967). Copyright 1967 Theodore Presser Company. Used by permission of the publisher.

VII. TEXTS USED IN THE WORKS WITH VOICE

Behold, My Servant (Everything That Lives Is Holy) for a cappella Mixed Chorus

Text by George Rochberg adapted from William Blake, *Isaiah*, and *Psalm 143*.

> Everything that lives is holy.
> Behold, my servant, whom I uphold;
> Mine elect, in whom mine soul delighteth.
> He shall bring forth.
> He shall not fail nor be discouraged.
> Till he have set judgement in the earth.
> For everything that lives is holy.
> Let them bring forth salvation.
> Let righteousness spring up together.
> For everything that lives is holy.
> Praise ye the Lord from the heavens;
> Praise ye him, in the heights.
> Praise ye him, all his angels;
> Praise ye him all his hosts.
> Praise ye him sun and moon;
> Praise ye him all ye stars of light.
> Praise ye him, ye heav'ns of heavens.

Blake Songs for Soprano and Chamber Ensemble

Texts from the poems *Ah! Sun-flower, Nurse's Song, The Fly*, and *The Sick Rose* from the *Songs of Experience* by William Blake.

I. Ah! Sunflower

Ah Sunflower! weary of time,
Who countest the steps of the Sun:
Seeking after that sweet golden clime
Where the travellers journey is done.

Where the Youth pined away with desire,
And the pale Virgin shrouded in snow:
Arise from their graves and aspire,
Where my Sun-flower wishes to go.

II. Nurse's Song

When the voices of children are heard on the green
And whisperings are in the dale:
The days of my youth rise fresh in my mind,
My face turns green and pale.

Then come home my children, the sun is gone
    down
And the dews of night arise
Your spring & your day are wasted in play
And your winter and night in disguise.

III. The Fly

Little Fly
Thy summers play
My thoughtless hand
Has brush'd away.

Am I not
A fly like thee?
Or art thou
A man like me?

For I dance
And drink & sing;
Till some blind hand
Shall brush my wing.

If thought is life
And strength & breath;
And the want
Of thought is death;

Then am I
A happy fly,
If I live
Or if I die.

V. *The Sick Rose*

O Rose thou art sick.
The invisible worm,
That flies in the night
In the howling storm:

Has found out thy bed
Of crimson joy:
And his dark secret love
Does thy life destroy.

The Book of Songs for Voice and Piano
There was an Aged King

Text from the poem *Es war ein alter König* by Heinrich Heine. Translated by Sir Theodore Martin.

There was an aged king,
His heart was heavy, his locks were grey;
This poor old king, he wedded
A maiden young and gay.

There was a pretty foot-page,
His looks were fair, and his heart was light,
The sammet train he carried
Of the queen so young and bright.

Don't know the old, old story?
So sweet is the telling, so sad to tell!
They had both to die, oh the pity!
They had loved each other too well.

With Rue My Heart is Laden

From a poem [untitled] by A.E. Housman.

> With rue my heart is laden
> For many golden friends I had,
> For many a rose-lipt maiden
> And many a light-foot lad.
>
> By brooks too broad for leaping
> The light-foot lads are laid;
> The rose-lipt girls are sleeping
> In fields where roses fade.
>
> > Copyright 1940 Henry Holt and Company.
> > Used by permission of the publisher.
> > Copyright 1969 Theodore Presser Company.
> > Used by permission of the publisher.

Warum sind denn die Rosen so blass?

Text from the poem *Warum sind den die Rosen so blass* by Heinrich Heine. Translated by Richard Garnett.

> O dearest, canst thou tell me why
> The rose should be so pale?
> And why the azure violet
> Should wither in the vale?
>
> And why the lark should in the cloud
> So sorrowfully sing?
> And why from loveliest balsam buds
> A scent of death should spring?
>
> And why the sun upon the mead
> So chillingly should frown?
> And why the earth should, like a grave,
> Be moldering and brown?
>
> And why it is that I myself
> So lanquishing should be?
> And why it is my heart of hearts
> That thou forsakest me?
>
> > Copyright 1969 Theodore Presser Company.
> > Used by permission of the publisher.

When I Am Dead, My Dearest

Text from the poem *Song* by Christina Georgina Rossetti.

When I am dead, my dearest,
    Sing no sad songs for me;
Plant thou no roses at my head,
    Nor shady cypress tree:
Be the green grass above me
    With showers and dewdrops wet:
And if thou wilt, remember,
    And if thou wilt, forget.

I shall not see the shadows,
    I shall not feel the rain;
I shall not hear the nightingale
    Sing on as if in pain:
And dreaming through the twilight
    That doth not rise nor set,
Haply I may remember,
    And haply I may forget.

Minnelied

Text from the poem *Mädchen mit dem roten Mündchen* by Heinrich Heine. Translated by Louis Untermeyer.

Girl whose mouth is red and laughing;
    Girl whose eyes are soft and bright,
All of my being moves about you,
    Thinking about you day and night.

To my lips I would be pressing,
    Love, your slender, tender hand;
And my tears would tremble, blessing
    That beloved and blessed hand.

Du bist wie eine Blume

Text from the poem *Du bist wie eine Blume* by Heinrich
Heine. Tranlsated by Sir Theodore Martin.

> Thou art even as a flower is,
> So gentle, and pure, and fair;
> I gaze on thee, and sadness
> Comes over my heart unaware.
>
> I feel as though I should lay, a sweet,
> My hands on thy head, with a prayer
> That God may keep thee alway, sweet,
> As gentle, and pure, and fair!
>> Copyright 1969 Theodore Presser Company.
>> Used by permission of the publisher.

Dirge

Text from the poem *A Dirge* by Percy Bysshe Shelley.

> Rough wind that moanest loud
> Grief too sad for songs;
> Wild wind when sullen cloud
> Knells all the night long:
> Sad storm whose tears are vain,
> Bare woods, whose branches strain,
> Deep caves and dreary main,
> Wail for the world's wrong!
>> Copyright 1969 Theodore Presser Company.
>> Used by permission of the publisher.

There Be None of Beauty's Daughters

Text from the poem *Stanzas for Music* by Lord Byron
[George Gordon Byron].

> There be none of Beauty's daughters
> With a magic like thee;
> And like music on the waters,
> Is thy sweet voice to me:
> When, as if its sound were causing
> The charmed ocean's pulsing,
> The waves lie still and gleaming
> And the lull'd winds seem dreaming:

And the midnight moon is weaving
      Her bright chain o'er the deep;
Whose breast is gently heaving,
      As an infant's asleep:
So the spirit bows before thee,
To listen and adore thee
With a full but soft emotion,
Like the smell of Summer's ocean.

Oh, My Love's Like a Red, Red Rose

Text from the poem *A Red, Red Rose* by Robert Burns.
      O, my luve is like a red, red rose,
            That's newly sprung in June.
      O, my luve is like the melodie,
            That's sweetly play'd in tune.

      As fair art thou my bonnie lass,
            So deep in luve am I,
      And I will luve thee still my dear,
            Till a' the seas gang dry.

      Till a' the seas gang dry my dear,
            And the rocks melt wi' the sun!
      And I will luve thee still, my dear,
            While the sands o' life shall run.
      And fare thee weel, my only luve,
            And fare thee well a while!

      And I will come again, my luve,
            Tho' it were ten thousand mile!

February Spring

      Text from the poem *February Spring* by Arnold Stein.
      In *Huertgen Wald* the dead men grow,
      Appearing one by one
      Beneath the February sun
      Out of the melting snow.
      In *Huertgen Wald* the dead men grow.

Ophelia's Song

Text from *Hamlet, Act IV, Scene V* by William Shakespeare.

And will he not come again?
No, no, he is dead,
Go to thy death-bed,
He will never come again.
His beard was white as snow,
All flaxen was his poll;
He is gone, he is gone,
And we cast away moan;
God ha' mercy on his soul!

Night Song at Amalfi

Text from the poem *Night Song at Amalfi* of the *Vignettes Overseas* by Sara Teasdale.

I asked the heav'n of stars
What I should give my love–
It answered me with silence,
Silence above.

I asked the darkened sea,
Down where the fishers go–
It answered me with silence,
Silence below.

Oh, I could give him weeping,
Or I could give him song–
But how can I give silence
My whole life long?

Song of Shadows

Text from the poem *The Song of Shadows* by Walter de la Mare.

Sweep thy faint strings, Musician,
With the long lean hand;
Downward the starry tapers burn,
Sinks soft the waning sand;
The old hound whimpers couched in sleep,
The embers smolder low;
Across the walls the shadows
Come and go.

Sweep softly thy strings, Musician,
The minutes mount to hours;
Frost on the windless casement weaves
A labyrinth of flowers;
Ghosts linger in the darkening air,
Hearken at the open door;
Music hath called them, dreaming,
Home once more.

No Fall of Tears

Text from the poem *To Bess* by Arnold Stein.

No fall of tears, no sigh;
We kiss and say goodbye
Cleanly and well.
And then there is nothing in the touch
Nor in the eye
To show how fiercely and how much
Squeezed hearts can swell.

The wheels turn and we tear
In two the roots we share.
We have no hands:
We are but ghosts, torn off from sense,
Moved by the bare

Spirit of love, sure and intense,
By thin strong strands.

Song of Day

Text from the poem *The Two Spirits: An Allegory* by Percy Bysshe Shelley.

SECOND SPIRIT

The deathless stars are bright above,
If I would cross the shade of night,
Within my heart is the lamp of love,
And that is day!
 And the moon will smile with gentle light,
Oh my golden plumes where'er they move;
The meteors will linger round my flight,
And make night day.

I see the light, and I hear the sound,
I'll sail on the flood of the tempest dark,
With the calm within and the light around,
Which makes night day:
And thou, when the gloom is deep and stark,
Look from the dull earth, slumber-bound,
My moon-light flight thou then mayst mark
On high, far away.

Du meine heilige Einsamkeit

Text from the poem *Du meine heilige Einsamkeit* by Rainer Maria Rilke.

Du meine heilige einsamkeit,
Du bist so reich und rein,
Und weit wie ein erwachender garten.

Meine heilige einsamkeit,
Du, halte die goldenen Turenzu,

Vor denen die Wunsche.

Lira-la-la

Text from the poem *I Go by Road* by Catulle Mendès.
Translated by Alice Meynell.

I go by road, I go by street–
    Lira, la, la!
O white high roads, ye know my feet!
A loaf I carry and, all told,
Three broad bits of lucky gold–
    Lira, la, la!
And oh, within my flowering heart,
(Sing, dear nightingale!) is my Sweet.

A poor man met me and begged for bread–
    Lira, la, la!
"Brother, take all the loaf," I said,
I shall but go with lighter cheer–
    Lira, la, la!
And oh, within my flowering heart
(Sing, sweet nightingale!) is my Dear.

A thief I met on the lonely way–
    Lira, la, la!
He took my gold; I cried to him, "Stay!
And take my pocket and make an end."
    Lira, la, la!
And oh, within my flowering heart
(Sing, soft nightingale!) is my Friend.

Now on the plain I have met with death–
    Lira, la, la!
My bread is gone, my gold, my breath.
But oh, this heart is not afraid–
    Lira, la, la!

For oh, within this lonely heart
(Sing, sad nightingale!) is my Maid.

Who Has Seen the Wind?

Text from a poem [untitled] by Christina Georgina Rossetti.
Who has seen the wind?
Neither I nor you:
But when the leaves hang trembling
The wind is passing thro'.

Who has seen the wind?
Neither you nor I:
But when the trees bow down their heads
The wind is passing by.

Sweetest Love

Text from the poem *Sweetest Love* by Arnold Stein.
Sweetest love, it is the eye
And not the heart deceiving.
Look with your heart and see that I
Return, I am not leaving.

See: from this train now moving slow
My face turned toward you, yearning
Closer with every yard I go
On the way to my returning.

I go to come: the myth is true:
The paths of love go wheeling
Round the curving earth: they do–
And yet this hopeless feeling...

Bright Cap and Streamers

Text from a poem [untitled] from *Chamber Music* by James Joyce.

> Bright cap and streamers,
>   He sings in the hollow:
>   Come follow, come follow,
> All you that love.
>
> Leave dreams to the dreamers
>   That will not after,
>   That song and laughter
> Do nothing move.
>
> With ribbons streaming,
>   He sings the bolder;
>   In troop at his shoulder
> The wild bees hum.
>
> And the time of dreaming
>   Dreams is over–
>   As lover to lover,
> Sweetheart I come.

The Blind Man at the Fair

Text from the poem *The Blind Man at the Fair* by Joseph Campbell.

> O to be blind!
> To know the darkness that I know.
> The stir I hear is empty wind,
> The people idly come and go.
>
> The sun is black, tho' warm and kind,
> The horsemen ride, the streamers blow
> Vainly in the fluky wind,
> For all is darkness where I go.

The cattle bellow to their kind,
The mummers dance, the jugglers throw,
The thimble-rigger speaks his mind—
But all is darkness where I go.

I feel the touch of womankind,
Their dresses flow as white as snow;
But beauty is a withered rind
For all is darkness where I go.

Last night the moan of Lammas shined,
Rising high and setting low;
But light is nothing to the blind—
All, all is darkness where they go.

White roads I walk with vacant mind,
White cloud shapes round me drifting slow,
White lilies waving in the wind—
And darkness ev'ry where I go.

Piping down the Valleys Wild

Text from the poem *Introduction* from the *Songs of Innocence* by William Blake.

Piping down the valleys wild
Piping songs of pleas and glee
On a cloud I saw a child.
And he laughing said to me.

Pipe a song about a Lamb;
So I piped with merry cheer,
Piper, pipe that song again—
So I piped, he wept to hear.

Drop thy pipe thy happy pipe
Sing thy song of happy cheer,
So I sung the same again
While he wept with joy to hear

Piper, sit thee down and write
In a book that all may read—

So he vanished from my sight.
And I plucked a hollow reed.

And I made a rural pen,
And I stained the water clear,
And I wrote my happy songs
Every child may joy to hear

Ecce Puer

Text from the poem *Ecce Puer* by James Joyce.

Of the dark past
A child is born;
With joy and grief
My heart is torn.

Calm in his cradle
The living lies.
May love and mercy
Unclose his eyes!

Young life is breathed
On the glass;
The world that was not
Comes to pass.

A child lies sleeping;
An old man gone.
Oh, father, forsaken,
Forgive your son!

Tyger! Tyger!

Text from the poem *The Tyger* from the *The Songs of Experience* by William Blake.

Tyger Tyger, burning bright,
In the forests of the night;

What immortal hand or eye,
Could frame thy fearful symmetry?

In what distant deeps or skies
Burnt the fire of thine eyes!
On what wings dare he aspire?
What the hand dare seize the fire?

 And what shoulder, & what art,
Could twist the sinews of thy heart?
And when thy heart began to beat,
What dread hand? & what dread feet?,

 What the hammer? what the chain?
In what furnace was thy brain?
What the anvil?   what dread grasp,
Dare its deadly terrors clasp?
When the stars threw down their spears
And watered heaven with their tears:
Did he smile his work to see?
Did he who made the Lamb make thee?

Tyger Tyger, burning bright,
In the forests of the night:
What immortal hand or eye,
Could frame thy fearful symmetry?

Cantes Flamencos for High Baritone

I. *Ven acá, mujer del mundo*

Based on *Martinetes* as sung by Rafael Romero in "Antologia del Cante Flamenco," Hispavox, S.A. Madrid.

¡Ven acá, mujer del mundo
convéncete a la razon!
¡Que no hay un hombre en la Tierra,
tan fijo como el neloj!

Dios, con ser Dios, le temio
a la muerte que viniera,
y yo por ti perderia
cien mil vidas que tuviera,
Y si no es verded,
Que Dios me mande la muerte
si me la quiere mander.

I. *Come Here, Woman of the World*

Come here, woman of the world
And be convinced
That there is no man on earth
Who can be as constant as a clock.

God, even God,
Feared the coming of death.
For you I would gladly lose
One hundred thousand lives.

If this is not true,
May God send me death,
If that is his wish.

II. *¡Ay, Deblica Bari!*

Based on *Debla* as sung by Rafael Romero in "Antologia del Cante Flamenco," Hispavox, S.A. Madrid.

En el barrio de Triana
ya no hay pluma ni tintero,
pa escribirte yo a mi mare,
Que hace tres años que no la reo.
¡Ay, Deblica Bari!

Yo Ya no era quien era,
ni quien yo soy ya seré.
¡Ay, Deblica Bari!

II. *Ay, Great Debla!*

In the district of Triana
There is no more pen or ink
So that I could write to my mother
Whom I haven't seen in three years.
Ay, Great Debla!

I am no longer who I used to be,
And who I am now, I shall no longer be.
Ay, Great Debla!

III. *Dale limosna, mujer*

Text taken from a poem by F.A. De Icaza. This poem is engraved on a stone set into the outside wall of a turret of the Alhambra overlooking the city of Grenada.

Dale limosna, mujer,
Que no hay en la vida nada
Como la pena de ser
Ciego en Granada.

III. *Give Alms, Wife*

Give alms, wife,
For there is nothing in life
Like the pain of being
Blind in Granada.

Used by permission of George Rochberg.

The Confidence Man, An Opera in Two Parts

Libretto by Gene Rochberg from Melville's play of the same title.

TIME: Mid-nineteenthth century, USA

PLACE: Crystal City, a riverboat town, on the Mississippi

PROLOGUE

ACT I

Scene 1 Main square, Crystal City on the Mississippi
Early morning, April 1

Scene 2 Same

Scene 3 Same

Scene 4 Town Square

Scene 5 Within a Magic Circle

Scene 6 In front of the Candle Shop

Scene 7 Same

ACT II

EPILOGUE

(A synopsis of *The Confidence Man* can be found on page 71)

CAST OF CHARACTERS

The Confidence Man	Baritone
China Aster	Tenor
Orchis	Tenor
Annabella, China Aster's wife	Soprano
The Angel of Bright Future	High Soprano
Old Plain Talk	Bass
Old Prudence	Bass
The Barber	Tenor
Mrs. Orchis	Mezzo-Soprano
A Young Peddler	Tenor
The Missourian	Bass
A Minister	Bass
A Charitable Lady	Speaking Part

Avatars of The Confidence Man:

The Man in the Snuff-Colored Surtout	Tenor
The Man in Grey with the White Ascot	Baritone

The Man in Grey with a   Bass
   Long Weed in his Hat and
   wearing White Gloves

Minstrel Show:
Bluebeard   Bass
Gripsack, Bluebeard's   Tenor
   sidekick
Fateema, Bluebeard's new   Tenor
   wife
Mafairy, Fateema's mother   Bass
Beppo, Fateema's brother   Baritone
Greppo, Fateema's brother   Baritone

Three Creditors (drawn from Chorus):
Creditor #1   Tenor
Creditor #2   Baritone
Creditor #3   Bass

Chorus of Townspeople and Travellers:

A reasonable ratio of men to women, old to young, an Indian or two, one or two Blacks. Also included in *Act I, Scene 1*, are the three Avatars of The Confidence Man, A Minister, A Charitable Lady, The Missourian, A Young Peddler, Old Plain Talk, Old Prudence, The Barber, his wife, and young daughters.

Same Chorus for *Act II, Scene 6 and 7*.

Reduced Chorus for the *Epilogue*.

PROLOGUE

CONFIDENCE MAN: *(Coming forward, all smiles and geniality.)*
Ladies and Gentlemen!
Gentlemen and Ladies!
I have here
The Good Samaritan Pain-Dissuader,
The pain killer par excellence,
Guaranteed to remove pain
Of every kind!

Only fifty cents a bottle.
Fifty cents–a small price
To pay for untold blessings.

You hold back.
You're not interested?
Ah, I see . . .
Perhaps you don't trust me.
You need to know
Who I am. *(Takes off surtout and is revealed as The Man in Grey. Avatar #1, A Man in a Snuff-Colored Surtout, appears in the background.)*

I am a COSMOPOLITAN.
A man of confidence.
A man of trust.
One who loves his fellow man.

But I see
You're still skeptical. *(Puts bottle into bag, rummages about, brings out flashy box which he holds aloft.)*

Drive away your pains
With the Omni-Balsamic Reinvigorator.
The balm of balms,
The medicinal psalm of psalms!
Only two dollars a box!

Two dollars seem too much?
Well, then take a dozen boxes!
At twenty dollars,
You'll be getting
FOUR for nothing! *(No response. He shrugs, puts box back in bag, takes out hat with long weed and puts it on. Takes out*

gloves and begins to draw them on. Avatar #2, the Man in
Grey with White Ascot, appears and joins Avatar #1, in a
"tableau vivant." Adjusts hat rakishly, and with a flourish:)

Ladies and Gentlemen!
Gentlemen and kind ladies!
You wouldn't turn away
An appeal
On behalf of
The Seminole Widow and Orphan Asylum
Now, would you?
What? You never heard of that charity?
Not surprising . . .
Only recently founded.

Is it not CHARITY
To ease human suffering?
To succor the poor?
To help the helpless?

Is it not CHARITY
To open your heart
And your purse
To save those in need,
And even worse?

I have a plan. *(Searches in bag; brings out accordion-fold*
pamphlet.)

Let me show you! *(Releases accordion-fold full length.)*
I have a plan, *(Waving plan about.)*
A plan for a
WORLD CHARITY ORGANIZATION.
W., C., O.!
An organization
Representing
Every single charity
That exists in the world today.
No more voluntary giving.
Away with the offerings
Of a generous heart.

Instead, my organization
Will TAX, yes, Ladies and Gentlemen,
TAX

Every man, woman and child
On this planet–
ONE DOLLAR.
Yes, only one dollar.
Why, with this fund
Properly distributed
The W.C.O. could disband
In . . . let's see . . .
Fourteen years.
By then, not a pauper or a heathen
Would be left
ANYWHERE
On the face of this globe. *(He has worked himself up to an ecstatic pitch, but becomes aware that listeners are not convinced.)*

But I see, my friends,
You still
Don't trust me. *(With mock pain.)*

Ah! *(Grandly removing his white ascot and jacket. Places them in carpet bag.)*

We should shut
Our ears to distrust!
And keep them open
Only for its opposite. *(Slips off grey trousers, puts them into bag. He is revealed in "white trousers of ample duck.")*

Careful everyone
Careful!
The spirit of distrust *(Sits to remove boots for "maroon colored slippers." Places boots in bag.)*
Can enter a mind
and lie dormant, *(He begins to rise slowly. When he reaches full height, he removes hat with weed and holds it high, revealing the "smoking cap" underneath. As he removes hat and gloves, Avatar #3, The Man with the Weed in his Hat and wearing White Gloves appears and joins the other two Avatars.)*
Only to ERUPT
Into terrible activity!
Ah. Confidence.

Sweet Confidence,
And shining benevolence.
Take them away
And all is lost. *(Reaches into bag for final item–the pipe.)*

You approve my
Style of dress? *(Turning completely around.)*
It's very much like
My style of thinking.
Why should men
Hide their light
Under the bushel
Of plain clothes? *(Lights pipe.)*
Let the radiance shine forth!
Life is a picnic
En costume! (Grandly.)

Now to the point.
To show you that
Nothing goes without confidence,
let me tell you
The story of a man,
A candle maker, a bringer of light.
Call him China Aster.
A man who built himself
A palace of moonbeams,
And when the moon set . . .
But, come, come with me
To Crystal City,
On the Mississippi! *(Picks up cape, puts it on inside out, re-vealing the "Emir's Robe." Picks up carpet bag, tucks stool under arm and together wit the three Avatars calls out:)*
CRYSTAL CITY! *(They move upstage and circulate among the crowd.)*

ACT I, SCENE 1

PEDDLER: Mesan, Mesan
            Read all about Mesan!
            Bandit of the Ohio!

            Moneybelts! Moneybelts for sale!
            Moneybelts for sale!

Protect your money!
Counterfeit bill detectors too!
Check your money!
Make sure it's good.

INDIVIDUAL CHORUS MEMBERS: Scoundrel!
Mississippi operator!
Shatterbrain!
You'll get nothing from me!
Scavenger! Parasite! *(Old Prudence shows keen interest in the Counterfeit Bill Detector. Young Peddler sells him one.)*

Read about Murrel.
Pirate of the Mississippi. *(Merchant buys moneybelt. As he turns away, Peddler picks his pocket.)*

PEDDLER: Read all about Mesan, *(Peddler works his way to exit.)*
Bandit of the Ohio.
Mesan, Mesan. *(Peddler exits.)*
Mesan, Mesan. *(Off-stage.)*

(During this the Confidence Man is getting his share of attention. First to approach is the Missourian. He wears a shaggy coat and high peaked racoon skin hat. On his legs are rawhide leggings, and he carries a double-barreled gun.)

MISSOURIAN: *(Approaching Confidence Man but addressing chorus.)*
And who
Of our fine fellow species
May this be?
Fine feathers
On foul meat!

CHORUS: Who can he be?
Quite an original!
Who can he be?

OLD PLAIN TALK: Uncommon countenance!

OLD PRUDENCE: Bless my soul!

CHORUS: Quite an original,
Who can be be?

MERCHANT: Green prophet from Utah!

MERCHANT'S WIFE: Strange fellow!

AVATAR #2: Odd fish!

MINISTER: Charity, my friends! *(Sanctimonious.)*

CHORUS: Quite an original
 Who can he be?
 Means something! *(Laughter, whispers, etc. Confidence
 Man moves about, interested in everything.)*
 As pine, beech, birch
 Ash, hemlock, and spruce
 Interweave their foliage
 In the natural wood,
 So we people
 Blend varieties of face and dress
 In the all-fusing
 Spirit of the West.

 And like the mighty Mississippi
 Uniting the streams
 From distant and opposite shores
 Pour forth in one grand
 Confident, cosmopolitan tide!

MISSOURIAN: Tell me, *(Looking the Confidence Man over with
 distaste.)*
 Did you ever see
 Signore Marzetti?

 In the Minstrel shows . . .
 In the African Pantomime?

CONFIDENCE MAN: No-o-o. *(Calmly; not at all offended.)*
 Good performer?

MISSOURIAN: Excellent!
 Plays the intelligent ape
 So well,
 He seems
 To be one!

 Saw him myself, once.

In New York.
But where's your tail? *(Circling Confidence Man.)*
Marzetti prides himself
On his!

CHORUS: Tell us,
     Tell us who,
     Who, in the name of
     The Great Chimpanzee,
     Who in thunder
     Are you?

CONFIDENCE MAN: I am
     A COSMOPOLITAN.
     A man of Confidence, a man of trust,
     One who loves his fellow man.
     As you can see, *(Confidence Man struts about showing off costume with a certain taste and elegance.)*
     I tie myself
     To no narrow tailor,
     But federate in my heart
     As in my costume,
     Something of all men.
     No man is strange to me.
     I approach all warm and trusting. *(As he says "trusting" the Barber hangs up a "NO TRUST" sign. Some in the crowd react; Confidence Man remains unperturbed.)*

     Some may be uncivil,
     But a true citizen of the world
     Returns good for ill.
     Man is a wine
     I never tire of sipping
     And comparing.

     As there are teetotal palates
     There must be teetotal souls
     Who can't enjoy
     The very best
     Brands of humanity

MISSOURIAN: And what society
     Of old drunks
     Hired you to lecture me?

MISSOURIAN and CHORUS: Yes, what society
  Of old drunks
  Hired you to lecture us?

MINISTER: Charity, good people
  Charity, my friends.

CONFIDENCE MAN: Let me tell you a story. *(Easy, jaunty manner.)*
  About a very moral, very moral,
  Very old woman,
  Who wouldn't even let her pigs
  Eat apples in the fall.
  Afraid the fruit
  Might ferment on their brains
  And make them swinish.

  One day she became very ill,
  And her good husband
  Sent for the doctor, etc. *(Signals Avatar #1 to join him. Confidence Man plays the husband and Avatar #1 plays the Doctor.)*

AVATAR #1 (Doctor): If you want your
  Wife cured,
  Get her a jug of rum.

CONFIDENCE MAN (Husband): Rum!
  My wife?
  Drink rum?

AVATAR #1 (Doctor): Either that
  Or she'll die!

CONFIDENCE MAN (Husband): But, but
  How much?

AVATAR #1 (Doctor): As much as she
  Can get down.

CONFIDENCE MAN (Husband): But, but
  She'll get drunk!

AVATAR #1 (Doctor): That's the cure!

CHORUS: That's the cure, that's the cure!
  As much as she can get down.

That's the cure, that's the cure!

CONFIDENCE MAN: Having broken the ice
    Of arid abstinence
    She never afterwards
    Kept herself
    A cup, a cup
    A cup too low!

MISSOURIAN: If I understand you correctly, sir,
    Man can't enjoy life
    Unless he gives up the sober view!
    Well, I'll take the cold water of truth any day
    Rather than the untruth of wine! *(Missourian begins to leave. Exits at "Too bad" of the chorus.)*

CONFIDENCE MAN: Too bad.
    You have no sense
    Of genial trust and confidence.

CHORUS and CONFIDENCE MAN: Too bad.
    You have no sense
    Of genial trust and confidence.

MINISTER: Charity, my friends!
    Charity, my friends.

CHORUS: Trust, trust, what trust
    Can you put in men?
    Why, what else but the trust
    Of perfect confidence! *(Chorus breaks into small groups.)*
    So we people
    Blend varieties of face and dress
    In the all-fusing spirit of the West.
    And like the mighty Mississippi
    Uniting streams from
    Distant and opposite shores
    Pour forth in one
    GRAND, CONFIDENT, COSMOPOLITAN
    TIDE!

AVATAR #3: *(Avatar #3, Man in the Grey Suit with the Weed in his Hat and wearing White Gloves, approaches Confidence Man confidentially, walking with him all the way to stage right, saying:)*

> Do I understand
> You are connected with
> The Black Rapids Coal Co.?

CONFIDENCE MAN: Yes, I happen to be
President and Transfer agent.

AVATAR #3: You are?

CONFIDENCE MAN: Yes, but what's it to you?
You don't want to invest
Do you?

AVATAR #3: Why, do you sell stock?

CONFIDENCE MAN: Some might be bought. *(Cagey.)*
Perhaps.

AVATAR #3: Could you do up the thing
For me right here and now?

CONFIDENCE MAN: Really sir, *(In amazement.)*
You are quite a businessman
Positively! I feel afraid of you!

AVATAR #3: Oh, no need of that!
Can I see the statement
Of your company?

(Confidence Man rummages about in his bag, brings out a pamphlet and hands it to Avatar #3 who studies it carefully, then returns it to the Confidence Man who returns it to the bag.)

> This tells a fine story!

CONFIDENCE MAN: So it does!
So it should! *(They finish deal in mime, Avatar #3 moves off into crowd and exits. Avatar #2 has been observing and as Avatar #3 exits he approaches the Confidence Man:)*

AVATAR #1: *(Avatar #1, Man in Snuff-colored Surtout, approaches Charitable Lady [stage left] and bows low:)*
Madam, pardon my freedom
But something in your face . . .

CHARITABLE LADY: *(Startled.)*
Why, really, you . . . you . . .

AVATAR #1: May I ask if you
Have confidence?

CHARITABLE LADY: Really sir,
Why sir, really–I . . .

AVATAR #1: Could you put confidence
In me, for instance?

CHARITABLE LADY: As much as one may
Wisely put
In a stranger.

AVATAR #1: Ah, who would be
A stranger?!
In vain I wander.
No one will have
Confidence in me.

CHARITABLE LADY: Can I, in any way
Befriend you?

AVATAR #1: No one can befriend me
Who has no confidence!

CHARITABLE LADY: But I, I have,
At least . . . to that degree . . .
I mean that . . .

AVATAR #1: No, no, you have none.
None at all!
Pardon, I see it!

CHARITABLE LADY: You are unfair, sir.
Believe me, I . . . yes. yes.
I may say . . . that–that

AVATAR #1: Prove it then.
Let me have $20.00

CHARITABLE LADY: *(Exploding.)*
T . . . Twenty dollars!

AVATAR #1: There, I told you,
You lack a warm
And trusting heart.

CHARITABLE LADY: Oh, sir, you are unkind!

Tell me,
Why do you want the money?

AVATAR #1: For the widowed,
And the fatherless.

CHARITABLE LADY: Ah, why didn't you
Say so at once?
Here, how could I
Hesitate?

AVATAR #1: *(Taking money, but not gratefully.)*
It's not very much *(Takes out little book and pencil.)*
But I'll register it here.
There is another register *(Pointing to sky.)*
Where is set down
The motive. *(Sanctimoniously as they leave separately.)*
Goodbye, dear lady.
You have confidence.
And thank you
For your trust! *(Exit.)*

AVATAR #2: *(Approaching.)*
Do you happen to know
Of any other good stock?

CONFIDENCE MAN: *(Sizing him up.)*
You wouldn't care to be
Concerned in the New Jerusalem
Would you?

AVATAR #2: New Jerusalem?

CONFIDENCE MAN: New City.
Way up in Northern Minnesota.
On the Mississippi. *(Rummages in bag, takes out rolled map.)*
Thriving!
There you see *(Using map.)*
The public buildings
The parks,
The Botanic gardens.
And see these 20 asterisks? *(Looking to see effect.)*
Those are the lyceums!

AVATAR #2: And are all these buildings

Now standing?

CONFIDENCE MAN: All standing!
Bona Fide!

AVATAR #2: These marginal squares here,
Are they water lots?

CONFIDENCE MAN: *(Insulted and walking away.)*
Water lots!?
In the City of New Jerusalem? *(Rolling up map and put-
ting it away.)*
All *terra firma*!

(They exit as Confidence Man says:)
Say, you wouldn't
Care to invest? *(Exit.)*

*(Chorus begins to exit by twos and threes, etc., until stage is
empty.)*

ACT I, SCENE 2

*(The window-counter of the Candle Shop is opened and China
Aster looks out. He is in his late twenties, at most early thirties.
He wears a leather apron, and tucked into its pocket is the greasy
hat of the candlemaker. There is an easy, natural charm about
him–honest, naive and gullible–something of the dreamer marks
his manner. He is devoted to his wife, Annabella, and to his work.
These qualities seem to have kept him where he is–just making
ends meet. He comes out the door of his shop in a cheerful
humor.)*

CHINA: The sky slides into blue.
The bluffs in bloom.
Wood and wave together,
And over all
An unsung tune.

And now the golden sun,
Higher and higher it rides!
Making a golden day.
Making me sing aloud
With joy!

(Annabella enters carrying boxes marked "WAX." She is a pretty woman in her middle twenties, with a spunky manner.)

CHINA: What a dream,
A dream of blue and gold
This would be,
If it were a dream!
But it's real,
And it's true.
And I have
A thousand things to do.

CHINA and ANNABELLA: And what a dream
A dream of blue and gold
This would be,
If it were a dream.
But it's real
An it's true
And I have a thousand things
To do!

ANNABELLA: Is the tallow ready?
Any candles done?

Yes, I really think
This week, things will be better!
If only, if only you were a better
Businessman,

You could light up this town.
You could light up this world.

CHINA: That's right. Yes!
It's my business
To make things bright
To chase away shadows
When darkness falls.
I could light up this town
I could light up this world.
But for now,
We don't have the money.
You know how it is,
I don't want to lend
And can't ask a friend.

ANNABELLA: You're such a good husband, *(Embracing.)*

How can you be
Such a bad businessman! *(Both laugh.)*
But we're so happy.

Spring is good to us.
All things warmed in
The landscape, leap!
Buds are blooming
Seeds are astir!
Time for work to be done.

CHINA: Then in winter
We can dream,
Dream in the rays
Of the candles shine.

CHINA and ANNABELLA: Dream of the love
That is yours,
That is mine!

ANNABELLA: You will light up the world
with your candles!

CHINA: And you, you will brighten
The world with your shining face.
In that world I dream of

When your eyes
Are a thousand stars.
Bella Anna, Annabella,
Bella Annabella.

CHINA and ANNABELLA: Our love will
Light up the world.
Days may grow dark
As sometimes they do,
But we'll keep them
Golden and bright.
With hearts full of love,
Things will go right.

(Orchis enters. Having won the lottery, he is ostentatiously dressed and keeps flicking and poking about with a gold-headed cane.)

Working together,
We'll make it happen.

Working together,
We'll make it happen!

ORCHIS: "Working together,
We'll make it happen!" *(In a pinched, sour tone.)*

Wake up! *(Shouting.)*
You're dreaming!
Nothing's going to happen.
Not while your capital
Is so small. *(Poking at boxes of WAX.)*
Get rid of this vile tallow!
Spermacetti is the thing to use,
Spermacetti is the thing to use,
Sperm–a–cet–ti!

CHINA: I've heard of spermacetti. *(Busy with his work, not looking at Orchis.)*

But just because you won the lottery
Doesn't mean you know the candle
Business.

ORCHIS: I call your attention to spermacetti
By way of acknowledging
Your goodness!
Remember my motive,
Remember my motive.
If you don't take my advice,
You'll be kicking yourself
With your own boot!

CHINA: Well, if I can do that,
I'll save you some shoe-leather,
Eh? Orchis?

ANNABELLA: Now that your money
Has raised you
From a cobbler's bench
To a sofa,
No wonder you're cock of the walk,

CHINA and ANNABELLA: No wonder you're
Cock of the walk!
Who would believe
We used to call you "Doleful Dumps!", etc.

(They burst out laughing.)

ORCHIS: "Doleful Dumps?"
　　With a sound digestion like mine,
　　Why would anyone call me that?

CHINA: Oh? Maybe you're the Happy Man
　　I keep hearing about.
　　There's someone out there
　　Looking for the Happy Man.

(Orchis is interested.)

ORCHIS: Yes, I'm happy.
　　My conscience is
　　Peaceful.

CHINA: Seems he wants to get hold of him,
　　Drill him, drop in the powder
　　And let him go, "POW!" *(China and Annabella laugh. Orchis manages a weak chuckle.)*

ORCHIS: Laugh, if you want to,
　　But I know that you need money.
　　Your capital,
　　Your capital is too small.

CHINA and ANNABELLA: We'll not quarrel about that.
　　We know that we need money.
　　And capital?
　　There's none, none at all! *(They laugh and enter shop.)*

ORCHIS: You're too honest!
　　You're too honest!
　　Capital?
　　Your capital's too small!

ORCHIS: I tell you what. *(Calling after them.)*
　　We're such good friends,
　　I'll give you a thousand dollars to extend with.

CHINA and ANNABELLA: APRIL FOOL! *(Appearing at window together.)*
　　(Laughing as they disappear.)

ORCHIS: No, no.
　　This isn't a joke.

I'm serious.

ANNABELLA: Enough of this nonsense! *(Appearing   at   door with boxes.)*
> You won the lottery?
> You have nothing better to do?
> We can't waste the morning talking.
> Good morning, Orchis. *(Annabella is leaving.   As she passes the window-counter, China appears with another box of candles.)*

CHINA: Just one more!

ANNABELLA: See you . . .
> Later . . .
>> *(She exits.)*

ACT I, SCENE 3

(China remains in shop. Orchis sits outside, relaxed.)

ORCHIS: I'm afraid, my friend,
> In leaning over your vats
> You've spilled out your brains! *(China laughs from inside. Orchis takes out checkbook with grand manner, goes to window and begins writing.)*

> Here, one thousand dollars! *(China comes to window.)*
> You can return the money
> Or not.
> Just as you please.

CHINA: One thousand dollars!
> So much money!

ORCHIS: Oh, by the way.
> It don't mean nothing–
> Just make out a little memorandum.
> Won't do any harm,
> You know.

> *(As though in a trance, China takes out paper and pen and writes a note.)*

> *(Orchis reads as China writes.)*

"I, China Aster, promise"

Mmmm, mmm, mmm,
"to pay"
Mmmm, mmm,
"on demand!?"
ON DEMAND!?
I told you *(Tearing up note.)*
I wasn't ever going
To make any demand.

I tell you what
Put it at four years.

*(China, still dazed, writes another note; and, just as he hands
it to Orchis, comes to his senses and tries unsuccessfully to get
it back.)*

CHINA: Four years!
Wait, stop! *(Coming out of shop.)*
Hold on!

ORCHIS: Four years
Is not a very long time.
Then you'll be rich!
You surely won't mind.

Four years! Four years!
You've got to try to risk it!
Things will go just fine.
In four years, you can tell.

CHINA: Four years! Four years!
It's not for me to risk it!
Things may not go too well.
In four years, who can tell?

Four years!
Can be a very long time.
I won't get rich
I'll lose everything!

ORCHIS: You have to take a chance!
Didn't I just do it?
Without a little risk,
I'd still be mending shoes!

Four years,
It's gone

Before you know it!

CHINA: I cannot take a chance!
        What if I should lose?
        With someone else's money,
        It isn't fair to do it!

ORCHIS: Four years
         It's gone
         Before you know it!

CHINA: Four years
        Can drag on
        Forever!

        Long enough
        To lose everything!
        Why put myself in
        A spot like that! *(Trying to return check.)*

ORCHIS: You're letting
         Your honesty get in your way.
         I'm your friend.
         I won't take it
         From you.

CHINA: Then take it from
        The pavement.
        There,
        It's not for me. *(Finds a stone and places it over check.)*

ORCHIS: Why, if you aren't
         The dolefullest creature alive!
         Why can't you be happy?
         Like me?
         Take the bright view!
         Show some confidence!

CHINA: I'm sure I don't know.
        But maybe not winning the lottery prize
        Makes the difference

ORCHIS: Hey day and high times!
         Before I knew anything
         About the prize,
         With my views
         And my digestion,

I was always cheerful,
Cheerful as a bird.
Always held the bright view.

CHINA: You did?
Bright view?
Remember, you were the one
We used to call "Doleful Dumps!"

ORCHIS: No matter.
The check can lie there!
But your note
Won't keep it company. *(Patting his pocket.)*

(Orchis heads toward the Barber Shop as the Confidence Man enters from the opposite direction. They greet each other, sit down, and mime a discussion as China struggles with himself over the check.)

ACT I, SCENE 4

(China Aster picks up check, is about to tear it up, but can't. Returns check to pavement and is about to enter Candle Shop. Changes his mind. Picks up check again and, this time, enters shop. Comes out without apron, hair brushed to one side, and full of resolve. He closes shop and heads toward Orchis and the Confidence Man, who seem to be enjoying a good joke. As China approaches, Orchis is saying:)

ORCHIS: "And let him
Go, POW!" *(Orchis and Confidence Man laugh.)*

CHINA: You must take your check. *(Nodding to Orchis and Confidence Man and getting right to the point.)*

Thank you,
But it's not for me.

ORCHIS: By any chance,
Are you getting advice
From those two old asses
The boys have named
"Old Plain Talk," that senile sinner–
And "Old Prudence," that dotard!

CHINA: They were my father's friends,
      And they're my friends, too.

ORCHIS: Friends?
      Save me from my friends!

      You ought to hear those two. *(Imitating Old Plain Talk and Old Prudence.)*

      Old Plain Talk wheezing out
      His sour old saws.
      And Old Prudence, standing by,
      Leaning on his staff
      And chiming in

      "Bless my soul,
      That's right!
      Indeed you did!"

      "Bless my soul,
      That's right!
      Indeed you did!"

      Why that Old Plain Talk is so stuffed
      With stale hay!
      He thinks it's wise
      To be a croaker! *(China is offended.)*

CONFIDENCE MAN: What is friendship
      If not the helping hand,
      The feeling heart.
      Take the check, my friend,
      Have confidence.

      Don't you see?
      Without confidence
      All business would run down
      And stop!
      Like an old clock.

      This is the age
      Of joint stock companies,
      And free and easies
      And we,
      We are the Golden Boys!

We Golden Boys, we moderns,
Can reap a bounty
Wide as the plains,
Broadcast like moonlight.
The bright future is ours,
Told in the stars.

ORCHIS: What a noble burst!
You can take him at his word.
What he says
Is true!

CONFIDENCE MAN: Ours is the reward,
Ours is the prize.
Are we not human?
Are we not men?
Comrades forever.

The bright future is ours,
Told in the stars

ORCHIS: Another noble burst!
You can take him at his word.
What he says
Is true!

CONFIDENCE MAN: And in days to come
with progress and plenty,
We'll have ease and refinement.

And the dreams we dream
Of riches and pleasure
Will bring joy in full measure.

We, we are the Golden Boys!
We Golden Boys, we moderns,
Can reap a bounty
Wide as the plains,
Broadcast like moonlight.

The bright future is ours
Told in the stars.

ORCHIS: Why feel twinges of misgivings?

CONFIDENCE MAN: Why hold back?
Take fiddle in hand
And set the tickled

World a-dancing!

CHINA: But, b ... *(Finding it difficult to speak.)*

CONFIDENCE MAN: No buts, my friend.

CHINA: I don't ...
I don't want you to think
I don't trust you.
But as a man I'm slow,
I'm cautious
But maybe ... your character ...
Your talk–maybe
Maybe, I ought to reconsider.

ORCHIS: Yes, yes, say what you mean!
And in English!

CHINA: How can I say what I mean?
I want to put a generous confidence
In what you say.

CONFIDENCE MAN and ORCHIS: Then do it!
Have confidence in that check.
For a special Providence.
Depend on us
To the last–
Depend on us
To the last! *(Beginning to exit.)*

CHINA: Goodbye. Goodbye. *(To himself rather than to Orchis and Confidence Man.)*
And may Providence
Have me in its
Good keeping.

CONFIDENCE MAN and ORCHIS: Be sure it will!
Be sure it will!
Be sure it will!
Be sure it will! *(They exit.)*

ACT I, SCENE 5

(China, left alone, puts check into wallet and hesitantly moves toward the Candle Shop. Lights slowly dim to total darkness. As the lights come up, the Angel of Bright Future is revealed, "with a lithe neck and maze of tawney gold." She begins singing in a whisper. China appears to be in a deep sleep.)

ANGEL: Out of the shadows I come, I come.
    Your Angel of Bright Future!
    Sent to testify
    The root and offspring of David
    The bright and morning star.
    Out of the shadows,
    Out of the shadows,
    The bright and morning star.

    Sent to show you the way *(China begins to rouse.)*
    To riches and gold!
    See, see the gold
    I carry! *(Gold is falling like rain as China watches, bewitched.)*

    Gold, Gold!
    Thick as kernels of corn,
    Fine as grains of wheat.

CHINA: This is another of my dreams.
    It can't be real!
    Where, where did she
    Come from!

ANGEL: Above all things
    Man needs the sun
    And the candle.

CHINA: Yes, yes,
    That's true!

ANGEL: Your trade has a share
    In a great mystery.
    Like the hosts of Heaven,
    You can make light.
    Now do what you must
    To make your future
    Shine bright!

ANGEL: Above all things
        Man needs the sun and the candle
        To light up the darkness,
        Bring warmth to his soul.
        Out of the shadows
        Come all kinds of wonders.
        Wonders have happened,
        But not without light.
        With light we can see . . .

CHINA: Above all things
        Man needs the sun and the cnadle
        To light up the darkness,
        Bring warmth to his soul.
        Out of the shadows
        Come all kinds of wonders.
        Wonders have happened,
        And why not for me?

ANGEL: See, see Bright Future
        Showers you with gold.

        Touch it! *(Golden rainfall continues. China holds back.)*

        Stretch out your hand.

        (Angel weaves around China in a sinuous dance.)

        China Aster, China Aster,
        China ASter, China Aster,
        Dare to change your life.

        (Stops dance to exhort China.)

        Drop this timid, cautious way
        And reappear
        A man! On his way to riches!

        Take your friend at his word.
        Cash the check
        And be rich.

        (Angel resumes dancing in an hypnotic, sensual fashion.)

        Gold in the mountain,
        Gold in the glen,
        Gold for the taking,

It's there for strong men.

Tell me where you choose to dwell–
In a Fool's Paradise,
Or in Wise Solomon's Hell?

ANGEL: Gold in the mountain,
Gold in the glen,
Gold for the taking
Gold for strong men.

CHINA: Fool's Paradise?
Wise Solomon's Hell?
This must be magic,
Can it be for me?

CHINA: Your song, *(By now China is completely undone. He is totally under the Angel's spell.)*

Hearing you sing . . .

When mermaid's songs move figureheads,
Then may glory, gold and women
Try their ways with me!

Ah, your sweet song,
It calls forth my every spike;
And my whole hull,
Like a ship
Sailing by magnetic rock
Caves in!

I must agree!

Even if my heart were stone,
It would crumble
Into gravel.

I can't hold back
Any longer!

ANGEL: Have confidence in me, *(Angel rings China in circle of golden light.)*

In yourself.
In me, in yourself.
Soon, soon, *(Lights dim very slowly.)*

You'll be rich.

(Angel is disappearing.)

Rich, rich, rich!

(She is gone.)

CHINA: This radiant angel
Could she deceive me?
No, No,
Never!
A fortune can
Be mine!

(Blackout.)

ACT I, SCENE 6

(Lights up on town square. Old Plain Talk and Old Prudence watch as Annabella sets a picnic table for lunch.)

ANNABELLA: And he offered us a check
For one thousand dollars!

OLD PLAIN TALK: Have nothing to do with
Him!
That Orchis is a fool!

ANNABELLA: A pretty smart fool,
I'd say!
He talks so pat,
So well.

OLD PLAIN TALK
A smart fool
Always talks well.

OLD PRUDENCE: That's right!
Bless my soul! That's right!
That Orchis is a fool!

ANNABELLA: Some might call him
"An original!"

OLD PLAIN TALK: Yes, maybe . . .
But I think he's cracked!

Him and his digestion . . .

Not much
originality about that!

You don't plan
To take that check,
Do you?

ANNABELLA: China will have
To answer that.

OLD PRUDENCE: Where is he?
I'm hungry!

ANNABELLA: Here open this
Have a little wine.

(Old Plain Talk opens bottle and pours.)

OLD PRUDENCE: Fruit of the vine
Tastes mighty fine!

OLD PLAIN TALK: One can't drink too much
Of good old wine.

OLD PRUDENCE and OLD PLAIN TALK: Let us drink of the
wine,
Let us drink of the vine,
Of the vine benign,
That sparkles warm
In Zanzovine.

Let us drink of the wine,
Let us drink of the vine,
The vine benign,
The vine divine,

The vine, the vine,
The vine divine,
The vine divine,
That sparkles warm
In Zanzovine,
That sparkles warm
In Zanzovine.

OLD PLAIN TALK: As I live,
A vine, A catawba vine,
Shall be planted
On my grave!

OLD PRUDENCE: Wine, you know,
    Opens the heart.

OLD PRUDENCE: Opens it?
    It thaws it right out!
    Every heart is frozen
    Till wine melts it.

OLD PRUDENCE, OLD PLAIN TALK, AND ANNABELLA: The
    vine divine,
    The vine, the vine,
    The vine divine,
    The vine, divine,
    That sparkles warm
    In Zanzovine,
    That sparkles warm
    In Zanzovine.

(China appears at door of shop, looking very strange.)

ANNABELLA: Is something wrong? *(Going to him.)*
    You look so stange.

CHINA: A spirit . . . *(Slightly disheveled and still under the spell
    of his dream.)*
    A spirit appeared to me . . .

OLD PRUDENCE: What?
    What's that he's saying?

OLD PLAIN TALK: He said, "A spirit."

CHINA: A radiant angel.

OLD PRUDENCE: Bless my soul!

CHINA: . . . In a dream–

OLD PLAIN TALK: Sounds like hocus-pocus to me.

CHINA: She had gold,
    Gold all round her,
    Thick as kernels of corn.
    She said: "Take your friend at his word,
    Cash the check.
    Be rich!"

OLD PLAIN TALK: Dreams are wonderful things,
    And many people think
    They come straight from heaven,
    But in matters ter-rest-try-al *(Pointing down.)*
    Don't be ruled
    By notions see-lest-chy-al. *(Pointing upward.)*

ANNABELLA, OLD PLAIN TALK, and OLD PRUDENCE:
    Careful, China,
    You're in a danger!, etc.
    The devil is very wise,
    He understands man
    Better than the One
    Who made him!

CHINA: You're turning
    Everything upside down!
    I won't listen!
    Stop your babble!

OLD PLAIN TALK: Go tell Orchis
    You'll have nothing to do
    With him.

    (Drinking along with Old Prudence.)

    Him and his digestion!
    I suspect him.

OLD PRUDENCE: This dream could explode *(With mouth full)*
    In your hand,
    And leave a scorching behind!

CHINA: Why, why must you always be so
    Suspicious?

OLD PLAIN TALK: Don't ask me to believe
    That black is white
    And white, black

CHINA: Never saw a minstrel show
    I suppose.

OLD PRUDENCE and OLD PLAIN TALK: We've seen 'em.
    Lot's of 'em.

OLD PLAIN TALK: They overdo the ebony

In my opinion.

CHINA: Maybe so, but white
Does become black.

OLD PLAIN TALK: Don't confuse life
With minstrel shows.
There it's white
Masquerading as black.

CHINA: You believe Orchis
Is out to hurt me, with money?

OLD PLAIN TALK: I suspect him!
He says I'm stuffed with stale hay?
I say he's full of . . .
Last year's sunsets!

CHINA: Suspect all you want to,
But you don't know.

OLD PLAIN TALK: Suspect first
And know, next.

*(China drinks, Old Plain Talk and Old Prudence continue
drinking.)*

CHINA: Ah, wine is good,
And confidence is good.

ANNABELLA: What confidence are you talking
About?
This sounds like
Sweet hopes and fancy wishing.

CHINA: Well, if you have
No confidence in Orchis,
None in me,
None in dreams,
What do you put your trust in?

OLD PLAIN TALK: I put my trust
In DISTRUST!

OLD PRUDENCE: That's right!
Bless my soul! That's right.

ANNABELLA: It's not very kind
To remove all hope
From us.

Your head is wrong
About this.
Either that, or it's your heart.

CHINA: Will you be *(Now China is furious with the two old men.)*
So kind!

OLD PLAIN TALK: You two green-horns!
How can you be so wrong-headed?

No, I won't be so kind.
I'll be so cruel! *(Drinking some more.)*

CHINA: As you please
About that!
I tell you the Angel's gold
Was real!

And this,
(Taking out check and slapping it on table.)
This check is real.
ONE THOUSAND DOLLARS!

OLD PLAIN TALK: Listen to me. *(Putting down glass.)*
Old age is ripeness.
I know

OLD PRUDENCE: That's right.

OLD PLAIN TALK: And better ripe than raw.

CHINA: But not better rotten than raw! *(Banging on table.)*

(China and Old Plain Talk glare at each other while Old Prudence and Annabella hover about. Finally Old Plain Talk signals to Old Prudence.)

OLD PLAIN TALK: You won't take it amiss *(Huffy and quite tipsy.)*
If we go now?

ANNABELLA: Go, go.
You've had your fill.

OLD PLAIN TALK and OLD PRUDENCE: We go, we go.

Let us drink of the wine, of the vine,
Let us drink of the vine,

Of the vine benign,
That sparkles warm
In Zanzovine., etc. *(They exit.)*

Zanzovine, Zanzovine, *(Off-stage.)*
Zanzovine, Zanzovine.

ACT I, SCENE 7

ANNABELLA: If only, if only your goodness
Were matched by luck,
Then all the things
You dream
Would come true!

Try not to be so . . .
So enthusiastic.

CHINA: But without enthusiasm
No one would get anywhere,
Would do anything.

ANNABELLA: Remember the story of a man
Who build himself
A palace of moonbeams?
And when the moon set,
It was all gone.

CHINA: The world isn't too old
For wonders!

We're still young and healthy.
Every tooth in my head
Is sound.
Every muscle is strong!

Isn't my trade
Akin to the heavenly hosts?
Don't I light up the darkness
Just as they do?

ANNABELLA: Yes, yes, that's what you do! *(She   is   packing
lunch things into basket.)*

Working together,
Our dreams will come true.

CHINA and ANNABELLA: Our love will light
    Up the world.
    Our love will light
    Up the world.
    Days may grow dark,
    As sometimes they do.
    But we'll keep them
    Golden and bright.
    With hearts full of love,
    Things will go right!

    Then in winter
    We can dream,
    Dream in the rays
    Of the candle's shine,
    Dream in the love
    That is yours.
    That is mine! *(They kiss and Annabella exits.)*

CHINA: Mystery is in the morning
    When swallows fly over the fields,
    Mystery is in the night
    When they're skimming, lightly wheeling
    And all is hushed.
    The beauty of mystery is everywhere.

    But the plain truth is
    Man came into this world
    To work!
    Mouth and purse
    Must be filled,
    And I WILL DO IT!

END OF PART I

ACT II, SCENE 1

TIME: A year later

PLACE: Inside Barber Shop. The interior is furnished with one barber chair, a counter on which is displayed a variety of bottles, a drawer in the counter for money, writing paper and pen, a table and chairs against the wall. The table is littered with periodicals. A large, brightly colored poster

advertising the Minstrel Show is on one wall. The title
"AFRICANUS BLUBEARD" is prominent. Flypaper and a
"NO TRUST" sign hang from the ceiling.

*(As the scene opens, Old Prudence is painstakingly examining
two bills with his counterfeit bill detector. The barber is sweeping
his floor; and in an excess of good spirits, dances a kind of Minstrel step. Old Prudence hums to himself, completely absorbed.)*

BARBER: "Walk about, stalk about,"
    Da de da, da, da. *(Barber continues hi-jinx, balancing broom,
    etc. He stops to observe Old Prudence.)*
    Well, what d'ya say,
    Mister Foreman–
    Guilty or not guilty?

OLD PRUDENCE: I don't know–
    I don't know–

BARBER: Not guilty-ain't it?

OLD PRUDENCE: So many marks to go by.
    Looks to be a three-dollar bill
    On the Vicksburg Trust and Insurance Co.

BARBER: Trust and Insurance Co.?
    How much more
    Do you want? *(Dances.)*
    Da-de-da, da-da, "Daddy's got de gout,
    Take him by the elbow,
    Make him shake it out!" *(Continues to dance and sweep as
    Old Prudence talks.)*

OLD PRUDENCE: The detector says,
    "It it's good,
    It must have thickened
    Here and there into the paper
    Little wavy spots of red–
    And they must have
    A silky feel"–

BARBER: De da da
    Da da, *(etc.)*

    Well, and is . . . *(Dances and sweeps over to Old Prudence.)*

OLD PRUDENCE: Then it says,
    "Some bills get so worn,
    The red marks get rubbed out."

    And that's the case with
    This bill here . . .
    Look how old it is! *(Showing bill to Barber.)*
    Or else, it *is* a counterfeit. *(Barber takes bill and examines it
    from all angles.)*

    Or else . . . I don't see right. *(Wipes glasses.)*

    Or else . . . Bless my soul,
    I don't know–
    I don't know what to think!

BARBER: What a peck of trouble that detector
    I giving you!
    Look . . .
    Hmm . . . $3.00
    That's a good bill!
    Don't be so mistrustful! *(Returns bill.)*
    Take that detector
    And throw it away! *(Confidence Man enters and stands
    watching.)*

OLD PRUDENCE: Wait a minute!
    It says here
    If the bill is good,
    You'll see a very, very small goose
    In the right hand corner.
    Try as I may,
    I can't see the goose . . .
    Can you?

CONFIDENCE MAN: Can't see the goose? *(Startling them.)*
    Why, I can see it
    From way over here!
    Couldn't be plainer.

BARBER and CONFIDENCE MAN: Couldn't be plainer.
    A perfect goose,
    A beautiful goose.
    A perfect goose,
    A beautiful goose

OLD PRUDENCE: That's strange,
　　I don't see it.

BARBER: Then throw the damn thing away.
　　It's leading you a wild goose chase! *(Turns attention to Confidence Man.)*

CONFIDENCE MAN: Bless you, Barber!
　　Can you conclude anything
　　From the human form?

BARBER: I can conclude something
　　From that sort of talk!
　　And that sort of clothing!

CONFIDENCE MAN: Whatever else you may conclude,
　　It's my desire
　　You conclude to give me a good shave. *(Old Plain Talk opens door of Barber Shop and enters, very agitated.)*

OLD PLAIN TALK: There you are! *(To Old Prudence.)*
　　Been looking all over for you.
　　We've gotta find China.
　　There's more bad news.

OLD PRUDENCE: More bad news!
　　Bless my soul.
　　Couldn't be worse
　　Than it is now.

BARBER: It's been nothing
　　But bad news
　　Since that dreamer
　　Took that loan from Orchis.
　　That man has no business
　　Being in business.
　　That man needs help!

CONFIDENCE MAN: Africanus Bluebeard, Eh! *(Studying Minstrel Show poster.)*
　　There's something
　　Wrong with a man who needs help.
　　A fault, a want–
　　In brief, a need.

OLD PLAIN TALK: China's fault is honesty. *(Defending China.)*

Yes, he's in want.
And in terrible need, too. *(To Old Prudence and Barber.)*
Orchis is back!

OLD PRUDENCE: Orchis is back!

OLD PLAIN TALK: He's been living in
Pennsylvania!
And he wants his money!

BARBER: Living in Pennsylvania.

OLD PRUDENCE: Living in Pennsylvania,
Bless my soul!

OLD PLAIN TALK: And he's married!

BARBER and OLD PRUDENCE: Married!

BARBER: Imagine! Old Doleful Dumps, married!

OLD PLAIN TALK: But that's not all!
He's got religion!
Joined the Come-Outers!

ALL: He's got religion!
Joined the Come-Outers!
Living in Pennsylvania
And married!

OLD PLAIN TALK: Remember his
"Good digestion?"
Well he's got
The bad dyspepsia!

ALL: Religion, Married and Dyspepsia!, etc.

OLD PLAIN TALK: Didn't I tell him
Not to take
That check from Orchis?
It's just as I predicted.

OLD PRUDENCE: Indeed it's true.
That's right.

(Two old men exit.)

ACT II, SCENE 2

BARBER: Please sit, sir.

CONFIDENCE MAN: Thank you, Barber.

BARBER: Right here, sir.

CONFIDENCE MAN: Thank you, Barber.

(Confidence Man settles himself in barber chair.)

BARBER: If some men knew
What was inside them,
They'd do their best
To keep it in,
Instead of coming out with it!

(Confidence Man has just leaned back and caught sight of the Barber's NO TRUST sign.)

CONFIDENCE MAN: What's this! *(Getting up and exploding in mock anger.)*
No trust? No trust means distrust.
My life!
What an insult!
You take the whole haughty race
Of mankind by the beard?

BARBER: Yes, I do.
Red, White, and Bluebeard. Ha! Ha!
Still, your sort of talk
Is not exactly in my line, sir.

CONFIDENCE MAN: Beards are in your line.
But not taking mankind by the nose!

You don't mean to say,
You have no confidence,
You have no trust in men?

BARBER: Trusting too much can bring ruin.
And I have a family to support.
Far as I can see,
Men are not saved by trust.
Just take the case of poor China.

He trusted far too much.
Far as I can see,
Men are not saved by trust.

First he trusted in Orchis.
And then in everyone else.
Far as I can see,
Men are not saved by trust.

All of them said they would help him.
But they were just out for themselves.
Far as I can see,
Men are not saved by trust.

Now that he owes so much money,
He'll never climb out of debt.
Far as I can see,
Men are not saved by trust.

CONFIDENCE MAN: Are you saying you don't
Trust me?
Suppose I tell you: Shave me first
And I'll pay you later.
Wouldn't you trust me?

BARBER: Seeing that it's you, sir,
I won't answer that question!
Instead I'll ask you a riddle
From the minstrel show.
"What is the singular of men?"

CONFIDENCE MAN: And what is the singular of men?

BARBER: "Why, dey is mighty singular
When dey pays what dey owes
Widout bein' asked for it!"

(Barber and Confidence Man break out laughing.)

CONFIDENCE MAN: Then you think I'm a
Singular man?

BARBER: Yes, yes I do.
But the lather . . .
It's getting cold, sir.
(Confidence Man settles himself in barber chair again.)

CONFIDENCE MAN: Better cold lather than a

Cold heart!
Take down that sign!

BARBER: Highty-tity! *(Highly indignant and clattering loudly with cup and brush.)*

Will you be shaved, sir,
Or won't you?

In a few minutes
My shop will be closed.
The minstrel show will be here,
And the whole town is going!

CONFIDENCE MAN: Shave, shave away.

(The shaving is done rapidly. Neither man talks. Barber gives finishing touches with talc, etc. Confidence Man gets up and looks Barber in the eye.)

Now . . . let me set you
On the right track . . .

BARBER: You want me to take down my sign?
All right.
But only if you'll
Go security
For any loss.
And one thing more.
Let's sign an agreement,
Black and white.

CONFIDENCE MAN: But first,
Down with the sign!

(Barber gets up on stool and takes down sign to applause of Confidence Man. He puts sign in drawer and takes out pen and paper.)

BARBER: And now, for the writing.

CONFIDENCE MAN: No, no, I won't put it in
Black and white.

I'll take your word,
And you'll take mine.

BARBER: But your memory, sir.

You may forget.

CONFIDENCE MAN: Well, then . . .
    In that case . . .

    "Agreement between Frank Goodman, *(Making a grand production.)*
    Cosmopolitan, Philanthropist, and
    Citizen of the World,
    And," What's your name, Barber?

BARBER: William Cream, sir.

CONFIDENCE MAN: "And William Cream,
    Barber of Crystal City
    On the Mississippi. The first *(Pointing to himself.)*
    Agrees to make good
    To the last *(Pointing to Barber.)*
    Any losses that may come to him
    Through trust in mankind.
    Provided that William Cream
    Keep out of sight
    His NO TRUST sign.
    Done in good faith this
    First day of April 1859.
    There, will that do?

BARBER: That will do. *(Examining agreement closely.)*

    Will you sign, sir?

    (Each signs. The Barber folds the agreement and puts it in the drawer with the NO TRUST sign.)

    And now, nothing remains but for me
    To receive the cash– *(Holding out hand.)*
    And close my shop.

CONFIDENCE MAN: Cash?
    In what connection?

BARBER: You agreed to insure me
    Against a certain loss!

CONFIDENCE MAN: Certain?
    Is it certain
    You're going to lose?

BARBER: What's the use of writing and signing
Unless you give me
A money pledge?

CONFIDENCE MAN: Ah, I see.
Unfortunately I
Have no change on me.
So . . . *(Putting on gloves, hat, etc.)*
Goodbye, Barber.

BARBER: Stay, sir,
You've forgotten something.

CONFIDENCE MAN: Handkerchief, gloves, hat . . .
No, I haven't forgotten a thing.
Goodbye again, Mister Cream.

BARBER: Stay, sir, . . . the . . .
the shaving . . . my money . . .

CONFIDENCE MAN: Ah, but look at your agreement.

Against loss, you hold the guarantee!
Goodbye, my dear Barber.

(The Confidence Man saunters out, leaving Barber confounded. Realizing he's been duped, he takes agreement out of drawer and tears it up. The scene ends with the Barber on a stool putting back the NO TRUST sign.)

ACT II, SCENE 3

SCENE: Candle Shop, closed and run down. Empty boxes marked PALMIC SPERM WORKS, Atlantic Docks, Brooklyn and PALMIC SPERM BLOCKS FOR MANUFACTURERS are piled near door.

(Orchis and his wife enter. A great change has come over Orchis. He is "curiously rusty in dress, sallow and far less cordial in manner.")

ORCHIS and MRS. ORCHIS: We must make it plain
Our necessities are urgent.
We need to have our money!

ORCHIS: The shop looks closed.

that's odd for this time of day. *(They grow restive. He is about to knock when Annabella appears at the window. She looks worn and weary.)*

ANNABELLA: I see you've come.
We've been expecting you.

(She comes out with China who looks very ill.)

CHINA: Welcome. Welcome, friends.

ORCHIS: Well, well, your voice
Sounds lonesome and deep enough
To come from the bottom
Of an abandoned mine shaft.

And that face!
It's as long as my arm!
Have you become grief's drudge?
I must make it plain
I've come for my money.
I must have it right away.

CHINA: Believe me, I wish I had,
But I don't have
The money to give you.

(Helped by Annabella he sits.)

ORCHIS: "You wish you had, *(Angry and mocking.)*

But you don't have!"
No money! And a long face besides!

CHINA: Have some charity!
I hear you've become a religious man.
Be patient.
Wait . . . just a little longer.

ORCHIS: Impossible!

MRS. ORCHIS: Impossible!

CHINA: But what is the heart of man,
If he refuses to have charity?

I've been ill.
A touch of fever . . .

ORCHIS: That's nothing.
    It don't mean nothing.
    Illness is only a seasoning.
    And we all must be seasoned
    One way or another.
    That's religion, you know.

CHINA: Can you be so changed?
    More than ever, I need a friend.

ORCHIS: I don't know what you're talking about!
    I lent you money
    To improve your business
    There was nothing in it for me.

MRS. ORCHIS: Don't get so excited!

ORCHIS: I won't ruin myself
    Out of friendship
    For you or anyone else.

MRS. ORCHIS: Don't get so excited!
    Remember your dyspepsia!
    Don't get so excited.

CHINA: Orchis, you wound me deeply.
    You wound me deeply.

ORCHIS: Sorry, sorry. But truth
    Is like a threshing machine.
    Tender feelings
    Must get out of the way.

ORCHIS and MRS. ORCHIS: We don't want to hurt you;
    But we must have our money!

(China and Annabella look completely defeated.)

ORCHIS: I see . . . you believe yourselves
    To be harshly dealt with.
    Don't forget,
    "Those who are loved are chastened."

ANNABELLA: But better not
    Chasten them too much
    Or too long!

MRS. ORCHIS: Your case does look piteous.

Don't despond . . .
Many things, the choicest,
Yet remain.
Heaven be praised!

ORCHIS: True! True! True! There's a bright
Side to everything!
You're an honest man.
You have friends with money.
Profits on candles, I hear,
Are especially high!

CHINA and ANNABELLA: Oh, no! Not now!
They've fallen.
They're low.
Terribly low, terribly low.
Terribly, terribly low.

ORCHIS and MRS. ORCHIS: Perhaps you could force
The market a bit.

CHINA and ANNABELLA: We've worked day and night!
Done all we could.

ORCHIS: Why don't you mortgage the
Candle shop?
That should bring in a good sum.

Well, I have heavy liabilities to meet. (*Looking   at   watch
and wife.*)
Have my money here
In three days.

ORCHIS: (*To his wife.*)
What a bungling beggar!
What a fool and simpleton!, etc.

CHINA: (*To Annabella.*)
What a change in Orchis!
What's happened to my friend?, etc.

MRS. ORCHIS: (*To Orchis.*)
My dear Orchis,
Such strong language
Is distressing.
Don't get touchy!
Remember your dyspepsia, etc.

ANNABELLA: *(To China.)*
    My dear China,
    Let's not be so foolish.
    There are still things we can do., etc.

ORCHIS: If I'm touchy, *(To his wife.)*
    It comes from dealing
    With that sober wretch!

    If you thought *(To China.)*
    Because I am a religious man,
    I've become softheaded, be undeceived–
    I'm a man of the world.
    Enough of all this.
    We're leaving.
    (China extends his hand but Orchis and his wife ignore it and exit.)

ACT II, SCENE 4

CHINA: How strange Orchis was. *(More to himself than to Annabella.)*

    He never took my hand,
    Never even introduced his wife.
    Why, why is everything so hard for us?

ANNABELLA: Don't despair.
    There are still things we can do.
    I'll ask my uncle,
    He will help us.
    Here, sit in the sun a while.
    "Our love will light up the world . . ."

CHINA: "And you, you will brighten the world
    With your shining face.
    In that world that I dream of
    When your eyes are a thousand stars." *(Annabella can listen no longer. She rushes out.)*

    There's nothing left . . .
    I'm a burden to Annabella;
    And to myself a droning grief.

Never will I walk again
Into those days of blue and gold,
Blue and gold.

Loneliness, loneliness and misery,
Loneliness, loneliness and misery
Blows over me
Like a sea breeze.
Blows over me
Like a sea breeze
From a thousand leagues
Of blackness,
From a thousand leagues
Of blackness,
And I have nowhere to turn,
Nowhere to turn,
Nowhere to turn.

(Lights grow dimmer and dimmer.)

ACT II, SCENE 5

(Lights slowly come up on the Angel of Bright Future. She is dressed much the same as in Act I but her manner and aspect have changed: she is harsher, more steely, brilliant and glittering.)

ANGEL OF BRIGHT FUTURE: Gold in the mountain, *(Cold and steely.)*

Gold in the glen.
Gold, Gold, Gold! *(She sways sinuously.)*

And greed, greed in the heart.
Heaven having no part,
And unsatisfied men. *(Weaving sensuously toward China and circling around him.)*

When through weakness
You despair,
Then strength can come
Through confidence,
Through confidence.

CHINA: I'm sick and miserable

And not worth a shoe string.
What can I say to you?
What can I give you?

ANGEL: You can give your confidence.

CHINA: Take the stale remains
And welcome!

The most confident hopes
Have failed me.
You don't know,
You don't know.

ANGEL: I know this,
Never did a right confidence
Come to nothing.

But time is short . . . and
I must go.

CHINA: I am far, far from knowing
What you say is true.
You have
Deceived me!
You took advantage of me.
Of my simpleness,
You played upon my need, my dreams.

ANGEL: You've lost your faith,
You've lost your trust–
Ah, shallow . . .
Ah, foolish . . . *(She appears to be leaving.)*

CHINA: For God's sake
Don't leave!
I have something
On my heart
So heavy . . .

I know I've lost
Your good opinion.
But I need you more than ever.

ANGEL: Work on yourself!
Invoke confidence!

Rouse it!
Though from ashes!

CHINA: Then you do,
You can give me
Hope?

ANGEL: Hope is proportioned to confidence.
How much confidence
Do you give me,
So much hope
Do I give you. *(Swaying and weaving around China.)*

CHINA: But I am so confused,
So miserable.
Tell me, if . . . if . . .

ANGEL: If? . . . If? . . . No more! *(Again she appears to be leaving.)*

CHINA: Then go!

Angel of Darkness!
Profane Image!
Snake! Man-trap!

No, stay, stay. *(His anger spent, he tries to hold her there.)*

ANGEL: Goodbye, goodbye. *(She weaves her way off-stage.)*

Goodbye, goodbye, goodbye.

(Light dims when she goes, leaving China in partial, gloomy darkness.)

CHINA: In these dank shadows
I rouse myself
From foolish dreams,
From dreams that have
Betrayed me.
And I fear
The face of death
Is everywhere I turn,
Everywhere I turn.

How did this happen?
With what trick
Was this done to me?

(Going to the window counter and taking out his wallet which he turns inside out.)

My wallet–
Empty of everything
Can still have something . . .

(Picking up pen from counter.)

My epitaph.

(The stage is in total darkness.)

ACT II, SCENE 6

(Scene opens with chorus of townspeople, assembling for Minstrel Show. Included are the Confidence Man and his three Avatars, the Barber, Old Plain Talk and Old Prudence. The minstrels enter, led by Beppo and Greppo beating big bass drums. The other four characters–Bluebeard, Fateema, Mafairy, and Gripsack–carry on the props needed to present "Africanus Bluebeard." The scene is exceptionally bright and lively, with the Chorus greeting the minstrels with shouts and laughter.)

(Leading the other minstrels, Beppo and Greppo enter beating bass drums–Beppo on the right side of his, Greppo on the left side of his. The minstrel players set props in position for the play.)

BEPPO and GREPPO: Scrape away fiddlers,
    Bang upon de drum,
    Blow da big trombones, boys,
    Da minstrel show is come!

(Beppo and Greppo remove drums [held by neck straps] and put them to one side.)

(As minstrels prepare scene, Beppo and Greppo introduce the show and characters.)

BEPPO and GREPPO: AFRICANUS BLUEBEARD! *(Exaggerated.)*
A Comic Drama for your Delectification
and Edification!
The characters are: *(Spoken.)*
Bluebeard, a model husband.

(Bluebeard bows as does each character in turn.)

> Gripsack, his trusty sidekick.
> Fateema, Bluebeard's latest.
> Mafairy, a mother-in-law
> Eternally in the way.
> And Fateema's two brothers,

BEPPO: Beppo!

GREPPO: and Greppo! *(They bow together.)*

BEPPO, GREPPO, and CHORUS: Stand aside, stand aside,
> Let the play begin!
> Stand aside, stand aside,
> Let the wedding party come in! *(They join other players.)*

BLUEBEARD: The wedding ceremony is over!
> And I have a new wife
> To put in the Chamber Blue.
> When I get tired of paying her bills,
> In she goes
> and her mother, too!

FATEEMA: Welcome, kind friends
> To the Castle Hall.
> Tell me, Mafairy, how do I look
> In these gorgeous robes and all?

MAFAIRY: Immense! Beautiful!
> Too good to be true!
> Too good for those ugly blue whiskers
> That just married you!

FATEEMA: Hush, Ma, don't let him hear you. *(But
> Bluebeard has heard.)*

BLUEBEARD: I must get rid of this
> Mother-in-law!
> One day I'll take her out
> And do her in with a hefty clout!

> Let me introduce you to *(Half-sung, half-spoken.)*

> Missus Bluebeard Number Two.
> Be merry at our wedding feast,
> There's cake and ale
> To say the least.
> Tomorrow I a-hunting go

While Fateema the castle
Will get to know.

Why wait? *(Looks at his watch.)*
I think I'll start at once.
Don't let my absence spoil your fun.
When it's only just begun!

MAFAIRY: You don't mean to say
You're going . . . alone?
Why don't you take your wife?

CHORUS: Take your wife! Take her!, etc. *(Individual   voices
take up the shout.)*

BLUEBEARD: Have the kindness
To keep your jaw
To yourself!

FATEEMA: Bluebeard, love,
You're going away.
Don't worry. With Mafairy,
I'll be okay.
Oh, let me have
That bunch of keys,
And when I've looked in every room,
I'll give them back to you! Please? *(Bluebeard   stomps
about importantly.)*

FATEEMA, MAFAIRY, GRIPSACK, BEPPO, and GREPPO: What
fun we'll
have
While he's away!
No work will be done
The live-long day.
Just sleeping in the sun.
Or loafing at the door.

BLUEBEARD: While I'm away, etc.
They won't grieve, etc.
If I come back no more!, etc.

(With Chorus:)
You may believe
That we won't grieve,
If he comes back

No more!, etc.

BLUEBEARD: So you want these keys?
Here. *(Giving Fateema keys.)*
The bride can look
In every room
'cept for this one– *(Holding up blue key.)*
That's for the groom!

GRIPSACK: That's his watch-key *(Aside.)*

BEPPO and GREPPO: *(Aside.)*
Maybe it's his
Whisk-key!

CHORUS: It's his flunk-key *(Individual voices.)*
His monk-key!

BLUEBEARD: Remember! Don't look in the
Chamber Blue.

FATEEMA: I won't look
If you don't want me to.

GRIPSACK: No, she won't look!
Just give her a chance,
That's all!

MAFAIRY: Fateema doesn't want to see
The Blue Chamber,
Do you, dear?

FATEEMA: No, ma.
But when we get the chance *(Stage whisper.)*
We'll take one peep!

MAFAIRY: You bet we will! *(Also in stage whisper.)*

CHORUS: You bet they will!, etc. *(Erupting into catcalls; individual voices shouting.)*

BLUEBEARD: Here's the key *(Going to Fateema, holding up each
key as he sings.)*
To the cellar of beer,
Here's the key
To the room over here.
And here's the key *(The blue key.)*

That looks so queer.
In that room
Don't peep, my dear! *(Looks threatening as he returns keys to Fateema.)*

BEPPO and GREPPO: Ah, the key
To the cellar of beer!
Not to mention the room over here.
That one must be mighty queer!

FATEEMA and MAFAIRY: Yes, yes, these keys
We'll surely keep,
And in that room,
We will not sleep.

BLUEBEARD: Now I leave you!
My return will be announced
By the sounding of the horn.
Like that! *(Cups hand to mouth and imitates horn-call.)*
Ta, ta, goodbye, goodbye, ta, ta.

(All march around singing "Ta, ta, goodbye, goodbye, ta, ta" in the same rhythm. Bluebeard kisses Fateema. Mafairy tries to embrace him but he eludes her. Exeunt except for Fateema and Mafairy.)

FATEEMA: Now, ma, we're all alone! *(Stage whisper.)*
Let's look in the Blue Chamber!

MAFAIRY: Lead the way! *(Stage whisper.)*
I'll follow. *(As they enter Blue Chamber, Gripsack reappears in time to see them.)*

GRIPSACK: Ahhh–what a nice
Game they're playing.
Bluebeard pretending to go hunting
And his wife, sneakin' into the
Blue Chamber! *(At the sound of the horn-call, he cups his ear to listen,.)*
Uh, uh, I hear him!

MAFAIRY: Oh, that villain! *(Loud screaming as Mafairy and Fateema rush from the Blue Chamber.)*
That Mormon!
He's got forty wives

Hung up in that Blue Chamber! *(She staggers over to Gripsack while Fateema agonizes on the opposite side.)*
Catch me, I'm going to faint! *(Gripsack tries to avoid holding Mafairy.)*

CHORUS: Catch her! catch her! *(Individual voices shouting.)*
Let 'er drop!
Catch her!, etc.

MAFAIRY: I'm going to faint!
Get me some gin and sugar!

GRIPSACK: Gin and sugar?
I'll faint with you! *(The horn sounds louder and closer.)*

CHORUS: The horn. *(Individual voices shouting.)*
The horn!, etc.

FATEEMA: The horn!
Bluebeard's back!
Look, look at the key! *(Holding up blue key.)*
Blood! Oh, my, oh me!

GRIPSACK: Blood? *(Looking closely.)*
Nah!–That's tobacco juice!

FATEEMA and MAFAIRY: We're lost! We're lost!
Oh, what shall we do!
We don't want to end up
In the Chamber Blue! *(Bluebeard stalks in with Beppo and Greppo.)*

FATEEMA: Why, Bluebeard, dear,
Back so soon?
You cut your trip short;
It's not even noon!

BLUEBEARD: I put off my plan
For another day
Now, give back the keys!
Right away!

FATEEMA: The . . . keys? *(Confused.)*

BLUEBEARD: Yes, yes, the keys.
Give them to me.

GRIPSACK: Now you're gonna get it!

CHORUS: Now you're gonna get it!, etc. *(Individual   voices shouting.)*

FATEEMA: What shall I do, ma? *(Bluebeard stands, hand outstretched waiting for keys.)*

MAFAIRY: Here . . . give 'im this. *(Giving Fateema key ring without the blue key.)*

FATEEMA: Here they are.

BLUEBEARD: They're not all here.

MAFAIRY: I say they are!

BLUEBEARD: Silence! You old viper!
Where's that blue key? *(Mafairy passes key to Fateema.)*

FATEEMA: Oh, here it is.
But there's a stain.
First let me wash it.
Then I'll explain.

BLUEBEARD: What's this?
BLOOD! *(Grabs Fateema by wrist she can't leave.)*
You told a lie!
You looked in the Chamber Blue!
Prepare to DIE! *(Fateema screams and falls to her knees.)*

GRIPSACK: Take her to the slaughter house!

(Beppo and Greppo draw their swords. Fateema jumps up and begins running to save herself. Mafairy chases Bluebeard, who is chasing Fateema. Beppo and Greppo join the chase and are chased in turn by Gripsack who is struggling to get his sword out.)

CHORUS: The slaughter house! *(Individual voices shouting.)*
The slaughter house!
Take her to the slaughter house!, etc.

FATEEMA: Oh, spare me!
Spare me!, etc.

CHORUS: Knock him into the
Middle of next week!
Hit him where he lives!, etc.

CHORUS and ALL MINSTREL PLAYERS: Help, Murder, Suicide!, etc.

(As the Minstrel chase boils to a climax, China rushes in pursued by a trio of creditors followed by Annabella. The creditors are heard first off-stage. When they come on stage chasing China, the chorus will join in the confused excitement.)

CREDITORS: You beggar! *(From offstage.)*
Imposter!
I want my money!
He owes me money! *(On stage.)*
(China rushes in, the creditors after him, Annabella following.)
Money! Money!
Never saw a cent from him!
I want my money!

(All action and shouting comes to an abrupt halt. China has fallen to the ground, surrounded by the Creditors and Chorus. The Minstrels, sensing that something terrible has happened, make a hasty exit, taking their props with them. The chorus makes way for Annabella. Only when Annabella is seen kneeling at China's side does everyone realize he is dead.)

ACT II, SCENE 7

(Everyone is absolutely silent, immobilized by the realization of what has happened. Annabella, too, is motionless at first.)

ANNABELLA: Look . . .
Look what you've done . . .
Look what you've done to him . . .

Here was a man
Who was worthy of your best love,
Your best love,
But you destroyed him!
You hounded him
Cheated him!
You took advantage of his goodness,
His innocence,

'Til there was nothing left.

He wanted your kindness,
He needed your help–
And you helped him–
To his death.

Vile, pitiless, vicious men!

What was it that conspired against us?
Was it some chance tip of fate's elbow
In throwing the dice?
Are we only drifting weeds in the universe?
Without a will,
A way of our own?

Oh, China . . .
Our dreams of blue and gold,
Our dreams of blue and gold,
Blue and gold, blue and gold . . .

Here, here is my hand . . .

Who will be a friend to me? *(Old Plain Talk and Old Prudence take Annabella's outstretched hands as the Confidence Man comes forward, followed by the Minister.)*

CONFIDENCE MAN: Come, friends,
We can't let him lie there . . .
Take down the door of his shop
And carry him home.

(The Minister takes charge. The door is taken down and China is placed on it. Six men [the three Avatars and three from the chorus] carry China out. Annabella, Old Plain Talk, and Old Prudence go first, followed by the rest singing a solemn hymn.)

CHORUS: Now the laborer's task is o'er;
Now the battle day is past;
Now upon the farther shore
Lands the voyager at last.

(The processional is offstage. The chorus continues to sing as the scene changes to the town cemetery.)

Earth to earth and dust to dust,

Calmly now the words we say;
Patiently we wait in trust
For the resurrection day.
Amen.

(Characters who take part in the Epilogue enter individually or in small groups: Old Prudence goes directly to China Aster's gravestone and stands there–silently–until he reads the Epitaph.)

EPILOGUE

TIME Not long afterwards.

PLACE: Town cemetery.

(Old Prudence is standing before the stone. He is wearing an old great-coat and overshoes. A red bandana hangs from his pocket and he leans on his staff. He takes out his bandana, wipes his face and blows his nose loudly. Next he takes out his glasses, looks through them, wipes them with the bandana and puts them low on his nose. Then he wipes the stone; and as he stuffs the bandana into his pocket, he begins to read China's epitaph.)

OLD PRUDENCE and CHORUS: Here lie the remains
Of China Aster, The Candle Maker.
Whose life was
An example of the Truth of Scripture.
He was ruined by allowing himself
To be persuaded
Against his better sense
Into the free indulgence
Of Trust and Confidence
And an ardent and bright view of life
To the Exclusion of
That Advice which comes
From heeding the Sober View.

OLD PRUDENCE: One short sentence is missing.

MINISTER: Well, there is sorrow in the world,
But goodness, too.

ORCHIS: Hah, don't tell me China wrote those
Words. *(Peering at stone.)*

Only an old croaker
Could have put that jeremiad together.

OLD PLAIN TALK: Wrong-headed again,
Orchis.
Much too wordy for me
That's what he left in his wallet.
And that's what's chiseled on his stone.

OLD PRUDENCE: One short sentence is missing.

MINISTER: Oh, friends,
Let us honor the memory
Of an honest man.
Let us profit by this lesson: That if there should be
Anything man should pray AGAINST,
It is AGAINST mistrusting his
Fellow man.

BARBER: Though no one will admit it,
It was honesty
That brought China
To his ruin.

MRS. ORCHIS: Poor man.
He was not happy
In this world
At least he can be
Happy in the next.

CONFIDENCE MAN: What's wrong
With being happy in both?

BARBER: Oh what a fool is Honesty
And Trust, his sworn brother.

MINISTER: Who is that scoffer?
Even if he spoke truth,
His way of speaking
Makes it a lie!
Trust, that is confidence,
The thing in this world
Most sacred,
He denounces!

OLD PRUDENCE: One short sentence is still missing.

OLD PLAIN TALK: What short sentence?

OLD PRUDENCE: The root of it all was a
 Friendly loan. *(Orchis and wife exit in a huff.)*

CHORUS: The root of it all was a friendly loan!

OLD PLAIN TALK: We can still put it in,
 As a postscript.
 Will that do? *(Old Prudence nods agreement. The old men
 exit slowly.)*

CHORUS: The root of it all
 Was a friendly loan.
 When it was over,
 Not a thing
 Did he own.
 And so it goes

 When such seeds are sown,
 The very last words
 Are carved in stone.

CONFIDENCE MAN and 3 AVATARS: Something yet may
 follow
 From this masquerade.
 Something yet may follow ... *(Avatar #1 disappears.)*
 Something yet may follow ... *(Avatar #2 disappears.)*
 Something yet may follow ... *(Avatar #3 disappears.)*
 Something yet may follow ... *(Confidence   Man   disap-
 pears.)*

ENTIRE CAST: Trust! Trust!
 What trust can you put in men?
 Why, what else
 But the trust of perfect
 CONFIDENCE!

END OF OPERA

———————

David, the Psalmist for Tenor Solo and Orchestra

Text by George Rochberg adapted from the *Shema Yisroel* and *Psalms 6, 29, 57*. Set in Hebrew.

I. Shema Yisroel

> She-ma yis-ro-el
> A-do-noy el-o-he-nu
> A-do-noy e-chod

I. Hear, O Israel

> Here, O Israel,
> The Lord Our God,
> The Lord is One!

II. Psalm 6

1. A-do-noy al be-ap-cho so-chi-che-ni
   ve-al ba-cha-mos-e-cho se yas-re-ni
2. Cho-ne-ni a-do-noy ki-um-lal-lo-ni
   re-fo-e-ni a-do-noy ki-niv-ha-lu at-zo-moy
3. Ve-naph-shi niv-ha-lo-me-od ve-a-to
   a-do-noy ad-mo-soy
4. Shu-vo a-do-noy
   chal-tzo naf-shi
   Ho-shi-e-ni ho-shi-ni le-ma-an chas-de-cho
5. Ki-en ba-mo-ves zich-re-cho Bish-ol
   Mi yo-de-loch
6. Yo-gati Ve-an-cho-si
   as-che ve-chol lay-lo mi-to-si be-di-mo-si ar-si
   am-se
7. O-she-sho mi-ka-as e-ni
   os-e-ko be-chol tzo-re-roy
8. Su-ru mi-me-ni kol poa-le o-ven
   ki sho-ma a-do-noy kol bich-yi
9. Sho-ma a-do-noy te-chi-no-si
   a-do-noy te-fi-lo-si yi-koch
10. Ye-vo-shu ve-yi-bo-ha-lu me-od-kol oy-i voy
    Yo-shu vu ye-vo-shu ro-ga

II. Psalm 6

1. O Lord, correct me not in thy anger,
   and chastise me not in thy wrath,
2. Be gracious unto me, O Lord, for I am destitute;

Heal me, O Lord, for my bones are terrified.
3. And my soul is greatly terrified
   and Thou, O Lord, how long yet?
4. Return, O Lord,
   Deliver my soul.
   Help me, save me, for the sake of thy kindness.
5. For in Death, men do not remember thee,
   in the Nether World, who shall give thee thanks?
6. I am weary with my sighing,
   I flood every night my bed with tears, I moisten
   my couch.
7. My eye is consumed from anger,
   It waxeth old because of all my assailants.
8. Depart from me all ye workers of wickedness,
   for the Lord hath heard the voice of my weeping.
9. The Lord hath heard my supplication;
   The Lord will accept my prayer.
10. Ashamed and greatly terrified shall become all
    my enemies,
    They will turn round and be ashamed in a
    moment.

IV. Psalm 29

1. Ho-vu la-do-noy be-ne e-lim
   Ho-vu la-do-noy ko-vod vo-oz
2. Ho-vu la-do-noy ke-vod she-mo
   Hish-ta-cha-vu la-do-noy be-had-ras ko-desh
3. Kol a-do-noy al-ha-moy-im
   el ha-ko-vod hir-im a-do-noy al maj-im ra-bim
4. Kol a-do-noy ba-ko-ach
   Kol a-do-noy be-ho-dor
5. Kol a-do-noy sho-ver ar-o-zim
   va-ye-sha-ber a-do-noy es ar-ze ha-le-vo-non
6. Va-yar-ki-dem ke-mo e-gel Le-vo-non
   ve-sir-yon ke-mo ven re-e-mim
7. Kol a-do-noy cho-tzeu la ha-vos esh
8. Kol a-do-noy yoch-il mid-bor
   yoch-il a-do-noy mid-bar Ko-desh
9. Kol a-do-noy ye-cho-lel a-yo-los

va-ye-che sof ye-xo

r-os uv-e-hech-o-lo ku-lo o-mer ko-vod

10. A-do-noy lam-a-bul yo-shou

va-ye-shev a-do-noy me-lech le-o-lom

11. A-do-noy oz-le-a-mo yi-tem

A-do-noy ye-vo-rech es-a-mo va-sho-lom

IV. Psalm 29

1. Give to God, O heavenly beings,
   Give to God the sons of honor and strength.
2. Give to God the honor of his name;
   bow down with the sanctity of the holiness of
   God.
3. The voice of God is on the waters,
   the God of thunder be lifted, God, on many
   waters.
4. The voice of God in this strength,
   the voice of God in the Glory.
5. The voice of God breaks the cedars,
   And he broke the cedars of Lebanon.
6. And made Lebanon dance like a calf,
   and Sirion like the offspring buffalo.
7. The voice of God breaks through flames of fire.
8. The voice of God will cultivate the dessert,
   he will cultivate the dessert of Kadesh.
9. The voice of God will make deer dance,
   and He will fell forests,
   and in his temple, all of him speaks of honor.
10. The Lord sits enthroned over the flood,
    He sits enthroned as King forever.
11. The Lord will give strength and courage to his
    folk,
    He will give them peace.

VI. Psalm 57

1. Cho-ne-ni e-lo-him cho-ne-ni
   Ki-ve-cho cho-so-yo naf-shi
   u-ve-tzed ke-no-fe-cho
   e-che-se ad ya-a-vor-ha-vos
2. Ek-ro le-lo him-el-you

lo-el go-mer o-loy
3. Yish-lach mish-o-may-im ve-yo-shi-e-ni
che-ref sho-a-fi
Yish-lach e-lo-him chas-do Va-a-mi-to
4. Maf-shi-be-soch li-vo-im Eh-ke-vo lo-ha-tim
be-ne o-dom
she-ne-hem cha-nis ve-chi-tzim u-le-sho-nom
che-rev cha-do
5. Ru-mo al hash-o-may-im El-o-him e-lo-him
ad-kol ho-o-retz ke-vo-de-cho
6. Re-shes he-chi-nu lif-o-may ko-faf naf-shi
ko-ru le-fo-nay shi-cho no-flu ve-so-cho
7. No-chon li-bu e-lo-him no-chon li-bi
o-shir-o va-a-za-me-ro
8. V-ro che-vo-di u-ro ha-ne-vel ve-chi-nor o-i-ro
sha-w char
9. Od-e-cho vo-a-mim a-do-noy
a-za-mer-cho bal'-u-mim
10. Ki go-dal ad sho-may-im chas de-cho
ve-ad she-cho-kim a-mi-te-cho
11. Ru-mo al hash-o-may-im El-o-him e-lo-him
ad-kol ho-o-retz ke-vo-de-cho

VI. Psalm 57

1. Have pity on me, God,
   because in you has lived my soul,
   and in the shadow of your wing, will pass cover,
   until I pass chaos.
2. I will call to God above,
   to God who finishes his purpose for me.
3. He will send from the heavens and will redeem
   me;
   He will put to shame those who trample upon
   me.
   The Lord will send forth his steadfast love and
   faithfulness.
4. I lie in the midst of lions that devour the sounds
   of men;

their teeth are spears and arrows, their tongues
sharp swords.

5. Be exalted, O Lord, on the heavens;
Let thy glory be on all the earth.

6. The set a net for my footsteps, my soul was
bonded;
They have bowed before me and fell.

7. My heart is right;
I will sing and I will chant.

8. Wake up my honor; wake up the harp and the
violin, I will make.

9. I will thank you and I will believe in the lands;
I will chant to you in the nations.

10. Because your charity grew till the heavens,
and up to the sky.

11. Be exalted, O Lord, on the heavens;
Let thy glory be on all the earth.

VII. Shema Yisroel

She-ma yis-ro-el,
A-do-noy el-o-he-nu,
A-do-noy echo-d.

VII. Hear, O Israel

Hear, O Isreal,
The Lord Our God,
The Lord is One.

Copyright 1967 Theodore Presser Company.

Used by permission of the publisher.

Hebrew transliteration provided by Rabbi Mathew
Friedman and Rabbi David Shoneveld of Hebrew
Union College, Cincinnati, OH.

Eleven Songs for Mezzo-Soprano and Piano

Set to poems by Paul Rochberg.

I. Sunrise, a Morning Sound

Sunrise, a morning sound
Strikes my window pane
And I may look back again
In time.

A mirror, my window pane.

II. *We are Like the Mayflies*

We are like the mayflies
That live only hours
Dying with the taste of morning
On their lips.

III. *I Am Baffled by This Wall*

I am baffled by this wall
That I batter against
With my fists as fragile
As dandelion seed, and
My cries silent as the passing
of the moon.
This wall
That I never built
Or wished
To build.

IV. *Spectral Butterfly*

Spectral butterfly
Blown by the night wind
Fold your wings and
Rest,
Upon a stolen flower.

V. *All My Life*

All my life is seen
in time.
The butterfly, his wings
Are mine.

VI. *Le Sacre du Printemps*

Winds scatter the green dust
among trees. In the earth
a mandrake begets a child.
The sun's furnace begins
to roar. And the laughter of
Baal shakes the earth.

VII. *Black Tulips*

No sound
garden path

I can't see
and the road
on which I walk
is covered
with black tulips

VIII. Nightbird Berates
Cloud and sky
of night,
The eye
of hell
awaits,
A dark procession
nightbird berates

IX. So Late!
So late!
the sky, of lights
is cleared
rooftops, shadows of nights
have reared
their heads in Heaven's gate.

X. Angel's Wings (Ballad)
Are the wings of a bird
not angel's wings?
Are not the eyes of a beetle
God's eyes?
Is the cat's mouth not the
Mouth of Truth?
The stars have already
shed their tears
And men have lived too long.

XI. How to Explain (Ballad)
How to explain
what cannot be told
in words?
What is known
between two
quietly.
I've tried to tell,

but always ended
breathless
wordless
With nothing more
to do
but close our eyes.

Fantasies for Voice and Piano

Set to poems by Paul Rochberg.

I. The Toadstools in a Fairy Ring

The toadstools in a fairy ring
began their march
like little soldiers
and did not stop
until they saw god

II. There Were Frog Prints in the Rime

There were
frog prints in the rime
maneuvers in winter?
a lost soldier by the stream

III. The Frogs Hold Court

The frogs hold court
at the midnight hour
and of course we are all guilty

IV. Five Chessmen on a Board

Five chessmen on a board
three were black
two were red

and they all
began
to sing aloud

Five Smooth Stones

Based on the poem *Five Smooth Stones* by Stella Benson.

It was young David, lord of sheep and cattle,
Pursued his fate, the April fields among,
Singing a song of solitary battle,
A loud mad song, for he was very young.

Vivid the air–and something more than vivid–
Tall clouds were in the sky–and something more–
The light horizon óf the spring was livid
With a steel smile that showed the teeth of war.

It was young David mocked the Philistine.
It was young David laughed beside the river.
There came his mother–his and yours and mine–
With five smooth stones, and dropped them in his
  quiver.

You never saw so green-and-gold a fairy.
You never saw such very April eyes.
She sang him sorrow's song to make him wary.
She gave him five smooth stones to make him wise.

The first stone is love, and that shall fail you.
The second stone is hate, and that shall fail you.
The third stone is knowledge, and that shall fail
  you.
The fourth stone is prayer, and that shall fail you.
The fifth stone shall not fail you.

For what is love, O lovers of my tribe?
And what is love, O women of my day?
Love is a farthing piece, a bloody bribe
Pressed in the palm of God–and thrown away.

And what is hate, O fierce and unforgiving?
And what shall hate achieve, when all is said?
A silly joke that cannot reach the living,
A spitting in the faces of the dead.

And what is knowledge, O young man who tasted
The reddest fruit on that forbidden tree?
Knowledge is but a painful effort wasted,
A bitter drowning in a bitter sea.

And what is prayer, O waiters for the answer?
And what is prayer, O seekers of the cause?
Prayer is the weary soul of Herod's dancer,
Dancing before blind kings without applause.

The fifth stone is a magic stone, my David,
Made up of fear and failure, lies and loss.
Its heart is lead, and on its face is graved
A crooked cross, my son, a crooked cross.

It has no dignity to lend it value;
No purity–alas, it bears a stain.
You shall not give it gratitude, nor shall you
Recall it all your days, except with pain.

Oh, bless your blindness, glory in your groping!
Mock at your betters with an upward chin!
And when the moment has gone by for hoping,
Sling your fifth stone, O son of mine, and win.

Grief do I give you, grief and dreadful laughter;
Sackcloth for banner, ashes in your wine.
Go forth, go forth, nor ask me what comes after;
The fifth stone shall not fail you, son of mine.

Go forth, go forth, and slay the Philistine.

Four Songs of Solomon for Voice and Piano

I. *Rise up, My Love,* text taken from the *Song of Solomon 2: 10-13). II. Come My Beloved,* text taken from the *Song of Solomon 7: 11-12). III. Set Me as a Seal* text taken from the *Song of Solomon 8: 6). IV. Behold! Thou Art Fair* text taken from the *Song of Solomon 4: 7, 9, 10).

I. Rise up, My Love

> Rise up, my love, my fair one, and come away.
> For, lo, the winter is past, the rain is over and gone.
> The flowers appear on the earth;
> and the voice of the turtle is heard in our land;
> and the vines in blossom give forth their fragrance.
> Arise, my love, my fair one, and come away.

II. Come My Beloved

> Come, my beloved, let us go forth into the field;
> let us lodge in the villages.
> Let us get up early to the vineyards;
> let us see whether the vine hath budded, whether
>   the vine blossoms be
> opened, and the pomegranates be in flower.
> There will I give you my love.

III. Set Me as a Seal

> Set me as a seal upon thy heart, as a seal upon thine
>   arm:
> for love is strong as death;
> jealousy cruel as the grave.
> The flashes thereof are flashes of fire,
> a very flame of the Lord.

IV. Behold! Thou Art Fair

> Behold! thou art fair, my love, thou art fair.
> Behold! thou art fair, thou hast ravished my heart
>   with one of thine eyes.
> How sweet is thy love, how much better thy love
>   than wine!
> Copyright 1949 Theodore Presser Company.
> Used by permission of the publisher.

Music for "The Alchemist" for Soprano and Eleven Players.

Text from *The Alchemist, Act IV, Scene III* by Ben Jonson.

CHARACTERS (from this Scene): Subtle, the Alchemist; Face, the Housekeeper; Dol Common, their Colleague; Sir Epicure Mammon, a Knight.

DOL COMMON: For, after Alexander's death–

SIR EPICURE MAMMON: Good Lady–

DOL COMMON: That Perdiccas and Antigonus were slain,
The two that stood, Seleuc', and Ptolemy–

SIR EPICURE MAMMON: Madam.

DOL COMMON: Made up the two legs, and the fourth beast,
That was Gog-north and Egypt-south which after
Was called Gog-iron-leg and South-iron-leg–

SIR EPICURE MAMMON: Lady–

DOL COMMON: And then Gog-horned. So was Egypt too:
Then, Egypt-clay-leg and Gog-clay-leg–

SIR EPICURE MAMMON: Sweet madam–

DOL COMMON: And last Gog-dust and Egypt-dust, which fall
In the last link of the fourth chain. And these
Be stars in story, which none see or look at–

SIR EPICURE MAMMON: What shall I do?

DOL COMMON: For, as he says, except
We call the rabbins, and the heathen Greeks–

SIR EPICURE MAMMON: Dear Lady–

DOL COMMON: To come from Salem and from Athens,
And teach the people of Great Britain– *(Enter   Face,
hastily, in his Servant's dress.)*

FACE: What's the matter, Sir?

SIR EPICURE MAMMON: Oh
She's in her fit.

DOL COMMON: We shall know nothing–

FACE: Death, sir,
We are undone.

DOL COMMON: Where then a learned linguist
Shall see the ancient used communion
Of vowels and consonants–

FACE: My master will hear!

DOL COMMON: A wisdom which Pythagoras held most high–

SIR EPICURE MAMMON: Sweet honourable lady!

DOL COMMON: To comprise
    All sound of voices, in few marks of letters–

FACE: Nay, you must never hope to lay her now. (*They all
    speak.*)

DOL COMMON: And so we may arrive at Talmud skill
    And profane Greek, to raise the building up
    Of Helen's house against the Ishmaelite,
    King of the Thorgarma, and his habergions
    Brimstony, blue, and fiery; and the force
    of King Abaddon, and the beast of Cittim:
    Which Rabbi David Kimchi, Onkelos,
    And Aben Ezra do interpret Rome.

FACE: How did you put her into't?

SIR EPICURE MAMMON: Alas! I talked
    Of a fifth monarchy I would erect,
    With the philosopher's stone, by chance, and she
    Falls on the other four straight.

FACE: Out of Broughton!
    I told you so. 'Slid, stop her mouth.

SIR EPICURE MAMMON: Is't best?

FACE: She'll never leave else. If the old man hear her–

SUBTLE: (*within.*)
    What's to do there?

FACE: Oh, we are lost! Now she hears him, she is quiet.

Passions [According to the Twentieth Century] for Actors, Dancers, Singers, Speakers, and Instrumentalists

Text by George Rochberg adapted from various sources.

LIST OF PERFORMERS:
SCENE A:

Herod the Great	Actor
Two Counsellors	Actors
Two Mixed Choruses	Jazz Quintet (Tpt, Tn Sax, Piano, Bass, Drums)

PASSION I:

Alto Solo	Singer
Cantor	Baritone, Singer
Small Chorus of Six Men	Singers
Three Male Speakers (Baritone, Bass, Basso profundo)	Actors
Two Mixed Choruses	Brass Ensemble (3 Tpt, 4 Hn, 3 Trb), Perc.

SCENE B:

Herod	Actor
Soldiers (small group of 4 to 8)	Actors
Two Mixed Choruses	
Men's Chorus (drawn from larger choruses)	Singers
	Brass Ensemble (3 Tpt, 4 Hn, 3 Trb), Perc.

PASSION II:

Soprano Solo	Singer
Alto Solo	Singer
Two Mixed Choruses	Brass Ensemble (3 Tpt, 4 Hn, 3 Trb), Piano, Perc.

SCENE C:

Actors/Dancers (for Three Dumb Shows)	
Soprano Voice (Andromache)	Actress
Tenor voice (Cain)	Actor
Baritone-bass voice (Oedipus)	Actor

PASSION III:

Soprano Solo	Singer
Alto Solo	Singer

Cantor (Baritone)	Singer
Two Mixed Choruses	
Six Men's Voices	Singers
Three Male Speakers	Actors
(Baritone, Bass, Basso	
profundo)	
Brass ensemble (3 Tpt, 4 Hn,	
3 Trb), Piano, Tape, Perc.	

SCENE D:

Herod	Actor
Soldiers	Actors
Two Mixed Choruses	
Small Men's Chorus	
Brass Ensemble (3 Tpt, 4 Hn,	
3 Trb), Perc.	
Jazz Quintet	

SCENE A-1

HEROD'S COURT: *Babble of voices, laughter, general discussion produced by two Choruses. Cutting through this stage noise, jazz improvisation (trumpet, tenor saxophone, piano, bass, drums) is heard–loud, forceful. Tempo is fast [♩ = ca. 200]; style is hard, gutty, assymmetric phrases with "hocket" off-beats; chromatic, i.e., quasi-"atonal" rather than "tonal". Improvisation continues throughout Herod's speech, backing his up and maintaining its intensity.*

The atmosphere of Herod's court is brassy, vulgar, "pagan". Costumes should reflect these qualities. Herod himself is a brutish, large, loud-mouthed physical type. His delivery is stylized: rhythmic, "jazzy"–matching the improvisation of the instrumentalists. There is an unrestrained, unmistakeable violence about his manner and delivery. His attitude says: "I will not be brooked". In the Scenes where he appears, Herod is essentially always the same.

HEROD: Stint brodels your dinyea, ev'ryone!
    I rode that ye harken to I be gone;
    For if I begin, I break ev'ry bone,

And pull from the skin the carcass anon,
Yea pardie!
Cease all this wonder,
And make us no blunder.
For I rive you asunder,
Be ye so hardy.

SCENE A-2

HEROD: Peace, both young and old, at my bidding, I rode,
For I have all in wold–in me stands life and dead.
Who that is so bold, I brain him through the head;
Speak no ere I have told what I will in this stead.

Ye wot not
All that I will move;
Stir not but ye have leave,
For if ye do, I cleave
You small as flesh to pot.

My mirths are turned to teen, my meekness to ire,
And all for one, I ween, within I fare as fire.
May I see him with een, I shall give him his hire;
But do as I mean, I were a full lewd sire.

In wones,
Had I that lad in hand,
As I am king in land
I should with this steel brand
Break all his bones.

My name springs far and near: the doughtiest, men me
call,
That ever ran with spear, a lord and king royal.
What joy is me to hear a lad to seize my stall!
If I this crown may bear, that boy shall buy for all.

I anger.
I wot not what devil me ails.
They teen me so with tales
That by God's dear nails,
I will peace no longer

SCENE A-3

HEROD: What devil! methinks I burst for anger and for teen;
I trow these kings be past, that here with me have been.
They promised me full fast 'ere now here to be seen,
For else I should have cast another sleight, I ween.

I tell you,
A boy they said they sought
With offering that they brought;
I moves my heart right nought
To break his neck in two.

But be they passed me, by Mahoun in heaven,
I shall, and that in hie, set all on six and seven.
Trow ye a kings as I will suffer them to neven
Any do have mastery but myself full even?

Nay lieve!–
The devil me hang and draw,
If I that losel know,
But I give him a blow
That life I shall him reave.

One spoke in mine ear a wonderful talking,
And said a maiden should bear another to be king.
Sirs, I pray you inquire in all writing,
In Virgil, in Homer, and all other thing
But legend.
Seek poesy tales,
Leave epistles and grales.
Mass, matins, nought avails–
All these I defend.

I pray you tell me handly now what ye find.

SCENE A-4:

FIRST COUNSELLOR: Truly, sir, prophecy, it is not blind.
We read thus by Isay: He shall be so kind
That a maiden, soothly, which never sinned,
Shall him bear:
Virgo consipict,
Natumque pariet.
"Emmanuel" is let,

His name for to lare:
"God is with us," that is for to say.

SECOND COUNSELLOR: And others say thus, trust me ye
may:
Of Bedlem a gracious lord shall spray,
That of Jeury mightious king shall be ay,
Lord mighty;
And him shall honour
Both king and emperor.

HEROD: Why, and should I to him cower?
Nay, there thou liest lightly!
Fie! the devil thee speed, and me, but I drink once!
This hast thou done, indeed, to anger me for the nonce;
And thou, knave, thou thy meed shall have, by Cock's
dear bones!
Thou canst not half thy creed! Out, thieves, from my
wones!

Fie, knaves!
Fie, dotty polls, with your books:
Go cast them in the brooks!
With such wiles and crooks
My wit away raves.

Heard I neve such a trant, that a knave so slight
Should come like a saint and reave me my right.
Nay, he shall aslant; I shall kill him down straight.
Were! I say, let me pant. Now think I to fight
For anger.
My guts will out-thring
But I this lad hang;
With out I have avenging
I may live no longer.

Should a carl in a cave but of one year of age
Thus make me to rave?

SCENE A-5

FIRST COUNSELLOR: Sir, peace this outrage!
Away let ye waive all such language.
You worship to save, is he aught but a page of a year?

We two shall him teen

With out wits between,
That, if ye do as I mean,
He shall die on a spear.

SECOND COUNSELLOR: For dread that he reign, do as we
  rede:
      Throughout Bedlem and ilk other stead
  Make knights ordain, and put unto deed
  All knave–children of two years' breed
  And within;
  This child may ye spill
  Thus at your own will.

HEROD: Now thou say'st here till
  A right noble gin.
  If I live in land good life, as I hope,
  This dare I thee warrant–to make the a pope.

  Oh my heart is risand now in a glope!
  For this noble tisand thou shalt have a drop
  Of my good grace: Marks, rents, and pounds,
  Great castles and grounds;
  Through all seas and sounds;
  I give thee the chase.

  Now I will proceed and take vengeance.
  All the flower of knighthood call to legeance.....

  Improvisation ends. Lights change to prepare Passion I.
  There is no perceptible break between end of Scene A and
  beginning of Passion I except through light transition. When
  Passion I begins, the stage is bathed in blue-white light– or
  anyother light combination effect which will detach events of
  Passion I from a worldly atmosphere and cause stage to seem to
  recede visually. A sufficient interval of silence should elapse so
  that the chaning of Six Men's Voices and echo effects of
  Choruses seem to emerge from a deep void.

PASSION I

SIX MEN'S VOICES: De-us cu-jus ho-di-er-na di-e
  prae-co-ni-um
  In-no-cen-tes Mar-ty-res non lo-quen-do sed
  mo-ri-en-do con-fe-ssi-sunt.

CANTOR: Ayl mo-lay rach-a-mim sho-chen ba-m'-ro-mim
ham-tzay
m'-nu-cho n'-cho-no
al kan-fay ha-sh'-chi-no
ho-ro-ki-a maz-hi-rim.

SECOND MALE SPEAKER: We are the prurient observers,
The guilty bystanders
who survived the terrors
of history.
We have survived,
but at what price,
with a knowledge
and participation in events
now
rigified
in the nightmare
of the past?
The way we smile,
our gestures,
our turns of speech,
the very lines of our faces
to the terror
grief
and guilt.

CHORUS I: And praised. Be. The Lord.

CHORUS II: Auschnitz
Maidanak
Treblinka
Buchenwald
Mauthausen
Belzec
Sobibar
Chelmno
Ponary
Theresienstadt
Warsaw
Vilna
Skarzysko
Bergon Belson
Jahow
Dora

Neuengamma
Pustkow

FIRST MALE SPEAKER: I shall never again believe what they
way
or what they think.

FIRST MALE SPEAKER: It is of men,
and of men only,
that one should always be frightened.

SECOND MALE SPEAKER: It is of men,
and of men only,
that one should always be frightened.

THIRD MALE SPEAKER: It is of men,
and of men only,
that one should always be frightened.

THREE MALE SPEAKERS: a swarming
demonic
presence

SIX MEN'S VOICES: It is done
it is finished
but we endure

FIRST MALE SPEAKER: Yes,
at times one's heart could break in sorrow.
But often, too,
preferably in the evening,
I can't help thinking that Ernie Levy,
dead six million times,
is still alive
somewhere,
I don't know where...

SECOND MALE SPEAKER: We see it int he demonic halflight
between living and dying
where there is little difference
between being live
and being dead.
The aftermath to the slaughter,
as in a nightmare,
silently magnifies the act,
dinning it into the consciousness.

THIRD MALE SPEAKER: The way we smile,
   our gestures,
   our turns of speech,
   the very lines of our faces,
   still bear witness
   to the terror,
   grief,
   and guilt.
   an overlapping of fact
   and dream,
   perhaps an aftermath of silence
   when the horror of what has happened begins to dawn.

ALTO SOLO AND SIX MEN'S VOICES: Ef-fe-de-runt
   san-gui-nem Sanc-to-rum ve-lut a-quam in cir-cu-i-tu
   Jer-rus-a-lem et non e-rat qui se-pe-li-ret

FIRST MALE SPEAKER: Yesterday,
   as I stood in the street
   trembling with despair,
   rooted to the spot,
   a drop of pity fell from above
   upon my face.
   But there was no breeze in the air,
   no cloud in the sky
   There was only
   a presence.

SECOND MALE SPEAKER: Here the victim children are caught
   in the midst of their terrible grief,
   and final suffering,
   with swollen head's enlarged against their small,
   useless,
   disappropriate hands
   as if they themselves have become the personification of
   the nightmare

   It is done,
   it is finished
   but we endure.

THIRD MALE SPEAKER: The solemnly murderers,
   skull-helmeted,
   encased killer figures

the slaughter of the innocents
the aftermath to the slaughter,
as in a mightmare,
silently magnifies the act,
dinning it into the consciouness
the embodiment of a wordless scream
retracted lips over horror-grinning teeth
the skull-helmet
slipping
down.

SIX MEN'S VOICES: Oh God,
Whose glory the Martyred Innocents did this day
confess not be speaking, but by dying.

FIRST MALE SPEAKER: Thou hast not betrayed me,
Lord:
of every grief
was...I...brought forth
first-born.

THREE MALE SPEAKERS: They have poured out the blood of
saints,
like water,
round about Jerusalem.
And there is none
to bring them.

CANTOR: Es nish-mos ha-k'-du shim v'-ha-t'-ho-rim
She-ne-her-gu
she-nish ch'-tu
she-nis r'-fu
she-nit b'-u
V'-she-ne chen-ku al ki-dush ha-sh'-ma-yin

FIRST MALE SPEAKER: a final irony,
...a skeleton-mounted Hitler figure in the act of
castrating itself faces the spectator
It is like catching the devil cutting off his own tail
...Now the blood that drips is the blood of the master
Executioner grim,
...self-absorbed,
...well-practiced,
...mechanistically sacrificed to his own ideology,
...half-sqatting,

cutting off his manhood as the spectre of death
...clamps down on him the lid-like cover of a bony-skull,
...with the decisiveness of someone covering a stuffed
garbage can.

SCENE B-1

Herod's Court again. To tune of Horst Wessel Song sung by Men's Chorus in unison and accompanied by Small Ensemble of Brasses and Percussion–loud, blatant, trife–Herod's Knights (Soldiers) march onto stage and come to a halt in front of Herod. Music stops.

HEROD: Welcome, lordings!

SOLDIERS AND CHORUSES: Sieg Heil!

HEROD: both great and small!

SOLDIERS AND CHORUSES: Sieg Heil!

HEROD: The cause now is this that I send for you all:
A lad, a knave, born is that should be king royal;
But I kill him

SOLDIERS AND CHORUSES: Sieg Heil!

HEROD: and his,

SOLDIERS AND CHORUSES: Sieg Heil!

HEROD: I wot I burst my gall.
Therefore, sirs
Vengeance shall yet take
All for that lad's sake,
And men I Shall you make
Where ye come ay where, sirs

SOLDIERS: Hail! doughfirst of all!

CHORUSES: Sieg Heil!

SOLDIERS: We are come at your call

CHORUSES: Sieg Heil!

SOLDIERS: For to do what we shall,

CHORUSES: Sieg Heil!

SOLDIERS: Your lust to fulfill.

CHORUSES: Sieg Heil!

HEROD: To Bedlem look ye go, and all the coast about.
    All knave-children ye slay–and lords ye shall he stout–
    of years if they be two and within. Of all that rout
    Alive leave none fo tho that lie in swaddle-clout,
    I rede you.
    Spare no tins blood,

SOLDIERS AND CHORUSES: Sieg Heil!

HEROD: If woman wax wood,
    I warm you, sirs, to speed you.
    Hence! Now go your way, that we were there.

SOLDIERS AND CHORUSES: Sieg Heil! Sieg Heil! Sieg Heil!

  *As Soldiers wheel and march off, lights change, siren begins,
  Soprano Solo screams and Passion II is underway. The whole
  transition is a matter of seconds only.*

<hr>

PASSION II

ALTO SOLO: Como fue?

CHORUSES: What happened?

ALTO SOLO: Una grieta en la mejilla

MEN'S AND WOMEN'S VOICES: Esso es todo!

SOPRANO SOLO: Una
    Que a-prie-ta el ta-llo
    Un al-fi-ler quebu-ce-a
    hast-a en-con-trar las rai-ci-llas del grit-to.
    y el mar
    de-ja de mo-ver-se

THIRD MALE SPEAKER: The monk who killed himself
    appeared to be in early 20's... seated in the street, he
    doused his robes with gasoline... and lit a match... three
    minutes later...

    The shaven-headed young monk drove up in a taxicab
    to the market's traffic circle at 12:30. He walked a few
    steps, squatted down with legs crossed in the Buddist

Lotus Blossom fashion... emptied a gasoline can he had carried in a robber bag... and lit a match...

He winced and grimaced briefly as the flames engulfed him... But he maintained his position of erect serenity, with his arms raised stiffly before him...

until his charred and blackened body toppled to the pavement...

TWO MALE SPEAKERS AND SIX MEN'S VOICES: De-jam-e! Stand aside!

WOMEN: De e-sa ma-ner-a?

ALTO SOLO: El sor-a-zon sa-li-o so-lo

SOPRANO SOLO: Ay, ay de mi!

CHORUSES: Mi-se-re-re no-bis

ALTO SOLO: Ag-nus De-i qui tol-lis pec-ca-ta mun-di

CHORUSES: Heaven help me!

FIRST MALE SPEAKER: It is the cry of Hecuba... Priam's Queen... and Hector's mother; Queen no more... nor mother. ...of Andromache, Hector's wife; But wife no more... nore mother... (Astyanax, little angel... Where were your wings when they made you leap from the tall towers, when you took the sick leap head downward from the heights of Troy?)

It is the cry of Electra... of Antigone for the father, for the brother struck down by the chavel-bone of Cain, death's storm-trooper, the man of ten-thousand names and ten-thousand faces...

The charred and blackened walk of Troy still smoke...
The broken body of Hiroshima will writhes in agony of sudden fire...
And the heart of Israel aches externally in the hands of God.

It is the Cry
that reverberates and echos in the marrow of man...
unquiet... unstilled...
It is the cry

that richochetes around the walls of eternity...
and will not stop...

A thorn-point to harass a stalk.
A pin-prick to dive till it touches the roots of a cry.
(And tears it from the heart's core...)

THIRD MALE SPEAKER: And the sea moves no more

WOMEN: De e-sa-ma-ner-a?

MEN: Was that how it happened?

ALTO SOLO: El car-a-zon sa-li-o so-lo

SOPRANO SOLO: Mary, mother of us where is your relief?

SCENE C-1

Three Dumb Shows are enacted simultaneously:

(1) Herod's Soldiers/Women of Bethlehem. This take place in center of stage. Action is violent. Soldiers attacking and killing methodically. Women in panic, silent screams, hair-rending, clothes in shreds–running, falling, defending their children, beating the floor with their hands, imploring gestures, etc.

(2) Murder at the Crossroads. Oedipus and Leius, his father and Lauis' servants and retainers. This takes place stage right, forward.

(3) Cain and Abel. Murder in the fields. This takes place stage left, forward.

These three pantomimes may be acted out or danced; or a combination of acting and dancing. No. 1 lends itself to dance better than to acting. No. 3 could be danced in highly stylized fashion, etc. In any case, the approach to each should vary sufficiently to permit maximum variety of visual projection.

There is no music during Scene C. However, three Actors speak simultaneously. They are off-stage. Their voices come over loud-speakers.

(1) Andromache: parallels "Herod's Soldiers/Women of Bethlehem".

(2) Oedipus: parallels "Murder at the Crossroads".

(3) Cain: parallels "Murder in the Fields".

Each delivers his (or her) lines differently, according to the inflection of the language used, the attitude (emotional sources) of each one's condition and situation. For example, Andromache is addressing her son, Astyanax, before handing him over to the Greeks; Oedipus is remembering his meeting with an old man who turns out to be Laius, his father–his impatience and irritation at the time, his present horror, etc.; Cain is just about to murder Abel *in the present.*

SCENE C-2

ANDROMACHE: Astyamax, mein Lieb, mein einzig Leben,
    Nun tragen sie dich fort–Ich kann micht mit.
    Weinst du, mein Lieb, vergiessest kleine Tranen,
    Und weisst doch nicht, was Klaglich deinen wartet!
    Hsangst dich an Mutters Kleiden, streckst die Handchen,
    Schupfst unter warme Flugel, sasses Vogelein?
    Du musst erbarmlich, kind, dein Leben lassen.
    Zum Todesturm schleppt dich ein grausen Landsknecht.
    O Sohn, in mutters weichen arm, Geliebtes,
    O Kleinen, sussen Atem mir am Munde!
    Kommt her, ihr armen Armchen, und unarmtmich,
    Zum letzemmel kusst mich, geliebte Luppen!!
    Hast du nich Lieb?
    O Griechen, Teufel,
    In allen marteru meister, ungeheure,
    Was tat dies kind, das ihr es musset morden?

OEDIPUS: I came in my flight to that very spot where you tell me this king perished. Now, lady, I will tell you the truth. When I had come close up to these three roads, I came upon a herald, and a man like him you have described seated in a carriage. The man who held the reins and the old man himself would not give me room, but thought to force me from the path, and I struck the driver in my anger. The old man, seeing what I had done, waited till I was passing him and then struck me upon the head. I paid him back in full, for I knocked him out of the carriage with a blow of my stick. He rolled on his back, and after that I killed them all. If this stranger were indeed Laius, is there a more miserable man in the world than the man before you? Is there a man more hated of Heaven? No stranger, no citizen, may receive him into his house, not a soul may speak to him, and no mouth but my own mouth has laid this curse upon me. Am I not wretched? May I be swept from this world before I have endured this doom! O! O! All brought to pass! All truth! Now O light, may I look my last upon you, having been found accursed in bloodshed, accursed in marriage, and in my coming into the world accursed!

CAIN: What, thou stinking losel, and is it so?
Doth God thee love and hateth me?
Thou shalt be dead, I shall thee slo:
Thy Lord, thy God thou shalt never see;
Tithing more shalt thou never slay thee.

Thy Death is dight, thy days be go.
Out of my hands shalt thou not flee;
With this stroke I thee kill.

Now this boy is slain and dead,
Of him I shall never more have dread.
He shall hereafter never eat bread;
With this grass I shall him kill.

As Dumb Shows and speeches end, lights change and provide transition to Passion III. Stage bathed in blue-white light for beginning of Passion III.

PASSION III

CHORUS: Deus cujus hodierna
Die praeconium
Innocentes Martyres no loquendo sed moriendo
confessisunt

ALTO SOLO: Non m'haitradito signore: d'ogni dolore son fatto primo nato.

SECOND MALE SPEAKER: Thou hast not betrayed me, Lord:

of every grief
was... I... brought forth
first-born.

TAPE: Seid umschlumgen, Millionem
Diesen Kuss der ganzen Welt.
Bruderi uberm sternenzelt
muss ein heber
Vater wohnen
Ahnest da den Schopfer, Welt?
Such ihn uberm sternenzelt!
Uber sternen muss er hownen
Seid umschlumgem
Freude, schonen.

CHORUS II: Day after day
Immerzu
Giorno dopo giorno

TWO VOICES FROM THE SIX MEN'S VOICES: Immerzu fahren
hire die leute zu ihren eigenes begrabnis...
Day after day
Immerzu
Giorno dopo giorno

TWO VOICES FROM THE SIX MEN'S VOICES: Day after day
the people leave here for their own funeral...
Giorno dopo giorno
Day after day
Immerzu

TWO VOICES FROM THE SIX MEN'S VOICES: Giorno dopo
giorno: parole maledetto e il sangue e l'oro...
Immerzu
Giorno dopo giorno
Day after day

SOPRANO SOLO: Dona eis requiem. Requiem Jempiternam.

CHORUS II: O ye millions! O ye millions! O ye millions!
Requiem

FIRST MALE SPEAKER: O nostra della terra
miei simili
vi riconosco

al vostro morso
e caduta: la pieta
e la croce gentile
ci he lasciate.
Uomo del mio tempo
T'ho visto
eri tu, con la tua scienze esatta
persuasa allo sterminio
senza amore
senza Cristo
Haiucciso ancora
come sempre
corne uccisero i padri
E questo sangue odora come nel giorno
quando il fratello
"Andiamo ai campi"

SECOND MALE SPEAKER: Monsters of the earth
my similars
I recognize you
at your bite
is pity fallen
and the gentle cross
has left us.
O Black Angel of Auschnitz
You are still the one with the
stone and the sling
man of my time
I have seen you
in the charis of fire
at the gallows
at the wheels of fortune
I have seen you
It was you with your exact science
persuaded to extermination
without love
without Christ
again you have killed
as always
as did your fathers fill
And this book smells as on the day
on brother told the other brother
"Let us go into the fields!"

ALTO SOLO, SOPRANO SOLO, CHORUSES: Agnus dei qui
   tollis peccata mundi.

SOPRANO SOLO: Ihr sturz nieder millionen

ALTO SOLO: Eli, Eli, lamazartani?

CHORUS I: Miserere, miserere

CHORUS II: O ye millions, O ye millions

THIRD MALE SPEAKER: Mein Gott,... Mein Gott,... warum
   hast du mich verlassen?

SIX MEN'S VOICES: five
   gallows
   torture
   science
   extermination

CHORUSES: Welt? Zelt

THIRD MALE SPEAKER: No, no, my friends

CHORUSES: Mes amis
   Amigos mies
   Meine freunde
   Amici miei
   My friends

BARITONE SOLO: nicht diese tone.

CHORUSES: nicht diese tone.

THIRD MALE SPEAKER: And he said to the children:
   We shall enter the kingdom together:
   ...In a little while we shall enter it...hand in hand...and
   there a banquet of old mines, of tasty foods, full of
   marrow and of old wines, clean and good...there my
   little lambs...Breathe deeply, my lambs... and quickly...

WOMEN'S VOICES: Then...I'll never see you again?...Never
   again?

SIX MEN'S VOICES: In a little while...I swear it...

FIRST MALE SPEAKER: Man, strip off thy garments

SECOND MALE SPEAKER: rend thy rainment

FIRST MALE SPEAKER: cover they head with ashes

SECOND MALE SPEAKER: run into the streets

FIRST AND SECOND MALE SPEAKERS: and dance in thy madness.

ALTO SOLO: Eli, Eli, lamazartani?

CHORUSES: O Mensch! O Mensch! O Mensch!

THIRD MALE SPEAKER: The master of Bonn's dream lies buried in the mass graves of Dulmo,...Riga,...Minsk,...still rides the death trains...rises in the smoke of Auschurtz...writhes in the agonies of Warsaw,...Vilna,...Kovno

SIX MEN'S VOICES: Aussiedlung [Evacuation]... Sonderbehandlung [Special Treatment]... Umsiedlung [Resettlement]... Endlosung [Final Solution]...

ALTO SOLO: E piu no posso tornare nel mio elisio... Alzermo tombe in riva al mare... sui campi dilaniati...

ALL WOMEN: O tochter aus Elysium

SOPRANO SOLO: Lebwohl, Mutter,...deine Tochten Ljubka geht fort in die feuche Erde...

CANTOR: Es nishmos ha-k'-do shim V'-ha-to'-ho rim
She-ne-her-gu
She-nish ch'-tu
She-nis r'-fu
She-nit b'-u
V'-shje-ne-chen-ku al ki-dush ha-shaym

WOMEN'S CHORUS: O Mutter, von so vielen kindern butter... Oh! So tu auch ich...und schlag...und schlag die Arde,...und rufe meinen Gotten in die Tiefe...verraten.

ALTO SOLO: O Erde, du die kinder nahrte!
O hort, ihr kinder unter, eure mutter!

...So wef ich meine knie auf die Erde...und schlag die
Erde, Sehlag mit beiden Handen...
und schlag...und schlag die Erde... verlorren...

SCENE D-1

*Herod's court again. General babble and vocal tumult
accompanies Horst Wessel Song which brings Soldiers on
stage again, marchin "victoriously". They have returned from
the Slaughter of the Innocents. They stand before Herod.
Horst Wessel Song continues through first part of Scene.*

SOLDIERS:

Hail (Heil), Herod our King!

SOLDIERS AND CHORUSES:

Sieg Heil! Sieg Heil!

FIRST SOLDIER: Full gald may ye be;

SECOND SOLDIER: Good tidings we bring.

THIRD SOLDIER: Harken now to me:

ALL SOLDIERS:

We have made riding throughout Jewry.
Well wit ye one thing, that mardered have we
Many thosands.

CHORUSES: Sieg Heil! Many thousands! Thousands,
Thousands! Sieg Heil! Yea, pardie! Many thousands!

HEROD: I was casten in care, so frightly afraid;
But I then not despair, for low is he laid
That I must dreaded ere, so have I him flayed;
And else wonder were–and so many strayed
In the street–
That one should be harmless
And scape away hafless,
Where so many childs
Their bales cannot beat.

A hundred thousand, I wot, and forty are slain,
And four thousand. Thereat me ought to be fain;
such a murder on a flat shall never be again.
Had I but one bat at that lurden
So young,

It should have been spoken: How I had me wroken,
Were I dead and rotten,
With many a tongue.

Thus shall I teach knaves example to take,
In their wits that raves, such mastery to make.
All wantonness waives; no language ye crack!
No sovereign you saves; your hecks shall I shake
Asunder.
No king ye on call
But on Herod

SOLDIERS AND CHORUSES: Sieg Heil!

HEROD: The royal

SOLDIERS AND CHORUSES: Sieg Heil!

HEROD: or else many one shall
upon your bodies wonder.

SOLDIERS AND CHORUSES: Sieg Heil!

HEROD: For if I hear it spoken when I come again,
Your brains be broken; therefore be ye bain.
Nothing be unlocken; it shall be so plain.
Begin I to reckon, I think all disdain
For-daunced.
Sirs, this is my counsel: Be not too cruel
But adien–to the devil!
I am no more French.

SOLDIERS AND CHORUSES: Sieg Heil! Yea Pardie!

> *Jazz improvisation continues past Herod's last lines and*
> *breaks off suddenly in midst of tumult and shouting of*
> *Choruses, Soldiers marching off stage, fragments of Horst*
> *Wessel Song, brilliant bursts of light–and final abrupt*
> *blackout. Finis.*
>
> 13 April 1967, George Rochberg.
>
> Copyright 1967 Theodore Presser Company.
>
> Used by permission of the publisher.
> passion tear my body limb from limb;

Phaedra, a Monodrama for Mezzo-Soprano and Orchestra

Texts adapted freely by Gene Rochberg from Robert Lowell's play based on Racine's *Phédra*.

(A synopsis of *Phaedra* may be found on page 113.)

I. Aria: "In May, in Brilliant Athens" (Phaedra)

> In May, in brilliant Athens, on my marriage day,
> I turned aside for shelter from the smile
> of Theseus. Death was frowning in an aisle–
> Hippolytus! I saw his face, turned white!
> I could not breathe or speak.
> I faced my flaming executioner,
> Aphrodite, my mother's murderer!
> I fled him, yet he stormed me in disguise,
> and seemed to watch me from his father's eyes.
> Each day I saw Hippolytus
> and felt my ancient
> passion tear my body limb from limb;
> naked Venus was clawing down her victim.
> What could I do? Each moment, terrified
> by wild emotions, now I cried
> for death to save my glory and expel
> my gloomy frenzy from this world, my hell.

II. Orchestral Interlude: Black Sails

III. Aria: "You Monster" (Phaedra)

> You monster! You understood me too well!
> Why do you hang there, speechless, petrified,
> polite! My mind whirls. What have I to hide?
> Phaedra in all her madness stands before you.
> Fool, I love you, I adore you!
> At first I fled you, and when this fell short
> of safety, I exiled you from court. I was afraid
> to kiss my husband lest I love his son.
> I made you fear me;
> you loathed me more, I ached for you no less.
> Misfortune magnified your loveliness.

Do you believe my passion
is voluntary? That my obscene confession
is some dark trick, some oily artifice?
Avenge yourself, invoke
your father; a worse monster threatens you
than any Theseus ever fought and slew
the wife of Theseus loves Hippolytus!
See, Prince! Look, this monster, ravenous
for her execution, will not flinch.
I want your sword's spasmodic final inch.

IV. Orchestral Interlude: Theseus' Homecoming

V. Supplication (Arioso): "Theseus, I Heard the Deluge of Your Voice" (Phaedra).

Theseus, I heard the deluge of your voice,
and stand here trembling. If there's still time for
     choice,
hold back your hand, still bloodless; spare your race!
I supplicate you, I kneel here for grace.
Oh, Theseus, will you drench the earth
with your own blood? his virtue, youth and birth
cry out for him–spare me this incestuous pain!

VI. Cabaletta (Aria): "My Last Calamity Has Come" (Phaedra)

My last calamity
has come. This is the bottom of the sea.
All that preceded this had little force–
the flames of lust, the horrors of remorse,
the prim refusal by my grim young master,
were only feeble hints of this disaster.
They love each other!
For them each natural impulse was allowed,
each day was summer and without a cloud.
     Ugh, they'll love forever–
even while I am talking, they embrace,
they scorn me, they are laughing in my face!
I hear them swear
they will be true forever, everywhere.
Have pity on my jealous rage;
I'll kill this happiness that jeers at age.

I'll summon Theseus; hate shall answer hate!
What am I saying? Have I lost my mind?
I am jealous, and call my husband! Imposture!
Incest! Murder! Bind me, gag me;
I am frothing with desire.
My husband is alive, and I'm on fire!
For whom? Hippolytus. When I have said
his name, blood fills my eyes, my heart stops dead.
My lover's lifeblood is my single good.
Nothing else will cool my murderous thirst for
    blood.
Yet I live on! I live, looked down upon
by my progenitor, the sacred sun,
by Zeus, by Europa, by the universe
of gods and stars, my ancestors. They curse
their daughter. In the great night
of Hades, I'll find shelter from their sight.
What am I saying? I've no place to turn:
Minos, my father, holds the judge's urn.
Will he not shake and curse his fatal star
that brings his daughter trembling to his bar?
His child by Pasiphae forced to tell
a thousand sins unclassified in hell?
Father, you'll be your own child's executioner!
You cannot kill me; look, my murderer is Venus.
I killed myself–and what was worse I wasted
my life for pleasures I have never tasted.
My lover flees me still, and my last gasp
is for the fleeting flesh I failed to clasp.

VII. *Orchestral Postlude: The Death of Hippolytus*

Sacred Song of Reconciliation (Mizmor l'Piyus) for Bass-Baritone and Small Orchestra

Text by George Rochberg based on texts from *Hosea*, *Isiah*, and *Genesis* which were suggested by its commissioner Madame Frier, founder of Testimonium.

I. Hu taraf

Hu taraf
V'yir-pa-e-nu
V'yakh b'-she-nu

I. He Tore [Destroyed]

He tore [destroyed]
And He will heal us
And He will conquer us

II. Ki hineni vore

Ki hi-ne-ni vo-re sha-ma-yim
Kha-da-sha
V'lo tiz-a-khar-na ha-rish-o-not
V'lo ta-a-le-na al-lev
Ki im ssi-ssa v-gi-la a-de-ad a-sher a-ni vo-re
Ki-ni-ne-ni vo-re et ye-ru-sha-la-yim

II. For Behold I Create

For behold I create the heaven [or sky] new
And do not forget the first ones
And do not pay attention [take it to heart]
For with joy and gladness forever and ever until I
    create
For behold I create Jerusalem

III. V'hay'ta

V'ha-y'-ta hak-ke-shet b'a-nan
U-r'-i-ti-ha liz-kor b-rit o-lam ben El-o-him
b'khob ba-sar
a-sher al-ha-a-rets

III. And it Was

And it was a rainbow
And I saw it to remember the eternal covenant
    between God
and all living creatures
that are on the earth

IV. Ki im ssi-ssu

> Ki im ssi-ssu v'gi-lu a-de-ad a-sher a-ni vo-re
> Ki hi-ne-ni vore et yi-ru-sha-la-yim

IV. For with Joy

> For with joy and gladness forever and ever until I
>   create
> For behold I create Jerusalem

V. Hu taraf

> Hu taraf
> V'yir-pa-e-nu
> V'yakh b'-she-nu

V. He Tore [Destroyed]

> He tore [destroyed]
> And He will heal us
> And he will conquer us
>
> > Hebrew transliteration.
> > Copyright 1971 Theodore Presser Company.
> > Used by permission of the publisher.
> > Translation provided by Rabbi Matthew Friedman
> >   and Rabbi David Schoneveld of Hebrew Union
> >   College, Cincinnati, OH.

Songs in Praise of Krishna for Soprano and Piano

Texts drawn from *In Praise of Krishna,* a small volume of poetry translated from the *Bengali* by Denise Levertov and Edward Dimock, Jr. The *Bengali* is a body of lyrics by Vaishnava poets of Bengal which were produced between the fourteenth and seventeenth centuries.

I. Hymn to Krishna (I): Radha Speaks

> It was in bitter maytime my lord
> renounced the world, and shaved his head,
> and took to the road with only a
> staff and a begging bowl.
> My heart sickens, tears
> sting my eyes. The hope of my life
> went with him.
> How long will my days drag on
> without him, my Gaura?

The springtime, when the world brims over
with joy, comes round again,
bitter to me.
My old love for my lord
aches in my heart, all I remember
makes life a noose
tight'ning about my throat.

II. Hymn to Krishna (II): Radha Speaks

After long sorrow, I am graciously
brought by fate to my Golden One,
my Gaura,
my treasury of virtue.
After long sorrow I am brought to joy,
my eyes learn what their vision is for,
looking into his face, bright moon.
A long time they were fasting, my eyes,
those thirsty chakora birds whose sole food
is moonbeams:
now they have found
the round moon itself!

III. Krishna Speaks

Her slender body like a flash of lightning,
her feet, color of dawn, stepping swiftly
among the other lotus petals...
Friend, tell me who she is! She plays
among her friends,
plays with my heart.
When she raises her eyebrows I see
the arching waves of the River Kalindi.
Her careless look lights on a leaf
and the whole forest flames into blue flowers.
When she smiles
a delicate sweetness fills me, fragrance
of lily and jasmine.

IV. Radha Speaks

As the mirror to my hand,
the flowers to my hair,
kohl to my eyes,

tambul to my mouth,
musk to my breast,
neck lace to my throat,
ecstasy to my flesh,
heart to my home–
as wing to bird,
water to fish,
life to the living–
so you to me.
But tell me,
Madhava, beloved,
who are you?
Who are you really?

V. Radha Speaks

O Madhava, how shall I tell you of my terror?
I could not describe my coming here
if I had a million tongues.
When I left my room and saw the darkness
I trembled:
I could not see the path,
there were snakes that writhed around my ankles!
I was alone, a woman; the night was so dark,
the forest so dense and gloomy,
and I had so far to go.
The rain was pouring down–
which path should I take?
My feet were muddy
and burning where thorns had scratched them.
But I had the hope of seeing you, none of it
    mattered,
and now my terror seems far away...
When the sound of your flute reaches my ears
it compels me to leave my home, my friends,
it draws me into the dark toward you.

IV. Radha Speaks

Lord of my heart, what have I dreamed...
how shall I go home, now that daylight has come?
My musk and sandalwood perfumes are faded,

the kohl smudged from my eyes, the vermilion line
drawn in the part of my hair paled.
O put the ornament
of your own body upon me,
take me with you down-glancing one.
Dress me in your own yellow robes,
smooth my disheveled hair,
wind round my throat your garland of forest
    flowers.
Thus, beloved, someone in Gokula entreats.

VII. Radha Speaks

I brought honey and drank it mixed with milk—
but where was its sweetness? I tasted gall.
I am steeped in bitterness, as the seed
of a bitter fruit in its juice.
My heart smolders.
A fire without is plain to be seen
but this fire flames within,
it sears my breast.
Desire burns the body—how can it be relieved?

VIII. Radha Speaks

My mind is not on housework.
Now I weep, now I laugh at the world's censure.
He draws me—to become
an outcast, a hermit woman in the woods!
He has bereft me of parents, brothers, sisters,
my good name. His flute
took my heart—
his, a thin bamboo trap enclosing me—
a cheap bamboo flute was Rhadha's ruin.
That hollow, simple stick—
fed nectar by his lips, but issuing
poison...
If you should find a clump of jointed reeds,
pull off their branches!
Tear them up by the roots!
Throw them
into the sea.

IX. The Old Woman Messenger Speaks

I place beauty spots on my sagging cheeks,
smudge kohl around my dulling eyes,
put flowers in my burned-white hair.
Yes, my vanity is absurd,
the years have slipped by,
I remember, and grieve for them;
my breasts hang limp,
my hips are bony.
Yet on this withered body
the god of Love plunges and rolls.

X. The Old Woman Messenger Speaks

Shining one, golden as the champa flower,
the god of fate has given your radiance to you
in sacred offering.
Fortunate one, blessed and golden one,
his dark body shall wed with yours.
Waste nothing of the light of youth,
go quickly with him.

XI. Krishna Speaks

My moon-faced one,
I am waiting
to make our bed ready,
to gather lotus petals–
your body will press them,
hidden from even friendly eyes...
Come,
the sweet breeze from the sandalwoods
senses our trusting place...

XII. Radha Speaks

Beloved, what more shall I say to you?
In life and in death, in birth after birth
you are the lord of my life.
A noose of love binds
my heart to your feet.
My mind fixed on you alone, I have offered you
    everything;
in truth, I have become your slave.

In this family, in that house, who is really mine?
Whom can I call my own?
It was bitter cold and I took refuge
at your lotus feet.
While my eyes blink, and I do not see you.
I feel the heart within me die.

XIII. Radha Speaks

Let the earth of my body be mixed with the earth
my beloved walks on.
Let the fire of my body be the brightness
in the mirror that reflects his face.
Let the water of my body join the waters
of the lotus pool he bathes in.
Let the breath of my body be air
lapping his tired limbs.
Let me be sky, and moving through me
that cloud-dark Shyama, my beloved.

XIV. Radha Speaks

O my friend, my sorrow is unending.
It is the rainy season, my house is empty,
the sky is filled with seething clouds,
the earth sodden with rain, and my love far away.
Cruel Kama pierces from me with his arrows: the
lightning flashes, the peacocks dance, frogs and
waterbirds, drunk with delight, call incessantly–and
my heart is heavy. Darkness on earth, the sky
intermittently lit with a sullen glare...

Songs of Inanna and Dumuzi for Contralto and Piano

Text by Francesca Rochberg-Halton translated from Sumerian liturgical texts originally written in cuneiform on clay tablets in ancient Mesopotamia around 2000 B.C. during the Third Dynasty of Ur. The texts were preserved in copies by scribes who lived several centuries later.

I. *ša lam-lam-ma (Luxuriant Heart)*

ša lam-lam-ma
ša i-bi-sa-sa ad nu-un-...
šeš-me he-me-en šeš-me-en he-...
šeš ka-e-gal-la-me he-me-en
u-mu-un-si ma-gur-me he-me-en
sahar gigir sar-re-me he-me-en
ad-da-uru di-ku-ru-me he-me-en
mi-us-sa gar mi-us-sa gar
šeš mi-us-sa ad-da-me he-me-en
mi-us-sa gu-zi-bi-me he-me-en
ama-me e-ne nig ze-ba hu-mu-gal me-en
im-ma-gin-na-zu na-am-ti-na-nam
e-a ku-ra-ma he-gal-la
da-na-da hul-la diri-mu
ze-ba-mu ba-na-da ze-ba an ze-em i-bi
bal-bal-e Inanna-kam

I. *ša lam-lam-ma (Luxuriant Heart)*

Luxuriant heart,
Heart, beautiful eyes, the father...
Be my brother, be my brother.
Be my brother at the gate of the palace.
Be the lord of my large boat.
Be the driver of my chariot.
Be the dust of the running chariots.
Be my city father, my judge.
Son-in-law, the chosen son-in-law,
Brother, be the son-in-law of my father.
Be my father's son-in-law.
May my mother have all good things for you.
You come bringing life,
Your entering the house brings abundance.
To lie with you is my utmost delight.
My sweet, I will lie with you, sweet...
Song of Inanna.

II. *He Blossoms, He Abounds (ba-lam ba-lam-lam)*

He blossoms, he abounds; He is like the watered
  lettuce.
Piled up in the shade of the garden; He is like the
  watered lettuce.
My barley, overflowing with loveliness in the
  furrow; He is like the
  watered lettuce.
My best apple tree, which bears fruit; He is like the
  watered lettuce.
Honey man, honey man, you are so sweet to me.
My lord, honey man of the gods, beauty of his
  mother.
His hand is honey, his foot is honey; You are so
  sweet to me.
His limbs are honey sweet; You are so sweet to me.
My most graceful lettuce...in the plain; He is like
  the watered lettuce.
Song of Inanna

II. *He Blossoms, He Abounds (ba-lam ba-lam-lam)*

ba-lam ba-lam-lam hi-iz-am a ba-an-dug
kiri gi-edin-na gu-gar-gar-ra-na hi-iz . . . a ba-an-de
še ab-sin-ba hi-li-a diri-mu hi-iz-am a ba-an-dug
haš-hur em-sag-ga gurun il-la-mu hi-iz-am a
  ba-an-dug
lu-lal-e lu-lal-e ga-a mu-ku-ku-de-en
en-mu lu-lal-e dingir-ra sa-ga ama-na-mu
šu-ni lal-e gir-ni lal-e ga-a mu-un-ku-ku-de-en
a-šu-gir-ni lal ku-ku-dam ga-a mu-un-ku-ku-de-en
li-dir šu-nigin tukum ku-ku-mu sa . . .
hi sa-sa edin-na e-ru-mu hi-iz-am a ba-an-dug

III. *She Calls for the Bed of Joy (Invocation I)*

She calls for the bed of joy!
To the sweetened bed she invites the king.
To the sweetened bed she invites the beloved.
She speaks to him of life and long days.
Nin-shu-bur, the faithful servant of E-an-na,
Takes his right hand

and leads him to the lap of Inanna.
May the lord, the love chosen by your own heart,
The king, your beloved husband, enjoy long days
    at your pure sweet thighs.

III. She Calls for the Bed of Joy (Invocation I)

ki-na-ša-hul-la al ba-an-dug ki-na al ba-an-dug
ki-na-ur-ze-ba al ba-an-dug ki-ns sl ba-an-dug
lugal ki-na-ze-ba-ni-še gumu-un-na-de-e
ki-ag ki-na-ze-ba-ni-še gunu-un-na-de-e
inim-ti inim-u-sud-ra gunu-un-na-de-e
ga-ša-an-šubur-ra sukkal-zi-e-an-na-ke
kišib-me-zi-da-na im-ma-an-dab
ur-ga-ša-an-na-še hi-li-a mu-ni-ku
u-mu-un-e am-ša-ge ba-e-pa-da-zu
lugal-e nitalam-ki-ag-zu ur-ku-nig-dug-zu
u ha-ba-ni-ib-sud-e-de

IV. he-tum-tum (May He Bring)

he-tum-tum he-tum-tum dig-dig-ga-bi ga-na
    he-tum-tum
i-da-lam gaba-me ba-du-du
i-da-lam gal-la-me sig ba-an-mu
ur-mu-ti-in-na-še di-di-de ba-ba
    ga-ba-hul-hul-le-en-de-en
gu-ud-an-ze-en gu-ud-an-ze-en
ba-u gal-la-ma-ke-eš ga-ba-hul-hul-le-en-de-en
gu-ud-an-ze-en gu-ud-an-ze-en
egir-bi in-na-sa in-na-sa
he-tum-tum he-tum-tum dig-dig-ga-bi ga-na
    he-tum-tum
bal-bal-e Inanna-kam

IV. he-tum-tum (May He Bring)

May he bring, may he bring, its laughter, come!
    may he bring.
Now my chest has grown bigger.
Now hair has grown on my vulva.
Going to the lap of the husband, oh! Let us rejoice!
Dance! Jump!
Oh! Oh! Let us rejoice over my vulva.

Dance! Jump!

Afterwards it will be pleasing to her.

Let him bring, let him bring, its laughter, come! Let him bring.

Song of Inanna.

V. lu-bi-mu lu-bi-mu (My Lubi, My Lubi)

My lubi, my lubi, my lubi,

My labi, my labi, my honey of her mother.

My wine, my sweet honey, sweet word of her mother.

The gaze of your eyes delights me, come, sister my love.

You who are so full of life, who are so full of life, swear to me it's true!

Brother, outside the city you who are so full of life, swear to me it's true!

Let me swear the oath for you, my brother, my beautiful brother.

You laid your right hand on my vulva.

You left hand (rested) on my head.

Your mouth came near to my mouth.

And then your lips rested on my head.

For this I will swear the oath.

My lubi, my lubi, sister my love.

V. lu-bi-mu lu-bi-mu (My Lubi, My Lubi)

lu-bi-mu lu-bi-mu lu-bi-mu

la-bi-mu la-bi-mu lal-ama-ugu-na-mu

gu-a-mu lal-ku-ku-mu ka-lal-ama-na-mu

igi-za igi-du-ru-na-bi ma-dug gin nin ki-ag-mu

mu-un-ti-le-na mu-un-ti-le-na na-am-erim-ma kud-de-en

šeš uru-bar-ra mu-un-ti-le-nam na-am-erim-ma kud-de-en

šeš-mu na-am-erim-ma du-mu-ra-an-mar-mar šeš i-bi-sa-sa-mu

šu-zi-da-zu gal-la-ga de-im-mar

gub-bu-zu sag-mu-uš im-ši-ri

ka-zu ka-ga um-me-te

šu-um-du-um-mu sag-za u-ba-e-ni-dab
za-e ur-ta na-am-erim-ma kud-de-en
lu-bi-mu la-bi-mu gin nin ki-ag-mu

VI. May the Tigris and the Euphrates (Invocation II)

May the Tigris and the Euphrates bring the
floodwaters.
Over all their banks may grass grow and fill the
meadows.
May the pure lady of grains gather there the piles
of grain.
My lady, mistress of heaven and earth, queen of the
universe,
May he live long at your thighs.

VI. May the Tigris and the Euphrates (Invocation II)

idigna buranun-na a-u-ba hu-mu-ni-ib-tum
gu-gu-ba hu-mu-ta-mu-mu a-gar he-en-si
gur-du-gur-maš ku-ga-ša-an-nidaba-ke gu
hu-mu-ni-gur-gur
ga-ša-an-mu nin-an-ki nin-an-ki-šu-a
ur-zu-še u ha-ba-ni-ib-su-e

VII. Luxuriant Heart (ša lam-lam-ma)

Luxuriant heart,
Heart, beautiful eyes, the father...
Be my brother, be my brother.
Be my brother at the gate of the palace.
Be the lord of my large boat.
Be the driver of my chariot.
Be the dust of the running chariots.
Be my city father, my judge.
Son-in-law, the chosen son-in-law,
Brother, be the son-in-law of my father.
Be my father's son-in-law.
May my mother have all good things for you.
You come bringing life,
Your entering the house brings abundance.
To lie with you is my utmost delight.
My sweet, I will lie with you, sweet...
Song of Inanna.

VII. Luxuriant Heart (ša lam-lam-ma)
> ša lam-lam-ma
> ša i-bi-sa-sa ad nu-un-...
> šeš-me he-me-en šeš-me-en he-...
> šeš ka-e-gal-la-me he-me-en
> u-mu-un-si ma-gur-me he-me-en
> sahar gigir sar-re-me he-me-en
> ad-da-uru di-ku-ru-me he-me-en
> mi-us-sa gar mi-us-sa gar
> šeš mi-us-sa ad-da-me he-me-en
> mi-us-sa gu-zi-bi-me he-me-en
> ama-me e-ne nig ze-ba hu-mu-gal me-en
> im-ma-gin-na-zu na-am-ti-na-nam
> e-a ku-ra-ma he-gal-la
> da-na-da hul-la diri-mu
> ze-ba-mu ba-na-da ze-ba an ze-em i-bi
> bal-bal-e Inanna-kam
>> Used by permission of Francesca Rochberg-Halton.
>> Copyright 1983 Theodore Presser Company.
>> Used by permission of the publisher.

String Quartet No. 2 with Soprano

Text drawn from the opening and closing stanzas of Rainer Maria Rilke's *Ninth Duino Elegy*. Translated by Harry Behn.
> Why do we treasure so highly our moment of being
>> that flutters
> away like leaves of the laurel, darker
> than all surrounding green, with little waves
> on ev'ry leaf (laughter of wind)–O why
> must we, so mortal, avoiding destiny,
> sigh after destiny?...
> Not because happiness is true,
> that unearned profit of certain loss.
> Not from curiosity, or to temper the heart,
> that still could live in the laurel...
> But simply because to live is important, and we
> are needed by all this here and now,
> these ephemera that oddly concern us.

We most ephemeral. Once
for everything, once only. Once, no more.
And we, too
once. And never again. But this
having been once only:
here on earth, can it ever again be no more?

Is this your wish, O Earth: invisible
emergence in us? Is this your subtle dream,
to become invisible? Earth!
What is your urgent command? to be
    transformed?
Earth, my adored, I obey. You need
no other Springs to win me, one
is more than my blood can endure.
I in your keep have been nameless for aeons.
You have always been right, and your holiest
    vision
friendly death.
Yet I live. On what? Neither my childhood
    nor my future
diminish.....Immeasurable being
wells in my heart.

String Quartet No. 7 with Baritone

Based on poems by Paul Rochberg.

I. The Beast of Night

The beast of night
Dark furred
Bares teeth and claws
Of leafless branches
Laps at the light
I carry.
Grows
On the agar of imaginings.

Swells with the gases
Of will o' the wisp swamps.
And again I am a child
Of fears and dread
Of the dark furred night.

And I cast no shadow
On waves or sand.

II. Floating in a Dream

Floating in a dream
I am lost in it
The world goes before me.
Floating in a dream
I am real in it
Real for the world
Of my dream.
Floating
Beyond unreality
To step from the mirror
I am.
Swimming in this life
I am.

III. Cavalry

Over the softly rolling hills
of rotted cereal boxes and baling wire
Come the calvary
The bugle sounds
and waving the banners slap readly at the
    whipping dust

Their steeds of blackened barrel staves
hooves of shiny new flatirons
leaving dead rats and broken lightbulbs
bloodied in the mire
Their redburning eyes of a monstrous dragonfly
bicycle reflectors stare out
turning to flaming blood all those under their gaze

Their uniforms proudly bear
crepe paper of the purple and the gold

A most impressive sight
their bottle tops and rivets
shoelaces and telephones
Their helmets porcelained
sightless behind shattered spectacles
brains wired to forgotten dress dummies
sauerkraut in plastic bags

Drive them on across the field of ***
to an unseen battle
sword of picket fences
they brandish in rusty eggbeaters
The lances railroads
topped by soup stained ascots
the lancers at attention
pierce the sky, their lances seagullroosted

The horses puff black clouds of flies
under the loading hook spurs
whose boots stovepipes

Nailed broomsticks
switch on charred backs
The general, highest on his,
tubercular calf locked
in a potbellied stove

red heat
a cat o'nine tails of rat's bones
and spitting cobras
Who would touch him

The charge
foe the horror
red in the sky black in the sky
green bloodfire close the stars
The battle
into the river shrank back quivering evaporating
burning hissing
unwilling to give ground
mixing hermit crabs and palpitating

orange peels
almost tearing
great stones piled up

And in the morning
a little girl's lost doll
thought in the new forest

hat we saw
and one dented stove pipe
with a hand

IV. And When the Dream Had Faded

And when the dream had faded
Into a yellow green cloud
I knew
That I had let
A thousand other lives
Fall from my hand
Like the cat, who this morning
Slipped through my arms–
A drop of mercury
That shattered on the floor
Into millions of stars
I could never recover.

And when the dream was red
I was a dragon
Who tore his cobweb bones
Into galaxies of needles
To sting myself,
And for one night only
To sharpen his claws
Against the gate of Heaven

And I cast no shadow
On waves or sand.

Symphony No. 3 for Double Chorus, Chamber Chorus, Soloists and Large Orchestra

Text comprised of excerpts from the Schütz *Symphonica Sacra, Saul, Saul, Saul, Was verfolgst du mich?*, the Bach Chorale *Durch Adams Fall ist ganz verderbt*, and the Beethoven *Missa Solemnis, Agnus Dei*.

Schütz

Saul, Saul, Saul, Was verfolgst du mich?
Es wird dir schwer werden wider den stachel zu
lochen.

J.S. Bach

Durch Adams fall ist ganz verderbt.

Beethoven

Agnus Dei, qui tolis peccata mundi, miserere nobis.
Copyright 1970 Theodore Presser Company.
Used by permission of the publisher.

Tableaux (Sound Pictures from "The Silver Talons of Piero Kostrov" by Paul Rochberg)

Text based on Paul Rochberg's story *The Silver Talons on Piero Kostrov* published in the magazine *Chelsea Seventeen* (August 1965).

PART I

1. Night Piece

("I heard a woman singing, singing with the voice of a child... I did not know the song, but in it the sun never set... I could hear her singing. Wordlessly, or I could not hear her words.")

Death's Mask.

2. Morning Bell Music

("Morning bells singing in my ears. Giant seashells, waves beating in them forever. Sing to the new sun...Sing to all.")

The world knows my joy!

3. The Cathedral

("In silence broods the cathedral.")

4. Night Piece

("Night, again night," He doesn't live here anymore.)

PART II

5. Silver Talon Music

("Those birds. Their reptilian talons, beaks, that tear away the flesh and grind the bones...They fly to heaven and tear the gods to pieces, everyone. There are new rulers on earth, in the sky.")

6. Echo Night Piece

("Night, again night.")

Why must it always return?"

7. The Chant

("I hear singing, chanting from far away...Every movement premeditated for ages. Singing; from the river, the cathedral, from under the earth.")

Miserere nobis.

8. The Light

("It flooded the sky with gold...")

[spoken concurrently]

Morning bells singing.	The cathedral how it rises
Giant seashells, waves	from the ground. It seems
beating in them forever.	to fly upward, to strain
Sing to the new sun...	against the stones...

PART III

9. Ballad

("If I were sure that your existence and mine were more than a shadow.

If I could be certain that you are not merely a mirage,

And I only a passing cloud.")

10. Night Piece

("We sleep, The night is warm. The sun shines through the earth.")

11. *The Eagle*

("A shapeless bundle like a human form shrieks once and sinks into the sea. There is a huge eagle in the middle of the stage clutching a shapeless bundle vaguely like a human form in its talons.

It screams once and flies out into the audience, up to the ceiling and vanishes,")

12. *n.t.*

("And yet you are, although you cannot be.")
> Copyright 1989 Mrs. George Rochberg.
> Used by permission of Mrs. George Rochberg.
> Copyright 1972 Theodore Presser Company.
> Used by permission of the publisher.

Three Psalms for a cappella Mixed Chorus

Hebrew transliteration by Alexander L. Ringer. Hebrew transliterations and English translations are both included in the score.

Psalm 23

1. The Lord is my shepherd; I shall not want.
2. He maketh me to lie down in green pastures;
   He leadeth me beside the still waters.
3. My soul restoreth;
   He guideth me in righteous paths for his name's sake.
4. Yea, though I walk the valley of the shadow, I will fear no evil;
   For thou art with me; Thy rod and staff they comfort.
5. Thou set before me a table, in the presence of mine enemies;
   Anointest my hand with oil; My cup runneth over.
6. Goodness and mercy surely shall follow me all my days;
   And I will dwell, In the house of the Lord forever!

Psalm 23

1. A-do-nai ro-ee lo ech-sar
2. Bi-not de-she yar-bee-tsay-nee
   al may me-nu-chot ye-na-ha-lay-nee
3. Naf-shee ye-sho-vayv
   yan-chay-nee ve-ma-g'lay tse-dek l'ma-an sh'-mo
4. Gam kee ay-laych b'-gay tsal-mo-vet lo ee-ra ra
   kee at ta-i-ma-dee
   shiv-t'-cha u-mish-an-te-cha hay-ma
   y'-na-cha-mu-nee
5. Ta-a-roch l'fa-nai shul-chan ne-ged tso-r'-rai
   Dish-an-ta va-she-men-ro-shee ko-see r'-va ya
6. Ach tov va-che-sed yir-d'-fu-nee kol ye-may
   cha-yai
   ye-shav-tee b'-vayt A-do-nai l'-o-rech ya-meem

Psalm 43

1. O God, be thou my judge,
   And plead my cause against an ungodly nation;
   Deliver me from deceitful and unjust man.
2. For thou art the God of my strength.
   Lord, why hast thou cast me off?
   Why go I bow'd down before th' oppression of
   the foe?
3. O send thy light and thy truth;
   Let them lead me;
   Let them bring me unto thy holy mountain,
   And to thy dwelling places.
4. Then I will go unto the altar of God,
   To God my exceeding joy;
   And praise thee upon the harp,
   O my God.
5. Why art thou cast down, O my soul?
   Why moanest thou within me?
   Hope thou, hope in God;
   For I shall praise my salvation,
   My countenance and my God!

Psalm 43

1. Shof-tayu-nee e-lo-heem
   v'-ree va ree-vee mig-goy la-cha-seed
   may-eesh mir-ma v'-av-la t'-fal-tay-tay-nee
2. Kee at-ta e-lo-hay ma-u-zee
   La-ma z'-nach-ta-nee,
   La-ma ko-dayr et-ha-laych b'-la-cahts o-yev
3. Sh'-lach or'-cha va-a-meet'-cha
   hay-ma yan-chu-nee
   y'-vee-u-nee el har kod-sh'-cha
   v'el mish-k'-no-to-cha
4. V'-a-vo-a el miz-bach el-o-heem
   El ayl sim-chat gee-lee
   V'-od-cha v'chin-nor
   El-o-heem el-o-hai
5. Ma tish-to-cha-chee naf shee
   U-ma te-he-mee a-lai
   Ho-chee-lee lay-lo-heem
   Kee od od-en-nu y'-shu-ot
   pa-nai vay-lo-hai

Psalm 150

1. Praise ye the Lord! Give him praises!
   Praise the Lord in his sanctuary.
2. Praise ye the Lord in the fullness of pow'r;
   Praise ye the Lord for mighty acts;
3. Praise ye the Lord with sounds of trumpets,
   Praise the Lord with psal'try and with harp.
4. Praise him with the timbrel and the dance;
   Praise him with string'd instruments and organs.
5. Praise ye the Lord upon the cymbals;
   Praise the Lord upon the high-sounding cymbals.
6. All things that have breath, let them praise him!
   Praise ye the Lord!

Psalm 150

1. Ha-l'-lu-ya Ha-l'-lu-ya
   Ha-l'-lu-ayl b'-kad-sho
2. Ha-l'-lu-hu bir-kee-ya u-zo
   Ha-l'-lu-hu big-vu-ro-tav

3. Ha-l'-lu-hu b'-tay-ka sho-far
   Ha-l'-lu-hu b'-nay-vel v'chi-nor
4. Ha-l'-lu-hu b'-tof u-ma-chol
   Ha-l'-lu-hu b'-mi-neem v'-u-gay
5. Ha-l'-lu-hu b'-tsil tse lay sha-ma
   Ha-l'-lu-hu b'-tsil-tse-lay t'-ru-a
6. Kol ha-n'-sha-ma t'-hal-layl-ya
   Ha-l'-lu-ya

Hebrew translation provided by Rabbi Matthew
   Friedman and Rabbi David Schonveld of Hebrew
   Union College, Cincinnati, OH.

PART TWO

THE DOCUMENTS

Plate 8: George Rochberg and Loren Maazel at a rehearsel of the
Sixth Symphony (Leningrad, 07 October 1989).

I. ARTICLES AND ESSAYS BY GEORGE ROCHBERG

The Aesthetics of Survival: A Composer's View of Twentieth Century Music, Introduction by William Bolcom. (Ann Arbor, MI: University of Michigan Press, 1984) 244 pp.

Tradition and Twelve-Tone Music (ca. 1955)

Indeterminacy in the New Music (1959)

Duration in Music (1960)

The New Image of Music (1963)

The Concepts of Musical Time and Space (1963)

In Search of Music (1964)

Aural Fact or Fiction: Or, Composing at the Seashore (1965)

The Avant-Garde and the Aesthetics of Survival (1969)

No Center (1969)

The Composer in Academia: Reflections on a Theme of Stravinsky (1970)

Humanism vs. Science (1970)

Reflections on Schönberg (1972)

Reflections on the Renewal of Music (1972)

The Fantastic and the Logical: Reflections on Science, Politics, and Art (1973)

The Structure of Time in Music (1973)

On the *Third String Quartet* (1974)

The Marvelous in Art (1982)

"Anton Webern: *Sechs Stücke, Opus 6* (pub. 1956)," *Notes: The Quarterly Journal of the Music Library Association* XV/4 (September 1958) 653-654.

"Arnold Schönberg: *Variations* (1955)," *Notes: The Quarterly Journal of the Music Library Association* XIV (March 1957) 197-198.

"The Avant-Garde and the Aesthetics of Survival," *New Literary History [University of Virginia]* III/1 (Autumn 1971) 71-92.

"Bernd Alois Zimmermann: *Perspektiven* (1956)," *Notes: The Quarterly Journal of the Music Library Association* XIV (March 1957) 197-198.

"Can the Arts Survive Modernism? A Discussion of the Characteristics, History and Legacy of Modernism," *Critical Inquiry* XI (December 1984) 317-40.

"The Composer in Academia: George Rochberg," *College Music Symposium* X (Fall 1970) 89-91.

"Composer Rochberg Challenges Ormandy's View of Orchestra's Role," *The Philadelphia Inquirer* (28 September 1969) V, 1 & 7.

"The Computer, The Brain and Music," Unpublished paper delivered as a "Slee Lecture" at the State University of New York [SUNY] at Buffalo, NY (Spring 1964).

"Contemporary Music in an Affluent Society," *ASCAP* I (1967) 10-11; reprinted in *Music Journal* LV/1 (September 1968) 60-62.

"Current Chronicle: Canada," *Musical Quarterly* LXVII/1 (1961) 103-105.

"Dika Newlin: *Piano Trio, Op. 2* (1948)," *Notes: The Quarterly Journal of the Music Library Association* XIII/4 (September 1956) 695-697.

"Direction and Continuity in Music," Unpublished paper delivered as a "Slee Lecture" at the State University of New York [SUNY] at Buffalo, NY (Spring 1964).

"Duration in Music," *The Modern Composer and His World*. (Toronto, Canada: University of Toronto Press, 1961) 56-64;

reprinted in *Nutida Musik [Stockholm]*; reprinted in *Melos [Germany]*.

Egon Wellesz: *Suite for Flute Solo* (1957), *Suite for Clarinet Solo* (1957), *Suite for Woodwind Quintet* (1956)," Notes: *The Quarterly Journal of the Music Library Association* XV (March 1958) 253.

"Elliott Carter: *String Quartet No. 1*," *Musical Quarterly* (n.d., ca. 1950's).

"Erich Itor Kahn: *Quartet for 2 Violins, Viola and Violoncello* (1953)," Notes: *The Quarterly Journal of the Music Library Association* XIII/4 (September 1956) 695-697.

"Ernst Krenek: *Suite for Flute and String Orchestra* (1957), *Suite for Clarinet and String Orchestra* (1957), *Suite for Woodwind Quintet* (1956)," Notes: *The Quarterly Journal of the Music Library Association* XV (March 1958) 253.

"Ethical and Aesthetic Values in Contemporary Music," Unpublished paper orginally delivered at "East - West in Music" Conference, Jerusalem, Israel (August 1963).

"[Review of] *A Fiddle, A Sword, and A Lady* by Albert Spalding, pub. Henry, Holt & Company," *The Philadelphia Inquirer* (n.d., ca. 1940's) 1p.

"Fiddlers and Fribbles, or, Is Art a Separate Reality?" *New Literary History [University of Virginia]* XVIII (1987) 257-79.

"George Perle: *Serial Composition and Atonality*," *Journal of the American Musicological Society* XVI/3 (Fall 1963) 413-418.

"*Grove's Dictionary of Music and Musicians*," *Etude* LXXIII/3 (March 1955) 8, 47.

"Guston and Me: Digression and Return," *Contemporary Music Review* (Forthcoming).

"The Harmonic Tendency of the Hexachord," *Journal of Music Theory* III/2 (November 1959) 208-230.

"Review of *Heritage and Obligation* by Paul Hindemith, pub. Yale University Press (1952)," *The Philadelphia Inquirer* (n.d., ca. 1940's) 1p.

The Hexachord and its Relation to the Twelve Tone Row. (Bryn Mawr, PA: Theodore Presser, 1956) 40pp.

"How I Work," Unpublished memo written on the occasion of the of induction of George Rochberg into the American Academy and Institute of Arts and Letters (1985).

"Hugo Weisgall," *Bulletin of the American Composers Alliance* VII/2 (1958) 2-5.

"Humanism vs. Science [selections]," *Music in the Western World*, compiled by Piero Weiss and Richard Taruskin. (New York, NY: Schirmer Books, A Division of Macmillan, Inc., 1984) 534-538.

"Iconography of the Mind: Inward Seeing and Iconic Thinking," Unpublished (1985-1986).

"In Search of Music," *Alumni Forum [Montclair State College, Montclair, NJ]* (1965), originally delivered at the Commencement exercises of the Philadelphia Musical Academy (June 1964).

"Indeterminacy in the New Music," *The Score* XXVI (January 1960) 9-19.

"Kramer vs. Kramer," *Critical Inquiry* II/3 (March 1985) 509-517.

"Letters: Stolen Theater," *High Fidelity/Musical America* XIX/12 (December 1969) 6.

"Luigi Dallapiccola: *Tartiniana Seconda, Divertimento per Violion e Pianoforte* (pub. 1957)," *Notes: The Quarterly Journal of the Music Library Association* XV/4 (September 1958) 654.

"Milton Babbitt: *Woodwind Quartet in One Movement*," *Notes: The Quarterly Journal of the Music Library Association* XIII/4 (September 1956) 695-697.

"Music Mailbag: Incoherent," *The New York Times* (27 July 1969) II, 14.

"The Music of Arnold Schönberg," *Columbia Records* M2S-767 [liner notes].

"New Devices and New Dimensions," *Cleveland Orchestra Program Notes* (21 & 23 January 1960) 475-477.

"New Devices and New Dimensions," *Cleveland Orchestra Program Notes* (15 February 1960) 9-10.

"The New Image of Music," *Perspectives of New Music* II/1 (Fall - Winter 1963) 1-10; originally delivered as a "Slee Lecture" and the State University of New York [SUNY] at Buffalo, NY (Spring 1964).

"New World of Sound," *Etude* LXXI/1 (January 1953) 19 & 50.

"News of the Culture or News of the Universe?," *Annals, AAPSS [American Academy of Political and Social Science]* 500 (November 1988) 116-126.

"Nikos Skalkottas: *Tender Melody for Cello and Piano, Sonatina for Cello and Piano, Passacaglia for Piano, Suite No. 4 for Piano*," *Notes: The Quarterly Journal of the Music Library Association* XIV (March 1957) 197-198.

"No Center," *Composer [USA]* I/2 (1969) 86-91; originally delivered at UCLA [University of California at Los Angeles] (January 1969).

"*Notes on Chromaticism*," Unpublished text housed at Theodore Presser Company (1971) 77pp.

"Observations on the Ph.D. in Composition," *College Music Symposium* III (Fall 1963) 64-65.

"Pierre Boulez: *Structures* (1955)," *Notes: The Quarterly Journal of the Music Library Association* XIV (March 1957) 197-198.

"Introduction," *Poems and Stories of Paul Rochberg.* (UK: Aquila Press, Ltd., 1989).

"Presumption and Responsibility in Art," Unpublished (ca. 1956).

"A Raid on the Infinite," Published in the Conference Proceedings of the Parasychology Foundation of New York, NY (1970); originally delivered at the 18th Annual International Conference of Parasychology in Le Piol, France (June 1969).

"Reflections on Schönberg," *Perspectives of New Music* XI/2 (Spring - Summer 1973) 56-83.

"Reflections on the Renewal of Music," *Current Musicology* XIII (1972) 75-82.

"Schönberg's American Period," *International Cyclopedia of Music and Musicians*. (New York, NY: Doud Mead, 1964).

"Stravinsky: A Composers' Memorial [untitled contribution by George Rochberg]," *Perspectives of New Music* IX/2 (Spring - Summer 1971), X/1 (Fall - Winter 1971) 32-33.

"The Study of Music at University: An American Composer's Standpoint," *Musical Times [Great Britain]* CXIV/1569 (November 1973) 1108-1109, 1111-1112.

"*Three Commentaries*," Unpublished document housed at Theodore Presser Company (1968 - 1978) 21pp.

"Three Levels of Creative Activity," *Philadelphia Music Dispatch* (1955).

"A Three-Way Mirror," Unpublished (1988).

"Tradition and Twelve-Tone Music," *Mandala Magazine [Philadelphia]* (1955).

"The War on Imagery: Speculations on Monotheism, Idolitry, Iconoclasm, and Ideology," Unpublished (1987).

"Webern: Master of Harmony," Unpublished paper (n.d., ca. late 1960's).

"Webern's Search for Harmonic Identity," *Journal of Music Theory* VI/1 (Spring 1962) 109-22.

"Whither Orchestras? Rochberg Challenges Ormandy," *American Musical Digest* I/2 (November 1969) 16-18.

"Wilbur Ogdon: *Intermezzo for Orchestra* (1953)," *Notes: The Quarterly Journal of the Music Library Association* XIII/4 (September 1956) 697.

II. LETTERS HOUSED IN PUBLIC COLLECTIONS

Copies of original letters to and from George Rochberg may be found in the following Libraries:

Library of Congress [LC] Collections:

Current Correspondence Collection [LC/CC].

Coolidge Foundation Correspondence Collection [LC/CF].

Damrosch-Mannes Collection [LC/DM].

De la Vega (ML94.V43) Collection [LC/DA].

Edward Steuermann Collection [LC/ES].

Koussevitsky Foundation Correspondence Collection [LC/KF].

Old Correspondence Collection [LC/OC].

Slonimsky Collection [LC/SL].

Harvard University, Houghton Library, Hans Moldenhauer Collection [HU].

New York Public Library [NYPL].

Copies of original letters to and from George Rochberg may be found in the following publications:

"Correspondencia entre Lan Adomián y George Rochberg, una polemica," *Heterofonia [México* XIV/73 (1981) 22-26.

La Voluntad de crear: Lan Adomián, Tomo I. (Ciudad Universitaria, México: Universidad Nacional Autónoma de México, 1980).

Adomián, Lan. Letter to George Rochberg (16 March 1960). "Correspondencia entre Lan Adomián y George Rochberg, una polemica," *Heterofonia [México* XIV/73 (1981) 23.

TOPIC: Adomián's *Symphony No. 2.*

Adomián, Lan. Letter to George Rochberg (22 June 1969). "Correspondencia entre Lan Adomián y George Rochberg, una polemica," *Heterofonia [México* XIV/73 (1981) 23.

TOPIC: Adomián's recent compositions.

NAMES: Gene Rochberg.

Adomián, Lan. Letter to George Rochberg (04 March 1974). "Correspondencia entre Lan Adomián y George Rochberg, una polemica," *Heterofonia [México* XIV/73 (1981) 23-24.

TOPIC: Lan questions Rochberg's change in style.

NAMES: Beethoven, Berg, Boulez, Gesualdo, Josquin, Mahler, Monteverdi, Max Plank, Wagner.

WORKS DISCUSSED: *String Quartet No. 3, Tableaux.*

Adomián, Lan. Letter to George Rochberg (12 August 1974). "Correspondencia entre Lan Adomián y George Rochberg, una polemica," *Heterofonia [México* XIV/73 (1981) 25.

TOPIC: serialism, opera.

NAMES: Bach, Boulez.

Adomián, Lan. Letter to George Rochberg (26 September 1975). "Correspondencia entre Lan Adomián y George Rochberg, una polemica," *Heterofonia [México* XIV/73 (1981) 26.

TOPIC: recordings.

WORKS DISCUSSED: *String Quartet No. 3.*

Adomián, Lan. Letter to George Rochberg (08 December 1975). "Correspondencia entre Lan Adomián y George Rochberg, una polemica," *Heterofonia [México* XIV/73 (1981) 26.

TOPIC: Adomián's recent compositions.

Adomián, Lan. Letter to George Rochberg (16 March 1960). *La Voluntad de crear: Lan Adomián, Tomo I.* (Ciudad Universitaria, México: Universidad Nacional Autónoma de México, 1980), 173-174.

TOPIC: Adomián's *Symphony No. 2*.

Adomián, Lan. Letter to George Rochberg (26 October 1961). *La Voluntad de crear: Lan Adomián, Tomo I*. (Ciudad Universitaria, México: Universidad Nacional Autónoma de México, 1980), 174.

TOPIC: Adomián's *Cantata* and *Tamayana*.

Adomián, Lan. Letter to George Rochberg (10 February 1962). *La Voluntad de crear: Lan Adomián, Tomo I*. (Ciudad Universitaria, México: Universidad Nacional Autónoma de México, 1980), 175.

TOPIC: twelve-tone music.

NAMES: Marius Flotuis.

Adomián, Lan. Letter to George Rochberg (03 September 1965). *La Voluntad de crear: Lan Adomián, Tomo I*. (Ciudad Universitaria, México: Universidad Nacional Autónoma de México, 1980), 175.

NAMES: Gene Rochberg, Francesca Rochberg.

Adomián, Lan. Letter to George Rochberg (22 June 1969). La Voluntad de crear: Lan Adomián, Tomo I. (Ciudad Universitaria, México: Universidad Nacional Autónoma de México, 1980), 175-176.

TOPIC: Adomián's recent compositions.

NAMES: Gene Rochberg.

Adomián, Lan. Letter to George Rochberg (04 March 1974). *La Voluntad de crear: Lan Adomián, Tomo I*. (Ciudad Universitaria, México: Universidad Nacional Autónoma de México, 1980), 176-178.

TOPIC: Lan questions Rochberg's change in style.

NAMES: Beethoven, Berg, Boulez, Gesualdo, Josquin, Mahler, Monteverdi, Max Plank, Wagner.

WORKS DISCUSSED: *String Quartet No. 3, Tableaux*.

Adomián, Lan. Letter to George Rochberg (12 August 1974). *La Voluntad de crear: Lan Adomián, Tomo I.* (Ciudad Universitaria, México: Universidad Nacional Autónoma de México, 1980), 178-179.

TOPIC: serialism, opera.

NAMES: Bach, Boulez.

Adomián, Lan. Letter to George Rochberg (26 September 1975). *La Voluntad de crear: Lan Adomián, Tomo I.* (Ciudad Universitaria, México: Universidad Nacional Autónoma de México, 1980), 180.

TOPIC: recordings.

WORKS DISCUSSED: *String Quartet No. 3.*

Adomián, Lan. Letter to George Rochberg (08 December 1975). *La Voluntad de crear: Lan Adomián, Tomo I.* (Ciudad Universitaria, México: Universidad Nacional Autónoma de México, 1980), 181.

TOPIC: Adomián's recent compositions.

Broido, Arnold. Letter to Donald L. Leavitt (02 October 1984) 1p. LC/CF.

WORKS DISCUSSED: *Trio [No. 2] for Violin, Cello, and Piano.*

PERFORMERS: Beaux Arts Trio.

Broido, Arnold. Letter to Donald L. Leavitt (02 October 1984) 1p. LC/CF.

WORKS DISCUSSED: *Trio [No. 2] for Violin, Cello, and Piano.*

PERFORMERS: Beaux Arts Trio.

Broido, Arnold. Letter to Donald L. Leavitt (22 January 1985) 1p. LC.

WORKS DISCUSSED: *Trio [No. 2] for Violin, Cello, and Piano.*

Broido, Arnold. Letter to Donald L. Leavitt (16 April 1985) 1p. LC.

WORKS DISCUSSED: *Trio [No. 2] for Violin, Cello, and Piano.*

PERFORMERS: Beaux Arts Trio.

Broido, Arnold. Letter to Donald L. Leavitt (23 April 1985) 1p. LC.

WORKS DISCUSSED: *Trio [No. 2] for Violin, Cello, and Piano.*
PERFORMERS: Beaux Arts Trio.

Caleb, Frank. Letter to George Rochberg (09 March 1988) 1p. LC.

WORKS DISCUSSED: *Sonata for Violin and Piano.*
NAMES: Maria Bachmann, Ellen Highstein.

Caleb, Frank. Letter to George Rochberg (06 April 1988) 1p. LC.

WORKS DISCUSSED: *Sonata for Violin and Piano.*
NAMES: Maria Bachmann, Ellen Highstein.

Clark, Hattie. Letter to George Rochberg (27 July 1984) 1p. LC.

WORKS DISCUSSED: *Trio No. 2 for Violin, Cello, and Piano.*
PERFORMERS: Beaux Arts Trio.

Crosby, John. Letter to George Rochberg (29 January 1982) 1p. NYPL.

WORKS DISCUSSED: *The Confidence Man.*

DeCray, Marcella. Letter to George Rochberg (30 September 1973) 1p. NYPL.

WORKS DISCUSSED: *Ukiyo-E.*

DeCray, Marcella. Letter to George Rochberg (04 October 1973) 1p. NYPL.

WORKS DISCUSSED: *Ukiyo-E.*

Godel, Kenneth. Letter to George Rochberg (27 January 1986) 1p. NYPL.

WORKS DISCUSSED: *To the Dark Wood.*

Grant, Margaret. Letter to George Rochberg (22 July 1957). 1p. LC.

TOPIC: Serge Koussevitzky Music Foundation commission.
WORKS DISCUSSED: *Dialogues.*

Leavitt, Donald L. Letter to George Rochberg (06 May 1981) 1p. LC.

WORKS DISCUSSED: *Quintet for String Quintet, Trio [No. 1] for Violin, Cello, and Piano.*

PERFORMERS: Beaux Arts Trio, Concord String Quartet.

Leavitt, Donald L. Letter to George Rochberg (26 April 1983) 1p. LC/CF.

WORKS DISCUSSED: *Sonata for Violin and Piano, Trio [No. 2] for Violin, Cello, and Piano.*

PERFORMERS: Beaux Arts Trio.

NAMES: Berg, Brahms, Busch, Elizabeth Sprague Coolidge, Leonora Jackson, Joachim, McKim, Serkin.

Leavitt, Donald L. Letter to George Rochberg (27 July 1984) 1p. LC/CF.

WORKS DISCUSSED: *Trio [No. 2] for Violin, Cello, and Piano.*

PERFORMERS: Beaux Arts Trio.

NAMES: Concord String Quartet, Hattie Clark.

Leavitt, Donald L. Letter to George Rochberg (27 July 1984) 1p. LC/CF.

WORKS DISCUSSED: *Trio [No. 2] for Violin, Cello, and Piano.*

PERFORMERS: Beaux Arts Trio.

Leavitt, Donald L. Letter to Arnold Broido (13 February 1985) 2pp. LC/CF.

WORKS DISCUSSED: *Trio [No. 2] for Violin, Cello, and Piano.*

Leavitt, Donald L. Letter to George Rochberg (28 June 1985) 1p. LC.

WORKS DISCUSSED: *Quartet for Violin, Viola, Cello, and Piano, Trio [No. 2] for Violin, Cello, and Piano.*

PERFORMERS: Beaux Arts Trio.

Moore, Ward. Letter to George Rochberg (16 January 1964) 1p. NYPL.

WORKS DISCUSSED: *Apocalyptica [I].*

Pruett, James W. Letter to George Rochberg (02 March 1988) 1p. LC.

WORKS DISCUSSED: *Sonata for Violin and Piano.*

NAMES: Maria Bachmann, Ellen Highstein.

Pruett, James W. Letter to George Rochberg (02 March 1988) 1p. LC.

WORKS DISCUSSED: *Sonata for Violin and Piano.*

NAMES: Maria Bachmann, Ellen Highstein.

Rochberg, George. Letter to Lan Adomián (08 September 1957). "Correspondencia entre Lan Adomián y George Rochberg, una polemica," *Heterofonia [México* XIV/73 (1981) 22.

TOPIC: twelve-tone music, Adomián's compositions.

NAMES: Gene Rochberg.

Rochberg, George. Letter to Lan Adomián (08 October 1961). "Correspondencia entre Lan Adomián y George Rochberg, una polemica," *Heterofonia [México* XIV/73 (1981) 23.

TOPIC: general.

NAMES: Gene Rochberg.

WORKS DISCUSSED: *Blake Songs, Symphony No. 2.*

Rochberg, George. Letter to Lan Adomián (31 May 1972). "Correspondencia entre Lan Adomián y George Rochberg, una polemica," *Heterofonia [México* XIV/73 (1981) 23.

TOPIC: artistic prosperity, working within oneself.

Rochberg, George. Letter to Lan Adomián (08 March 1974). "Correspondencia entre Lan Adomián y George Rochberg, una polemica," *Heterofonia [México* XIV/73 (1981) 25.

TOPIC: serialism and his change in style.

NAMES: Bach, Beethoven.

WORKS DISCUSSED: *String Quartet No. 3, Tableaux.*

Rochberg, George. Letter to Lan Adomián (27 June 1975). "Correspondencia entre Lan Adomián y George Rochberg, una polemica," *Heterofonia [México* XIV/73 (1981) 25-26.

TOPIC: the twentieth-century's "new period", and "reclaiming the past".

NAMES: Beethoven, Mozart.

Rochberg, George. Letter to Lan Adomián (17 November 1975). "Correspondencia entre Lan Adomián y George Rochberg, una polemica," *Heterofonia [México* XIV/73 (1981) 26.

TOPIC: twentieth-century music.

NAMES: Haydn, Matisse, Picasso, Verdi.

WORKS DISCUSSED: *String Quartet No. 3.*

Rochberg, George. Letter to Lan Adomián (08 September 1957). *La Voluntad de crear: Lan Adomián, Tomo I.* (Ciudad Universitaria, México: Universidad Nacional Autónoma de México, 1980), 173.

TOPIC: twelve-tone music, Adomián's compositions.

NAMES: Gene Rochberg.

Rochberg, George. Letter to Lan Adomián (08 October 1961). *La Voluntad de crear: Lan Adomián, Tomo I.* (Ciudad Universitaria, México: Universidad Nacional Autónoma de México, 1980), 174.

TOPIC: general.

NAMES: Gene Rochberg.

WORKS DISCUSSED: *Blake Songs, Symphony No. 2.*

Rochberg, George. Letter to Lan Adomián (10 January 1962). *La Voluntad de crear: Lan Adomián, Tomo I.* (Ciudad Universitaria, México: Universidad Nacional Autónoma de México, 1980), 174.

TOPIC: compositional style.

NAMES: Paul Rochberg.

Rochberg, George. Letter to Lan Adomián (25 August 1965). *La Voluntad de crear: Lan Adomián, Tomo I.* (Ciudad Universitaria, México: Universidad Nacional Autónoma de México, 1980), 175.

TOPIC: returing to composing.

NAMES: Paul and Francesca Rochberg.

Rochberg, George. Letter to Lan Adomián (31 May 1972). La Voluntad de crear: Lan Adomián, Tomo I. (Ciudad Universitaria, México: Universidad Nacional Autónoma de México, 1980), 176.

TOPIC: artistic prosperity, working within oneself.

Rochberg, George. Letter to Lan Adomián (08 March 1974). *La Voluntad de crear: Lan Adomián, Tomo I.* (Ciudad Universitaria, México: Universidad Nacional Autónoma de México, 1980), 178.

TOPIC: serialism and his change in style.

NAMES: Bach, Beethoven.

WORKS DISCUSSED: *String Quartet No. 3, Tableaux.*

Rochberg, George. Letter to Lan Adomián (27 June 1975). La Voluntad de crear: Lan Adomián, Tomo I. (Ciudad Universitaria, México: Universidad Nacional Autónoma de México, 1980), 179-180.

TOPIC: the twentieth-century's "new period", and "reclaiming the past".

NAMES: Beethoven, Mozart.

Rochberg, George. Letter to Lan Adomián (17 November 1975). *La Voluntad de crear: Lan Adomián, Tomo I.* (Ciudad Universitaria, México: Universidad Nacional Autónoma de México, 1980), 180-181.

TOPIC: twentieth-century music.

NAMES: Haydn, Matisse, Picasso, Verdi.

WORKS DISCUSSED: *String Quartet No. 3.*

Rochberg, George. Letter to Lan Adomián (26 August 1977). *La Voluntad de crear: Lan Adomián, Tomo I.* (Ciudad Universitaria, México: Universidad Nacional Autónoma de México, 1980), 181.

TOPIC: brief note.

NAMES: Gene Rochberg.

Rochberg, George. Letter to the Beaux Arts Trio, c/o Donald L. Leavitt (29 March 1981) 1p. LC.

WORKS DISCUSSED: *Trio [No. 1] for Violin, Cello, and Piano, Trio [No. 2] for Violin, Cello, and Piano.*

NAMES: Donald L. Leavitt.

Rochberg, George. Letter to John Crosby (06 February 1981) 1p. NYPL.

WORKS DISCUSSED: *The Confidence Man.*

Rochberg, George. Letter to John Crosby (01 March 1981) 1p. NYPL.

WORKS DISCUSSED: *The Confidence Man.*

Rochberg, George. Letter to John Crosby (08 August 1981) 1p. NYPL.

WORKS DISCUSSED: *The Confidence Man.*

Rochberg, George. Letter to Aurelio de la Vega (16 December 1963) 2pp. LC/AD.

NAMES: Gene Rochberg.

Rochberg, George. Letter to Aurelio de la Vega (15 April 1965) 4pp. LC/AD.

WORKS DISCUSSED: *Contra Mortem et Tempus.*

PERFORMERS: Aeolian Quartet.

Rochberg, George. Letter to Aurelio de la Vega (25 May 1965) 4pp. LC/AD.

WORKS DISCUSSED: *Apocalyptica [I], Contra Mortem et Tempus.*

PERFORMERS: Aeolian Quartet.

NAMES: Francesca Rochberg.

Rochberg, George. Letter to Aurelio de la Vega (25 July 1972) 2pp. HU.

Rochberg, George. Letter to Aurelio de la Vega (23 January 1983) 1p. HU.

Rochberg, George. Letter to Aurelio de la Vega (Christmas card, 1983). HU.

Rochberg, George. Letter to Aurelio de la Vega (28 July 1984) 1p. HU.

Rochberg, George. Letter to Clarence Foy (n.d.) 1p. LC/SL.

Rochberg, George. Letter to Margaret Grant (26 July 1957) 2pp. LC/KF.
TOPIC: Serge Koussevitzky Music Foundation commission.
WORKS DISCUSSED: *Dialogues.*

Rochberg, George. Letter to Margaret Grant (05 December 1957) 1p. LC/KF.
TOPIC: Serge Koussevitzky Music Foundation commission.
WORKS DISCUSSED: *Dialogues.*

Rochberg, George. Letter to Richard Hill (01 November 1955) 1p. LC/OC.
TOPIC: Theodore Presser business.
NAMES: Milton Babbitt.

Rochberg, George. Letter to Donald L. Leavitt (28 March 1983) 2pp. LC/CF.
WORKS DISCUSSED: *Trio [No. 2] for Violin, Cello, and Piano.*

Rochberg, George. Letter to Donald L. Leavitt (28 June 1984) 1p. LC/CF.
WORKS DISCUSSED: *Trio [No. 2] for Violin, Cello, and Piano.*

Rochberg, George. Letter to Donald L. Leavitt (13 April 1985) 1p. LC/CF.
WORKS DISCUSSED: *Trio [No. 2] for Violin, Cello, and Piano.*
NAMES: Arnold Broido, Hattie Clark.
PERFORMERS: Beaux Arts Trio.

Rochberg, George. Letter to Hans Moldenhauer (30 April 1969) 2pp. HU.

Rochberg, George. Letter to Hans Moldenhauer (28 March 1972) 2pp. HU.

Rochberg, George. Letter to Hans Moldenhauer (30 May 1972) 2pp. HU.

Rochberg, George. Letter to Hans Moldenhauer (04 July 1972) 2pp. HU.

Rochberg, George. Letter to Hans Moldenhauer (24 August 1972) 2pp. HU.

TOPIC: Schönberg.

Rochberg, George. Letter to Hans Moldenhauer (17 September 1972) 4pp. HU.

Rochberg, George. Letter to Hans Moldenhauer (05 December 1976) 1p. HU.

WORKS DISCUSSED: *Partita Variations, String Quartet No. 2, Waltz Serenade.*

Rochberg, George. Letter to Hans Moldenhauer (08 December 1984) 2pp. HU.

WORKS DISCUSSED: *Concerto for Oboe and Orchestra.*

Rochberg, George. Letter to Hans Moldenhauer (22 January 1985) 1p. HU.

WORKS DISCUSSED: *Symphony No. 1.*

Rochberg, George. Letter to Hans Moldenhauer (n.d.). HU.

WORKS DISCUSSED: *Concerto for Oboe and Orchestra, Quintet for String Quintet, Symphony No. 2, Symphony No. 4.*

Rochberg, George. Letter to James W. Pruett (08 March 1988) 2pp. LC.

WORKS DISCUSSED: *Sonata for Violin and Piano, Trio [No. 2] for Violin, Cello, and Piano.*

NAMES: Frank Caleb, Beaux Arts Trio.

Rochberg, George. Letter to Sol Schoenbach (n.d., ca. 09 January 1968) 1p. NYPL.

WORKS DISCUSSED: *Fanfares.*

Rochberg, George. Letter to Harold Spivacke (16 December 1957) 2pp. LC/KF.

WORKS DISCUSSED: *Dialogues.*

PERFORMERS: Eric Simon.

Rochberg, George. Letter to Harold Spivacke (26 December 1957) 1p. LC/KF.

WORKS DISCUSSED: *Dialogues.*

PERFORMERS: Eric Simon.

Rochberg, George. Letter to Harold Spivacke (07 January 1958) 1p. LC/KF.

WORKS DISCUSSED: *Dialogues.*

PERFORMERS: Eric Simon.

Rochberg, George. Letter to Harold Spivacke (14 January 1958) 1p. LC/KF.

WORKS DISCUSSED: *Dialogues.*

PERFORMERS: Eric Simon.

Rochberg, George. Letter to Harold Spivacke (07 April 1958) 1p. LC.

WORKS DISCUSSED: *Dialogues.*

Rochberg, George. Letter to Harold Spivacke (20 February 1962) 1p. LC.

NAMES: Dr. Otto Albrecht.

Rochberg, George. Letter to Harold Spivacke (21 February 1968) 1p. LC.

TOPIC: Library of Congress cataloging error.

Rochberg, George. Letter to Edward Steuermann (17 October 1955) 1p. LC/ES.

TOPIC: Arnold Schönberg Society concert.

Rochberg, George. Letter to Edward Steuermann (12 December 1955) 1p. LC/ES.

TOPIC: Arnold Schönberg Society concert.

Rochberg, George. Letter to Edward Steuermann (27 April 1956) 1p. LC/ES.

TOPIC: concert of music by Edward Steuermann.

WORKS DISCUSSED: *String Quartet No. 1.*

Rochberg, George. Letter to Edward Steuermann (01 November 1956) 1p. LC/ES.

WORKS DISCUSSED: *Sonata-Fantasia.*

Rochberg, George. Letter to Edward Steuermann (27 November 1956) 1p. LC/ES.

WORKS DISCUSSED: *Sonata-Fantasia, Twelve Bagatelles.*

NAMES: William Masselos.

Rochberg, George. Letter to Edward Steuermann (29 October 1957) 1p. LC/ES.

WORKS DISCUSSED: *Sonata-Fantasia.*

NAMES: Howard Lebow, Max Pollikoff, Henry Weinberg.

Rochberg, George. Letter to Edward Steuermann (22 April 1959) 1p. LC/ES.

WORKS DISCUSSED: *Sonata-Fantasia.*

NAMES: Howard Lebow.

Rochberg, George. Letter to Edward N. Waters (22 October 1961) 4pp. LC/KF.

WORKS DISCUSSED: *Dialogues.*

NOTE: Includes performance suggestions.

NAMES: Paul Rochberg.

Rochberg, George. Letter to Edward N. Waters (30 October 1961) 2pp. LC/KF.

WORKS DISCUSSED: *Dialogues.*

NAMES: Paul Rochberg.

Rochberg, George. Letter to Edward N. Waters (12 November 1961) 1p. LC/KF.

WORKS DISCUSSED: *Dialogues.*

Rochberg, George. Letter to Edward N. Waters (02 December 1961) 1p. LC/KF.

WORKS DISCUSSED: *Dialogues.*

NAMES: Paul Rochberg.

Rochberg, George. Letter to Edward N. Waters (28 February 1962) 1p. LC.

NAMES: Dr. Otto Albrecht, Paul Rochberg.

Rochberg, George. Letter to Edward N. Waters (24 February 1964) 1p. LC.

WORKS DISCUSSED: *Serenata d'estate.*

Rochberg, George. Letter to Edward N. Waters (03 March 1964) 2pp. LC.

WORKS DISCUSSED: *Time-Span II.*

NAMES: Boulez, Foss, Stockhausen, Xenakis, Paul Rochberg.

Rochberg, George. Letter to Edward N. Waters (01 April 1964) 1p. LC.

WORKS DISCUSSED: *Passions [According to the Twentieth Century].*

Rochberg, George. Letter to Edward N. Waters (08 April 1964) 3pp. LC.

WORKS DISCUSSED: *Passions [According to the Twentieth Century].*

Rochberg, George. Letter to Edward N. Waters (26 October 1964) 1p. LC.

TOPIC: Dallapiccola concert.

Spivacke, Harold. Letter to George Rochberg (11 December 1957) 1p. LC/KF.

WORKS DISCUSSED: *Dialogues.*

Spivake, Harold. Letter to George Rochberg (02 January 1958) 1p. LC/KF.

WORKS DISCUSSED: *Dialogues.*

PERFORMERS: Eric Simon.

Spivake, Harold. Letter to George Rochberg (17 January 1958) 1p. LC/KF.

WORKS DISCUSSED: *Dialogues.*

PERFORMERS: Eric Simon.

Spivake, Harold. Letter to George Rochberg (16 April 1958) 1p. LC/KF.

WORKS DISCUSSED: *Dialogues.*

Spivake, Harold. Letter to George Rochberg (01 March 1962) 1p. LC.

NAMES: Dr. Otto Albrecht.

Spivake, Harold. Letter to George Rochberg (05 March 1968) 1p. LC.

TOPIC: Library of Congress cataloging error.

Steuermann, Edward. Letter to George Rochberg (n.d., ca. January 1956) 1p. LC/ES.

TOPIC: Arnold Schönberg Society concert.

Steuermann, Edward. Letter to George Rochberg (n.d., ca. November 1956) 1p. LC/ES.

WORKS DISCUSSED: *Sonata-Fantasia.*

Steuermann, Edward. Letter to George Rochberg (n.d., ca. April-May 1959) 1p. LC/ES.

NAMES: Howard Lebow.

Waters, Edward N. Letter to George Rochberg (18 October 1961) 1p. LC/KF.

WORKS DISCUSSED: *Dialogues.*

Waters, Edward N. Letter to George Rochberg (25 October 1961) 1p. LC/KF.

WORKS DISCUSSED: *Dialogues.*

NAMES: Melvin Kaplan, Paul Rochberg.

PERFORMERS: Charles Russo, Harriett Wingreen.

Waters, Edward N. Letter to George Rochberg (14 November 1961) 1p. LC/KF.

WORKS DISCUSSED: *Dialogues.*

NAMES: William Roach, Paul Rochberg.

Waters, Edward N. Letter to George Rochberg (21 November 1961) 1p. LC/KF.

WORKS DISCUSSED: *Dialogues.*

NAMES: Paul Rochberg.

Waters, Edward N. Letter to George Rochberg (21 February 1962) 1p. LC.

NAMES: Dr. Otto Albrecht, Paul Rochberg.

Waters, Edward N. Letter to George Rochberg (28 February 1964) 1p. LC.

WORKS DISCUSSED: *Serenata d'estate.*

Waters, Edward N. Letter to George Rochberg (06 April 1964) 1p. LC.

WORKS DISCUSSED: *Passions [According to the Twentieth Century].*

Waters, Edward N. Letter to George Rochberg (14 April 1964) 1p. LC.

WORKS DISCUSSED: *Passions [According to the Twentieth Century].*

Wood, Jennings. Letter to George Rochberg (27 December 1957) 1p. LC/KF.

WORKS DISCUSSED: *Dialogues.*

Plate 9: (L to R) Igor Kipnis, George Rochberg, Melvin Strauss, May 1989.

III. DISCOGRAPHY AND LINER NOTES

Between Two Worlds (Ukiyo-e III) for Flute and Piano

Performed by Sue Ann Kahn, flute and Andrew Willis, piano. CRI 531 (1982). Liner notes by Sue Ann Kahn include quotes by George Rochberg.

Black Sounds (Apocalyptica II) for 17 Winds

Performed by the Oberlin Wind Ensemble, Kenneth Moore conducting. Grenadilla 1019 (1977). Liner notes by George Rochberg.

Blake Songs for Soprano and Chamber Ensemble

Performed by Jan DeGaetani, mezzo-soprano and the Contemporary Chamber Ensemble, Arthur Weisberg conducting. Nonesuch 71302 (1974). Liner notes by Charles Wuorinen.

La Bocca Della Verità for Oboe and Piano

Performed by James Ostryniec, oboe and Charles Wuorinen, piano. CRI 423 (1980). Liner notes unattributed.

Performed by James Ostryniec, oboe and Charles Wuorinen, piano. CRI Anthology Series ACS 6013 (1985) [Original release: CRI 423 (Recorded 1979)]. Liner notes by George Rochberg.

Performed by Ronald Roseman, oboe and Gilbert Kalish, piano. Ars Nova/Ars Antigua, AN 1008 (ca. 1971). Liner notes by George Rochberg.

Caprice Variations for Unaccompanied Violin

[*Twenty-three Variations*] performed by Gidon Kremer, violin. DG 415484 (1974). Liner notes by Peter Cosse.

[Complete *Variations*] performed by Zvi Zeitlin, violin. MHS 3719 (1977). Liner notes by Michael Walsh.

Carnival Music Suite for Piano Solo

Performed by Alan Mandel, piano. Grenadilla 1019 (1977). Liner notes by George Rochberg.

Chamber Symphony for Nine Instruments

Performed by the Oberlin Chamber Orchestra, Kenneth Moore conducting. Desto 6444 (1975). Liner notes by George Rochberg.

Concerto for Oboe and Orchestra

Performed by Joseph Robinson, oboe and the New York Philharmonic, Zubin Mehta conducting. New World 335 (1984). Liner notes by Michael Walsh.

Concerto for Violin and Orchestra

Performed by Isaac Stern, violin and the Pittsburgh Symphony Orchestra, Andre Previn conducting. CBS M-35149 (1979). Liner notes adapted from unattributed program notes of the Pittsburgh Symphony Orchestra.

Contra Mortem et Tempus for Flute, Clarinet, Violin, and Piano

Performed by the Aeolian Chamber Players (Lewis Kaplan, violin, Thomas Nyfenger, flute, Lloyd Greenberg, clarinet, Gilbert Kalish, piano). CRI 231 (1967). Liner notes by George Rochberg.

Performed by the Aeolian Chamber Players (Lewis Kaplan, violin, Thomas Nyfenger, flute, Lloyd Greenberg, clarinet, Gilbert Kalish, piano). CRI Anthology Series ACS 6013 (1985) [Original release: CRI 231 (Recorded 1967)]. Liner notes by George Rochberg.

Performed by the University of New South Wales [Australia] Ensemble (John Harding, violin, Geoffrey Collins, flute, Murray Khouri, clarinet, David Stanhope, piano). Music Broadcasting Society of New South Wales Cooperative Ltd., Australia, MBS 5 (1982). Liner notes by Grahman Hair.

Dialogues for Clarinet and Piano

Performed by John Russo, clarinet, and Lydia Russo, piano. Capra 1204 (1976). Liner notes by George Rochberg.

Performed by the University of New South Wales [Australia] Ensemble (Murray Khouri, clarinet and David Bollard, piano). Music Broadcasting Society of New South Wales Cooperative Ltd., Australia, MBS 5 (1982). Liner notes by Grahman Hair.

Duo Concertante for Violin and Cello

Performed by Mark Sokol, violin and Norman Fischer, cello. CRI 337 (1975). Liner notes by George Rochberg.

Performed by Mark Sokol, violin and Norman Fischer, cello. CRI Anthology Series ACS 6013 (1985) [Original release: CRI 337 (Recorded 1974)]. Liner notes by George Rochberg.

Performed by Daniel Kobialka, violin, and Jan Kobialka, cello. Advance Records, FGR-6C (1969). Liner notes by George Rochberg.

Electrikaleidoscope for Amplified Flute, Clarinet, Cello, Piano, and Electric Piano

Performed by the Twentieth Century Consort. The Smithsonian Collection (NO22A) #1022, CONSORT I (1979). Liner notes by Christopher Kendall and Bill Bennett.

Eleven Songs for Mezzo-Soprano and Piano

Performed by Sharon Mabry, soprano and Patsy Wade, piano. Owl Recordings, Owl-28 (1983). Liner notes by George Rochberg.

Music for the Magic Theater

Performed by the Oberlin Orchestra, Kenneth Moore conducting. Desto 6444 (1975). Liner notes by George Rochberg.

Nach Bach, Fantasy for Harpsichord or Piano

Performed by Igor Kipnis, harpsichord. Grenadilla 1019 (1968). Liner notes by George Rochberg.

Night Music for Orchestra

Performed by the Louisville Orchestra, Robert Whitney conducting. LOU 623 (ca. 1961). Liner notes by Fanny Brandeis include quotes by George Rochberg.

Quartet for Violin, Viola, Cello, and Piano

Forthcoming.

Quintet for Piano and String Quartet

Performed by Alan Marks, piano and the Concord String Quartet. Nonesuch 71396 (1980). Liner notes by Claude Baker.

Ricordanza (Soliloquy) for Cello and Piano

Performed by Norman Fischer, cello and George Rochberg, piano. CRI 337 (1975). Liner notes by George Rochberg.

Performed by Norman Fischer, cello and George Rochberg, piano. CRI Anthology Series ACS 6013 (1985) [Original release: CRI 337 (Recorded 1974)]. Liner notes by George Rochberg.

Serenata d'estate for Flute, Harp, Guitar, Violin, Viola, and Cello

Performed by the Contemporary Chamber Ensemble, Arthur Weisberg conducting. Nonesuch 71220 (ca. 1970). Liner notes by Eric Salzmann.

Performed by the Contemporary Chamber Ensemble, Arthur Weisberg conducting. Nonesuch Compact Disc (Forthcoming).

Slow Fires of Autumn (Ukiyo-e II) for Flute and Harp

Performed by Carol Wincenc, flute and Nancy Allen, harp. CRI 436 (1980). Liner notes by George Rochberg.

Performed by Carol Wincenc, flute and Nancy Allen, harp. CRI Anthology Series ACS 6013 (1985) [Original release: CRI 436 (Recorded 1979)]. Liner notes by George Rochberg.

Sonata for Violin and Piano

Forthcoming.

Songs in Praise of Krishna for Soprano and Piano

Performed by Neva Pilgrim, soprano and George Rochberg, piano. CRI 360 (1972). Liner notes by George Rochberg.

String Quartet No. 1

Performed by the Concord String Quartet. CRI 337 (1975). Liner notes by George Rochberg.

String Quartet No. 2 with Soprano

Performed by Janice Harsanyi, soprano and the Philadelphia String Quartet. CRI 164 (1963). Liner notes by Edwin London include quotes by George Rochberg.

Performed by Phyllis Bryn-Julson, soprano and the Concord String Quartet. Turnabout TV-S 34524 (1974). Liner notes by George Rochberg.

String Quartet No. 3

Performed by the Concord String Quartet. Nonesuch H-71283 (1973). Liner notes by George Rochberg.

String Quartets Nos. 4, 5 and 6, "The Concord Quartets"

Performed by the Concord String Quartet. RCA ARL2-4198 (1984). Liner notes by Theodore Libbey, Jr., and Mark Sokol.

String Quartet No. 7 with Baritone

Performed by Leslie Guinn, baritone and the Concord String Quartet. Nonesuch 78017 (1983). Liner notes by Phillip Ramey include quotes by George Rochberg.

Symphony No. 1 for Orchestra

[Three movement version] performed by the Louisville Orchestra, Robert Whitney conducting. LOU 634 (ca. 1963). Liner notes (unattributed) include quotes by George Rochberg.

Symphony No. 2 for Orchestra

Performed by the New York Philharmonic, Werner Torkanowsky conducting. Columbia ML 5779 and Columbia MS 6379 (1962). Liner notes by Edward Downes.

Performed by the New York Philharmonic, Werner Torkanowsky conducting. CRI 492 (1983) [Original release: Columbia ML 5779 (1962)]. Liner notes by Robert Carl.

Tableaux (Sound Pictures from "The Silver Talons of Piero Kostrov," by Paul Rochberg) for Soprano, Two Actors' Voices, Small Mens' Chorus, and Twelve Players

Jan DeGaetani, mezzo-soprano and the Penn Contemporary Players, Richard Wernick conducting. Turnabout TV-S 34492 (1973). Liner notes (unattributed) include quotes by George Rochberg.

Three Psalms for a cappella Mixed Chorus

[Psalm 23 only] performed by the Choir of Trinity Church, New York City, Larry King conducting. Available from the Music Office of Trinity Church, 74 Trinity Place, New York City 10006 (n.d.). Liner notes by William Hays.

[Psalm 150 only] performed by the Oberlin College Choir, Robert Fountain conducting. Oberlin College Choir Recording Series IX (1959). Liner notes unattributed.

To the Dark Wood, Music for Woodwind Quintet

Forthcoming.

Trio for Clarinet, Horn, and Piano

Performed by Larry Combs, clarinet, Gail Williams, horn, and Mary Ann Covert, piano. Crystal Records 731 (1986). Liner notes by Arrand Parsons and Larry Combs.

Trio [No. 1] for Violin, Cello, and Piano

Performed by Kees Kooper, violin, Fred Sherry, cello, and Mary Louise Boehm, piano. Turnabout TV-S 34520 (1973). Liner notes (unattributed) include quotes by George Rochberg.

Twelve Bagatelles for Piano Solo

Performed by David Burge, piano. Advance Recordings, FGR-3 (1966). Liner notes by George Rochberg.

Two Preludes and Fughettas from the Book of Contrapuntal Pieces for Keyboard Instruments

[Excerpts only] performed by Bradford Gowen, piano. Record included in Piano Quarterly CXXII (Summer 1983).

Ukiyo-e (Pictures of the Floating World) for Solo Harp

Performed by Marcella DeCray, harp. Grenadilla 1063 (1982). Liner notes by Christopher Fulkerson.

Performed by Susan Allen, harp. 1750 Arch Records, S-1787 (1982). Liner notes by Mel Powell.

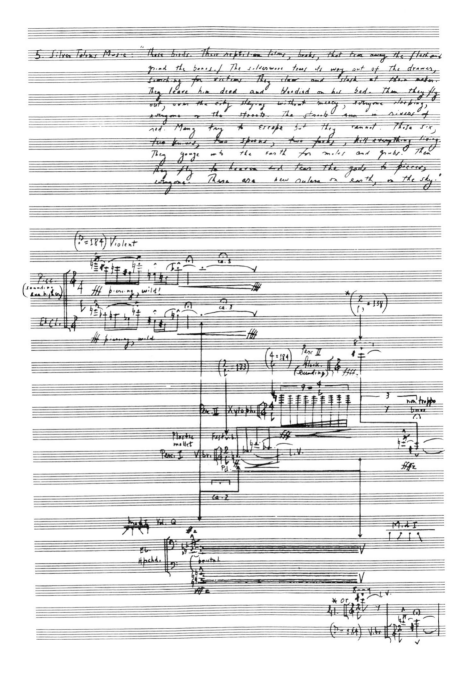

Plate 10: Autograph of page 20 of *Tableaux (Sound Pictures from the "Silver Talons of Piero Kostrov," by Paul Rochberg)* (1968). Copyright 1972 Theodore Presser Company. Userd by permission of the publisher.

IV. ORIGINAL MANUSCRIPTS AND DOCUMENTS HOUSED AT THE LIBRARY OF CONGRESS

[*Author's note*] Manuscript/document descriptions have been provided by the Library of Congress (Music Division).

Black Sounds (Apocalyptica II) for 17 Winds

Holograph copy of final version, full-score.
Ml045.R65B6, Folio.

Chamber Symphony for Nine Instruments

Holograph copy of final version, full-score.
M962.R62C5.

Capriccio for Orchestra

Holograph copy of final version, full-score.
Ml045.R65C3.

Concerto for Violin and Orchestra

Holograph copy of final version, full-score.
Ml012.R67, Folio.

David, the Psalmist for Tenor Solo and Orchestra

Holograph copy of final version, full-score.
M2l03.R65D4, Folio.

Dialogues for Clarinet and Piano

Original sketches, draft copies, and final version.
ML30.3c.R62, No. 1, Case.

Electrikaleidoscope for Amplified Flute, Clarinet, Cello, Piano, and Electric Piano

Holograph copy of final version, full-score.
M522.R57E4.

Fanfares for Massed Trumpets, Horns, and Trombones

Holograph copy of final version, full-score.
M1270.R68F3, Folio.

Four Short Sonatas for Piano Solo

Original sketches, draft version, pencil tissues (final score).
United States Information Agency [USIA] manuscripts.

I Can't Forget

Copyright office listing: E unpub. 76264 (12 September 1933).

Imago Mundi for Large Orchestra

Holograph copy of final version, full-score.
M1045.R65I5, Folio.

March of the Halberds (261st Infantry March)

Copy of the final version.
Copyright office listing: E unpub. 356212 (03 December 1943).

Music for "The Alchemist", for Soprano and Eleven Players

Holograph copy of final version, full-score.
M1510.R67A4, Case.

Phaedra, a Monodrama in Seven Scenes for Mezzo-Soprano and Orchestra

Holograph copy of final version, full-score.
M1500.R628P5, Case.

Sacred Song of Reconciliation (Mizmur l'Piyus) for Bass-Baritone and Small Orchestra

Holograph copy of final version, full-score.
M2l03.R65S2, Folio.

Songs in Praise of Krishna for Soprano and Piano

Holograph copy of final version, full-score.
Ml621.4.R, Case.

Song of the Doughboy

Copy of the final version.
Copyright office listing: E unpub. 371709 (17 April 1944).

Symphony No. 3 for Vocal Soloists, Chamber Chorus, Double Chorus, and Large Orchestra

Holograph copy of final version, full-score.
Ml00l.R68, No.3, Folio.

Symphony No. 4 for Large Orchestra

Holograph copy of final version, full-score.
Ml00l.R68, No.4, Folio

Trio [No. 2] for Violin, Cello, and Piano

Original sketches, draft copies, and final version.
ML29c.R63, No. 1 & 2, Case.

261st Infantry Song

Copy of the final version.
Copyright office listing: E unpub. 357306 (02 December 1943).

Waltz Serenade for Orchestra

Holograph copy of final version, full-score.
Ml049.R67W3.

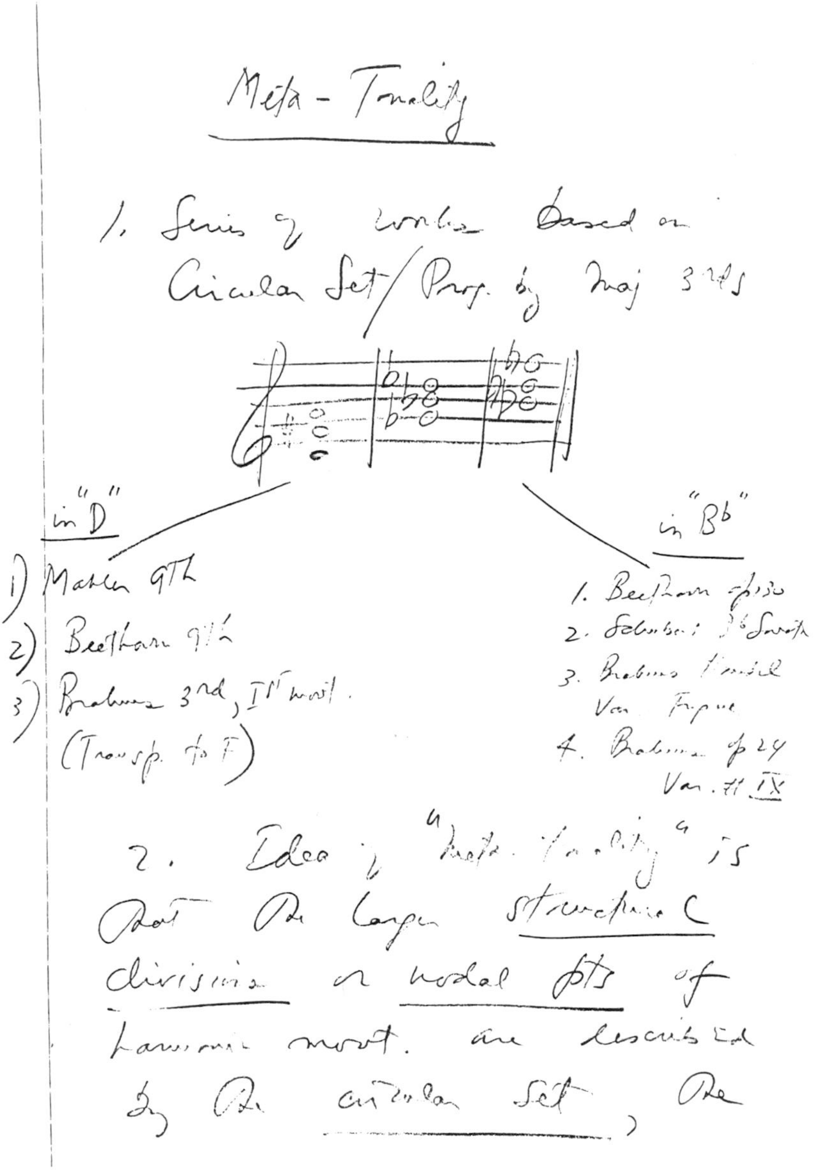

Meta-Tonality

1. Series of works based on
Circular Set/Prog. by Maj 3rds

in "D"

1) Mahler 9th
2) Beethoven 9th
3) Brahms 3rd, IInd movt.
(Transp. to F)

in "Bb"

1. Beethoven op. 130
2. Schubert Bb Sonata
3. Brahms Handel Var. Fugue
4. Brahms op 24 Var. # IX

2. Idea of "meta-tonality" is that the larger structural divisions or nodal pts of harmonic movt. are described by the circular set, the

Plate 11: Autograph of page from notes on *Meta-Tonality* (ca. 1970). Used by permission of George Rochberg.

V. ORIGINAL MANUSCRIPTS AND DOCUMENTS HOUSED AT THE NEW YORK PUBLIC LIBRARY (LINCOLN CENTER)

[*Author's note*] Item designations and descriptions have been provided by the New York Public Library (Music Division).

ITEM 1

TITLE: *Quintet for Piano and String Quartet.*

PUBLISHED: Bryn Mawr, PA: TP, ca. 1984.

CALL NUMBER: JNG 88-381.

ITEM 2

TITLE: *Waltz Serenade for Orchestra* (Sound recording).

CALL NUMBER: LT-7 1982.

ITEM 3

TITLE: *Symphony No. 1 for Orchestra* (Sound recording).

CALL NUMBER: LT-7 1981.

ITEM 4

TITLE: *Symphony No. 2 for Orchestra* (Sound recording).

CALL NUMBER: LT-7 2058.

ITEM 5

TITLE: *Concerto for Oboe and Orchestra.*

PUBLISHED: Bryn Mawr, PA: TP, ca. 1985.

CALL NUMBER: JNG 87-153.

ITEM 6

AUTHOR: Rochberg-Halton, Eugene.

TITLE: *Meaning and Modernity: Social Theory in the Pragmatic Attitude.*

PUBLISHED: Chicago, IL: University of Chicago Press, 1986.

CALL NUMBER: JLE 87-1425.

ITEM 7

TITLE: *Concerto for Violin and Orchestra (Epilogue).*

PUBLISHED: 1974.

CALL NUMBER: JPB 86-18, No. 74.

ITEM 8

TITLE: *Concerto for Violin and Orchestra* (Selections).

PUBLISHED: 1974.

CALL NUMBER: JPB 88-18, No. 73.

ITEM 9

TITLE: *Language, Literature, and History: Philological and Historical Studies Presented to Erica Reiner, edited by Francesca Rochberg-Halton.*

PUBLISHED: New Haven, CT: American Oriental Society, 1987.

CALL NUMBER: OAC (American Oriental Series), Volume 67.

ITEM 10

TITLE: *Two Preludes and Fughettas* from the *Book of Contrapuntal Pieces for Keyboard Instruments.*

PUBLISHED: Bryn Mawr, PA: TP, ca. 1980.

CALL NUMBER: Music-Am. (Sheet) 84-621.

CALL NUMBER: AMC M25 R672 B7.

ITEM 11

TITLE: *String Quartet No. 1.*

PUBLISHED: Bryn Mawr, PA: TP, ca. 1986.

CALL NUMBER: JNF 87-58.

ITEM 12

TITLE: *Quartet for Violin, Viola, Cello, and Piano.*
PUBLISHED: Bryn Mawr, PA: TP, ca. 1985.
CALL NUMBER: JNG 87-56.

ITEM 13

TITLE: *Caprice Variations for Unaccompanied Violin.*
COMPLETED: 16 January 1970.
DESCRIPTION: 136 leaves of MS, 28 x 38 cm.
NOTES: Holograph, in pencil, on green paper. Includes sketches of an earlier version for violin and piano.
PUBLISHED: New York, NY: Galaxy Music, 1973.
SUBJECTS: 1. Rochberg, George—Manuscripts. 2. Variations (Violin).
CALL NUMBER: JPB 86-18, No. 45.

ITEM 14

TITLE: *Ricordanza (Soliloquy) for Cello and Piano.*
COMPLETED: 03 November 1972.
DESCRIPTION: 1 MS score, 88 pp., 28 x 37 cm.
NOTES: Holograph sketches, chiefly on green paper.
PUBLISHED: Bryn Mawr, PA: TP, 1974.
SUBJECTS: 1. Rochberg, George—Manuscripts.
CALL NUMBER: JPB 86-18, No. 63.

ITEM 15

TITLE: *Quintet for Piano and String Quartet* (Sketches).
COMPLETED: 18 October 1975.
DESCRIPTION: 1 MS score, ca. 250 leaves, 28 x 38 cm.
NOTES: Holograph sketches, chiefly on green paper.
PUBLISHED: Bryn Mawr, PA: TP, 1975.
SUBJECTS: 1. Rochberg, George—Manuscripts.
CALL NUMBER: JPB 86-18, No. 62.

ITEM 16

TITLE: *Apocalyptica [I] for Wind Ensemble.*
COMPLETED: 14 July 1964.
DESCRIPTION: 1 MS score, 300 leaves, 34 cm. or smaller.

NOTES: Holograph sketches. Accompanied by letter dated January 16, 1964 from Ward Moore to the composer.

PUBLISHED: Bryn Mawr, PA: TP, 1966.

SUBJECTS: 1. Rochberg, George—Manuscripts.

CALL NUMBER: JPB 86-18, No. 44.

ITEM 17

TITLE: *String Quartet No. 2 with Soprano.*

COMPLETED: 26 August 1963.

DESCRIPTION: 1 MS score, 95 pp., 38 cm.

NOTES: Holograph (photocopy) with markings in red pencil.

PUBLISHED: Bryn Mawr, PA: TP, 1971.

SUBJECTS: 1. Rilke, Rainer Maria, 1875-1926—Musical Settings. 2. Rochberg, George—Manuscripts—Facsimiles. 3. String Quartets—Scores. 4. Songs (High Voice) with Instrumental Ensemble—Scores.

OTHER HEADINGS: I. Rilke, Rainer Maira, 1875-1926. *Duineger Elegien*. English.

CALL NUMBER: JPB 86-18, No. 61.

ITEM 18

TITLE: *Three Black Pieces for Orchestra* from *Zodiac, I, V, VII.*

COMPLETED: 05 August 1965.

DESCRIPTION: 1 MS score, 34 pp., 27 x 35 cm.

NOTES: Holograph signed, in pencil.

SUBJECTS: 1. Rochberg, George—Manuscripts. 2. Orchestral Music, Arranged—Scores.

OTHER HEADINGS: I. *Three Black Pieces*. II. *Black Pieces*. III. *Zodiac*.

CALL NUMBER: JPB 86-18, No. 43.

ITEM 19

TITLE: *Phaedra, A Monodrama for Mezzo-Soprano and Orchestra* (Sketches).

COMPLETED: 23 March 1974.

DESCRIPTION: 1 MS score, ca. 250 pp., 27 x 34 cm.

NOTES: Holograph sketches. Accompanied by synopsis and composer's notes, 68 leaves.

SUBJECTS: 1. Rochberg, George—Manuscripts.

CALL NUMBER: JPB 86-18, No. 59.

ITEM 20

TITLE: *Phaedra, A Monodrama for Mezzo-Soprano and Orchestra* (Selections).

COMPLETED: 18 March 1974.

DESCRIPTION: 1 MS score, 52 leaves, 28 x 38 cm.

NOTES: Holograph, in pencil. "Began orchestration Jan. 24, 1974."

SUBJECTS: 1. Rochberg, George—Manuscripts. 2. Songs (High Voice) with Orchestra—Excerpts—Scores.

OTHER HEADINGS: I. Racine, Jean, 1639-1699. *Phaedre*. English. II. Rochberg, Gene.

CALL NUMBER: JPB 86-18, No. 60.

ITEM 21

TITLE: *Zodiac for Orchestra*.

COMPLETED: 22 August 1964.

DESCRIPTION: 1 MS score, 107 pp., 34 cm.

NOTES: Holograph signed, in pencil, with emendations in ink. Accompanied by a published copy of the *Twelve Bagatelles for Piano Solo* with note on cover "Orchestral version," which contains orchestration markings by the composer.

SUBJECTS: 1. Rochberg, George—Manuscripts. 2. Orchestral Music, Arranged—Scores.

CALL NUMBER: JPB 85-18, No. 42.

ITEM 22

TITLE: *Waltz Serenade for Orchestra*.

COMPLETED: 08 February 1957.

DESCRIPTION: 1 MS score, 61 pp., 34 cm.

NOTES: Holograph signed, in pencil. "A revision of *Ballet Music for Strings* (or *Waltzes for Strings*), which I am withdrawing. Begun Jan. 24, 1957."

SUBJECTS: 1. Rochberg, George—Manuscripts. 2. Waltzes (Orchestra)—Scores.

CALL NUMBER: JPB 86-18, No. 41.

ITEM 23

TITLE: *Variations on an Original Theme for String Quartet.*

COMPLETED: 15 May 1946.

DESCRIPTION: 1 MS score, 15pp., and 3 MS parts, 35 cm.

NOTES: Holograph signed in ink.

SUBJECTS: 1. Rochberg, George—Manuscripts. 2. Variations (String Quartet)—Scores and Parts.

CALL NUMBER: JPB 86-18, No. 40.

ITEM 24

TITLE: *Music for "The Alchemist" (A Play by Ben Jonson)* (Sketches).

COMPLETED: 06 September 1966.

DESCRIPTION: 1 MS score, 92pp., 27 x 35 cm.

NOTES: Holograph sketches. Accompanied by scenario (46 pp.) and composer's notes (7 leaves). Includes design ground plan for the Repertory Theatre of Lincoln Center (1 sheet, 65 x 46 cm.).

SUBJECTS: 1. Rochberg, George—Manuscripts.

OTHER HEADINGS: I. Jonson, Ben, 1573?-1637. *The Alchemist.* II. Vivian Beaumont Theater. III. *Alchemist Music.*

CALL NUMBER: JPB 86-18, No. 57.

ITEM 25

TITLE: *Music for "The Alchemist" (A Play by Ben Jonson).*

COMPLETED: 12 August 1968.

DESCRIPTION: 1 MS score, ca. 200pp., 38 cm. or smaller.

NOTES: Holograph (photocopy) with additions in pencil. "Comprising references to quotations from and side-glances at the music of the Renaissance, Elizabethan England and today." Accompanied by partial score (56 leaves) on transparent paper, photocopy of other scores (32 pp.) with note "These not used in final collage version as is, but as music—all included except #13. Aug. 12, 1968."

PUBLISHED: Bryn Mawr, PA: TP.

SUBJECTS: 1. Rochberg, George—Manuscripts. 2. Music, Incidental—Scores.

OTHER HEADINGS: I. Jonson, Ben, 1573?-1637. *The Alchemist.* II. *Alchemist Music.*

CALL NUMBER: JPB 86-18, No. 58.

ITEM 26

TITLE: *Hymn and Jubilation (Fantasy and Fugue) for Orchestra.*

COMPLETED: 194-?.

DESCRIPTION: 1 MS score, 90pp., 34 cm.

NOTES: Holograph.

SUBJECTS: 1. Rochberg, George—Manuscripts. 2. Orchestral Music—Scores.

CALL NUMBER: JPB 86-18, No. 56.

ITEM 27

TITLE: *Cantes Flamencos* (Sketches).

COMPLETED: 03 August 1969.

DESCRIPTION: 37 leaves of MS, 28 x 39 cm.

NOTES: Holograph sketches. Accompanied by texts (5 leaves).

SUBJECTS: 1. Rochberg, George—Manuscripts.

CALL NUMBER: JPB 86-18, No. 55.

ITEM 28

TITLE: *Five Smooth Stones, for Orchestra, Mixed Chorus, and Soprano Solo.*

COMPLETED: 09 June 1949.

DESCRIPTION: 1 MS score, 179pp., 34 cm.

NOTES: Holograph signed. Accompanied by 6 leaves of transparent paper, cheifly blank.

SUBJECTS: 1. Benson, Stella, 1892-1933—Musical Settings. 2. Rochberg, George—Manuscripts. 3. Cantatas, Secular—Scores.

OTHER HEADINGS: I. Benson, Stella, 1892-1933. *Five Smooth Stones*. II. *Five Smooth Stones*. III. *Smooth Stones*.

CALL NUMBER: JPB 86-18, No. 54.

ITEM 29

TITLE: *Trio [No. 2] for Violin, Cello, and Piano.*

PUBLISHED: Bryn Mawr, PA: TP, 1985.

DESCRIPTION: 1 score, 73 leaves, 36 cm.

NOTES: Publisher's second proofs, with corrections by the composer, and note from the engraver in caption. Accompanied by note, July 8, 1985, from the composer.

SUBJECTS: 1. Piano Trios—Scores.

CALL NUMBER: JPB 86-18, No. 39.

ITEM 30

TITLE: *Fantasies for Voice and Piano* (Sketches).

COMPLETED: 02 - 20 August 1971.

DESCRIPTION: 1 MS score, 24pp., 27 x 34 cm.

NOTES: Holograph sketches. Poems by Paul Rochberg. Accompanied by text (3 leaves). Accompanied by partial score (leaves 11-12) on transparent paper.

PUBLISHED: Bryn Mawr, PA: TP., 1975.

SUBJECTS: 1. Rochberg, George—Manuscripts. 2. Rochberg, Paul, 1944-1964—Musical Settings.

OTHER HEADINGS: I. Rochberg, Paul, 1944-1964.

CALL NUMBER: JPB 86-18, No. 53.

ITEM 31

TITLE: *Electrikaleidoscope for Violin, Flute, Cello, Clarinet, Piano, and Electric Piano.*

COMPLETED: 27 August 1972.

DESCRIPTION: 1 MS score, 126 leaves, 28 x 39 cm.

NOTES: Holograph signed, in pencil, chiefly on green paper. "Began sometime after July 25/26, 1972." "Aug. 5-27, 1972, Newtown Square, PA."

SUBJECTS: 1. Rochberg, George—Manuscripts. 2. Quintets (piano, clarinet, flute, violin, cello)—Scores.
CALL NUMBER: JPB 86-18, No. 52.

ITEM 32
TITLE: *Trio for Horn, Clarinet, and Piano.*
COMPLETED: 12 March 1980.
DESCRIPTION: 1 MS score, 79pp., 36 cm.
NOTES: Holograph (photocopy) accompanied by partial score (8 leaves, 28 x 37 cm.) containing new section in 1st movement.
PUBLISHED: Bryn Mawr, PA: TP, 1981.
SUBJECTS: 1. Rochberg, George—Manuscripts. 2. Trios (piano, clarinet, horn)—Scores.
CALL NUMBER: JPB 86-18, No. 38.

ITEM 33
TITLE: *Dialogues for Clarinet and Piano.*
COMPLETED: 14 July 1958.
DESCRIPTION: 1 MS, 61pp., 34cm, and 2 MS parts, 37 cm.
NOTES: Holograph signed, in pencil. Some portions photocopied from earlier versions. "Final version."
PUBLISHED: Bryn Mawr, PA: TP, 1959.
SUBJECTS: 1. Rochberg, George—Manuscripts. 2. Clarinet and Piano music—Scores and parts.
CALL NUMBER: JPB 86-18, No. 51.

ITEM 34
TITLE: *Dialogues for Clarinet and Piano.*
COMPLETED: 29 May 1958.
DESCRIPTION: 1 MS score, 58pp., 34 cm.
NOTES: Holograph signed, in pencil. "Revised May 10, 1958." Accompanied by photocopy of 1 MS score (31 pp.), with revisions by the composer, dated Sept. 21-Dec. 5, 1957.
SUBJECTS: 1. Rochberg, George—Manuscripts. 2. Clarinet and Piano music—Scores.
CALL NUMBER: JPB 86-18, No. 50.

ITEM 35

TITLE: *Dialogues for Clarinet and Piano.*

COMPLETED: 29 May 1958.

DESCRIPTION: 1 MS score, 30pp., 32 cm. and 2 MS parts, 20pp. each, 37cm.

NOTES: Holograph (photocopy). Includes parts for A and B-flat clarinet. Accompanied by 2 additional parts (13 pp. each) marked "1st version," and sketchbook score (30 pp., 15 cm.) marked "Revisions, *Clarinet Sonata.*"

SUBJECTS: 1. Rochberg, George—Manuscripts—Facsimiles. 2. Rochberg, George—Manuscripts. 3. Clarinet and Piano music—Scores and parts.

CALL NUMBER: JPB 86-18, No. 49.

ITEM 36

TITLE: *Concerto (or Concert piece) for Two Pianos and Orchestra.*

COMPLETED: 1951.

DESCRIPTION: 1 MS score, 75pp., 40 cm.

NOTES: Holograph, in pencil.

SUBJECTS: 1. Rochberg, George—Manuscripts. 2. Concertos (two pianos)—Scores.

OTHER HEADINGS: I. *Concert Piece.*

CALL NUMBER: JPB 86-18, No. 48.

ITEM 37

TITLE: *Concerto for Violin and Orchestra.*

COMPLETED: 06 December 1974.

DESCRIPTION: 1 MS score, 221 pp., 49 cm.

NOTES: Holograph (photocopy) with emendations in pencil.

PUBLISHED: Bryn Mawr, PA: TP, ca. 1977.

SUBJECTS: 1. Rochberg, George—Manuscripts—Facsimiles. 2. Concertos (Violin)—Scores.

CALL NUMBER: JPB 86-18, No. 72.

ITEM 38

TITLE: *Ukiyo-E (Pictures of the Floating World) for Flute and Harp* (Sketches).

COMPLETED: 05 September 1973.

DESCRIPTION: 3 leaves of MS, 28 x 39 cm.

NOTES: Holograph sketches, on green paper. Accompanied by photocopy of these sketches (10 leaves), letter, 9/30/(73), and note, 10/4/73 from Marcella DeCray.

PUBLISHED: Bryn Mawr, PA: TP, 1976.

SUBJECTS: 1. Rochberg, George—Manuscripts.

OTHER HEADINGS: I. DeCray, Marcella. II. *Pictures of the Floating World*. III. *End of Summer*.

CALL NUMBER: JPB 86-18, No. 71.

ITEM 39

TITLE: *Eleven Songs for Voice and Piano* (Sketches).

COMPLETED: 26 November 1969.

DESCRIPTION: 1 MS score, 69 leaves, 28 x 38 cm.

NOTES: Holograph sketches, on green paper.

PUBLISHED: Bryn Mawr, PA: TP, 1973.

SUBJECTS: 1. Rochberg, George—Manuscripts. 2. Rochberg, Paul, 1944-1964—Musical Settings.

OTHER HEADINGS: I. Rochberg, Paul, 1944-1964.

CALL NUMBER: JPB 86-18, No. 66.

ITEM 40

TITLE: *Sacred Song of Reconciliation (Mizmor 1'piyus) for Baritone and Chamber Orchestra* (Sketches).

COMPLETED: 14 March 1970.

DESCRIPTION: 1 MS score, 91 leaves, 28 x 38 cm.

NOTES: Holograph sketches, on green paper. Hebrew (romanized) words.

SUBJECTS: 1. Rochberg, George—Manuscripts.

OTHER HEADINGS: I. *Sacred Song of Reconciliation*. II. *Mizmor l'piyus*.

CALL NUMBER: JPB 86-18, No. 64.

ITEM 41

TITLE: *Three Commentaries* (Sketches).

COMPLETED: 1968-1978.

DESCRIPTION: 68pp. of MS, 27 x 34 cm.

NOTES: Holograph sketches. Accompanied by copy of Richard Rodger's *Lover* (2 leaves, 35 cm.), and a copy of John Dowland's *Forlorn Hope Fancy* (3 leaves, 35 cm.).

SUBJECTS: 1. Rochberg, George—Manuscripts.

OTHER HEADINGS: I. Commentaries.

CALL NUMBER: JPB 86-18, No. 47.

ITEM 42

TITLE: *Carnival Music, Suite for Piano Solo.*

COMPLETED: 29 June 1971.

DESCRIPTION: 86pp. of MS, 27 x 35 cm.

NOTES: Holograph, in pencil. "*Transformations.*" Added title, crossed out. "*Based on a Bach Motif and Related Motifs.*" "*Commentaries on J.S. Bach Sinfonia No. 9 (Three-part Invention in f minor),* which became *Suite for Piano: Carnival Music,* June 1971." Additional materials dated July 22, 1968. Accompanied by sketches (8 leaves).

SUBJECTS: 1. Rochberg, George—Manuscripts. 2. Suites (Piano).

OTHER HEADINGS: I. Rochberg, George. *Commentaries.* II. Bach, Johann Sebastian, 1685-1750. *Inventions, harpsichord, BWV 795, f minor.*

CALL NUMBER: JPB 86-18, No. 46.

ITEM 43

TITLE: *Trio for Horn, Clarinet, and Piano.*

COMPLETED: 22 April 1948.

DESCRIPTION: 1 MS score, 117pp., 32 cm.

NOTES: Holograph signed, in ink, with pencil emendations. Revised in 1980.

SUBJECTS: 1. Rochberg, George—Manuscripts. 2. Trios (piano, clarinet, horn)—Scores.

CALL NUMBER: JPB 86-18, No. 37.

ITEM 44

TITLE: *To the Dark Wood, Music for Woodwind Quintet* (Sketches).

COMPLETED: 08 October 1985.

DESCRIPTION: 1 MS score, 85 leaves, 28 x 39 cm.

NOTES: Holograph sketches, on green paper.

PUBLISHED: Bryn Mawr, PA: TP, 1986.

SUBJECTS: 1. Rochberg, George—Manuscripts.

CALL NUMBER: JPB 86-18, No. 69.

ITEM 45

TITLE: *To the Dark Wood, Music for Woodwind Quintet.*

COMPLETED: 10 October 1985.

DESCRIPTION: 1 MS score, 96 leaves, 28 x 39 cm.

NOTES: Holograph signed, in pencil, on green paper. Accompanied by a photocopy of this score (28 x 43 cm.). Includes performance notes.

PUBLISHED: Bryn Mawr, PA: TP, 1986.

SUBJECTS: 1. Rochberg, George—Manuscripts. 2. Rochberg, George—Manuscripts—Facsimiles. 3. Wind Quintets (bassoon, clarinet, flute, horn, oboe)—Scores.

CALL NUMBER: JPB 86-18, No. 70.

ITEM 46

TITLE: *To the Dark Wood, Music for Woodwind Quintet.*

PUBLISHED: Bryn Mawr, PA: TP, ca. 1985.

DESCRIPTION: 1 score, 38 leaves, 36 cm.

NOTES: Publisher's second proofs (1/29/86) with corrections by the composer. Includes performance notes.

SUBJECTS: 1. Wind Quintets (bassoon, clarinet, flute, horn, oboe)—Scores.

CALL NUMBER: JPB 86-18, No. 36.

ITEM 47

TITLE: *To the Dark Wood, Music for Woodwind Quintet.*

PUBLISHED: Bryn Mawr, PA: TP, ca. 1985.

DESCRIPTION: 1 score, 38 leaves, 36 cm.

NOTES: Publisher's first proofs, with corrections by the composer. Accompanied by letter, 1/27/86, from Kenneth Godel to the composer (1 leaf, 28 cm.). Includes performance notes.

SUBJECTS: 1. Wind Quintets (Bassoon, clarinet, flute, horn, oboe)—Scores.

CALL NUMBER: JPB 86-18, No. 35.

ITEM 48

TITLE: *Time-Span II for Orchestra.*

COMPLETED: 1962.

DESCRIPTION: 1 MS score, 37pp., 46 cm.

NOTES: Holograph (photocopy), with numerous corrections in pencil.

PUBLISHED: New York, NY: Leeds Music, 1985.

SUBJECTS: 1. Rochberg, George—Manuscripts—Facsimiles. 2. Orchestral Music—Scores.

OTHER HEADINGS: I. *Time-Span II.*

CALL NUMBER: JPB 86-18, No. 68.

ITEM 49

TITLE: *Time-Span I for Orchestra.*

COMPLETED: 16 May 1960.

DESCRIPTION: 1 MS score, 29pp., 36 x 54 cm. folded to 36 x 27 cm.

NOTES: Holograph signed, in pencil. "Orchestration completed May 16, 1960." "Withdrawn and revised in 1962, subsequently titled *Time-Span II.*"

SUBJECTS: 1. Rochberg, George—Manuscripts.

CALL NUMBER: JPB 86-18, No. 34.

ITEM 50

TITLE: *Time-Span I for Orchestra* (Sketches).

COMPLETED: 25 April 1960.

DESCRIPTION: 1 MS score, 48pp., 25 x 35 cm.

NOTES: Holograph sketches. Accompanied by sketches titled "*St. Louis II*" (7 pp., 30 cm.).

SUBJECTS: 1. Rochberg, George—Manuscripts.

OTHER HEADINGS: I. *Time-Span I.* II. *Time-Span.* III. *St. Louis II.*

CALL NUMBER: JPB 86-18, No. 33.

ITEM 51

TITLE: *Tableaux (Sound Pictures from The Silver Talons of Piero Kostrov by Paul Rochberg) for Soprano, Two Actors' Voices, Small Mens' Chorus, and Twelve Players* (Sketches).

COMPLETED: 02 September 1968.

DESCRIPTION: 97pp. of MS, 27 x 34 cm.

NOTES: Holograph sketches. Accompanied by text (3 leaves, 34 cm.), instrumentation notes (1 leaf, 28 cm.), partial score (1 leaf, 47 cm.) on transparent paper, and sketch of July 27, 1967 (1 leaf, 28 cm.).

PUBLISHED: Bryn Mawr, PA: TP, 1972.

SUBJECTS: 1. Rochberg, George—Manuscripts.

OTHER HEADINGS: I. Rochberg, Paul, 1944-1964. *Silver Talons of Piero Kostrov.* II. *Sound Pictures from The Silver Talons of Piero Kostrov.* III. *Silver Talons of Piero Kostrov.*

CALL NUMBER: JPB 86-18, No. 32.

ITEM 52

TITLE: *Songs in Praise of Krishna for Soprano and Piano* (Sketches).

COMPLETED: June - August 1970.

DESCRIPTION: 1 MS score, 150 leaves, 28 x 38 cm.

NOTES: Holograph sketches, on green paper. Worksheets (8 pp., 22-38 cm.) laid in.

PUBLISHED: Bryn Mawr, PA: TP, 1980.

SUBJECTS: 1. Rochberg, George—Manuscripts.

CALL NUMBER: JPB 86-18, No. 67.

ITEM 53

TITLE: *Songs in Praise of Krishna for Soprano and Piano.*

COMPLETED: 04 October 1971.

DESCRIPTION: 1 MS score, 88 leaves, 28 cm.

NOTES: Holograph (photocopy). Copy used for recording session, with annotations in ink and yellow marker.

PUBLISHED: Bryn Mawr, PA: TP, 1980.

SUBJECTS: 1. Krishna—Songs and music. 2. Rochberg, George—Manuscripts—Facsimiles. 3. Song Cycles. 4. Songs (High Voice) with Piano.

CALL NUMBER: JPB 86-18, No. 31.

ITEM 54

TITLE: *Instrumental Music* (Sketches). Sketches and tissues (*String Quartet No. 1*). Other pieces written during War in England, France, Germany.

COMPLETED: 1942-1951.

DESCRIPTION: 256 pp. of MS, 40 cm. or smaller.

NOTES: Holograph sketches, in part on transparent paper. Contents: *String Trio, Chorale-canon, Music for Paul and Gene, Scherzando for Woodwind Quartet, Little Suite for Piano, Two Sketches for Piano, String Quartet No. 1*, three notebooks.

SUBJECTS: 1. Rochberg, George—Manuscripts.

CALL NUMBER: JPB 86-18, No. 65.

ITEM 55

TITLE: *Instrumental Music* (Sketches).

COMPLETED: 1958-1961.

DESCRIPTION: 72pp. of MS, 32 cm.

NOTES: Holograph sketches. Partial Contents: *Oboe-piano Music* (23 August 1958), *String Quartet No. 2* (1959), *St. Louis (Time-Span I), String Quartet No. 2* (07 July 1961).

SUBJECTS: 1. Rochberg, George—Manuscripts.

CALL NUMBER: JPB 86-18, No. 30.

ITEM 56

TITLE: *Instrumental Music* (Sketches). Rows, scraps & bits of things.

COMPLETED: 1956 - 1960.

DESCRIPTION: 1 MS score, 92pp., 36 cm. or smaller.

NOTES: Holograph sketches. Partial Contents: *Cheltenham Concerto* (1958), row forms, *Sonata-Fantasia, String Quartet* (17 August 1956), *Oboe Sonata* (02 May), *Clarinet Sonata* (14 September 1957), *String Quartet* (1959-1960).

SUBJECTS: 1. Rochberg, George—Manuscripts.

CALL NUMBER: JPB 86-18, No. 29.

ITEM 57

TITLE: *Quartet for Jazz Combo* (Sketches).

COMPLETED: 01 November 1958.

DESCRIPTION: 1 MS score, 26pp., 31cm.

NOTES: Holograph sketches. "Begun Aug. '58." Accompanied by *"Three Jazz Sketches for Piano Solo"* (2 pp., 34 cm.).

SUBJECTS: 1. Rochberg, George—Manuscripts.

OTHER HEADINGS: I. Rochberg, George. *Jazz Sketches*.

CALL NUMBER: JPB 86-18, No. 28.

ITEM 58

TITLE: *Nach Bach, Fantasy for Harpsichord or Piano* (Sketches).

COMPLETED: 06 July 1966.

DESCRIPTION: 66pp. of MS, 28 cm.

NOTES: Holograph sketches (27 x 34 cm).

PUBLISHED: Bryn Mawr, PA: TP, 1967.

SUBJECTS: 1. Rochberg, George—Manuscripts.

CALL NUMBER: JPB 86-18, No. 27.

ITEM 59

TITLE: *Music for the Magic Theater* (Sketches).

COMPLETED: 26 September 1965.

DESCRIPTION: 1 MS score, 130pp., 28 cm. or smaller.

NOTES: Holograph sketches. Accompanied by 1 MS score (1 leaf) on transparent paper.

PUBLISHED: Bryn Mawr, PA: TP, 1972.

SUBJECTS: 1. Rochberg, George—Manuscripts.

OTHER HEADINGS: I. *Magic Theater*.

CALL NUMBER: JPB 86-18, No. 26.

ITEM 60

TITLE: *Chamber Symphony, Music for Nine Instruments.*

COMPLETED: 14 December 1953.

DESCRIPTION: 1 MS score, 230pp., 32 cm.

NOTES: Holograph, in pencil. "Begun July 3, 1953 (New-town Square, PA)." "Completed Dec. 14, 1953 (Newtown Square, PA)." Accompanied by sketch (2pp., 18 x 27 cm.).

PUBLISHED: Bryn Mawr, PA: TP, 1978.

SUBJECTS: 1. Rochberg, George—Manuscripts. 2. Nonets (bassoon, clarinet, horn, oboe, trombone, trumpet, violin, viola, violoncello)—Scores.

CALL NUMBER: JPB 86-18, No. 25.

ITEM 61

TITLE: *Fanfares for Massed Trumpets, Horns, and Trombones.*

COMPLETED: 12 January 1968.

DESCRIPTION: 1 MS score, 28 leaves, 27 x 34 cm.

NOTES: Holograph, in pencil. Accompanied by sketches (Jan. 9, 1968, 28pp.), schematics, letter from Sol Schoenbach to the composer, and letter to Sol Schoenbach (composer's draft).

PUBLISHED: Bryn Mawr, PA: TP.

SUBJECTS: 1. Rochberg, George—Manuscripts. 2. Brass Ensembles—Scores. 3. Fanfares.

CALL NUMBER: JPB 86-18, No. 23.

ITEM 62

TITLE: *Duo Concertante for Violin and Cello.*

COMPLETED: 28 May 1955.

DESCRIPTION: 1 MS score, 45pp., 20 x 24 cm.

NOTES: Holograph, in pencil.

PUBLISHED: Bryn Mawr, PA: TP, 1960.

SUBJECTS: 1. Rochberg, George—Manuscripts. 2. Violin and Violoncello music—Scores.

CALL NUMBER: JPB 86-18, No. 22.

ITEM 63

TITLE: *David, the Psalmist for Tenor Solo and Orchestra.*

COMPLETED: 21 July 1955.

DESCRIPTION: 1 MS score, 80pp., 32 cm.

NOTES: Holograph in pencil, with ink emendations. Hebrew words romanized. "Composed April 26 - July 21, 1955."

PUBLISHED: Bryn Mawr, PA: TP.

SUBJECTS: 1. Rochberg, George—Manuscripts. 2. Solo Cantatas, Sacred (High Voice)—Scores. 3. Psalms (Music).

OTHER HEADINGS: I. *David, the Psalmist.* II. *Shema Yisroel.*

CALL NUMBER: JPB 86-18, No. 21.

ITEM 64

TITLE: *Contra Mortem et Tempus for Flute, Clarinet, Violin, and Piano* (Sketches).

COMPLETED: 17 March 1965.

DESCRIPTION: 1 MS score, 31 leaves, 25 x 36 cm.

NOTES: Holograph sketches.

PUBLISHED: Bryn Mawr, PA: TP, 1967.

SUBJECTS: 1. Rochberg, George—Manuscripts.

CALL NUMBER: JPB 86-13, No. 20.

ITEM 65

TITLE: *Music for Oboe and String Trio* (Sketches).

COMPLETED: 05 December 1952.

DESCRIPTION: 1 MS score, 14pp. 32 cm.

NOTES: Holograph sketches.

SUBJECTS: 1. Rochberg, George—Manuscripts.

CALL NUMBER: JPB 86-18, No. 19.

ITEM 66

TITLE: *Chamber Symphony for Nine Instruments* (Sketches).

COMPLETED: 21 October 1953.

DESCRIPTION: 1 MS score, 250pp., 32-34 cm.

NOTES: Holograph sketches. Accompanied by sketches for a *String Quartet*, and a work for 2 pianos (2 leaves).

PUBLISHED: Bryn Mawr, PA: TP, 1978.
SUBJECTS: 1. Rochberg, George—Manuscripts.
CALL NUMBER: JPB 86-18, No. 18.

ITEM 67

AUTHOR: Scheidt, Samuel, 1587-1654. Transcribed by George Rochberg.
TITLE: *Cantio Sacra, Warum betrubst du dich, mein Herz.*
COMPLETED: 19 April 1953.
DESCRIPTION: 1 MS score, 84pp., 33 cm.
NOTES: Originally for organ. Rochberg's holograph, in pencil. Accompanied by 2 copies of the original music.
PUBLISHED: Philadelphia, PA: Fleischer Collection.
SUBJECTS: 1. Rochberg, George—Manuscripts. 2. Chamber Orchestra Music, Arranged—Scores.
OTHER HEADINGS: I. Rochberg, George. II. *Warum betrubst du duch, mein Herz?.*
CALL NUMBER: JPB 86-18, No. 17.

ITEM 68

TITLE: *Behold, My Servant (Everything that Lives Is Holy) for a cappella Mixed Chorus.*
COMPLETED: 07 August 1973.
DESCRIPTION: 1 MS score, 14pp., 27 x 34 cm.
NOTES: Holograph in pencil. Accompanied by sketches and texts (17pp.).
PUBLISHED: Bryn Mawr, PA: TP, 1974.
SUBJECTS: 1. Blake, William, 1757-1827—Musical Settings. 2. Rochberg, George—Manuscripts. 3. Choruses, Sacred (Mixed Voices, four-parts), Unaccompanied. 4. Psalms (Music).
OTHER HEADINGS: I. Blake, William, 1757-1827. II. *Everything that Lives Is Holy.*
CALL NUMBER: JPB 86-18, No. 16.

ITEM 69

TITLE: *La Bocca della Verità, Music for Oboe and Piano.*
COMPLETED: April 1959.

DESCRIPTION: 1 MS score, 31pp., 25 x 36 cm.

NOTES: Holograph signed, in pencil. Accompanied by 1 MS score (1 leaf) on transparent paper.

SUBJECTS: 1. Rochberg, George—Manuscripts. 2. Oboe and Piano music—Scores.

CALL NUMBER: JPB 86-18, No. 15.

ITEM 70

TITLE: *La Bocca della Verità, Music for Oboe and Piano.*

COMPLETED: April 1959.

DESCRIPTION: 1 MS score, 31pp., 25 x 36 cm.

NOTES: Holograph signed, in pencil. Accompanied by 1 MS score (1 leaf) on transparent paper.

SUBJECTS: 1. Rochberg, George—Manuscripts. 2. Oboe and Piano music—Scores.

CALL NUMBER: JPB 86-18, No. 15.

ITEM 71

TITLE: *Book of Songs, Ecce Puer.*

COMPLETED: 19 May 1957.

DESCRIPTION: 1 MS score, 7 leaves, 36 cm.

NOTES: Holograph, on transparent paper. "This version May 17-19, 1957, Mexico City."

SUBJECTS: 1. Joyce, James, 1882-1941—Musical Settings. 2. Rochberg, George—Manuscripts. 3. Songs (Low Voice) with Instrumental Ensemble—Scores.

OTHER HEADINGS: I. Joyce, James, 1882-1941. *Ecce puer.* II. *Ecce Puer.* III. *Behold the Child.*

CALL NUMBER: JPB 86-18, No. 14.

ITEM 72

TITLE: *Blake Songs, Tyger! Tyger!*

COMPLETED: 19 July 1957.

DESCRIPTION: 1 MS score, 31 leaves, 36 cm.

NOTES: Holograph, on transparent paper. "Mexico City, June 22-July 19, 1957."

SUBJECTS: 1. Blake, William, 1757-1827—Musical Settings. 2. Rochberg, George—Manuscripts. 3. Songs (Medium Voice) with Instrumental Ensemble—Scores.

OTHER HEADINGS: I. Blake, William, 1757-1827. *Songs of Innocence and Experience.* II. *Tyger! Tyger!*

CALL NUMBER: JPB 86-18, No. 13.

ITEM 73

TITLE: *Blake Songs, Tyger! Tyger!*

COMPLETED: 19 July 1957.

DESCRIPTION: 1 MS score, 44pp., 34 cm.

NOTES: Holograph signed, in pencil. "Mexico City, June 22-July 19, 1957."

SUBJECTS: 1. Blake, William, 1757-1827—Musical Settings. 2. Rochberg George—Manuscripts. 3. Songs (Medium Voice) with Instrumental Ensemble—Scores.

OTHER HEADINGS: I. Blake, William, 1757-1827. *Songs Innocence and Experience.* II. *Tyger! Tyger!*

CALL NUMBER: JPB 86-18, No. 10.

ITEM 74

TITLE: *Blake Songs, The Sick Rose.*

COMPLETED: 26 May 1957.

DESCRIPTION: 1 score, 15 leaves, 34 cm.

NOTES: Engraved copy. "May 26, 1957, Mexico City."

PUBLISHED: New York, NY: Leeds [MCA], 1963.

SUBJECTS: 1. Blake, William, 1757-1827—Musical Settings. 2. Songs (High Voice) with Instrumental Ensemble—Scores.

OTHER HEADINGS: I. Blake, William, 1757-1827. *Songs of Innocence and Experience.* II. *The Sick Rose.*

CALL NUMBER: JPB 86-18, No. 11.

ITEM 75

TITLE: *Blake Songs, The Sick Rose.*

COMPLETED: 26 May 1957.

DESCRIPTION: 1 MS score, 17pp., 34 cm.

NOTES: Holograph signed, in pencil. "May 26, 1957, Mexico City."

PUBLISHED: New York, NY: Leeds [MCA], 1963.

SUBJECTS: 1. Blake, William, 1757-1827—Musical Settings. 2. Rochberg, George—Manuscripts. 3. Songs (High Voice) with Instrumental Ensemble—Scores.

OTHER HEADINGS: I. Blake, William, 1757-1827. *Songs of Innocence and Experience.* II. *The Sick Rose.*

CALL NUMBER: JPB 86-18, No. 9.

ITEM 76

TITLE: *Blake Songs, The Fly.*

COMPLETED: 21 - 24 May 1957.

DESCRIPTION: 1 MS score, 18pp., 34 cm.

NOTES: Holograph signed, in pencil. "May 21-24, 1957, Mexico City."

PUBLISHED: New York, NY: Leeds [MCA], 1963.

SUBJECTS: 1. Blake, William, 1757-1827—Musical Settings. 2. Rochberg, George—anuscripts. 3. Songs (High Voice) with Instrumental Ensemble—Scores.

OTHER HEADINGS: I. Blake, William, 1757-1827. *Songs of Innocence and Experience.* II. *The Fly.*

CALL NUMBER: JPB 86-18, No. 8.

ITEM 77

TITLE: *Blake Songs, Nurse's Song.*

COMPLETED: 04 - 10 June 1957.

DESCRIPTION: 1 MS score, 15pp., 34 cm.

NOTES: Holograph signed, in pencil. "June 4-10, 1957, Mexico City, 2nd version."

PUBLISHED: New York, NY: Leeds [MCA], 1963.

SUBJECTS: 1. Blake, William, 1757-1827—Musical Settings. 2. Rochberg, George—Manuscripts. 3. Songs (High Voice) with Instrumental Ensemble—Scores.

OTHER HEADINGS: I. Blake, William, 1757-1827. *Songs of Innocence and Experience.* II. *Nurse's Song.*

CALL NUMBER: JPB 86-18, No. 7.

ITEM 78

TITLE: *Blake Songs, Ah! Sun-flower.*

COMPLETED: 04 July 1957.

DESCRIPTION: 1 MS score, 19pp., 34 cm.

NOTES: Holograph signed, in pencil. "June 15-24, 1957, Mexico City. Second version, touched-up, July 4, 1957."

SUBJECTS: 1. Blake, William, 1757-1827—Musical Settings. 2. Rochberg, George—Manuscripts. 3. Songs (High Voice) with Instrumental Ensemble—Scores.

OTHER HEADINGS: I. Blake, William, 1757-1827. *Songs of Innocence and Experience.* II. *Ah! Sun-flower.*

CALL NUMBER: JPB 86-18, No. 6.

ITEM 79

TITLE: *Blake Songs for Soprano and Chamber Ensemble.*

COMPLETED: 07 January 1961.

DESCRIPTION: 1 MS score, 58pp., 36 cm.

NOTES: Holograph signed, in pencil. "This notebook contains a setting of *Tyger! Tyger!*, never published or performed." Accompanied by sketch of *Ah! Sun-flower* (1 leaf) "Nov. 12, 1960."

PUBLISHED: New York, NY: Leeds [MCA], 1963.

SUBJECTS: 1. Blake, William, 1757-1827—Musical Settings. 2. Rochberg, George—Manuscripts. 3. Songs (High Voice) with Instrumental Ensemble—Scores.

OTHER HEADINGS: I. Blake, William, 1757-1827. *Songs of Innocence and Experience.* II. *Ah! Sun-flower.* III. *The Fly.* IV. *Tyger! Tyger!* V. *Nurse's Song.* VI. *The Sick Rose.*

CALL NUMBER: JPB 86-18, No. 5.

ITEM 80

TITLE: *Black Sounds (Apocalyptica II) for Small Orchestra.*

COMPLETED: 19 June 1965.

DESCRIPTION: 1 MS score, 85pp., 27 x 34 cm.

NOTES: Holograph signed, in pencil. Accompanied by sketches (46 pp., 22 x 28 cm.), and typewritten scenario (photocopy) titled *"Far Rockaway"* (12 leaves, 28 cm.).

SUBJECTS: 1. Rochberg, George—Manuscripts. 2. Ballets—Scores.

OTHER HEADINGS: I. Sokolow, Anna. *The Act.* II. *The Act* (Television program).

CALL NUMBER: JPB 86-18, No. 4.

ITEM 81

TITLE: *Ballade for Piano Solo.*

COMPLETED: January 1939.

DESCRIPTION: 3pp. of MS, 32 cm.

NOTES: Holograph, in ink.

SUBJECTS: 1. Rochberg, George—Manuscripts. 2. Piano Music.

CALL NUMBER: JPB 86-18, No. 3.

ITEM 82

TITLE: *Twelve Bagatelles for Piano Solo.*

COMPLETED: 19 September 1952.

DESCRIPTION: 50pp. of MS, 32 cm.

NOTES: Holograph signed, in pencil. Includes emendations. Accompanied by tone row (1 leaf). "*Paul's Marching Song* 11/28/52." "Completed Sept. 19 on the eve of Gene's birthday, Rosh Hashana."

PUBLISHED: Bryn Mawr, PA: TP, 1955.

SUBJECTS: 1. Rochberg, George—Manuscripts. 2. Piano Music.

OTHER HEADINGS: I. Rochberg, Paul, 1944-1964. *Marching Song.*

CALL NUMBER: JPB 86-18, No. 2.

ITEM 83

TITLE: *Apocalyptica [I] for Wind Ensemble.*

COMPLETED: 22 July 1964.

DESCRIPTION: 1 MS score, 128pp., 34 cm.

NOTES: Holograph signed, in pencil. Performance instructions (7 pp.) laid in. Accompanied by sketches for the percussion set-up (4 leaves).

PUBLISHED: Bryn Mawr, PA: TP, 1966.

SUBJECTS: 1. Rochberg, George—Manuscripts. 2. Band Music—Scores.

CALL NUMBER: JPB 86-18, No. 1.

ITEM 84

TITLE: *Sonata-Fantasia for Piano Solo.*

PUBLISHED: Bryn Mawr, PA: TP, 1958.

DESCRIPTION: 32pp. of MS, 30 cm.

NOTES: "Newtown Square, July 19 - October 30, 1956."

SUBJECTS: 1. Sonatas (Piano).

CALL NUMBER: AMC M25 R696 F6, No. 1-2.

ITEM 85

TITLE: *Trio for Violin, Cello, and Piano.*

PUBLISHED: Bryn Mawr, PA: TP, ca. 1986.

DESCRIPTION: 1 score, 74pp., 31 cm.

SUBJECTS: 1. Piano Trios—Scores.

OTHER HEADINGS: I. Library of Congress. Elizabeth Sprague Coolidge Foundation.

CALL NUMBER: JNG 87-57.

ITEM 86

TITLE: *Introduction and Rondo for String Orchestra.*

COMPLETED: 1942.

DESCRIPTION: 1 MS score, 18pp., 27 x 35 cm.

NOTES: Holograph, signed. "Completed March 23, 1942; New York City."

SUBJECTS: 1. Rochberg, George—Manuscripts. 2. String Orchestra Music—Scores.

CALL NUMBER: JPB 82-61.

ITEM 87

TITLE: *Four Short Sonatas for Piano Solo.*

PUBLISHED: Bryn Mawr, PA: TP, ca. 1986.

DESCRIPTION: 20 pp of MS, 31 cm.

SUBJECTS: 1. Sonatas (Piano).

CALL NUMBER: AMC M23 R672 S5.

ITEM 88

TITLE: *Carnival Music, Suite for Piano Solo.*
PUBLISHED: Bryn Mawr, PA: TP, ca. 1975.
DESCRIPTION: 39pp., 31 cm.
SUBJECTS: 1. Suites (Piano).
CALL NUMBER: JNG 76-146.
CALL NUMBER: AMC M24 R672 C2.

ITEM 89

TITLE: *Quintet for String Quintet.*
PUBLISHED: Bryn Mawr, PA: TP, ca. 1983.
DESCRIPTION: 1 score, 92pp., 31 cm.
NOTES: Publisher's No.: 114-40297.
SUBJECTS: 1. String Quintets—Scores.
CALL NUMBER: AMC M552 R672 O7.
CALL NUMBER: JNG 85-231.

ITEM 90

TITLE: *Quintet for String Quintet.*
COMPLETED: 1981.
CALL NUMBER: JPB 82-69.

ITEM 91

TITLE: *Trio for Horn, Clarinet, and Piano.*
PUBLISHED: Bryn Mawr, PA: TP, ca. 1981.
CALL NUMBER: AMC M317 R672 T8.
CALL NUMBER: JNG 85-137.

ITEM 92

AUTHOR: Esherick, Wharton.
TITLE: *Drawings by Wharton Esherick,* compiled, edited, and with an introduction by Gene Rochberg.
PUBLISHED: New York, NY: Van Nostrand Reinhold, ca. 1978.
CALL NUMBER: 3-MGO (Esherick) 79-1548.

ITEM 93

AUTHOR: Csikszentmihalyi, Mihaly and Eugene Rochberg-Halton.

TITLE: *The Meaning of Things: Domestic Symbols and the Self.*

PUBLISHED: Cambridge, England: Cambridge University Press, 1981.

CALL NUMBER: JFE 81-2724.

ITEM 94

AUTHOR: Rochberg, Gene.

TITLE: *The Confidence Man, An Opera in Two Parts (Libretto).*

PUBLISHED: Bryn Mawr, PA: TP, ca. 1982.

CALL NUMBER: JNF 82-135.

ITEM 95

AUTHOR: Rochberg, George.

TITLE: *The Aesthetics of Survival: A Composer's View of Twentieth-Century Music,* edited and with an introduction by William Bolcom.

PUBLISHED: Ann Arbor, MI: University of Michigan Press, ca. 1984.

CALL NUMBER: JME 84-181.

ITEM 96

AUTHOR: San Francisco Contemporary Music Players.

TITLE: *The San Francisco Contemporary Music Players* (Sound recording).

PUBLISHED: New York, NY: Grenadilla Enterprises, ca. 1982.

CALL NUMBER: LSRX 13838 (C).

ITEM 97

TITLE: *Waltz Serenade for Orchestra* (Sound recording).

CALL NUMBER: LTK-7 37.

ITEM 98

TITLE: *Symphony No. 1 for Orchestra* (Sound recording).

CALL NUMBER: LTK-7 36.

ITEM 99

TITLE: *Symphony No. 2 for Orchestra* (Sound recording).
CALL NUMBER: LTK-7 113.

ITEM 100

TITLE: *Three Sides of George Rochberg* (Sound recording).
PUBLISHED: New York, NY: Grenadilla Records, ca. 1977.
CALL NUMBER: LSRX 4665.

ITEM 101

TITLE: *Caprice Variations for Unaccompanied Violin* (Sound recording).
PUBLISHED: New York, NY: Musical Heritage Society MHS 3719, 1978.
CALL NUMBER: LSRX 4062.

ITEM 102

TITLE: *Eleven Songs for Mezzo-Soprano and Piano.*
PUBLISHED: Bryn Mawr, PA: TP, 1973.
CALL NUMBER: AMC M1621 R672 S6 1973.

ITEM 103

TITLE: *Ukiyo-e (Pictures of the Floating World) for Solo Harp.*
PUBLISHED: Bryn Mawr, PA: TP, ca. 1976.
CALL NUMBER: JNG 76-487.

ITEM 104

TITLE: *Twelve Bagatelles for Piano Solo.*
PUBLISHED: Bryn Mawr, PA: TP, ca. 1955.
CALL NUMBER: AMC M25 R672 B2.

ITEM 105

TITLE: *Sonata for Viola and Piano.*
PUBLISHED: Bryn Mawr, PA: TP, ca. 1979.
CALL NUMBER: AMC M226 R672 S6.
CALL NUMBER: JNG 83-71.

ITEM 106

TITLE: *Duo for Oboe and Bassoon.*
PUBLISHED: Bryn Mawr, PA: TP, ca. 1980.
CALL NUMBER: AMC M289 R673 D8.
CALL NUMBER: JNG 83-91.

ITEM 107

TITLE: *String Quartet No. 4.*
PUBLISHED: Bryn Mawr, PA: TP, ca. 1979.
CALL NUMBER: JNG 81-251.

ITEM 108

TITLE: *Slow Fires of Autumn (Ukiyo-e III) for Flute and Harp.*
PUBLISHED: Bryn Mawr, PA: TP, 1980.
CALL NUMBER: JNG 82-283.
CALL NUMBER: AMC M297 R672 S6.

ITEM 109

TITLE: *Trio [No. 1] for Violin, Cello, and Piano* (Sketches).
COMPLETED: 1963.
CALL NUMBER: JPB 82-73.

ITEM 110

TITLE: *Time-Span [II] for Orchestra.*
COMPLETED: 1960.
CALL NUMBER: JPB 82-72.

ITEM 111

TITLE: *Songs in Praise of Krishna for Soprano and Piano* (Sketches).
COMPLETED: September 1970.
CALL NUMBER: JPB 82-71.

ITEM 112

TITLE: *Quintet for String Quintet* (Sketches).
COMPLETED: 1981.
CALL NUMBER: JPB 82-70.

ITEM 113

TITLE: *String Quartet No. 5* (Sketches).

COMPLETED: 1978.

CALL NUMBER: JPB 82-67.

ITEM 114

TITLE: *String Quartet No. 6* (Sketches).

COMPLETED: 1978.

CALL NUMBER: JPB 82-68.

ITEM 115

TITLE: *String Quartet No. 4* (Sketches).

COMPLETED: 1977.

CALL NUMBER: JPB 82-66.

ITEM 116

TITLE: *String Quartet No. 2* (Sketches).

COMPLETED: 1960.

CALL NUMBER: JPB 82-65.

ITEM 117

TITLE: *Oboe-Piano Music.*

COMPLETED: 19—.

CALL NUMBER: JPB 82-64.

ITEM 118

TITLE: *Octet, A Grand Fantasia for Flute, Clarinet, Horn, Violin, Viola, Cello, Bass, and Piano.*

COMPLETED: 1980.

CALL NUMBER: JPB 82-63.

ITEM 119

TITLE: *Music for the Magic Theater for Small Orchestra.*

COMPLETED: 1965.

CALL NUMBER: JPB 82-62.

ITEM 120

TITLE: *The Confidence Man, An Opera in Two Parts (Prologue, Act I) (Vocal Score).*

COMPLETED: 1980.
CALL NUMBER: JPB 82-60.

ITEM 121

AUTHOR: Rochberg, Gene.
TITLE: *The Confidence Man, An Opera in Two Parts (Libretto).*
COMPLETED: 1980.
CALL NUMBER: JPB 82-59.

ITEM 122

TITLE: *Concerto for Violin and Orchestra.*
COMPLETED: 1974.
CALL NUMBER: JPB 82-58.

ITEM 123

TITLE: *Songs in Praise for Krishna for Soprano and Piano.*
PUBLISHED: Bryn Mawr, PA: TP, ca. 1981.
CALL NUMBER: JNG 81-390.
CALL NUMBER: AMC M1621 R672 S6.

ITEM 124

TITLE: *The Confidence Man, An Opera in Two Parts (Vocal Score).*
PUBLISHED: Bryn Mawr, PA: TP, ca. 1982.
CALL NUMBER: AMC M1503 R672 C7.

ITEM 125

TITLE: *Quintet for Piano and String Quartet.*
PUBLISHED: Bryn Mawr, PA: TP, 1975.
CALL NUMBER: AMC M512 R672.

ITEM 126

TITLE: *Chamber Symphony for Nine Instruments.*
PUBLISHED: Bryn Mawr, PA: TP, ca. 1978.
CALL NUMBER: JNG 81-45.

ITEM 127

TITLE: *Partita-Variations for Piano Solo.*
PUBLISHED: Bryn Mawr, PA: TP, ca. 1977.

ITEM 128

TITLE: *String Quartet No. 5.*
PUBLISHED: Bryn Mawr, PA: TP, ca. 1979.

ITEM 129

TITLE: *String Quartet No. 6.*
PUBLISHED: Bryn Mawr, PA: TP, ca. 1979.

ITEM 130

TITLE: *Music for the Magic Theater for a Chamber Ensemble of Fifteen Players.*
PUBLISHED: Bryn Mawr, PA: TP, 1972.

ITEM 131

TITLE: *Zodiac for Orchestra.*
PUBLISHED: Bryn Mawr, PA: TP, ca. 1974.

ITEM 132

TITLE: *Music for the Magic Theater for Small Orchestra.*
COMPLETED: 1965.

ITEM 133

TITLE: *Concerto for Violin and Orchestra (Piano reduction).*
PUBLISHED: Bryn Mawr, PA: TP, ca. 1977.

ITEM 134

TITLE: *David, the Psalmist for Tenor and Orchestra.*
COMPLETED: 1954.

ITEM 135
>   TITLE: *Imago Mundi for Large Orchestra.*
>   COMPLETED: 1973.
>   CALL NUMBER: AMC M1045 R672I3.

ITEM 136
>   TITLE: *Transcendental Variations for String Orchestra.*
>   PUBLISHED: New York, NY: Galaxy Music Corp., ca. 1977.
>   CALL NUMBER: JNG 79-77.

ITEM 137
>   TITLE: *Symphony No. 2 for Orchestra.*
>   PUBLISHED: Bryn Mawr, PA: TP, ca. 1958.
>   CALL NUMBER: AMC M1001 R672, No. 2.

ITEM 138
>   TITLE: *Phaedra, A Monodrama for Mezzo-Soprano and Orchestra.*
>   COMPLETED: 1974.
>   CALL NUMBER: AMC M1613 R672P6.

ITEM 139
>   TITLE: *Concerto for Violin and Orchestra (Piano reduction).*
>   PUBLISHED: Bryn Mawr, PA: TP, ca. 1977.
>   CALL NUMBER: JNG 79-132.

ITEM 140
>   TITLE: *Night Music for Orchestra.*
>   COMPLETED: 1949.
>   CALL NUMBER: JNH 79-6.

ITEM 141
>   TITLE: *String Quartet No. 3.*
>   PUBLISHED: New York, NY: Galaxy Music Corp., ca. 1976.
>   CALL NUMBER: JNG 76-307.

ITEM 142
>   TITLE: *Fantasies for Voice and Piano.*
>   PUBLISHED: Bryn Mawr, PA: TP, ca. 1975.

ITEM 143

TITLE: *Zodiac for Orchestra.*
PUBLISHED: Bryn Mawr, PA: TP, ca. 1974.

ITEM 144

TITLE: *Four Songs of Solomon for Voice and Piano.*
PUBLISHED: Bryn Mawr, PA: TP, ca. 1949.

ITEM 145

TITLE: *Caprice Variations for Unaccompanied Violin.*
PUBLISHED: New York, NY: Galaxy Music Corp., 1973.

ITEM 146

TITLE: *Contra Mortem et Tempus, for Flute, Clarinet, Violin, and Piano.*
PUBLISHED: Bryn Mawr, PA: TP, ca. 1967.

ITEM 147

TITLE: *Ricordanza (Soliloquy) for Cello and Piano.*
PUBLISHED: Bryn Mawr, PA: TP, 1974.

ITEM 148

TITLE: *Tableaux (Sound Pictures from The Silver Talons of Piero Kostrov, by Paul Rochberg), for Soprano, Two Actors' Voices, Small Mens' Chorus, and Twelve Players.*
PUBLISHED: Bryn Mawr, PA: TP, ca. 1972.

ITEM 149

TITLE: *Music for the Magic Theater, for a Chamber Ensemble of Fifteen Players.*
PUBLISHED: Bryn Mawr, PA: TP, 1972.

ITEM 150

TITLE: *Two Songs from "Tableaux" [for Soprano and Piano]*.
PUBLISHED: Bryn Mawr, PA: TP, 1971.

ITEM 151

TITLE: *Apocalyptica [I] for Wind Ensemble*.
PUBLISHED: Bryn Mawr, PA: TP, ca. 1966.

VI. ORIGINAL MANUSCRIPTS AND DOCUMENTS HOUSED AT HARVARD UNIVERSITY, HOUGHTON LIBRARY, HANS MOLDENHAUER COLLECTION

[*Author's note*] Manuscript/document descriptions are those of Hans Moldenhauer and have been provided by Harvard University (Houghton LIbrary).

Concerto for Oboe and Orchestra

Dated 1983. Document signed. Piano reduction. Blueprint score with autograph corrections in red ink and pencil. 27 (26) pp. 33.5 x 28 cm. Spiral bound. Oboe part. Document. Blueprint, with autograph corrections in red ink and pencil. 10 (9) pp. 33 x 25.5 cm.

Partita Variations for Piano Solo

Dated 1967. Sketches, 92 pp. (85 pp. 28 x 38 cm.; 7 pp. various sizes.)

Phaedra, a Monodrama in Seven Scenes for Mezzo-Soprano and Orchestra

Document signed. Blueprint of the full score, with autograph dedication. 272 pp. 38 x 29 cm. Also autograph page giving title, instrumentation, and other details of the score.

Quartet for Piano, Violin, Viola, and Cello

Dated 1983. Document. Printer's proofs with autograph corrections in red ink. 62 pp. 35 x 28 and 28 x 21.5 cm.

String Quartet No. 2 with Soprano

Dated 1961. Autograph manuscript. Full score. 101 pp. 35.5 x 26.5 cm.

String Quartet No. 2 with Soprano

Autograph manuscript. Sketches. 218 pp. Various sizes, plus 2 pages of the Rilke text used within the work. 28 x 21.5 cm.

String Quartet No. 3

Dated 1972. Autograph manuscript. Complete draft. 230 pp. 28 x 38.5 cm.

String Quartet No. 3

Autograph manuscript. Miscellaneous sketches. 70 pp. 28 x 38.5 cm. plus 3 p. 33 x 22 cm.

Symphony No. 1 fort Orchestra

Document signed. Full score, blueprint, with ink and pencil corrections. Four movements. 273 pp. 43 x 30 and 34.5 x 27 cm. Bound in cloth.

Symphony No. 1 for Orchestra

Autograph manuscript. Third movement, *Capriccio*. Master sheets of miscellaneous wind parts. 95 pp. 32 x 34 cm.

Symphony No. 1 for Orchestra

Dated 1949-1955. Document signed. First and second movements. Full score. Blueprint, with autograph corrections and a prefatory page of instructions to the printer. 90 pp. 44.5 x 32 cm. Spiral bound.

Symphony No. 1 for Orchestra

Dated 1948-1957. Document. Third movement, *Capriccio*. Full score, blueprint, with autographed corrections. 81 pp. 44.5 x 32 cm. Spiral bound.

Symphony No. 4 for Large Orchestra

Dated 1976. Autograph manuscript. For orchestra, sketches for all three movements (mvts. I and III condensed score; mvt. II full score). 199 pp. (157 pp. 28 x 38 cm.; 12 pp. various sizes) (Sketches to the second movement kept with blueprint of the *Waltz Serenade*).

Symphony No. 5 for Orchestra

Dated 1984. Autograph manuscript. "Rough sketches" (Rochberg). In pencil, with several dates, beginning April, and compositional concepts. 157 pp. 28 x 38.5 cm.

Symphony No. 5 for Orchestra

Dated 1984. Autograph manuscript. Pencil sketches. Full score. On closing page: "Laus Deo, Oct. 10, 1984. Newtown Square, PA." 140 pp. 28 x 38.5 cm.

Waltz Serenade for Orchestra

Dated 1957. Document. Blueprint score, with many changes and additions. 50 pp. 56 x 32 cm.

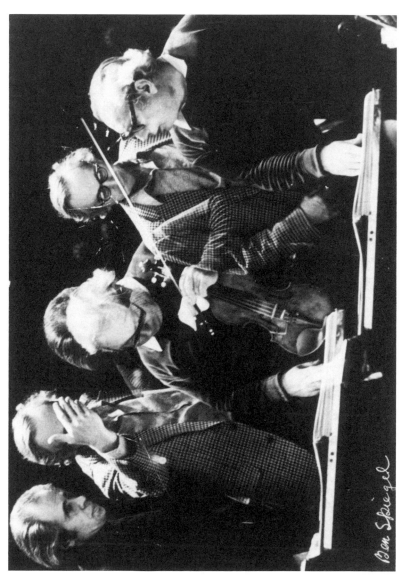

Plate 12: [L to R] David Johanes, George Rochberg, and Isaac Stern at a rehearsal of the *Concerto for Violin and Orchestra* (04 April 1975).

VII. ORIGINAL MANUSCRIPTS AND DOCUMENTS HOUSED AT THEODORE PRESSER COMPANY

Apocalyptica [I] for Large Wind Ensemble

Arioso for Piano Solo

Bartokiana for Piano Solo

Behold, My Servant (Everything That Lives Is Holy) for a cappella Mixed Chorus

Between Two Worlds (Ukiyo-e III) Five Images for Flute and Piano

Black Sounds (Apocalyptica II) for Seventeen Winds

La Bocca della Veritá, Music for Oboe and Piano

La Bocca della Veritá, Music for Violin and Piano

Book of Contrapuntal Pieces for Keyboard Instruments

Book of Songs for Voice and Piano

Cantes Flamencos for High Baritone

Cantio Sacra for Chamber Orchestra

Carnival Music, Suite for Piano Solo

Chamber Symphony for Nine Instruments

Cheltenham Concerto for Small Orchestra

Concerto for Oboe and Orchestra
    Full-score.

Concerto for Oboe and Orchestra
    Piano Reduction.

Concerto for Violin and Orchestra

Full-score.

Concerto for Violin and Orchestra
Piano Reduction.

The Confidence Man (A Comic Fable), Opera in Two Parts

Contra Mortem et Tempus for Flute, Clarinet, Violin, and Piano

David, the Psalmist, for Tenor Solo and Orchestra
Full-score.

David, the Psalmist for Tenor Solo and Orchestra
Piano Reduction.

Dialogues for Clarinet and Piano

Duo for Oboe and Bassoon.

Duo Concertante for Violin and Cello

Electrikaleidoscope for Amplified Flute, Clarinet, Violin, Cello, Piano, and Electric Piano

Eleven Songs for Mezzo-Soprano and Piano

Fanfares for Massed Trumpets, Horns, and Trombones

Fantasies for Voice and Piano

Four Short Sonatas for Piano Solo

Four Songs of Solomon for Voice and Piano

Imago Mundi (Image of the World) for Large Orchestra

Music for "The Alchemist" for Soprano and Eleven Players

Music for the Magic Theater for a Chamber Ensemble of Fifteen Players
Original version.

Music for the Magic Theater for Small Orchestra
Orchestral version.

Nach Bach, Fantasy for Harpsichord or Piano

Night Music for Orchestra

Notes on Chromaticism

Text. Unpublished (1971) 77pp.

Octet, A Grand Fantasia for Flute, Clarinet, Horn, Violin, Viola, Cello, Bass, and Piano

Partita-Variations for Piano Solo

Phaedra, Monodrama for Mezzo-Soprano and Orchestra
Full-score.

Phaedra, Monodrama for Mezzo-Soprano and Orchestra
Piano Reduction.

Prelude on "Happy Birthday" for Almost Two Pianos

Quartet for Piano, Violin, Viola, and Cello

Quintet for Piano and String Quartet

Quintet for String Quintet

Ricordanza (Soliloquy) for Cello and Piano ·

Sacred Song of Reconciliation (Mizmur l'Piyus) for Bass-Baritone and Small Orchestra

Slow Fires of Autumn (Ukiyo-e II) for Flute and Harp

Sonata for Viola and Piano

Sonata for Violin and Piano

Sonata-Fantasia for Piano Solo

Songs in Praise of Krishna for Soprano and Piano

Songs of Inanna and Dumuzi for Contralto and Piano

String Quartet No. 1

String Quartet No. 2 with Soprano

String Quartet No. 4, "The Concord Quartets"

String Quartet No. 5, "The Concord Quartets"

String Quartet No. 6, "The Concord Quartets"

String Quartet No. 7 with Baritone

Suite No. 1 (Based on the Opera The Confidence Man) for Large Orchestra

Suite No. 2 (Based on the Opera The Confidence Man) for Solo Voices, Chorus, and Orchestra

Symphony No. 1 for Orchestra
Three-movement version.

Symphony No. 1 for Orchestra
Five-movement version.

Symphony No. 2 for Orchestra

Symphony No. 3 for Vocal Soloists, Chamber Chorus, Double Chorus, and Large Orchestra

Symphony No. 4 for Large Orchestra

Symphony No. 5 for Orchestra

Symphony No. 6 for Orchestra

Tableaux (Sound Pictures from the "Silver Talons of Piero Kostrov," by Paul Rochberg) for Soprano, Two Actors' Voices, Small Mens' Chorus, and Twelve Players

Three Cadenzas for Mozart's Concerto for Oboe, K. 314

Three Commentaries
Text. Unpublished (1978) 21pp.

Three Psalms for a cappella Mixed Chorus

To the Dark Wood, Music for Woodwind Quintet

Trio for Clarinet, Horn, and Piano

Trio [No. 1] for Violin, Cello, and Piano

Trio [No. 2] for Violin, Cello, and Piano

Twelve Bagatelles for Piano Solo

Two Preludes and Fughettas from the Book of Contrapuntal Pieces for Keyboard Instruments

Two Songs from "Tableaux" [for Soprano and Piano]

Ukiyo-e (Pictures of the Floating World) for Solo Harp

Zodiac for Orchestra

BIBLIOGRAPHY

EDITORIAL PRINCIPLES

The entries in the first section of the BIBLIOGRAPHY entitled GENERAL BIBLIOGRAPHY, have been selected because they deal with the work and interests of George Rochberg from a wide perspective. They have been organized alphabetically by author's last name. The second section, entitled BIBLIOGRAPHY BY SUBJECT contains articles, reviews, and other m,aterials dealing with a specific work and is organized (1) alphabetically by title of the work, and then (2) alphabetically by author's last name.

All bibliographic entries are annotated and include descriptions as to the:

(1) TYPE [of article], *e.g.*, review, record review, score review, article (general), analysis, interview [with George or Gene Rochberg], interview [with someone other than the Rochbergs], upcoming première, upcoming performance(s), abstract, announcement of award, or letter to the editor;

(2) PERFORMERS participating in the performance being discussed;

(3) NAMES of all composers, authors, and musicians mentioned in the article (performers excluded);

(4) OTHER WORKS [by Rochberg] DISCUSSED in the same article;

(5) OTHER WORKS [by Rochberg] MENTIONED briefly in the same article but not discussed.

GENERAL BIBLIOGRAPHY

n.a. *"The Aesthetics of Survival*: Schriften des amerikanischen Komponisten George Rochberg," *Neue Zurcher Zeitung [Zurich]* 1 (03 January 1986) 33.

TYPE: review.

NAMES: Bolcom.

BOOKS DISCUSSED: *The Aesthetics of Survival.*

Blaustein, Susan. "The Survival of Aesthetics: Books by Boulez, DeLio, Rochberg," *Perspectives of New Music* XXVII/1 (Winter 1989) 272-303.

TYPE: article, review.

WORKS DISCUSSED: *String Quartet No. 3, String Quartet No. 4, String Quartet No. 5, String Quartet No. 6.*

BOOKS DISCUSSED: *The Aesthetics of Survival.*

Block, Steven D. "George Rochberg—Progressive or Master Forger?" *Perspectives of New Music* XXI/1-2 (Fall-Winter 1982/Spring-Summer 1983) 407-409.

TYPE: article.

NAMES: many.

WORKS DISCUSSED: *String Quartet No. 3, String Quartet No. 4, String Quartet No. 5, String Quartet No. 6.*

Boehm, Yohanan. "Tonalities and Textures," *The Jerusalem Post Magazine* (05 November 1982).

TYPE: article, review, record review, interview.

WORKS DISCUSSED: *Concerto for Violin and Orchestra, The Confidence Man, Sacred Song of Reconciliation.*

Bookspan, Martin. "Mozart's *Clarinet Quintet*," *Stereo Review* (October 1975) 46.

TYPE: record review.

Boyd, Karen Kumler. "Composer Award Concert March 1, 2: Symphony Honors George Rochberg," *New Era [Lancaster, PA]* (17 February 1986) 23, 24.

TYPE: article, announcement of award, interview.

WORKS DISCUSSED: *Imago Mundi, Symphony No. 2.*

Boyd, Karen Kumler. "Plus Two Local Soloists: Works by Haydn, and Strauss at Symphony's Next Concert," *New Era [Lancaster, PA]* (17 February 1986) 24.

TYPE: article, announcement of award, interview.

WORKS DISCUSSED: *Imago Mundi.*

Burge, David. "Contemporary Piano: Repertoire, Part II," *Contemporary Keyboard* (March–April 1976) 44.

TYPE: article.

WORKS DISCUSSED: *Sonata-Fantasia.*

Burge, David. *Twentieth-Century Piano Music.* (New York, NY: Schirmer, Forthcoming).

Carlson, Effie B. *A Bio-Bibliographical Dictionary of Twelve-Tone and Serial Composers.* (Metuchen, NJ: Scarecrow Press, Inc., 1970) 149-151.

TYPE: article, bibliography.

NAMES: Schönberg, Webern.

WORKS DISCUSSED: *Sonata-Fantasia, Symphony No. 1, Twelve Bagatelles.*

BOOKS DISCUSSED: *The Hexachord and Its Relation to the Twelve-Tone Row.*

n.a. "C-CM [Cincinnati College-Conservatory of Music] Books Music Exposition," *Cincinnati Post* (14 April 1965).

TYPE: residency.

Clarkson, Austin. "Rochberg, George," *New Grove Dictionary of Music and Musicians,* ed. Stanley Sadie. (London: Macmillian, 1980) XVI, 80-81.

TYPE: biography.

NAMES: many.

WORKS DISCUSSED: many.

Commanday, Robert Paul. "Graffitti on the Taj Mahal," *American Musical Digest* I (December 1969) 8-10.

TYPE: article.

NAMES: Eugene Ormandy.

n.a. "Composer Honored (Brandeis Creative Arts Award)," *Musical Opinion* CVIII/1294 (September 1985) 339.

TYPE: announcement of award.

WORKS DISCUSSED: *Symphony No. 5, Trio [No. 2] for Violin, Cello, and Piano.*

n.a. "Correspondencia entre Lan Adomian y George Rochberg, una polemica," *Heterofonia* XIV/73 (1981) 22-26.

TYPE: letters.

Custer, Arthur. "Current Chronicle: Philadelphia," *Musical Quarterly* LIII/2 (April 1967) 251.

TYPE: article.

Danuser, Hermann. "Zur Kritik der musikalischen Postmoderne," *Neue Zeitschrift fur Musik* CXLIX/12 (December 1988) 4-9.

TYPE: article, analysis.

WORKS DISCUSSED: *Contra Mortem et Tempus, Music for the Magic Theater, Quintet for Piano and String Quartet, String Quartet No. 2, String Quartet No. 3, Trio [No. 1] for Violin, Cello, and Piano.*

BOOKS DISCUSSED: *The Aesthetics of Survival.*

Darling, Henry R. "New Courses and Twelve-Tone Composition Put Zip in Penn's Music Department," *The Sunday Bulletin [Philadelphia]* (30 September 1962) 15.

TYPE: article, interview.

WORKS DISCUSSED: *Night Music, Symphony No. 1.*

WORKS MENTIONED: *Chamber Symphony, String Quartet No. 1, String Quartet No. 2, Time Span, Twelve Bagtelles.*

Drone, Jeanette. "George Rochberg," *Pan Pipes of Sigma Alpha Iota* LXXIII/2 (Winter 1981) 41.

TYPE: announcement of premières, performances, commissions, awards.

WORKS DISCUSSED: *The Confidence Man, Quintet for Piano and String Quartet, Slow Fires of Autumn, Sonata for Viola and Piano, String Quartet No. 4, String Quartet No. 5, String Quartet No. 6, String Quartet No. 7.*

Drone, Jeanette. "George Rochberg," *Pan Pipes of Sigma Alpha Iota* LXXIV/2 (Winter 1982) 41.

TYPE: announcement of premières, performances, publications, recordings, commissions, residencies.

WORKS DISCUSSED: *The Confidence Man, Imago Mundi, Phaedra, Quintet for Piano and String Quartet, Quintet for String Quintet, Song in Praise of Krishna, String Quartet No. 4, String Quartet No. 5, String Quartet No. 6, String Quartet No. 7, Symphony No. 4, Trio for Clarinet, Horn, and Piano.*

Drone, Jeanette. "George Rochberg," *Pan Pipes of Sigma Alpha Iota* LXXV/2 (Winter 1983) 39.

TYPE: announcement of performances, publications, recordings, commissions, residencies.

WORKS DISCUSSED: *Concerto for Oboe and Orchestra, Concerto for Violin and Orchestra, String Quartet No. 7.*
BOOKS DISCUSSED: *The Aesthetics of Survival.*

Dufallo, Richard. *Conversations with Composers.* (London: Oxford University Press, Forthcoming).
TYPE: interview.

Eckert, Thor Jr. "The Sovering Seventies: The Arts: Beyond Reviews and Revenues," *The Christian Science Monitor* (02 January 1980) 13-14.
TYPE: article.

n.a. Eighteen Grants Awarded by Institute of Arts and Letters," *The New York Times* (04 May 1962) 22.
TYPE: announcement of National Institute of Arts & Letters Grants.

Ewen, David, ed. *Composers Since 1900: A Biographical Critical Guide: First Supplement.* (New York, NY: The H. W. Wilson Company, 1981) 235-241.
TYPE: biography.
NAMES: many.
WORKS DISCUSSED: many.

Felton, James. "Composers Are Sane But the World Isn't, Says Penn [University of Pennsylvania at Philadelphia] Rochberg," *The Sunday Bulletin [Philadelphia]* (13 February 1966) 11.
TYPE: article, interview.
NAMES: many.
WORKS DISCUSSED: *Contra Mortem et Tempus, Music for the Magic Theater, Night Music, String Quartet No. 2, Symphony No. 1, Symphony No. 2, Symphony No. 3, Zodiac.*

Felton, James. "Music Beat: Rochberg Composing Opera; Wife Is Librettist," *The Sunday Bulletin [Philadelphia]* (16 July 1978) 2-EA.
TYPE: article, interview, upcoming performance.
WORKS DISCUSSED: *Caprice Varations, Concerto for Violin and Orchestra, Phaedra, String Quartet No. 4, String Quartet No. 5, String Quartet No. 6.*

Fogel, Henry. "George Rochberg: A Rapproachment with the Past," *Syracuse Guide* V (January 1976) 24-26, 42.
TYPE: article.
NAMES: many.

WORKS DISCUSSED: *Concerto for Violin and Orchestra, Phaedra, String Quartet No. 3, Symphony No. 3.*

Fogel, Henry. "A Conversation with George Rochberg," *Syracuse Guide* (March 1976) 27-28, 36.

TYPE: interview.

NAMES: many.

WORKS DISCUSSED: *Phaedra, String Quartet No. 3.*

Foss, Lukas. "Contemporary Music Observations from Those Who Create It," *Music and Artists* V/3 (June–July 1972) 13.

TYPE: interview.

n.a. "$407,276 in Grants to Go to Composers," *The New York Times* (11 February 1974) I, 46.

TYPE: announcement of National Endowment for the Arts awards.

WORKS DISCUSSED: *Imago Mundi, Phaedra.*

Freedman, Guy. "Metamorphosis of a Twentieth-Century Composer," *Music Journal* XXXIV/3 (March 1976) 12-13, 38.

TYPE: interview.

NAMES: many.

WORKS DISCUSSED: *Quintet for Piano and String Quartet, Symphony No. 3.*

Frumpkin, Cary. "Interlake Profiles," Radio interview with George Rochberg. (WFMT-FM, Chicago, IL: 04 December 1980).

TYPE: taped interview.

NAMES: many.

WORKS DISCUSSED: many.

Gagne, Cole and Tracy Caras. *Soundpieces: Interviews with American Composers.* (Metuchen, NJ: Scarecrow Press, Inc., 1982) 337-354.

TYPE: interview.

NAMES: many.

WORKS DISCUSSED: many.

n.a. "George Rochberg," *Composers of the Americas* X (1964) 85-90.

TYPE: biography.

NAMES: many.

WORKS DISCUSSED: many.

n.a. "George Rochberg," *Pan Pipes of Sigma Alpha Iota* LXVIII/2 (January 1976) 70.

TYPE: announcement of premières and performances.

WORKS DISCUSSED: *La Bocca della Verità, Concerto for Violin and Orchestra, Phaedra.*

n.a. "George Rochberg," *Pan Pipes of Sigma Alpha Iota* LXVIX/2 (January 1977) 68.

TYPE: announcement of premières, performances, publications, recordings.

WORKS DISCUSSED: *Caprice Variations, Concerto for Violin and Orchestra, Dialogues, Partita Variations, Phaedra, Quintet for Piano and String Quartet, Songs in Prasie of Krishna, Symphony No. 4, Twelve Bagatelles, Ukiyo-e.*

n.a. "George Rochberg," *Pan Pipes of Sigma Alpha Iota* LXX/2 (January 1978) 59.

TYPE: announcement of performances, commissions.

n.a. "George Rochberg," *Pan Pipes of Sigma Alpha Iota* LXXII/2 (Winter 1980) 40.

TYPE: announcement of premières, performances, recordings, commissions.

WORKS DISCUSSED: *Concerto for Violin and Orchestra, The Confidence Man, Duo Concertante, Quintet for Piano and String Quartet, Ricordanza, Slow Fires of Autumn, Sonata for Viola and Piano, String Quartet No. 4, String Quartet No. 5, String Quartet No. 6.*

Giffin, Glenn. "Music," *The Sunday Denver Post* (23 July 1972) 10.

TYPE: article, interview.

NAMES: Aspen Conference on Contemporary Music.

Goodman, H. "Unorthodox Combinations," *New Leader* LXV (09-23 August 1982) 22-23.

TYPE: article.

Griffiths, Paul. *Modern Music: A Concise History from Debussy to Boulez.* (New York, NY: Thames and Hudson, Inc., 1985) 200, 201.

TYPE: discussion.

NAMES: Beethoven, Mahler.

WORKS DISCUSSED: *Contra Mortem et Tempus, String Quartet No. 3.*

Grimes, Ev. "Conversations with American Composers: Ev Grimes Interviews George Rochberg," *Music Educators Journal* LXXIII/1 (September 1986) 42-44, 46-49.

TYPE: interview.

Hardy, Owen. "'Foremost Is Life,' A Musical Rebel Feels," *The Courier-Journal [Louisville, KY]* (16 April 1980).

TYPE: article, interview.

WORKS DISCUSSED: *Music for the Magic Theater, Ricordanza.*

Hasty, Christopher F. "On the Problem of Succession and Continuity in Twentieth-Century Music," *Music Theory Spectrum* VIII (1986) 58-73.

TYPE: article.

NAMES: Leonard Meyer, Schönberg, Webern.

Henehan, Donal J. "An Apostate Questions Modernist Pietes with Gusto," *The New York Times* (03 June 1984) II, 21-22.

TYPE: article.

BOOKS DISCUSSED: *The Aesthetics of Survival.*

WORKS DISCUSSED: *Serenata d'estate, String Quartet No. 3.*

Henahan, Donal J. "Music: Rochberg Work," *The New York Times* (09 May 1973) 43.

TYPE: article.

NAMES: many.

WORKS DISCUSSED: many.

Henahan, Donal J. "Tommorrow's Music: Something Old, Something New," *The New York Times* (28 May 1972) II, 11.

TYPE: article.

WORKS DISCUSSED: *Music for the Magic Theater, String Quartet No. 3.*

Hillerman, Anne. "Santa Fe Festival Hosts Rochberg," *The New Mexican [Santa Fe, NM]* (18 July 1979).

TYPE: review, interview.

WORKS DISCUSSED: Duo Concertante, Ricordanza.

Hinson, Maurice. *Guide to the Pianist's Repertoire.* (Bloomington, IN: Indiana University Press, 1973) 527.

TYPE: review.

NAMES: Bach.

WORKS DISCUSSED: *Arioso, Bartokiana, Nach Bach, Sonata-Fantasia, Twelve Bagatelles.*

Hinson, Maurice. *Guide to the Pianist's Repertoire: Supplement.* (Bloomington, IN: Indiana University Press, 1979) 257.

TYPE: review.

NAMES: Bach, Steven D. Jones.

WORKS DISCUSSED: *Arioso, Bartokiana, Carnival Music, Nach Bach, Partita Variations, Prelude on "Happy Birthday," Sonata-Fantasia, Twelve Bagatelles.*

Hinson, Maurice. *Guide to the Pianist's Repertoire, Second, Revised and Enlarged Edition*. (Bloomington, IN: Indiana University Press, 1987) 598-599.

TYPE: review.

NAMES: Bach, Brahms, David Burge.

WORKS DISCUSSED: *Arioso, Bartokiana, Carnival Music, Nach Bach, Partita Variations, Prelude on "Happy Birthday," Sonata-Fantasia, Twelve Bagatelles, Two Preludes and Fughettas from The Book of Contrapuntal Pieces for Keyboard Instruments.*

Hinson, Maurice. *Music for Piano and Orchestra: An Annotated Guide*. (Bloomington, IN: Indiana University Press, 1981) 248.

TYPE: review.

WORKS DISCUSSED: *Concert Piece for Two Pianos and Orchestra.*

Hinson, Maurice. *The Piano in Chamber Ensemble*. (Bloomington, IN: Indiana University Press, 1978) 156, 336, 442.

TYPE: review.

WORKS DISCUSSED: *Contra Mortem et Tempus, Ricordanza, Trio [No. 1] for Violin, Cello, and Piano.*

Horn, Daniel Paul. "*Carnival Music*: An Introduction to the Piano Music of George Rochberg," *Clavier* XXVII/9 (November 1988) 17-21.

TYPE: article.

NAMES: many.

WORKS DISCUSSED: *Arioso, Bartokiana, Book of Contrapuntal Pieces for Keyboard Instruments, Carnival Music, Four Short Sonatas, Nach Bach, Partita Variations, Prelude on "Happy Birthday," Sonata No. 1 for Piano Solo, Sonata No. 2 for Piano Solo, Sonata-Fantasia, Twelve Bagatelles, Two Preludes and Fughettas from The Book of Contrapuntal Pieces for Keyboard Instruments.*

Huebner, W. Michael. "Composer Pursues *Aesthetics of Survival* in Modern Music," *The Kansas City Star* (12 August 1984) 7F.

TYPE: review.

NAMES: Berg, Bolcom, Boulez, Schönberg.

WORKS DISCUSSED: *String Quartet No. 3.*

BOOKS DISCUSSED: *The Aesthetics of Survival.*

Isacoff, Stuart. "New Music Corner," *Keyboard Classics* (September–October 1985) 34-36.

TYPE: article, interview.

WORKS DISCUSSED: *Partita Variations.*

BOOKS DISCUSSED: *The Aesthetics of Survival.*

Johnson, Wayne. "Orchestras on Way Out?," *The Seattle Times* (02 November 1969) A-7.

TYPE: article.

Kanny, Mark. "Rochberg Sets Tone for New Composing Style," *The Pittsburgh Post-Gazette* (16 October 1987).

TYPE: interview.

WORKS DISCUSSED: *Symphony No. 1, Symphony No. 2.*

Kimmelman, Michael. "A Composer Airs His Philosophy," *The Philadelphia Inquirer* (05 September 1985) 10C.

TYPE: WGBH-Boston, WHYY-Philadelphia film.

WORKS DISCUSSED: *Between Two Worlds, String Quartet No. 5.*

Kolodin, Irving. "Berio, Rochberg and the Musical Quote," *The Saturday Review* (08 February 1975) 36-38.

TYPE: article.

Kramer, Jonathan D. "Can Moderism Survive George Rochberg?" *Critical Inquiry* XI (December 1984) 341-54.

TYPE: article.

Lawrence, Michael R., and Timothy Wolfe. *The Mind of Music [Documentary Film].* (Peabody Conservatory of Music, Baltimore, MD: 1980) 30-minutes.

TYPE: film.

CAST: Yehudi Menuhin, George Rochberg, Dr. Lewis Thomas, Gunther Schuller, Eugene Helm, Elliott Galkin.

n.a. "Leisure Lines: On the Scene: The Art of Offering the Arts: 'Y' [92nd Street, New York City] Arts Council at 21," *The Jewish Exponent* (16 February 1979).

TYPE: article.

Levy, Bertram. "Urbana: Report from the University of Illinois," *Perspectives of New Music* IV/2 (Spring– Summer 1966) 181-183.

TYPE: article.

NAMES: Alexander L. Ringer.

McLaughlin, Patricia. "Three Penn Composers: Professor Crumb, Rochberg, and Wernick Are All Major Figures in Contemporary Music," *The Pennsylvania Gazette* LXXVI/3 (December 1977).

TYPE: article, interview, discography.

NAMES: many.

WORKS DISCUSSED: many.

n.a. "Music and Dance: Ormandy Back from Europe; Rochberg Concert at Curtis," *The Evening Bulletin [Philadelphia]* (04 February 1977) 29, 31.

TYPE: upcoming performance.

WORKS DISCUSSED: *Dialogues, Partita-Variations, Quintet for Piano and String Quartet.*

n.a. "*Music Journal's* 1972 Annual Gallery of Living Composers: George Rochberg," *Music Journal* XXX (Annual 1972) 56.

TYPE: biography.

WORKS DISCUSSED: many.

BOOKS DISCUSSED: *The Hexachord and its Relation to the Twelve-Tone Row.*

Myers, Ken. "Whatever Happened to Classical Music?" *Eternity* (November 1986) 23-26.

TYPE: article.

NAMES: Mozart, Schönberg.

Owens, David. "Avant-Garde: What Does it Mean Today?," *The Christian Science Monitor* (24 August 1983) 20.

TYPE: article.

Owens, David. "The 'Great American *Symphony*': Aaron Copland's Third," *The Christian Science Monitor* (19 July 1983) 20.

TYPE: article.

Owens, David. "Inside Twentieth-Century Music," *The Christian Science Monitor* (24 February 1982) 20.

TYPE: article.

Owens, David. "Inside Twentieth-Century Music," *The Christian Science Monitor* (16 July 1981) 21.

TYPE: article.

Owens, David. "Turning from Twelve-Tone: Inside Twentieth-Century Music," *The Christian Science Monitor* (03 May 1984) 39.

TYPE: article.

WORKS DISCUSSED: *Concerto for Violin and Orchestra, String Quartet No. 4, String Quartet No. 5, String Quartet No. 6, Symphony No. 1, Symphony No. 2.*

Page, Tim. "Apostate Modernist," *The New York Times Magazine* (29 May 1983) 24-25.

TYPE: article, interview.

NAMES: Beethoven, Dallapiccola, Del Tredici, Haydn, Mahler, Mozart, Schönberg.

WORKS DISCUSSED: *String Quartet No. 3, String Quartet No. 4, String Quartet No. 5, String Quartet No. 6.*

Page, Tim. "A Channel 13 Documentary on the Composer Rochberg," *The New York Times* (08 August 1986).

TYPE: article on film.

Page, Tim. "Music Notes: Concord Disbanding," *The New York Times* (18 January 1987) Sec. II, 23, 26.

TYPE: article.

PERFORMERS: Concord String Quartet.

WORKS DISCUSSED: *String Quartet No. 3, String Quartet No. 4, String Quartet No. 5, String Quartet No. 6.*

Parsons, Aaron. "Interlake Profiles," Radio interview with George Rochberg. (WFMT-FM, Chicago, IL: 30 October 1981).

TYPE: taped interview.

NAMES: many.

WORKS DISCUSSED: many.

Perle, George. "George Rochberg: *The Hexachord and Its Relation to the Twelve-Tone Row,*" *Journal of the American Musicological Society* X/1 (Spring 1957) 55-59.

TYPE: review.

NAMES: many.

BOOKS DISCUSSED: *The Hexachord and Its Relation to the Twelve-Tone Row.*

Plush, Vincent. Taped Interview with George Rochberg. (New Haven, CT: Yale University, Oral History, American Music, 12 October 1983) two and one-half 90-minute tapes.

TYPE: taped interview, transcript available.

Porter, Andrew. "Musical Events: Questions," *The New Yorker* (12 February 1979) 109-115.

TYPE: article.

NAMES: many.

WORKS DISCUSSED: *Concerto for Violin and Orchestra, Duo Concertante, Music for the Magic Theater, Ricordanza, String Quartet No. 1, String Quartet No. 3, String Quartet No. 4, String Quartet No. 5, String Quartet No. 6.*

Porter, Andrew. "Questions," *The New Yorker* (16 August 1979) 109-110.

TYPE: article.

Reise, Jay. "Rochberg the Progressive," *Perspectives of New Music* XIX/1 (Fall–Winter 1980) XIX/2 (Spring–Summer 1981) 395-407.

TYPE: article, analysis.

NAMES: many.

WORKS DISCUSSED: *Contra Mortem et Tempus, String Quartet No. 3, Symphony No. 2, Tableaux.*

von Rhein, John. "Music: The 'Concord' Debut to Mark a Return to the Romantic," *The Chicago Tribune* (20 January 1980).

TYPE: article, interview.

NAMES: many.

WORKS DISCUSSED: *Concerto for Violin and Orchestra, The Confidence Man, Music for the Magic Theater, String Quartet No. 3, String Quartet No. 4, String Quartet No. 5, String Quartet No. 6, String Quartet No. 7.*

Ringer, Alexander L. "Current Chronicle: United States: Cleveland," *Musical Quarterly* XLV/2 (April 1959) 230-234.

TYPE: article.

WORKS DISCUSSED: *Chamber Symphony, David, the Psalmist, Sonata-Fantasia, String Quartet No. 1, Symphony No. 1, Symphony No. 2, Twelve Bagatelles, Three Psalms.*

BOOKS DISCUSSED: *The Hexachord and Its Relation to the Twelve-Tone Row.*

Ringer, Alexander L. "The Music of George Rochberg," *Musical Quarterly* LII/4 (October 1966) 409-430.

TYPE: article.

NAMES: many.

WORKS DISCUSSED: many.

BOOKS DISCUSSED: *The Hexachord and Its Relation to the Twelve-Tone Row.*

Ringer, Alexander L., John Vinton editor. *Dictionary of Contemporary Music.* (New York, NY: E.P. Dutton & Co., Inc., 1974) 629-630.

TYPE: biography.

NAMES: many.

WORKS DISCUSSED: many.

Rochberg, George, Herbert Deutsch, Walter Sears, Rosalyn Tureck. *Bach and Electronic Media: A Discussion and Demonstration of the Moog Synthesizer [tape].* (Center for Cassette Studies, Hollywood, CA: 1973) 65 minutes, with 6pp. program.

TYPE: tape.

NAMES: many.

n.a. "Rochberg, George," *Current Biography* XLVI/9 (September 1985) 33-36.

TYPE: biography.

NAMES: many.

WORKS DISCUSSED: many.

Rochberg, George. "n.t.," *The Christian Science Monitor* (13 December 1982) 21.

TYPE: quote.

Rochberg-Halton, Eugene. "George Rochberg," *Meaning and Modernity: Social Theory in the Pragmatic Attitude.* (Chicago, IL: University of Chicago Press, 1986) 131-132, 218, 233, 238, 247, 254, 259-263.

TYPE: book.

BOOKS DISCUSSED: *The Aesthetics of Survival.*

Rousuek, J. Wynn. "Film Explores Music's Essence: Film Tries to Express the Essence of Music in World, Images," *The Sun [Baltimore]* (16 November 1980) D-1, D-10.

TYPE: review of film.

Saal, Hubert. "Rochberg's Rebirth," *Newsweek* XCIII/8 (19 February 1979) 70, 73, 73C.

TYPE: article, inteview.

WORKS DISCUSSED: *String Quartet No. 4, String Quartet No. 5, String Quartet No. 6.*

WORKS MENTIONED: *Concerto for Violin and Orchestra, String Quartet No. 3.*

Sabin, R. "Some Younger American Composers," *Tempo* LXIV (Spring 1963) 28.

TYPE: article.

NAMES: Stravinsky.

Sandow, G. "Music: 'Y' [92nd Street, New York] Contemporary Music Conference?" *Village Voice* XXVI (11 February 1981) 78.

TYPE: article.

Scanlon, Roger. "Spotlight on Contemporary American Composers—George Rochberg," *National Association of Teachers of Singing Bulletin* (October 1976) 48-49, 53-54.

TYPE: article.

WORKS DISCUSSED: *Blake Songs, David, the Psalmist, Eleven Songs, Fantasies, Four Songs of Solomon, Music for "The Alchemist," Phaedra, Sacred Song of Reconciliation, Songs in Praise of Krishna, String Quartet No. 2, Symphony No. 3, Two Songs from "Tableaux," Tableaux.*

Schonberg, Harold C. "Neo-Romantic Music Warms a Public Chilled by the Avant-Garde," *The New York Times* (20 March 1977) II, 1, 17.
TYPE: article.
NAMES: many.
WORKS DISCUSSED: *Concerto for Violin and Orchestra.*

Siegel, Sol Louis. "Rochberg: Classic Opinions," *Electricity* (06–12 August 1981) 5.
TYPE: interview.
WORKS DISCUSSED: *Concerto for Violin and Orchestra, Quintet for Piano and String Quartet, String Quartet No. 3.*

Sloniminsky, Nicolas. "Rochberg, George," *Baker's Biographical Dictionary of Music and Musicians, Seventh Edition.* (New York, NY: Schirmer, 1984).
TYPE: biography.
NAMES: many.
WORKS DISCUSSED: many.

Smith, Patrick J. "UMHA Conference on Contemporary Music," *High Fidelity/Musical America* XXXI/6 (June 1981) MA-23, MA-39.
TYPE: article.

Stewart, Paul. *A Discussion of George Rochberg's Music.* (Louisville, KY: Meetings International, April 1986) Cassette MTNA-329. [A Lecture Recital on Rochberg's *Carnival Music*, recorded at the 1986 MTNA Convention; April 1986; Portland, Oregon.]
TYPE: lecture recital.
NAMES: many.
WORKS DISCUSSED: *Arioso, Bartokiana, Book of Contrapuntal Pieces for Keyboard Instruments, Carnival Music, Four Short Sonatas, Nach Bach, Partita Variations, Prelude on "Happy Birthday," Sonata-Fantasia, Twelve Bagatelles, Two Preludes and Fughettas from The Book of Contrapuntal Pieces for Keyboard Instruments.*

Stewart, Paul. "The Piano Music of George Rochberg and the New Romanticism," *The American Music Teacher* XXVIII/3 (January 1989) 24-27, 62.
TYPE: lecture recital transcript.
NAMES: many.

WORKS DISCUSSED: *Arioso, Bartokiana, Book of Contrapuntal Pieces for Keyboard Instruments, Carnival Music, Four Short Sonatas, Nach Bach, Partita Variations, Prelude on "Happy Birthday," Sonata-Fantasia, Twelve Bagatelles, Two Preludes and Fughettas from The Book of Contrapuntal Pieces for Keyboard Instruments.*

n.a. "Thirteen at Penn [University of Pennsylvania at Philadelphia] Given Guggenheim Grants," *The Philadelphia Inquirer* (04 April 1966) 5.

TYPE: announcement of Guggenheim awards.

Valdes, Lesley. "A Birthday Salute to Rochberg," *The Philadelphia Inquirer* (17 April 1988) 1-L, 10-L.

TYPE: interview, upcoming performance.

WORKS DISCUSSED: *Duo Concertante, Serenata d'estate, Slow Fires of Autumn, String Quartet No. 3, String Quartet No. 7, To the Dark Wood, Trio [No. 2] for Violin, Cello, and Piano.*

WORKS MENTIONED: *Concerto for Violin and Orchestra, Sonata for Violin and Piano, Symphony No. 5, Symphony No. 6.*

Webster, Daniel. "George Rochberg: American Music's Bellwether," *The Philadelphia Inquirer* (25 July 1982) 1-K, 13-K.

TYPE: article, interview.

WORKS DISCUSSED: *The Confidence Man, Phaedra, Symphony No. 2.*

Webster, Daniel. "George Rochberg: His First Opera, to be Premièred Next Month Turns a New Stylistic Corner," *High Fidelity/Musical America* XXXII/6 (June 1982) Cover, MA-4, MA-5, MA-39.

TYPE: article, interview.

WORKS DISCUSSED: *The Confidence Man.*

Webster, Daniel. "In Honor of Rochberg, Three Nights Devoted to His Works," *The Philadelphia Inquirer* (17 January 1979).

TYPE: review.

WORKS DISCUSSED: *Duo Concertante, Quintet for Piano and String Quartet, Ricordanza, String Quartet No. 1, String Quartet No. 2, String Quartet No. 3, String Quartet No. 4, String Quartet No. 5, String Quartet No. 6.*

Webster, Daniel. "At Irvine Auditorium: Penn's [University of Pennsylvania at Philadelphia] Conductor 'Sums Up'," *The Philadelphia Inquirer* (27 April 1968) 12.

TYPE: review.

PERFORMERS: George Rochberg, University of Pennsylvania [at Philadelphia] Orchestra.

NAMES: Beethoven, Brahms, Mozart, Verdi.

Webster, Daniel. "On the Changing Rhythms in the Life of a Composer," *The Philadelphia Inquirer* (16 January 1979) D1, D3.

TYPE: article, interview.

NAMES: many.

WORKS DISCUSSED: *Concerto for Violin and Orchestra, The Confidence Man, Slow Fires of Autumn, String Quartet No. 4, String Quartet No. 5, String Quartet No. 6.*

Webster, Daniel. "Once More with Feeling: A Hearing for New Romanticism," *The Philadelphia Inquirer* (09 June 1983) 1-E, 6-E.

TYPE: article.

Webster, Daniel. "A Symphony Out of the Past: George Rochberg's Music Gets a Philadelphia Hearing," *The Philadelphia Inquirer* (10 March 1985) I-11.

TYPE: interview, upcoming performance.

WORKS DISCUSSED: *Symphony No. 1, Symphony No. 2, Symphony No. 3, Symphony No. 5, Trio [No. 1] for Violin, Cello, and Piano.*

Webster, Daniel. "Taking His Leave of Penn [University of Pennsylvania at Philadelphia] to Pen More Music," *The Philadelphia Inquirer* (27 March 1983) 1-H, 10-H, 11-H.

TYPE: article, interview.

WORKS DISCUSSED: *Concerto for Oboe and Orchestra, The Confidence Man, Imago Mundi.*

n.a. "Who's Here," *Keshet: Cultural News from Israel [Jerusalem]* VI (December 1982).

TYPE: announcement of residency.

Woodford, Bruce. "Some Noteable Thoughts," *The Santa Fe Reporter [Santa Fe, NM]* (11 July 1984) 27.

TYPE: review.

NAMES: Bolcom.

WORKS DISCUSSED: *The Confidence Man.*

BOOKS DISCUSSED: *The Aesthetics of Survival.*

Youngren, William H. "Ear Versus Mind," *The Atlantic* CCLVI/3 (September 1985) 112-114.

TYPE: review.

NAMES: many.

BOOKS DISCUSSED: *The Aesthetics of Survival.*

BIBLIOGRAPHY BY SUBJECT

Apocalyptica [I] for Large Wind Ensemble

Gagne, Cole and Tracy Caras. *Soundpieces: Interviews with American Composers.* (Metuchen, NJ: Scarecrow Press, Inc., 1982).

TYPE: interview.

OTHER WORKS DISCUSSED: *Black Sounds, Concerto for Violin and Orchestra, The Confidence Man, Contra Mortem et Tempus, Electrikaleidoscope, Music for the Magic Theater, Octet, Quintet for Piano and String Quartet, Ricordanza, Sonata No. 2 for Piano Solo, String Quartet No. 3, String Quartet No. 4, String Quartet No. 5, String Quartet No. 6, Twelve Bagatelles.*

OTHER WORKS MENTIONED: many.

Moore, David W. "Rochberg: *Carnival Music, Black Sounds, Nach Bach,*" *American Record Guide* XLI/9 (July 1978) 25-26.

TYPE: record review.

NAMES: Ives.

OTHER WORKS DISCUSSED: *Black Sounds, Carnival Music, Nach Bach, String Quartet No. 3.*

n.a. "Bulletin Board," *Music Educators' Journal* LI/5 (April–May 1965) 135.

TYPE: upcoming première.

PERFORMERS: Ward Moore, Montclair State College Band.

n.a. "Paterson Native's Work Will Highlight Concert," *The Morning News [Paterson, NJ]* (18 May 1965).

TYPE: upcoming première.

PERFORMERS: Ward Moore, Montclair State College Band.

OTHER WORKS MENTIONED: *Sonata No. 1 for Piano Solo, Sonata No. 2 for Piano Solo, String Quartet No. 1, Symphony No. 1.*

Ringer, Alexander L. "The Music of George Rochberg," *Musical Quarterly* LII/4 (October 1966) 409-430.

TYPE: article.

PERFORMERS: Ward Moore, Montclair State College Band.

NAMES: Varèse, Shakespeare.

OTHER WORKS DISCUSSED: *Black Sounds, Blake Songs, La Bocca della Verità, Cantio Sacra, Capriccio for Two Pianos, Chamber Symphony, Theltenham Concerto, Concert Piece for Two Pianos and Orchestra, Contra Mortem et Tempus, David, the Psalmist, Dialogues, Duo Concertante, Four Songs of Solomon, Music for the Magic Theater, Nach*

Bach, Night Music, Passions [According to the Twentieth Century], Serenata d'estate, Sonata-Fantasia, String Quartet No. 1, String Quartet No. 2, Symphony No. 1, Symphony No. 2, Three Psalms, Time-Span, Trio for Clarinet, Horn, and Piano, Trio [No. 1] for Violin, Cello, and Piano, Twelve Bagatelles, Zodiac.

OTHER WORKS MENTIONED: *Arioso, Bartokiana, Five Smooth Stones, Sonata No. 1 for Piano Solo, Sonata No. 2 for Piano Solo, Waltz Serenade.*

BOOKS DISCUSSED: *The Hexachord and Its Relation to the Twelve-Tone Row.*

Arioso for Piano Solo

Hinson, Maurice. *Guide to the Pianist's Repertoire: An Annotated Guide.* (Bloomington, IN: Indiana University Press, 1973) 527.

TYPE: score review.

OTHER WORKS DISCUSSED: *Bartokiana, Nach Bach, Sonata-Fantasia, Twelve Bagatelles.*

Hinson, Maurice. *Guide to the Pianist's Repertoire: An Annotated Guide, Supplement.* (Bloomington, IN: Indiana University Press, 1979) 275.

TYPE: score review.

OTHER WORKS DISCUSSED: *Bartokiana, Carnival Music, Nach Bach, Partita Variations, Prelude on "Happy Birthday," Sonata-Fantasia, Twelve Bagatelles.*

Hinson, Maurice. *Guide to the Pianist's Repertoire: An Annotated Guide, Second, Revised, and Enlarged Edition.* (Bloomington, IN: Indiana University Press, 1987) 598-599.

TYPE: score review.

OTHER WORKS DISCUSSED: *Bartokiana, Carnival Music, Nach Bach, Partita Variations, Prelude on "Happy Birthday," Sonata-Fantasia, Twelve Bagatelles, Two Preludes and Fughettas from The Book of Contrapuntal Pieces.*

Horn, Daniel Paul. *"Carnival Music*: An Introduction to the Piano Music of George Rochberg," *Clavier* XXVII/9 (November 1988) 17-21.

TYPE: article.

OTHER WORKS DISCUSSED: *Bartokiana, Book of Contrapuntal Pieces for Keyboard Instruments, Carnival Music, Four Short Sonatas, Nach Bach, Partita Variations, Prelude on "Happy Birthday," Sonata-Fantasia, Twelve Bagatelles.*

OTHER WORKS MENTIONED: *Sonata No. 1 for Piano Solo, Sonata No. 2 for Piano Solo.*

Stewart, Paul. "The Piano Music of George Rochberg and the New Romanticism," *American Music Teacher* XXXVIII/3 (January 1989) 24-27, 62.

TYPE: article.

OTHER WORKS DISCUSSED: *Bartokiana, Book of Contrapuntal Pieces for Keyboard Instruments, Carnival Music, Four Short Sonatas, Nach Bach, Partita Variations, Prelude on "Happy Birthday," Sonata-Fantasia, Twelve Bagatelles, Two Preludes and Fughettas.*

Bartokiana for Piano Solo

Hinson, Maurice. *Guide to the Pianist's Repertoire: An Annotated Guide.* (Bloomington, IN: Indiana University Press, 1973) 527.

TYPE: score review.

OTHER WORKS DISCUSSED: *Arioso,   Nach   Bach,   Sonata-Fantasia, Twelve Bagatelles.*

Hinson, Maurice. *Guide to the Pianist's Repertoire: An Annotated Guide, Supplement.* (Bloomington, IN: Indiana University Press, 1979) 275.

TYPE: score review.

OTHER WORKS DISCUSSED: *Arioso, Carnival Music, Nach Bach, Partita Variations, Prelude on "Happy Birthday," Sonata-Fantasia, Twelve Bagatelles.*

Hinson, Maurice. *Guide to the Pianist's Repertoire: An Annotated Guide, Second, Revised, and Enlarged Edition.* (Bloomington, IN: Indiana University Press, 1987) 598-599.

TYPE: score review.

OTHER WORKS DISCUSSED: *Arioso, Carnival Music, Nach Bach, Partita Variations, Prelude on "Happy Birthday," Sonata-Fantasia, Twelve Bagatelles, Two Preludes and Fughettas from The Book of Contrapuntal Pieces.*

Horn, Daniel Paul. "*Carnival Music*: An Introduction to the Piano Music of George Rochberg," *Clavier* XXVII/9 (November 1988) 17-21.

TYPE: article.

NAMES: Bartók.

OTHER WORKS DISCUSSED: *Arioso, Book of Contrapuntal Pieces for Keyboard Instruments, Carnival Music, Four Short Sonatas, Nach Bach,*

Partita Variations, Prelude on "Happy Birthday," Sonata-Fantasia, Twelve Bagatelles.

OTHER WORKS MENTIONED: *Sonata No. 1 for Piano Solo, Sonata No. 2 for Piano Solo.*

Stewart, Paul. "The Piano Music of George Rochberg and the New Romanticism," *American Music Teacher* XXXVIII/3 (January 1989) 24-27, 62.

TYPE: article.

NAMES: Bartók.

OTHER WORKS DISCUSSED: *Arioso, Book of Contrapuntal Pieces for Keyboard Instruments, Carnival Music, Four Short Sonatas, Nach Bach, Partita Variations, Prelude on "Happy Birthday," Sonata-Fantasia, Twelve Bagatelles, Two Preludes and Fughettas.*

Between Two Worlds (Ukiyo-e III), Five Images for Flute and Piano

Hasden, Nikki C. "The Record Column: Latest Classical Recordings Highlight Music for Flute and Piano," *The Chattanooga Times [Chattanooga, TN]* (14 February 1987) B5.

TYPE: review.

PERFORMERS: Sue Ann Kahn, Andrew Willis.

OTHER WORKS DISCUSSED: *Concerto for Oboe and Orchestra.*

Kimmelman, Michael. "A Composer Airs His Philosophy," *The Philadelphia Inquirer* (05 September 1985).

TYPE: review.

PERFORMERS: Sue Ann Kahn, Andrew Willis.

OTHER WORKS DISCUSSED: *String Quartet No. 5.*

Page, Tim. "A Channel 13 Documentary on the Composer Rochberg," *The New York Times* (08 August 1986) III, 26.

TYPE: upcoming television program.

PERFORMERS: Sue Ann Kahn, Andrew Willis.

Black Sounds (Apocalyptica II) for Seventeen Winds

Aikin, Jim. "Records: Three Sides of George Rochberg," *Contemporary Keyboard* IV/9 (September 1978) 62.

TYPE: record review.

PERFORMERS: Kenneth Moore, Oberlin Wind Ensemble.

OTHER WORKS DISCUSSED: *Carnival Music, Nach Bach.*

Bronston, Levering. "Three Sides of George Rochberg," *The New Records* XLVI/5 (July 1978) 7.

TYPE: record review.

PERFORMERS: Kenneth Moore, Oberlin Wind Ensemble.

NAMES: Anna Sokolow, Varèse.

OTHER WORKS DISCUSSED: *Carnival Music, Nach Bach, String Quartet No. 3.*

Frank, Peter. "Rochberg: *Carnival Music, Black Sounds, Nach Bach,*" *Fanfare* I/6 (July–August 1978) 75-76.

TYPE: record review.

PERFORMERS: Kenneth Moore, Oberlin Wind Ensemble.

NAMES: Henry Brant, Lou Harrison, Varèse.

OTHER WORKS DISCUSSED: *Carnival Music, Nach Bach.*

Gagne, Cole and Tracy Caras. *Soundpieces: Interviews with American Composers.* (Metuchen, NJ: Scarecrow Press, Inc., 1982).

TYPE: interview.

OTHER WORKS DISCUSSED: *Apocalyptica [I], Concerto for Violin and Orchestra, The Confidence Man, Contra Mortem et Tempus, Electrikaleidoscope, Music for the Magic Theater, Octet, Quintet for Piano and String Quartet, Ricordanza, Sonata No. 2 for Piano Solo, String Quartet No. 3, String Quartet No. 4, String Quartet No. 5, String Quartet No. 6, Twelve Bagatelles.*

OTHER WORKS MENTIONED: many.

Moore, David W. "Rochberg: *Carnival Music, Black Sounds, Nach Bach,*" *American Record Guide* XLI/9 (July 1978) 25-26.

TYPE: record review.

PERFORMERS: Kenneth Moore, Oberlin Wind Ensemble.

NAMES: Ives, Varèse.

OTHER WORKS DISCUSSED: *Apocalyptica [I], Carnival Music, Nach Bach, String Quartet No. 3.*

Ringer, Alexander L. "The Music of George Rochberg," *Musical Quarterly* LII/4 (October 1966) 409-430.

TYPE: article.

PERFORMERS: Lincoln Center.

NAMES: Varèse.

OTHER WORKS DISCUSSED: *Apocalyptica [I], Blake Songs, La Bocca della Verità, Cantio Sacra, Capriccio for Two Pianos, Chamber Symphony, Cheltenham Concerto, Concert Piece for Two Pianos and Orchestra, Contra Mortem et Tempus, David, the Psalmist, Dialogues,*

Duo Concertante, Four Songs of Solomon, Music for the Magic Theater, Nach Bach, Night Music, Passions [According to the Twentieth Century], Serenata d'estate, Sonata-Fantasia, String Quartet No. 1, String Quartet No. 2, Symphony No. 1, Symphony No. 2, Three Psalms, Time-Span, Trio for Clarinet, Horn, and Piano, Trio [No. 1] for Violin, Cello, and Piano, Twelve Bagatelles, Zodiac.

OTHER WORKS MENTIONED: *Arioso, Bartokiana, Five Smooth Stones, Sonata No. 1 for Piano Solo, Sonata No. 2 for Piano Solo, Waltz Serenade.*

BOOKS DISCUSSED: *The Hexachord and Its Relation to the Twelve-Tone Row.*

Salzman, Eric. "Rochberg: *Carnival Music, Black Sounds, Nach Bach,*" *Stereo Review* XL/4 (October 1978) 160.

TYPE: record review.

PERFORMERS: Kenneth Moore, Oberlin Wind Ensemble.

NAMES: Anna Sokolow, Varèse.

OTHER WORKS DISCUSSED: *Carnival Music, Nach Bach.*

Blake Songs for Soprano and Chamber Ensemble

Bernstein, Bob. "Spectrum: New American Music," *Business Review* (02–08 August 1975).

TYPE: record review.

PERFORMERS: Jan DeGaetani, Arthur Weisberg, Contemporary Chamber Ensemble.

OTHER WORKS DISCUSSED: *String Quartet No. 3.*

Cohn, Arthur, Shirley Fleming, Russell Kerr, Igor Kipnis, Ralph Lewando, J. Robertson. "New York: Philharmonic Opens Season with Cleopatre," *The Music Magazine: Musical Courier* CLXIII/12 (November 1961) 31-33.

TYPE: review.

NAMES: Berg.

Diether, Jack. " International Society of Contemporary Music [ISCM] Concert," *Musical America* LXXXI/11 (November 1961) 55-56.

TYPE: review.

PERFORMERS: Shirley Sudock, Ralph Shapey, Hartt Chamber Players.

NAMES: William Blake, Webern.

Griffiths, Paul. "Rochberg: *Blake Songs,*" *Musical Times [Great Britain]* CXVII/1597 (March 1976) 237.

TYPE: record review.

PERFORMERS: Jan DeGaetani, Arthur Weisberg, Contemporary Chamber Ensemble.

NAMES: William Blake, Trakl, Webern.

Harvey, James E. "On Record: Nonesuch Issues Brave New Music," *The Flint Journal [Flint, MI]* (15 December 1975).

TYPE: record review.

PERFORMERS: Jan DeGaetani, Arthur Weisberg, Contemporary Chamber Ensemble.

NAMES: William Blake.

Hoffman, W. L. "Arts and Entertainment: US [United States] Composer on Canberra Stint," *The Canberra Times [Australia]* (20 October 1986).

TYPE: upcoming performances.

PERFORMERS: Jane Manning, Christopher Lyndon Gee.

OTHER WORKS DISCUSSED: *Octet, Quintet for Piano and String Quartet, Songs in Praise of Krishna, Symphony No. 4, To the Dark Wood.*

OTHER WORKS MENTIONED: *Concerto for Violin and Orchestra, Symphony No. 5.*

Hoffman, W. L. "Music: Rochberg: Positive First Half," *The Canberra Times [Australia]* (22 October 1986) 29.

TYPE: review.

PERFORMERS: Jane Manning, Christopher Lyndon Gee.

OTHER WORKS DISCUSSED: *Octet, Quintet for Piano and String Quartet, To the Dark Wood.*

Mootz, William. "Rochberg's Works Offer Constant Allures," *The Courier Journal [Louisville, KY]* (16 April 1980) C4.

TYPE: review.

PERFORMERS: Marilyn Shepherd, Constance Moore.

NAMES: Berg, William Blake.

OTHER WORKS DISCUSSED: *Contra Mortem et Tempus, Quintet for Piano and String Quartet, Ricordanza.*

Potter, Keith. "Rochberg: *String Quartet No. 1, Duo Concertante, Ricordanza*," *Records and Recordings [Great Britain]* (March 1977) 72-73.

TYPE: record review.

OTHER WORKS DISCUSSED: *Contra Mortem et Tempus, Duo Concertante, Ricordanza, String Quartet No. 1, String Quartet No. 2, String Quartet No. 3.*

Ringer, Alexander L. "The Music of George Rochberg," *Musical Quarterly* LII/4 (October 1966) 409-430.

TYPE: article.

OTHER WORKS DISCUSSED: *Apocalyptica [I], Black Sounds, La Bocca della Verità, Cantio Sacra, Capriccio for Two Pianos, Chamber Symphony, Cheltenham Concerto, Concert Piece for Two Pianos and Orchestra, Contra Mortem et Tempus, David, the Psalmist, Dialogues, Duo Concertante, Four Songs of Solomon, Music for the Magic Theater, Nach Bach, Night Music, Passions [According to the Twentieth Century], Serenata d'estate, Sonata-Fantasia, String Quartet No. 1, String Quartet No. 2, Symphony No. 1, Symphony No. 2, Three Psalms, Time-Span, Trio for Clarinet, Horn, and Piano, Trio [No. 1] for Violin, Cello, and Piano, Twelve Bagatelles, Zodiac.*

OTHER WORKS MENTIONED: *Arioso, Bartokiana, Five Smooth Stones, Sonata No. 1 for Piano Solo, Sonata No. 2 for Piano Solo, Waltz Serenade.*

BOOKS DISCUSSED: *The Hexachord and Its Relation to the Twelve-Tone Row.*

Roosevelt, Oliver. "Melodiya-Columbia Agreement Brings New Disks to U.S.," *The Birmingham News [Birmingham, AL]* (01 December 1974) 6E.

TYPE: record review.

PERFORMERS: Jan DeGaetani, Arthur Weisberg, Contemporary Chamber Ensemble.

NAMES: William Blake.

Salzman, Eric. "Music: At New School: Organization for Contemporary Music Opens Series of Concerts Here," *The New York Times* (07 October 1961) 15.

TYPE: review.

PERFORMERS: Shirley Sudock, Ralph Shapey, Hartt Chamber Players.

NAMES: Webern.

Salzman, Eric. "New Music: Uptown and Downtown," *Stereo Review* XXXIV/6 (June 1975) 110-111.

TYPE: record review.

PERFORMERS: Jan DeGaetani, Arthur Weisberg, Contemporary Chamber Ensemble.

NAMES: William Blake.

Scanlan, Roger. "Spotlight on Contemporary American Composers," *The NATS [National Association of Teachers of Singing] Bulletin* XXXIII/1 (October 1976) 48-49, 53-54.

TYPE: article.

OTHER WORKS DISCUSSED: *David, The Psalmist, Eleven Songs, Fantasies, Four Songs of Solomon, Music for "The Alchemist," Phaedra, Sacred Song of Reconciliation, Songs in Praise of Krishna, String Quartet No. 2, Symphony No. 3, Tableaux, Two Songs from "Tableaux".*

OTHER WORKS MENTIONED: many.

Shupp Jr., E. E. "Rochberg: *Blake Songs,*" *The New Records* XLII/11 (January 1975) 6.

TYPE: record review.

PERFORMERS: Jan De Gaetani, Arthur Weisberg, Contemporary Chamber Ensemble.

NAMES: William Blake.

n.a. "Spectrum: New American Music, Volume IV," *Record World* XXX/1437 (04 January 1975) 35.

TYPE: record review.

PERFORMERS: Jan DeGaetani, Arthur Weisberg, Contemporary Chamber Ensemble.

NAMES: William Blake.

Stacey, Truman. "Five Composers Basis for Nonesuch Volumes," *The Lake Charles American Press [Lake Charles, LA]* (21 June 1975).

TYPE: record review.

PERFORMERS: Jan DeGaetani, Arthur Weisberg, Contemporary Chamber Ensemble.

NAMES: William Blake.

Wells, Tilden. "Rochberg, Crumb, and Wuorinen Featured: Record Label Promotes Americans," *The Columbus Dispatch [Columbus, OH]* (24 August 1975) Entertainment Guide, 27.

TYPE: record review.

PERFORMERS: Jan DeGaetani, Arthur Weisberg, Contemporary Chamber Ensemble.

NAMES: William Blake, Schönberg.

La Bocca della Veritá for Oboe/Violin and Piano

Felton, James. "Rochberg's Chamber Music Is Aired at the Art Alliance," *The Evening Bulletin [Philadelphia]* (16 February 1966) 27.

TYPE: review.

PERFORMERS: Aeolian Chamber Players.

NAMES: Webern.

OTHER WORKS DISCUSSED: *Contra Mortem et Tempus, Dialogues, Night Music, Symphony No. 1, Symphony No. 2, Trio [No. 1] for Violin, Cello, and Piano.*

Gelles, George. "Bowdoin Festival: Accent on the New," *The Boston Globe* (15 August 1966) 15.

TYPE: review.

PERFORMERS: Gilbert Kalish, George Rochberg.

OTHER WORKS DISCUSSED: *Contra Mortem et Tempus, Nach Bach, Trio [No. 1] for Violin, Cello, and Piano.*

Johnston, Ben. "Reports: Letter from Urbana," *Perspectives of New Music* XX/1 (Fall–Winter 1963) 137-141.

TYPE: review.

Hughes, Allen. "American Music Played at N.Y.U. [New York University]: Serial Style Predominates in Contemporary Works," *The New York Times* (07 April 1965).

TYPE: review.

PERFORMERS: Lewis Kaplan, Gilbert Kalish.

NAMES: Mel Powell.

Ringer, Alexander L. "The Music of George Rochberg," *Musical Quarterly* LII/4 (October 1966) 409-430.

TYPE: article.

NAMES: David Tudor, Josef Marx.

OTHER WORKS DISCUSSED: *Apocalyptica [I], Black Sounds, Blake Songs, Cantio Sacra, Capriccio for Two Pianos, Chamber Symphony, Cheltenham Concerto, Concert Piece for Two Pianos and Orchestra, Contra Mortem et Tempus, David, the Psalmist, Dialogues, Duo Concertante, Four Songs of Solomon, Music for the Magic Theater, Nach Bach, Night Music, Passions [According to the Twentieth Century], Serenata d'estate, Sonata-Fantasia, String Quartet No. 1, String Quartet No. 2, Symphony No. 1, Symphony No. 2, Three Psalms, Time-Span, Trio for Clarinet, Horn, and Piano, Trio [No. 1] for Violin, Cello, and Piano, Twelve Bagatelles, Zodiac.*

OTHER WORKS MENTIONED: *Arioso, Bartokiana, Five Smooth Stones, Sonata No. 1 for Piano Solo, Sonata No. 2 for Piano Solo, Waltz Serenade.*

BOOKS DISCUSSED: *The Hexachord and Its Relation to the Twelve-Tone Row.*

Seay, Albert. "George Rochberg: *La Bocca della Verità, Music for Oboe and Piano*," *Notes: Quarterly Journal of the Music Library Association* XXIII/3 (March 1967) 612-613.

TYPE: score review.

NAMES: David Tudor, Josef Marx.

Webster, Daniel. "At the Art Alliance: Aeolian Players Shine Spotlight on Rochberg," *The Philadelphia Inquirer* (16 February 1966) 27.

TYPE: review.

PERFORMERS: Aeolian Chamber Players.

NAMES: Webern.

OTHER WORKS DISCUSSED: *Contra Mortem et Tempus, Dialogues, Trio [No. 1] for Violin, Cello, and Piano.*

Book of Contrapuntal Pieces for Keyboard Instruments

Horn, Daniel Paul. "*Carnival Music*: An Introduction to the Piano Music of George Rochberg," *Clavier* XXVII/9 (November 1988) 17-22.

TYPE: article.

OTHER WORKS DISCUSSED: *Arioso, Bartokiana, Carnival Music, Four Short Sonatas, Nach Bach, Partita Variations, Prelude on "Happy Birthday," Sonata-Fantasia, Twelve Bagatelles.*

OTHER WORKS MENTIONED: *Sonata No. 1 for Piano Solo, Sonata No. 2 for Piano Solo.*

Stewart, Paul. "The Piano Music of George Rochberg and the New Romanticism," *American Music Teacher* XXXVIII/3 (January 1989) 24-27, 62.

TYPE: article.

OTHER WORKS DISCUSSED: *Arioso, Bartokiana, Carnival Music, Four Short Sonatas, Nach Bach, Partita Variations, Prelude on "Happy Birthday," Sonata-Fantasia, Twelve Bagatelles, Two Preludes and Fughettas.*

Cantio Sacra for Chamber Orchestra

Ringer, Alexander L. "The Music of George Rochberg," *Musical Quarterly* LII/4 (October 1966) 409-430.

TYPE: article.

NAMES: Scheidt.

OTHER WORKS DISCUSSED: *Apocalyptica [I], Black Sounds, Blake Songs, La Bocca della Verità, Capriccio for Two Pianos, Chamber Symphony, Cheltenham Concerto, Concert Piece for Two Pianos and Orchestra, Contra Mortem et Tempus, David, the Psalmist, Dialogues, Duo Concertante, Four Songs of Solomon, Music for the Magic Theater, Nach Bach, Night Music, Passions [According to the Twentieth Century], Serenata d'estate, Sonata-Fantasia, String Quartet No. 1, String Quartet No. 2, Symphony No. 1, Symphony No. 2, Three Psalms, Time-Span, Trio for Clarinet, Horn, and Piano, Trio [No. 1] for Violin, Cello, and Piano, Twelve Bagatelles, Zodiac.*

OTHER WORKS MENTIONED: *Arioso, Bartokiana, Five Smooth Stones, Sonata No. 1 for Piano Solo, Sonata No. 2 for Piano Solo, Waltz Serenade.*

BOOKS DISCUSSED: *The Hexachord and Its Relation to the Twelve-Tone Row.*

Capriccio for Two Pianos

Ringer, Alexander L. "The Music of George Rochberg," *Musical Quarterly* LII/4 (October 1966) 409-430.

TYPE: article.

NAMES: Bartók.

OTHER WORKS DISCUSSED: *Apocalyptica [I], Black Sounds, Blake Songs, La Bocca della Verità, Cantio Sacra, Chamber Symphony, Cheltenham Concerto, Concert Piece for Two Pianos and Orchestra, Contra Mortem et Tempus, David, the Psalmist, Dialogues, Duo Concertante, Four Songs of Solomon, Music for the Magic Theater, Nach Bach, Night Music, Passions [According to the Twentieth Century], Serenata d'estate, Sonata-Fantasia, String Quartet No. 1, String Quartet No. 2, Symphony No. 1, Symphony No. 2, Three Psalms, Time-Span, Trio for Clarinet, Horn, and Piano, Trio [No. 1] for Violin, Cello, and Piano, Twelve Bagatelles, Zodiac.*

OTHER WORKS MENTIONED: *Arioso, Bartokiana, Five Smooth Stones, Sonata No. 1 for Piano Solo, Sonata No. 2 for Piano Solo, Waltz Serenade.*

BOOKS DISCUSSED: *The Hexachord and Its Relation to the Twelve-Tone Row.*

Caprice Variations for Unaccompanied Violin

Barbier, Pierre E. "Gidon Kremer, Violin," *Diapson/Harmonie [Paris]* (June 1986).

TYPE: record review.

PERFORMERS: Gidon Kremer.

NAMES: Isaac Stern.

OTHER WORKS MENTIONED: *Concerto for Violin and Orchestra.*

Beaujean, Alfred. "A Paganini: Werke von Nathan Milstein, Alfred Schnittke, Heinrich Wilhelm Ernst, George Rochberg," *Stereoplay [Stuttgart]* (April 1986).

TYPE: record review.

PERFORMERS: Gidon Kremer.

Blanks, Fred. "Violin Lovers Take Heart," *The Sydney Morning Herald [Australia]* (23 May 1977).

TYPE: review.

PERFORMERS: Zvi Zeitlin.

Bloch, Robert. "George Rochberg: *Caprice Variations,*" *Notes: Quarterly Journal of the Music Library Association* XXXI/2 (December 1974) 398.

TYPE: score review.

NAMES: Bartók, Beethoven, Brahms, Dallapiccola, Liszt, Mahler, Milhaud, Paganini, Rachmaninoff, Scarlatti, Schubert, Stravinsky, Mark Twain, Webern.

Buell, Richard. "The Arts: Zeitlin Shows Versatility at MIT [Massachusetts Institute of Technology] Concert," *The Boston Globe* (03 December 1974) 20.

TYPE: review.

PERFORMERS: Zvi Zeitlin.

NAMES: Bach, Beethoven, Mahler, Schubert, Ed Sullivan, Mark Weber.

OTHER WORKS DISCUSSED: *String Quartet No. 3.*

Commanday, Robert P. "Music World: A Violinist with Consummate Virtuosity," *The San Francisco Chronicle* (10 December 1974) 42.

TYPE: review.

PERFORMERS: Zvi Zeitlin.

NAMES: Bartók, Beethoven, Fritz Kreisler, Mahler, Schubert, Webern.

Cossé, Peter. "A Paganini: Virtuose Musik für Violine: Milstein, Schnittke, Ernst, Rochberg," *Fono Forum [Munich, ermany]* V (May 1986) 51.

TYPE: record review.

PERFORMERS: Gidon Kremer.

Cossé, Peter. "Paganini: Virtuose Musik für Violine von Milstein, Schnittke, Ernst, Rochberg," *Stereo [Munich, Germany]* (May 1986) 152.

TYPE: record review.

PERFORMERS: Gidon Kremer.

Doucelin, Jacques. "Violon à l'américaine," *Le Figaro* (30 March 1977).

TYPE: review.

PERFORMERS: Robert Brown.

Evett, Robert. "Candidates for Oblivion," *Washington Star-News [Washington, D.C.]* (03 March 1974) G3.

TYPE: review.

PERFORMERS: Donna Lerew.

Felton, James. "Music Beat: Rochberg Composing Opera; Wife Is Librettist," *The Sunday Bulletin [Philadelphia]* (16 July 1978) 2-EA.

TYPE: article, interview.

NAMES: Paganini.

OTHER WORKS DISCUSSED: *Concerto for Violin and Orchestra, The Confidence Man, Phaedra, String Quartet No. 4, String Quartet No. 5, String Quartet No. 6.*

Frank, Peter. "Rochberg: *Caprice Variations,*" *Fanfare* I/5 (May–June 1978) 76.

TYPE: record review.

PERFORMERS: Zvi Zeitlin.

NAMES: Bach, Bartók, Beethoven, George Crumb, Mahler, Paganini, Schubert, Webern.

Helleu, Claude. "Gidon Kremer et Valery Afanassiev: Hallucinations," *Le Quotidien de Paris* 1723 (07 June 1985).

TYPE: review.

PERFORMERS: Gidon Kremer.

NAMES: Paganini.

Hoffmann, Stephan. "A Paganini—Virtuose Music für Violine," *HiFi Vision [Stuttgart]* (April 1986).

TYPE: record review.

PERFORMERS: Gidon Kremer.

Hudson, Sue. "Paganini Pot-Pourri: Virtuoso Compositions for Solo Violin in Tribute to Paganini by Nathan Milstein, Alfred Schnittke, Heinrich Wilhelm Ernst, George Rochberg," *HiFi News* 31/5 (May 1986) 135.

TYPE: record review.

PERFORMERS: Gidon Kremer.

Hughes, Allen. "Music: Adroit *Variations*: Zvi Zeitlin, Violinist Offers Debut Here of Rochberg's 22 *Caprice Pieces*," *The New York Times* (10 February 1975) 21.

TYPE: review.

PERFORMERS: Zvi Zeitlin.

NAMES: Beethoven, Mahler, Paganini, Schubert, Webern.

Methuen-Campbell, James. "Virtuoso Violin Music Inspired by Paganini," *Gramophone [Great Britain]* LXIII/755 (April 1986) 1305.

TYPE: record review.

PERFORMERS: Gidon Kremer.

McLellan, Joseph. *"Violin Caprice,"* The Washington Post *[Washington, D.C.]* (21 January 1974) B11.

TYPE: review.

PERFORMERS: Donna Lerew.

NAMES: Beethoven, Brahms, Paganini, Webern.

n.a. "Musique," *L'Express [Paris]* (28 March–03 April 1977) 10.

TYPE: upcoming performance.

PERFORMERS: Robert Brown.

Petit-Castelli, Claude. "...et le Stradivarius d'Einstein," *Le Matin de Paris* (28 March 1977).

PERFORMERS: Robert Brown.

NAMES: Paganini, Brahms, Mahler, Webern.

Pittenger, Mabel. "Fine Debut for Concert Series," *The Mill Valley Record [Kentfiled, CA]* (20 October 1976).

TYPE: review.

PERFORMERS: Donna Lerew.

NAMES: Paganini.

von Rhein, John. "Chamber Music Chicago Begins Concert Series on Rewarding Note," *The Chicago Tribune* (26 October 1988) C9.

TYPE: review.

PERFORMERS: Gidon Kremer.

NAMES: Paganini.

DeRhen, Andrew. "Zvi Zeitlin, Violin," *High Fidelity/Musical America* XXV/6 (June 1975) MA-33.

TYPE: review.

PERFORMERS: Zvi Zeitlin.

NAMES: Paganini, Stravinsky, Tchaikovsky, Webern.

Rockwell, John. "Music: Debuts in Review: Soviet-Trained Violinist," *The New York Times* (07 October 1984) I, 84.
TYPE: review.
PERFORMERS: Mischa Lefkowitz.
NAMES: Paganini.

Syöqvist, Gunnar. "Nutida Häxmästare," *Musikrevy [Stockholm]* (March 1986).
TYPE: record review.
PERFORMERS: Gidon Kremer.
NAMES: Beethoven, Brahms, Mahler, Webern.

Tircuit, Heuwell. "A Night for American Music," *The San Francisco Chronicle* (01 November 1976) 46.
TYPE: review.
PERFORMERS: Donna Lerew.

Turok, Paul. "New and Noteworthy: A Survey of Interesting New Recordings," *Ovation* VIII/1 (February 1987) 49.
TYPE: record review.
PERFORMERS: Gidon Kremer.

Walsh, Michael. "New Music We Should Know and Love," *The Rochester Democrat and Chronicle [Rochester, NY]* (13 October 1974) 1-H, 4-H.
TYPE: review.
OTHER WORKS DISCUSSED: *Serenata d'estate, String Quartet No. 3.*

Walsh, Michael. "Zeitlin Opens Concert Seasons," *The Rochester Democrat and Chronicle [Rochester, NY]* (20 September 1974) 4C.
TYPE: review.
PERFORMERS: Zvi Zeitlin.
NAMES: Bartók, Beethoven, Brahms, Mahler, Schubert, Stravinsky.
OTHER WORKS DISCUSSED: *String Quartet No. 3.*

Wagner, Rainer. "Bogen-Streiche: Paganini und Chaplin," *Deutches Allgem, Sonntagsblatt [Hamburg, Germany]* (11 May 1986).
TYPE: record review.
PERFORMERS: Gidon Kremer.

Wagner, Rainer. "Noch ein Teufelsgeiger?: Gidon Kremers Produktion 'A Paganini'," *Hannoversche Allgem, Zeitung [Hannover, Germany]* (02 April 1986).
TYPE: record review.
PERFORMERS: Gidon Kremer.

Webster, Daniel. "At Annenberg Center: Variation Abounds in Virtuoso Works for Violin, Cello," *The Philadelphia Inquirer* (01 March 1973) 8-B.

TYPE: review.

PERFORMERS: Jerome Wigler.

NAMES: Paganini.

Carnival Music for Piano Solo

Aikin, Jim. "Records: Three Sides of George Rochberg," *Contemporary Keyboard* IV/9 (September 1978) 62.

TYPE: record review.

PERFORMERS: Alan Mandel.

OTHER WORKS DISCUSSED: *Black Sounds, Nach Bach.*

Bronston, Levering. "Three Sides of George Rochberg," *The New Records* XLVI/5 (July 1978) 7.

TYPE: record review.

PERFORMERS: Alan Mandel.

NAMES: Jerome Lowenthal.

OTHER WORKS DISCUSSED: *Black Sounds, Nach Bach, String Quartet No. 3.*

Burge, David. "Contemporary Piano: Best Pieces of the '70s," *Contemporary Keyboard* V/11 (November 1979) 75.

TYPE: article.

NAMES: Brahms.

Burge, David. "George Rochberg: *Carnival Music, Suite for Piano Solo,*" *Notes: The Quarterly Journal of Music Library Association* XXXIII/2 (December 1976) 414, 415.

TYPE: score review.

NAMES: Barber, Bartók, Mahler, Stravinsky.

OTHER WORKS MENTIONED: *Concerto for Violin and Orchestra, Sonata-Fantasia, String Quartet No. 3, Twelve Bagatelles.*

Frank, Peter. "Rochberg: *Carnival Music, Black Sounds, Nach Bach,*" *Fanfare* I/6 (July–August 1978) 75-76.

TYPE: record review.

PERFORMERS: Alan Mandel.

NAMES: Bach, Chopin, Jerome Lowenthal, Stravinsky.

OTHER WORKS DISCUSSED: *Black Sounds, Nach Bach.*

Felton, James. "At the Academy: Lowenthal Recital: Strong Penn [University of Pennsylvania at Philadelphia] Influence," *The Evening Bulletin [Philadelphia]* (05 May 1972) 35.

TYPE: review.

PERFORMER: Jerome Lowenthal.

NAMES: Bach.

Hinson, Maurice. *Guide to the Pianist's Repertoire: An Annotated Guide, Supplement.* (Bloomington, IN: Indiana University Press, 1979) 275.

TYPE: score review.

OTHER WORKS DISCUSSED: *Arioso, Bartokiana, Nach Bach, Partita Variations, Prelude on "Happy Birthday," Sonata-Fantasia, Twelve Bagatelles.*

Hinson, Maurice. *Guide to the Pianist's Repertoire: An Annotated Guide, Second, Revised, and Enlarged Edition.* (Bloomington, IN: Indiana University Press, 1987) 598-599.

TYPE: score review.

OTHER WORKS DISCUSSED: *Arioso, Bartokiana, Nach Bach, Partita Variations, Prelude on "Happy Birthday," Sonata-Fantasia, Twelve Bagatelles, Two Preludes and Fughettas from The Book of Contrapuntal Pieces.*

Horn, Daniel Paul. "*Carnival Music*: An Introduction to the Piano Music of George Rochberg," *Clavier* XXVII/9 (November 1988) 17-22.

TYPE: article.

NAMES: Bach, Brahms, Ives, Joplin, Mahler, Stravinsky.

OTHER WORKS DISCUSSED: *Arioso, Bartokiana, Book of Contrapuntal Pieces for Keyboard Instruments, Four Short Sonatas, Nach Bach, Partita Variations, Prelude on "Happy Birthday," Sonata-Fantasia, Twelve Bagatelles.*

OTHER WORKS MENTIONED: *Sonata No. 1 for Piano Solo, Sonata No. 2 for Piano Solo.*

Levin, Monroe. "Notes on Music," *Jewish Exponent* (12 May 1972).

TYPE: review.

OTHER WORKS DISCUSSED: *Music for the Magic Theater.*

Mandel, Alan. "*Carnival Music, Suite for Piano Solo* by George Rochberg," *Piano Quarterly* XCIII (Spring 1976) 10, 12.

TYPE: score review.

NAMES: Crumb, Gershwin, Ives.

Margrave, Wendell. "Alan Mandel," *The Washington Post [Washington, D.C.]* (31 January 1977) C7.

    TYPE: review.

    PERFORMERS: Alan Mandel.

Moore, David W. "Rochberg: *Carnival Music, Black Sounds, Nach Bach,*" *American Record Guide* XLI/9 (July 1978) 25-26.

    TYPE: record review.

    PERFORMERS: Alan Mandel.

    NAMES: Ives.

    OTHER WORKS DISCUSSED: *Apocalyptica [I], Black Sounds, Nach Bach, String Quartet No. 3.*

n.a. "News and Honors," *ASCAP Today* VI/1 (July 1972) 31.

    TYPE: announcement of premières.

    OTHER WORKS DISCUSSED: *String Quartet No. 3.*

Salzmann, Eric. "Rochberg: *Carnival Music, Black Sounds, Nach Bach,*" *Stereo Review* XL/4 (October 1978) 160.

    TYPE: record review.

    PERFORMERS: Alan Mandel.

    NAMES: Bach, Brahms.

    OTHER WORKS DISCUSSED: *Black Sounds, Nach Bach.*

Stewart, Paul. "The Piano Music of George Rochberg and the New Romanticism," *American Music Teacher* XXXVIII/3 (January 1989) 24-27, 62.

    TYPE: article.

    NAMES: Barber, Brahms, Debussy, Gershwin, Schumann, Wagner.

    OTHER WORKS DISCUSSED: *Arioso, Bartokiana, Book of Contrapuntal Pieces for Keyboard Instruments, Four Short Sonatas, Nach Bach, Partita Variations, Prelude on "Happy Birthday," Sonata-Fantasia, Twelve Bagatelles, Two Preludes and Fughettas.*

Webster, Daniel. "Lowenthal Comfortable with New Work," *The Philadelphia Inquirer* (05 May 1972) 23.

    TYPE: review.

    PERFORMERS: Jerome Lowenthal.

    NAMES: Beethoven, Berg, Schumann.

Chamber Symphony for Nine Instruments

Archibald, Bruce. "Rochberg: *Chamber Symphony, Duo Concertante, Music for the Magic Theater, Ricordanza, String Quartet No. 1,"* *Musical Quarterly* LXII/4 (October 1976) 613-615.

TYPE: record review.

PERFORMERS: Kenneth Moore, Oberlin Chamber Orchestra.

OTHER WORKS DISCUSSED: *Contra Mortem et Tempus, Duo Concertante, Music for the Magic Theater, Ricordanza, String Quartet No. 1.*

Bronston, Levering. "Rochberg: *Chamber Symphony, Duo Concertante, Music for the Magic Theater, Ricordanza, String Quartet No. 1,"* *The New Records* XLIII/11 (January 1976) 7-8.

TYPE: record review.

PERFORMERS: Kenneth Moore, Oberlin Chamber Orchestra.

OTHER WORKS DISCUSSED: *Duo Concertante, Music for the Magic Theater, Ricordanza, String Quartet No. 1.*

Dixon, Joan DeVee. "George Rochberg's *Nach Bach, A Fantasy for Harpsichord or Piano,"* Unpublished (June 1988) 13pp.

TYPE: article, interviews with George Rochberg and Igor Kipnis.

NAMES: Dallapiccola.

OTHER WORKS DISCUSSED: *Contra Mortem et Tempus, Music for the Magic Theater, Nach Bach, Partita Variations, Sonata-Fantasia, Symphony No. 3.*

Oliva, Mark. "Classical Record Review," *The Nevada State Journal* (18 January 1976) 11.

TYPE: record review.

PERFORMERS: Kenneth Moore, Oberlin Chamber Orchestra.

OTHER WORKS DISCUSSED: *Duo Concertante, Music for the Magic Theater, Ricordanza, String Quartet No. 1.*

Porter, Andrew. "Rochberg: Chamber Works," *High Fidelity/Musical America* XXVI/5 (May 1976) 90-92.

TYPE: record reviews.

PERFORMERS: Kenneth Moore, Oberlin Chamber Orchestra.

OTHER WORKS DISCUSSED: *Concerto for Violin and Orchestra, Duo Concertante, Music for the Magic Theater, Ricordanza, String Quartet No. 1.*

Porter, Andrew. "Musical Events: Questions," *The New Yorker* (12 February 1979) 109-115.

TYPE: article.

OTHER WORKS DISCUSSED: *Concerto for Violin and Orchestra, Duo Concertante, Music for the Magic Theater, Ricordanza, String Quartet No. 1, String Quartet No. 2, String Quartet No. 3, String Quartet No. 4, String Quartet No. 5, String Quartet No. 6.*

Potter, Keith. "Rochberg: *Chamber Symphony, Duo Concertante, Music for the Magic Theater, Ricordanza, String Quartet No. 1*," *Records and Recordings [Great Britain]* (March 1977) 72-73.

TYPE: record review.

PERFORMERS: Kenneth Moore, Oberlin Chamber Orchestra.

OTHER WORKS DISCUSSED: *Duo Concertante, Music for the Magic Theater, Ricordanza, String Quartet No. 1, String Quartet No. 3.*

Ringer, Alexander L. "Current Chronicle: United States: Cleveland," *Musical Quarterly* XLV/2 (April 1959) 230-234.

TYPE: article, review.

OTHER WORKS DISCUSSED: *David, The Psalmist, Sonata-Fantasia, String Quartet No. 1, Symphony No. 1, Symphony No. 2, Three Psalms, Twelve Bagatelles.*

BOOKS DISCUSSED: *The Hexachord and Its Relation to the Twelve-Tone Row.*

Ringer, Alexander L. "The Music of George Rochberg," *Musical Quarterly* LII/4 (October 1966) 409-430.

TYPE: article.

PERFORMERS: Hugo Weisgall, Baltimore Chamber Society.

NAMES: Dallapiccola, Schönberg.

OTHER WORKS DISCUSSED: *Apocalyptica [I], Black Sounds, Blake Songs, La Bocca della Verità, Cantio Sacra, Capriccio for Two Pianos, Cheltenham Concerto, Concert Piece for Two Pianos and Orchestra, Contra Mortem et Tempus, David, the Psalmist, Dialogues, Duo Concertante, Four Songs of Solomon, Music for the Magic Theater, Nach Bach, Night Music, Passions [According to the Twentieth Century], Serenata d'estate, Sonata-Fantasia, String Quartet No. 1, String Quartet No. 2, Symphony No. 1, Symphony No. 2, Three Psalms, Time-Span, Trio for Clarinet, Horn, and Piano, Trio [No. 1] for Violin, Cello, and Piano, Twelve Bagatelles, Zodiac.*

OTHER WORKS MENTIONED: *Arioso, Bartokiana, Five Smooth Stones, Sonata No. 1 for Piano Solo, Sonata No. 2 for Piano Solo, Waltz Serenade.*

BOOKS DISCUSSED: *The Hexachord and Its Relation to the Twelve-Tone Row.*

Salzman, Eric. "Rochberg: *Chamber Symphony, Duo Concertante, Music for the Magic Theater, Ricordanza, String Quartet No. 1,*" *Stereo Review* XXXVII/1 (July 1976) 111.

TYPE: record review.

PERFORMERS: Kenneth Moore, Oberlin Chamber Orchestra.

OTHER WORKS DISCUSSED: *Duo Concertante, Music for the Magic Theater, Ricordanza, String Quartet No. 1.*

Singer, Samuel L. "Penn Turns to Its Own Composers," *The Philadelphia Inquirer* (28 April 1975) 4B.

TYPE: review.

PERFORMERS: Richard Wernick, Penn [University of Pennsylvania at Philadelphia] Contemporary Players.

Veilleux, C. Thomas. "Chamber Music Roundup Reveals Three Fine Records," *The Sunday Post [Bridgeport, CT]* (10 October 1976) E14.

TYPE: record review.

PERFORMERS: Kenneth Moore, Oberlin Chamber Orchestra.

OTHER WORKS DISCUSSED: *Duo Concertante, Music for the Magic Theater, Ricordanza, String Quartet No. 1.*

Webster, Daniel. "Stylistic Odyssey of George Rochberg," *The Philadelphia Inquirer* (15 February 1976) 7H.

TYPE: record review.

PERFORMERS: Kenneth Moore, Oberlin Chamber Orchestra.

NAMES: Dallapiccola.

OTHER WORKS DISCUSSED: *Duo Concertante, Music for the Magic Theater, Ricordanza, String Quartet No. 1.*

Cheltenham Concerto for Small Orchestra

Henahan, Donal J. "Montclair Chamber Orchestra Excels in First of Three Concerts," *The New York Times* (08 February 1977) 25.

TYPE: review.

PERFORMERS: Gerald Schwartz, Montclair State College Chamber Orchestra.

NAMES: Webern.

Parmenter, Ross. "World of Music: Fresh Look at Theories: Hemidemisemiquavers," *The New York Times* (10 May 1959) 9.

TYPE: announcement of International Society of Contemporary Music [ISCM] prize.

Ringer, Alexander L. "The Music of George Rochberg," *Musical Quarterly* LII/4 (October 1966) 409-430.

TYPE: article.

PERFORMERS: Cheltenham Art Center.

NAMES: Beethoven, Webern.

OTHER WORKS DISCUSSED: *Apocalyptica [I]*, *Black Sounds*, *Blake Songs*, *La Bocca della Verità*, *Cantio Sacra*, *Capriccio for Two Pianos*, *Chamber Symphony*, *Concert Piece for Two Pianos and Orchestra*, *Contra Mortem et Tempus*, *David, the Psalmist*, *Dialogues*, *Duo Concertante*, *Four Songs of Solomon*, *Music for the Magic Theater*, *Nach Bach*, *Night Music*, *Passions [According to the Twentieth Century]*, *Serenata d'estate*, *Sonata-Fantasia*, *String Quartet No. 1*, *String Quartet No. 2*, *Symphony No. 1*, *Symphony No. 2*, *Three Psalms*, *Time-Span*, *Trio for Clarinet, Horn, and Piano*, *Trio [No. 1] for Violin, Cello, and Piano*, *Twelve Bagatelles*, *Zodiac*.

OTHER WORKS MENTIONED: *Arioso*, *Bartokiana*, *Five Smooth Stones*, *Sonata No. 1 for Piano Solo*, *Sonata No. 2 for Piano Solo*, *Waltz Serenade*.

BOOKS DISCUSSED: The Hexachord and Its Relation to the Twelve-Tone Row.

Singer, Samuel L. "Cheltenham Art Center Concert: Chamber Group Plays Première," *The Philadelphia Inquirer* (19 May 1958) 11.

TYPE: review.

PERFORMERS: Herbert Fiss, Philadelphia Chamber Music Society.

NAMES: Bach, Mozart.

Concert Piece for Two Pianos and Orchestra

Hinson, Maurice. *Music for Piano and Orchestra: An Annotated Guide.* (Bloomington, IN: Indiana University Press, 1981) 248.

TYPE: review.

Ringer, Alexander L. "The Music of George Rochberg," *Musical Quarterly* LII/4 (October 1966) 409-430.

TYPE: article.

NAMES: Bartók.

OTHER WORKS DISCUSSED: *Apocalyptica [I]*, *Black Sounds*, *Blake Songs*, *La Bocca della Verità*, *Cantio Sacra*, *Capriccio for Two Pianos*, *Chamber Symphony*, *Cheltenham Concerto*, *Contra Mortem et Tempus*, *David, the Psalmist*, *Dialogues*, *Duo Concertante*, *Four Songs of Solomon*, *Music for the Magic Theater*, *Nach Bach*, *Night Music*, *Passions [According to the Twentieth Century]*, *Serenata d'estate*, *Sonata-Fantasia*, *String Quartet No. 1*, *String Quartet No. 2*, *Symphony No. 1*, *Symphony No. 2*, *Three Psalms*, *Time-Span*, *Trio for Clarinet, Horn, and Piano, Trio [No. 1] for Violin, Cello, and Piano, Twelve Bagatelles, Zodiac.*

OTHER WORKS MENTIONED: *Arioso, Bartokiana, Five Smooth Stones, Sonata No. 1 for Piano Solo, Sonata No. 2 for Piano Solo, Waltz Serenade.*

BOOKS DISCUSSED: *The Hexachord and Its Relation to the Twelve-Tone Row.*

Concerto for Oboe and Orchestra

Eckert, Thor Jr. "A Case for Playing 'Disappointing' New Music," *The Christian Science Monitor* (15 May 1985) 23.

TYPE: review.

PERFORMERS: Joseph Robinson, Zubin Mehta, New York Philharmonic.

Ellis, Stephen W. "Rochberg: *Concerto*," *Fanfare* X/4 (March–April 1987) 192-193.

TYPE: record review.

PERFORMERS: Joseph Robinson, Zubin Mehta, New York Philharmonic.

NAMES: Barber, Becker, Sendak.

Finn, Robert. "Druckman's *Prism* Views Older Works as Current," *The Plain Dealer [Cleveland, OH]* (16 November 1986) 4H.

TYPE: record review.

PERFORMERS: Joseph Robinson, Zubin Mehta, New York Philharmonic.

NAMES: Berg, Mahler.

Grueninger, Walter F. "Recorded Music in Review," *Consumers' Research Magazine* LXX/10 (October 1987) 43.

TYPE: record review.

PERFORMERS: Joseph Robinson, Zubin Mehta, New York Philharmonic.

Guinn, John. "Getting Critical: Classics: Four Works by Americans," *The Detroit Free Press* (05 January 1987).

TYPE: record review.

PERFORMERS: Joseph Robinson, Zubin Mehta, New York Philharmonic.

Guregian, Elaine. "New Records," *The Instrumentalist* XLI/5 (December 1986) 84.

TYPE: record review.

PERFORMERS: Joseph Robinson, Zubin Mehta, New York Philharmonic.

NAMES: Mahler.

Hasden, Nikki C. "The Record Column: Latest Classical Recordings Highloight Music for Flute and Oboe," *The Chattanooga Times [Chattanooga, TN]* (14 February 1987) B5.

TYPE: record review.

PERFORMERS: Joseph Robinson, Zubin Mehta, New York Philharmonic.

NAMES: Prokofiev, Wagner.

Henahan, Donal J. "Philharmonic: A Rochberg Première," *The New York Times* (14 December 1984) III, 4.

TYPE: review.

PERFORMERS: Joseph Robinson, Zubin Mehta, New York Philharmonic.

NAMES: Berg, Prokofiev, Strauss.

Henahan, Donal J. "The Philharmonic Marks Some Musical Birthdays," *The New York Times* (01 April 1984) II, 25.

TYPE: upcoming première.

PERFORMERS: Joseph Robinson, Zubin Mehta, New York Philharmonic.

Milsom, John. "George Rochberg: *Oboe Concerto*," *Gramophone [Great Britain]* LXV/772 (September 1987) 404-405.

TYPE: record review.

PERFORMERS: Joseph Robinson, Zubin Mehta, New York Philharmonic.

NAMES: Berg, Prokofiev, Stravinsky.

Metcalf, Steve. "Record Reviews: Classical," *The Hartford Courant [Hartford, CT]* (04 December 1986) Calendar, 8.

TYPE: record review.

PERFORMERS: Joseph Robinson, Zubin Mehta, New York Philharmonic.

Monson, Karen. "Rochberg: *Concerto*," *Ovation* VIII/5 (June 1987) 40.

TYPE: record review.

PERFORMERS: Joseph Robinson, Zubin Mehta, New York Philharmonic.

NAMES: Prokofiev, Wagner.

n.a. "1984-1985 Season Premières," *Symphony Magazine* XXXV/5 (October–November 1984) 38.

TYPE: upcoming première.

PERFORMERS: Joseph Robinson, Zubin Mehta, New York Philharmonic.

Reilly, Robert R. "Classical Reviews: Rochberg," *High Fidelity* XXXVIII/1 (January 1988) 62.

TYPE: record review.

PERFORMERS: Joseph Robinson, Zubin Mehta, New York Philharmonic.

NAMES: Beethoven, Mahler, Schönberg.

Rockwell, John. "New York Philharmonic Under Various Batons," *The New York Times* (18 January 1987) 25, 32.

TYPE: record review.

PERFORMERS: Joseph Robinson, Zubin Mehta, New York Philharmonic.

Salzman, Eric. "Rochberg: *Oboe Concerto,*" *Stereo Review* LII/2 (February 1987) 180.

TYPE: record review.

PERFORMERS: Joseph Robinson, Zubin Mehta, New York Philharmonic.

NAMES: Bartók, Berg, Mahler, Prokofiev, Sibelius.

Schwartz, K. Robert. "Rochberg: *Oboe Concerto,*" *High Fidelity/Musical America* XXXV/4 (April 1985) MA-20, MA-22.

TYPE: review.

PERFORMERS: Joseph Robinson, Zubin Mehta, New York Philharmonic.

NAMES: Berg, Mahler.

Silverton, Mike. "Random Noise," *Fanfare* XI/2 (November - December 1987) 355-356.

TYPE: record review.

PERFORMERS: Joseph Robinson, Zubin Mehta, New York Philharmonic.

NAMES: Schuman.

Ward, Charles. "Rochberg: *Oboe Concerto,*" *The Houston Chronicle* (26 April 1987) Zest, 13.

TYPE: record review.

PERFORMERS: Joseph Robinson, Zubin Mehta, New York Philharmonic.

Webster, Daniel. "Taking His Leave of Penn [University of Pennsylvania at Philadelphia] to Pen More Music," *The Philadelphia Inquirer* (27 March 1983) 1H, 10H, 11H.

TYPE: article, interview.

PERFORMERS: Joseph Robinson, Zubin Mehta, New York Philharmonic.

OTHER WORKS DISCUSSED: *The Confidence Man, Imago Mundi.*

OTHER WORKS MENTIONED: *String Quartet No. 1, String Quartet No. 2, String Quartet No. 3, String Quartet No. 4, String Quartet No. 5, String Quartet No. 6.*

Zakariasen, Bill. "*Oboe Concerto* Makes a Debut," *The Daily News [New York]* (15 December 1984) 13.

TYPE: review.

PERFORMERS: Joseph Robinson, Zubin Mehta, New York Philharmonic.

NAMES: Berg.

Concerto for Violin and Orchestra

Anthony, Michael. "Stern, Orchestra Perform," *The Minneapolis Tribune* (25 March 1976) 5-B.

TYPE: review.

PERFORMERS: Isaac Stern, Stanislaw Skrowaczewski, Minnesota Orchestra.

Apone, Carl. "Composer's 'High Note' of Birthday Celebrations," *The Pittsburgh Press* (30 March 1975) F7.

TYPE: upcoming première, interview.

PERFORMERS: Isaac Stern, Donald Johanos, Pittsburgh Symphony Orchestra.

NAMES: Bartók, Mozart, Donald Steinfirst, Schönberg.

Apone, Carl. "Surprise: New Work Gets Ovation," *The Pittsburgh Press* (05 April 1975) 8.

TYPE: review.

PERFORMERS: Isaac Stern, Donald Johanos, Pittsburgh Symphony Orchestra.

NAMES: Brahms, Hindemith, Mozart, Sibelius, Donald Steinfirst.

Belt, Byron. "Isaac Stern Premières New Rochberg *Concerto*," *The Staten Island Advance* (16 April 1975); reprinted: "Stern Plays Rochberg," *The Jersey Journal* (16 April 1975) 14; reprinted: "Stern's Rochberg Glitters," *The Long Island Press* (16 April 1975).

TYPE: review.

PERFORMERS: Isaac Stern, Donald Johanos, Pittsburgh Symphony Orchestra.

NAMES: Berg, Chausson, Korngold, Karen Monson, William Steinberg, Donald Steinfirst, Vaughan Williams.

Boehm, Yohanan. "Tonalities and Textures," *The Jerusalem Post Magazine* (05 November 1982).

TYPE: article, review, record review, interview.

PERFORMERS: Isaac Stern, Andre Previn, Pittsburgh Symphony Orchestra.

NAMES: William Steinberg.

OTHER WORKS DISCUSSED: *The Confidence Man, Sacred Song of Reconciliation.*

Carr, Jay. "An Eloquent Stern Performance," *The Detroit News* (19 March 1976) 7-C.

TYPE: review.

PERFORMERS: Isaac Stern, Aldo Ceccato, Detroit Symphony Orchestra.

NAMES: Berg.

OTHER WORKS MENTIONED: *String Quartet No. 2, Symphony No. 3.*

Carr, Jay. "Sharing a Sense of Loss with Rochberg," *The Detroit News* (29 January 1980) B5.

TYPE: review.

OTHER WORKS DISCUSSED: *String Quartet No. 3, String Quartet No. 4, String Quartet No.5, String Quartet No. 6, String Quartet No. 7.*

Close, Roy M. "Simple Themes Build Strength in *Concerto,*" *The Minneapolis Star* (25 March 1976) 5-C.

TYPE: review.

PERFORMERS: Isaac Stern, Stanislaw Skrowaczewski, Minnesota Orchestra.

Collins, Simon. "Issac Stern," *The Strad* LXXXVIII/1048 (August 1977) 291-297.

TYPE: review, interview with Isaac Stern.

PERFORMERS: Isaac Stern.

NAMES: Bach, Berg, Donald Johanos, William Steinfirst.

Covell, Roger. "Lack of Scope Sees a Change in Style," *The Sydney Morning Herald [Australia]* (18 October 1986).

TYPE: review, interview.

PERFORMERS: Isaac Stern.

OTHER WORKS DISCUSSED: *Ricordanza, String Quartet No. 3, Symphony No. 5, To the Dark Wood.*

Croan, Robert. "Classical Record Reviews: Copland Celebration: Music of George Rochberg," *The Pittsburgh Post-Gazette* (07 May 1976) 34.

TYPE: review.

PERFORMERS: Isaac Stern, Donald Johanos, Pittsburgh Symphony Orchestra.

OTHER WORKS DISCUSSED: *Duo Concertante, Ricordanza, String Quartet No. 1.*

Croan, Robert. "Late *P-G [Pittsburgh Post-Gazette]* Writer Honored: *Concerto's* Première Hails Critic Steinfirst," *The Pittsburgh Post-Gazette* (05 April 1975) 1, 22.

TYPE: review.

PERFORMERS: Isaac Stern, Donald Johanos, Pittsburgh Symphony Orchestra.

NAMES: William Steinberg, Donald Steinfirst.

Croan, Robert. "As Symphony Honors Donald Steinfirst: Rochberg Work to Première Here," *The Pittsburgh Post-Gazette* (31 March 1975) 15.

TYPE: upcoming première, interview.

PERFORMERS: Isaac Stern, Donald Johanos, Pittsburgh Symphony Orchestra.

NAMES: William Steinberg, Donald Steinfirst.

Dickinson, Peter. "Rochberg, George," *Music and Letters* LXVI/1 (January 1984) 130.

TYPE: score review.

PERFORMERS: Isaac Stern.

NAMES: Berg.

OTHER WORKS DISCUSSED: *The Confidence Man, Slow Fires of Autumn, Sonata for Viola and Piano, Songs in Praise of Krishna.*

n.a. "Entertainment Calendar: Symphony Honors Late Critic," *The Pittsburgh Post-Gazette* (04 April 1975) V, 2.

TYPE: review.

PERFORMERS: Isaac Stern.

NAMES: Donald Steinfirst.

Felton, James. "Music Beat: Rochberg Composing Opera; Wife Is Librettist," *The Sunday Bulletin [Philadelphia]* (16 July 1978) 2-EA.

TYPE: upcoming performance, article, interview.

NAMES: Isaac Stern, Philadelphia Orchestra.

OTHER WORKS DISCUSSED: *Caprice Variations, The Confidence Man, Phaedra, String Quartet No. 4, String Quartet No. 5, String Quartet No. 6.*

Felton, James. "Philadephia Composers . . . And Two From Vienna," *The Sunday Bulletin [Philadelphia]* (13 April 1975).

TYPE: upcoming première.

PERFORMERS: Isaac Stern, Donald Johanos, Pittsburgh Symphony Orchestra.

Fogel, Henry. "George Rochberg: A Raproachment with the Past," *The Syracuse Guide* V (January 1976) 24-26, 42.

TYPE: article.

NAMES: Sibelius.

PERFORMERS: Isaac Stern.

OTHER WORKS DISCUSSED: *Phaedra, String Quartet No. 3, Symphony No. 3.*

Frank, Andrew. "George Rochberg: *Concerto for Violin and Orchestra,*" *Notes: The Quarterly Journal of the Music Library Association* XXXV/1 (September 1978) 170-171.

TYPE: score review.

NAMES: Bartók, Berg, Isaac Stern.

Fried, Alexander. "A Fine, New *Violin Concerto,*" *The San Francisco Examiner* (08 May 1975) 1, 29.

TYPE: review.

PERFORMERS: Isaac Stern, Seiji Ozawa, San Francisco Symphony.

NAMES: William Steinberg.

Gagne, Cole and Tracy Caras. *Soundpieces: Interviews with American Composers.* (Metuchen, NJ: Scarecrow Press, Inc., 1982).

TYPE: interview.

OTHER WORKS DISCUSSED: *Apocalyptica [I], Black Sounds, The Confidence Man, Contra Mortem et Tempus, Electrikaleidoscope, Music for the Magic Theater, Octet, Quintet for Piano and String Quartet, Ricordanza, Sonata No. 2 for Piano Solo, String Quartet No. 3, String Quartet No. 4, String Quartet No. 5, String Quartet No. 6, Twelve Bagatelles.*

OTHER WORKS MENTIONED: many.

Greenfield, Edward. "LSO [London Symphony Orchestra]/Previn," *The Guardian [London]* (18 March 1977).

TYPE: review.

PERFORMERS: Isaac Stern, Andre Previn, London Symphony Orchestra.

NAMES: Donald Steinfirst.

Guinn, John. "At the Symphony: New *Concerto* Gets Stern's Best Effort," *The Detroit Free Press* (20 March 1976) 6B.

TYPE: review.

PERFORMERS: Isaac Stern, Aldo Ceccato, Detroit Symphony Orchestra.

NAMES: Bartók, Beethoven.

Guinn, John. "Issac Stern's Bullish On a New *Concerto*," *The Detroit Free Press* (19 March 1976) 7-B.

TYPE: upcoming première, interview with Isaac Stern.

PERFORMERS: Isaac Stern, Aldo Ceccato, Detroit Symphony Orchestra.

Guinn, John. "Rochberg's *Violin Concerto*: Symphony Concert Highlight," *The Detroit Free Press* (19 March 1976) 7-B.

TYPE: review.

PERFORMERS: Isaac Stern, Aldo Ceccato, Detroit Symphony Orchestra.

Henagow, Raymond. "Composer Bows With Stern, Solti As New *Concerto* Triumphs," *The Rogers Park-Edgewater News [Chicago]* (16 April 1975); reprinted: "Composer Bows With Stern, Solti As New *Concerto* Triumphs," *Life [Glenview, IL]* (17 April 1975); reprinted: "Composer Bows With Stern, Solti As New *Concerto* Triumphs," *Life [Skokie, IL]* (17 April 1975).

TYPE: review.

PERFORMERS: Isaac Stern, Sir Georg Solti, Chicago Symphony Orchestra.

NAMES: Khachaturian, Prokofiev.

OTHER WORKS MENTIONED: *Black Sounds, Imago Mundi, Music for the Magic Theater, Night Music, String Quartet No. 1, String Quartet No. 3, Symphony No. 2, Symphony No. 3, Symphony No. 4.*

Henahan, Donal J. "Critic's Notebook: G.O.P. [Grand Old Party (The Republican Party)] and Tanglewood in Tune," *The New York Times* (23 August 1976) 20.

TYPE: review.

PERFORMERS: Isaac Stern, Seiji Ozawa, Boston Symphony Orchestra.

NAMES: Bartók.

Henahan, Donal J. "Stern Plays Rochberg, A Tanglewood Success," *The New York Times* (17 August 1976) 24.

TYPE: review.

PERFORMERS: Isaac Stern, Seiji Ozawa, Boston Symphony Orchestra.

NAMES: Bartók, Mozart, Prokofiev, Schönberg, Webern.

OTHER WORKS MENTIONED: *String Quartet No. 3.*

Hite, Rosemary Curtin. "Wolfgang Would Have Loved It: Isaac Stern Performance Shows Master of Extremes," *The Citizen-Journal [Columbus, OH]* (03 April 1976) 6.

TYPE: review.

PERFORMERS: Isaac Stern, Evan Whallon, Columbus Symphony Orchestra.

Holland, Bernard. "Premières: Forward Regress," *The Pittsburgh Forum* (11 April 1975).

TYPE: review.

PERFORMERS: Isaac Stern, Donald Johanos, Pittsburgh Symphony Orchestra.

NAMES: Rachmaninoff.

Hughes, Robert. "On the Line: *Concerto for Violin and Orchestra,*" *Time* CV/18 (05 May 1975) 57.

TYPE: review, interview.

PERFORMERS: Isaac Stern.

NAMES: Bach, Prokofiev, Gene Rochberg, Paul Rochberg, Sibelius, Webern.

Hume, Paul. "Praise for New Music," *The Washington Post [Washington, D.C.]* (10 November 1976) B-11.

TYPE: review.

PERFORMERS: Isaac Stern, Antal Dorati, National Symphony Orchestra.

NAMES: Berg, Donald Steinfirst.

Jacobs, Arthur. "Festival Hall: Issac Stern," *The Financial Times [London]* (18 March 1977).

TYPE: review.

PERFORMERS: Isaac Stern, Andre Previn, London Symphony Orchestra.

NAMES: Bartók, Bloch, Mozart, Schönberg, Donald Steinfirst.

Johnson, Harriett. "Words & Music: Almost Worthy," *The New York Post* (16 April 1975) 45.

TYPE: review.

PERFORMERS: Isaac Stern, Donald Johanos, Pittsburgh Symphony Orchestra.

NAMES: William Steinberg, Donald Steinfirst.

Kay, Norman. "Concerts: Royal Festival Hall: LSO [London Symphony Orchestra]/Previn/Stern," *The Daily Telegraph [London]* (18 March 1977).

TYPE: review.

PERFORMERS: Isaac Stern, Andre Previn, London Symphony Orchestra.

NAMES: Bartók, Berg, Schönberg.

Krebs, Betty Dietz. "Country's Symphony Orchestras 'Wind Down' for Summer Whirl," *The Dayton Daily News [Dayton, OH]* (04 April 1975) 42.

TYPE: upcoming première.

PERFORMERS: Isaac Stern, Donald Johanos, Pittsburgh Symphony Orchestra.

NAMES: William Steinberg, Donald Steinfirst.

Krebs, Betty Dietz. "Rochberg *Concerto* Fine Sample of His Talents," *The Dayton Daily News [Dayton, OH]* (07 April 1975) 16.

TYPE: review.

PERFORMERS: Isaac Stern, Donald Johanos, Pittsburgh Symphony Orchestra.

NAMES: William Steinberg, Richard Strauss.

Kriegsman, Alan M. "Bicentennial Commissions," *The St. Louis Globe-Democrat* (19 April 1975) 10E.

TYPE: review, interview.

PERFORMERS: Isaac Stern, Donald Johanos, Pittsburgh Symphony Orchestra.

NAMES: Robert Bernat, Ralph Rizzolo, William Steinberg, Donald Steinfirst, Stravinsky.

Kriegsman, Alan M. "First of Bicentennial Works Is Premièred," *The Peninsula Herald [Monterey, CA]* (20 April 1975).

TYPE: review.

PERFORMERS: Isaac Stern, Donald Johanos, Pittsburgh Symphony Orchestra.

NAMES: William Steinberg, Donald Steinfirst.

Kriegsman, Alan M. "The Tip of the 200-Year Iceberg: The Tip of the Bicentennial Musical Iceberg," *The Washington Post [Washington, D.C.]* (07 April 1975) B1-B2.

TYPE: review, interview.

PERFORMERS: Isaac Stern, Donald Johanos, Pittsburgh Symphony Orchestra.

NAMES: Robert Bernat, Ralph Rizzolo, William Steinberg, Donald Steinfirst, Stravinsky.

La Fave, Kenneth. "Music Scene: Composer George Rochberg: Melody Above the Storm," *The Chicago Tribune* (28 April 1988).

TYPE: article, interview.

NAMES: Isaac Stern.

OTHER WORKS DISCUSSED: *Night Music, String Quartet No. 4, String Quartet No. 5, String Quartet No. 6, Symphony No. 1, Symphony No. 6.*

Lange, Art. "Rochberg: *Quintet,*" *American Record Guide* XLV/3 (December 1981) 24-25.

TYPE: record review.

NAMES: Bartók.

OTHER WORKS DISCUSSED: *Music for the Magic Theater, Quintet for Piano and String Quartet, String Quartet No. 2, String Quartet No. 3, String Quartet No. 4, String Quartet No. 5, String Quartet No. 6.*

Levin, Monroe. "Notes on Music," *Jewish Exponent* (09 May 1975).

TYPE: review.

PERFORMERS: Isaac Stern, Donald Johanos, Pittsburgh Symphony Orchestra.

NAMES: Bartók, Brahms, Tchaikovsky.

Lowens, Irving. "Dorati Work Is Premièred," *The Washington Star [Washington, D.C.]* (10 November 1976) E5.

TYPE: review.

PERFORMERS: Isaac Stern, Antal Dorati, National Symphony Orchestra.

NAMES: Mahler, Donald Steinfirst.

OTHER WORKS DISCUSSED: *Tableaux.*

Malitz, Nancy. "Stern Creates Magic with *Concerto,*" *The Cincinnati Enquirer* (21 December 1975) A-8.

TYPE: review.

PERFORMERS: Isaac Stern, Eduardo Mata, Cincinnati Symphony Orchestra.

NAMES: Babbitt, Donald Steinfirst.

Marsh, Robert C. "Rochberg Success a Tribute to a Critic," *The Chicago Sun-Times* (11 April 1975) 70.

TYPE: review.

PERFORMERS: Isaac Stern, Sir Georg Solti, Chicago Symphony Orchestra.

NAMES: Donald Steinfirst.

Mayer, William. "Modern Music Makes a Breakthrough," *Horizon* XX/1 (September 1977) 52-58.

TYPE: article, review.

NAMES: Brahms, Isaac Stern, Harold Schonberg.

Monson, Karen. "Symphony Program Suffers From '76 Spread," *The Chicago Daily News* (11 April 1975) 24.

TYPE: review.

PERFORMERS: Isaac Stern, Sir Georg Solti, Chicago Symphony Orchestra.

NAMES: Donald Steinfirst.

Monson, Karen. "Rochberg: *Concerto for Violin and Orchestra*," *High Fidelity/Musical America* XXIX/9 (September 1979) 123.

TYPE: record review.

PERFORMERS: Isaac Stern, Andre Previn, Pittsburgh Symphony Orchestra.

Northcott, Bayan. "Massenet Idol," *The Sunday Telegraph [London]* (20 March 1977).

TYPE: review.

PERFORMERS: Isaac Stern, Andre Previn, London Symphony Orchestra.

Owens, David. "Turning from Twelve-Tone: Inside Twentieth-Century Music," *The Christian Science Monitor* (03 May 1984) 39.

TYPE: article.

PERFORMERS: Isaac Stern, Andre Previn, Pittsburgh Symphony Orchestra.

OTHER WORKS DISCUSSED: *String Quartet No. 4, String Quartet No. 5, String Quartet No. 6, Symphony No. 1, Symphony No. 2.*

Pernick, Ben. "The New Rochberg," *Fanfare* II/6 (July - August 1979) 80.

TYPE: record review.

PERFORMERS: Isaac Stern, Andre Previn, Pittsburgh Symphony Orchestra.

NAMES: Bartók, Berg, Hindemith, Prokofiev, Shostakovich.

Peters, Frank. "Isaac Stern Plays Rochberg *Concerto*," *The St. Louis Post-Dispatch* (13 December 1975) 3-A.

TYPE: review.

PERFORMERS: Isaac Stern, Walter Susskind, St. Louis Symphony Orchestra.

OTHER WORKS MENTIONED: *String Quartet No. 3*.

Pincus, Andrew. "Tanglewood Review: American Composers Take Bows with BSO [Boston Symphony Orchestra]," *The Berkshire Eagle [Pittsfield, MA]* (16 August 1976) 10.

TYPE: review.

PERFORMERS: Isaac Stern, Seiji Ozawa, Boston Symphony Orchestra.

NAMES: Prokofiev, Schönberg, Stravinsky.

Porter, Andrew. "Musical Events: Questions," *The New Yorker* (12 February 1979) 109-115.

TYPE: article.

PERFORMERS: Isaac Stern.

OTHER WORKS DISCUSSED: *Chamber Symphony, Duo Concertante, Music for the Magic Theater, Ricordanza, String Quartet No. 1, String Quartet No. 2, String Quartet No. 3, String Quartet No. 4, String Quartet No. 5, String Quartet No. 6*.

Porter, Andrew. "Rochberg: Chamber Works," *High Fidelity/Musical America* XXVI/5 (May 1976) 90-92.

TYPE: review.

PERFORMERS: Isaac Stern.

OTHER WORKS DISCUSSED: *Chamber Symphony, Duo Concertante, Music for the Magic Theater, Ricordanza, String Quartet No. 1*.

von Rhein, John. "Music: The 'Concord' Debut to Mark a Return to the Romantic," *The Chicago Tribune* (20 January 1980) VI, 23.

TYPE: article, interview.

PERFORMERS: Isaac Stern, Sir Georg Solti, Chicago Symphony Orchestra.

OTHER WORKS DISCUSSED: *The Confidence Man, Music for the Magic Theater, Octet, String Quartet No. 3, String Quartet No. 4, String Quartet No. 5, String Quartet No. 6, String Quartet No. 7*.

Rice, Patricia. "Isaac Stern: Fiddler Extraordinare," *The St. Louis Post-Dispatch* (12 December 1975) 2-F.

TYPE: upcoming performance, interview with Stern.

PERFORMERS: Isaac Stern, St. Louis Symphony Orchestra.

n.a. "Rochberg *Concerto* to be Unveiled," *The Evening Bulletin [Philadelphia]* (19 March 1975) 44.

TYPE: upcoming première.

PERFORMERS: Isaac Stern, Donald Johanos, Pittsburgh Symphony Orchestra.

OTHER WORKS DISCUSSED: *Symphony No. 4.*

Salzman, Eric. "Festival: Issac Stern," *Stereo Review* XLIII/1 (July 1979) 103.

TYPE: record review.

PERFORMERS: Isaac Stern, Andre Previn, Pittsburgh Symphony Orchestra.

NAMES: Bartók, Berg, Prokofiev.

Schonberg, Harold C. "Concert: Issac Stern," *The New York Times* (16 April 1975) 54.

TYPE: review.

PERFORMERS: Isaac Stern, Donald Johanos, Pittsburgh Symphony Orchestra.

NAMES: Bloch, Brahms, Prokofiev, William Steinberg, Donald Steinfirst.

Schonberg, Harold C. "Neo-Romantic Music Warms a Public Chilled by the Avant-Garde," *The New York Times* (20 March 1977) II, 1, 17.

TYPE: article.

PERFORMERS: Isaac Stern.

NAMES: Brahms.

Shainman, Irwin. "A Musical Dichotomy," *The Berkshire Eagle [Pittsfield, MA]* (04 September 1976) 8.

TYPE: review.

PERFORMERS: Isaac Stern, Seiji Ozawa, Boston Symphony Orchestra.

NAMES: Bartók, Berg, Prokofiev.

Siegel, Sol Louis. "Rochberg: Classic Opinions," *Electricity* (06–12 August 1981) 5.

TYPE: review, interview.

PERFORMERS: Isaac Stern, Donald Johanos, Pittsburgh Symphony Orchestra.

OTHER WORKS DISCUSSED: *Quintet for Piano and String Quartet, String Quartet No. 3.*

Smith, Patrick J. "Tanglewood's Festival of Contemporary Music: Brains Count More Than Feelings," *High Fidelity/Music America* XXVI/12 (December 1976) MA-20.

TYPE: review.

PERFORMERS: Isaac Stern, Seiji Ozawa, Boston Symphony Orchestra.

Stearns, Dave. "Eastman Gets in on Major American Opera," *The Rochester Times-Union [Rochester, NY]* (11 December 1981) 1C, 4C.

TYPE: article.

PERFORMERS: Isaac Stern.

OTHER WORKS DISCUSSED: *The Confidence Man.*

Steinberg, Michael. "Leaning on Unearned Income," *The Boston Globe* (27 March 1975) 24.

TYPE: review.

PERFORMERS: Norman Fischer, Jean E. Fischer.

NAMES: Beech, Beethoven, Brahms, Britten, Eskins, Foote, Mahler, MacDowell, Schönberg.

OTHER WORKS DISCUSSED: *Ricordanza, String Quartet No. 3.*

n.a. "Stern Billed with Chicago Symphony," *The South End Reporter [Chicago]* (03 April 1975); reprinted: *The Southtown Economist [Chicago]* (02 April 1975).

TYPE: review.

PERFORMERS: Isaac Stern, Sir Georg Solti, Chicago Symphony Orchestra.

NAMES: Bartók, Mozart, Schönberg.

n.a. "Thrilling Première of *Concerto,*" *The St Louis Globe-Democrat* (13 December 1975) 6-D.

TYPE: review.

PERFORMERS: Isaac Stern, Walter Susskind, St. Louis Symphony Orchestra.

Tircuit, Heuwell. "At the Symphony: *Violin Concerto* About Concertos," *The San Francisco Chronicle* (09 May 1975).

TYPE: review.

PERFORMERS: Isaac Stern, Seiji Ozawa, San Francisco Symphony.

NAMES: Bloch, Messiaen, Paganini, Prokofiev, Sessions, Symanowski, Vieuxtemp.

OTHER WORKS DISCUSSED: *String Quartet No. 3, Symphony No. 2.*

van Vugt, Harry. "Stern Brilliant in New *Concerto*," *The Windsor Star [Windsor, Ontario, Canada]* (19 March 1976).

TYPE: review.

PERFORMERS: Isaac Stern, Aldo Ceccato, Detroit Symphony Orchestra.

Walsh, Michael. "Kronos Quartet Passes the Test," *The San Francisco Examiner* (28 March 1980) 31.

TYPE: review.

PERFORMERS: Kronos String Quartet.

OTHER WORKS DISCUSSED: *String Quartet No. 2, String Quartet No. 3, String Quartet No. 4, String Quartet No. 5, String Quartet No. 6.*

Webster, Daniel. "On the Changing Rhythms in the Life of a Composer," *The Philadelphia Inquirer* (16 January 1979) D1, D3.

TYPE: article, interview.

PERFORMERS: Isaac Stern, Philadelphia Orchestra.

OTHER WORKS DISCUSSED: *The Confidence Man, Slow Fires of Autumn, String Quartet No. 4, String Quartet No. 5, String Quartet No. 6.*

Webster, Daniel. "Pittsburgh Symphony: Rochberg Première," *High Fidelity/Musical America* XXV/8 (August 1975) MA-25, MA-37.

TYPE: review.

PERFORMERS: Isaac Stern, Donald Johanos, Pittsburgh Symphony Orchestra.

NAMES: William Steinberg, Donald Steinfirst.

Webster, Daniel. "Rochberg *Concerto* Sparkles," *The Philadelphia Inquirer* (09 April 1975) 9D.

TYPE: review.

PERFORMERS: Isaac Stern, Donald Johanos, Pittsburgh Symphony Orchestra.

Webster, Daniel. "Rochberg's *Concerto* Sticks with Tradition," *The Philadelphia Inquirer* (03 April 1975) 4C.

TYPE: review.

PERFORMERS: Isaac Stern, Donald Johanos, Pittsburgh Symphony Orchestra.

OTHER WORKS DISCUSSED: *Symphony No. 3.*

n.a. "Who's Here," *Keshet: Cultural News from Israel [Jerusalem]* VI (December 1982) 6.

TYPE: upcoming performance.

PERFORMERS: Jerusalem Symphony Orchestra.

Wierzbicki, James. "Music: 'Conservative' *Concerto*," *The Cincinnati Post* (22 December 1975) 29.

TYPE: review.

PERFORMERS: Isaac Stern, Eduardo Mata, Cincinnati Symphony Orchestra.

NAMES: Donald Steinfirst.

Wierzbicki, James. "George Rochberg," *The St. Louis Globe-Democrat* (30 August 1980) 6B.

TYPE: record review.

OTHER WORKS DISCUSSED: *Slow Fires of Autumn, Ukiyo-e.*

Wierzbicki, James. "Up the River," *The Cincinnati Post* (16 April 1975) 22.

TYPE: review.

PERFORMERS: Isaac Stern, Donald Johanos, Pittsburgh Symphony Orchestra.

NAMES: Donald Steinfirst.

Willis, Thomas. "The Symphony: Memory and Music Served," *The Chicago Tribune* (11 April 1975) III, 7.

TYPE: review.

PERFORMERS: Isaac Stern, Sir Georg Solti, Chicago Symphony Orchestra.

NAMES: Bartók, Mahler, Schönberg, William Walton.

Zakariasen, Bill. "A Gift for Fiddlers," *The New York Daily News* (17 April 1975) 105.

TYPE: review.

PERFORMERS: Isaac Stern, Donald Johanos, Pittsburgh Symphony Orchestra.

NAMES: Bartók, Korngold, Prokofiev, Respighi, Donald Steinfirst, Szymanowski.

The Confidence Man   (A Comic Fable), Opera in Two Parts

Alyo. "Opera Reviews: *The Confidence Man* (Santa Fe Opera)," *Variety* CCCVIII (08 September 1982) 120.

TYPE: review.

PERFORMERS: Santa Fe Opera.

NAMES: Melville.

Barnheimer, Martin. "World Première: Rochberg's *Confidence Man* Staged in Santa Fe," *The Los Angeles Times* (07 August 1982) V (Calendar), 1, 7; reprinted: "Santa Fe Opera," *Opera Canada* XXIII/4 (1982) 28-29.

TYPE: review.

PERFORMERS: Santa Fe Opera.

NAMES: Hindemith, Melville, Menotti, Puccini, Strauss, Wagner, Verdi.

Baxter, Robert. "Music: Work Première to Mark Group's Birthday," *The Courier-Post [Philadelphia]* (03 January 1982).

TYPE: upcoming première, interview with the Concord String Quartet.

OTHER WORKS DISCUSSED: *Quintet for String Quintet.*

Belsom, J. "Santa Fe: A Première and an Absorbing Repertoire," *Opera* XXXIII (Autumn 1982) 119-120.

TYPE: review.

Boehm, Yohanan. "Tonalities and Textures," *The Jerusalem Post Magazine* (05 November 1982).

TYPE: article, review, record review, interview.

PERFORMERS: Santa Fe Opera.

NAMES: Britten, Melville.

OTHER WORKS DISCUSSED: *Concerto for Violin and Orchestra Sacred Song of Reconciliation.*

Cunningham, Carl. "Opera: *The Confidence Man,*" *The Houston Post* (01 August 1982) AA-13.

TYPE: review.

PERFORMERS: Santa Fe Opera.

NAMES: Melville, Mozart, Gene Rochberg, Stravinsky.

Davis, Peter G. "Music: Lost in the Desert," *New York* XV (23 August 1982) 79-80.

TYPE: review.

PERFORMERS: Santa Fe Opera.

NAMES: Berg, Britten, Melville, Menotti, Monteverdi, Poulenc, Gene Rochberg.

Davis, Peter G. "Rochberg Finishing His First Opera," *The New York Times* (21 May 1981) III, 24.

TYPE: upcoming première, interview.

PERFORMERS: Santa Fe Opera.

NAMES: Emerson, Hawthorne, Melville, Gene Rochberg, Shakespeare, Verdi.

Dickinson, Peter. "Rochberg, George," *Music and Letters* LXVI/1 (January 1984) 130.

TYPE: score review.

PERFORMERS: Santa Fe Opera.

OTHER WORKS DISCUSSED: *Concerto for Violin and Orchestra, Slow Fires of Autumn, Sonata for Viola and Piano, Songs in Praise of Krishna.*

Dunning, William. "Satisfied Exhilaration," *The Santa Fe Reporter* (02 August 1979).

TYPE: review, inteview.

PERFORMERS: Santa Fe Opera.

NAMES: Melville.

OTHER WORKS DISCUSSED: *Quintet for Piano and String Quartet, Ricordanza, String Quartet No. 4, String Quartet No. 5, String Quartet No. 6.*

OTHER WORKS MENTIONED: *String Quartet No. 1, String Quartet No. 2, String Quartet No. 3.*

Eckert, Thor Jr. "Santa Fe: A Place for the New and Obscure in Opera: Rochberg's Effort Lacks Unitym While Strauss' Opera Proves Its Worth," *The Christian Science Monitor* (23 August 1982) 17.

TYPE: review.

PERFORMERS: Santa Fe Opera.

NAMES: Melville, Gene Rochberg.

OTHER WORKS MENTIONED: *Concerto for Violin and Orchestra, Quintet for Piano and String Quartet, Quintet for String Quintet, String Quartet No. 4, String Quartet No. 5, String Quartet No. 6.*

Eckert, Thor Jr. "Two Contrasting Festivals and What They Say About Standards Today," *The Christian Science Monitor* (01 September 1982) 18.

TYPE: review.

PERFORMERS: Santa Fe Opera.

OTHER WORKS DISCUSSED: *Quintet for String Quintet.*

Feder, Susan. "Santa Fe," *Musical Times [Great Britain]* CXXIII/1676 (October 1982) 713.

TYPE: review.

PERFORMERS: Santa Fe Opera.

NAMES: Melville, Gene Rochberg.

OTHER WORKS DISCUSSED: *Quintet for String Quintet.*

Felton, James. "Music Beat: Rochberg Composing Opera; Wife Is Librettist," *The Sunday Bulletin [Philadelphia]* (16 July 1978) 2-EA.

TYPE: article, interview.

PERFORMERS: Santa Fe Opera.

NAMES: Hermann Hesse, Melville, Gene Rochberg.

OTHER WORKS DISCUSSED: *Caprice Variations, Concerto for Violin and Orchestra, Phaedra, String Quartet No. 4, String Quartet No. 5, String Quartet No. 6.*

n.a. "A First Opera from Rochberg," *Ovation* III/5 (June 1982) 7.

TYPE: upcoming première.

PERFORMERS: Richard Pearlman, Santa Fe Opera.

NAMES: Melville, Gene Rochberg.

Gagne, Cole and Tracy Caras. *Soundpieces: Interviews with American Composers.* (Metuchen, NJ: Scarecrow Press, Inc., 1982).

TYPE: interview.

PERFORMERS: Santa Fe Opera.

NAMES: Menotti.

OTHER WORKS DISCUSSED: *Apocalyptica [I], Black Sounds, Concerto for Violin and Orchestra, Contra Mortem et Tempus, Electrikaleidoscope, Music for the Magic Theater, Octet, Quintet for Piano and String Quartet, Ricordanza, Sonata No. 2 for Piano Solo, String Quartet No. 3, String Quartet No. 4, String Quartet No. 5, String Quartet No. 6, Twelve Bagatelles.*

OTHER WORKS MENTIONED: many.

Goldsmith, Diane. "Santa Fe: Rochberg's First Opera: A Tenth Anniversary," *Ovation* III/10 (November 1982) 36-37.

TYPE: review.

PERFORMERS: Santa Fe Opera.

NAMES: Debussy, Melville, Gene Rochberg.

OTHER WORKS DISCUSSED: *Quintet for String Quintet.*

Henahan, Donal J. "Music View: Focusing on the Vexing Libretto Problem," *The New York Times* (15 August 1982) II, 15.

TYPE: review.

PERFORMERS: Santa Fe Opera.

NAMES: Berg, William Gaddis, James Joyce, Thomas Mann, Gene Rochberg, Nathaniel West.

Henahan, Donal J. "Opera: Melville's *Confidence Man* in Santa Fe," *The New York Times* (02 August 1982) III, 14.

TYPE: review.

PERFORMERS: Santa Fe Opera.

NAMES: Melville, Puccini, Gene Rochberg, Tchaikovsky, Verdi.

Jacobson, Robert. "Santa Fe," *Opera News* XLVII/5 (November 1982) 38, 40, 42.

TYPE: review.

PERFORMERS: Santa Fe Opera.

NAMES: Boulez, Hindemith, Jerome Kern, Mahler, Melville, Gene Rochberg.

Kerner, Leighton. "Music: The Salome of the Golden West," *Voice* XXXVII (31 August 1982) 68.

TYPE: Mreview.

PERFORMERS: Santa Fe Opera.

NAMES: Berg, Sigmund Romberg, Weill.

OTHER WORKS MENTIONED: *Concerto for Violin and Orchestra, String Quartet No. 1, String Quartet No. 2, String Quartet No. 3, String Quartet No. 4, String Quartet No. 5, String Quartet No. 6.*

LaFave, Kenneth. "Odyssey to Opera," *Opera News* XLVII/1 (July 1982) 14-16.

TYPE: article, interview.

PERFORMERS: Santa Fe Opera.

NAMES: Berg, Melville, Mozart, Gene Rochberg, Rossini, Strauss, Verdi, Wagner.

OTHER WORKS MENTIONED: *Chamber Symphony, Contra Mortem et Tempus, Music for the Magic Theater, String Quartet No. 3, String Quartet No. 4, String Quartet No. 5, String Quartet No. 6, String Quartet No. 7, Twelve Bagatelles.*

Larson, Tom. "Musical Festival Gives Rare Musical Gift," *The New Mexican [Santa Fe, NM]* (29 July 1982) A-4.

TYPE: upcoming première.

PERFORMERS: Santa Fe Opera.

OTHER WORKS DISCUSSED: *Quintet for String Quintet.*

OTHER WORKS MENTIONED: *String Quartet No. 3, String Quartet No. 4, String Quartet No. 5, String Quartet No. 6, String Quartet No. 7.*

Levin, Monroe. "Notes on Music," *Jewish Exponent* (15 January 1982).

TYPE: upcoming première.

PERFORMERS: Santa Fe Opera.

OTHER WORKS DISCUSSED: *Quintet for String Quintet.*

McLellean, Joseph. "*Confidence Man* Opera Reflects Composer's Shift to New Lyricism," *The Philadelphia Inquirer* (03 August 1982) 6-D.

TYPE: review.

PERFORMERS: Santa Fe Opera.

NAMES: Melville, Gene Rochberg.

Oppens, Kurt. "Raritäten: Rochberg's *Confidence Man* and Strauss' *Liebe der Danae* in Santa Fe," *Opernwelt* XXIII/10 (October 1982) 36-38.

TYPE: review.

PERFORMERS: Santa Fe Opera.

NAMES: Berg, James Joyce, Melville, Gene Rochberg, Weill.

Porter, Andrew. "Musical Events: A Frail Bark," *The New Yorker* (16 August 1982) 66-68.

TYPE: review.

PERFORMERS: Santa Fe Opera.

NAMES: Emerson, Elizabeth Foster, Thomas Mann, Melville, Hershel Parker, Puccini, Gene Rochberg, Tchaikovsky, Thoreau, Carl van Vechten, Mark Winsome.

OTHER WORKS DISCUSSED: *Quintet for String Quintet, String Quartet No. 3.*

von Rhein, John. "Music: The 'Concord' Debut to Mark a Return to the Romantic," *The Chicago Tribune* (20 January 1980) VI, 23.

TYPE: article, interview.

PERFORMERS: Santa Fe Opera.

NAMES: Melville, Gene Rochberg.

OTHER WORKS DISCUSSED: *Concerto for Violin and Orcehestra, Music for the Magic Theater, Octet, String Quartet No. 3, String Quartet No. 4, String Quartet No. 5, String Quartet No. 6, String Quartet No. 7.*

von Rhein, John. "*Confidence Man* a Lifeless Disaster," *The Chicago Tribune* (03 August 1982) II, 4.

TYPE: review.

PERFORMERS: Santa Fe Opera.

NAMES: Berg, Mahler, Melville, Puccini, Gene Rochberg, Weill.

OTHER WORKS DISCUSSED: *String Quartet No. 4, String Quartet No. 5, String Quartet No. 6.*

von Rhein, John. "Two New Opera–One Good, One Less than Grand," *The Chicago Tribune* (22 August 1982) Arts and Books: VI, 8, 9.

TYPE: review.

PERFORMERS: Santa Fe Opera.

NAMES: Boulez, Gene Rochberg, Weill.

n.a. "The Rochbergs Have Turned to Melville for Their First Opera,"
The Pennsylvania Gazette (June 1982) 17-18.

TYPE: upcoming première, interview.

PERFORMERS: Santa Fe Opera.

NAMES: Melville, Gene Rochberg, Wagner.

Smith, Patrick J. "Rochberg's *The Confidence Man*," *High Fidelity/Musical America* XXXII/11 (November 1982) MA-30, MA-32.

TYPE: review.

PERFORMERS: Santa Fe Opera.

NAMES: Melville, Sigmund Romberg, Gene Rochberg.

Stearns, Dave. "Eastman Gets in on Major American Opera," *The Rochester Times-Union [Rochester, NY]* (11 December 1981) 1C, 4C.

TYPE: article, upcoming première, interview.

PERFORMERS: Richard Pearlman, Santa Fe Opera.

NAMES: Herman Hesse, Melville, Gene Rochberg.

OTHER WORKS DISCUSSED: *Concerto for Violin and Orchestra*.

Walsh, Michael. "In Santa Fe, A Worthy Failure: Rochberg's *Confidence Man* Challengingly Evokes an Older Idiom," *Time* CXX/7 (16 August 1982) 64.

TYPE: review.

PERFORMERS: Santa Fe Opera.

NAMES: Melville, Gene Rochberg.

OTHER WORKS MENTIONED: *Concerto for Violin and Orchestra*, *String Quartet No. 3*, *String Quartet No. 4*, *String Quartet No. 5*, *String Quartet No. 6*.

Webster, Daniel. "Concord Quartet: Rochberg *Quintet* Première," *High Fidelity/Musical America* XXXII/5 (May 1982) MA-34, MA-36.

TYPE: review.

PERFORMERS: Santa Fe Opera.

OTHER WORKS DISCUSSED: *Quintet for String Quintet*.

Webster, Daniel. "George Rochberg: American Music's Bellwether," *The Philadelphia Inquirer* (25 July 1982) 1-K, 13-K.

TYPE: article, interview.

PERFORMERS: Santa Fe Opera.

NAMES: John Crosby, Hermann Hesse, Melville, Mozart, Puccini, Gene Rochberg.

OTHER WORKS DISCUSSED: *Phaedra, Symphony No. 2*.

OTHER WORKS MENTIONED: many.

Webster, Daniel. "George Rochberg: His First Opera, to be Premièred Next Month Turns a New Stylistic Corner," *High Fidelity/Musical America* XXXII/6 (June 1982) Cover, MA-4, MA-5, MA-39.

TYPE: upcoming première, interview.

PERFORMERS: Santa Fe Opera.

NAMES: Hermann Hesse, Melville, Mozart, Puccini, Gene Rochberg, Wagner.

Webster, Daniel. "On the Changing Rhythms in the Life of a Composer," *The Philadelphia Inquirer* (16 January 1979) D1, D3.

TYPE: article, interview.

PERFORMERS: Santa Fe Opera.

OTHER WORKS DISCUSSED: *Concerto for Violin and Orchestra, Slow Fires of Autumn, String Quartet No. 4, String Quartet No. 5, String Quartet No. 6.*

Webster, Daniel. "A Quartet Will Ring Out the Old by Stringing in the New," *The Philadephia Inquirer* (03 January 1982).

TYPE: article, upcoming première, interview with the Concord String Quartet.

PERFORMERS: Santa Fe Opera.

OTHER WORKS DISCUSSED: *Quintet for String Quintet, String Quartet No. 3, String Quartet No. 4, String Quartet No. 5, String Quartet No. 6.*

Webster, Daniel. "Rochberg *Quintet*: A Pictorial Prelude to the Opera," *The Philadelphia Inquirer* (07 January 1982).

TYPE: review.

PERFORMERS: Santa Fe Opera.

OTHER WORKS DISCUSSED: *Quintet for String Quintet.*

Webster, Daniel. "Taking His Leave of Penn [University of Pennsylvania at Philadelphia] to Pen More Music," *The Philadelphia Inquirer* (27 March 1983) 1H, 10H, 11H.

TYPE: article, interview.

PERFORMERS: Santa Fe Opera.

OTHER WORKS DISCUSSED: *Concerto for Oboe and Orchestra, Imago Mundi.*

OTHER WORKS MENTIONED: *String Quartet No. 1, String Quartet No. 2, String Quartet No. 3, String Quartet No. 4, String Quartet No. 5, String Quartet No. 6.*

Woodford, Bruce. "Some Noteable Thoughts," *The Santa Fe Reporter* (11 July 1984) 27.

TYPE: review.

PERFORMERS: Santa Fe Opera.

BOOKS DISCUSSED: *The Aesthetics of Survival.*

Young, Allen. "Big Voices, Risky Rep Mark Santa Fe Opera; Walk-outs on Melville," *Variety* (18 August 1982).

TYPE: review.

PERFORMERS: Santa Fe Opera.

NAMES: Melville.

Contra Mortem et Tempus for Flute, Clarinet, Violin, and Piano

Archibald, Bruce. "Rochberg: *Chamber Symphony, Duo Concertante, Music for the Magic Theater, Ricordanza, String Quartet No. 1*," *Musical Quarterly* LXXII/4 (October 1976) 613-615.

TYPE: record review.

NAMES: Berg, Berio, Boulez, Ives, Varèse.

OTHER WORKS DISCUSSED: *Chamber Symphony, Duo Concertante, Music for the Magic Theater, Ricordanza, String Quartet No. 1.*

Bowen, Meirion. "Purcell Room: American Music," *The Guardian [London]* (05 March 1982).

TYPE: review.

PERFORMERS: Lysis [Ensemble].

NAMES: Berlioz, Boulez, Ives, Varèse.

Danuser, Hermann. "Zur Kritik der musikalischen Postmoderne," *Neue Zeitschrift fur Musik* CXLIX/12 (December 1988) 4-9.

TYPE: article.

OTHER WORKS DISCUSSED: *Music for the Magic Theater, Quintet for Piano and String Quartet, String Quartet No. 2, String Quartet No. 3, Trio [No. 1] for Violin, Cello, and Piano.*

BOOKS DISCUSSED: *The Aesthetics of Survival.*

Dixon, Joan DeVee. "George Rochberg's *Nach Bach, A Fantasy for Harpsichord or Piano*," Unpublished (June 1988) 13pp.

TYPE: article, interviews with George Rochberg and Igor Kipnis.

OTHER WORKS DISCUSSED: *Chamber Symphony, Music for the Magic Theater, Nach Bach, Partita Variations, Sonata-Fantasia, Symphony No. 3.*

D., P. W. "Lysis Ensemble," *The Daily Telegraph [London]* (05 March 1982).

TYPE: review.

PERFORMERS: Lysis Ensemble.

NAMES: Webern.

Felton, James. "Composers Are Sane But the World Isn't, Says Penn Rochberg," *The Sunday Bulletin [Philadelphia]* (13 February 1966) 11.

TYPE: interview.

PERFORMERS: Aeolian Chamber Players.

OTHER WORKS DISCUSSED: *Music for the Magic Theater, Night Music, String Quartet No. 2, Symphony No. 1, Symphony No. 2, Symphony No. 3, Zodiac.*

Gagne, Cole and Tracy Caras. *Soundpieces: Interviews with American Composers.* (Metuchen, NJ: Scarecrow Press, Inc., 1982).

TYPE: interview.

OTHER WORKS DISCUSSED: *Apocalyptica [I], Black Sounds, Concerto for Violin and Orchestra, The Confidence Man, Electrikaleidoscope, Music for the Magic Theater, Octet, Quintet for Piano and String Quartet, Ricordanza, Sonata No. 2 for Piano Solo, String Quartet No. 3, String Quartet No. 4, String Quartet No. 5, String Quartet No. 6, Twelve Bagatelles.*

OTHER WORKS MENTIONED: many.

Gelles, George. "Bowdoin Festival: Accent on the New," *The Boston Globe* (15 August 1966) 15.

TYPE: review.

PERFORMERS: Aeolian Chamber Players.

OTHER WORKS DISCUSSED: *La Bocca della Verità, Nach Bach, Trio [No. 1] for Violin, Cello, and Piano.*

Griffiths, Paul. *Modern Music: A Concise History from Debussy to Boulez.* (New York, NY: Thames and Hudson, Inc., 1978) 200-201.

TYPE: article.

NAMES: Beethoven, Mahler.

OTHER WORKS DISCUSSED: *String Quartet No. 3.*

Hinson, Maurice. *The Piano in Chamber Ensemble: An Annotated Guide.* (Bloomington, IN: Indiana University Press, 1978) 442.

TYPE: review.

NAMES: Berio, Boulez, Ives, Varèse.

OTHER WORKS DISCUSSED: *Dialogues, Ricordanza, Trio [No. 1] for Violin, Cello, and Piano.*

Jack, Adrian. *"Contra Mortem et Tempus,"* *Records and Recordings [Great Britain]* XVIII/9 (June 1975) 45-46.

TYPE: review.

PERFORMERS: Aeolian Chamber Players.

NAMES: Webern, Charles Wuorinen.

Johnson, Wayne. "Rochberg Will Hear Rochberg this Friday," *The Seattle Times* (29 October 1969) 20.

TYPE: upcoming performance.

PERFORMERS: William O. Smith, Robert Suderberg, University of Washington Contemporary Group, Philadelphia String Quartet, Soni Ventorum.

OTHER WORKS DISCUSSED: *Music for "The Alchemist," Music for the Magic Theater, Tableaux.*

Johnson, Wayne. "U. W. [University of Washington] Group Plays Great Concert," *The Seattle Times* (03 November 1969) 22.

TYPE: review.

PERFORMERS: William O. Smith, Robert Suderberg, University of Washington Contemporary Group, Philadelphia String Quartet, Soni Ventorum.

NAMES: Berg, Mozart.

OTHER WORKS DISCUSSED: *Music for "The Alchemist," Music for the Magic Theater, Tableaux.*

Klein, Howard. "A New Look for an Old Label," *The New York Times* (23 March 1969) IV, 32-33.

TYPE: record review.

PERFORMERS: Aeolian Chamber Players.

Mootz, William. "Rochberg's Works Offer Constant Allures," *The Courier Journal [Louisville, KY]* (16 April 1980) C4.

TYPE: review.

PERFORMERS: Francis Fuge, Dallas Tidwell, David Updegraff, John Craig.

OTHER WORKS DISCUSSED: *Blake Songs, Quintet for Piano and String Quartet, Ricordanza.*

Potter, Keith. "Rochberg: *String Quartet No. 1, Duo Concertante, Ricordanza,"* *Records and Recordings [London]* (March 1977) 72-73.

TYPE: record review.

OTHER WORKS DISCUSSED: *Blake Songs, Duo Concertante, Ricordanza, String Quartet No. 1, String Quartet No. 2, String Quartet No. 3.*

Putnam, Thomas. "Composer Hears *Magic Theater*: Played by Philharmonic with Melvin Conducting," *The Buffalo Courier Express* (26 January 1969).

TYPE: review, interview.

NAMES: Berg, Hermann Hesse, Ives, Mahler, Mozart, Varèse, Webern.

OTHER WORKS DISCUSSED: *Music for the Magic Theater, Symphony No. 3, Time-Span.*

Reise, Jay. "Rochberg the Progressive," *Perspectives of New Music* XIX/1-2 (Fall-Winter 1980/Spring-Summer 1981) 395-407.

TYPE: article, analysis.

NAMES: Berg, Steven Block.

OTHER WORKS DISCUSSED: *String Quartet No. 3, Symphony No. 2, Tableaux.*

Ringer, Alexander L. "The Music of George Rochberg," *Musical Quarterly* LII/4 (October 1966) 409-430.

TYPE: article.

PERFORMERS: Aeolian Chamber Players.

NAMES: Berg, Berio, Boulez, Ives, Varèse.

OTHER WORKS DISCUSSED: *Apocalyptica [I], Black Sounds, Blake Songs, La Bocca della Verità, Cantio Sacra, Capriccio for Two Pianos, Chamber Symphony, Cheltenham Concerto, Concert Piece for Two Pianos and Orchestra, David, the Psalmist, Dialogues, Duo Concertante, Four Songs of Solomon, Music for the Magic Theater, Nach Bach, Night Music, Passions [According to the Twentieth Century], Serenata d'estate, Sonata-Fantasia, String Quartet No. 1, String Quartet No. 2, Symphony No. 1, Symphony No. 2, Three Psalms, Time-Span, Trio for Clarinet, Horn, and Piano, Trio [No. 1] for Violin, Cello, and Piano, Twelve Bagatelles, Zodiac.*

OTHER WORKS MENTIONED: *Arioso, Bartokiana, Five Smooth Stones, Sonata No. 1 for Piano Solo, Sonata No. 2 for Piano Solo, Waltz Serenade.*

BOOKS DISCUSSED: *The Hexachord and Its Relation to the Twelve-Tone Row.*

Salzman, Eric. "Rochberg: *Contra Mortem et Tempus*," *Stereo Review* XXII/4 (April 1969) 100.

TYPE: record review.

PERFORMERS: Aeolian Chamber Players.

OTHER WORKS DISCUSSED: *Music for the Magic Theater.*

Schwartz, Elliott. "Current Chronicle: United States: Brunswick, Maine," *Musical Quarterly* LI/4 (October 1965) 680-687.

TYPE: review.

PERFORMERS: Aeolian Chamber Players.

NAMES: Berg, Meyer Kupforman, Ives, Morton Subotnick, Varèse, Webern.

Spaeth, Sigmund. "Contemporary Music at Bowdoin College," *Music Educators' Journal* LII/3 (January 1966) 96.

TYPE: announcement of ASCAP award.

PERFORMERS: Aeolian Chamber Players.

Speath, Sigmund. "Contemporary Music Festival," *Music Journal* XXIII/8 (November 1965) 28, 61-62.

TYPE: review.

PERFORMERS: Aeolian Chamber Players.

NAMES: Berg, Ives, Varèse, Webern.

Steinberg, Michael. "Festival at Bowdoin Features New Concerts," *The Boston Globe* (19 August 1965) 24.

TYPE: review.

PERFORMERS: Aeolian Chamber Players.

NAMES: Berg, Ives, Varèse, Webern.

Steinberg, Michael. "Fromm Free Program Intense, Almost Violent," *The Boston Globe* (06 November 1972) 23.

TYPE: review.

OTHER WORKS DISCUSSED: *String Quartet No. 3.*

Stromberg, Rolf. "Two Young Musicians Gifted," *The Seattle Post-Intelligencer* (03 November 1969) S*45.

TYPE: review.

PERFORMERS: William O. Smith, Robert Suderberg, University of Washington Contemporary Group, Philadelphia String Quartet, Soni Ventorum.

OTHER WORKS DISCUSSED: *Music for "The Alchemist," Music for the Magic Theater, Tableaux.*

Stronglin, Theodore. "Aeolian Chamber Players Offer Bowdoin-Commissioned Works," *The New York Times* (11 May 1966) 42.

TYPE: review.

PERFORMERS: Aeolian Chamber Players.

Thorne, Michael. "Rochberg: *Contra Mortem et Tempus*," *HiFi News* (December 1975).

TYPE: Review

PERFORMERS: Aeolian Chamber Players.

OTHER WORKS DISCUSSED: *String Quartet No. 3.*

Webster, Daniel. "At the Art Alliance: Aeolian Players Shine Spotlight on Rochberg," *The Philadelphia Inquirer* (16 February 1966) 27.

TYPE: review.

PERFORMERS: Aeolian Chamber Players.

NAMES: Berg, Ives, Varèse, Webern.

OTHER WORKS DISCUSSED: *La Bocca della Verità, Dialogues, Trio [No. 1] for Violin, Cello, and Piano.*

Webster, Daniel. "Rochberg's Chamber Music Is Aired at the Art Alliance," *The Evening Bulletin [Philadelphia]* (16 February 1966).

TYPE: review.

PERFORMERS: Aeolian Chamber Players.

NAMES: Webern.

OTHER WORKS DISCUSSED: *La Bocca della Verità, Dialogues, Night Music, Symphony No. 1, Symphony No. 2, Trio [No. 1] for Violin, Cello, and Piano.*

David, The Psalmist for Tenor Solo and Orchestra

Diehl, George K. "At Philadelphia Civic Center: Première of *David, The Psalmist,*" *The Evening Bulletin [Philadelphia]* (09 December 1966) B-53.

TYPE: review.

PERFORMERS: David Page, Melvin Strauss.

NAMES: Schönberg.

n.a. "Honoring the American Composer," *International Musician* LIX/7 (January 1961) 44.

TYPE: première.

PERFORMERS: Frederic Prausnitz, Juilliard Orchestra.

Manges, Edyth. "George Rochberg, Newtown, Is Prize-Winning Composer," *The Upper Darby News [Upper Darby, PA]* XXII/17 (11 November 1954) 1.

OTHER WORKS DISCUSSED: *Night Music.*

Ringer, Alexander L. "Current Chronicle: New York, Jerusalem, and Urbana, Illinois," *Musical Quarterly* LVIII/1 (January 1972) 128-132.

TYPE: review.

PERFORMERS: United States Cultural Centers in Tel Aviv and Jerusalem.

OTHER WORKS MENTIONED: *Sacred Song of Reconciliation, Songs in Praise of Krishna, Symphony No. 3.*

Ringer, Alexander L. "Current Chronicle: United States: Cleveland," *Musical Quarterly* XLV/2 (April 1959) 230-234.

TYPE: article, review.

OTHER WORKS DISCUSSED: *Chamber Symphony, Sonata-Fantasia, String Quartet No. 1, Symphony No. 1, Symphony No. 2, Three Psalms, Twelve Bagatelles.*

BOOKS DISCUSSED: *The Hexachord and Its Relation to the Twelve-Tone Row.*

Ringer, Alexander L. "The Music of George Rochberg," *Musical Quarterly* LII/4 (October 1966) 409-430.

TYPE: article.

NAMES: Schönberg.

OTHER WORKS DISCUSSED: *Apocalyptica [I], Black Sounds, Blake Songs, La Bocca della Verità, Cantio Sacra, Capriccio for Two Pianos, Chamber Symphony, Cheltenham Concerto, Concert Piece for Two Pianos and Orchestra, Contra Mortem et Tempus, Dialogues, Duo Concertante, Four Songs of Solomon, Music for the Magic Theater, Nach Bach, Night Music, Passions [According to the Twentieth Century], Serenata d'estate, Sonata-Fantasia, String Quartet No. 1, String Quartet No. 2, Symphony No. 1, Symphony No. 2, Three Psalms, Time-Span, Trio for Clarinet, Horn, and Piano, Trio [No. 1] for Violin, Cello, and Piano, Twelve Bagatelles, Zodiac.*

OTHER WORKS MENTIONED: *Arioso, Bartokiana, Five Smooth Stones, Sonata No. 1 for Piano Solo, Sonata No. 2 for Piano Solo, Waltz Serenade.*

BOOKS DISCUSSED: *The Hexachord and Its Relation to the Twelve-Tone Row.*

Scanlan, Roger. "Spotlight on Contemporary American Composers," *The NATS [National Association of Teachers of Singing] Bulletin* XXXIII/1 (October 1976) 48-49, 53-54.

TYPE: article.

OTHER WORKS DISCUSSED: *Blake Songs, Eleven Songs, Four Songs of Solomon, Fantasies, Music for "The Alchemist," Phaedra, Sacred Song of Reconciliation, Songs in Praise of Krishna, String Quartet No. 2, Symphony No. 3, Tableaux, Two Songs from "Tableaux".*

OTHER WORKS MENTIONED: many.

Dialogues for Clarinet and Piano

Felton, James. "Rochberg's Chamber Music Is Aired at the Art Alliance," *The Evening Bulletin [Philadelphia]* (16 February 1966) 27.

TYPE: review.

PERFORMERS: Aeolian Chamber Players.

NAMES: Webern.

OTHER WORKS DISCUSSED: *La Bocca della Verità, Contra Mortem et Tempus, Night Music, Symphony No. 1, Symphony No. 2, Trio [No. 1] for Violin, Cello, and Piano.*

Hinson, Maurice. *The Piano in Chamber Ensemble: An Annotated Guide.* (Bloomington, IN: Indiana University Press, 1978) 442.

TYPE: review.

OTHER WORKS DISCUSSED: *Contra Mortem et Tempus, Ricordanza, Trio [No. 1] for Violin, Cello, and Piano.*

n.a. "Music and Dance: Ormandy Back from Europe; Rochberg Concert at Curtis," *The Evening Bulletin [Philadelphia]* (04 February 1977) 29, 31.

TYPE: upcoming performance.

PERFORMERS: John Russo, Lydia Ignacio.

OTHER WORKS DISCUSSED: *Partita Variations, Quintet for Piano and String Quartet.*

Ringer, Alexander L. "The Music of George Rochberg," *Musical Quarterly* LII/4 (October 1966) 409-430.

TYPE: article.

PERFORMERS: Eric Simon, Alicia Schachter.

OTHER WORKS DISCUSSED: *Apocalyptica [I], Black Sounds, Blake Songs, La Bocca della Verità, Cantio Sacra, Capriccio for Two Pianos, Chamber Symphony, Cheltenham Concerto, Concert Piece for Two Pianos and Orchestra, Contra Mortem et Tempus, David, The Psalmist, Duo Concertante, Four Songs of Solomon, Music for the Magic Theater, Nach Bach, Night Music, Passions [According to the Twentieth Century], Serenata d'estate, Sonata-Fantasia, String Quartet No. 1, String Quartet No. 2, Symphony No. 1, Symphony No. 2, Three Psalms, Time-Span, Trio for Clarinet, Horn, and Piano, Trio [No. 1] for Violin, Cello, and Piano, Twelve Bagatelles, Zodiac.*

OTHER WORKS MENTIONED: *Arioso, Bartokiana, Five Smooth Stones, Sonata No. 1 for Piano Solo, Sonata No. 2 for Piano Solo, Waltz Serenade.*

BOOKS DISCUSSED: *The Hexachord and Its Relation to the Twelve-Tone Row.*

Schonberg, Harold C. "Concert Marked by Novel Sounds: Fourth Music in Our Time Program Given at 'Y'—Electronic Work Heard," *The New York Times* (13 March 1959).

TYPE: review.

PERFORMERS: Herbert Tichman, Ruth Tichman.

Simek, Julius Franz. "New Music Concert," *Musical America* LXXVIII/6 (May 1958) 26.

TYPE: review.

PERFORMERS: Eric Simon, Alicia Schachter.

Webster, Daniel. "At the Art Alliance: Aeolian Players Shine Spotlight on Rochberg," *The Philadelphia Inquirer* (16 February 1966) 27.

TYPE: review.

PERFORMERS: Aeolian Chamber Players.

NAMES: Webern.

OTHER WORKS DISCUSSED: *La Bocca della Verità, Contra Mortem et Tempus, Trio [No. 1] for Violin, Cello, and Piano.*

Duo for Oboe and Bassoon

Staltzer, Frank. "*Duo for Oboe and Bassoon*," *Woodwind * Brass & Percussion* XXVII/7 (December 1981) 29.

TYPE: score review.

NAMES: Sol Schoenbach.

Webster, Daniel. "Swarthmore Festival Fills Void," *The Philadelphia Inquirer* (28 June 1983).

TYPE: review.

Duo Concertante for Violin and Cello

Archibald, Bruce. "Rochberg: *Chamber Symphony, Duo Concertante, Music for the Magic Theater, Ricordanza, String Quartet No. 1*," *Musical Quarterly* LXXII/4 (October 1976) 613-615.

TYPE: record review.

PERFORMERS: Mark Sokol, Norman Fischer.

NAMES: Berg, Schönberg.

OTHER WORKS DISCUSSED: *Chamber Symphony, Contra Mortem et Tempus, Music for the Magic Theater, Ricordanza, String Quartet No. 1.*

Bronston, Levering. "Rochberg: *Chamber Symphony, Duo Concertante, Music for the Magic Theater, Ricordanza, String Quartet No. 1,*" *The New Records* XLIII/11 (January 1976) 7-8.

TYPE: record review.

PERFORMERS: Mark Sokol, Norman Fischer.

OTHER WORKS DISCUSSED: *Chamber Symphony, Music for the Magic Theater, Ricordanza, String Quartet No. 1.*

n.a. "Chamber Music Fest to Feature Rochberg," *The Albuquerque Journal* (01 April 1979) D-13.

TYPE: upcoming performances.

PERFORMERS: Mark Sokol, Norman Fischer.

OTHER WORKS DISCUSSED: *Quintet for Piano and String Quartet, Ricordanza, String Quartet No. 4, String Quartet No. 5, String Quartet No. 6.*

n.a. "Composer Rochberg Featured in Santa Fe Chamber Music," *The Los Alamos Monitor [Los Alamos, NM]* (18 April 1979).

TYPE: upcoming performances.

PERFORMERS: Mark Sokol, Norman Fischer.

OTHER WORKS DISCUSSED: *Quintet for Piano and String Quartet, Ricordanza, String Quartet No. 4, String Quartet No. 5, String Quartet No. 6.*

Croan, Robert. "Classical Record Reviews: Copland Celebration: Music of George Rochberg," *The Pittsburgh Post-Gazette* (07 May 1976) 34.

TYPE: record review.

PERFORMERS: Mark Sokol, Norman Fischer.

OTHER WORKS DISCUSSED: *Concerto for Violin and Orchestra, Ricordanza, String Quartet No. 1.*

Dunning, William. "Records Are Foretaste of Santa Fe Festival," *The Los Alamos Monitor [Los Alamos, NM]* (27 April 1979).

TYPE: record reviews.

PERFORMERS: Mark Sokol, Norman Fischer.

OTHER WORKS DISCUSSED: *Ricordanza, Song in Praise of Krishna, String Quartet No. 1, String Quartet No. 4, String Quartet No. 5, String Quartet No. 6.*

Dunning, William. "Rochberg Honors Past," *The Los Alamos Monitor [Los Alamos, NM]* (02 August 1979).

TYPE: review, interview.

PERFORMERS: Mark Sokol, Norman Fischer.

OTHER WORKS DISCUSSED: *Quintet for Piano and String Quartet, Ricordanza, String Quartet No. 4, String Quartet No. 5, String Quartet No. 6.*

Dunning, William. "Rochberg Records: Summer Glimpse," *The Santa Fe Reporter* (27 April 1979).

TYPE: record reviews.

PERFORMERS: Mark Sokol, Norman Fischer.

OTHER WORKS DISCUSSED: *Ricordanza, Song in Praise of Krishna, String Quartet No. 1, String Quartet No. 4, String Quartet No. 5, String Quartet No. 6.*

Dunning, William. "Santa Fe Chamber Music Festival Scheduled," *The Los Alamos Monitor [Los Alamos, NM]* (06 April 1979).

TYPE:

upcoming performances.

PERFORMERS: Mark Sokol, Norman Fischer.

OTHER WORKS DISCUSSED: *Quintet for Piano and String Quartet, Ricordanza, String Quartet No. 4, String Quartet No. 5, String Quartet No. 6.*

Henahan, Donal J. "Zukofsky, Violinist Plays New Works," *The New York Times* (13 February 1969) 52.

TYPE: review.

PERFORMERS: Paul Zukofsky, Robert Sylvester.

Hillerman, Anne. "Santa Fe Festival Hosts Rochberg," *The New Mexican [Santa Fe, NM]* (18 July 1979).

TYPE: review, interview.

PERFORMERS: Mark Sokol, Norman Fischer.

OTHER WORKS DISCUSSED: *Ricordanza.*

La Mariana, Angelo. "The String Clearing House: Duets: *Duo Concertante*," *The School Musician* XXXII/3 (November 1960) 22, 74-75.

TYPE: review.

Oliva, Mark. "Classical Record Reviews," *The Nevada State Journal* (18 January 1976) 11.

TYPE: record review.

PERFORMERS: Mark Sokol, Norman Fischer.

OTHER WORKS DISCUSSED: *Chamber Symphony, Music for the Magic Theater, Ricordanza, String Quartet No. 1.*

Porter, Andrew. "Musical Events: Questions," *The New Yorker* (12 February 1979) 109-115.

TYPE: article, review.

OTHER WORKS DISCUSSED: *Concerto for Violin and Orchestra, Music for the Magic Theater, Ricordanza, String Quartet No. 1, String Quartet No. 2, String Quartet No. 3, String Quartet No. 4, String Quartet No. 5, String Quartet No. 6.*

Porter, Andrew. "Rochberg: Chamber Works," *High Fidelity/Musical America* XVI/5 (May 1976) 90-92.

TYPE: record reviews.

PERFORMERS: Mark Sokol, Norman Fischer.

OTHER WORKS DISCUSSED: *Chamber Symphony, Concerto for Violin and Orchestra, Music for the Magic Theater, Ricordanza, String Quartet No. 1.*

Potter, Keith. "Rochberg: *String Quartet No. 1, Duo Concertante, Ricordanza,*" *Records and Recordings [Great Britain]* (March 1977) 72-73.

TYPE: record review.

PERFORMERS: Mark Sokol, Norman Fischer.

OTHER WORKS DISCUSSED: *Blake Songs, Contra Mortem et Tempus, Ricordanza, String Quartet No. 1, String Quartet No. 2, String Quartet No. 3.*

Ringer, Alexander L. "The Music of George Rochberg," *Musical Quarterly* LII/4 (October 1966) 409-430.

TYPE: article.

NAMES: Schönberg.

OTHER WORKS DISCUSSED: *Apocalyptica [I], Black Sounds, Blake Songs, La Bocca della Verità, Cantio Sacra, Capriccio for Two Pianos, Chamber Symphony, Cheltenham Concerto, Concert Piece for Two Pianos and Orchestra, Contra Mortem et Tempus, David, the Psalmist, Dialogues, Four Songs of Solomon, Music for the Magic Theater, Nach Bach, Night Music, Passions [According to the Twentieth Century], Serenata d'estate, Sonata-Fantasia, String Quartet No. 1, String Quartet No. 2, Symphony No. 1, Symphony No. 2, Three Psalms, Time-Span, Trio for Clarinet, Horn, and Piano, Trio [No. 1] for Violin, Cello, and Piano, Twelve Bagatelles, Zodiac.*

OTHER WORKS MENTIONED: *Arioso, Bartokiana, Five Smooth Stones, Sonata No. 1 for Piano Solo, Sonata No. 2 for Piano Solo, Waltz Serenade.*

BOOKS DISCUSSED: *The Hexachord and Its Relation to the Twelve-Tone Row.*

n.a. "Rochberg: Fundamentally Affirmative," *The Silver City Daily Press [Silver City, NM]* (05 April 1979).

TYPE: upcoming performances, article.

PERFORMERS: Mark Sokol, Norman Fischer.

OTHER WORKS DISCUSSED: *Quintet for Piano and String Quartet, Ricordanza, String Quartet No. 4, String Quartet No. 5, String Quartet No. 6.*

Salzman, Eric. "Rochberg: *Chamber Symphony, Duo Concertante, Music for the Magic Theater, Ricordanza, String Quartet No. 1,*" *Stereo Review* XXXVII/1 (July 1976) 111.

TYPE: record review.

PERFORMERS: Mark Sokol, Norman Fischer.

OTHER WORKS DISCUSSED: *Chamber Symphony, Music for the Magic Theater, Ricordanza, String Quartet No. 1.*

Sargeant, Winthrop. "Concert Records: Romantic and Gothic," *The New Yorker* (26 January 1976) 91-93.

TYPE: record review.

PERFORMERS: Mark Sokol, Norman Fisher.

OTHER WORKS DISCUSSED: *Ricordanza, String Quartet No. 1.*

Valdes, Lesley. "A Birthday Salute to Rochberg," *The Philadelphia Inquirer* (17 April 1988) 1-L, 10-L.

TYPE: upcoming performance, article, interview.

PERFORMERS: Curtis Institute of Music.

OTHER WORKS DISCUSSED: *Serenata d'estate, Slow Fires of Autumn, String Quartet No. 3, To the Dark Wood, Trio [No. 2] for Violin, Cello, and Piano.*

OTHER WORKS MENTIONED: *Concerto for Violin and Orchestra, Sonata for Violin and Piano, Symphony No. 5, Symphony No. 6.*

Veilleux, C. Thomas. "Chamber Music Roundup Reveals Three Fine Records," *The Sunday Post [Bridgeport, CT]* (10 October 1976) E-14.

TYPE: record review.

PERFORMERS: Mark Sokol, Norman Fischer.

OTHER WORKS DISCUSSED: *Chamber Symphony, Music for the Magic Theater, Ricordanza, String Quartet No. 1.*

Webster, Daniel. "In Honor Of Rochberg, Three Nights Devoted to His Works," *The Philadelphia Inquirer* (17 January 1979).

TYPE: review, upcoming performances.

PERFORMERS: Mark Sokol, Norman Fischer.

OTHER WORKS DISCUSSED: *Quintet for Piano and String Quartet, Ricordanza.*

OTHER WORKS MENTIONED: *String Quartet No. 1, String Quartet No. 2, String Quartet No. 3, String Quartet No. 4, String Quartet No. 5, String Quartet No. 6.*

Webster, Daniel. "Stylistic Odyssey of George Rochberg," *The Philadelphia Inquirer* (15 February 1976) 7H.

TYPE: record review.

PERFORMERS: Mark Sokol, Norman Fischer.

OTHER WORKS DISCUSSED: *Chamber Symphony, Music for the Magic Theater, Ricordanza, String Quartet No. 1.*

Electrikaleidoscope for Amplified Flute, Clarinet, Violin, Cello, Piano, and Electric Piano

Gagne, Cole and Tracy Caras. *Soundpieces: Interviews with American Composers.* (Metuchen, NJ: Scarecrow Press, Inc., 1982).

TYPE: interview.

NAMES: Jacob Druckman.

OTHER WORKS DISCUSSED: *Apocalyptica [I], Black Sounds, Concerto for Violin and Orchestra, The Confidence Man, Contra Mortem et Tempus, Music for the Magic Theater, Octet, Quintet for Piano and String Quartet, Ricordanza, Sonata No. 2 for Piano Solo, String Quartet No. 3, String Quartet No. 4, String Quartet No. 5, String Quartet No. 6, Twelve Bagatelles.*

OTHER WORKS MENTIONED: many.

Hiemenz, Jack. "Aeolian Chamber Players," *High Fidelity/Musical America* XXIII/4 (April 1973) MA-16.

TYPE: review.

PERFORMERS: Aeolian Chamber Players.

NAMES: Beethoven, Stravinsky.

Hughes, Allen. "Music: Sharp Contrast," *The New York Times* (21 December 1972) 29.

TYPE: review.

PERFORMERS: Aeolian Chamber Players.

NAMES: Beethoven, Stravinsky.

Johnson, Tom. "Music," *The Village Voice* (28 December 1972) 26-27.

TYPE: review.

PERFORMERS: Aeolian Chamber Players.

NAMES: Bach, Beethoven, Berio, Foss, Mahler, Stravinsky.

Kozinn, Allan. "Recitals and Miscellany: Twentieth-Century Consort," *High Fidelity/Musical America* XXXII/7 (July 1982) 62.

TYPE: record review.

PERFORMERS: Twentieth Century Consort.

NAMES: Beethoven, Copland, Susato.

Eleven Songs for Mezzo-Soprano and Piano

Boyer, D. Royce. "Rochberg: *Eleven Songs,*" *The Sonneck Society Bulletin* (Summer 1988).

TYPE: record review.

PERFORMERS: Sharon Mabry, Patsy Wade.

NAMES: Paul Rochberg.

Bridges, John. "'London Songs' Première Fine 'Dimensions' Opener," *The Tennessean [Nashville, TN]* (12 November 1981) 39.

TYPE: review.

PERFORMERS: Sharon Mabry.

NAMES: Paul Rochberg.

Bridges, John. "For the Record," *The Tennessean [Nashville, TN]* (17 June 1984) 7F.

TYPE: record review.

PERFORMERS: Sharon Mabry, Patsy Wade.

NAMES: Paul Rochberg.

Brookhouser, Frank. "A Dead Son Lives on in Father's Music," *The Evening Bulletin [Philadelphia]* (05 November 1970).

TYPE: upcoming première.

PERFORMERS: George Rochberg.

NAMES: Paul Rochberg.

OTHER WORKS MENTIONED: *Sacred Song of Reconciliation, Symphony No. 3.*

Felton, James. "At St. Mary's Church: Most Perfect Chamber Recital of a Decade," *The Evening Bulletin [Philadelphia]* (02 April 1970) 17.

TYPE: review.

PERFORMERS: Neva Pilgrim, George Rochberg.

NAMES: Paul Rochberg, Berg.

Finn, Robert. "Oberlin Concert Makes Poor Affair with Fare and Where," *The Plain Dealer [Cleveland]* (22 March 1970) 11B.

TYPE: review.

PERFORMERS: Darlen Wiley, Wilbur Price.

NAMES: Paul Rochberg.

Frank, Andrew. "George Rochberg: *Eleven Songs*," *Notes: The Quarterly Journal of the Music Library Association* XXII/3 (March 1976) 643-644.

TYPE: score review.

NAMES: Paul Rochberg.

OTHER WORKS MENTIONED: *Concerto for Violin and Orchestra, String Quartet No. 2, String Quartet No. 3, Trio [No. 1] for Violin, Cello, and Piano.*

George, Earl. "Concert Features Quartet, Soprano," *The Syracuse Herald* (23 April 1979) 7.

TYPE: review.

PERFORMERS: Neva Pilgrim, George Rochberg.

NAMES: Paul Rochberg.

OTHER WORKS DISCUSSED: *String Quartet No. 5.*

Hasden, Nikki C. "A Mezzo-Soprano from Tennessee Makes Impressive Record Debut," *The Chattanooga Times [Chattanooga, TN]* (05 May 1984) B8.

TYPE: review.

PERFORMERS: Sharon Mabry.

NAMES: Paul Rochberg.

Holland, Bernard. "Music: Bartók and Rochberg Songs," *The New York Times* (03 February 1985) I, 54.

TYPE: review.

PERFORMERS: Margaret Ahrens, Paul Alan Levi.

NAMES: Paul Rochberg.

Legge-Wilkinson, Margaret. "Music: A Mixed Bag of Images and Sounds," *The Canberra Times [Australia]* (25 October 1986) B7.

TYPE: review.

PERFORMERS: Jane Manning, Christopher Lyndon Gee.

NAMES: Billie Holiday, Paul Rochberg.

Miller, Karl F. "Rochberg: *Eleven Songs*," *American Record Guide* XLVII/6 (July 1984) 66-67.

TYPE: record review.

OTHER WORKS DISCUSSED: *Symphony No. 2, Symphony No. 3.*

Page, Tim. "Music: Debuts in Review," *The New York Times* (15 May 1983) I, 48.

TYPE: review.

PERFORMERS: Margaret Ahrens, Paul Alan Levi.

NAMES: Paul Rochberg.

Passarella, Lee. "Vocal: Rochberg," *The New Records* LII/2 (April 1984) 10-11.

TYPE: record review.

PERFORMERS: Sharon Mabry, Patsy Wade.

NAMES: Paul Rochberg.

Robinson, Martha. "Soprano Soars After Stumbling Start," *The Vancouver Sun [Vancouver, Canada]* (14 October 1971) 42.

TYPE: review.

PERFORMERS: Judith Mass, Peggy Schofield.

NAMES: Paul Rochberg.

n.a. "Rochberg Songs: Pilgrim to Perform," *The Syracuse Herald* (15 April 1979) 7.

TYPE: upcoming performance.

PERFORMERS: Neva Pilgrim, George Rochberg.

NAMES: William Blake, Paul Rochberg.

OTHER WORKS MENTIONED: *Songs in Praise of Krishna, String Quartet No. 5.*

Scanlan, Roger. "Spotlight on Contemporary American Composers," *The NATS [National Association of Teachers of Singing] Bulletin* XXXIII/1 (October 1976) 48-49, 53-54.

TYPE: article.

OTHER WORKS DISCUSSED: *Blake Songs, David, The Psalmist, Four Songs of Solomon, Fantasies, Music for "The Alchemist," Phaedra, Sacred Song of Reconciliation, Songs in Praise of Krishna, String Quartet No. 2, Symphony No. 3, Tableaux, Two Songs from "Tableaux".*

OTHER WORKS MENTIONED: many.

Simmons, Walter. "Rochberg: *Eleven Songs*," *Fanfare* VII/6 (July–August 1984).

TYPE: record review.

PERFORMERS: Sharon Mabry, Patsy Wade.

NAMES: Paul Rochberg.

Singer, Samuel L. "At St. Mary's Church: New Music Juxtaposed With Renaissance Fare at Chamber Concert," *The Philadelphia Inquirer* (02 April 1970) 35.

TYPE: review.

PERFORMERS: Neva Pilgrim, George Rochberg.

NAMES: Paul Rochberg.

Singer, Samuel L. "Composers' Forum Program Both Innovative and Perplexing," *The Philadelphia Inquirer* (23 November 1970).

TYPE: review.

PERFORMERS: Neva Pilgrim, George Rochberg.

NAMES: Paul Rochberg.

Toms, John. "Rochberg," *Tulsa Tribune* (11 July 1984).

TYPE: record review.

PERFORMERS: Sharon Mabry, Patsy Wade.

NAMES: Paul Rochberg.

Fanfares for Massed Trumpets, Horns, and Trombones

Felton, James. "Concert Set March 17: *Fanfare for 144 Brass Horns,*" *The Philadelphia Inquirer* (03 March 1968).

TYPE: upcoming première, interview.

NAMES: Sol Schoenbach.

OTHER WORKS DISCUSSED: *Symphony No. 3, Zodiac.*

Felton, James. "Settlement School's 60th Birthday: Rochberg's New *Fanfare* Is Impressive," *The Evening Bulletin [Philadelphia]* (18 March 1968) 21.

TYPE: review.

PERFORMERS: Sigmund Hering, Settlement Music School.

NAMES: Berlioz, Gabrieli, Mahler, Penderecki.

Fantasies for Voice and Piano

Espina, Noni. "Music Review: Solo: *Fantasies,*" *The NATS [National Association of Teachers of Singing] Bulletin* XXXIII/2 (December 1976) 42.

TYPE: score review.

Scanlan, Roger. "Spotlight on Contemporary American Composers," *The NATS [National Association of Teachers of Singing] Bulletin* XXXIII/1 (October 1976) 48-49, 53-54.

TYPE: article.

OTHER WORKS DISCUSSED: *Blake Songs, David, The Psalmist, Four Songs of Solomon, Eleven Songs,* Music for *"The Alchemist," Phaedra, Sacred Song of Reconciliation, Songs in Praise of Krishna,* String Quartet No. 2, Symphony No. 3, Tableaux, *Two Songs from "Tableaux".*

OTHER WORKS MENTIONED: many.

Four Short Sonatas for Piano Solo

Cacioppo, Curt. "Guns and Beethoven," *Piano Quarterly* XXXV/139 (Fall 1987) 68.

TYPE: première.

Espagnet, Andrea Rossi. "Villa Pignatelli, Michael Caldwell al Pianoforte: Un don Pasqulate Tutto USA," *Napolinotte [Naples, Italy]* (11 June 1984).

TYPE: review.

PERFORMERS: Michael Caldwell.

Holland, Bernard. "Music Diplomacy," *The New York Times* (29 January 1984) II, 17-18.

TYPE: upcoming première.

PERFORMERS: Michael Caldwell.

NAMES: United States Information Agency Artistic Ambassador Program.

Horn, Daniel Paul. "*Carnival Music*: An Introduction to the Piano Music of George Rochberg," *Clavier* XXVII/9 (November 1988) 17-22.

TYPE: article.

OTHER WORKS DISCUSSED: *Arioso, Bartokiana, Book of Contrapuntal Pieces for Keyboard Instruments, Carnival Music, Nach Bach, Partita Variations, Prelude on "Happy Birthday," Sonata-Fantasia, Twelve Bagatelles.*

OTHER WORKS MENTIONED: *Sonata No. 1 for Piano Solo, Sonata No. 2 for Piano Solo.*

Iannone, di Massino. "A Villa Pignatelli il Pianista Statunitense: La Musicalita Italiana di Michael Caldwell," *Napoli Oggi [Naples, Italy]* (21 June 1984).

TYPE: review.

PERFORMERS: Michael Caldwell.

Stewart, Paul. "The Piano Music of George Rochberg and the New Romanticism," *American Music Teacher* XXXVIII/3 (January 1989) 24-27, 62.

TYPE: article.

NAMES: Mahler, Mozart.

OTHER WORKS DISCUSSED: *Arioso, Bartokiana, Book of Contrapuntal Pieces for Keyboard Instruments, Carnival Music, Nach Bach, Partita Variations, Prelude on "Happy Birthday," Sonata-Fantasia, Twelve Bagatelles, Two Preludes and Fughettas.*

Four Songs of Solomon for Voice and Piano

Davis, Peter G. "Recital: Maria Rangel," *The New York Times* (12 June 1978) III, 18.

TYPE: review.

PERFORMERS: Maria Luisa Rangel, Miguel Pinto.

Espina, Noni. "Music Review: Solo: *Four Songs of Solomon*," *The NATS [National Association of Teachers of Singing] Bulletin* XXXIII/2 (December 1976) 42.

TYPE: score review.

Johnson, Harriett. "Music: Sixteen Tongues End in Babel," *The New York Post* (12 June 1978) 21.

TYPE: review.

PERFORMERS: Maria Luisa Rangel, Miguel Pinto.

Ringer, Alexander L. "The Music of George Rochberg," *Musical Quarterly* LII/4 (October 1966) 409-430.

TYPE: article.

PERFORMERS: David Lloyd.

NAMES: Schönberg.

OTHER WORKS DISCUSSED: *Apocalyptica [I], Black Sounds, Blake Songs, La Bocca della Veritá, Cantio Sacra, Capriccio for Two Pianos, Chamber Symphony, Cheltenham Concerto, Concert Piece for Two Pianos and Orchestra, Contra Mortem et Tempus, David, the Psalmist, Dialogues, Duo Concertante, Music for the Magic Theater, Nach Bach, Night Music, Passions [According to the Twentieth Century], Serenata d'estate, Sonata-Fantasia, String Quartet No. 1, String Quartet No. 2, Symphony No. 1, Symphony No. 2, Three Psalms, Time-Span, Trio for Clarinet, Horn, and Piano, Trio [No. 1] for Violin, Cello, and Piano, Twelve Bagatelles, Zodiac.*

OTHER WORKS MENTIONED: *Arioso, Bartokiana, Five Smooth Stones, Sonata No. 1 for Piano Solo, Sonata No. 2 for Piano Solo, Waltz Serenade.*

BOOKS DISCUSSED: *The Hexachord and Its Relation to the Twelve-Tone Row.*

Scanlan, Roger. "Spotlight on Contemporary American Composers," *The NATS [National Association of Teachers of Singing] Bulletin* XXXIII/1 (October 1976) 48-49, 53-54.

TYPE: article.

OTHER WORKS DISCUSSED: *Blake Songs, David, The Psalmist, Eleven Songs, Fantasies, Music for "The Alchemist," Phaedra, Sacred Song of*

Reconciliation, Songs in Praise of Krishna, String Quartet No. 2, Symphony No. 3, Tableaux, Two Songs from "Tableaux".
OTHER WORKS MENTIONED: many.

Imago Mundi (Image of the World) for Large Orchestra

Boyd, Karen Kumler. "Composer Award-Concert March 1, 2: Symphony Honors George Rochberg," *New Era [Lancaster, PA]* (17 February 1986) 23, 24.

TYPE: article, upcoming performance, announcement of award, interview.

PERFORMERS: Stephen Gunzenhauser, Lancaster Symphony Orchestra.

Boyd, Karen Kumler. "Plus Two Local Soloists: Works by Haydn and Strauss at Symphony's Next Concert," *New Era [Lancaster, PA]* (17 Feburary 1986) 24.

TYPE: upcoming performance.

PERFORMERS: Stephen Gunzenhauser, Lancaster Symphony Orchestra.

Cera, Stephen. "Beethoven Dwarfs Other BSO [Baltimore Symphony Orchestra] Offerings," *The Sun [Baltimore, MD]* (01 April 1983) B5.

TYPE: review.

PERFORMERS: Sergiu Comissiona, Baltimore Symphony Orchestra.

NAMES: Bartók, Messiaen, Stravinsky, Varèse.

Cooklis, Ray. "Review: Pianist Evokes One-Handed Complexities," *The Cincinnati Enquirer* (10 January 1987) D-3.

TYPE: review.

PERFORMERS: David Loebel, Cincinnati Symphony Orchestra.

Haynes, Alfred. "Beethoven: Shlomo Mintz Plays a Marvelous Concerto," *The Evening Sun [Baltimore]* (01 April 1983).

TYPE: review.

PERFORMERS: Sergiu Comissiona, Baltimore Symphony Orchestra.

Holland, Bernard. "Philharmonic: Festival of Moderns," *The New York Times* (12 June 1983) I, 66.

TYPE: review.

PERFORMERS: New York Philharmonic.

NAMES: Bartók, Stravinsky.

Hughes, Allen. "Music: *Imago Mundi*: Comissiona Leads Baltimore in Work Reminiscent of Japanese Composer," *The New York Times* (12 May 1974) 49.

TYPE: review.

PERFORMERS: Sergiu Comissiona, Baltimore Symphony Orchestra.

NAMES: George Balanchine, Toshiro Mayuzumi.

Hutton, Mary Ellyn. "Symphony's Guest Artist Gives Masterful Performance," *The Cincinnati Post* (10 January 1987) 5B.

TYPE: review.

PERFORMERS: David Loebel, Cincinnati Symphony Orchestra.

Jenkins, Speight. "Itzhak Perlman Is Soloist with Baltimore Symphony," *The New York Post* (11 May 1974) 16.

TYPE: review.

PERFORMERS: Sergiu Comissiona, Baltimore Symphony Orchestra.

NAMES: Stravinsky.

Little, Barbara. "Rochberg Honored at Fulton Program," *The Lancaster Intellegencer Journal [Lancaster, PA]* (03 March 1986).

TYPE: review, announcement of award, interview.

PERFORMERS: Stephen Gunzenhauser, Lancaster Symphony Orchestra.

Marsh, Robert C. "Perlman, Solti and Tchaikovsky: The Spirit of Perfection," *The Chicago Sun-Times* (30 October 1981) 68.

TYPE: review.

PERFORMERS: Sir Georg Solti, Chicago Symphony Orchestra.

NAMES: Barber, Mahler, Stravinsky, Wagner.

Neilson, James. "Where Do You Stand . . . : About the 'Uncommon' Man Dwelling in a 'Common' World," *The School Musician* LIII/10 (June–July 1982) 4-5.

TYPE: review.

PERFORMERS: Sir Georg Solti, Chicago Symphony Orchestra.

n.a. "Notes on Music," *The Philadelphia Inquirer* (23 December 1986).

TYPE: upcoming performance, announcement of award.

PERFORMERS: Stephen Gunzenhauser, Delaware Symphony Orchestra.

n.a. "Penn [University of Pennsylvania at Philadelphia] Professor to Get Composer Award," *The News-Journal [Wilmington, DE]* (11 December 1986) D7.

TYPE: upcoming performance, announcement of award.

PERFORMERS: Stephen Gunzenhauser, Delaware Symphony Orchestra.

n.a. "Rochberg Work," *The School Musician* (June–July 1982) 5.

TYPE: review.

PERFORMERS: Sir Georg Solti, Chicago Symphony Orchestra.

Rockwell, John. "The Philharmonic Looks at Contemporary Music," *The New York Times* (29 May 1983) 17.

TYPE: upcoming performance.

von Rhein, John. "The Symphony: Solti's CSO [Chicago Symphony Orchestra] Return Radiates Optimism," *The Chicago Tribune* (30 October 1981) III.

TYPE: review.

PERFORMERS: Sir Georg Solti, Chicago Symphony Orchestra.

NAMES: Bartók, Shostakovich, Stravinsky.

n.a. "Symphonic Highlights: Premières," *International Musician* LXXII/12 (June 1974) 12; reprinted: *Symphony News* XXV/3 (June 1974) 26–27.

TYPE: review.

PERFORMERS: Sergiu Comissiona, Baltimore Symphony Orchestra.

Webster, Daniel. "Taking His Leave of Penn [University of Pennsylvania at Philadelphia] to Pen More Music," *The Philadelphia Inquirer* (27 March 1983) 1H, 10H, 11H.

TYPE: article, interview.

PERFORMERS: New York Philharmonic.

OTHER WORKS DISCUSSED: *Concerto for Oboe and Orchestra, The Confidence Man.*

OTHER WORKS MENTIONED: *String Quartet No. 1, String Quartet No. 2, String Quartet No. 3, String Quartet No. 4, String Quartet No. 5, String Quartet No. 6.*

Music for "The Alchemist" for Soprano and Eleven Players

Brustein, Robert. "Sepulchral Odors at Lincoln Center," *The New Republic* (29 October 1966).

TYPE: review.

PERFORMERS: The Repertory Theater of Lincoln Center.

NAMES: Ben Jonson.

Hobe. "Show on Broadway: *The Alchemist*," *Variety* (19 October 1966).

TYPE: review.

PERFORMERS: The Repertory Theater of Lincoln Center.

NAMES: Ben Jonson.

Johnson, Wayne. "Rochberg Will Hear Rochberg this Friday," *The Seattle Times* (29 October 1969) 20.

TYPE: upcoming performance.

PERFORMERS: William O. Smith, Robert Suderburg, Elizabeth Suderberg, University of Washington Contemporary Group.

NAMES: Ben Jonson.

OTHER WORKS DISCUSSED: *Contra Mortem et Tempus, Music for the Magic Theater, Tableaux.*

Johnson, Wayne. "U. W. [University of Washington] Group Plays Great Concert," *The Seattle Times* (03 November 1969) 22.

TYPE: review.

PERFORMERS: William O. Smith, Robert Suderburg, Elizabeth Suderberg, University of Washington Contemporary Group, Philadelphia String Quartet, Soni Ventorum.

NAMES: Ben Jonson, Stravinsky.

OTHER WORKS DISCUSSED: *Contra Mortem et Tempus, Music for the Magic Theater, Tableaux.*

Scanlan, Roger. "Spotlight on Contemporary American Composers," *The NATS [National Association of Teachers of Singing] Bulletin* XXXIII/1 (October 1976) 48-49, 53-54.

TYPE: article.

OTHER WORKS DISCUSSED: *Blake Songs, David, The Psalmist, Eleven Songs, Fantasies, Four Songs of Solomon, Phaedra, Sacred Song of Reconciliation, Songs in Praise of Krishna, String Quartet No. 2, Symphony No. 3, Tableaux, Two Songs from "Tableaux".*

OTHER WORKS MENTIONED: many.

Stromberg, Rolf. "Two Young Musicians Gifted," *The Seattle Post-Intelligencer* (03 November 1969) S*45.

TYPE: review.

PERFORMERS: William O. Smith, Robert Suderberg, Elizabeth Suderberg, University of Washington Contemporary Group, Philadelphia String Quartet, Soni Ventorum.

NAMES: Ben Jonson.

OTHER WORKS DISCUSSED: *Contra Mortem et Tempus, Music for the Magic Theater, Tableaux.*

Music for the Magic Theater

Archibald, Bruce. "Rochberg: *Chamber Symphony, Duo Concertante, Music for the Magic Theater, Ricordanza, String Quartet No. 1,*" *Musical Quarterly* LXXII/4 (October 1976) 613-615.

TYPE: record review.

PERFORMERS: Kenneth Moore, Oberlin Orchestra.

OTHER WORKS DISCUSSED: *Chamber Symphony, Contra Mortem et Tempus, Duo Concertante, Ricordanza, String Quartet No. 1.*

Ashforth, Alden. "Is Music Just Around the Corner?," *Cultural Affairs [Published by the Associated Councils of the Arts]* IX (Winter 1970) 27-33.

TYPE: article.

Bronston, Levering. "Rochberg: *Chamber Symphony, Duo Concertante, Music for the Magic Theater, Ricordanza, String Quartet No. 1,*" *The New Records* XLIII/11 (January 1976) 7-8.

TYPE: record review.

PERFORMERS: Kenneth Moore, Oberlin Orchestra.

OTHER WORKS DISCUSSED: *Chamber Symphony, Duo Concertante, Ricordanza, String Quartet No. 1.*

Danuser, Hermann. "Zur Kritik der musikalischen Postmoderne," *Neue Zeitschrift fur Musik* CXLIX/12 (December 1988) 4-9.

TYPE: article.

OTHER WORKS DISCUSSED: *Contra Mortem et Tempus, Quintet for Piano and String Quartet, String Quartet No. 2, String Quartet No. 3, Trio [No. 1] for Violin, Cello, and Piano.*

BOOKS DISCUSSED: *The Aesthetics of Survival.*

Dixon, Joan DeVee. "George Rochberg's *Nach Bach, A Fantasy for Harpsichord or Piano,*" Unpublished (June 1988) 13pp.

TYPE: article, interviews with George Rochberg and Igor Kipnis.

OTHER WORKS DISCUSSED: *Chamber Symphony, Contra Mortem et Tempus, Nach Bach, Partita Variations, Sonata-Fantasia, Symphony No. 3.*

Dwyer, John. "The Philharmonic: Erica Morini Displays True Violin Virtuosity In Intensive Program," *The Buffalo Evening News* (20 January 1969) I, 10.

TYPE: review.

PERFORMERS: Albert Pratz, Gilbert Kalish, Buffalo Symphony Orchestra.

NAMES: Beethoven, Hermann Hesse, Mahler, Mozart, Rabindranath Tagore, Varèse.

Felton, James. "Composers Are Sane But the World Isn't, Says Penn Rochberg," *The Sunday Bulletin [Philadelphia]* (13 February 1966) 11.

TYPE: interview.

PERFORMERS: Ralph Shapey, Contemporary Chamber Players [University of Chicago].

NAMES: Mozart.

WORKS DISCUSSED: *Contra Mortem et Tempus, Night Music, String Quartet No. 2, Symphony No. 1, Symphony No. 2, Symphony No. 3, Zodiac.*

Felton, James. "Penn [University of Pennsylvania at Philadelphia] Contemporary Players: Avant-Garde Concert Is Praised," *The Evening Bulletin [Philadelphia]* (22 April 1967) 9.

TYPE: review.

PERFORMERS: Melvin Strauss, Penn [University of Pennsylvania at Phildelphia] Contemporary Players.

NAMES: Beethoven, Mozart, Peter Schickele [P.D.Q. Bach].

Gagne, Cole and Tracy Caras. *Soundpieces: Interviews with American Composers.* (Metuchen, NJ: Scarecrow Press, Inc., 1982).

TYPE: interview.

NAMES: Mahler, Mozart.

OTHER WORKS DISCUSSED: *Apocalyptica [I], Black Sounds, Concerto for Violin and Orchestra, The Confidence Man, Contra Mortem et Tempus, Electrikaleidoscope, Octet, Quintet for Piano and String Quartet, Ricordanza, Sonata No. 2 for Piano Solo, String Quartet No. 3, String Quartet No. 4, String Quartet No. 5, String Quartet No. 6, Twelve Bagatelles.*

OTHER WORKS MENTIONED: many.

George, Earl. "Government-Subsidized Concert Provides Modern Music Babel," *The Syracuse Herald-Journal* (15 March 1975).

TYPE: review.

PERFORMERS: David Loebel, Syracuse Symphony Orchestra.

NAMES: Mahler, Mozart.

Giffin, Glenn. "Musical Sparks Fly at Aspen Performance," *The Denver Post* (17 July 1972).

TYPE: review.

PERFORMERS: Richard Dufallo, Aspen Music Festival Ensemble.

NAMES: Mahler, Mozart.

Goldberg, Albert. "Music Review: Evening Concerts Opener," *The Los Angeles Times* (10 October 1973) 16.

TYPE: review.

PERFORMERS: Gerhard Samuel, Cal-Arts Faculty Ensemble.

NAMES: Mahler, Mozart.

Hardy, Owen. "'Foremeost Is Life,' A Musical Rebel Feels," *The Courier-Journal [Louisville, KY]* (16 April 1980) C1.

TYPE: article, interview.

NAMES: Mozart.

OTHER WORKS DISCUSSED: *Ricordanza*.

Heimenz, Jack. "Juilliard: Rochberg, Ligeti," *High Fidelity/Musical America* XXV/3 (March 1975) MA-28.

TYPE: review.

PERFORMERS: Richard Dufallo, Juilliard Student Ensemble.

NAMES: Mahler, Mozart, Stravinsky.

OTHER WORKS MENTIONED: *String Quartet No. 3.*

Henahan, Donal J. "Current Chronicle: United States: Chicago," *Musical Quarterly* LIII/1 (January 1967) 246-250.

TYPE: review.

PERFORMERS: Ralph Shapey, Contemporary Chamber Players [University of Chicago].

NAMES: Beethoven, Mahler, Mozart, Varèse.

Henahan, Donal J. "Music: Aspen's Resident Composers: Pieces by Druckman and Rochberg Given: Works Are Marked by a Personal Vision," *The New York Times* (19 July 1972) 25.

TYPE: review.

PERFORMERS: Richard Dufallo, Aspen Music Festival Ensemble.

NAMES: Brahms, Jacob Druckman, Ives, Mahler, Mozart, Schönberg.

Henahan, Donal J. "Music: Rochberg Work by National Orchestra," *The New York Times* (19 July 1972) 25.

TYPE: review.

OTHER WORKS DISCUSSED: *String Quartet No. 3.*

Henahan, Donal J. "Tommorrow's Music: Something Old, Something New," *The New York Times* (28 May 1972) II, 11.

TYPE: article.

NAMES: Beethoven, Mahler, Mozart.

OTHER WORKS DISCUSSED: *String Quartet No. 3.*

Johnson, Wayne. "Rochberg Will Hear Rochberg this Friday," *The Seattle Times* (29 October 1969) 20.

TYPE: upcoming performance.

PERFORMERS: William O. Smith, Robert Suderburg, University of Washington Contemporary Group, Philadelphia String Quartet, Soni Ventorum.

NAMES: Hermann Hesse.

OTHER WORKS DISCUSSED: *Contra Mortem et Tempus, Music for "The Alchemist," Tableaux.*

Johnson, Wayne. "U. W. [University of Washington] Group Plays Great Concert," *The Seattle Times* (03 November 1969) 22.

TYPE: review.

PERFORMERS: William O. Smith, Robert Suderburg, University of Washington Contemporary Group, Philadelphia String Quartet, Soni Ventorum.

NAMES: Berg, Hermann Hesse, Mozart.

OTHER WORKS DISCUSSED: *Contra Mortem et Tempus, Music for "The Alchemist," Tableaux.*

Kolodin, Irving. "Music to My Ears: Berio, Rochberg, and the Musical Quote," *Saturday Review* (08 February 1975) 36-38.

TYPE: article.

NAMES: Mahler, Mozart.

Lange, Art. "Rochberg: *Quintet*," *American Record Guide* XLV/3 (December 1981) 24-25.

TYPE: record review.

NAMES: Beethoven, Ives, Mahler, Mozart, Wagner.

OTHER WORKS DISCUSSED: *Concerto for Violin and Orchestra, Quintet for Piano and String Quartet, String Quartet No. 2, String Quartet No. 3, String Quartet No. 4, String Quartet No. 5, String Quartet No. 6.*

Levin, Monroe. "Notes on Music," *Jewish Exponent* (12 May 1972).

TYPE: review.

OTHER WORKS DISCUSSED: *Carnival Music.*

Marsh, Robert C. "U. of C. [University of Chicago] Anniversary Concert Strikes an Argumentative Note," *The Chicago Sun-Times* (25 January 1967) 36.

TYPE: review.

PERFORMERS: Ralph Shapey, Contemporary Chamber Players [University of Chicago].

NAMES: Beethoven, Mahler, Mozart.

Marsh, Robert C. "University of Chicago: Four Premières," *High Fidelity/Musical America* XVII/4 (April 1967) MA-11.

TYPE: review.

PERFORMERS: Ralph Shapey, Contemporary Chamber Players [University of Chicago].

NAMES: Beethoven, Mahler, Mozart.

Porter, Andrew. "Musical Events: Questions," *The New Yorker* (12 February 1979) 109-115.

TYPE: article, review.

NAMES: Beethoven, Goethe, Hermann Hesse, Mahler, Mozart, Varèse, Webern.

OTHER WORKS DISCUSSED: *Duo Concertante, Ricordanza, String Quartet No. 1, String Quartet No. 2, String Quartet No. 3, String Quartet No. 4, String Quartet No. 5, String Quartet No. 6.*

Porter, Andrew. "Rochberg: Chamber Works," *High Fidelity/Musical America* XXVI/5 (May 1976) 90-92.

TYPE: record review.

PERFORMERS: Kenneth Moore, Oberlin Orchestra.

NAMES: Beethoven, Goethe, Hermann Hesse, Mahler, Mozart, Varèse, Wagner, Webern.

OTHER WORKS DISCUSSED: *Chamber Symphony, Concerto for Violin and Orchestra, Duo Concertante, Ricordanza, String Quartet No. 1.*

Potter, Keith. "Rochberg: *Chamber Symphony, Duo Concertante, Music for the Magic Theater, Ricordanza, String Quartet No. 1,*" *Records and Recordings [Great Britain]* (March 1977) 72-73.

TYPE: record review.

PERFORMERS: Kenneth Moore, Oberlin Orchestra.

OTHER WORKS DISCUSSED: *Chamber Symphony, Duo Concertante, Ricordanza, String Quartet No. 1.*

Putnam, Thomas. "Composer Hears *Magic Theater*: Played by Philharmonic with Melvin Conducting," *The Buffalo Courier Express* (26 January 1969).

TYPE: review, interview.

PERFORMERS: Melvin Strauss, Buffalo Philharmonic Orchestra.

NAMES: Hermann Hesse, Mahler, Mozart.

OTHER WORKS MENTIONED: *Contra Mortem et Tempus, Symphony No. 3, Time-Span.*

Putnam, Thomas. "Review: Philharmonic Presents Clever Mozart Program," *The Buffalo Courier Express* (20 January 1969).

TYPE: review.

PERFORMERS: Melvin Strauss, Buffalo Philharmonic Orchestra.

NAMES: Mahler, Mozart.

Putnam, Thomas. "Strauss to Introduce Two Works Here," *The Buffalo Courier Express* (20 October 1968).

TYPE: upcoming performance.

PERFORMERS: Melvin Strauss, Buffalo Philharmonic Orchestra.

von Rhein, John. "Music: The 'Concord' Debut to Mark a Return to the Romantic," *The Chicago Tribune* (20 January 1980) VI, 23.

TYPE: article, interview.

OTHER WORKS DISCUSSED: *Concerto for Violin and Orchestra, The Confidence Man, Octet, String Quartet No. 3, String Quartet No. 4, String Quartet No. 5, String Quartet No. 6, String Quartet No. 7.*

Ringer, Alexander L. "The Music of George Rochberg," *Musical Quarterly* LII/4 (October 1966) 409-430.

TYPE: article.

PERFORMERS: Ralph Shapey, Contemporary Chamber Players [University of Chicago].

NAMES: J.S. Bach, Miles Davis, Hermann Hesse, Mahler, Mozart, Stockhausen.

OTHER WORKS DISCUSSED: *Apocalyptica [I], Black Sounds, Blake Songs, La Bocca della Verità, Cantio Sacra, Capriccio for Two Pianos, Chamber Symphony, Cheltenham Concerto, Concert Piece for Two Pianos and Orchestra, Contra Mortem et Tempus, David, the Psalmist, Dialogues, Duo Concertante, Four Song of Solomon, Nach Bach, Night Music, Passions [According to the Twentieth Century], Serenata d'estate, Sonata-Fantasia, String Quartet No. 1, String Quartet No. 2, Symphony No. 1, Symphony No. 2, Three Psalms, Time-Span, Trio for Clarinet, Horn, and Piano, Trio [No. 1] for Violin, Cello, and Piano, Twelve Bagatelles, Zodiac.*

OTHER WORKS MENTIONED: *Arioso, Bartokiana, Five Smooth Stones, Sonata No. 1 for Piano Solo, Sonata No. 2 for Piano Solo, Waltz Serenade.*

BOOKS DISCUSSED: *The Hexachord and Its Relation to the Twelve-Tone Row.*

Salzman, Eric. "Rochberg: *Chamber Symphony, Duo Concertante, Music for the Magic Theater, Ricordanza, String Quartet No. 1,*" *Stereo Review* XXVII/1 (July 1976) 111.

TYPE: record review.

PERFORMERS: Kenneth Moore, Oberlin Orchestra.

NAMES: Beethoven, Hermann Hesse, Mahler, Mozart, Varèse, Webern.

OTHER WORKS DISCUSSED: *Chamber Symphony, Duo Concertante, Ricordanza, String Quartet No. 1.*

Salzman, Eric. "Rochberg: *Contra Mortem et Tempus,*" *Stereo Review* XXII/4 (April 1969) 100.

TYPE: record review.

PERFORMERS: Aeolian Chamber Players.

OTHER WORKS DISCUSSED: *Contra Mortem et Tempus.*

Stromberg, Rolf. "Two Young Musicians Gifted," *The Seattle Post-Intelligencer* (03 November 1969) S*45.

TYPE: review.

PERFORMERS: William O. Smith, Robert Suderberg, University of Washington Contemporary Group, Philadelphia String Quartet, Soni Ventorum.

NAMES: Hermann Hesse.

OTHER WORKS DISCUSSED: *Contra Mortem et Tempus, Music for "The Alchemist," Tableaux.*

Strongin, Theodore. "Music: Symphonists Accept Moderns: But That's in Chicago at Campus Concert: University Musicians' Works Get Hearings," *The New York Times* (26 January 1967) 25.

TYPE: review.

PERFORMERS: Ralph Shapey, Contemporary Chamber Players [University of Chicago].

NAMES: Beethoven, Mahler, Mozart, Varèse.

Tatham, D.F. "Good and Bad Effects in Challenging Music," *The Syracuse Post-Standard* (15 March 1975) 7.

TYPE: review.

PERFORMERS: David Loebel, Syracuse Symphony Orchestra.

NAMES: Mozart.

n.a. "U. of C. [University of Chicago] Plans Music at 75th Anniversary: Eight Composers to Write Original Works," *The Chicago Tribune* (06 November 1966) F4.

TYPE: upcoming première.

PERFORMERS: Ralph Shapey, Contemporary Chamber Players [University of Chicago].

Veilleux, C. Thomas. "Chamber Music Roundup Reveals Three Fine Records," *The Sunday Post [Bridgeport, CT]* (10 October 1976) E-14.

TYPE: record review.

PERFORMERS: Kenneth Moore, Oberlin Orchestra.

OTHER WORKS DISCUSSED: *Chamber Symphony, Duo Concertante, Ricordanza, String Quartet No. 1.*

Webster, Daniel. "At Curtis Hall: Contemporary Works Played by Two Groups," *The Philadelphia Inquirer* (20 April 1967).

TYPE: review.

PERFORMERS: Melvin Strauss, Buffalo Philharmonic Orchestra.

NAMES: Beethoven, Mozart, Varèse.

Webster, Daniel. "Stylistic Odyssey of George Rochberg," *The Philadelphia Inquirer* (15 February 1976) 7H.

TYPE: record review.

PERFORMERS: Kenneth Moore, Oberlin Orchestra.

NAMES: Beethoven, Mahler, Mozart, Varèse, Webern.

OTHER WORKS DISCUSSED: *Chamber Symphony, Duo Concertante, Ricordanza, String Quartet No. 1.*

Nach Bach, Fantasy for Harpsichord or Piano

Aikin, Jim. "Records: Three Sides of George Rochberg," *Contemporary Keyboard* IV/9 (September 1978) 62.

TYPE: record review.

PERFORMERS: Igor Kipnis.

OTHER WORKS DISCUSSED: *Black Sounds, Carnival Music.*

Bennis, W. J. "Igor Kipnis: een Bezeten Musicus," *Algemeen Dagblad [Rotterdam]* (11 November 1967).

TYPE: review.

PERFORMERS: Igor Kipnis.

NAMES: Bach.

Bronston, Levering. "Three Sides of George Rochberg," *The New Records* XLVI/5 (July 1978) 7.

TYPE: record review.

PERFORMERS: Igor Kipnis.

NAMES: Bach.

OTHER WORKS DISCUSSED: *Black Sounds, Carnival Music, String Quartet No. 3.*

Cudworth, Charles. "Igor Kipnis," *Musical Times [Great Britain]* CVIII/1498 (December 1967) 1133.

TYPE: review.

PERFORMERS: Igor Kipnis.

Davis, Peter G. "Harpsichord Gets Electronic Voice: Stanley Lock and Joel Spiegelman Perform," *The New York Times* (22 April 1968) 58.

TYPE: review.

PERFORMERS: Joel Spiegelman.

Dixon, Joan DeVee. "George Rochberg's *Nach Bach, A Fantasy for Harpsichord or Piano,*" *The Iowa Music Teacher* XLV/2 (Spring - May 1988) 4-9.

TYPE: article, interviews with George Rochberg and Igor Kipnis.

NAMES: Bach, Brahms, Chopin, Igor Kipnis, Scriabin, Melvin Strauss.

OTHER WORKS DISCUSSED: *Partita Variations, Sonata-Fantasia.*

Dixon, Joan DeVee. "George Rochberg's *Nach Bach, A Fantasy for Harpsichord or Piano,*" Unpublished (June 1988) 13pp.

TYPE: article, interviews with George Rochberg and Igor Kipnis.

NAMES: Bach, Brahms, Chopin, Igor Kipnis, Scriabin, Melvin Strauss.

OTHER WORKS DISCUSSED: *Chamber Symphony, Contra Mortem et Tempus, Music for the Magic Theater, Partita Variations, Sonata-Fantasia, Symphony No. 3.*

Elsner, Carmen. "Harpsichordist Kipnis Discovers Hundreds of Allies at Concert," *The Wisconsin State Journal [Madison, WI]* (08 March 1967).

TYPE: review.

PERFORMERS: Igor Kipnis.

Felton, James. "Penn [University of Pennsylvania at Philadelphia] Contemporary Group Austere in New Music," *The Evening Bulletin [Philadelphia]* (28 January 1967) 9.

TYPE: review.

PERFORMERS: Igor Kipnis.

NAMES: Bach.

Frank, Peter. "Rochberg: *Carnival Music, Black Sounds, Nach Bach,*" *Fanfare* I/6 (July–August 1978) 75-76.

TYPE: review.

PERFORMERS: Igor Kipnis.

OTHER WORKS DISCUSSED: *Black Sounds, Carnival Music.*

Finn, Robert. "Fresh Sounds at Oberlin Give Relief," *The Plain Dealer [Cleveland, OH]* (17 July 1969) 7C.

TYPE: review.

PERFORMERS: Richard Bunger.

NAMES: Bach, Webern.

Gelles, George. "Bowdoin Festival: Accent on the New," *The Boston Globe* (15 August 1966) 15.

TYPE: review.

PERFORMERS: George Rochberg.

NAMES: Bach, Berg, Chopin.

OTHER WORKS DISCUSSED: *La Bocca della Verità, Contra Mortem et Tempus, Trio [No. 1] for Violin, Cello, and Piano.*

Goldsmith, Harris. "Etsuko Tazaki, piano," *High Fidelity/Musical America* XXVII/5 (May 1977) MA-26.

TYPE: review.

PERFORMERS: Etsuko Tazaki.

OTHER WORKS DISCUSSED: *Partita Variations.*

Henry, Derrick. "Spontaneity and Warmth from Igor Kipnis," *The Boston Globe* (27 April 1984) 54.

TYPE: review.

PERFORMERS: Igor Kipnis.

NAMES: Bach.

Hinson, Maurice. *Guide to the Pianist's Repertoire: An Annotated Guide.* (Bloomington, IN: Indiana University Press, 1973) 527.

TYPE: score review.

NAMES: Bach.

OTHER WORKS DISCUSSED: *Arioso,   Bartokiana,   Sonata-Fantasia, Twelve Bagatelles.*

Hinson, Maurice. *Guide to the Pianist's Repertoire: An Annotated Guide, Supplement.* (Bloomington, IN: Indiana University Press, 1979) 275.

TYPE: score review.

NAMES: Bach.

OTHER WORKS DISCUSSED: *Arioso, Bartokiana, Carnival Music, Partita Variations, Prelude on "Happy Birthday," Sonata-Fantasia, Twelve Bagatelles.*

Hinson, Maurice. *Guide to the Pianist's Repertoire: An Annotated Guide, Second, Revised, and Enlarged Edition.* (Bloomington, IN: Indiana University Press, 1987) 598-599.

TYPE: score review.

NAMES: Bach.

OTHER WORKS DISCUSSED: *Arioso, Bartokiana, Carnival Music, Partita Variations, Prelude on "Happy Birthday," Sonata-Fantasia, Twelve Bagatelles, Two Preludes and Fughettas from The Book of Contrapuntal Pieces.*

Horn, Daniel Paul. *"Carnival Music:* An Introduction to the Piano Music of George Rochberg," *Clavier* XXVII/9 (November 1988) 17-22.

TYPE: article.

NAMES: Bach, Igor Kipnis.

OTHER WORKS DISCUSSED: *Arioso, Bartokiana, Book of Contrapuntal Pieces for Keyboard Instruments, Carnival Music, Four Short Sonatas, Partita Variations, Prelude on "Happy Birthday," Sonata-Fantasia, Twelve Bagatelles.*

OTHER WORKS MENTIONED: *Sonata No. 1 for Piano Solo, Sonata No. 2 for Piano Solo.*

Hughes, Allen. "Bach Unit Weighs Electronic Media: Society's Study Group Finds Little Effect on Works," *The New York Times* (18 July 1969) 15.

TYPE: review.

PERFORMERS: Rosalyn Tureck.

Hume, Paul. "Lowenthal Leads 'Musical Tour'," *The Washington Post [Washington, D.C.]* (08 December 1969) C9.

TYPE: review.

PERFORMERS: Jerome Lowenthal.

NAMES: Bach.

Loveless, Robert C. "Ambassador for Musical Revolt: Avant-Garde Pianist Performs," *The Honolulu Star-Bulletin* (20 November 1970) C-4.

TYPE: review.

PERFORMERS: Richard Bunger.

Lyne, William. "Letters to *R & R* [*Records and Recordings*]: Kipnis Recital," *Records and Recordings [Great Britain]* (November 1967).

TYPE: upcoming performance.

PERFORMERS: Igor Kipnis.

NAMES: Charles Cudworth.

Moore, David W. "Rochberg: *Carnival Music, Black Sounds, Nach Bach*," *American Record Guide* XLI/9 (July 1978) 25-26.

TYPE: record review.

PERFORMERS: Igor Kipnis.

OTHER WORKS DISCUSSED: *Apocalyptica [I], Black Sounds, Carnival Music, String Quartet No. 3.*

Ringer, Alexander L. "The Music of George Rochberg," *Musical Quarterly* LII/4 (October 1966) 409-430.

TYPE: article.

NAMES: J.S. Bach, Miles Davis, Hermann Hesse, Mahler, Mozart, Stockhausen.

OTHER WORKS DISCUSSED: *Apocalyptica [I], Black Sounds, Blake Songs, La Bocca della Verità, Cantio Sacra, Capriccio for Two Pianos, Chamber Symphony, Cheltenham Concerto, Concert Piece for Two Pianos and Orchestra, Contra Mortem et Tempus, David, the Psalmist, Dialogues, Duo Concertante, Four Songs of Solomon, Music for the Magic Theater, Night Music, Passions [According to the Twentieth Century], Serenata d'estate, Sonata-Fantasia, String Quartet No. 1, String Quartet No. 2, Symphony No. 1, Symphony No. 2, Three Psalms, Time-Span, Trio for Clarinet, Horn, and Piano, Trio [No. 1] for Violin, Cello, and Piano, Twelve Bagatelles, Zodiac.*

OTHER WORKS MENTIONED: *Arioso, Bartokiana, Five Smooth Stones, Sonata No. 1 for Piano Solo, Sonata No. 2 for Piano Solo, Waltz Serenade.*

BOOKS DISCUSSED: *The Hexachord and Its Relation to the Twelve-Tone Row.*

Sadie, Stanley. "A Striking Music Personality," *The Times Saturday Review [London]* (04 November 1967) 19.

TYPE: review.

PERFORMERS: Igor Kipnis.

NAMES: Bach.

Salisbury, Wilma. "Half a Piano Recital Lifts Lid on Part Two of Oberlin Festival," *The Plain Dealer [Cleveland, OH]* (20 March 1970).

TYPE: review.

OTHER WORKS DISCUSSED: *Prelude on "Happy Birthday," Tableaux.*

Salzman, Eric. "Rochberg: *Carnival Music, Black Sounds, Nach Bach*," *Stereo Review* XL/4 (October 1978).

TYPE: review.

PERFORMERS: Igor Kipnis.

NAMES: Bach.

OTHER WORKS DISCUSSED: *Black Sounds, Carnival Music.*

Scher, Valerie. "Retrospective Concert Surveys Talents of Composer Rochberg," *The Philadelphia Inquirer* (26 March 1983).

TYPE: review.

PERFORMERS: Jerome Lowenthal.

NAMES: Bach.

OTHER WORKS DISCUSSED: *Partita Variations, Sonata-Fantasia, Variations on an Original Theme.*

Schoff, F.G. "Kipnis on Harpsichord Good Listening at MSC [Moorehead State College]," *The Forum [Fargo, ND and Moorehead, MN]* (09 March 1967) 16.

TYPE: review.

PERFORMERS: Igor Kipnis.

NAMES: Bach, Webern.

Singer, Samuel. "Lowenthal Plays 'Birds and B's' in Recital at Settlement School," *The Philadelphia Inquirer* (14 February 1971).

TYPE: review.

PERFORMERS: Jerome Lowenthal.

NAMES: Bach, Sol Schoenbach.

Staff, Charles. "Kipnis and His Harpsichord Charm Music Fete Audience," *The Indianapolis News* (08 July 1975).

TYPE: review.

PERFORMERS: Igor Kipnis.

NAMES: Bach.

Starreveld, Rogier. "Igor Kipnis: Bijzonder Clavecinist," *Het Parool* (11 November 1967) 11.

TYPE: review.

PERFORMERS: Igor Kipnis.

NAMES: Bach.

Stewart, Paul. "The Piano Music of George Rochberg and the New Romanticism," *American Music Teacher* XXXVIII/3 (January 1989) 24-27, 62.

TYPE: article.

NAMES: Bach.

OTHER WORKS DISCUSSED: *Arioso, Bartokiana, Book of Contrapuntal Pieces for Keyboard Instruments, Carnival Music, Four Short Sonatas,*

Partita Variations, Prelude on "Happy Birthday," Sonata-Fantasia, Twelve Bagatelles, Two Preludes and Fughettas.

Webster, Daniel. "At U. of P. [University of Pennsylvania at Philadelphia]: Concert Offers Modern Works," *The Philadelphia Inquirer* (28 January 1967).

TYPE: review.

PERFORMERS: Igor Kipnis.

NAMES: Bach.

Young, Blyth. "Evening of Harpsichord Provides Soothing Balm," *The Ottawa Journal [Ottawa, Ontario, Canada]* (20 January 1969).

TYPE: review.

PERFORMERS: Igor Kipnis.

NAMES: Bach.

Night Music for Orchestra

Affelder, Paul. "Milstein Earns Plaudits in Prokofiev *Concerto*," *The Brooklyn Eagle* (24 April 1953) 11.

TYPE: review.

PERFORMERS: Dmitri Mitropoulos, New York Philharmonic-Symphony Orchestra.

NAMES: Laszlo Barga.

Berger, Arthur. "Concert and Recital: The Philharmonic," *The New York Herald-Tribune* (24 April 1953) 23.

TYPE: review.

PERFORMERS: Dmitri Mitropoulos, New York Philharmonic-Symphony Orchestra.

Biancolli, Louis. "Music: Milstein Fills Demands of Prokofiev," *The New York World-Telegram and Sun* (24 April 1953) 23.

TYPE: review.

PERFORMERS: Dmitri Mitropoulos, New York Philharmonic-Symphony Orchestra.

NAMES: Berg, Schönberg.

Brozen, Michael. "Debuts and Reappearances: Composers and Musicians for Peace," *High Fidelity/Musical America* XVIII/8 (August 1968) MA-11.

TYPE: review.

PERFORMERS: Izler Solomon.

Darling, Henry R. "New Courses and Twevle-Tone Composition Put Zip in Penn's [University of Pennsylvania at Philadelphia] Music

Department," *The Sunday Bulletin [Philadelphia]* (30 September 1962) 15.

TYPE: article, interview.

PERFORMERS: New York Philharmonic.

OTHER WORKS DISCUSSED: *Symphony No. 1.*

OTHER WORKS MENTIONED: *Chamber Symphony, String Quartet No. 1, String Quartet No. 2, Time-Span, Twelve Bagatelles.*

Frankenstein, Alfred. "Rochberg: *Night Music*," *High Fidelity* XII/8 (August 1962) 83.

TYPE: record review.

PERFORMERS: Robert Whitney, Louisville Orchestra.

Felton, James. "Composers Are Sane But the World Isn't, Says Penn Rochberg," *The Sunday Bulletin [Philadelphia]* (13 February 1966) 11.

TYPE: interview.

PERFORMERS: Dmitri Mitropoulos, New York Philharmonic-Symphony Orchestra.

WORKS DISCUSSED: *Contra Mortem et Tempus, Music for the Magic Theater, String Quartet No. 2, Symphony No. 1, Symphony No. 2, Symphony No. 3, Zodiac.*

Felton, James. "Rochberg's Chamber Music Is Aired at the Art Alliance," *The Evening Bulletin [Philadelphia]* (16 February 1966).

TYPE: review.

NAMES: Webern.

OTHER WORKS DISCUSSED: *La Bocca della Verità, Contra Mortem et Tempus, Dialogues, Symphony No. 1, Symphony No. 2, Trio for Violin, Cello, and Piano.*

Gelles, George. "At Symphony: Superb Performances from Leinsdorf, BSO [Boston Symphony Orchestra]," *The Boston Globe* (18 December 1965).

TYPE: review.

PERFORMERS: Erich Leinsdorf, Boston Symphony Orchestra.

NAMES: Jules Eskin, Laurence Thorstenberg.

n.a. "George Rochberg Wins George Gershwin Memorial Contest," *Musical America* LXXIII/1 (01 January 1953) 25.

TYPE: announcement of Gershwin Competition prize.

Johnson, Harriett. "Philharmonic in Final Week," *The New York Post* (24 April 1953) 66.

TYPE: review.

PERFORMERS: Dimitri Mitropoulos, New York Philharmonic-Symphony Orchestra.

Katzenstein, Larry. "Guest Conductor Chooses Old Favorites, Dark Score," *The St. Louis Post-Dispatch* (03 April 1988).

TYPE: review.

PERFORMERS: Raymond Leppard, St. Louis Symphony Orchestra.

La Fave, Kenneth. "Music Scene: Composer George Rochberg: Melody Above the Storm," *The Chicago Tribune* (28 April 1988).

TYPE: article, interview.

NAMES: Raymond Leppard.

OTHER WORKS DISCUSSED: *Concerto for Violin and Orchestra, String Quartet No. 4, String Quartet No. 5, String Quartet No. 6, Symphony No. 1, Symphony No. 6.*

Manges, Edyth. "George Rochberg, Newtown, Is Prize-Winning Composer," *The Upper Darby News [Upper Darby, PA]* XXII/17 (11 November 1954) 1.

TYPE: article.

NAMES: Gene, Frances, and Paul [Rochberg].

OTHER WORKS DISCUSSED: *David, the Psalmist.*

Ringer, Alexander L. "The Music of George Rochberg," *Musical Quarterly* LII/4 (October 1966) 409-430.

TYPE: article.

PERFORMERS: Dimitri Mitropoulos, New York Philharmonic-Symphony Orchestra.

NAMES: Bartók, Stravinsky.

OTHER WORKS DISCUSSED: *Apocalyptica [I], Black Sounds, Blake Songs, La Bocca della Verità, Cantio Sacra, Capriccio for Two Pianos, Chamber Symphony, Cheltenham Concerto, Concert Piece for Two Pianos and Orchestra, Contra Mortem et Tempus, David, the Psalmist, Dialogues, Duo Concertante, Four Songs of Solomon, Music for the Magic Theater, Nach Bach, Passions [According to the Twentieth Century], Serenata d'estate, Sonata-Fantasia, String Quartet No. 1, String Quartet No. 2, Symphony No. 1, Symphony No. 2, Three Psalms, Time-Span, Trio for Clarinet, Horn, and Piano, Trio [No. 1] for Violin, Cello, and Piano, Twelve Bagatelles, Zodiac.*

OTHER WORKS MENTIONED: *Arioso, Bartokiana, Five Smooth Stones, Sonata No. 1 for Piano Solo, Sonata No. 2 for Piano Solo, Waltz Serenade.*

BOOKS DISCUSSED: *The Hexachord and Its Relation to the Twelve-Tone Row.*

n.a. "Rochberg Receives Naumburg Award," *The New York Times* (26 July 1961) 37.

TYPE: annoucement of Naumburg Recording Award.

OTHER WORKS DISCUSSED: *Symphony No. 2.*

de Schauensee, Max. "Music Tempo Brisk this Week: Lorne Munroe and French Pianist Soloists at Two Orchestra Concerts," *The Evening Bulletin [Philadelphia]* (29 October 1961) V, 12.

TYPE: upcoming performance, interview.

PERFORMERS: Eugene Ormandy, Lorne Munroe, Philadelphia Orchestra.

de Schauensee, Max. "Philadelphia: Operatic War," *Musical America* LXXXII/1 (January 1962) 133-134.

TYPE: review.

PERFORMERS: Eugene Ormandy, Lorne Munroe, Philadelphia Orchestra.

Schloss, Edwin H. "Orchestra to Play Rochberg Work: Munroe Is Soloist," *The Philadelphia Inquirer* (29 October 1961) 1, 5.

TYPE: upcoming performance, interview.

PERFORMERS: Eugene Ormandy, Lorne Munroe, Philadelphia Orchestra.

OTHER WORKS MENTIONED: *Chamber Symphony, Cheltenham Conceto, String Quartet No. 1, String Quartet No. 2, Symphony No. 1, Symphony No. 2, Time-Span.*

Taubman, Howard. "*Night Music* Given by Philharmonic," *The New York Times* (24 April 1953) 29.

TYPE: review.

PERFORMERS: Dimitri Mitropoulos, New York Philharmonic-Symphony Orchestra.

Watt, Douglas. "Man with a Past," *The New Yorker* (02 May 1953) 80-82.

TYPE: review.

PERFORMERS: Dimitri Mitropoulos, New York Philharmonic-Symphony Orchestra.

OTHER WORKS DISCUSSED: *Symphony No. 1.*

n.a. "World of Music: George Rochberg," *Etude* LXXI/2 (February 1953) 8.

TYPE: upcoming première, announcement of Gershwin award.

PERFORMERS: Dimitri Mitropoulos, New York Philharmonic-Symphony Orchestra.

Octet, A Grand Fantasia for Flute, Clarinet, Horn, Violin, Viola, Cello, Bass, and Piano

n.a. "Chamber Society's Plans," *The New York Times* (27 April 1978) III, 21.

TYPE: upcoming performance.

PERFORMERS: Chamber Music Society of Lincoln Center.

Gagne, Cole and Tracy Caras. *Soundpieces: Interviews with American Composers.* (Metuchen, NJ: Scarecrow Press, Inc., 1982).

TYPE: interview.

OTHER WORKS DISCUSSED: *Apocalyptica [I], Black Sounds, Concerto for Violin and Orchestra, The Confidence Man, Contra Mortem et Tempus, Electrikaleidoscope, Music for the Magic Theater, Quintet for Piano and String Quartet, Ricordanza, Sonata No. 2 for Piano Solo, String Quartet No. 3, String Quartet No. 4, String Quartet No. 5, String Quartet No. 6, Twelve Bagatelles.*

OTHER WORKS MENTIONED: many.

Hoffman, W. L. "Arts and Entertainment: US [United States] Composer on Canberra Stint," *The Canberra Times [Australia]* (20 October 1986).

TYPE: upcoming performances.

OTHER WORKS DISCUSSED: *Blake Songs, Quintet for Piano and String Quartet, Songs in Praise of Krishna, Symphony No. 4, To the Dark Wood.*

OTHER WORKS MENTIONED: *Concerto for Violin and Orchestra, Symphony No. 5.*

Hoffman, W.L. "Music: Rochberg: Positive First Half," *The Canberra Times [Australia]* (22 October 1986) 29.

TYPE: review.

OTHER WORKS DISCUSSED: *Blake Songs, Quintet for Piano and String Quartet, To the Dark Wood.*

Jenkins, Speight. "World Première of Rochberg's *Octet,*" *The New York Post* (26 April 1980) 16.

TYPE: review.

PERFORMERS: Chamber Music Society of Lincoln Center.

NAMES: Mahler, Wagner.

Reinthaler, Joan. "Chamber Music Society," *The Washington Post* (28 April 1980) B9.

TYPE: review.

PERFORMERS: Chamber Music Society of Lincoln Center.

von Rhein, John. "Music: The 'Concord' Debut to Mark a Return to the Romantic," *The Chicago Tribune* (20 January 1980) VI, 23.

TYPE: article, interview.

PERFORMERS: Chamber Music Society of Lincoln Center.

OTHER WORKS DISCUSSED: *Concerto for Violin and Orchestra, The Confidence Man, Music for the Magic Theater, String Quartet No. 3, String Quartet No. 4, String Quartet No. 5, String Quartet No. 6, String Quartet No. 7.*

Schonberg, Harold C. "Music: Chamber Music Society in New Rochberg *Octet*," *The New York Times* (27 April 1980) 68.

TYPE: review.

PERFORMERS: Chamber Music Society of Lincoln Center.

NAMES: Rachmaninoff.

OTHER WORKS DISCUSSED: *String Quartet No. 4, String Quartet No. 5, String Quartet No. 6.*

Smith, Patrick J. "New York: Chamber Music Society: Rochberg Première," *High Fidelity/Musical America* XXX/8 (August 1980) MA-22.

TYPE: review.

PERFORMERS: Chamber Music Society of Lincoln Center.

NAMES: Mahler, Rachmaninoff, Schönberg.

Partita Variations for Piano Solo

n.a. "n.t.," *The Curtis Institue of Music Alumni Association Newsletter* III/4 (Winter 1977) 4.

TYPE: review.

PERFORMERS: Arthur Fennimore.

OTHER WORKS DISCUSSED: *Dialogues, Quintet for Piano and String Quartet.*

Dixon, Joan DeVee. "George Rochberg's *Nach Bach, A Fantasy for Harpsichord or Piano*," *The Iowa Music Teacher* XLV/2 (Spring - May 1988) 4-9.

TYPE: article, interviews with George Rochberg and Igor Kipnis.

OTHER WORKS DISCUSSED: *Nach Bach, Sonata-Fantasia.*

Dixon, Joan DeVee. "George Rochberg's *Nach Bach, A Fantasy for Harpsichord or Piano*," Unpublished (June 1988) 13pp.

TYPE: article, interviews with George Rochberg and Igor Kipnis.

OTHER WORKS DISCUSSED: *Chamber Symphony, Contra Mortem et Tempus, Music for the Magic Theater, Nach Bach, Sonata-Fantasia, Symphony No. 3.*

Ericson, Raymond. "Etsko Tazaki, Pianist on Grand Scale, at 'Y'," *The New York Times* (19 September 1980) III, 5.

TYPE: upcoming recital, interview with Etsuko Tazaki.

PERFORMERS: Etsuko Tazaki.

Eyer, Ron. "Dictionary Anyone?," *The Daily News [New York]* (15 December 1976) 30.

TYPE: review.

PERFORMERS: Etsuko Tazaki.

NAMES: Bach, Chopin.

Goldsmith, Harris. "Etsuko Tazaki, Piano," *High Fidelity/Musical America* XXVII/5 (May 1977) MA-26.

TYPE: review.

PERFORMERS: Etsuko Tazaki.

NAMES: Brahms, Busoni, Mussorgsky, Prokofiev, Schubert.

OTHER WORKS DISCUSSED: *Nach Bach.*

Henahan, Donal. "Recital: Tazaki Piano Does Rochberg Proud," *The New York Times* (15 December 1976) II, 17.

TYPE: review.

PERFORMERS: Etsuko Tazaki.

NAMES: Bellini, Chopin, Cowell, Liszt, Mozart, Scriabin, Schönberg.

Hinson, Maurice. *Guide to the Pianist's Repertoire: An Annotated Guide, Supplement.* (Bloomington, IN: Indiana University Press, 1979) 275.

TYPE: score review.

OTHER WORKS DISCUSSED: *Arioso, Bartokiana, Carnival Music, Nach Bach, Prelude on "Happy Birthday", Sonata-Fantasia, Twelve Bagatelles.*

Hinson, Maurice. *Guide to the Pianist's Repertoire: An Annotated Guide, Second, Revised, and Enlarged Edition.* (Bloomington, IN: Indiana University Press, 1987) 598-599.

TYPE: score review.

OTHER WORKS DISCUSSED: *Arioso, Bartokiana, Carnival Music, Nach Bach, Prelude on "Happy Birthday", Sonata-Fantasia, Twelve Bagatelles, Two Preludes and Fughettas from The Book of Contrapuntal Pieces.*

Horn, Daniel Paul. "*Carnival Music*: An Introduction to the Piano Music of George Rochberg," *Clavier* XXVII/9 (November 1988) 17-22.

TYPE: article.

NAMES: Beethoven, Chopin, Etsuko Tazaki.

OTHER WORKS DISCUSSED: *Arioso, Bartokiana, Book of Contrapuntal Pieces for Keyboard Instruments, Carnival Music, Four Short Sonatas, Nach Bach, Prelude on "Happy Birthday", Sonata-Fantasia, Twelve Bagatelles.*

OTHER WORKS MENTIONED: *Sonata No. 1 for Piano Solo, Sonata No. 2 for Piano Solo.*

Hume, Paul. "Piano," *The Washington Post* [Washington, D.C.] (06 December 1976) B6.

TYPE: review.

PERFORMERS: Etsuko Tasaki.

Isacoff, Stuart. "New Music Corner: George Rochberg," *Keyboard Classics* (September–October 1985).

TYPE: article, interview.

Lowens, Irving. "Rochberg *Variations* Is Premièred," *The Washington Star* [Washington, D.C.] (06 December 1976) D3.

TYPE: review.

PERFORMERS: Etsuko Tazaki.

NAMES: Bach, Beethoven, Edyth Bush, Schumann.

Kimball, Robert. "Odyssey of Rochberg Aided by Etsuko Tazaki," *The New York Post* (14 December 1976) 47.

TYPE: review.

PERFORMERS: Etsuko Tazaki.

NAMES: Beethoven, Chopin, Rachmaninoff.

n.a. "Music and Dance: Ormandy Back from Europe; Rochberg Concert at Curtis," *The Evening Bulletin* [Philadelphia] (04 February 1977) 29, 31.

TYPE: upcoming performance.

PERFORMERS: Arthur Fennimore.

OTHER WORKS DISCUSSED: *Dialogues, Quintet for Piano and String Quartet.*

O'Reilly, F. Warren. "Music: A Prodigious Talent at Festival," *The Washington Times* [Washington, D.C.] (24 April 1984).

TYPE: review.

PERFORMERS: Sylvia Glickman.

Page, Tim. "Music: Debuts in Review: A Cellist and Four Pianists Are Recitalists," *The New York Times* (16 January 1983) I, 48.

TYPE: review.

PERFORMERS: Elizabeth Wright.

Peters, Frank. "Review: Pianist Etsuko Tazaki," *The St. Louis Post* (04 April 1977).

TYPE: review.

PERFORMERS: Etsuko Tazaki.

NAMES: Beethoven, Chopin, Liszt, Rachmaninoff.

OTHER WORKS MENTIONED: Concerto for Violin and Orchestra.

Scher, Valerie. "Retrospective Concert Surveys Talents of Composer Rochberg," *The Philadelphia Inquirer* (26 March 1983).

TYPE: review.

PERFORMERS: Jerome Lowenthal.

NAMES: Chopin, Haydn.

OTHER WORKS DISCUSSED: *Nach Bach, Sonata-Fantasia, Variations on an Original Theme.*

Schuller, K. G. "Pianist's Performance Is Brilliant," *The St. Louis Globe* (04 April 1977).

TYPE: review.

PERFORMERS: Etsuko Tazaki.

NAMES: Chopin, Mozart, Schumann.

Stewart, Paul. "The Piano Music of George Rochberg and the New Romanticism," *American Music Teacher* XXXVIII/3 (January 1989) 24-27, 62.

TYPE: article.

NAMES: Brahms, Debussy.

OTHER WORKS DISCUSSED: *Arioso, Bartokiana, Book of Contrapuntal Pieces for Keyboard Instruments, Carnival Music, Four Short Sonatas, Nach Bach, Prelude on "Happy Birthday", Sonata-Fantasia, Twelve Bagatelles, Two Preludes and Fughettas.*

Webster, Daniel. "Rochberg's Indian Love Song Pulsing, Vital," *The Philadelphia Inquirer* (31 January 1978) 7-A.

TYPE: review.

PERFORMERS: Arthur Fennimore.

NAMES: Bach, Chopin, Debussy, Schumann.

Passions *[According to the Twentieth Century] for Actors, Dancers, Singers, Choruses, Speakers, and Instrumentalists*

Ringer, Alexander L. "The Music of George Rochberg," *Musical Quarterly* LII/4 (October 1966) 409-430.

TYPE: article.

OTHER WORKS DISCUSSED: *Apocalyptica [I], Black Sounds, Blake Songs, La Bocca della Verità, Cantio Sacra, Capriccio for Two Pianos, Chamber Symphony, Cheltenham Concerto, Concert Piece for Two Pianos and Orchestra, Contra Mortem et Tempus, David, the Psalmist, Dialogues, Duo Concertante, Four Songs of Solomon, Music for the Magic Theater, Nach Bach, Night Music, Serenata d'estate, Sonata-Fantasia, String Quartet No. 1, String Quartet No. 2, Symphony No. 1, Symphony No. 2, Three Psalms, Time-Span, Trio for Clarinet, Horn, and Piano, Trio [No. 1] for Violin, Cello, and Piano, Twelve Bagatelles, Zodiac.*

OTHER WORKS MENTIONED: *Arioso, Bartokiana, Five Smooth Stones, Sonata No. 1 for Piano Solo, Sonata No. 2 for Piano Solo, Waltz Serenade.*

BOOKS DISCUSSED: *The Hexachord and Its Relation to the Twelve-Tone Row.*

Phaedra , *Monodrama for Mezzo-Soprano and Orchestra*

Felton, James. "Music Beat: Rochberg Composing Opera; Wife is Librettist," *The Sunday Bulletin [Philadelphia]* (16 July 1978) 2-EA.

TYPE: article, interview.

PERFORMERS: Syracuse Contemporary Art Group.

NAMES: Hermann Hesse, Robert Lowell.

OTHER WORKS DISCUSSED: *Caprice Variations, Concerto for Violin and Orchestra, The Confidence Man, String Quartet No. 4, String Quartet No. 5, String Quartet No. 6.*

Fogel, Henry. "A Conversation with George Rochberg," *The Syracuse Guide* (March 1976) 27-28, 36.

TYPE: interview.

NAMES: many.

PERFORMERS: David Loebel, Neva Pilgrim, Syracuse Symphony Orchestra.

OTHER WORKS DISCUSSED: *String Quartet No. 3.*

Fogel, Henry. "George Rochberg: A Raproachment with the Past," *The Syracuse Guide* V (January 1976) 24-26, 42.

TYPE: article.

NAMES: many.

PERFORMERS: David Loebel, Neva Pilgrim, Syracuse Symphony Orchestra.

OTHER WORKS DISCUSSED: *Concerto for Violin and Orchestra, String Quartet No. 3, Symphony No. 3.*

n.a. "$407,276 in Grants To Go To Composers," *The New York Times* (11 February 1974) 46.

TYPE: announcement of NEA [National Endowment for the Arts] awards.

Grey, Gene. "*Phaedra* Fascinates with Its Drama," *The Sunday Press* [Binghamton, NY] (15 November 1981).

TYPE: review.

PERFORMERS: David Loebel, Lucy Shelton, Binghamton Symphony Orchestra.

Grey, Gene. "Symphony to Perform Rochberg's *Phaedra*," *The Binghamton Press* [Binghamton, NY] (23 November 1981).

TYPE: upcoming performance.

PERFORMERS: David Loebel, Lucy Shelton, Binghamton Symphony Orchestra.

Grey, Gene. "What's Up: Festival to Feature Cultures," *The Binghamton Press* [Binghamton, NY] (13 November 1981).

TYPE: upcoming performance.

PERFORMERS: David Loebel, Lucy Shelton, Binghamton Symphony Orchestra.

Nugent, George. "Syracuse Symphony: *Phaedra* Somber Musical Première," *The Syracuse Post-Standard* (10 January 1976).

TYPE: review.

PERFORMERS: David Loebel, Neva Pilgrim, Syracuse Symphony Orchestra.

NAMES: Prokofiev, Racine, Gene Rochberg, Strauss.

Ranallo, Ronald J. "In Rehearsal," *The Syracuse Herald-Journal* (08 January 1976) 35.

TYPE: upcoming première.

PERFORMERS: David Loebel, Neva Pilgrim, Syracuse Symphony Orchestra.

Ranallo, Ronald J. "*Phaedra* called 'Forceful Work'," *The Syracuse Her-ald-Journal* (10 January 1976) 11.

TYPE: review.

PERFORMERS: David Loebel, Neva Pilgrim, Syracuse Symphony Orchestra.

NAMES: Racine, Gene Rochberg.

Ranallo, Ronald J. "Syracuse Symphony: Rochberg Première: *Phae-dra*," *High Fidelty/Musical America* XXVI/4 (April 1976) MA-36.

TYPE: review.

PERFORMERS: David Loebel, Neva Pilgrim, Syracuse Symphony Orchestra.

NAMES: Racine, Gene Rochberg.

Scanlan, Roger. "Spotlight on Contemporary American Composers," *The NATS [National Association of Teachers of Singing] Bulletin* XXXIII/1 (October 1976) 48-49, 53-54.

TYPE: article.

OTHER WORKS DISCUSSED: *Blake Songs, David, The Psalmist, Eleven Songs, Four Songs of Solomon, Fantasies, Music for "The Alchemist", Phaedra, Sacred Song of Reconciliation, Songs in Praise of Krishna, String Quartet No. 2, Symphony No. 3, Tableaux, Two Songs from "Tableaux".*

OTHER WORKS MENTIONED: many.

Svejda, Jim. "What's Happened . . . : Syracuse Symphony Orchestra, David Loebel, conducting," *Syracuse Guide* VII (March 1976) 8.

TYPE: review.

PERFORMERS: David Loebel, Neva Pilgrim, Syracuse Symphony Orchestra.

NAMES: Janacek, Lowell, Mahler, Stravinsky.

Walsh, Michael. "A Major New Work," *The Rochester Democrat and Chronicle [Rochester, NY]* (18 January 1976) 1-G, 4-G.

TYPE: review.

PERFORMERS: David Loebel, Neva Pilgrim, Syracuse Symphony Orchestra.

NAMES: Lowell, Racine, Gene Rochberg.

OTHER WORKS MENTIONED: *Concerto for Violin and Orchestra, String Quartet No. 3.*

Webster, Daniel. "George Rochberg: American Music's Bellwether," *The Philadelphia Inquirer* (25 July 1982) 1-K, 13-K.

TYPE: article, interview.

NAMES: Gene Rochberg.

OTHER WORKS DISCUSSED: *The Confidence Man, Symphony No. 2.*

Prelude on "Happy Birthday" for Almost Two Pianos

Harvey, John H. "Toy Piano Gets into the Act at Rug Concert," *The St. Paul Pioneer Press Dispatch* (18 June 1975) 15.

TYPE: review.

PERFORMERS: Leonard Slatkin, Vladimir Levitski.

NAMES: Chopin.

Hinson, Maurice. *Guide to the Pianist's Repertoire: An Annotated Guide, Supplement.* (Bloomington, IN: Indiana University Press, 1979) 275.

TYPE: score review.

OTHER WORKS DISCUSSED: *Arioso, Bartokiana, Carnival Music, Nach Bach, Partita Variations, Sonata-Fantasia, Twelve Bagatelles.*

Hinson, Maurice. *Guide to the Pianist's Repertoire: An Annotated Guide, Second, Revised, and Enlarged Edition.* (Bloomington, IN: Indiana University Press, 1987) 598-599.

TYPE: score review.

OTHER WORKS DISCUSSED: *Arioso, Bartokiana, Carnival Music, Nach Bach, Partita Variations, Sonata-Fantasia, Twelve Bagatelles, Two Preludes and Fughettas from The Book of Contrapuntal Pieces.*

Horn, Daniel Paul. "*Carnival Music*: An Introduction to the Piano Music of George Rochberg," *Clavier* XXVII/9 (November 1988) 17-22.

TYPE: article.

OTHER WORKS DISCUSSED: *Arioso, Bartokiana, Book of Contrapuntal Pieces for Keyboard Instruments, Carnival Music, Four Short Sonatas, Nach Bach, Partita Variations, Sonata-Fantasia, Twelve Bagatelles.*

OTHER WORKS MENTIONED: *Sonata No. 1 for Piano Solo, Sonata No. 2 for Piano Solo.*

Salisbury, Wilma. "Half a Piano Recital Lifts Lid on Part Two of Oberlin Festival," *The Plain Dealer [Cleveland, OH]* (20 March 1970) 7C.

TYPE: review.

OTHER WORKS DISCUSSED: *Nach Bach, Tableaux.*

Stewart, Paul. "The Piano Music of George Rochberg and the New Romanticism," *American Music Teacher* XXXVIII/3 (January 1989) 24-27, 62.

TYPE: article.

NAMES: Bach.

OTHER WORKS DISCUSSED: *Arioso, Bartokiana, Book of Contrapuntal Pieces for Keyboard Instruments, Carnival Music, Four Short Sonatas, Nach Bach, Partita Variations, Sonata-Fantasia, Twelve Bagatelles, Two Preludes and Fughettas.*

Quartet for Piano, Violin, Viola and Cello

Floyd, Jerry. "Rochberg *Quartet* Premières," *The Washington Times* [Washington, D.C.] (20 June 1985) 2B.

TYPE: review.

PERFORMERS: Alexis Galpherine, Miles Hoffman, Christopher Riley, Peter Wiley.

NAMES: Shostakovich, Stravinsky.

Tuck, Lon. "The Stuff of Virtuosity," *The Washington Post* [Washington, D.C.] (19 June 1985) B8.

TYPE: review.

PERFORMERS: Alexis Galpherine, Miles Hoffman, Christopher Riley, Peter Wiley.

Quintet for Piano and String Quartet

n.a. "American Music: George Rochberg," *The Newsreal* [Tucson, AZ] (10 July–13 August 1981) 12-18.

TYPE: record review.

PERFORMERS: Concord String Quartet, Alan Marks.

OTHER WORKS DISCUSSED: *Slow Fires of Autumn.*

Blechner, Mark. "New York: Concord String Quartet: Three Premières," *High Fidelity/Musical America* XXVI/7 (July 1976) MA-30, MA-31.

TYPE: review.

PERFORMERS: Concord String Quartet, Jerome Lowenthal.

NAMES: Beethoven, Brahms, Mendelssohn, Schumann.

Canby, Edward Tatnall. "Classical Reviews: Musical Collage," *Audio* (September 1982) 24.

TYPE: record review.

PERFORMERS: Concord String Quartet, Alan Marks.

NAMES: Bartók, Beethoven, Brahms, Schumann, Stravinsky.

n.a. "Chamber Music Fest to Feature Rochberg," *The Albuquerque Journal* (01 April 1979) D-13.

TYPE: upcoming performances.

PERFORMERS: Norman Fischer, George Rochberg.

OTHER WORKS DISCUSSED: *Duo Concertante, Ricordanza, String Quartet No. 4, String Quartet No. 5, String Quartet No. 6.*

n.a. "Composer Rochberg Featured in Santa Fe Chamber Music," *The Los Alamos Monitor [Los Alamos, NM]* (18 April 1979).

TYPE: upcoming performances.

PERFORMERS: Norman Fischer, George Rochberg.

OTHER WORKS DISCUSSED: *Duo Concertante, Ricordanza, String Quartet No. 4, String Quartet No. 5, String Quartet No. 6.*

Danuser, Hermann. "Zur Kritik der musikalischen Postmoderne," *Neue Zeitschrift fur Musik* CXLIX/12 (December 1988) 4-9.

TYPE: article, analysis.

OTHER WORKS DISCUSSED: *Contra Mortem et Tempus, Music for the Magic Theater, String Quartet No. 2, String Quartet No. 3, Trio [No. 1] for Violin, Cello, and Piano.*

BOOKS DISCUSSED: *The Aesthetics of Survival.*

Dunning, William. "Reviewer Lauds Sound, Performers," *The Los Alamos Monitor [Los Alamos, NM]* (06 July 1982).

TYPE: record review.

PERFORMERS: Concord String Quartet, Alan Marks.

NAMES: Ives, Varèse.

Dunning, William. "Rochberg Honors Past," *The Los Alamos Monitor [Los Alamos, NM]* (02 August 1979).

TYPE: review, interview.

PERFORMERS: Concord String Quartet, Alan Marks.

NAMES: Brahms, Dvorak, Martinu.

OTHER WORKS DISCUSSED: *Duo Concertante, Ricordanza, String Quartet No. 4, String Quartet No. 5, String Quartet No. 6.*

Dunning, William. "Santa Fe Chamber Music Festival Scheduled," *The Los Alamos Monitor [Los Alamos, NM]* (06 April 1979).

TYPE: upcoming performances.

PERFORMERS: Concord String Quartet, Alan Marks.

OTHER WORKS DISCUSSED: *Duo Concertante, Ricordanza, String Quartet No. 4, String Quartet No. 5, String Quartet No. 6.*

Dunning, William. "Satisfied Exhilaration," *The Santa Fe Reporter* (02 August 1979).

TYPE: review, interivew.

PERFORMERS: Concord String Quartet, Alan Marks.

NAMES: Brahms, Dvorak, Martinu.

OTHER WORKS DISCUSSED: *The Confidence Man, Ricordanza, String Quartet No. 4, String Quartet No. 5, String Quartet No. 6.*

OTHER WORKS MENTIONED: *String Quartet No. 1, String Quartet No. 2, String Quartet No. 3.*

Freed, Richard. "Rochberg *Quintet for Piano and Strings*," *Stereo Review* XLVI/11 (November 1981) 92, 94.

TYPE: record review.

PERFORMERS: Concord String Quartet, Alan Marks.

NAMES: Mahler.

OTHER WORKS MENTIONED: *String Quartet No. 3, String Quartet No. 4, String Quartet No. 5, String Quartet No. 6.*

Freedman, Guy. "Metamorphosis of a 20th Century Composer," *Music Journal* XXXIV/3 (March 1976) 12, 13, 38.

TYPE: interview.

OTHER WORKS DISCUSSED: *Symphony No. 3.*

Gagne, Cole and Tracy Caras. *Soundpieces: Interviews with American Composers.* (Metuchen, NJ: Scarecrow Press, Inc., 1982).

TYPE: interview.

OTHER WORKS DISCUSSED: *Apocalyptica [I], Black Sounds, Concerto for Violin and Orchestra, The Confidence Man, Contra Mortem et Tempus, Electrikaleidoscope, Music for the Magic Theater, Octet, Ricordanza, Sonata No. 2 for Piano Solo, String Quartet No. 3, String Quartet No. 4, String Quartet No. 5, String Quartet No. 6, Twelve Bagatelles.*

OTHER WORKS MENTIONED: many.

Hahn, Kathy. "Journal Reviews," *Music Journal* XXIV/5 (May 1976) 31, 41-42.

TYPE: review.

PERFORMERS: Concord String Quartet, Jerome Lowenthal.

Haskell, Harry. "Quartet Explores Composer's Depths: Classical Records," *The Kansas City Star* (27 September 1981) 11G.

TYPE: record review.

PERFORMERS: Concord String Quartet, Alan Marks.

NAMES: Brahms.

Henahan, Michael. "Recordings: *Quintet for Piano and String Quartet*," *Newsweek* XCVIII/24 (14 December 1981) 119.

TYPE: record review.

PERFORMERS: Concord String Quartet, Alan Marks.

NAMES: Beethoven.

Hillerman, Anne. "Performances Set," *The New Mexican [Santa Fe, NM]* (18 July 1979).

TYPE: upcoming performances.

PERFORMERS: Concord String Quartet, Alan Marks.

OTHER WORKS DISCUSSED: *String Quartet No. 4, String Quartet No. 5, String Quartet No. 6.*

Hoffman, W. L. "Arts and Entertainment: US [United States] Composer on Canberra Stint," *The Canberra Times [Australia]* (20 October 1986).

TYPE: upcoming performances.

OTHER WORKS DISCUSSED: *Blake Songs, Octet, Songs in Praise of Krishna, Symphony No. 4, To the Dark Wood.*

OTHER WORKS MENTIONED: *Concerto for Violin and Orchestra, Symphony No. 5.*

Hoffman, W. L. "Music: Rochberg: Positive First Half," *The Canberra Times [Australia]* (22 October 1986) 29.

TYPE: review.

NAMES: Britten, Brahms, Mahler, Shostakovich.

OTHER WORKS DISCUSSED: *Blake Songs, Octet, To the Dark Wood.*

Lange, Art. "Rochberg: *Quintet*," *American Record Guide* XLV/3 (December 1981) 24-25.

TYPE: record review.

PERFORMERS: Concord String Quartet, Alan Marks.

NAMES: Bartók, Beethoven, Mendelssohn.

OTHER WORKS DISCUSSED: *Concerto for Violin and Orchestra, Music for the Magic Theater,String Quartet No. 2, String Quartet No. 3, String Quartet No. 4, String Quartet No. 5, String Quartet No. 6.*

Levin, Monroe. "Notes on Music," *Jewish Exponent* (26 March 1976).

TYPE: review.

PERFORMERS: Concord String Quartet, Jerome Lowenthal.

NAMES: Bartók, Mahler.

OTHER WORKS MENTIONED: *Concerto for Violin and Orchestra.*

Mootz, William. "Rochberg's Works Offer Constant Allures," *The Courier Journal [Louisville, KY]* (16 April 1980) C4.

TYPE: review.

PERFORMERS: Louisville String Quartet, Constance Moore.

NAMES: Beethoven, Mahler.

OTHER WORKS DISCUSSED: *Blake Songs, Contra Mortem et Tempus, Ricordanza.*

n.a. "Music and Dance: Ormandy Back from Europe; Rochberg Concert at Curtis," *The Evening Bulletin [Philadelphia]* (04 February 1977) 29, 31.

TYPE: upcoming performance.

PERFORMERS: Concord String Quartet, Vladimir Sokoloff.

OTHER WORKS DISCUSSED: *Dialogues, Partita Variations.*

Pontzious, Richard. "Spotlighting Unfamiliar Works," *The San Francisco Examiner* (06 October 1981) E7.

TYPE: record review.

PERFORMERS: Concord String Quartet, Alan Marks.

n.a. "Rochberg: Fundamentally Affirmative," *The Silver City Daily Press [Silver City, NM]* (05 April 1979).

TYPE: upcoming performances.

PERFORMERS: Concord String Quartet, Alan Marks.

OTHER WORKS DISCUSSED: *Duo Concertante, Ricordanza, String Quartet No. 4, String Quartet No. 5, String Quartet No. 6.*

Rockwell, John. "Music: Concord Strings: Quartet Performs Pieces by Johnston, Foss, and Rochberg at Tully Hall," *The New York Times* (17 March 1976).

TYPE: review.

PERFORMERS: Concord String Quartet, Jerome Lowenthal.

NAMES: Brahms.

Saal, Hubert. "Evangelistic Strings," *Newsweek* LXXXVII/13 (29 March 1976) 97-98.

TYPE: article, review.

PERFORMERS: Concord String Quartet, Jerome Lowenthal.

OTHER WORKS DISCUSSED: *String Quartet No. 3.*

Saal, Hubert. "Recordings: A Musical Offering: Classical: *Quintet for Piano and String Quartet,*" *Newsweek* XCVIII/24 (14 December 1981) 119.

TYPE: record review.

PERFORMERS: Concord String Quartet, Alan Marks.

NAMES: Beethoven.

Siegel, Sol Louis. "Rochberg: Classic Opinions," *Electricity* LXXVIII (06–12 August 1981) 5.

TYPE: record review, interview.

PERFORMERS: Concord String Quartet, Alan Marks.

OTHER WORKS DISCUSSED: *Concerto for Violin and Orchestra, String Quartet No. 3.*

n.a. "Spotlight," *Music Journal* XXXIV/2 (February 1976) 39.

TYPE: upcoming première.

PERFORMERS: Concord String Quartet, Jerome Lowenthal.

Toms, John. "Concord Quartet Plays Faultlessly," *The Tulsa Tribune* (28 April 1982) 9B.

TYPE: record review.

PERFORMERS: Concord String Quartet, Alan Marks.

OTHER WORKS DISCUSSED: *String Quartet No. 4, String Quartet No. 5, String Quartet No. 5.*

Trotter, Herman. "Records: Classical: Rochberg Strikes a Happy Modern Medium," *The Buffalo News* (09 October 1981) 36.

TYPE: record review.

PERFORMERS: Concord String Quartet, Alan Marks.

NAMES: Beethoven, Liszt, Saint-Saens.

OTHER WORKS DISCUSSED: *Quintet for Piano and String Quartet, String Quartet No. 3, String Quartet No. 4, Trio [No. 1] for Violin, Cello, and Piano.*

Ward, Charles. "Rochberg: *Piano Quintet,*" *The Houston Chronicle* (06 September 1981).

TYPE: record review.

PERFORMERS: Concord String Quartet, Alan Marks.

Webster, Daniel. "In Honor of Rochberg, Three Nights Devoted to His Works," *The Philadelphia Inquirer* (17 January 1979).

TYPE: review, upcoming performances.

PERFORMERS: Alan Marks, Concord String Quartet.

OTHER WORKS DISCUSSED: *Duo Concertante, Ricordanza.*

OTHER WORKS MENTIONED: *String Quartet No. 1, String Quartet No. 2, String Quartet No. 3, String Quartet No. 4, String Quartet No. 5, String Quartet No. 6.*

Quintet for String Quintet

Baxter, Robert. "Music: World Première to Mark Group's Birthday," *The Courier-Post [Philadelphia]* (03 January 1982).

TYPE: upcoming première, interview with the Concord String Quartet.

PERFORMERS: Concord String Quartet, Bonnie Thron.

OTHER WORKS DISCUSSED: *The Confidence Man.*

n.a. "Concord String Night," *The New York Times* (05 February 1982) III, 15.

TYPE: upcoming performance.

PERFORMERS: Concord String Quartet, Anthony Elliott.

Eckert, Thor Jr. "Two Contrasting Festivals and What They Say About Standards Today," *The Christian Science Monitor* (01 September 1982) 18.

TYPE: review.

PERFORMERS: Concord String Quartet, Nathaniel Rosen.

OTHER WORKS DISCUSSED: *The Confidence Man.*

Feder, Susan. "Santa Fe," *Musical Times [Great Britain]* CXXIII/1676 (October 1982) 713.

TYPE: review.

PERFORMERS: Concord String Quartet, Nathaniel Rosen.

OTHER WORKS DISCUSSED: *The Confidence Man.*

Goldsmith, Diane. "Santa Fe: Rochberg's First Opera; a Tenth Anniversary," *Ovation* III/10 (November 1982) 36-37.

TYPE: review.

PERFORMERS: Concord String Quartet, Nathaniel Rosen.

NAMES: Beethoven, Mahler.

OTHER WORKS DISCUSSED: *The Confidence Man.*

Holland, Bernard. "Strings: Rochberg Première," *The New York Times* (09 February 1982) III, 8.

TYPE: review.

PERFORMERS: Concord String Quartet, Anthony Elliott.

NAMES: Beethoven.

Holland, Bernard. "When Politics Intrude into Programming," *The New York Times* (04 April 1982) II, 19.

TYPE: article, interview with the Concord String Quartet.

Kimball, Robert. "Music Beat: Rochberg & Elliott," *The New York Post* (11 February 1982) 44.

TYPE: review.

PERFORMERS: Concord String Quartet, Anthony Elliott.

NAMES: Bartók, Beethoven, Berg, Mahler, Shostakovich.

Kupferberg, Herbert. "The Concord Quartet Embarks upon Its Second Decade," *Ovation* III/11 (December 1982) 12, 13, 36.

TYPE: article, interview with the Concord String Quartet.

PERFORMERS: Concord String Quartet.

OTHER WORKS DISCUSSED: *String Quartet No. 4, String Quartet No. 5, String Quartet No. 6.*

Larson, Tom. "Musical Festival Gives Rare Musical Gift," *The New Mexican [Santa Fe, NM]* (29 July 1982) A-4.

TYPE: review.

PERFORMERS: Concord String Quartet, Nathaniel Rosen.

NAMES: Bartók, Beethoven, Brahms.

OTHER WORKS DISCUSSED: *The Confidence Man.*

OTHER WORKS MENTIONED: *String Quartet No. 3, String Quartet No. 4, String Quartet No. 5, String Quartet No. 6, String Quartet No. 7.*

Levin, Monroe. "Notes on Music," *Jewish Exponent* (15 January 1982).

TYPE: review.

PERFORMERS: Concord String Quartet, Bonnie Thron.

OTHER WORKS DISCUSSED: *The Confidence Man.*

Maldonado, Charles. "Two Nights of Rain: Music Festival Delights Audiences," *The Albuquerque Journal* (30 July 1982).

TYPE: review.

PERFORMERS: Concord String Quartet, Nathaniel Rosen.

Porter, Andrew. "Musical Events: A Frail Bark," *The New Yorker* (16 August 1982) 66-69.

TYPE: review.

PERFORMERS: Concord String Quartet, Nathaniel Rosen.

OTHER WORKS DISCUSSED: *The Confidence Man, String Quartet No. 3.*

Rockwell, John. "Music: The Concord String Quartet," *The New York Times* (24 February 1985) I, 46.

TYPE: review.

PERFORMERS: Concord String Quartet, Sharon Robinson.

Tatton, Thomas. "*Quintet* by George Rochberg," *American String Teacher* XXXV/1 (Winter 1985) 85.

TYPE: score review.

PERFORMERS: Concord String Quartet.

NAMES: Schubert.

Webster, Daniel. "Concord Quartet: Rochberg *Quintet* Première," *High Fidelity/Musical America* XXXII/5 (May 1982) MA-34, MA-35, MA-36.

TYPE: review.

PERFORMERS: Concord String Quartet, Bonnie Thron.

OTHER WORKS MENTIONED: *The Confidence Man.*

Webster, Daniel. "A Quartet Will Ring Out the Old by Stringing in the New," *The Philadephia Inquirer* (03 January 1982).

TYPE: upcoming première, interview with the Concord String Quartet.

PERFORMERS: Concord String Quartet, Anthony Elliott, Nathaniel Rosen, Bonnie Thron.

NAMES: Beethoven, Schubert.

OTHER WORKS DISCUSSED: *The Confidence Man, String Quartet No. 3, String Quartet No. 4, String Quartet No. 5, String Quartet No. 6.*

Webster, Daniel. "Rochberg *Quintet*: A Pictorial Prelude to Opera," *The Philadelphia Inquirer* (07 January 1982) 12-A.

TYPE: review.

PERFORMERS: Concord String Quartet, Bonnie Thron.

NAMES: Britten.

OTHER WORKS DISCUSSED: *The Confidence Man.*

Rhapsody and Prayer for Violin and Piano

Patrick, Corbin. "Richest Violin Competition Unveiled," *The Indianapolis Star* (17 January 1988) E1, E8.

TYPE: upcoming commission and première.

NAMES: Josef Gingold.

Ricordanza (Soliloquy) for Cello and Piano

Archibald, Bruce. "Rochberg: *Chamber Symphony, Duo Concertante, Music for the Magic Theater, Ricordanza, String Quartet No. 1*," *Musical Quarterly* LXXII/4 (October 1976) 613-615.

TYPE: record review.

PERFORMERS: Norman Fischer, George Rochberg.

NAMES: Beethoven, Brahms, Mahler.

OTHER WORKS DISCUSSED: *Chamber Symphony, Contra Mortem et Tempus, Duo Concertante, Music for the Magic Theater, String Quartet No. 1.*

Bronston, Levering. "Rochberg: *Chamber Symphony, Duo Concertante, Music for the Magic Theater, Ricordanza, String Quartet No. 1*," *The New Records* XLIII/11 (January 1976) 7-8.

TYPE: record review.

PERFORMERS: Norman Fischer, George Rochberg.

NAMES: Beethoven, Mahler.

OTHER WORKS DISCUSSED: *Chamber Symphony, Duo Concertante, Music for the Magic Theater, String Quartet No. 1.*

n.a. "Chamber Music Fest to Feature Rochberg," *The Albuquerque Journal* (01 April 1979) D-13.

TYPE: upcoming performances.

PERFORMERS: Norman Fischer, George Rochberg.

OTHER WORKS DISCUSSED: *Duo Concertante, Quintet for Piano and String Quartet, String Quartet No. 4, String Quartet No. 5, String Quartet No. 6.*

n.a. "Composer Rochberg Featured in Santa Fe Chamber Music," *The Los Alamos Monitor [Los Alamos, NM]* (18 April 1979).

TYPE: upcoming performances.

PERFORMERS: Norman Fischer, George Rochberg.

NAMES: Beethoven.

OTHER WORKS DISCUSSED: *Duo Concertante, Quintet for Piano and String Quartet, String Quartet No. 4, String Quartet No. 5, String Quartet No. 6.*

Covell, Roger. "Lack of Scope Sees a Change in Style," *The Sydney Morning Herald [Australia]* (18 October 1986).

TYPE: review, interview.

OTHER WORKS DISCUSSED: *Concerto for Violin and Orchestra, String Quartet No. 3, Symphony No. 5, To the Dark Wood.*

Croan, Robert. "Classical Record Reviews: Copland Celebration: Music of George Rochberg," *The Pittsburgh Post-Gazette* (07 May 1976) 34.

TYPE: record review.

PERFORMERS: Norman Fischer, George Rochberg.

OTHER WORKS DISCUSSED: *Concerto for Violin and Orchestra, Duo Concertante, Ricordanza.*

Davis, Peter G. "Music: Rudikov, Cellist," *The New York Times* (10 May 1976).

TYPE: review.

PERFORMERS: Michael Rudikov, Evelyne Crochet.

Davis, Peter G. "Music: Recent Rochberg," *The New York Times* (26 April 1974) 26.

TYPE: review.

PERFORMERS: Norman Fischer, George Rochberg.

NAMES: Brahms, Mahler.

OTHER WORKS DISCUSSED: *String Quartet No. 3.*

Donner, Jay M. "Electronic Music: Computer Music from Colgate," *The New Records* (February 1981) 15.

TYPE: record review.

NAMES: Robert Boyer.

Dunning, William. "Records Are Foretaste of Santa Fe Festival," *The Los Alamos Monitor [Los Alamos, NM]* (27 April 1979).

TYPE: record reviews.

PERFORMERS: Norman Fischer, George Rochberg.

NAMES: Beethoven.

OTHER WORKS DISCUSSED: *Duo Concertante, Song in Praise of Krishna, String Quartet No. 1, String Quartet No. 4, String Quartet No. 5, String Quartet No. 6.*

Dunning, William. "Rochberg Honors Past," *The Los Alamos Monitor [Los Alamos, NM]* (02 August 1979).

TYPE: review, interview.

PERFORMERS: Norman Fischer, George Rochberg.

OTHER WORKS DISCUSSED: *Duo Concertante, Quintet for Piano and String Quartet, String Quartet No. 4, String Quartet No. 5, String Quartet No. 6.*

Dunning, William. "Rochberg Records: Summer Glimpse," *The Santa Fe Reporter* (27 April 1979).

TYPE: record reviews.

PERFORMERS: Norman Fischer, George Rochberg.

NAMES: Beethoven.

OTHER WORKS DISCUSSED: *Duo Concertante, Song in Praise of Krishna, String Quartet No. 1, String Quartet No. 4, String Quartet No. 5, String Quartet No. 6.*

Dunning, William. "Santa Fe Chamber Music Festival Scheduled," *The Los Alamos Monitor [Los Alamos, NM]* (06 April 1979).

TYPE: upcoming performances.

PERFORMERS: Norman Fischer, George Rochberg.

OTHER WORKS DISCUSSED:

Duo Concertante, Quintet for Piano and String Quartet, String Quartet No. 4, String Quartet No. 5, String Quartet No. 6.

Dunning, William. "Satisfied Exhilaration," *The Santa Fe Reporter* (02 August 1979).

TYPE: review, interview.

PERFORMERS: Norman Fischer, George Rochberg.

OTHER WORKS DISCUSSED: *The Confidence Man, Duo Concertante, String Quartet No. 4, String Quartet No. 5, String Quartet No. 6.*

Fullman, Mary Jane. "Bargers of Carversville Carry on Cultural Exchange," *The Daily Intelligencer [Doylestown, PA]* (14 November 1973).

TYPE: review.

PERFORMERS: Norman Fischer, Jean E. Fischer.

Gagne, Cole and Tracy Caras. *Soundpieces: Interviews with American Composers.* (Metuchen, NJ: Scarecrow Press, Inc., 1982).

TYPE: interview.

PERFORMERS: Michael Rudiakov.

OTHER WORKS DISCUSSED: *Apocalyptica [I], Black Sounds, Concerto for Violin and Orchestra, The Confidence Man, Contra Mortem et Tempus, Electrikaleidoscope, Music for the Magic Theater, Octet, Quintet for Piano and String Quartet, Sonata No. 2 for Piano Solo, String Quartet No. 3, String Quartet No. 4, String Quartet No. 5, String Quartet No. 6, Twelve Bagatelles.*

OTHER WORKS MENTIONED: many.

Hardy, Owen. "'Foremost Is Life,' A Musical Rebel Feels," *The Courier-Journal [Louisville, KY]* (16 April 1980) C1.

TYPE: article, interview.

OTHER WORKS DISCUSSED: *Music for the Magic Theater.*

Henahan, Donal J. "Music: Recent Rochberg," *The New York Times* (26 April 1974) 26.

TYPE: review.

PERFORMERS: Norman Fischer, George Rochberg.

OTHER WORKS DISCUSSED: *String Quartet No. 3.*

Hillerman, Anne. "Santa Fe Festival Host Rochberg," *The New Mexican [Santa Fe, NM]* (18 July 1979).

TYPE: review, interview.

PERFORMERS: Norman Fischer, George Rochberg.

OTHER WORKS DISCUSSED: *Duo Concertante.*

Hinson, Maurice. *The Piano in Chamber Ensemble: An Annotated Guide.* (Bloomington, IN: Indiana University Press, 1978) 156.

TYPE: review.

NAMES: Beethoven, Wagner.

OTHER WORKS DISCUSSED: *Contra Mortem et Tempus, Dialogues, Trio [No. 1] for Violin, Cello, and Piano.*

Jenkins, Speight. "Record World: Classical: A Home for the Composer," *Record World* XXXI/1502 (03 April 1976) 48-49.

TYPE: record review.

PERFORMERS: Norman Fischer, George Rochberg.

OTHER WORKS DISCUSSED: *String Quartet No. 1.*

Jenkins, Speight. "Concord String Quartet Plays Music by Rochberg," *The New York Post* (26 April 1974) 56.

TYPE: review.

PERFORMERS: Norman Fischer, George Rochberg.

OTHER WORKS DISCUSSED: *String Quartet No. 3.*

Mootz, William. "Rochberg's Works Offer Constant Allures," *The Courier Journal [Louisville, KY]* (16 April 1980) C4.

TYPE: review.

PERFORMERS: Susannah Onwood, Constance Moore.

OTHER WORKS DISCUSSED: *Blake Songs, Contra Mortem et Tempus, Quintet for Piano and String Quartet.*

Oliva, Mark. "Classical Record Reviews," *The Nevada State Journal* (18 January 1976) 11.

TYPE: record review.

PERFORMERS: Norman Fischer, George Rochberg.

OTHER WORKS DISCUSSED: *Chamber Symphony, Duo Concertante, Music for the Magic Theater, String Quartet No. 1.*

Porter, Andrew. "Musical Events: Questions," *The New Yorker* (12 February 1979) 109-115.

TYPE: article, review.

NAMES: Beethoven.

OTHER WORKS DISCUSSED: *Concerto for Violin and Orchestra, Duo Concertante, Music for the Magic Theater, String Quartet No. 1, String Quartet No. 2, String Quartet No. 3, String Quartet No. 4, String Quartet No. 5, String Quartet No. 6.*

Porter, Andrew. "Rochberg: Chamber Works," *High Fidelity/Musical America* XVI/5 (May 1976) 90-92.

TYPE: record review.

PERFORMERS: Norman Fischer, George Rochberg.

NAMES: Beethoven, Wagner, Tchaikovsky.

OTHER WORKS DISCUSSED: *Chamber Symphony, Concerto for Violin and Orchestra, Duo Concertante, Music for the Magic Theater, String Quartet No. 1.*

Potter, Keith. "Rochberg: *String Quartet No. 1, Duo Concertante, Ricordanza,*" *Records and Recordings [Great Britain]* (March 1977) 72-73.

TYPE: record review.

PERFORMERS: Norman Fischer, George Rochberg.

NAMES: Beethoven, Cardew, Crumb, Davies, Lentz, Rzewski, West.

OTHER WORKS DISCUSSED: *Blake Songs, Contra Mortem et Tempus, Duo Concertante, String Quartet No. 1, String Quartet No. 2, String Quartet No. 3.*

Powell, Verna. "Reviews: Instruments: *Ricordanza,*" *American Music Teacher* XIV/5 (April–May 1975) 53-54.

TYPE: score review.

n.a. "Rochberg: Fundamentally Affirmative," *The Silver City Daily Press [Silver City, NM]* (05 April 1979).

TYPE: upcoming performances.

PERFORMERS: Norman Fischer, Alan Marks.

OTHER WORKS DISCUSSED: *Duo Concertante, Quartet for Piano and String Quartet, String Quartet No. 4, String Quartet No. 5, String Quartet No. 6.*

Salzman, Eric. "Rochberg: *Chamber Symphony, Duo Concertante, Music for the Magic Theater, Ricordanza, String Quartet No. 1,*" *Stereo Review* XXXVII/1 (July 1976) 111.

TYPE: record review.

PERFORMERS: Norman Fischer, George Rochberg.

NAMES: Beethoven.

OTHER WORKS DISCUSSED: *Chamber Symphony, Duo Concertante, Music for the Magic Theater, String Quartet No. 1.*

Sargeant, Winthrop. "Concert Records: Romantic and Gothic," *The New Yorker* (26 January 1976) 91-93.

TYPE: review.

PERFORMERS: Norman Fischer, George Rochberg.

NAMES: Boulanger.

OTHER WORKS DISCUSSED: *Duo Concertante, String Quartet No. 1.*

Smith, G. Jean. "String Clinic: Try Something New: Rochberg, George," *The Instrumentalist* XXX/10 (May 1976) 62.

TYPE: score review.

Steinberg, Michael. "Leaning on Unearned Income," *The Boston Globe* (27 March 1975) 24.

TYPE: review.

PERFORMERS: Norman Fischer, Jean E. Fischer.

NAMES: Beech, Beethoven, Brahms, Britten, Eskins, Foote, Mahler, MacDowell, Schönberg.

OTHER WORKS DISCUSSED: *Concerto for Violin and Orchestra, String Quartet No. 3.*

Veilleux, C. Thomas. "Chamber Music Roundup Reveals Three Fine Records," *The Sunday Post [Bridgeport, CT]* (10 October 1976) E14.

TYPE: record review.

PERFORMERS: Norman Fischer, George Rochberg.

OTHER WORKS DISCUSSED: *Chamber Symphony, Duo Concertante, Music for the Magic Theater, String Quartet No. 1.*

Webster, Daniel. "In Honor of Rochberg, Three Nights Devoted to His Works," *The Philadelphia Inquirer* (17 January 1979).

TYPE: review, upcoming performances.

PERFORMERS: George Rochberg, Norman Fischer.

OTHER WORKS DISCUSSED: *Duo Concertante, Quintet for Piano and String Quartet.*

OTHER WORKS MENTIONED: *String Quartet No. 1, String Quartet No. 2, String Quartet No. 3, String Quartet No. 4, String Quartet No. 5, String Quartet No. 6.*

Webster, Daniel. "Stylistic Odyssey of George Rochberg," *The Philadelphia Inquirer* (15 February 1976) 7H.

TYPE: record review.

PERFORMERS: George Rochberg, Norman Fischer.

NAMES: Beethoven.

OTHER WORKS DISCUSSED: *Chamber Symphony, Duo Concertante, Music for the Magic Theater, String Quartet No. 1.*

Sacred Song of Reconciliation (Mizmur l'Piyus) for Bass-Baritone and Small Orchestra

Boehm, Yohanan. "Music in Israel: Composers, Critics, Audience," *League of Composers in Israel: Israel Music Week [Jerusalem]* (30 November–31 December 1969) 8-14.

TYPE: announcement of commission.

Boehm, Yohanan. "Tonalities and Textures," *The Jerusalem Post Magazine* (05 November 1982).

TYPE: article, review, record review, interview.

PERFORMERS: Testimonium [Jerusalem].

OTHER WORKS DISCUSSED: *Concerto for Violin and Orchestra, The Confidence Man.*

Brookhouser, Frank. "A Dead Son Lives on in Father's Music," *The Evening Bulletin [Philadelphia]* (05 November 1970).

TYPE: article.

PERFORMERS: Testimonium [Jerusalem].

NAMES: Hebrew University.

OTHER WORKS DISCUSSED: *Eleven Songs.*

Harran, Don. "Report from Israel: Testimonium II, 1971," *Current Musicology* XV (1973) 38-43.

TYPE: article, review.

PERFORMERS: Testimonium [Jerusalem].

NAMES: Roman Haubenstock-Ramati, Foss, Recha Frier.

OTHER WORKS MENTIONED: *Night Music.*

Pataki, Lanislaus. "Israeli Musik-Wochen," *Das Orchester* XIX/3 (March 1971) 150.

TYPE: review.

PERFORMERS: Testamonium [Jerusalem].

NAMES: Recha Frier.

Ringer, Alexander L. "Current Chronicle: New York, Jerusalum, and Urbana, Illinois," *Musical Quarterly* LVIII/1 (January 1972) 128-132.

TYPE: review.

PERFORMERS: Testimonium [Jerusalem].

NAMES: Recha Frier.

OTHER WORKS DISCUSSED: *David, the Psalmist, Songs in Praise of Krishna, Symphony No. 3.*

Scanlan, Roger. "Spotlight on Contemporary American Composers," *The NATS [National Association of Teachers of Singing] Bulletin* XXXIII/1 (October 1976) 48-49, 53-54.

TYPE: article.

OTHER WORKS DISCUSSED: *Blake Songs, David, The Psalmist, Eleven Songs, Four Songs of Solomon, Fantasies, Music for "The Alchemist", Phaedra, Songs in Praise of Krishna, String Quartet No. 2, Symphony No. 3, Tableaux, Two Songs from "Tableaux".*

OTHER WORKS MENTIONED: many.

Serenata d'estate for Flute, Harp, Guitar, Violin, Viola, and Cello

Campbell, R. M. "SSO's [Seattle Symphony Orchestra's] New Music Series Offers Quite a Mixture," *The Seattle Post-Intelligencer* (18 September 1986) C9.

TYPE: review.

PERFORMERS: Gerard Schwarz, members of the Seattle Symphony Orchestra.

Ericson, Raymond. "Flutist: Sue Ann Kahn," *The New York Times* (20 March 1980) C14.

TYPE: review.

PERFORMERS: Sue Ann Kahn, Ronald Oakland, Jacob Glick, Chris Finckel, Susan Jolles, David Starobin.

Flanagan, William. "Nonesuch's Spectrum: New American Music," *Stereo Review* XXIII/2 (August 1969) 94-95.

TYPE: review.

Henahan, Donal J. "An Apostate Questions Modernist Pieties with Gusto," *The New York Times* (03 June 1984) II, 21-22.

TYPE: article.

OTHER WORKS DISCUSSED: *String Quartet No. 3.*

BOOKS DISCUSSED: The Aesthetics of Survival.

Horowitz, Joseph. "Music: Brooklyn Philharmonia Plays a Modern American Bill," *The New York Times* (23 February 1980) 11.

TYPE: review.

PERFORMERS: Lucas Foss, members of the Brooklyn Philharmonia.

NAMES: Webern.

McQuilkin, Terry. "Composer's Choice Series Opens at UCLA [University of California at Los Angeles]," *The Los Angeles Times* (15 January 1981) VI, 10.

TYPE: review.

PERFORMERS: William Bolcom, members of the Los Angeles Philharmonic.

Miller, Philip L. "The New 'Spectrum' Series from Nonesuch," *American Record Guide* XXXV/10 (June 1969) 940-941.

TYPE: record review.

PERFORMERS: Arthur Weisberg, Contemporary Chamber Ensemble.

NAMES: Webern.

Morgan, Robert P. "Fresh Music from the University 'Laboratory'," *High Fidelity* XIX/6 (June 1969) 75-76.

TYPE: record review.

PERFORMERS: Arthur Weisberg, Contemporary Chamber Ensemble.

NAMES: Schönberg.

Page, Tim. "Concert: Music Today Plays Work by Stephan," *The New York Times* (30 November 1986) I, 95.

TYPE: review.

PERFORMERS: Gerard Schwarz, Music Today.

Ringer, Alexander L. "The Music of George Rochberg," *Musical Quarterly* LII/4 (October 1966) 409-430.

TYPE: article.

PERFORMERS: Arthur Winograd, "Music in Our Time".

OTHER WORKS DISCUSSED: *Apocalyptica [I], Black Sounds, Blake Songs, La Bocca della Verità, Cantio Sacra, Capriccio for Two Pianos, Chamber Symphony, Cheltenham Concerto, Concert Piece for Two Pianos and Orchestra, Contra Mortem et Tempus, David, the Psalmist, Dialogues, Duo Concertante, Four Songs of Solomon, Music for the Magic Theater, Nach Bach, Night Music, Passions [According to the Twentieth Century], Sonata-Fantasia, String Quartet No. 1, String Quartet No. 2, Symphony No. 1, Symphony No. 2, Three Psalms, Time-Span, Trio for Clarinet, Horn, and Piano, Trio [No. 1] for Violin, Cello, and Piano, Twelve Bagatelles, Zodiac.*

OTHER WORKS MENTIONED: *Arioso, Bartokiana, Five Smooth Stones, Sonata No. 1 for Piano Solo, Sonata No. 2 for Piano Solo, Waltz Serenade.*

BOOKS DISCUSSED: *The Hexachord and Its Relation to the Twelve-Tone Row.*

Valdes, Lesley. "A Birthday Salute to Rochberg," *The Philadelphia Inquirer* (17 April 1988) 1-L, 10-L.

TYPE: upcoming performance, article, interview.

PERFORMERS: Curtis Institute of Music.

OTHER WORKS DISCUSSED: *Duo Concertante, Slow Fires of Autumn, String Quartet No. 3, To the Dark Wood, Trio [No. 2] for Violin, Cello, and Piano.*

OTHER WORKS MENTIONED: *Concerto for Violin and Orchestra, Sonata for Violin and Piano, Symphony No. 5, Symphony No. 6.*

Walsh, Michael. "New Music We Should Know and Love," *The Rochester Democrat and Chronicle [Rochester, NY]* (13 October 1974) 1-H, 4-H.

TYPE: review.

OTHER WORKS DISCUSSED: *Caprice Variations, String Quartet No. 3.*

Slow Fires of Autumn (Ukiyo-e II) for Flute and Harp

n.a. "American Music: George Rochberg," *The Newreal [Tucson, AZ]* (10 July–13 August 1981) 12-18.

TYPE: record review.

PERFORMERS: Carol Wincenc, Nancy Allen.

OTHER WORKS DISCUSSED: *Quintet for Piano and String Quartet.*

Dickinson, Peter. "Rochberg, George," *Music and Letters* LXVI/1 (January 1984) 130.

TYPE: score review.

PERFORMERS: Cage, Cowell.

OTHER WORKS DISCUSSED: *Concerto for Violin and Orchestra, The Confidence Man, Sonata for Viola and Piano, Songs in Praise of Krishna, String Quartet No. 3.*

Ditsky, John. "*Slow Fires of Autumn,*" *Fanfare* IV/3 (January–February 1981) 120.

TYPE: record review.

PERFORMERS: Carol Wincenc, Nancy Allen.

Ericson, Raymond. "Music Notes: A Flutist Takes a Solo Flight," *The New York Times* (22 April 1979) II, 23.

TYPE: upcoming première.

PERFORMERS: Carol Wincenc, Nancy Allen.

Henahan, Donal J. "Concert, Carol Wincenc, Flutist," *The New York Times* (24 April 1979) III, 10.

TYPE: review.

PERFORMERS: Carol Wincenc, Nancy Allen.

Jenkins, Speight. "n.t.," *The New York Post* (24 April 1979) 56.

TYPE: review.

PERFORMERS: Carol Wincenc.

OTHER WORKS DISCUSSED: *Ricordanza, String Quartet No. 3.*

McCurdy, Charles. "Music: Works of Rochberg and Schubel at Art Alliance," *The Philadelphia Inquirer* (20 February 1984) 6-C.

TYPE: review.

PERFORMERS: Patricia Kendell, Jude Mollenauer.

OTHER WORKS DISCUSSED: *Songs of Inanna and Dumuzi, Ukiyo-e.*

Moore, David W. "Rochberg: *Slow Fires of Autumn,*" *American Record Guide* XLIV/4 (April 1981) 24-25.

TYPE: record review.

PERFORMERS: Carol Wincenc, Nancy Allen.

OTHER WORKS DISCUSSED: *Concerto for Violin and Orchestra, Night Music, String Quartet No. 1, String Quartet No. 3, Symphony No. 1, Symphony No. 2.*

Moore, J. S. "Naumburg Performing Award Winners," *The New Records* XLVIII/9 (November 1980) 6.

TYPE: record review.

PERFORMERS: Carol Wincenc, Nancy Allen.

de Rhen, Andrew. "New York: Carol Wincenc, Flute," *High Fidelity/Musical America* XXIX/10 (October 1979) 33-34.

TYPE: review.

PERFORMERS: Carol Wincenc, Nancy Allen.

Rothstein, Joel. "John Harbison, George Rochberg," *Down Beat* XLVIII/7 (July 1981) 47-48.

TYPE: record review.

PERFORMERS: Carol Wincenc, Nancy Allen.

Schwartz, Jerry. "Classical Reviews," *The Atlanta Journal/The Atlanta Constitution* (30 August 1980) Leisure, 32.

TYPE: record review.

PERFORMERS: Carol Wincenc, Nancy Allen.

Shirakawa, Sam H. "Luring Listeners to the Music of the Harp," *The New York Times* (27 September 1981) II, 24.

TYPE: record review.

PERFORMERS: Carol Wincenc, Nancy Allen.

Trotter, Herman. "Records: Classical: The *Three Concord Quartets* Best Exemplify George Rochberg's Return to Tonal Composition," *The Buffalo News* (04 June 1982).

TYPE: review.

OTHER WORKS DISCUSSED: *String Quartet No. 4, String Quartet No. 5, String Quartet No. 6.*

Underwood, T. Jervis. "Flute Review," *Woodwind * Brass & Percussion* XX/7 (December 1981) 28.

TYPE: score review.

NAMES: Carol Wincenc.

Valdes, Lesley. "A Birthday Salute to Rochberg," *The Philadelphia Inquirer* (17 April 1988) 1-L, 10-L.

TYPE: upcoming performance, article, interview.

PERFORMERS: Curtis Institute of Music.

OTHER WORKS DISCUSSED: *Duo Concertante, Serenata d'estate, String Quartet No. 3, To the Dark Wood, Trio [No. 2] for Violin, Cello, and Piano.*

OTHER WORKS MENTIONED: *Concerto for Violin and Orchestra, Sonata for Violin and Piano, Symphony No. 5, Symphony No. 6.*

Webster, Daniel. "On the Changing Rhythms in the Life of a Composer," *The Philadelphia Inquirer* (16 January 1979) D1, D3.

TYPE: article, interview.

OTHER WORKS DISCUSSED: *Concerto for Violin and Orchestra, The Confidence Man, String Quartet No. 4, String Quartet No. 5, String Quartet No. 6.*

Wierzbicki, James. "George Rochberg," *The St. Louis Globe-Democrat* (30 August 1980) 6B.

TYPE: record review.

PERFORMERS: Carol Wincenc, Nancy Allen.

OTHER WORKS DISCUSSED: *Concerto for Violin and Orchestra, Ukiyo-e.*

Sonata No. 2 for Piano Solo

Gagne, Cole and Tracy Caras. *Soundpieces: Interviews with American Composers.* (Metuchen, NJ: Scarecrow Press, Inc., 1982).

TYPE: interview.

NAMES: Dallapiccola.

OTHER WORKS DISCUSSED: *Apocalyptica [I], Black Sounds, Concerto for Violin and Orchestra, Contra Mortem et Tempus, The Confidence Man, Electrikaleidoscope, Music for the Magic Theater, Octet, Quintet for Piano and String Quartet, Ricordanza, String Quartet No. 3, String Quartet No. 4, String Quartet No. 5, String Quartet No. 6, Twelve Bagatelles.*

OTHER WORKS MENTIONED: many.

Sonata for Viola and Piano

Berlinski, Herman. "Musical Notes: Rochberg's Return to Neo-Romanticism," *The Jewish Week [Washington, D.C.]* (17–23 April 1980) 30.

TYPE: review.

PERFORMERS: Yizhak Schotten, Katherine Collier.

NAMES: Brahms, Hindemith, Prokofiev.

OTHER WORKS DISCUSSED: *Concerto for Violin and Orchestra.*

Carpenter, Howard. "Strings: *Sonata for Viola and Piano*," *American Music Teacher* XXXI/5 (April–May 1982) 53.

TYPE: score review.

NAMES: Joseph de Pasquale, William Primrose.

Clements, Andrew. "Wigmore Hall Recitals: Ann Woodward," *The Financial Times [London]* (28 April 1980).

TYPE: review.

PERFORMERS: Ann Woodward, Roger Vignoles.

NAMES: Mahler.

Cunningham, Carl. "Music: Syzygy," *The Houston Post* (29 September 1982) 8B.

TYPE: review.

PERFORMERS: Wayne Crouse, John Schneider.

Dickinson, Peter. "Rochberg, George," *Music and Letters* LXVI/1 (January 1984) 130.

TYPE: score review.

NAMES: Berg, Brahms, Ives, Telemann.

OTHER WORKS DISCUSSED: *Concerto for Violin and Orchestra, The Confidence Man, Slow Fires of Autumn, Songs in Praise of Krishna, String Quartet No. 3.*

Goodfellow, William S. "Seventh International Viola Congress Honors William Primrose: A Major Talent Emerges in Competition for Violists," *High Fidelity/Musical America* XXIX/12 (December 1979) 22-24.

TYPE: review.

PERFORMERS: Joseph de Pasquale, Vladimir Sokoloff.

Goodwin, Noel. "London Debuts," *The Times [London]* (30 April 1980).

TYPE: review.

PERFORMERS: Ann Woodward, Roger Vignoles.

Hume, Paul. "Performing Arts: Schotten-Collier," *The Washington Post [Washington, D.C.]* (14 April 1980) C9.

TYPE: review.

PERFORMERS: Yizhak Schotten, Katherine Collier.

NAMES: William Primrose.

Mullmann, Bernd. "Entdeckungsreise: Werke von vier US-Komponisten in der Musikakademie," *Hessesche/Niedersachsische Allgemeine* (28 October 1982).

TYPE: review.

PERFORMERS: Wayne Crouse, John Schneider.

NAMES: Bartók, Menotti.

Shaw, Fred. "Concert Platform: Viola and the Piano," *The Huddersfield Examiner [Huddersfield, Great Britain]* (15 October 1982).

TYPE: review.

PERFORMERS: Wayne Crouse, John Schneider.

NAMES: William Primrose.

Smith, G. Jean. "Rochberg, George," *American String Teacher* XXXI/2 (Spring 1981) 56.

TYPE: score review.

NAMES: Joseph de Pasquale, William Primrose, Vladimir Sokoloff.

Ward, Charles. "Review: Crouse Program Is Bright with Polished Playing," *The Houston Chronicle* (29 September 1982) II, 14.

TYPE: review.

PERFORMERS: Wayne Crouse, John Schneider.

Sonata for Violin and Piano

McQuilkin, Terry. "Music Review: Maria Bachmann at Ambassador," *The Los Angeles Times* (13 April 1989).

TYPE: review.

PERFORMERS: Maria Bachmann, Jon Klibonoff.

Rockwell, John. "Review/Music: New Violin Sonata in Recital," *The New York Times* (25 May 1989).

TYPE: review.

PERFORMERS: Maria Bachmann, Jon Klibonoff.

NAMES: Brahms.

Salisbury, Wilma. "Entertainment: Violinist, Pianist Perform Superbly," *The Plain Dealer [Cleveland, OH]* (05 June 1989) 5C.

TYPE: review.

PERFORMERS: Maria Bachmann, Jon Klibonoff.

Sonata-Fantasia for Piano Solo

Burge, David. "Contemporary Piano: Repertoire, Part II," *Contemporary Keyboard* (March–April 1976) 44.

TYPE: article.

Crump, Peter N. "Reviews of Music," *Music and Letters* XL/2 (April 1959) 200, 202.

TYPE: score review.

NAMES: Schönberg.

OTHER WORKS DISCUSSED: *Twelve Bagatelles*.

Dixon, Joan DeVee. "George Rochberg's *Nach Bach, A Fantasy for Harpsichord or Piano*," *The Iowa Music Teacher* XLV/2 (Spring - May 1988) 4-9.

TYPE: article, interviews with George Rochberg and Igor Kipnis.

OTHER WORKS DISCUSSED: *Nach Bach, Partita Variations*.

Dixon, Joan DeVee. "George Rochberg's *Nach Bach, A Fantasy for Harpsichord or Piano*," Unpublished (June 1988) 13pp.

TYPE: article, interviews with George Rochberg and Igor Kipnis.

OTHER WORKS DISCUSSED: *Chamber Symphony, Contra Mortem et Tempus, Music for the Magic Theater, Nach Bach, Partita Variations, Symphony No. 3*.

Doerr, Alan. "Lebow Excels in Recital of Taxing Piano Works," *The Washington Post [Washington, D.C.]* (03 May 1965).

TYPE: review.

PERFORMERS: Howard Lebow.

NAMES: Berg, Schönberg.

Hinson, Maurice. *Guide to the Pianist's Repertoire: An Annotated Guide.* (Bloomington, IN: Indiana University Press, 1973) 527.

TYPE: score review.

OTHER WORKS DISCUSSED: *Arioso, Bartokiana, Nach Bach, Twelve Bagatelles*.

Hinson, Maurice. *Guide to the Pianist's Repertoire: An Annotated Guide, Supplement.* (Bloomington, IN: Indiana University Press, 1979) 275.

TYPE: score review.

OTHER WORKS DISCUSSED: *Arioso, Bartokiana, Carnival Music, Nach Bach, Partita Variations, Prelude on "Happy Birthday", Twelve Bagatelles.*

Hinson, Maurice. *Guide to the Pianist's Repertoire: An Annotated Guide, Second, Revised, and Enlarged Edition.* (Bloomington, IN: Indiana University Press, 1987) 598-599.

TYPE: score review.

NAMES: Brahms.

OTHER WORKS DISCUSSED: *Arioso, Bartokiana, Carnival Music, Nach Bach, Partita Variations, Prelude on "Happy Birthday", Twelve Bagatelles, Two Preludes and Fughettas from The Book of Contrapuntal Pieces.*

Horn, Daniel Paul. "*Carnival Music*: An Introduction to the Piano Music of George Rochberg," *Clavier* XXVII/9 (November 1988) 17-22.

TYPE: article.

NAMES: Schönberg.

OTHER WORKS DISCUSSED: *Arioso, Bartokiana, Book of Contrapuntal Pieces for Keyboard Instruments, Carnival Music, Four Short Sonatas, Nach Bach, Partita Variations, Prelude on "Happy Birthday", Twelve Bagatelles.*

OTHER WORKS MENTIONED: *Sonata No. 1 for Piano Solo, Sonata No. 2 for Piano Solo.*

Knessl, Lothar. "Wiener Schule aus den USA," *Neues Osterreich* 4481 (02 February 1960).

TYPE: review.

PERFORMERS: Howard Lebow.

Newman, William S. "George Rochberg: *Sonata-Fantasia for Piano Solo*," *Notes: The Quarterly Journal of the Music Library Association* XV/4 (September 1958) 662-663.

TYPE: score review.

NAMES: Boulez, Schönberg.

Page, Tim. "Concert: Washington Square," *The New York Times* (10 October 1982) 83.

TYPE: review.

PERFORMERS: James Primosch.

Ringer, Alexander L. "Current Chronicle: United States: Cleveland," *Musical Quarterly* XLV/2 (April 1959) 230-234.

TYPE: article, review.

OTHER WORKS DISCUSSED: *Chamber Symphony, David, The Psalmist, String Quartet No. 1, Symphony No. 1, Symphony No. 2, Three Psalms, Twelve Bagatelles.*

BOOKS DISCUSSED: *The Hexachord and Its Relation to the Twelve-Tone Row.*

Ringer, Alexander L. "The Music of George Rochberg," *Musical Quarterly* LII/4 (October 1966) 409-430.

TYPE: article.

PERFORMERS: Howard Lebow.

NAMES: Schönberg.

OTHER WORKS DISCUSSED: *Apocalyptica [I], Black Sounds, Blake Songs, La Bocca della Verità, Cantio Sacra, Capriccio for Two Pianos, Chamber Symphony, Cheltenham Concerto, Concert Piece for Two Pianos and Orchestra, Contra Mortem et Tempus, David, the Psalmist, Dialogues, Duo Concertante, Four Songs of Solomon, Music for the Magic Theater, Nach Bach, Night Music, Passions [According to the Twentieth Century], Serenata d'estate, String Quartet No. 1, String Quartet No. 2, Symphony No. 1, Symphony No. 2, Three Psalms, Time-Span, Trio for Clarinet, Horn, and Piano, Trio [No. 1] for Violin, Cello, and Piano, Twelve Bagatelles, Zodiac.*

OTHER WORKS MENTIONED: *Arioso, Bartokiana, Five Smooth Stones, Sonata No. 1 for Piano Solo, Sonata No. 2 for Piano Solo, Waltz Serenade.*

BOOKS DISCUSSED: *The Hexachord and Its Relation to the Twelve-Tone Row.*

Scher, Valerie. "Retrospective Concert Surveys Talents of Composer Rochberg," *The Philadelphia Inquirer* (26 March 1983).

TYPE: review.

PERFORMERS: Jerome Lowenthal.

OTHER WORKS DISCUSSED: *Nach Bach, Partita Variations, Variations on an Original Theme.*

Singer, Samuel. "Contemporary Music Festival: Newer Works Make Bartók Sound Old Hat," *The Philadelphia Inquirer* (14 May 1959).

TYPE: review.

PERFORMERS: Howard Lebow.

Stewart, Paul. "The Piano Music of George Rochberg and the New Romanticism," *American Music Teacher* XXXVIII/3 (January 1989) 24-27, 62.

TYPE: article.

NAMES: Schönberg.

OTHER WORKS DISCUSSED: *Arioso, Bartokiana, Book of Contrapuntal Pieces for Keyboard Instruments, Carnival Music, Four Short Sonatas, Nach Bach, Partita Variations, Prelude on "Happy Birthday", Twelve Bagatelles, Two Preludes and Fughettas.*

Vinton, John. "Medium Hurts Lebow Recital," *The Washington Evening Star [Washington, D.C.]* (03 May 1965) A15.

TYPE: review.

PERFORMERS: Howard Lebow.

Songs in Praise of Krishna for Soprano and Piano

n.a. "At Krannet Tuesday: *Krishna* Poems Celebrate Love," *The Champaign-Urbana Courier [Champaign-Urbana, IL]* (15 March 1971) 15.

TYPE: upcoming concert.

PERFORMERS: Neva Pilgrim, George Rochberg.

NAMES: Edward Dimock.

Cook, David. "Recording Surveys Electronic Music," *The Tallahassee Democrat* (13 February 1977) 10E.

TYPE: record review.

PERFORMERS: Neva Pilgrim, George Rochberg.

Davis, Peter G. "Neva Pilgrim Offers Song-Cycle Premières," *The New York Times* (11 December 1973) 55.

TYPE: review.

PERFORMERS: Neva Pilgrim, George Rochberg.

NAMES: Mahler.

OTHER WORKS DISCUSSED: *String Quartet No. 3.*

Dickinson, Peter. "Rochberg, George," *Music and Letters* LXVI/1 (January 1984) 130.

TYPE: score review, record review.

PERFORMERS: Neva Pilgrim, George Rochberg.

NAMES: Barber, Copland.

OTHER WORKS DISCUSSED: *Concerto for Violin and Orchestra, The Confidence Man, Slow Fires of Autumn, Sonata for Viola and Piano, String Quartet No. 3.*

Dunning, William. "Records Are Foretaste of Santa Fe Festival," *The Los Alamos Monitor [Los Alamos, NM]* (27 April 1979).

TYPE: record reviews.

PERFORMERS: Neva Pilgrim, George Rochberg.

NAMES: Thomas Pasatieri.

OTHER WORKS DISCUSSED: *Duo Concertante, Ricordanza, String Quartet No. 1, String Quartet No. 4, String Quartet No. 5, String Quartet No. 6.*

Dunning, William. "Rochberg Records: Summer Glimpse," *The Santa Fe Reporter* (27 April 1979).

TYPE: record reviews.

PERFORMERS: Neva Pilgrim, George Rochberg.

NAMES: Thomas Pasatieri.

OTHER WORKS DISCUSSED: *Duo Concertante, Ricordanza, String Quartet No. 1, String Quartet No. 4, String Quartet No. 5, String Quartet No. 6.*

Finn, Robert. "Supple Soprano Is Splendid at CIM [Cleveland Institute of Music] Recital," *The Plain Dealer [Cleveland, OH]* (14 February 1972) 8D.

TYPE: review.

PERFORMERS: Neva Pilgrim, Theodore Ganger.

Frank, Andrew. "Vocal Music: George Rochberg," *Notes: Quarterly Journal of the Music Library Association* XXXVIII/4 (June 1982) 948.

TYPE: score review.

NAMES: Neva Pilgrim, George Rochberg.

Frazier, Larry R. "*Songs in Praise of Krishna*," *The Opera Journal* X/2 (1977) 27.

TYPE: record review.

PERFORMERS: Neva Pilgrim, George Rochberg.

George, Earl. "Concert Features Quartet, Soprano," *The Syracuse Herald* (23 April 1979) 7.

TYPE: review.

PERFORMERS: Neva Pilgrim.

OTHER WORKS DISCUSSED: *String Quartet No. 5.*

Grueninger, Walter F. "Recorded Music in Review," *Consumers' Research Magazine* LXX/7 (July 1977) 43.

TYPE: record review.

PERFORMERS: Neva Pilgrim, George Rochberg.

Handte, Jerry. "Former Tri-Cities Star Records Rochberg Music," *The Binghamton Press [Binghamton, NY]* (28 November 1976).

TYPE: record review.

PERFORMERS: Neva Pilgrim, George Rochberg.

Harvey, James E. "On Record: Electronics Looms Big in New Music," *The Flint Journal [Flint, MI]* (16 January 1977).

TYPE: record review.

PERFORMERS: Neva Pilgrim, George Rochberg.

Hoffman, W. L. "Arts and Entertainment: US [United States] Composer on Canberra Stint," *The Canberra Times [Australia]* (20 October 1986).

TYPE: upcoming performances.

PERFORMERS: Jane Manning, Chritopher Lyndon Gee.

OTHER WORKS DISCUSSED: *Blake Songs, Octet, Quintet for Piano and String Quartet, Symphony No. 4, To the Dark Wood.*

OTHER WORKS MENTIONED: *Concerto for Violin and Orchestra, Symphony No. 5.*

Horowitz, Joseph. "Rochberg's Songs Praise Krishna," *The New York Times* (31 January 1978) 14.

TYPE: review.

PERFORMERS: Neva Pilgrim, Dennis Helmrich.

Jenkins, Speight. "End of the Year Thoughts and New Records," *Record World* XXXIII/1539 (25 December 1976) 138, 205.

TYPE: record review.

PERFORMERS: Neva Pilgrim, George Rochberg.

Johnson, Tom. "Pilgrim, Dunkel, Gottlieb, Schumann, and Hoyle," *Village Voice* (13 February 1978).

TYPE: review.

PERFORMERS: Neva Pilgrim, Dennis Helmrich.

Levin, Monroe. "Notes on Music," *Jewish Exponent* (05 November 1971).

TYPE: review.

PERFORMERS: Neva Pilgrim, George Rochberg.

NAMES: Berg, Mahler, Schönberg, Webern.

Newton, George. "*Songs in Praise of Krishna*," *The NATS [National Association of Teachers of Singing] Bulletin* XXXVIII/5 (May–June 1982) 33.

TYPE: review.

PERFORMERS: Neva Pilgrim, George Rochberg.

NAMES: Edward C. Dimrock, Jr., Denise Levertov.

Oliva, Mark. "Oliva's Opus: Emotion of Life," *The Reno Gazette-Journal [Reno, NV]* (06 March 1977) 7A.

TYPE: record review.

PERFORMERS: Neva Pilgrim, George Rochberg.

Rabinowitz, Peter. "Rochberg: *Songs in Praise of Krishna*," *Syracuse Guide* (September 1977) 31.

TYPE: record review.

PERFORMERS: Neva Pilgrim, George Rochberg.

NAMES: Berg, Messiaen, Ravel, Schubert, Schumann, Scriabin.

Reinthaler, Joan. "Neva Pilgrim," *The Washington Post [Washington, D.C.]* (10 April 1978) B-9.

TYPE: review.

PERFORMERS: Neva Pilgrim, Dennis Helmrich.

Ringer, Alexander L. "Current Chronicle: New York, Jerusalem, and Urbana, Illinois," *Musical Quarterly* LVIII/1 (January 1972) 128-132.

TYPE: review.

PERFORMERS: Neva Pilgrim, George Rochberg.

NAMES: Mahler.

OTHER WORKS DISCUSSED: *David, the Psalmist, Sacred Song of Reconciliation, Symphony No. 3.*

n.a. "Rochberg Songs: Pilgrim to Perform," *The Syracuse Herald* (15 April 1979) 7.

TYPE: upcoming concert.

PERFORMERS: Neva Pilgrim, George Rochberg.

OTHER WORKS DISCUSSED: *Eleven Songs, String Quartet No. 5.*

Salzmann, Eric. "Recording of Special Merit: George Rochberg: *Songs in Praise of Krishna*," *Stereo Review* XXXIX/4 (October 1977) 144.

TYPE: record review.

PERFORMERS: Neva Pilgrim, George Rochberg.

NAMES: Edward C. Dimrock, Jr., Denise Levertov, Schönberg, Scriabin.

Scanlan, Roger. "Spotlight on Contemporary American Composers," *The NATS [National Association of Teachers of Singing] Bulletin* XXXIII/1 (October 1976) 48-49, 53-54.

TYPE: article.

OTHER WORKS DISCUSSED: *Blake Songs, David, The Psalmist, Eleven Songs, Four Songs of Solomon, Fantasies, Music for "The Alchemist", Phaedra, Sacred Song of Reconciliation, String Quartet No. 2, Symphony No. 3, Tableaux, Two Songs from "Tableaux".*

OTHER WORKS MENTIONED: many.

Thornton, H. Frank. "Rochberg: *Songs in Praise of Krishna*," *The New Records* XLV/2 (April 1977) 12.

TYPE: record review.

PERFORMERS: Neva Pilgrim, George Rochberg.

Songs of Inanna and Dumuzi for Contralto and Piano

McCurdy, Charles. "Music: Works of Rochberg and Schubel at Art Alliance," *The Philadelphia Inquirer* (20 February 1984) 6-C.

TYPE: review.

NAMES: Francesca Rochberg-Halton.

OTHER WORKS DISCUSSED: *Slow Fires of Autumn, Ukiyo-e.*

Paton, John Glenn. "George Rochberg: *Songs of Inanna and Dumuzi for Contralto and Piano,*" *Notes: The Quarterly Journal of the Msuci Library Association* XLI/2 (December 1984) 393.

TYPE: score review.

NAMES: Francesca Rochberg-Halton.

Webster, Daniel. "Rochberg's Indian Love Songs Pulsing, Vital," *The Philadelphia Inquirer* (31 January 1978) 7-A.

TYPE: review.

PERFORMERS: Katherine Ciesinski, George Reeves.

NAMES: Francesca Rochberg-Halton.

OTHER WORKS DISCUSSED: *Partita Variations, Ukiyo-e.*

String Quartet No. 1

Archibald, Bruce. "Rochberg: *Chamber Symphony, Duo Concertante, Music for the Magic Theater, Ricordanza, String Quartet No. 1,*" *Musical Quarterly* LXXII/4 (October 1976) 613-615.

TYPE: record review.

PERFORMERS: Concord String Quartet.

NAMES: Bartók, Berg.

OTHER WORKS DISCUSSED: *Chamber Symphony, Contra Mortem et Tempus, Duo Concertante, Music for the Magic Theater, Ricordanza.*

Bronston, Levering. "Rochberg: *Chamber Symphony, Duo Concertante, Music for the Magic Theater, Ricordanza, String Quartet No. 1,*" *The New Records* XLIII/11 (January 1976) 7-8.

TYPE: record review.

PERFORMERS: Concord String Quartet.

OTHER WORKS DISCUSSED: *Chamber Symphony, Duo Concertante, Music for the Magic Theater, Ricordanza.*

Brunner, Lance W. "George Rochberg: *The Concord Quartets*," *Notes: The Quarterly Journal of the Music Library Association* XVIII/8 (December 1981) 423-426.

TYPE: score review, article.

NAMES: many.

OTHER WORKS DISCUSSED: *String Quartet No. 2, String Quartet No. 3, String Quartet No. 4, String Quartet No. 5, String Quartet No. 6.*

Clarke, Henry Leland. "Current Chronicle: United States: Seattle," *Musical Quarterly* LIII/8 (July 1967) 397-400.

TYPE: review.

PERFORMERS: Philadelphia String Quartet.

Croan, Robert. "Classical Record Reviews: Copland Celebration: Music of George Rochberg," *The Pittsburgh Post-Gazette* (07 May 1976) 34.

TYPE: record review.

PERFORMERS: Concord String Quartet.

OTHER WORKS DISCUSSED: *Concerto for Violin and Orchestra, Duo Concertante, Ricordanza.*

Danuser, Hermann. "Zur Kritik der musikalischen Postmoderne," *Neue Zeitschrift fur Musik* CXLIX/12 (December 1988) 4-9.

TYPE: article.

OTHER WORKS DISCUSSED: *Contra Mortem et Tempus, Music for the Magic Theater, Quintet for Piano and String Quartet, String Quartet No. 3, Trio [No. 1] for Violin, Cello, and Piano.*

Dunning, William. "Records Are Foretaste of Santa Fe Festival," *The Los Alamos Monitor [Los Alamos, NM]* (27 April 1979).

TYPE: record reviews.

PERFORMERS: Concord String Quartet.

NAMES: Schönberg.

OTHER WORKS DISCUSSED: *Duo Concertante, Ricordanza, Songs in Praise of Krishna, String Quartet No. 4, String Quartet No. 5, String Quartet No. 6.*

Dunning, William. "Rochberg Records: Summer Glimpse," *The Santa Fe Reporter* (27 April 1979).

TYPE: record review.

PERFORMERS: Concord String Quartet.

NAMES: Schönberg.

OTHER WORKS DISCUSSED: *Duo Concertante, Ricordanza, Songs in Praise of Krishna, String Quartet No. 4, String Quartet No. 5, String Quartet No. 6.*

Jenkins, Speight. "Record World: Classical: A Home for the Composer," *Record World* XXXI/1502 (03 April 1976) 48-49.

TYPE: record review.

PERFORMERS: Concord String Quartet.

OTHER WORKS DISCUSSED: *Ricordanza.*

Kraehenbuehl, David. "Chamber Music: George Rochberg: *String Quartet,*" *Notes: The Quarterly Journal of the Music Library Association* XV/1 (December 1957) 147.

TYPE: score review.

NAMES: Bartók, Berg.

Oliva, Mark. "Classical Record Review," *Nevada State Journal* (18 January 1976) 11.

TYPE: record review.

PERFORMERS: Concord String Quartet.

OTHER WORKS DISCUSSED: *Chamber Symphony, Duo Concertante, Music for the Magic Theater, Ricordanza.*

Porter, Andrew. "Musical Events: Questions," *The New Yorker* (12 February 1979) 109-115.

TYPE: article, review.

OTHER WORKS DISCUSSED: *Concerto for Violin and Orchestra, Duo Concertante, Music for the Magic Theater, Ricordanza, String Quartet No. 2, String Quartet No. 3, String Quartet No. 4, String Quartet No. 5, String Quartet No. 6.*

Porter, Andrew. "Rochberg: Chamber Works," *High Fidelity/Musical America* XVI/5 (May 1976) 90-92.

TYPE: record review.

PERFORMERS: Concord String Quartet.

OTHER WORKS DISCUSSED: *Chamber Symphony, Concerto for Violin and Orchestra, Duo Concertante, Music for the Magic Theater, Ricordanza.*

Potter, Keith. "Rochberg: *String Quartet No. 1, Duo Concertante, Ricordanza,*" *Records and Recordings [Great Britain]* (March 1977) 72-73.

TYPE: record review.

PERFORMERS: Concord String Quartet.

NAMES: Bartók, Beethoven, Berg.

OTHER WORKS DISCUSSED: *Blake Songs, Contra Mortem et Tempus, Duo Concertante, Ricordanza, String Quartet No. 2, String Quartet No. 3.*

Ringer, Alexander L. "Current Chronicle: United States: Cleveland," *Musical Quarterly* XLV/2 (April 1959) 230-234.

TYPE: article, review.

NAMES: Bartók.

OTHER WORKS DISCUSSED: *Chamber Symphony, David, The Psalmist, Sonata-Fantasia, Symphony No. 1, Symphony No. 2, Three Psalms, Twelve Bagatelles.*

BOOKS DISCUSSED: *The Hexachord and Its Relation to the Twelve-Tone Row.*

Ringer, Alexander L. "The Music of George Rochberg," *Musical Quarterly* LII/4 (October 1966) 409-430.

TYPE: article.

PERFORMERS: Galimir String Quartet.

NAMES: Bartók.

OTHER WORKS DISCUSSED: *Apocalyptica [I], Black Sounds, Blake Songs, La Bocca della Verità, Cantio Sacra, Capriccio for Two Pianos, Chamber Symphony, Cheltenham Concerto, Concert Piece for Two Pianos and Orchestra, Contra Mortem et Tempus, David, the Psalmist, Dialogues, Duo Concertante, Four Songs of Solomon, Music for the Magic Theater, Nach Bach, Night Music, Passions [According to the Twentieth Century], Serenata d'estate, Sonata-Fantasia, String Quartet No. 2, Symphony No. 1, Symphony No. 2, Three Psalms, Time-Span, Trio for Clarinet, Horn, and Piano, Trio [No. 1] for Violin, Cello, and Piano, Twelve Bagatelles, Zodiac.*

OTHER WORKS MENTIONED: *Arioso, Bartokiana, Five Smooth Stones, Sonata No. 1 for Piano Solo, Sonata No. 2 for Piano Solo, Waltz Serenade.*

BOOKS DISCUSSED: *The Hexachord and Its Relation to the Twelve-Tone Row.*

Salzman, Eric. "Rochberg: *Chamber Symphony, Duo Concertante, Music for the Magic Theater, Ricordanza, String Quartet No. 1,*" *Stereo Review* XXXVII/1 (July 1976) 111.

TYPE: record review.

PERFORMERS: Concord String Quartet.

OTHER WORKS DISCUSSED: *Chamber Symphony, Duo Concertante, Music for the Magic Theater, Ricordanza.*

Sargeant, Winthrop. "Concert Records: Romantic and Gothic," *The New Yorker* (26 January 1976) 93.

TYPE: review.

PERFORMERS: Concord String Quartet.

OTHER WORKS DISCUSSED: *Duo Concertante, Ricordanza.*

Veilleux, C. Thomas. "Chamber Music Roundup Reveals Three Fine Records," *The Sunday Post [Bridgeport, CT]* (10 October 1976) E14.

TYPE: record review.

PERFORMERS: Concord String Quartet.

OTHER WORKS DISCUSSED: *Chamber Symphony, Duo Concertante, Music for the Magic Theater, Ricordanza.*

Webster, Daniel. "Stylistic Odyssey of George Rochberg," *The Philadelphia Inquirer* (15 February 1976) 7H.

TYPE: record review.

PERFORMERS: Concord String Quartet.

OTHER WORKS DISCUSSED: *Chamber Symphony, Duo Concertante, Music for the Magic Theater, Ricordanza.*

String Quartet No. 2 with Soprano

Brunner, Lance W. "George Rochberg: *The Concord Quartets,*" *Notes: The Quarterly Journal of the Music Library Association* XVIII/8 (December 1981) 423-426.

TYPE: score review, article.

NAMES: many.

OTHER WORKS DISCUSSED: *String Quartet No. 1, String Quartet No. 3, String Quartet No. 4, String Quartet No. 5, String Quartet No. 6.*

Chase, Gilbert. "*String Quartet No. 2,*" *Musical Quarterly* L/1 (January 1964) 122-124.

TYPE: record review.

PERFORMERS: Janice Harsanyi, Philadelphia String Quartet.

NAMES: Rilke.

n.a. "Composers World," *Musical America* LXXXII/5 (May 1962) 47.

TYPE: review.

PERFORMERS: Janice Harsanyi, Philadelphia String Quartet.

Danuser, Hermann. "Zur Kritik der musikalischen Postmoderne," *Neue Zeitschrift fur Musik* CXLIX/12 (December 1988) 4-9.

TYPE: article.

OTHER WORKS DISCUSSED: *Contra Mortem et Tempus, Music for the Magic Theater, Quintet for Piano and String Quartet, String Quartet No. 2, Trio [No. 1] for Violin, Cello, and Piano.*

BOOKS DISCUSSED: *The Aesthetics of Survival.*

Felton, James. "Composers Are Sane But the World Isn't, Says Penn Rochberg," *The Sunday Bulletin [Philadelphia]* (13 February 1966) 11.

TYPE: interview.

PERFORMERS: Janice Harsanyi, Philadelphia String Quartet.

OTHER WORKS DISCUSSED: *Contra Mortem et Tempus, Music for the Magic Theater, Night Music, Symphony No. 1, Symphony No. 2, Symphony No. 3, Zodiac.*

Flanagan, William. "CRI [Composers' Recordings Incorporated] Comes of Age," *Stereo Review* XI/5 (November 1963) 84.

TYPE: record review.

PERFORMERS: Janice Harsanyi, Philadelphia String Quartet.

Hauptfuhrer, Fred. "Philadelphia String Quartet Finds Old Friends Abroad," *The Evening Bulletin [Philadelphia]* (04 June 1965) B-23.

TYPE: review.

PERFORMERS: Janice Harsanyi, Philadelphia String Quartet.

Henahan, Donal J. "Music: American Range," *The New York Times* (18 March 1976).

TYPE: review.

PERFORMERS: Clamma Dale, Riverside String Quartet.

NAMES: Rilke.

Henahan, Donal J. "Music: Rochberg Work," *The New York Times* (09 May 1973) 43.

TYPE: review.

PERFORMERS: Susan Davenny Wyner, Concord String Quartet.

NAMES: Bartók, Rilke, Schönberg.

Lange, Art. "Rochberg: *Quintet*," *American Record Guide* XLV/3 (December 1981) 24-25.

TYPE: record review.

NAMES: Schönberg.

OTHER WORKS DISCUSSED: *Concerto for Violin and Orchestra, Music for the Magic Theater, Quintet for Piano and String Quartet, String Quartet No. 3, String Quartet No. 4, String Quartet No. 5, String Quartet No. 6.*

Miller, Philip L. "Rochberg: *String Quartet No. 2*," *American Record Guide* XXIX/12 (August 1963) 943-944.

TYPE: record review.

PERFORMERS: Janice Harsanyi, Philadelphia String Quartet.

NAMES: Harry Behn, Rilke.

Montagu, George. "Philadelphia String Quartet," *Musical Opinion* LXXXVIII/1053 (July 1965) 587-588.

TYPE: review.

PERFORMERS: Janice Harsanyi, Philadelphia String Quartet.

NAMES: Rilke.

Morgan, Robert P. "Rochberg: *String Quartet No. 2*," *High Fidelity/Musical America* XXIV/11 (November 1974) 117-118.

TYPE: record review.

PERFORMERS: Phyllis Bryn-Julson, Concord String Quartet.

NAMES: Rilke.

OTHER WORKS MENTIONED: *String Quartet No. 3.*

Porter, Andrew. "Musical Events: Questions," *The New Yorker* (12 February 1979) 109-115.

TYPE: article, review.

PERFORMERS: Janice Harsanyi, Philadelphia String Quartet, Phyllis Bryn-Julson, Concord String Quartet.

OTHER WORKS DISCUSSED: *Concerto for Violin and Orchestra, Duo Concertante, Music for the Magic Theater, Ricordanza, String Quartet No. 1, String Quartet No. 3, String Quartet No. 4, String Quartet No. 5, String Quartet No. 6.*

Potter, Keith. "Rochberg: *String Quartet No. 1, Duo Concertante, Ricordanza*," *Records and Recordings [Great Britain]* (March 1977) 72-73.

TYPE: record review.

NAMES: Schönberg.

OTHER WORKS DISCUSSED: *Blake Songs, Contra Mortem et Tempus, Duo Concertante, Ricordanza, String Quartet No. 1, String Quartet No. 3.*

Rich, Alan. "Records: Innovators New and Old," *The New York Times* (23 June 1963) 12.

TYPE: record review.

PERFORMERS: Janice Harsanyi, Philadelphia String Quartet.

NAMES: Berg, Rilke.

Ringer, Alexander L. "The Music of George Rochberg," *Musical Quarterly* LII/4 (October 1966) 409-430.

TYPE: article.

PERFORMERS: Janice Harsanyi, Philadelphia String Quartet.

NAMES: Ives.

OTHER WORKS DISCUSSED: *Apocalyptica [I], Black Sounds, Blake Songs, La Bocca della Verità, Cantio Sacra, Capriccio for Two Pianos, Chamber Symphony, Cheltenham Concerto, Concert Piece for Two Pianos and Orchestra, Contra Mortem et Tempus, David, the Psalmist, Dialogues, Duo Concertante, Four Songs of Solomon, Music for the Magic Theater, Nach Bach, Night Music, Passions [According to the Twentieth Century], Serenata d'estate, Sonata-Fantasia, String Quartet No. 1, Symphony No. 1, Symphony No. 2, Three Psalms, Time-Span, Trio for Clarinet, Horn, and Piano, Trio [No. 1] for Violin, Cello, and Piano, Twelve Bagatelles, Zodiac.*

OTHER WORKS MENTIONED: *Arioso, Bartokiana, Five Smooth Stones, Sonata No. 1 for Piano Solo, Sonata No. 2 for Piano Solo, Waltz Serenade.*

BOOKS DISCUSSED: *The Hexachord and Its Relation to the Twelve-Tone Row.*

Robison, Judith. "Musical Highlights About Town," *The Music Magazine* CLXIV/6 (July 1962) 24.

TYPE: review.

PERFORMERS: Janice Harsanyi, Beaux Arts Trio.

NAMES: Rilke.

Salzman, Eric. "The Philadelphia School," *Stereo Review* XXXIV/1 (January 1975) 106.

TYPE: record review.

PERFORMERS: Phyllis Bryn-Julson, Concord String Quartet.

NAMES: Rilke.

Sargeant, Winthrop. "The Current Cinema," *The New Yorker* (19 May 1962) 181-185.

TYPE: review.

Scanlan, Roger. "Spotlight on Contemporary American Composers," *The NATS [National Association of Teachers of Singing] Bulletin* XXXIII/1 (October 1976) 48-49, 53-54.

TYPE: article.

OTHER WORKS DISCUSSED: *Blake Songs, David, The Psalmist, Eleven Songs, Four Songs of Solomon, Fantasies, Music for "The Alchemist", Phaedra, Sacred Song of Reconciliation, Songs in Praise of Krishna, Symphony No. 3, Tableaux, Two Songs from "Tableaux".*

OTHER WORKS MENTIONED: many.

Walsh, Michael. "Kronos Quartet Passes the Test," *The San Francisco Examiner* (28 March 1980) 31.

TYPE: review.

PERFORMERS: Kronos String Quartet.

NAMES: Bartók.

OTHER WORKS DISCUSSED: *Concerto for Violin and Orchestra, String Quartet No. 3, String Quartet No. 4, String Quartet No. 5, String Quartet No. 6.*

Webster, Daniel. "Quartet Home, Happy," *The Philadelphia Inquirer* (20 June 1965) V, 5.

TYPE: review.

PERFORMERS: Janice Harsanyi, Philadelphia String Quartet.

Webster, Daniel. "A Rochberg *Quartet* of Poetry, Intensity," *The Philadelphia Inquirer* (12 June 1983) 5-H.

TYPE: record review.

PERFORMERS: Leslie Guinn, Concord String Quartet.

NAMES: Paul Rochberg.

OTHER WORKS DISCUSSED: *String Quartet No. 7.*

OTHER WORKS MENTIONED: *String Quartet No. 4, String Quartet No. 5, String Quartet No. 6.*

String Quartet No. 3

Artner, Alan G. "n.t.," *The Chicago Tribune* (09 December 1973) VI, 9.

TYPE: review.

PERFORMERS: Concord String Quartet.

NAMES: Mahler.

Backas, James. "n.t.," *The Washington Evening Star [Washington, D.C.]* (09 September 1972) A-11.

TYPE: review.

PERFORMERS: Concord String Quartet.

NAMES: Bartók, Mahler.

Bernstein, Bob. "Spectrum: New American Music," *Business Review* (02–08 April 1975).

TYPE: record review.

PERFORMERS: Concord String Quartet.

OTHER WORKS DISCUSSED: *Blake Songs.*

Blaustein, Susan. "The Survival of Aesthetics: Books by Boulez, DeLio, Rochberg," *Perspectives of New Music* XXVII/1 (Winter 1989) 272-303.

TYPE: article, review.

OTHER WORKS DISCUSSED: *String Quartet No. 4, String Quartet No. 5, String Quartet No. 6.*

BOOKS DISCUSSED: *The Aesthetics of Survival.*

Block, Steven D. "George Rochberg—Progressive or Master Forgot?" *Perspectives of New Music* XXI/1-2 (Fall-Winter 1982/Spring-Summer 1983) 407-409.

TYPE: article.

NAMES: Bartók, Beethoven, Haydn, Mahler, Jay Reise, Schubert.

OTHER WORKS DISCUSSED: *String Quartet No. 4, String Quartet No. 5, String Quartet No. 6.*

Bridges, John. "Concord Quartet: Marked by Audacious Energy," *The Tennessean [Nashville, TN]* (05 March 1982) 46.

TYPE: upcoming performance, interview.

PERFORMERS: Concord String Quartet.

OTHER WORKS DISCUSSED: *String Quartet No. 4, String Quartet No. 5, String Quartet No. 6.*

Bronston, Levering. "Rochberg: *String Quartet No. 3,*" *The New World Records* XLVI/6 (August 1973) 5.

TYPE: record review.

PERFORMERS: Concord String Quartet.

NAMES: Beethoven, Mahler.

Bronston, Levering. "Three Sides of George Rochberg," *The New Records* XLVI/5 (July 1978) 7.

TYPE: record review.

PERFORMERS: Concord String Quartet.

OTHER WORKS DISCUSSED: *Black Sounds, Carnival Music, Nach Bach.*

Brunner, Lance W. "George Rochberg: *The Concord Quartets,*" *Notes: The Quarterly Journal of the Music Library Association* XVIII/8 (December 1981) 423-426.

TYPE: score review, article.

NAMES: many.

OTHER WORKS DISCUSSED: *String Quartet No. 1, String Quartet No. 2, String Quartet No. 4, String Quartet No. 5, String Quartet No. 6.*

Buell, Richard. "The Arts: Zeitlin Shows Versatility at MIT [Massachusetts Institute of Technology] Concert," *The Boston Globe* (03 December 1974) 20.

TYPE: review.

OTHER WORKS DISCUSSED: *Caprice Variations.*

Bull, John V. R. "Dancers Are Skillful But Tepid," *The Philadelphia Inquirer* (25 February 1978) 3-B.

TYPE: review.

PERFORMERS: Raymond Johnson Dance Company.

Cambell, R. M. "Mahler's Funeral Songs Live On," *The Seattle Post-Intelligencer* (16 May 1979) E2.

TYPE: review.

OTHER WORKS DISCUSSED: *Transcendental Variations.*

Carr, Jay. "Rochberg: *String Quartet No. 3*," *The Detroit Sunday News* (02 December 1973) H, 22.

TYPE: record review.

PERFORMERS: Concord String Quartet.

NAMES: Beethoven, Mahler.

Carr, Jay. "Sharing a Sense of Loss with Rochberg," *The Detroit News* (29 January 1980) B5.

TYPE: review.

PERFORMERS: Concord String Quartet.

OTHER WORKS DISCUSSED: *Concerto for Violin and Orchestra, String Quartet No. 4, String Quartet No. 5, String Quartet No. 6, String Quartet No. 7.*

Cera, Stephen. "George Rochberg: *String Quartet No. 3*," *The Los Angeles Times* (16 June 1974) Calendar, 55.

TYPE: record review.

PERFORMERS: Concord String Quartet.

NAMES: Beethoven, Mahler.

Chambers, John W. "Quartet Performs Difficult Works with Great Style," *The Times [Huntsville, AL]* (05 March 1974) 13.

TYPE: record review.

PERFORMERS: Concord String Quartet.

Covell, Roger. "Lack of Scope Sees a Change in Style," *The Sydney Morning Herald [Australia]* (18 October 1986).

TYPE: review, interview.

OTHER WORKS DISCUSSED: *Concerto for Violin and Orchestra, Ricordanza, Symphony No. 5, To the Dark Wood.*

Davis, Peter G. "Music: Recent Rochberg," *The New York Times* (26 April 1974) 26.

TYPE: review.

PERFORMERS: Concord String Quartet.

OTHER WORKS DISCUSSED: *Ricordanza.*

Dean, Jeff. "String Quartet Excels in Berg Composition," *The Phoenix* (05 October 1973) 2.

TYPE: review.

PERFORMERS: Concord String Quartet.

NAMES: Barber.

Dickinson, Peter. "Rochberg, George," *Music and Letters* LXVI/1 (January 1984) 130.

TYPE: review.

PERFORMERS: Brahms, Mahler.

OTHER WORKS DISCUSSED: *Concerto for Violin and Orchestra, The Confidence Man, Slow Fires of Autumn, Sonata for Viola and Piano, Songs in Praise of Krishna.*

Dyer, Richard. "A Serious Composer Who Likes to Have Fun," *The Boston Globe* (11 July 1981) 19, 21.

TYPE: review.

NAMES: Mahler.

Felton, James. "At the Art Alliance: Concordians Play Rochberg *String Quartet*," *The Evening Bulletin [Philadelphia]* (19 February 1973) 12-B.

TYPE: review.

PERFORMERS: Concord String Quartet.

NAMES: Mahler.

Freed, Richard. "Recording of Special Merit: Rochberg: *String Quartet No. 3*," *Stereo Review* XXXI/5 (November 1973) 122, 124.

TYPE: record review.

PERFORMERS: Concord String Quartet.

NAMES: Beethoven, Mahler.

Fleming, Shirley. "Musician of the Month: Jacob Druckman," *High Fidelity/Music America* XXII/8 (August 1972) MA-4, MA-5.

TYPE: review.

Fogel, Henry. "A Conversation with George Rochberg," *The Syracuse Guide* (March 1976) 27-28, 36.

TYPE: article.

NAMES: Beethoven, Mahler.

OTHER WORKS DISCUSSED: *Phaedra.*

Fogel, Henry. "George Rochberg: A Raproachment with the Past," *The Syracuse Guide* V (January 1976) 24-26, 42.

TYPE: article.

OTHER WORKS DISCUSSED: *Concerto for Violin and Orchestra, Phaedra, Symphony No. 3.*

Fried, Alexander. "A Wild, Driving *String Quartet*," *The San Francisco Examiner* (19 July 1973) 29.

TYPE: review.

PERFORMERS: Concord String Quartet.

NAMES: Schumann, Schubert, Mahler.

Gagne, Cole and Tracy Caras. *Soundpieces: Interviews with American Composers.* (Metuchen, NJ: Scarecrow Press, Inc., 1982).

TYPE: interview.

OTHER WORKS DISCUSSED: *Apocalyptica [I], Black Sounds, Concerto for Violin and Orchestra, Contra Mortem et Tempus, The Confidence Man, Electrikaleidoscope, Music for the Magic Theater, Octet, Quintet for Piano and String Quartet, Ricordanza, Sonata No. 2 for Piano Solo, String Quartet No. 4, String Quartet No. 5, String Quartet No. 6, Twelve Bagatelles.*

OTHER WORKS MENTIONED: many.

Griffiths, Paul. *Modern Music: A Concise History from Debussy to Boulez.* (New York, NY: Thames and Hudson, Inc., 1978) 200-201.

TYPE: article.

NAMES: Beethoven, Mahler.

OTHER WORKS DISCUSSED: *Contra Mortem et Tempus.*

Gudel, Paul. "Eclectic Chords," *The Grey City Journal [Chicago]* (08 March 1974) 3.

TYPE: review.

PERFORMERS: Concord String Quartet.

NAMES: Bartók, Beethoven, Mahler, Mozart, Stravinsky.

NOTE: a response by Gene Rochberg-Halton appears in a later edition.

Harrison, Max. "Rags to Rochberg," *The Times [London]* (20 April 1974).

TYPE: record review.

PERFORMERS: Concord String Quartet.

NAMES: Bartók.

OTHER WORKS DISCUSSED: *Contra Mortem et Tempus, String Quartet No. 2, Symphony No. 3.*

Hawthorne, Maggie. "Concord Quartet: Remarkable Strings," *The Seattle Post-Intelligencer* (05 May 1973) A-8.

TYPE: review.

PERFORMERS: Concord String Quartet.

Henahan, Donal J. "An Apostate Questions Modernist Pieties with Gusto," (03 June 1984) II, 21-22.
TYPE: article.
OTHER WORKS DISCUSSED: *Serenata d'estate.*
BOOKS DISCUSSED: *The Aesthetics of Survival.*

Henahan, Donal J. "Are They Returning to Melody?," *The New York Times* (15 July 1973) II, 20.
TYPE: record review.
PERFORMERS: Concord String Quartet.
NAMES: Bartók, Beethoven, Mahler.

Henahan, Donal J. "Music: Recent Rochberg," *The New York Times* (26 April 1974) 26.
TYPE: review.
PERFORMERS: Concord String Quartet.
NAMES: Beethoven, Brahms, Mahler.
OTHER WORKS DISCUSSED: *Ricordanza.*

Henahan, Donal J. "Music: Rochberg Work by National Orchestra," *The New York Times* (17 April 1985) III, 18.
TYPE: review.
NAMES: Bartók, Beethoven, Mahler, Stravinsky.
OTHER WORKS DISCUSSED: *Music for the Magic Theater.*

Henahan, Donal J. "A Rare New Work Played by Quartet," *The New York Times* (17 May 1972) 38.
TYPE: review.
PERFORMERS: Concord String Quartet.
NAMES: Bartók, Beethoven, Mahler.

Henahan, Donal J. "Tommorrow's Music: Something Old, Something New," *The New York Times* (28 May 1972) II, 11.
TYPE: review.
NAMES: Bartók, Beethoven, Mahler, Stravinsky.
OTHER WORKS DISCUSSED: *Music for the Magic Theater.*

Hiemenz, Jack. "Concord String Quartet: Rochberg," *High Fidelity/Musical America* XXII/8 (August 1972) MA-13, 16.
TYPE: review.
PERFORMERS: Concord String Quartet.
NAMES: Bartók, Hesse, McLuhan.

Hiemenz, Jack. "Juilliard: Rochberg, Ligeti," *High Fidelity/Musical America* XXV/3 (March 1975) MA-28.

TYPE: review.

PERFORMERS: Concord String Quartet.

NAMES: Brahms, Mahler.

OTHER WORKS DISCUSSED: *Music for the Magic Theater.*

Huebner, W. Michael. "Composer Pursues *Aesthetics of Survival* in Modern Music," *The Kansaas City Star* (12 August 1984) 7F.

TYPE: review.

PERFORMERS: Concord String Quartet.

NAMES: Brahms, Mahler.

BOOKS DISCUSSED: *The Aesthetics of Survival.*

Jenkins, Speight. "Concord String Quartet Plays Rochberg," *The New York Post* (26 April 1974).

TYPE: review.

PERFORMERS: Concord String Quartet.

NAMES: Brahms, Mahler.

OTHER WORKS DISCUSSED: *Ricordanza.*

Jones, Art. "Weill, Milhaud Splendid," *The Virginian-Pilot [Norfolk, VA]* (16 September 1973).

TYPE: record review.

PERFORMERS: Concord String Quartet.

NAMES: Stravinsky.

Kriegsman, Alan M. "Crosscurrents: The Arts at Year's End: An Air of Retrenchment Gathering?," *The Washington Post [Washington, D.C.]* (31 December 1972) F-1.

TYPE: review.

PERFORMERS: Concord String Quartet.

Kriegsman, Alan M. "Crosscurrents: A Courageous Display of Will," *The Washington Post [Washington, D.C.]* (17 September 1972) K-1, K-2.

TYPE: review.

PERFORMERS: Concord String Quartet.

Kriegsman, Alan M. "Peak Upon Peak of Excellence," *The Washington Post [Washington, D.C.]* (09 September 1972) C-9.

TYPE: review.

PERFORMERS: Concord String Quartet.

NAMES: Bartók, Beethoven, Brahms, Mahler.

Lange, Art. "Rochberg: *Quintet,*" *American Record Guide* XLV/3 (December 1981) 24-25.

TYPE: record review.

OTHER WORKS DISCUSSED: *Concerto for Violin and Orchestra, Music for the Magic Theater, Quintet for Piano and String Quartet, String Quartet No. 2, String Quartet No. 4, String Quartet No. 5, String Quartet No. 6.*

Levin, Monroe. "Notes on Music," *Jewish Exponent* (23 February 1973) 79.

TYPE: review.

PERFORMERS: Concord String Quartet.

NAMES: Beethoven, Brahms, Mahler.

Levinson, Mara. "Raymond Johnson Dance Company 'Zaps' Berg Audience with Energy, Force," *The Morning Call [Allentown, PA]* (04 November 1976).

TYPE: review.

PERFORMERS: Raymond Johnson Dance Company.

McCall, Joseph. "George Rochberg: *String Quartet No. 3,*" *The Cresset* (September 1973) 26.

TYPE: record review.

PERFORMERS: Concord String Quartet.

NAMES: Brahms.

McLellan, Joseph. "Four *Quartets,*" *The Washington Post [Washington, D.C.]* (15 July 1973) Book World, 11.

TYPE: record review.

PERFORMERS: Concord String Quartet.

NAMES: Debussy, Ravel.

Moore, David W. "Rochberg: *Carnival Music, Black Sounds, Nach Bach,*" *American Record Guide* XLI/9 (July 1978) 25-26.

TYPE: record review.

NAMES: Ives.

OTHER WORKS DISCUSSED: *Apocalyptica [I], Black Sounds, Carnival Music, Nach Bach.*

Morgan, Robert P. "Rochberg: *String Quartet No. 3,*" *High Fidelity/Musical America* XXIII/11 (November 1973) 115-116.

TYPE: record review.

PERFORMERS: Concord String Quartet.

NAMES: Beethoven, Jorge Luis Borge, John Cage, Cervantes, Ives, Mahler, Stravinsky.

OTHER WORKS MENTIONED: *Music for the Magic Theater, Nach Bach.*

Mundy, Harold G. "Vigor and Sensitivity Mark Audubon Opener," *The Scranton Times [Scranton, PA]* (27 September 1979) 8.

TYPE: review.

PERFORMERS: Audubon Quartet.

NAMES: Bartók, Beethoven, Ives, Mahler, Stravinsky.

Di Nardo, Tom. "Johnson Dance Troupe Puzzling," *The Evening Bulletin [Philadelphia]* (25 February 1978) 6-A.

TYPE: review.

PERFORMERS: Raymond Johnson Dance Company.

n.a. "News and Honors," *ASCAP Today* VI/1 (July 1972) 31.

TYPE: announcement of première.

OTHER WORKS DISCUSSED: *Carnival Music.*

Page, Tim. "Apostate Modernist," *The New York Times Magazine* (29 May 1983) 24-25.

TYPE: article.

NAMES: Mahler.

OTHER WORKS DISCUSSED: *String Quartet No. 4, String Quartet No. 5, String Quartet No. 6.*

Page, Tim. "Music Notes: Concord Disbanding," *The New York Times* (18 January 1987) II, 23 & 26.

TYPE: article.

PERFORMERS: Concord String Quartet.

OTHER WORKS DISCUSSED: *String Quartet No. 4, String Quartet No. 5, String Quartet No. 6.*

Porter, Andrew. "Musical Events: A Frail Bark," *The New Yorker* (16 August 1982) 66-69.

TYPE: review.

OTHER WORKS DISCUSSED: *The Confidence Man, Quintet for String Quintet.*

Porter, Andrew. "Musical Events: Questions," *The New Yorker* (12 February 1979) 109-115.

TYPE: article, review.

NAMES: Franck.

OTHER WORKS DISCUSSED: *Concerto for Violin and Orchestra, Duo Concertante, Music for the Magic Theater, Ricordanza, String Quartet No. 1, String Quartet No. 2, String Quartet No. 4, String Quartet No. 5, String Quartet No. 6.*

Potter, Keith. "Rochberg: *String Quartet No. 1, Duo Concertante, Ricordanza*," *Records and Recordings [Great Britain]* (March 1977) 72-73.

TYPE: record review.

NAMES: Beethoven, Cardew, Crumb, Davies, Lentz, Rzewski, West.

OTHER WORKS DISCUSSED: *Blake Songs, Contra Mortem et Tempus, Duo Concertante, Ricordanza, String Quartet No. 1, String Quartet No. 2.*

n.a. "Premières," *Music Educators' Journal* LIX/1 (September 1972) 111.

TYPE: announcement of première.

PERFORMERS: Concord String Quartet.

Rayment, Malcom. "Rochberg: *String Quartet No. 3*," *Records and Recordings [Great Britain]* (June 1974).

TYPE: record review.

PERFORMERS: Concord String Quartet.

NAMES: Bartók, Beethoven, Berg, Darwin, Ives, Mahler.

Reise, Jay. "Rochberg the Progressive," *Perspectives of New Music* XIX/1-2 (Fall-Winter 1980/Spring Summer 1981) 395-407.

TYPE: article, analysis.

NAMES: Beethoven, Steven Block, Bruckner, Mahler.

OTHER WORKS DISCUSSED: *Contra Mortem et Tempus, Symphony No. 2, Tableaux.*

von Rhein, John. "Music: The 'Concord' Debut to Mark a Return to the Romantic," *The Chicago Tribune* (20 January 1980) VI, 23.

TYPE: article, interview.

PERFORMERS: Concord String Quartet.

OTHER WORKS DISCUSSED: *Concerto for Violin and Orchestra, The Confidence Man, Music for the Magic Theater, Octet, String Quartet No. 4, String Quartet No. 5, String Quartet No. 6, String Quartet No. 7.*

n.a. "Rochberg: *String Quartet No. 3*," *Consumers Digest* XII/6 (November–December 1973) 13.

TYPE: record review.

PERFORMERS: Concord String Quartet.

NAMES: Beethoven, Mahler, Schönberg.

n.a. "Rochberg: *String Quartet No. 3*," *Consumers Reports* (January 1974) 95.

TYPE: record review.

PERFORMERS: Concord String Quartet.

NAMES: Beethoven, Mahler, Sibelius, Schönberg.

Rockwell, John. "What's New?," *High Fidelity/Musical America* XXIV/1 (January 1974) MA-10, MA-11, MA-32.

TYPE: article.

NAMES: Beethoven, Mahler, Robert P. Morgan.

Saal, Hubert. "Evangelistic Strings," *Newsweek* LXXXVII/13 (29 March 1976) 97-98.

TYPE: article, review.

PERFORMERS: Concord String Quartet.

OTHER WORKS DISCUSSED: *Quintet for Piano and String Quartet.*

Sargeant, Winthrop. "Concert Records: Wholesale and Retail," *The New Yorker* (21 January 1974) 74-78.

TYPE: record review.

PERFORMERS: Concord String Quartet.

NAMES: Beethoven, Mahler.

Schaphorst, Kenneth W. "The *Third String Quartet* of George Rochberg," Unpublished paper, Swarthmore College (25 May 1981) 16pp.

TYPE: term paper, interview.

Segal, Lewis. "Monday Evening Bing Concert," *The Los Angeles Times* (19 November 1975) IV, 19.

TYPE: review.

PERFORMERS: Arraiga String Quartet.

NAMES: Bartók, Beethoven, Mahler.

Shuster, Lewis. "Rochberg Befriended in Alternate Review," *The Phoenix* (05 October 1973) 2.

TYPE: review.

PERFORMERS: Concord String Quartet.

NAMES: Barber.

Siegel, Sol Louis. "Rochberg: Classic Opinion," *Electricity* (06–12 August 1981) 5.

TYPE: review, interview.

PERFORMERS: Concord String Quartet.

OTHER WORKS DISCUSSED: *Concerto for Violin and Orchestra, Quintet for Piano and String Quartet.*

Simon, Jeff. "This is About an Avant-Garde Recording that Runs Wild Sometimes, or Soft, and Includes the Works of UB [University of Buffalo] Composers . . . Lejaren Hiller . . . Morton Feldman," *The Buffalo Evening News* (18 August 1973) B9.

TYPE: article.

NAMES: Beethoven, Norman Brown, Ives, Mahler, Schönberg, Stravinsky.

Simon, Richard. "Modern Dance Finally Makes It, So Do Viewers," *The Sacramento Union* (24 February 1974) A-14.

TYPE: review.

PERFORMERS: Sacramento Ballet Company.

NAMES: Tance Johnson.

Stacey, Truman. "Jazz Based Suites Recorded," *The Lake Charles American Press [Lake Charles, LA]* (08 December 1973) FOCUS, 6.

TYPE: record review.

PERFORMERS: Concord String Quartet.

NAMES: Beethoven, Mahler.

Steinberg, Michael. "Opening Shriek Drives some from Hall: Fromm Free Program Intense, Almost Violent," *The Boston Globe* (06 November 1972) 23.

TYPE: review.

PERFORMERS: Concord String Quartet.

NAMES: Bartók, Beethoven, Bernstein, Mahler.

OTHER WORKS DISCUSSED: *Contra Mortem et Tempus.*

Steinberg, Michael. "Leaning on Unearned Income," *The Boston Globe* (27 March 1975) 24.

TYPE: review.

NAMES: Beethoven, Britten, Mahler, Schönberg.

OTHER WORKS DISCUSSED: *Concerto for Violin and Orchestra, Ricordanza.*

Thorne, Michael. "Rochberg: *Contra Mortem et Tempus,*" *HiFiNews* (December 1975).

TYPE: review.

OTHER WORKS DISCUSSED: *Contra Mortem et Tempus.*

Tircuit, Heuwell. "At the Symphony: *Violin Concerto* About Concertos," *The San Francisco Chronicle* (09 May 1975) 46.

TYPE: review.

NAMES: Beethoven, Mahler.

OTHER WORKS DISCUSSED: *Concerto for Violin and Orchestra, Symphony No. 2.*

Thorne, Michael. "Rochberg: *String Quartet No. 3,*" *HiFiNews* XIX/7 (July 1974) 109.

TYPE: record review.

PERFORMERS: Concord String Quartet.

NAMES: Brahms.

Tircuit, Heuwell. "The Avant-Grade Returns to Keys," *The San Francisco Chronicle* (03 July 1973) 38.

TYPE: record review.

PERFORMERS: Concord String Quartet.

NAMES: Bartók, Boulez.

Tircuit, Heuwell. "Concord String Quartet: Salaams for Very Young Group," *The San Fransisco Chronicle* (20 July 1973) 47.

TYPE: record review.

PERFORMERS: Concord String Quartet.

NAMES: Bartók, Beethoven, Dvorak, Mahler.

Trotter, Herman. "Records: Classical: Rochberg Strikes a Happy Modern Medium," *The Buffalo News* (09 October 1981) 36.

TYPE: record review.

OTHER WORKS DISCUSSED: *Quintet for Piano and String Quartet, String Quartet No. 4, Trio [No. 1] for Violin, Cello, and Piano.*

Tucker, Marilyn. "Composer Won't be the Messiah," *The San Francisco Chronicle* (08 May 1975) 47.

TYPE: review.

PERFORMERS: Concord String Quartet.

OTHER WORKS DISCUSSED: *Concerto for Violin and Orchestra.*

Turok, Paul. "Alice Tully Hall," *Music Journal* XXX/8 (October 1972) 60.

TYPE: review.

PERFORMERS: Concord String Quartet.

NAMES: Bartók, Beethoven, Mahler.

Valdes, Lesley. "A Birthday Salute to Rochberg," *The Philadelphia Inquirer* (17 April 1988) 1-L, 10-L.

TYPE: upcoming performance, article, interview.

NAMES: Beethoven.

OTHER WORKS DISCUSSED: *Duo Concertante, Serenata d'estate, Slow Fires of Autumn, To the Dark Wood, Trio [No. 2] for Violin, Cello, and Piano.*

OTHER WORKS MENTIONED: *Concerto for Violin and Orchestra, Sonata for Violin and Piano, Symphony No. 5, Symphony No. 6.*

Walsh, Michael. "Follow this Record for Direction in Contemporary Composition," *The Rochester Democrat and Chronicle [Rochester, NY]* (06 January 1974) 11-E.

TYPE: record review.

PERFORMERS: Concord String Quartet.

Walsh, Michael. "Kronos Quartet Passes the Test," *The San Francisco Examiner* (28 March 1980) 31.

TYPE: review.

PERFORMERS: Kronos String Quartet.

NAMES: Bartók.

OTHER WORKS DISCUSSED: *Concerto for Violin and Orchestra, String Quartet No. 2, String Quartet No. 4, String Quartet No. 5, String Quartet No. 6.*

Walsh, Michael. "New Music We Should Know and Love," *The Rochester Democrat and Chronicle [Rochester, NY]* (13 October 1974) 1-H, 4-H.

TYPE: review.

OTHER WORKS DISCUSSED: *Caprice Variations, Serenata d'estate.*

Walsh, Michael. "Zeitlin Opens Concert Seasons," *The Rochester Democrat and Chronicle [Rochester, NY]* (20 September 1974) 4C.

TYPE: review.

OTHER WORKS DISCUSSED: *Caprice Variations.*

Webster, Daniel. "A Quartet Will Ring Out the Old by Stringing in the New," *The Philadephia Inquirer* (03 January 1982).

TYPE: @FOLLOWER = review.

PERFORMERS: Concord String Quartet.

OTHER WORKS DISCUSSED: *The Confidence Man, Quintet for String Quintet, String Quartet No. 4, String Quartet No. 5, String Quartet No. 6.*

Webster, Daniel. "Impressive Musical Debut Offered by Chamber Groups," *The Philadelphia Inquirer* (19 February 1973) 9-A.

TYPE: review.

PERFORMERS: Concord String Quartet.

NAMES: Beethoven, Brahms.

OTHER WORKS DISCUSSED: *Symphony No. 3.*

Willis, Thomas. "Music: Past Becomes Powerful Now," *The Chicago Tribune* (04 March 1974) II, 18.

TYPE: review.

PERFORMERS: Concord String Quartet.

NAMES: Bartók, Beethoven, Mahler.

Wood, Hugh. "Thoughts on a Modern *Quartet*," *Tempo* CXI (December 1974) 23-26.

TYPE: article.

NAMES: Bartók, Beethoven, Ives, Mahler, Schönberg, Stravinsky, Webern.

String Quartet No. 4, *"The Concord Quartets"*

Bargreen, Melinda. "Music: Concord's Success Is Spectacular," *The Seattle Times* (29 October 1980) B11.

TYPE: upcoming performance.

PERFORMERS: Concord String Quartet.

OTHER WORKS DISCUSSED: *String Quartet No. 5*, *String Quartet No. 6*.

Blaustein, Susan. "The Survival of Aesthetics: Books by Boulez, DeLio, Rochberg," *Perspectives of New Music* XVII/1 (Winter 1989) 272-303.

TYPE: article, review.

OTHER WORKS DISCUSSED: *String Quartet No. 3*, *String Quartet No. 5*, *String Quartet No. 6*.

BOOKS DISCUSSED: *The Aesthetics of Survival*.

Block, Steven D. "George Rochberg—Progressive or Master Forger?" *Perspectives of New Music* XXI/1-2 (Fall-Winter 1982/ Spring-Summer 1983) 407-409.

TYPE: article.

NAMES: Bartók, Beethoven, Haydn, Mahler, Jay Reise, Schubert.

OTHER WORKS DISCUSSED: *String Quartet No. 3*, *String Quartet No. 5*, *String Quartet No. 6*.

Bridges, John. "Concord Quartet: Marked by Audacious Energy," *The Tennessean [Nashville, TN]* (05 March 1982) 46.

TYPE: upcoming performance, interview.

PERFORMERS: Concord String Quartet.

OTHER WORKS DISCUSSED: *String Quartet No. 3*, *String Quartet No. 5*, *String Quartet No. 6*.

Brunner, Lance W. "George Rochberg, *The Concord Quartets*," *Notes: The Quarterly Journal of the Music Library Association* XVIII/8 (December 1981) 423-426.

TYPE: score review, article.

NAMES: Ives.

OTHER WORKS DISCUSSED: *String Quartet No. 1, String Quartet No. 2, String Quartet No. 3, String Quartet No. 5, String Quartet No. 6.*

von Buchau, Stephanie. "High Notes: The Five Best Recent Releases," *Esquire* XCVIII/3 (September 1982) 206.

TYPE: review.

PERFORMERS: Concord String Quartet.

NAMES: Beethoven, Berg, Mahler, Mozart, Pachelbel, Schubert, Webern.

OTHER WORKS DISCUSSED: *String Quartet No. 5, String Quartet No. 6.*

Carr, Jay. "Sharing a Sense of Loss with Rochberg," *The Detroit News* (29 January 1980) B5.

TYPE: review.

PERFORMERS: Concord String Quartet.

OTHER WORKS DISCUSSED: *Concerto for Violin and Orchestra, String Quartet No. 3, String Quartet No. 5, String Quartet No. 6, String Quartet No. 7.*

Cera, Stephen. "Concord Quartet Displays Brilliance," *The Sun [Baltimore]* (15 December 1980) B-6.

TYPE: review.

PERFORMERS: Concord String Quartet.

OTHER WORKS DISCUSSED: *String Quartet No. 5, String Quartet No. 6.*

n.a. "Chamber Music Fest to Feature Rochberg," *The Albuquerque Journal* (01 April 1979) D-13.

TYPE: upcoming performances.

PERFORMERS: Concord String Quartet.

OTHER WORKS DISCUSSED: *Duo Concertante, Quintet for Piano and String Quartet, Ricordanza, String Quartet No. 5, String Quartet No. 6.*

n.a. "Composer Rochberg in Santa Fe Chamber Music Festival," *The Los Alamos Monitor [Los Alamos, NM]* (18 April 1979).

TYPE: upcoming performances.

PERFORMERS: Concord String Quartet.

NAMES: Stravinsky.

OTHER WORKS DISCUSSED: *Duo Concertante, Quintet for Piano and String Quartet, Ricordanza, String Quartet No. 5, String Quartet No. 6.*

n.a. "Composer to Join Quartet at Hamilton," *The Observer-Dispatch [Utica, NY]* (17 February 1980).

TYPE: upcoming performance.

PERFORMERS: Concord String Quartet.

OTHER WORKS DISCUSSED: *String Quartet No. 5, String Quartet No. 6.*

n.a. "Concord String Quartet Gets Rave Reviews," *The Dominion-Post [Morgantown, WV]* (17 November 1979).

TYPE: upcoming performance.

PERFORMERS: Concord String Quartet.

OTHER WORKS DISCUSSED: *String Quartet No. 5, String Quartet No. 6.*

n.a. "Contemporary Festival Charts Five-Day Schedule," *The Sunday Oklahoman [Oklahoma City]* (10 February 1980) Leisure, 18.

TYPE: upcoming performance.

PERFORMERS: Concord String Quartet.

OTHER WORKS DISCUSSED: *String Quartet No. 5, String Quartet No. 6.*

Corr, John. "Composer Wins Award," *The Philadelpha Inquirer* (18 September 1979) 6-B.

TYPE: announcement of Freidheim award.

Davis, Peter G. "Two Win American-Music Competition," *The New York Times* (17 September 1979) C-14.

TYPE: review.

PERFORMERS: Concord String Quartet.

OTHER WORKS DISCUSSED: *String Quartet No. 5, String Quartet No. 6.*

Ditsky, John. "Rochberg: *Quartets Nos. 4, 5, and 6,*" *Fanfare* V/5 (May–June 1982) 193-194.

TYPE: record review.

PERFORMERS: Concord String Quartet.

NAMES: Beethoven, Berg, Ives.

OTHER WORKS DISCUSSED: *String Quartet No. 5, String Quartet No. 6.*

Dunning, William. "Records Are Foretaste of Santa Fe Festival," *The Los Alamos Monitor [Los Alamos, NM]* (27 April 1979).

TYPE: record review.

PERFORMERS: Concord String Quartet.

OTHER WORKS DISCUSSED: *Duo Concertante, Ricordanza, Song in Praise of Krishna, String Quartet No. 1, String Quartet No. 5, String Quartet No. 6.*

Dunning, William. "Rochberg Honors Past," *The Los Alamos Monitor [Los Alamos, NM]* (02 August 1979).

TYPE: review, interview.

PERFORMERS: Concord String Quartet.

OTHER WORKS DISCUSSED: *Duo Concertante, Quintet for Piano and String Quartet, Ricordanza, String Quartet No. 5, String Quartet No. 6.*

Dunning, William. "Rochberg Records: Summer Glimpse," *The Santa Fe Reporter* (27 April 1979).

TYPE: record review.

PERFORMERS: Concord String Quartet.

OTHER WORKS DISCUSSED: *Duo Concertante, Ricordanza, Song in Praise of Krishna, String Quartet No. 1, String Quartet No. 5, String Quartet No. 6.*

Dunning, William. "Santa Fe Chamber Music Festival Scheduled," *The Los Alamos Monitor [Los Alamos, NM]* (06 April 1979).

TYPE: upcoming performances.

PERFORMERS: Concord String Quartet.

OTHER WORKS DISCUSSED: *Duo Concertante, Quintet for Piano and String Quartet, Ricordanza, String Quartet No. 5, String Quartet No. 6.*

Dunning, William. "Satisfied Exhilaration," *The Santa Fe Reporter* (02 August 1979).

TYPE: review, interview.

PERFORMERS: Concord String Quartet.

OTHER WORKS DISCUSSED: *The Confidence Man, Quintet for Piano and String Quartet, Ricordanza, String Quartet No. 5, String Quartet No. 6.*

OTHER WORKS MENTIONED: *String Quartet No. 1, String Quartet No. 2, String Quartet No. 3.*

Dwyer, John. "Mary Seaton Room: Concord Quartet Plays Up to Its High Standards," *The Buffalo Evening News* (14 October 1981) B8.

TYPE: review.

PERFORMERS: Concord String Quartet.

OTHER WORKS DISCUSSED: *String Quartet No. 5, String Quartet No. 6.*

Ericson, Raymond. "*The Concord Quartets,*" *The New York Times* (23 January 1979) III, 9.

TYPE: review.

PERFORMERS: Concord String Quartet.

NAMES: Beethoven, Mahler.

OTHER WORKS DISCUSSED: *String Quartet No. 5, String Quartet No. 6.*

Ericson, Raymond. "Rochberg Writes *Quartets* by Threes," *The New York Times* (21 January 1979) II, 15, 28.

TYPE: review, interview.

PERFORMERS: Concord String Quartet.

OTHER WORKS DISCUSSED: *String Quartet No. 5, String Quartet No. 6.*

Felton, James. "Music Beat: Rochberg Composing Opera; Wife Is Librettist," *The Sunday Bulletin [Philadelphia]* (16 July 1978) 2-EA.

TYPE: article, interview.

PERFORMERS: Concord String Quartet.

OTHER WORKS DISCUSSED: *Caprice Variations, Concerto for Violin and Orchestra, Phaedra, String Quartet No. 5, String Quartet No. 6.*

n.a. "Festival's Schedule Busy," *The Norman Transcript [Norman, OK]* (10 February 1980) 21.

TYPE: upcoming performance.

PERFORMERS: Concord String Quartet.

OTHER WORKS DISCUSSED: *String Quartet No. 5, String Quartet No. 6.*

Finn, Robert. "Quartet's New Direction Is in the Old Style," *The Plain Dealer [Cleveland, OH]* (22 February 1979) 1-B, 8-B.

TYPE: review.

PERFORMERS: Concord String Quartet.

NAMES: Beethoven, Brahms, Bruckner, Mahler, Mozart, Schönberg.

OTHER WORKS DISCUSSED: *String Quartet No. 5, String Quartet No. 6.*

Fleming, Shirley. "Concord String Quartet Plays an Evening of George Rochberg," *The New York Post* (23 January 1979) 40.

TYPE: review.

PERFORMERS: Concord String Quartet.

NAMES: Beethoven.

OTHER WORKS DISCUSSED: *String Quartet No. 5, String Quartet No. 6.*

OTHER WORKS MENTIONED: *String Quartet No. 3.*

n.a. "Freidheim Winners to be Broadcast," *The Sun [Baltimore]* (19 September 1979) B, 7.

TYPE: announcement of Freidheim Award.

PERFORMERS: Concord String Quartet.

Gagne, Cole and Tracy Caras. *Soundpieces: Interviews with American Composers*. (Metuchen, NJ: Scarecrow Press, Inc., 1982).

TYPE: interview.

OTHER WORKS DISCUSSED: *Apocalyptica [I], Black Sounds, Concerto for Violin and Orchestra, The Confidence Man, Contra Mortem et Tempus, Electrikaleidoscope, Music for the Magic Theater, Octet, Quintet for Piano and String Quartet, Ricordanza, Sonata No. 2 for Piano Solo, String Quartet No. 3, String Quartet No. 5, String Quartet No. 6, Twelve Bagatelles.*

OTHER WORKS MENTIONED: many.

n.a. "George Rochberg: *Quartets Nos. 4, 5, and 6*," People [Magazine] Weekly (19 April 1982).

TYPE: record review.

PERFORMERS: Concord String Quartet.

NAMES: Mozart, Schubert.

OTHER WORKS DISCUSSED: *String Quartet No. 5, String Quartet No. 6.*

Guinn, John. "Sound Judgement: Classics: Champions of Contemporary Music," *The Detroit Free Press* (21 March 1982) 4G.

TYPE: record review.

PERFORMERS: Concord String Quartet.

NAMES: Mahler.

OTHER WORKS DISCUSSED: *String Quartet No. 5, String Quartet No. 6.*

Hillerman, Anne. "Performances Set," *The The New Mexican [Santa Fe, NM]* (18 July 1979).

TYPE: upcoming performances.

PERFORMERS: Concord String Quartet.

OTHER WORKS DISCUSSED: *Quintet for Piano and String Quartet, String Quartet No. 5, String Quartet No. 6.*

Kupferberg, Herbert. "The Concord Quartet Embarks Upon Its Second Decade," *Ovation* III/11 (December 1982) 12-13, 36.

TYPE: review, interview with the Concord String Quartet.

PERFORMERS: Concord String Quartet.

OTHER WORKS DISCUSSED: *Quintet for String Quintet, String Quartet No. 5, String Quartet No. 6.*

Kupferberg, Herbert. "A Ring of *Quartets* to Crown a Jubilee," *The Detroit News* (28 January 1979) 4G.

TYPE: interview with George Rochberg and the Concord String Quartet.

PERFORMERS: Concord String Quartet.

OTHER WORKS DISCUSSED: *String Quartet No. 5, String Quartet No. 6.*

La Fave, Kenneth. "Music Scene: Composer George Rochberg: Melody Above the Storm," *The Chicago Tribune* (28 April 1988).

TYPE: article, interview.

NAMES: Beethoven, Haydn.

OTHER WORKS DISCUSSED: *Concerto for Violin and Orchestra, Night Music, String Quartet No. 5, String Quartet No. 6, Symphony No. 1, Symphony No. 6.*

Lange, Art. "Rochberg: *Quintet*," *American Record Guide* XLV/3 (December 1981) 24-25.

TYPE: record review.

NAMES: Haydn, Mozart.

OTHER WORKS DISCUSSED: *Concerto for Violin and Orchestra, Music for the Magic Theater, Quintet for Piano and String Quartet, String Quartet No. 2, String Quartet No. 3, String Quartet No. 5, String Quartet No. 6.*

Libby, Theodore W., Jr. "The Concord Quartets," *The Washington Star [Washington, D.C.]* (13 March 1981) D2.

TYPE: upcoming performance.

PERFORMERS: Concord String Quartet.

NAMES: Beethoven.

OTHER WORKS DISCUSSED: *String Quartet No. 5, String Quartet No. 6.*

Libby, Theodore W., Jr. "Music About Music," *The Washington Star [Washington, D.C..]* (14 March 1981).

TYPE: review.

PERFORMERS: Concord String Quartet.

NAMES: Beethoven, Berg, Mahler.

OTHER WORKS DISCUSSED: *String Quartet No. 5, String Quartet No. 6.*

McCoy, W. U. " A View from the Audience," *The Sunday Oklahoman [Oklahoma City]* (10 February 1980) Leisure, 2.

TYPE: upcoming performance.

PERFORMERS: Concord String Quartet.

OTHER WORKS DISCUSSED: *String Quartet No. 5, String Quartet No. 6.*

McCoy, W. U. "Musical Pinnacle Reached," *The Saturday Oklahoman and Times [Oklahoma City]* (16 February 1980) 36.

TYPE: upcoming performance.

PERFORMERS: Concord String Quartet.

OTHER WORKS DISCUSSED: *String Quartet No. 5, String Quartet No. 6.*

Moore, David W. "Rochberg: *String Quartet Nos. 4, 5, & 6,*" *American Record Guide* XLV/9 (July–August 1982) 28-29.

TYPE: record review.

PERFORMERS: Concord String Quartet.

NAMES: Beethoven.

OTHER WORKS DISCUSSED: *String Quartet No. 5, String Quartet No. 6.*

n.a. "Name: George Rochberg," *Music Journal* XXXVII/7 (November–December 1979) 39.

TYPE: announcement of Freidheim Award.

Owens, David. "Turning from Twelve-Tone: Inside Twentieth-Century Music," *The Christian Science Monitor* (03 May 1984) 39.

TYPE: article.

PERFORMERS: Concord String Quartet.

OTHER WORKS DISCUSSED: *Concerto for Violin and Orchestra, String Quartet No. 5, String Quartet No. 6, Symphony No. 1, Symphony No. 2.*

Page, Tim. "Apostate Modernist," *The New York Times Magazine* (29 May 1983) 24-25.

TYPE: article.

NAMES: Bartók, Beethoven, Haydn, Mahler, Mozart, Schönberg.

OTHER WORKS DISCUSSED: *String Quartet No. 3, String Quartet No. 5, String Quartet No. 6.*

Page, Tim. "Music Notes: Concord Disbanding," *The New York Times* (18 January 1987) II, 23 & 26.

TYPE: article.

PERFORMERS: Concord String Quartet.

OTHER WORKS DISCUSSED: *String Quartet No. 3, String Quartet No. 5, String Quartet No. 6.*

Porter, Andrew. "Musical Events: Questions," The New Yorker (12 February 1979) 109-115.

TYPE: article, review.

PERFORMERS: Concord String Quartet.

NAMES: Berg.

OTHER WORKS DISCUSSED: *Concerto for Violin and Orchestra, Duo Concertante, Music for the Magic Theater, Ricordanza, String Quartet No. 1, String Quartet No. 2, String Quartet No. 3, String Quartet No. 5, String Quartet No. 6.*

von Rhein, John. "Music: The 'Concord' Debut to Mark a Return to the Romantic," *The Chicago Tribune* (20 January 1980) VI, 23.

TYPE: article, interview.

PERFORMERS: Concord String Quartet.

OTHER WORKS DISCUSSED: *Concerto for Violin and Orchestra, The Confidence Man, Music for the Magic Theater, Octet, String Quartet No. 3, String Quartet No. 5, String Quartet No. 6, String Quartet No. 7.*

n.a. "Rochberg: Fundamentally Affirmative," *The Silver City Daily Press [Silver City, NM]* (05 April 1979).

TYPE: upcoming performances, article.

PERFORMERS: Concord String Quartet, Alan Marks, George Rochberg.

OTHER WORKS DISCUSSED: *Duo Concertante, Quintet for Piano and String Quartet, Ricordanza, String Quartet No. 5, String Quartet No. 6.*

Roosevelt, Oliver. "Concord Ranks with Very Best," *The Birmingham News [Birmingham, AL]* (01 March 1982) 7A.

TYPE: review.

PERFORMERS: Concord String Quartet.

NAMES: Beethoven, Brahms, Mahler, Ravel.

Saal, Hubert. "Rochberg's Rebirth," *Newsweek* XCIII/8 (19 February 1979) 70, 73, 73C.

TYPE: article, interview.

PERFORMERS: Concord String Quartet.

OTHER WORKS DISCUSSED: *String Quartet No. 5, String Quartet No. 6.*

OTHER WORKS MENTIONED: *Concerto for Violin and Orchestra, String Quartet No. 3.*

Salzman, Eric. "Stereo Review's Selection of Recordings of Special Merit: Best of the Month: Rochberg: *String Quartets Nos. 4, 5, and 6," Stereo Review* XLVII/9 (September 1982) 80-81.

TYPE: record review.

PERFORMERS: Concord String Quartet.

NAMES: Bartók, Beethoven, Mahler, Schönberg, Schubert.

OTHER WORKS DISCUSSED: *String Quartet No. 5, String Quartet No. 6.*

Schonberg, Harold C. "Chamber Music Festival Praised," *The Gallup New Mexico Independent* (02 August 1979) 21.

TYPE: review.

PERFORMERS: Concord String Quartet.

NAMES: Bartók, Beethoven, Franck, Haydn, Mahler, Schönberg, Schubert.

OTHER WORKS DISCUSSED: *String Quartet No. 5, String Quartet No. 6.*

Schonberg, Harold C. "Music: Chamber Music Society in New Rochberg *Octet," The New York Times* (27 April 1980) 68.

TYPE: review.

PERFORMERS: Concord String Quartet.

OTHER WORKS DISCUSSED: *String Quartet No. 5, String Quartet No. 6.*

Schonberg, Harold C. "Music: Santa Fe Chamber Festival Attains Big Time," *The New York Times* (31 July 1979) III, 8.

TYPE: review.

PERFORMERS: Concord String Quartet.

NAMES: Bartók, Beethoven, Franck, Haydn, Mahler, Schönberg, Schubert.

OTHER WORKS DISCUSSED: *String Quartet No. 5, String Quartet No. 6.*

Smith, Patrick. "New York: Concord String Quartet: Henze *Quartet No. 3," High Fidelity/Musical America* XXXII/8 (August 1982) MA-26.

TYPE: review.

PERFORMERS: Concord String Quartet.

OTHER WORKS DISCUSSED: *String Quartet No. 5, String Quartet No. 6.*

Smith, Tim. "Concord String Quartet," *The Washington Post [Washington, D.C.]* (17 March 1981) B2.

TYPE: review.

PERFORMERS: Concord String Quartet.

OTHER WORKS DISCUSSED: *String Quartet No. 5, String Quartet No. 6.*

n.a. *"String Quartets Nos. 4, 5, 6,"* The American String Teacher XXX/3 (Summer 1980) 48.

TYPE: score review.

PERFORMERS: Concord String Quartet.

OTHER WORKS DISCUSSED: *String Quartet No. 5, String Quartet No. 6.*

Toms, John. "Concord Quartet Plays Faultlessly," *The Tulsa Tribune* (28 April 1982) 9B.

TYPE: record review.

PERFORMERS: Concord String Quartet.

OTHER WORKS DISCUSSED: *Quintet for Piano and String Quartet, String Quartet No. 5, String Quartet No. 6.*

Trotter, Herman. "Records: Classical: Rochberg Strikes a Happy Modern Medium," *The Buffalo News* (09 October 1981) 36.

TYPE: upcoming performance.

OTHER WORKS DISCUSSED: *Quintet for Piano and String Quartet, String Quartet No. 3, Trio [No. 1] for Violin, Cello, and Piano.*

Trotter, Herman. "Records: Classical: *The Three Concord Quartets* Best Exemplify George Rochberg's Return to Tonal Composition," *The Buffalo News* (04 June 1982) Gusto, 29.

TYPE: record review.

PERFORMERS: The Concord String Quartet.

NAMES: Beethoven, Haydn.

OTHER WORKS DISCUSSED: *Slow Fires of Autumn, String Quartet No. 5, String Quartet No. 6.*

Warren, Jill. "Concord Celebrates Its Tenth Year," *The Indianapolis Star* (14 March 1982) VIII, 5.

TYPE: record review.

PERFORMERS: Concord String Quartet.

NAMES: Bartók, Beethoven, Mahler, Mozart, Schönberg, Schubert.

OTHER WORKS DISCUSSED: *String Quartet No. 5, String Quartet No. 6.*

Webster, Daniel. "On the Changing Rhythms in the Life of a Composer," *The Philadelphia Inquirer* (16 January 1979) D1, D3.

TYPE: article, interview, upcoming performance.

PERFORMERS: Concord String Quartet.

OTHER WORKS DISCUSSED: *Concerto for Violin and Orchestra, The Confidence Man, Slow Fires of Autumn, String Quartet No. 5, String Quartet No. 6.*

Webster, Daniel. "Philadelphia: Concord String Quartet: Three Premières by George Rochberg," *High Fidelity/Musical America* XXIX/5 (May 1979) MA-29, MA-30.

TYPE: review.

PERFORMERS: Concord String Quartet.

OTHER WORKS DISCUSSED: *String Quartet No. 5, String Quartet No. 6.*

Webster, Daniel. "A Quartet Will Ring Out the Old by Stringing in the New," *The Philadephia Inquirer* (03 January 1982).

TYPE: review.

PERFORMERS: Concord String Quartet.

OTHER WORKS DISCUSSED: *The Confidence Man, Quintet for String Quintet, String Quartet No. 3, String Quartet No. 5, String Quartet No. 6.*

Webster, Daniel. "Rochberg's *Concord Quartets*: Three Compelling Compositions," *The Philadelphia Inquirer* (22 January 1979) 3-A.

TYPE: review.

PERFORMERS: Concord String Quartet.

OTHER WORKS DISCUSSED: *String Quartet No. 5, String Quartet No. 6.*

String Quartet No. 5, "The Concord Quartets"

Bargreen, Melinda. "Music: Concord's Success Is Spectacular," *The Seattle Times* (29 October 1980).

TYPE: upcoming performance.

PERFORMERS: Concord String Quartet.

OTHER WORKS DISCUSSED: *String Quartet No. 4, String Quartet No. 6.*

Blaustein, Susan. "The Survival of Aesthetics: Books by Boulez, DeLio, Rochberg," *Perspectives of New Music* XVII/1 (Winter 1989) 272-303.

TYPE: article, review.

OTHER WORKS DISCUSSED: *String Quartet No. 3, String Quartet No. 4, String Quartet No. 6.*

BOOKS DISCUSSED: *The Aesthetics of Survival.*

Block, Steven D. "George Rochberg—Progressive or Master Forger?" *Perspectives of New Music* XXI/1-2 (Fall-Winter 1982/Spring Summer 1983) 407-409.

TYPE: article.

NAMES: Bartók, Beethoven, Haydn, Mahler, Jay Reise, Schubert.

OTHER WORKS DISCUSSED: *String Quartet No. 3, String Quartet No. 4, String Quartet No. 6.*

Bridges, John. "Concord Quartet: Marked by Audacious Energy," *The Tennessean [Nashville, TN]* (05 March 1982) 46.

TYPE: upcoming performance, interview.

PERFORMERS: Concord String Quartet.

OTHER WORKS DISCUSSED: *String Quartet No. 3, String Quartet No. 4, String Quartet No. 6.*

Brunner, Lance W. "George Rochberg, *The Concord Quartets,*" *Notes: The Quarterly Journal of the Music Library Association* XVIII/8 (December 1981) 423-426.

TYPE: score review, article.

OTHER WORKS DISCUSSED: *String Quartet No. 1, String Quartet No. 2, String Quartet No. 3, String Quartet No. 4, String Quartet No. 6.*

von Buchau, Stephanie. "High Notes: The Five Best Recent Releases," *Esquire* XCVIII/3 (September 1982) 206.

TYPE: review.

PERFORMERS: Concord String Quartet.

NAMES: Beethoven, Berg, Mahler, Mozart, Pachelbel, Schubert, Webern.

OTHER WORKS DISCUSSED: *String Quartet No. 4, String Quartet No. 5.*

Carr, Jay. "Sharing a Sense of Loss with Rochberg," *The Detroit News* (29 January 1980) B5.

TYPE: review.

PERFORMERS: Concord String Quartet.

OTHER WORKS DISCUSSED: *Concerto for Violin and Orchestra, String Quartet No. 3, String Quartet No. 4, String Quartet No. 6, String Quartet No. 7.*

Cera, Stephen. "Concord Quartet Displays Brilliance," *The Sun [Baltimore]* (15 December 1980) B-6.

TYPE: review.

PERFORMERS: Concord String Quartet.

NAMES: Mahler.

OTHER WORKS DISCUSSED: *String Quartet No. 4, String Quartet No. 6.*

n.a. "Chamber Music Fest to Feature Rochberg," *The Albuquerque Journal* (01 April 1979) D-13.

TYPE: upcoming performances.

PERFORMERS: Concord String Quartet.

OTHER WORKS DISCUSSED: *Duo Concertante, Quintet for Piano and String Quartet, Ricordanza, String Quartet No. 4, String Quartet No. 6.*

n.a. "Composer Rochberg in Santa Fe Chamber Music Festival," *The Los Alamos Monitor [Los Alamos, NM]* (18 April 1979).

TYPE: upcoming performances.

PERFORMERS: Concord String Quartet.

NAMES: Stravinsky.

OTHER WORKS DISCUSSED: *Duo Concertante, Quintet for Piano and String Quartet, Ricordanza, String Quartet No. 4, String Quartet No. 6.*

n.a. "Composer to Join Quartet at Hamilton," *The Observer-Dispatch [Utica, NY]* (17 February 1980).

TYPE: upcoming performance.

PERFORMERS: Concord String Quartet.

OTHER WORKS DISCUSSED: *String Quartet No. 4, String Quartet No. 6.*

n.a. "Concord String Quartet Gets Rave Reviews," *The Dominion-Post [Morgantown, WV]* (17 November 1979).

TYPE: upcoming performance.

PERFORMERS: Concord String Quartet.

OTHER WORKS DISCUSSED: *String Quartet No. 4, String Quartet No. 6.*

n.a. "Contemporary Festival Charts Five-Day Schedule," *The Sunday Oklahoman [Oklahoma City]* (10 February 1980) Leisure, 18.

TYPE: upcoming performance.

PERFORMERS: Concord String Quartet.

OTHER WORKS DISCUSSED: *String Quartet No. 4, String Quartet No. 6.*

Davis, Peter G. "Two Win American-Music Competition," *The New York Times* (17 September 1979) C-14.

TYPE: review.

PERFORMERS: Concord String Quartet.

OTHER WORKS DISCUSSED: *String Quartet No. 4, String Quartet No. 6.*

Ditsky, John. "Rochberg: *Quartets Nos. 4, 5, and 6*," *Fanfare* V/5 (May–June 1982) 193-194.

TYPE: record review.

PERFORMERS: Concord String Quartet.

NAMES: Beethoven, Ives.

OTHER WORKS DISCUSSED: *String Quartet No. 4, String Quartet No. 6.*

Dunning, William. "Records Are Foretaste of Santa Fe Festival," *The Los Alamos Monitor [Los Alamos, NM]* (27 April 1979).

TYPE: record review.

PERFORMERS: Concord String Quartet.

OTHER WORKS DISCUSSED: *Duo Concertante, Ricordanza, Song in Praise of Krishna, String Quartet No. 1, String Quartet No. 4, String Quartet No. 6.*

Dunning, William. "Rochberg Honors Past," *The Los Alamos Monitor [Los Alamos, NM]* (02 August 1979).

TYPE: review, interview.

PERFORMERS: Concord String Quartet.

OTHER WORKS DISCUSSED: *Duo Concertante, Quintet for Piano and String Quartet, Ricordanza, String Quartet No. 4, String Quartet No. 6.*

Dunning, William. "Rochberg Records: Summer Glimpse," *The Santa Fe Reporter* (27 April 1979).

TYPE: record review.

PERFORMERS: Concord String Quartet.

OTHER WORKS DISCUSSED: *Duo Concertante, Ricordanza, Song in Praise of Krishna, String Quartet No. 1, String Quartet No. 4, String Quartet No. 6.*

Dunning, William. "Santa Fe Chamber Music Festival Scheduled," *The Los Alamos Monitor [Los Alamos, NM]* (06 April 1979).

TYPE: upcoming performances.

PERFORMERS: Concord String Quartet.

OTHER WORKS DISCUSSED: *Duo Concertante, Quintet for Piano and String Quartet, Ricordanza, String Quartet No. 4, String Quartet No. 6.*

Dunning, William. "Satisfied Exhilaration," *The Santa Fe Reporter* (02 August 1979).

TYPE: review, interview.

PERFORMERS: Concord String Quartet.

OTHER WORKS DISCUSSED: *The Confidence Man, Quintet for Piano and String Quartet, Ricordanza, String Quartet No. 4, String Quartet No. 6.*

OTHER WORKS MENTIONED: *String Quartet No. 1, String Quartet No. 2, String Quartet No. 3.*

Dwyer, John. "Mary Seaton Room: Concord Quartet Plays Up to Its High Standards," *The Buffalo Evening News* (14 October 1981) B8.

TYPE: review.

PERFORMERS: Concord String Quartet.

OTHER WORKS DISCUSSED: *String Quartet No. 4, String Quartet No. 6.*

Ericson, Raymond. "*The Concord Quartets*," *The New York Times* (23 January 1979) III, 9.

TYPE: review.

PERFORMERS: Concord String Quartet.

NAMES: Beethoven, Mahler.

OTHER WORKS DISCUSSED: *String Quartet No. 4, String Quartet No. 6.*

Ericson, Raymond. "Rochberg Writes *Quartets* by Threes," *The New York Times* (21 January 1979) II, 15, 28.

TYPE: review, interview.

PERFORMERS: Concord String Quartet.

OTHER WORKS DISCUSSED: *String Quartet No. 4, String Quartet No. 6.*

Felton, James. "Music Beat: Rochberg Composing Opera; Wife Is Librettist," *The Sunday Bulletin [Philadelphia]* (16 July 1978) 2-EA.

TYPE: article, interview.

PERFORMERS: Concord String Quartet.

OTHER WORKS DISCUSSED: *Caprice Variations, Phaedra, String Quartet No. 4, String Quartet No. 6.*

OTHER WORKS MENTIONED: *Concerto for Violin and Orchestra.*

n.a. "Festival's Schedule Busy," *The Norman Transcript [Norman, OK]* (10 February 1980) 21.

TYPE: upcoming performance.

PERFORMERS: Concord String Quartet.

OTHER WORKS DISCUSSED: *String Quartet No. 4, String Quartet No. 6.*

Finn, Robert. "Quartet's New Direction Is in the Old Style," *The Plain Dealer [Cleveland, OH]* (22 February 1979) 1-B, 8-B.

TYPE: review.

PERFORMERS: Concord String Quartet.

NAMES: Beethoven, Brahms, Bruckner, Dvorak, Mahler, Mozart, Schönberg.

OTHER WORKS DISCUSSED: *String Quartet No. 4, String Quartet No. 6.*

Fleming, Shirley. "Concord String Quartet Plays an Evening of George Rochberg," *The New York Post* (23 January 1979) 40.

TYPE: review.

PERFORMERS: Concord String Quartet.

NAMES: Haydn, Mahler.

OTHER WORKS DISCUSSED: *String Quartet No. 4, String Quartet No. 6.*

Gagne, Cole and Tracy Caras. *Soundpieces: Interviews with American Composers.* (Metuchen, NJ: Scarecrow Press, Inc., 1982).

TYPE: interview.

OTHER WORKS DISCUSSED: *Apocalyptica [I], Black Sounds, Concerto for Violin and Orchestra, The Confidence Man, Contra Mortem et Tempus, Electrikaleidoscope, Music for the Magic Theater, Octet, Quintet for Piano and String Quartet, Ricordanza, Sonata No. 2 for Piano Solo, String Quartet No. 3, String Quartet No. 4, String Quartet No. 6, Twelve Bagatelles.*

OTHER WORKS MENTIONED: many.

George, Earl. "Concert Features Quartet, Soprano," *The Syracuse Herald-Journal* (23 April 1979) 7.

TYPE: review.

PERFORMERS: Concord String Quartet.

OTHER WORKS DISCUSSED: *Eleven Songs.*

n.a. "George Rochberg: *Quartets Nos. 4, 5, and 6,*" *People [Magazine] Weekly* (19 April 1982).

TYPE: record review.

PERFORMERS: Concord String Quartet.

NAMES: Mozart, Schubert.

OTHER WORKS DISCUSSED: *String Quartet No. 4, String Quartet No. 6.*

Guinn, John. "Sound Judgement: Classics: Champions of Contemporary Music," *The Detroit Free Press* (21 March 1982) 4G.

TYPE: record review.

PERFORMERS: Concord String Quartet.

NAMES: Haydn.

OTHER WORKS DISCUSSED: *String Quartet No. 4, String Quartet No. 6.*

Hambleton, Ronald. "Composer Shares Beethoven Tradition," *The Toronto Star [Toronto, Canada]* (26 January 1981) D-4.

TYPE: review.

PERFORMERS: Concord String Quartet.

Hillerman, Anne. "Performances Set," *The New Mexican [Santa Fe, NM]* (18 July 1979).

TYPE: upcoming performances.

PERFORMERS: Concord String Quartet.

OTHER WORKS DISCUSSED: *Quintet for Piano and String Quartet, String Quartet No. 4, String Quartet No. 6.*

Kimmelman, Michael. "A Composer Airs His Philosophy," *The Philadelphia Inquirer* (05 September 1985).

TYPE: review.

PERFORMERS: Concord String Quartet.

OTHER WORKS DISCUSSED: *Between Two Worlds.*

Kupferberg, Herbert. "The Concord Quartet Embarks Upon Its Second Decade," *Ovation* III/11 (December 1982) 12-13, 36.

TYPE: review, interview with the Concord String Quartet.

PERFORMERS: Concord String Quartet.

OTHER WORKS DISCUSSED: *Quintet for String Quintet, String Quartet No. 4, String Quartet No. 6.*

Kupferberg, Herbert. "A Ring of Quartets to Crown a Jubilee," *The Detroit News* (28 January 1979) 4G.

TYPE: interview with George Rochberg and the Concord String Quartet.

PERFORMERS: Concord String Quartet.

OTHER WORKS DISCUSSED: *String Quartet No. 4, String Quartet No. 6.*

La Fave, Kenneth. "Music Scene: Composer George Rochberg: Melody Above the Storm," *The Chicago Tribune* (28 April 1988).

TYPE: article, interview.

NAMES: Beethoven, Haydn.

OTHER WORKS DISCUSSED: *Concerto for Violin and Orchestra, Night Music, String Quartet No. 4, String Quartet No. 6, Symphony No. 1, Symphony No. 6.*

Lange, Art. "Rochberg: *Quintet*," *American Record Guide* XLV/3 (December 1981) 24-25.

TYPE: record review.

NAMES: Haydn, Mozart.

OTHER WORKS DISCUSSED: *Concerto for Violin and Orchestra, Music for the Magic Theater, Quintet for Piano and String Quartet, String Quartet No. 2, String Quartet No. 3, String Quartet No. 4, String Quartet No. 6.*

Libby, Theodore W., Jr. "*The Concord Quartets*," *The Washington Star* [Washington, D.C.] (13 March 1981).

TYPE: upcoming performance.

PERFORMERS: Concord String Quartet.

NAMES: Beethoven.

OTHER WORKS DISCUSSED: *String Quartet No. 4, String Quartet No. 6.*

Libby, Theodore W., Jr. "Music About Music," *The Washington Star* [Washington, D.C.] (14 March 1981) D2.

TYPE: review.

PERFORMERS: Concord String Quartet.

NAMES: Beethoven, Mahler, Schubert.

OTHER WORKS DISCUSSED: *String Quartet No. 4, String Quartet No. 6.*

MacClelland, Scott. "Opinion: Reviews: Franciscan Quartet," *Pacific Monthly/Prelude* (February 1989) 50.

TYPE: review.

PERFORMERS: Franciscan String Quartet.

McCoy, W. U. "A View from the Audience," *The Sunday Oklahoman* [Oklahoma City] (10 February 1980) Leisure, 2.

TYPE: upcoming performance.

PERFORMERS: Concord String Quartet.

OTHER WORKS DISCUSSED: *String Quartet No. 4, String Quartet No. 6.*

McCoy, W. U. "Musical Pinnacle Reached," *The Saturday Oklahoman and Times [Oklahoma City]* (16 February 1980) 36.

TYPE: upcoming performance.

PERFORMERS: Concord String Quartet.

OTHER WORKS DISCUSSED: *String Quartet No. 4, String Quartet No. 6.*

Moore, David W. "Rochberg: *String Quartet Nos. 4, 5, & 6,*" *American Record Guide* XLV/9 (July–August 1982) 28-29.

TYPE: record review.

PERFORMERS: Concord String Quartet.

NAMES: Beethoven.

OTHER WORKS DISCUSSED: *String Quartet No. 4, String Quartet No. 6.*

Murphy, Tom. "Review: Chester String Quartet Shines Especially in Rochberg's Piece," *Charleston Daily Mail* (16 January 1984) 6B.

TYPE: review.

PERFORMERS: Chester String Quartet.

Owens, David. "Turning from Twelve-Tone: Inside Twentieth-Century Music," *The Christian Science Monitor* (03 May 1984) 39.

TYPE: article.

PERFORMERS: Concord String Quartet.

OTHER WORKS DISUCSSED: *Concerto for Violin and Orchestra, String Quartet No. 4, String Quartet No. 6, Symphony No. 1, Symphony No. 2.*

Page, Tim. "Apostate Modernist," *The New York Times Magazine* (29 May 1983) 24-25.

TYPE: article.

NAMES: Bartók, Beethoven, Haydn, Mahler, Mozart, Schönberg.

OTHER WORKS DISCUSSED: *String Quartet No. 3, String Quartet No. 4, String Quartet No. 6.*

Page, Tim. "Music Notes: Concord Disbanding," *The New York Times* (18 January 1987) II, 23 & 26.

TYPE: article.

PERFORMERS: Concord String Quartet.

OTHER WORKS DISCUSSED: *String Quartet No. 3, String Quartet No. 4, String Quartet No. 6.*

Porter, Andrew. "Musical Events: Questions," *The New Yorker* (12 February 1979) 109-115.

TYPE: article, review.

PERFORMERS: Concord String Quartet.

NAMES: Beethoven, Haydn, Janacek, Mahler.

OTHER WORKS DISCUSSED: *Concerto for Violin and Orchestra, Duo Concertante, Music for the Magic Theater, Ricordanza, String Quartet No. 1, String Quartet No. 2, String Quartet No. 3, String Quartet No. 4, String Quartet No. 6.*

von Rhein, John. "Music: The 'Concord' Debut to Mark a Return to the Romantic," *The Chicago Tribune* (20 January 1980) VI, 23.

TYPE: article, interview.

PERFORMERS: Concord String Quartet.

OTHER WORKS DISCUSSED: *Concerto for Violin and Orchestra, The Confidence Man, Music for the Magic Theater, Octet, String Quartet No. 3, String Quartet No. 4, String Quartet No. 6, String Quartet No. 7.*

n.a. "Rochberg: Fundamentally Affirmative," *The Silver City Daily Press [Silver City, NM]* (05 April 1979).

TYPE: upcoming performances, article.

PERFORMERS: Concord String Quartet, Alan Marks, George Rochberg.

OTHER WORKS DISCUSSED: *Duo Concertante, Quintet for Piano and String Quartet, Ricordanza, String Quartet No. 4, String Quartet No. 6.*

n.a. "Rochberg Songs: Pilgrim to Perform," *The Syracuse Herald* (15 April 1979) 7.

TYPE: review, upcoming performance.

PERFORMERS: Concord String Quartet.

OTHER WORKS DISCUSSED: *Eleven Songs, Songs in Praise of Krishna.*

Saal, Hubert. "Rochberg's Rebirth," *Newsweek* XCIII/8 (19 February 1979) 70, 73, 73C.

TYPE: article, interview.

PERFORMERS: Concord String Quartet.

OTHER WORKS DISCUSSED: *String Quartet No. 4, String Quartet No. 6.*

Salzman, Eric. "Stereo Review's Selection of Recordings of Special Merit: Best of the Month: Rochberg: *String Quartets Nos. 4, 5, and 6," Stereo Review* XLVII/9 (September 1982) 80-81.

TYPE: record review.

PERFORMERS: Concord String Quartet.

NAMES: Bartók, Beethoven, Mahler, Schönberg, Schubert.

OTHER WORKS DISCUSSED: *String Quartet No. 4, String Quartet No. 6.*

Schonberg, Harold C. "Chamber Music Festival Praised," *The Gallup New Mexico Independent* (02 August 1979) 21.

TYPE: review.

PERFORMERS: Concord String Quartet.

NAMES: Bartók, Beethoven, Franck, Haydn, Mahler, Schönberg, Schubert.

OTHER WORKS DISCUSSED: *String Quartet No. 4, String Quartet No. 6.*

Schonberg, Harold C. "Music: Chamber Music Society in New Rochberg *Octet*," *The New York Times* (27 April 1980) 68.

TYPE: review.

PERFORMERS: Concord String Quartet.

OTHER WORKS DISCUSSED: *String Quartet No. 4, String Quartet No. 6.*

Schonberg, Harold C. "Music: Santa Fe Chamber Festival Attains Big Time," *The New York Times* (31 July 1979) III, 8.

TYPE: review.

PERFORMERS: Concord String Quartet.

NAMES: Bartók, Beethoven, Franck, Haydn, Mahler, Schönberg, Schubert.

OTHER WORKS DISCUSSED: *String Quartet No. 4, String Quartet No. 6.*

Smith, Patrick. "New York: Concord String Quartet: Henze *Quartet No. 3*," *High Fidelity/Musical America* XXXII/8 (August 1982) MA-26.

TYPE: review.

PERFORMERS: Concord String Quartet.

OTHER WORKS DISCUSSED: *String Quartet No. 4, String Quartet No. 6.*

Smith, Tim. "Concord String Quartet," *The Washington Post [Washington, D.C.]* (17 March 1981) B2.

TYPE: review.

PERFORMERS: Concord String Quartet.

OTHER WORKS DISCUSSED: *String Quartet No. 4, String Quartet No. 6.*

n.a. "*String Quartets Nos. 4, 5, 6,*" *The American String Teacher* XXX/3 (Summer 1980) 48.

    TYPE: score review.

    PERFORMERS: Concord String Quartet.

    NAMES: Morton Newman.

    OTHER WORKS DISCUSSED: *String Quartet No. 4, String Quartet No. 6.*

Toms, John. "Concord Quartet Plays Faultlessly," *The Tulsa Tribune* (28 April 1982) 9B.

    TYPE: record review.

    PERFORMERS: Concord String Quartet.

    OTHER WORKS DISCUSSED: *Quintet for Piano and String Quartet, String Quartet No. 4, String Quartet No. 6.*

Trotter, Herman. "Records: Classical: *The Three Concord Quartets* Best Exemplify George Rochberg's Return to Tonal Composition," *The Buffalo News* (04 June 1982) Gusto, 29.

    TYPE: record review.

    PERFORMERS: The Concord String Quartet.

    NAMES: Beethoven, Haydn.

    OTHER WORKS DISCUSSED: *Slow Fires of Autumn, String Quartet No. 4, String Quartet No. 6.*

Warren, Jill. "'Concord' Celebrates Its Tenth Year," *The Indianapolis Star* (14 March 1982) VIII, 5.

    TYPE: record review.

    PERFORMERS: Concord String Quartet.

    NAMES: Bartók, Beethoven, Mahler, Mozart, Schönberg, Schubert.

    OTHER WORKS DISCUSSED: *String Quartet No. 4, String Quartet No. 6.*

Webster, Daniel. "On the Changing Rhythms in the Life of a Composer," *The Philadelphia Inquirer* (16 January 1979) D1, D3.

    TYPE: article, interview, upcoming performance.

    PERFORMERS: Concord String Quartet.

    OTHER WORKS DISCUSSED: *Concerto for Violin and Orchestra, The Confidence Man, Slow Fires of Autumn, String Quartet No. 4, String Quartet No. 6.*

Webster, Daniel. "Philadelphia: Concord String Quartet: Three Premières by George Rochberg," *High Fidelity/Musical America* XXIX/5 (May 1979) MA-29-30.

TYPE: review.

PERFORMERS: Concord String Quartet.

NAMES: Haydn.

OTHER WORKS DISCUSSED: *String Quartet No. 4, String Quartet No. 6.*

Webster, Daniel. "A Quartet Will Ring Out the Old by Stringing in the New," *The Philadephia Inquirer* (03 January 1982).

TYPE: review.

PERFORMERS: Concord String Quartet.

OTHER WORKS DISCUSSED: *The Confidence Man, Quintet for String Quintet, String Quartet No. 3, String Quartet No. 4, String Quartet No. 6.*

Webster, Daniel. "Rochberg's *Concord Quartets*: Three Compelling Compositions," *The Philadelphia Inquirer* (22 January 1979) 3-A.

TYPE: review.

PERFORMERS: Concord String Quartet.

NAMES: Haydn.

OTHER WORKS DISCUSSED: *String Quartet No. 4, String Quartet No. 6.*

String Quartet No. 6, "The Concord Quartets"

Bargreen, Melinda. "Music: Concord's Success Is Spectacular," *The Seattle Times* (29 October 1980).

TYPE: upcoming performance.

PERFORMERS: Concord String Quartet.

OTHER WORKS DISCUSSED: *String Quartet No. 4, String Quartet No. 5.*

Blaustein, Susan. "The Survival of Aesthetics: Books by Boulez, DeLio, Rochberg," *Perspectives of New Music* XVII/1 (Winter 1989) 272-303.

TYPE: article, review.

OTHER WORKS DISCUSSED: *String Quartet No. 3, String Quartet No. 4, String Quartet No. 5.*

BOOKS DISCUSSED: *The Aesthetics of Survival.*

Block, Steven D. "George Rochberg—Progressive or Master Forger?" *Perspectives of New Music* XXI/1-2 (Fall-Winter 1982/Spring-Summer 1983) 407-409.

TYPE: article.

NAMES: Bartók, Beethoven, Haydn, Mahler, Jay Reise, Schubert.

OTHER WORKS DISCUSSED: *String Quartet No. 3, String Quartet No. 4, String Quartet No. 5.*

Bridges, John. "Concord Quartet: Marked by Audacious Energy," *The Tennessean [Nashville, TN]* (05 March 1982) 46.

TYPE: upcoming performance, interview.

PERFORMERS: Concord String Quartet.

OTHER WORKS DISCUSSED: *String Quartet No. 3, String Quartet No. 4, String Quartet No. 5.*

Brunner, Lance W. "George Rochberg, *The Concord Quartets*," *Notes: The Quarterly Journal of the Music Library Association* XVIII/8 (December 1981) 423-426.

TYPE: score review, article.

NAMES: Pachelbel.

OTHER WORKS DISCUSSED: *String Quartet No. 1, String Quartet No. 2, String Quartet No. 3, String Quartet No. 4, String Quartet No. 5.*

von Buchau, Stephanie. "High Notes: The Five Best Recent Releases," *Esquire* XCVIII/3 (September 1982) 206.

TYPE: review.

PERFORMERS: Concord String Quartet.

NAMES: Beethoven, Berg, Mahler, Mozart, Pachelbel, Schubert, Webern.

OTHER WORKS DISCUSSED: *String Quartet No. 4, String Quartet No. 6.*

Carr, Jay. "Sharing a Sense of Loss with Rochberg," *The Detroit News* (29 January 1980) B5.

TYPE: review.

PERFORMERS: Concord String Quartet.

OTHER WORKS DISCUSSED: *Concerto for Violin and Orchestra, String Quartet No. 3, String Quartet No. 4, String Quartet No. 5, String Quartet No. 7.*

Cera, Stephen. "Concord Quartet Displays Brilliance," *The Sun [Baltimore]* (15 December 1980) B-6.

TYPE: review.

PERFORMERS: Concord String Quartet.

OTHER WORKS DISCUSSED: *String Quartet No. 4, String Quartet No. 5.*

n.a. "Chamber Music Fest to Feature Rochberg," *The Albuquerque Journal* (01 April 1979) D-13.

TYPE: upcoming performances.

PERFORMERS: Concord String Quartet.

OTHER WORKS DISCUSSED: *Duo Concertante, Quintet for Piano and String Quartet, Ricordanza, String Quartet No. 4, String Quartet No. 5.*

n.a. "Composer Rochberg in Santa Fe Chamber Music Festival," *The Los Alamos Monitor [Los Alamos, NM]* (18 April 1979).

TYPE: upcoming performances.

PERFORMERS: Concord String Quartet.

NAMES: Stravinsky.

OTHER WORKS DISCUSSED: *Duo Concertante, Quintet for Piano and String Quartet, Ricordanza, String Quartet No. 4, String Quartet No. 5.*

n.a. "Composer to Join Quartet at Hamilton," *The Observer-Dispatch [Utica, NY]* (17 February 1980).

TYPE: upcoming performance.

PERFORMERS: Concord String Quartet.

OTHER WORKS DISCUSSED: *String Quartet No. 4, String Quartet No. 5.*

n.a. "Concord String Quartet Gets Rave Reviews," *The Dominion-Post [Morgantown, WV]* (17 November 1979).

TYPE: upcoming performance.

PERFORMERS: Concord String Quartet.

OTHER WORKS DISCUSSED: *String Quartet No. 4, String Quartet No. 6.*

n.a. "Contemporary Festival Charts Five-Day Schedule," *The Sunday Oklahoman [Oklahoma City]* (10 February 1980) Leisure, 18.

TYPE: upcoming performance.

PERFORMERS: Concord String Quartet.

OTHER WORKS DISCUSSED: *String Quartet No. 4, String Quartet No. 5.*

Davis, Peter G. "Two Win American-Music Competition," *The New York Times* (17 September 1979) C-14.

TYPE: review.

PERFORMERS: Concord String Quartet.

OTHER WORKS DISCUSSED: *String Quartet No. 4, String Quartet No. 5.*

Ditsky, John. "Rochberg: *Quartets Nos. 4, 5, and 6,*" *Fanfare* V/5 (May–June 1982) 193-194.

TYPE: record review.

PERFORMERS: Concord String Quartet.

NAMES: Beethoven, Ives, Pachelbel.

OTHER WORKS DISCUSSED: *String Quartet No. 4, String Quartet No. 5.*

Dunning, William. "Records Are Foretaste of Santa Fe Festival," *The Los Alamos Monitor [Los Alamos, NM]* (27 April 1979).

TYPE: record review.

PERFORMERS: Concord String Quartet.

OTHER WORKS DISCUSSED: *Duo Concertante, Ricordanza, Song in Praise of Krishna, String Quartet No. 1, String Quartet No. 4, String Quartet No. 5.*

Dunning, William. "Rochberg Honors Past," *The Los Alamos Monitor [Los Alamos, NM]* (02 August 1979).

TYPE: review, interview.

PERFORMERS: Concord String Quartet.

OTHER WORKS DISCUSSED: *Duo Concertante, Quintet for Piano and String Quartet, Ricordanza, String Quartet No. 4, String Quartet No. 6.*

Dunning, William. "Rochberg Records: Summer Glimpse," *The Santa Fe Reporter* (27 April 1979).

TYPE: record reviews.

PERFORMERS: Concord String Quartet.

NAMES: Beethoven, Pachelbel.

OTHER WORKS DISCUSSED: *Duo Concertante, Ricordanza, Song in Praise of Krishna, String Quartet No. 1, String Quartet No. 4, String Quartet No. 5.*

Dunning, William. "Santa Fe Chamber Music Festival Scheduled," *The Los Alamos Monitor [Los Alamos, NM]* (06 April 1979).

TYPE: upcoming performances.

PERFORMERS: Concord String Quartet.

OTHER WORKS DISCUSSED: *Duo Concertante, Quintet for Piano and String Quartet, Ricordanza, String Quartet No. 4, String Quartet No. 5.*

Dunning, William. "Satisfied Exhilaration," *The Santa Fe Reporter* (02 August 1979).

TYPE: review, interview.

PERFORMERS: Concord String Quartet.

OTHER WORKS DISCUSSED: *The Confidence Man, Quintet for Piano and String Quartet, Ricordanza, String Quartet No. 4, String Quartet No. 5.*

OTHER WORKS MENTIONED: *String Quartet No. 1, String Quartet No. 2, String Quartet No. 3.*

Ericson, Raymond. "*The Concord Quartets,*" *The New York Times* (23 January 1979) III, 9.

TYPE: review.

PERFORMERS: Concord String Quartet.

NAMES: Beethoven, Mahler.

OTHER WORKS DISCUSSED: *String Quartet No. 4, String Quartet No. 5.*

Ericson, Raymond. "Rochberg Writes *Quartets* by Threes," *The New York Times* (21 January 1979) II, 15, 28.

TYPE: review, interview.

PERFORMERS: Concord String Quartet.

OTHER WORKS DISCUSSED: *String Quartet No. 4, String Quartet No. 5.*

Felton, James. "Music Beat: Rochberg Composing Opera; Wife Is Librettist," *The Sunday Bulletin [Philadelphia]* (16 July 1978) 2-EA.

TYPE: article, interview.

PERFORMERS: Concord String Quartet.

OTHER WORKS DISCUSSED: *Caprice Variations, Phaedra, String Quartet No. 4, String Quartet No. 5.*

OTHER WORKS MENTIONED: *Concerto for Violin and Orchestra.*

n.a. "Festival's Schedule Busy," *The Norman Transcript [Norman, OK]* (10 February 1980) 21.

TYPE: upcoming performance.

PERFORMERS: Concord String Quartet.

OTHER WORKS DISCUSSED: *String Quartet No. 4, String Quartet No. 5.*

Finn, Robert. "Quartet," *The Plain Dealer [Cleveland, OH]* (22 February 1979) 1-B, 8-B.

TYPE: review.

PERFORMERS: Concord String Quartet.

NAMES: Beethoven, Brahms, Bruckner, Mahler, Mozart, Pachelbel, Schönberg.

OTHER WORKS DISCUSSED: *String Quartet No. 4, String Quartet No. 5.*

Fleming, Shirley. "Concord String Quartet Plays an Evening of George Rochberg," *The New York Post* (23 January 1979) 40.

TYPE: review.

PERFORMERS: Concord String Quartet.

NAMES: Beethoven, Mozart.

OTHER WORKS DISCUSSED: *String Quartet No. 4, String Quartet No. 5.*

Gagne, Cole and Tracy Caras. *Soundpieces: Interviews with American Composers.* (Metuchen, NJ: Scarecrow Press, Inc., 1982).

TYPE: interview.

OTHER WORKS DISCUSSED: *Apocalyptica [I], Black Sounds, Concerto for Violin and Orchestra, The Confidence Man, Contra Mortem et Tempus, Electrikaleidoscope, Music for the Magic Theater, Octet, Quintet for Piano and String Quartet, Ricordanza, Sonata No. 2 for Piano Solo, String Quartet No. 3, String Quartet No. 4, String Quartet No. 6, Twelve Bagatelles.*

OTHER WORKS MENTIONED: many.

n.a. "George Rochberg: *Quartets Nos. 4, 5, and 6,*" *People [Magazine] Weekly* (19 April 1982).

TYPE: record review.

PERFORMERS: Concord String Quartet.

NAMES: Beethoven, Mozart, Pachelbel, Schubert.

OTHER WORKS DISCUSSED: *String Quartet No. 4, String Quartet No. 5.*

Guinn, John. "Sound Judgement: Classics: Champions of Contemporary Music," *The Detroit Free Press* (21 March 1982) 4G.

TYPE: record review.

PERFORMERS: Concord String Quartet.

NAMES: Mahler.

OTHER WORKS DISCUSSED: *String Quartet No. 4, String Quartet No. 6.*

Hillerman, Anne. "Performances Set," *The New Mexican [Santa Fe, NM]* (18 July 1979).

TYPE: upcoming performances.

PERFORMERS: Concord String Quartet.

OTHER WORKS DISCUSSED: *Quintet for Piano and String Quartet, String Quartet No. 4, String Quartet No. 5.*

Kupferberg, Herbert. "The Concord Quartet Embarks Upon Its Second Decade," *Ovation* III/11 (December 1982) 12-13, 36.

TYPE: review, interview with the Concord String Quartet.

PERFORMERS: Concord String Quartet.

OTHER WORKS DISCUSSED: *Quintet for String Quintet, String Quartet No. 4, String Quartet No. 5.*

Kupferberg, Herbert. "A Ring of Quartets to Crown a Jubilee," *The Detroit News* (28 January 1979) 4G.

TYPE: interview with George Rochberg and the Concord String Quartet.

PERFORMERS: Concord String Quartet.

OTHER WORKS DISCUSSED: *String Quartet No. 4, String Quartet No. 5.*

La Fave, Kenneth. "Music Scene: Composer George Rochberg: Melody Above the Storm," *The Chicago Tribune* (28 April 1988).

TYPE: article, interview.

NAMES: Beethoven, Haydn.

OTHER WORKS DISCUSSED: *Concerto for Violin and Orchestra, Night Music, String Quartet No. 4, String Quartet No. 5, Symphony No. 1, Symphony No. 6.*

Lange, Art. "Rochberg: Quintet," *American Record Guide* XLV/3 (December 1981) 24-25.

TYPE: record review.

NAMES: Haydn, Mozart.

OTHER WORKS DISCUSSED: *Concerto for Violin and Orchestra, Music for the Magic Theater, Quintet for Piano and String Quartet, String Quartet No. 2, String Quartet No. 3, String Quartet No. 4, String Quartet No. 5.*

Libby, Theodore W., Jr. "The Concord Quartets," *The Washington Star [Washington, D.C.]* (13 March 1981).

TYPE: review.

PERFORMERS: Concord String Quartet.

NAMES: Beethoven.

OTHER WORKS DISCUSSED: *String Quartet No. 4, String Quartet No. 5.*

Libby, Theodore W., Jr. "Music About Music," *The Washington Star [Washington, D.C.]* (14 March 1981) D2.

TYPE: review.

PERFORMERS: Concord String Quartet.

NAMES: Beethoven, Mahler, Pachelbel.

OTHER WORKS DISCUSSED: *String Quartet No. 4, String Quartet No. 5.*

McCoy, W. U. " A View from the Audience," *The Sunday Oklahoman [Oklahoma City]* (10 February 1980) Leisure, 2.

TYPE: upcoming performance.

PERFORMERS: Concord String Quartet.

OTHER WORKS DISCUSSED: *String Quartet No. 4, String Quartet No. 5.*

McCoy, W. U. "Musical Pinnacle Reached," *The Saturday Oklahoman and Times [Oklahoma City]* (16 February 1980) 36.

TYPE: upcoming performance.

PERFORMERS: Concord String Quartet.

OTHER WORKS DISCUSSED: *String Quartet No. 4, String Quartet No. 5.*

Moore, David W. "Rochberg: *String Quartet Nos. 4, 5, & 6,*" *American Record Guide* XLV/9 (July–August 1982) 28-29.

TYPE: record review.

PERFORMERS: Concord String Quartet.

NAMES: Beethoven, Mozart, Pachelbel, Schönberg, Schubert.

OTHER WORKS DISCUSSED: *String Quartet No. 4, String Quartet No. 5.*

Owens, David. "Turning from Twelve-Tone: Inside Twentieth-Century Music," *The Christian Science Monitor* (03 May 1984) 39.

TYPE: article.

PERFORMERS: Concord String Quartet.

OTHER WORKS DISCUSSED: *Concerto for Violin and Orchestra, String Quartet No. 4, String Quartet No. 5, Symphony No. 1, Symphony No. 2.*

Page, Tim. "Apostate Modernist," *The New York Times Magazine* (29 May 1983) 24-25.

TYPE: article.

NAMES: Bartók, Beethoven, Haydn, Mahler, Mozart, Schönberg.

OTHER WORKS DISCUSSED: *String Quartet No. 3, String Quartet No. 4, String Quartet No. 5.*

Page, Tim. "Music Notes: Concord Disbanding," *The New York Times* (18 January 1987) II, 23 & 26.

TYPE: article.

PERFORMERS: Concord String Quartet.

OTHER WORKS DISCUSSED: *String Quartet No. 3, String Quartet No. 4, String Quartet No. 5.*

Porter, Andrew. "Musical Events: Questions," *The New Yorker* (12 February 1979) 109-115.

TYPE: article, review.

PERFORMERS: Concord String Quartet.

NAMES: Berg, Mahler, Pachelbel, Tchaikovsky.

OTHER WORKS DISCUSSED: *Concerto for Violin and Orchestra, Duo Concertante, Music for the Magic Theater, Ricordanza, String Quartet No. 1, String Quartet No. 2, String Quartet No. 3, String Quartet No. 4, String Quartet No. 5.*

von Rhein, John. "Music: The 'Concord' Debut to Mark a Return to the Romantic," *The Chicago Tribune* (20 January 1980) VI, 23.

TYPE: article, interview.

PERFORMERS: Concord String Quartet.

OTHER WORKS DISCUSSED: *Concerto for Violin and Orchestra, The Confidence Man, Music for the Magic Theater, Octet, String Quartet No. 3, String Quartet No. 4, String Quartet No. 5, String Quartet No. 7.*

n.a. "Rochberg: Fundamentally Affirmative," *Silver City Daily Press [Silver City, NM]* (05 April 1979).

TYPE: upcoming performances, article.

PERFORMERS: Concord String Quartet, Alan Marks, George Rochberg.

OTHER WORKS DISCUSSED: *Duo Concertante, Quintet for Piano and String Quartet, Ricordanza, String Quartet No. 4, String Quartet No. 5.*

Saal, Hubert. "Rochberg's Rebirth," *Newsweek* XCIII/8 (19 February 1979) 70, 73, 73C.

TYPE: article, interview.

PERFORMERS: Concord String Quartet.

NAMES: Beethoven, Pachelbel.

OTHER WORKS DISCUSSED: *String Quartet No. 4, String Quartet No. 5.*

Salzman, Eric. "Stereo Review's Selection of Recordings of Special Merit: Best of the Month: Rochberg: *String Quartets Nos. 4, 5, and 6*," *Stereo Review* XLVII/9 (September 1982) 80-81.

TYPE: record review.

PERFORMERS: Concord String Quartet.

NAMES: Bartók, Beethoven, Mahler, Pachelbel, Schönberg, Schubert.

OTHER WORKS DISCUSSED: *String Quartet No. 4, String Quartet No. 5.*

Schonberg, Harold C. "Chamber Music Festival Praised," *The Gallup New Mexico Independent* (02 August 1979) 21.

TYPE: review.

PERFORMERS: Concord String Quartet.

NAMES: Bartók, Beethoven, Franck, Haydn, Mahler, Schönberg, Schubert.

OTHER WORKS DISCUSSED: *String Quartet No. 4, String Quartet No. 5.*

Schonberg, Harold C. "Music: Chamber Music Society in New Rochberg *Octet*," *The New York Times* (27 April 1980) 68.

TYPE: review.

PERFORMERS: Concord String Quartet.

OTHER WORKS DISCUSSED: *String Quartet No. 4, String Quartet No. 5.*

Schonberg, Harold C. "Music: Santa Fe Chamber Festival Attains Big Time," *The New York Times* (31 July 1979) III, 8.

TYPE: review.

PERFORMERS: Concord String Quartet.

NAMES: Bartók, Beethoven, Franck, Haydn, Mahler, Schönberg, Schubert.

OTHER WORKS DISCUSSED: *String Quartet No. 4, String Quartet No. 5.*

Smith, Patrick. "New York: Concord String Quartet: Henze *Quartet No. 3*," *High Fidelity/Musical America* XXXII/8 (August 1982) MA-26.

TYPE: review.

PERFORMERS: Concord String Quartet.

OTHER WORKS DISCUSSED: *String Quartet No. 4, String Quartet No. 5.*

Smith, Tim. "Concord String Quartet," *The Washington Post [Washington, D.C.]* (17 March 1981) B2.

TYPE: review.

PERFORMERS: Concord String Quartet.

NAMES: Pachelbel.

OTHER WORKS DISCUSSED: *String Quartet No. 4, String Quartet No. 5.*

n.a. *"String Quartets Nos. 4, 5, 6,"* The American String Teacher XXX/3 (Summer 1980) 48.

TYPE: score review.

PERFORMERS: Concord String Quartet.

NAMES: Pachelbel, Isaac Stern.

OTHER WORKS DISCUSSED: *String Quartet No. 4, String Quartet No. 5.*

Toms, John. "Concord Quartet Plays Faultlessly," *The Tulsa Tribune* (28 April 1982) 9B.

TYPE: record review.

PERFORMERS: Concord String Quartet.

OTHER WORKS DISCUSSED: *Quintet for Piano and String Quartet, String Quartet No. 4, String Quartet No. 5.*

Trotter, Herman. "Records: Classical: *The Three Concord Quartets* Best Exemplify George Rochberg's Return to Tonal Composition," *The Buffalo News* (04 June 1982) Gusto, 29.

TYPE: record review.

PERFORMERS: The Concord String Quartet.

NAMES: Beethoven, Haydn, Pachelbel.

OTHER WORKS DISCUSSED: *Slow Fires of Autumn, String Quartet No. 4, String Quartet No. 5.*

Warren, Jill. "'Concord' Celebrates Its Tenth Year," *The Indianapolis Star* (14 March 1982) VIII, 5.

TYPE: record review.

PERFORMERS: Concord String Quartet.

NAMES: Bartók, Beethoven, Mahler, Mozart, Schönberg, Schubert.

OTHER WORKS DISCUSSED: *String Quartet No. 4, String Quartet No. 5.*

Webster, Daniel. "On the Changing Rhythms in the Life of a Composer," *The Philadelphia Inquirer* (16 January 1979) D1, D3.

TYPE: article, interview, upcoming performance.

PERFORMERS: Concord String Quartet.

OTHER WORKS DISCUSSED: *Concerto for Violin and Orchestra, The Confidence Man, Slow Fires of Autumn, String Quartet No. 4, String Quartet No. 5.*

Webster, Daniel. "Philadelphia: Concord String Quartet: Three Premiâres by George Rochberg," *High Fidelity/Musical America* XXIX/5 (May 1979) MA-29-30.

TYPE: review.

PERFORMERS: Concord String Quartet.

NAMES: Pachelbel.

OTHER WORKS DISCUSSED: *String Quartet No. 4, String Quartet No. 5*.

Webster, Daniel. "A Quartet Will Ring Out the Old by Stringing in the New," *The Philadephia Inquirer* (03 January 1982).

TYPE: review.

PERFORMERS: Concord String Quartet.

OTHER WORKS DISCUSSED: *The Confidence Man, Quintet for String Quintet, String Quartet No. 3, String Quartet No. 4, String Quartet No. 5*.

Webster, Daniel. "Rochberg's *Concord Quartets*: Three Compelling Compositions," *The Philadelphia Inquirer* (22 January 1979) 3-A.

TYPE: review.

PERFORMERS: Concord String Quartet.

NAMES: Pachelbel.

OTHER WORKS DISCUSSED: *String Quartet No. 4, String Quartet No. 5*.

String Quartet No. 7 with Baritone

Carr, Jay. "Sharing a Sense of Loss with Rochberg," *The Detroit News* (29 January 1980) B5.

TYPE: review.

PERFORMERS: Leslie Guinn, Concord String Quartet.

NAMES: Paul Rochberg.

OTHER WORKS DISCUSSED: *Concerto for Violin and Orchestra, String Quartet No. 3, String Quartet No. 4, String Quartet No. 5, String Quartet No. 6*.

Dyer, Richard. "Concord Quartet Opens Fromm Series," *The Boston Globe* (17 October 1980) 21.

TYPE: review.

PERFORMERS: Leslie Guinn, Concord String Quartet.

NAMES: Prokofiev.

Gilman, J.L. "Rochberg: *String Quartet No. 7*," *American Record Guide* XLVIII/1 (November 1984) 18-19.

TYPE: review.

PERFORMERS: Leslie Guinn, Concord String Quartet.

NAMES: Paul Rochberg.

OTHER WORKS MENTIONED: *Quintet for Piano and String Quartet, String Quartet No. 1, String Quartet No. 3, String Quartet No. 4, String Quartet No. 5, String Quartet No. 6.*

Guregian, Elaine. "Rochberg Work the Highlight," *The Ann Arbor News [Ann Arbor, MI]* (28 January 1980) B-6.

TYPE: review.

PERFORMERS: Leslie Guinn, Concord String Quartet.

NAMES: Paul Rochberg.

Page, Tim. "Recordings: Time Barnishes Barber's *Antony and Cleopatra*," *The New York Times* (04 November 1984) II, 25.

TYPE: record review.

PERFORMERS: Leslie Guinn, Concord String Quartet.

von Rhein, John. "Music: The 'Concord' Debut to Mark a Return to the Romantic," *The Chicago Tribune* (20 January 1980) VI, 23.

TYPE: article, interview.

PERFORMERS: Leslie Guinn, Concord String Quartet.

OTHER WORKS DISCUSSED: *Concerto for Violin and Orchestra, The Confidence Man, Music for the Magic Theater, Octet, String Quartet No. 3, String Quartet No. 4, String Quartet No. 5, String Quartet No. 7.*

n.a. "Rochberg Centennial Commission," *Music at Michigan [University of Michigan, Ann Arbor, MI]* XIII/7 (January 1980) 2.

TYPE: upcoming premiåre.

PERFORMERS: Leslie Guinn, Concord String Quartet.

Simmons, Walter. "Rochberg: *String Quartet No. 7*," *Fanfare* VI/5 (May–June 1983) 92.

TYPE: record review.

PERFORMERS: Leslie Guinn, Concord String Quartet.

NAMES: Berg, Paul Rochberg.

Rockwell, John. "Chamber Music With Few Big Names Fills Concert Halls," *The New York Times* (09 January 1981) III, 1 & 20.

TYPE: upcoming performance.

PERFORMERS: Leslie Guinn, Concord String Quartet.

Sockerson, Edward. "Rochberg: *String Quartet No. 7*," *Classical Music* CCXXV (11 June 1983) 21.

TYPE: review.

PERFORMERS: Leslie Guinn, Concord String Quartet.

Webster, Daniel. "A Rochberg *Quartet* of Poetry, Intensity," *The Philadelphia Inquirer* (12 June 1983) 5-H.

TYPE: record review.

PERFORMERS: Leslie Guinn, Concord String Quartet.

NAMES: Paul Rochberg.

OTHER WORKS DISCUSSED: *String Quartet No. 2.*

OTHER WORKS MENTIONED: *String Quartet No. 4, String Quartet No. 5, String Quartet No. 6.*

Symphony No. 1 for Orchestra

Barrett, Marjorie. "Contemporary Music Concert Well Received," *The Rocky Mountain News [Denver, CO]* (12 November 1958) 68.

TYPE: review.

NAMES: Saul Caston, Denver Symphony Orchestra.

Boros, Ethel. "Pianists Fill Guest Book," *The Cleveland News* (21 February 1959).

TYPE: upcoming performance.

NAMES: George Szell, Cleveland Orchestra.

OTHER WORKS DISCUSSED: *Symphony No. 2.*

Darling, Henry R. "New Courses and Twelve-Tone Composition Put Zip in Penn's [University of Pennsylvania at Philadelphia] Music Department," *The Sunday Bulletin [Philadelphia]* (30 September 1962) 15.

TYPE: article, interview.

PERFORMERS: New York Philharmonic.

OTHER WORKS DISCUSSED: *Night Music.*

OTHER WORKS MENTIONED: *Chamber Symphony, String Quartet No. 1, String Quartet No. 2, Time-Span, Twelve Bagatelles.*

Felton, James. "Composers Are Sane But the World Isn't, Says Penn Rochberg," *The Sunday Bulletin [Philadelphia]* (13 February 1966) 11.

TYPE: interview.

PERFORMERS: Eugene Ormandy, Philadelphia Orchestra, Robert Whitney, Louisville Orchestra.

OTHER WORKS DISCUSSED: *Contra Mortem et Tempus, Music for the Magic Theater, Night Music, String Quartet No. 2, Symphony No. 2, Symphony No. 3, Zodiac.*

Felton, James. "Rochberg's Chamber Music Is Aired at the Art Alliance," *The Evening Bulletin [Philadelphia]* (16 February 1966) 27.

TYPE: review.

NAMES: Webern.

OTHER WORKS DISCUSSED: *La Bocca della Veritá, Contra Mortem et Tempus, Dialogues, Night Music, Symphony No. 2, Trio [No. 1] for Violin, Cello, and Piano.*

Johnson, Harriett. "Words and Music: Ormandy Features Three Premieèes," *The New York Post* (02 April 1958).

TYPE: review.

NAMES: Eugene Ormandy, Philadelphia Orchestra.

Kanny, Mark. "Rochberg Sets Tone for New Composing Style," *The Pittsburgh Post-Gazette* (16 October 1987) Weekend, 2.

TYPE: article.

NAMES: Mahler, Stravinsky.

OTHER WORKS DISCUSSED: *Symphony No. 2.*

Klein, Howard. "Louisville Carries On," *The New York Times* (10 November 1963).

TYPE: record review.

PERFORMERS: Robert Whitney, Louisville Orchestra.

NAMES: Bartók, Schönberg, Stravinsky.

LaFave, Kenneth. "Music Scene: Composer George Rochberg: Melody Above the Storm," *The Chicago Tribune* (28 April 1988).

TYPE: article, interview.

OTHER WORKS DISCUSSED: *Concerto for Violin and Orchestra, Night Music, String Quartet No. 4, String Quartet No. 5, String Quartet No. 6, Symphony No. 6.*

Lang, Paul Henry. "Music: Philadelphia Orchestra," *The New York Herald Tribune* (03 April 1958).

TYPE: review.

PERFORMERS: Eugene Ormandy, Philadelphia Orchestra.

NAMES: Mahler.

Lindstrom, Walt. "Denver Symphony: New Music Wins Warm Response," *The Denver Post* (12 November 1958) 45.

TYPE: review.

PERFORMERS: Saul Creston, Denver Symphony Orchestra.

Milburn, Frank Jr. "Rochberg *Symphony* Played by Philadelphians," *Musical America* LXXVIII/5 (May 1958) 18.

TYPE: review.

PERFORMERS: Eugene Ormandy, Philadelphia Orchestra.

NAMES: Bartók, Schönberg.

Owens, David. "Turning from Twelve-Tone: Inside Twentieth-Century Music," *The Christian Science Monitor* (03 May 1984) 39.

TYPE: article.

PERFORMERS: Robert Whitney, Louisville Orchestra.

OTHER WORKS DISCUSSED: *Concerto for Violin and Orchestra, String Quartet No. 4, String Quartet No. 5, String Quartet No. 6, Symphony No. 2.*

Ringer, Alexander. "Current Chronicle: United States: Cleveland," *Musical Quarterly* XLV/2 (April 1959) 230-234.

TYPE: article, review.

OTHER WORKS DISCUSSED: *Chamber Symphony, David, The Psalmist, Sonata-Fantasia, String Quartet No. 1, Symphony No. 2, Three Psalms, Twelve Bagatelles.*

BOOKS DISCUSSED: *The Hexachord and Its Relation to the Twelve-Tone Row.*

Ringer, Alexander L. "The Music of George Rochberg," *Musical Quarterly* LII/4 (October 1966) 409-430.

TYPE: article.

PERFORMERS: Eugene Ormandy, Philadelphia Orchestra.

NAMES: Bartók, Hindemith, Stravinsky.

OTHER WORKS DISCUSSED: *Apocalyptica [I], Black Sounds, Blake Songs, La Bocca della Veritá, Cantio Sacra, Capriccio for Two Pianos, Chamber Symphony, Cheltenham Concerto, Concert Piece for Two Pianos and Orchestra, Contra Mortem et Tempus, David, the Psalmist, Dialogues, Duo Concertante, Four Songs of Solomon, Music for the Magic Theater, Nach Bach, Night Music, Passions [According to the Twentieth Century], Serenata d'estate, Sonata-Fantasia, String Quartet No. 1, String Quartet No. 2, Symphony No. 2, Three Psalms, Time-Span, Trio for Clarinet, Horn, and Piano, Trio [No. 1] for Violin, Cello, and Piano, Twelve Bagatelles, Zodiac.*

OTHER WORKS MENTIONED: *Arioso, Bartokiana, Five Smooth Stones, Sonata No. 1 for Piano Solo, Sonata No. 2 for Piano Solo, Waltz Serenade.*

BOOKS DISCUSSED: *The Hexachord and Its Relation to the Twelve-Tone Row.*

Roy, Klaus George. "Rochberg's New *Symphony* in Première," *The Christian Science Monitor* (21 March 1959) 10.

TYPE: review.

PERFORMERS: Eugene Ormandy, Philadelphia Orchestra.

OTHER WORKS DISCUSSED: *Symphony No. 2.*

de Schauensee, Max. "The Philadelphia Orchestra: Superb Program Features Première of Three Works," *The Evening Bulletin [Philadelphia]* (29 March 1958) 16.

TYPE: review.

PERFORMERS: Eugene Ormandy, Philadelphia Orchestra.

Schloss, Edwin H. "Philadelphia Orchestra: Three Works Given Première Here," *The Philadelphia Inquirer* (29 March 1958) 11.

TYPE: review.

PERFORMERS: Eugene Ormandy, Philadelphia Orchestra.

NAMES: William Blake.

Taubman, Howard. "Music: A Bounty of Unfamiliar Works: Philadelphians Present Three Local Premières: Scores by Rochberg, Rosza and Prokofiev," *The New York Times* (03 April 1958).

TYPE: review.

PERFORMERS: Eugene Ormandy, Philadelphia Orchestra.

NAMES: Schönberg.

Watt, Douglas. "Man with a Past," *The New Yorker* (02 May 1953) 80-82.

TYPE: review.

PERFORMERS: Dimitri Mitropoulos, New York Philharmonic-Symphony Orchestra.

OTHER WORKS DISCUSSED: *Night Music.*

Webster, Daniel. "A *Symphony* Out of the Past: George Rochberg's Music Gets a Philadelphia Hearing," *The Philadelphia Inquirer* (10 March 1985) I, 11.

TYPE: article, interview, upcoming performance.

PERFORMERS: Werner Torkanowsky, New York Philharmonic, Eugene Ormandy, Philadelphia Orchestra.

OTHER WORKS DISCUSSED: *Symphony No. 2, Symphony No. 3, Symphony No. 5, Trio [No. 2] for Violin, Cello, and Piano, Variations on an Original Theme.*

Symphony No. 2 for Orchestra

Biancolli, Louis. "Music: Mozart *Concerto* Gets Unforgettable Treatment," *The New York World-Telegram and Sun* (16 February 1960) 17.

TYPE: review.

PERFORMERS: George Szell, Cleveland Orchestra.

Biancolli, Louis. "Music: Philharmonic Presents More Prize Winners," *The New York World-Telegram and Sun* (02 January 1962) 12.
TYPE: review.
PERFORMERS: Werner Torkanowsky, New York Philharmonic.

Boros, Ethel. "The Music Beat: Szell, Orchestra Play Rochberg Première," *The Cleveland News* (27 February 1959).
TYPE: review.
PERFORMERS: George Szell, Cleveland Orchestra.
NAMES: Wagner.

Boros, Ethel. "Pianists Fill Guest Book," *The Cleveland News* (21 February 1959).
TYPE: upcoming performance.
PERFORMERS: George Szell, Cleveland Orchestra.
OTHER WORKS DISCUSSED: *Symphony No. 1.*

Briggs, John. "Naumburg Award Winners in Philharmonic Concert," *The New York Post* (02 January 1962) 16.
TYPE: review.
PERFORMERS: Werner Torkanowsky, New York Philharmonic.

Calvin, Robert E. "Modern Art: It Has Snob Appeal," *The Plain Dealer [Cleveland, OH]* (15 December 1959) 16.
TYPE: letter to the editor.

Darack, Arthur. "Cataclysmic Music," *The Cincinnati Enquirer* (03 March 1959) 4D.
TYPE: review.
PERFORMERS: George Szell, Cleveland Orchestra.
NAMES: Adrian Leverkuhn, Thomas Mann, Stravinsky.

Ellis, Stephen W. "Rochberg: *Symphony No. 2*," *Fanfare* VII/4 (March–April 1984) 237.
TYPE: record review.
PERFORMERS: Werner Torkanowsky, New York Philharmonic.
OTHER WORKS MENTIONED: *Night Music, String Quartet No. 2, Symphony No. 1.*

Elwell, Herbert. "Orchestra Introduces New, Absorbing American Work," *The Plain Dealer [Cleveland, OH]* (27 February 1959) 24.
TYPE: review.
PERFORMERS: George Szell, Cleveland Orchestra.

Ericson, Raymond. "Music: Three Prize Winners: Torkanowsky Leads the Philharmonic in Rochberg Work—Silverstein Plays," *The New York Times* (01 January 1962) 15.

TYPE: review.

PERFORMERS: Werner Torkanowsky, New York Philharmonic.

Evans, Peter A. *"Symphony No. 2," Music and Letters* LXIII/3 (April 1962) 286-287.

TYPE: review.

Eyer, Ronald. "Music: New York Philharmonic," *The New York Herald Tribune* (01 January 1962) 6.

TYPE: review.

PERFORMERS: Werner Torkanowsky, New York Philharmonic.

Felton, James. "Composers Are Sane But the World Isn't, Says Penn [University of Pennsylvania at Philadelphia] Rochberg," *The Sunday Bulletin [Philadelphia]* (13 February 1966) 11.

TYPE: interview.

PERFORMERS: George Szell, Cleveland Orchestra, Werner Torkanowsky, New York Philharmonic.

OTHER WORKS DISCUSSED: *Contra Mortem et Tempus, Music for the Magic Theater, Night Music, String Quartet No. 2, Symphony No. 1, Symphony No. 3, Zodiac.*

Felton, James. "Rochberg's Chamber Music Is Aired at the Art Alliance," *The Evening Bulletin [Philadelphia]* (16 February 1966) 27.

TYPE: review.

NAMES: Webern.

OTHER WORKS DISCUSSED: *La Bocca della Verità, Contra Mortem et Tempus, Dialogues, Night Music, Symphony No. 1, Trio [No. 1] for Violin, Cello, and Piano.*

Harrison, Jay S. "Leon Fleisher Is Soloist with the Cleveland Orchestra," *The New York Herald Tribune* (16 February 1960).

TYPE: review.

PERFORMERS: George Szell, Cleveland Orchestra.

Holtkamp, Rena C. "Orchestra and Rubenstein Excel," *The Plain Dealer [Cleveland, OH]* (22 January 1960) 18.

TYPE: review.

PERFORMERS: George Szell, Cleveland Orchestra.

NAMES: Beethoven.

Holtkamp, Rena C. "Orchestra Will Present New American *Symphony," The Plain Dealer [Cleveland, OH]* (22 February 1959) 14F.

TYPE: upcoming première.

PERFORMERS: George Szell, Cleveland Orchestra.

Hruby, Frank. "Pianist Firkusny, Orchestra Play in Perfect Harmony," *The Cleveland Press* (27 February 1959) 30.
TYPE: review.
PERFORMERS: George Szell, Cleveland Orchestra.

Hruby, Frank. "Rochberg *Symphony* Première Acclaimed in Cleveland," *Musical America* LXXIX/4 (April 1959) 11.
TYPE: review.
PERFORMERS: George Szell, Cleveland Orchestra.

Hruby, Frank. "Rubenstein Improves with the Years," *The Cleveland Press* (22 January 1960) 17.
TYPE: review.
PERFORMERS: George Szell, Cleveland Orchestra.

Johnson, Harriett. "Words and Music: *Nocturne* and Rochberg *No. 2*," *The New York Post* (16 February 1960) 18.
TYPE: review.
PERFORMERS: George Szell, Cleveland Orchestra.
NAMES: Berg.

Kanny, Mark. "Rochberg Sets Tone for New Composing Style," *The Pittsburgh Post-Gazette* (16 October 1987) Weekend, 2.
TYPE: article.
NAMES: Mahler, Stravinsky.
OTHER WORKS DISCUSSED: *Symphony No. 1.*

Kastensieck, Miles. "At Carnegie Hall: Rochberg Played by Clevelanders," *The New York Journal—American* (16 February 1960) 13.
TYPE: review.
PERFORMERS: George Szell, Cleveland Orchestra.

Kastensieck, Miles. "At Carnegie Hall: Silverstein in Fine Tune," *The New York Journal—American* (02 January 1962).
TYPE: review.
PERFORMERS: Werner Torkanowsky, New York Philharmonic.

Locklair, Winston. "Cleveland Series Introduces American Works: Rochberg *Symphony* Given New York Debut," *Musical America* LXXX/3 (March 1960) 26.
TYPE: review.
PERFORMERS: George Szell, Cleveland Orchestra.

Miller, Karl F. "Rochberg: *Eleven Songs*," *American Record Guide* XLVII/6 (July 1984) 66-67.
TYPE: record review.

OTHER WORKS DISCUSSED: *Eleven Songs, Symphony No. 3.*

Miller, Karl F. "Rochberg: *Symphony No. 2,*" *American Record Guide* XLVIII/1 (November 1984) 19-20.

TYPE: record review.

PERFORMERS: Werner Torkanowsky, New York Philharmonic.

n.a. "Miscellaneous Disks: Rochberg: *Symphony No. 2,*" *The New York Times* (23 June 1963) 14.

TYPE: record review.

PERFORMERS: Werner Torkanowsky, New York Philharmonic.

Mooney, Paul. "Orchestra's Key Is B Sharp," *The Cleveland Press* (21 February 1959) 13.

TYPE: upcoming première.

PERFORMERS: George Szell, Cleveland Orchestra.

n.a. "Music: Mid-West Orchestra and Five American Composers in Spotlight this Week," *The New York Times* (14 February 1960) 9.

TYPE: upcoming première.

PERFORMERS: George Szell, Cleveland Orchestra.

n.a. "Naumburg Recording Award—Rochberg," *Pan Pipes [Magazine of Sigma Alpha Iota]* LIV/2 (January 1962) 10.

TYPE: announcement of award.

PERFORMERS: Werner Torkanowsky, New York Philharmonic.

Owens, David. "Turning from Twelve-Tone: Inside Twentieth-Century Music," *The Christian Science Monitor* (03 May 1984) 39.

TYPE: article.

PERFORMERS: Werner Torkanowsky, New York Philharmonic.

OTHER WORKS DISCUSSED: *Concerto for Violin and Orchestra, String Quartet No. 4, String Quartet No. 5, String Quartet No. 6, Symphony*

Parmenter, Ross. "Music: Large-Scale *Symphony* with a Twelve-Tone Row: Rochberg's *Second* Makes Deep Impression: Clevelanders Introduce Work at Carnegie Hall," *The New York Times* (16 February 1960)._
Times (16 February 1960).

TYPE: review.

PERFORMERS: George Szell, Cleveland Orchestra.

n.a. "Premières," *Time* LXXIII/10 (09 March 1959) 50.

TYPE: review.

PERFORMERS: George Szell, Cleveland Orchestra.

NAMES: Herbert Elwell, Schönberg, Stavinsky.

Raynor, Henry. "*Symphony No. 2*," *Music Review* XXIII/4 (1962) 337-338.

TYPE: score review.

PERFORMERS: George Szell, Cleveland Orchestra.

Reise, Jay. "Rochberg the Progressive," *Perspectives of New Music* XIX/1-2 (Fall-Winter 1980/Spring-Summer 1981) 395-407.

TYPE: article, analysis.

NAMES: Berg, Steven Block.

OTHER WORKS DISCUSSED: *Contra Mortem et Tempus, String Quartet No. 3, Tableaux.*

Ringer, Alexander L. "Current Chronicle: St. Louis," *Musical Quarterly* LXVII/1 (January 1961) 101-103.

TYPE: review.

PERFORMERS: St. Louis Symphony Orchestra.

NAMES: Mozart, Webern.

OTHER WORKS DISCUSSED: *Time-Span.*

Ringer, Alexander L. "Current Chronicle: United States: Cleveland," *Musical Quarterly* XLV/2 (April 1959) 230-234.

TYPE: article, review.

PERFORMERS: George Szell, Cleveland Orchestra.

NAMES: Berlioz, Mahler, Webern.

OTHER WORKS DISCUSSED: *Chamber Symphony, David, The Psalmist, Sonata-Fantasia, String Quartet No. 1, Symphony No. 1, Three Psalms, Twelve Bagatelles.*

BOOKS DISCUSSED: *The Hexachord and Its Relation to the Twelve-Tone Row.*

Ringer, Alexander L. "The Music of George Rochberg," *Musical Quarterly* LII/4 (October 1966) 409-430.

TYPE: article.

PERFORMERS: George Szell, Cleveland Orchestra.

NAMES: Berg.

OTHER WORKS DISCUSSED: *Apocalyptica [I], Black Sounds, Blake Songs, La Bocca della Verità, Cantio Sacra, Capriccio for Two Pianos, Chamber Symphony, Cheltenham Concerto, Concert Piece for Two Pianos and Orchestra, Contra Mortem et Tempus, David, the Psalmist, Dialogues, Duo Concertante, Four Songs of Solomon, Music for the Magic Theater, Nach Bach, Night Music, Passions [According to the Twentieth Century], Serenata d'estate, Sonata-Fantasia, String Quartet No. 1, String Quartet No. 2, Symphony No. 1, Three Psalms, Time-*

Span, Trio for Clarinet, Horn, and Piano, Trio [No. 1] for Violin, Cello, and Piano, Twelve Bagatelles, Zodiac.

OTHER WORKS MENTIONED: *Arioso, Bartokiana, Five Smooth Stones, Sonata No. 1 for Piano Solo, Sonata No. 2 for Piano Solo, Waltz Serenade.*

BOOKS DISCUSSED: *The Hexachord and Its Relation to the Twelve-Tone Row.*

n.a. "Rochberg Receives Naumburg Award," *The New York Times* (26 July 1961) 37.

TYPE: announcement of Naumburg Recoring Award.

PERFORMERS: Werner Torkanowsky, New York Philharmonic.

OTHER WORKS DISCUSSED: *Night Music.*

Roy, Klaus George. "Rochberg's New *Symphony* in Première," *The Christian Science Monitor* (21 March 1959).

TYPE: review.

PERFORMERS: George Szell, Cleveland Orchestra.

OTHER WORKS DISCUSSED: *Symphony No. 1.*

Sabin, Robert. "Naumburg Winners with Philharmonic," *Musical America* LXXXII/2 (February 1962) 31.

TYPE: review.

PERFORMERS: Werner Torkanowsky, New York Philharmonic.

Sisley, E. Lucretia. "The Cleveland Orchestra," *Musical Courier* CLXI/3 (March 1960) 17-18.

TYPE: review.

PERFORMERS: George Szell, Cleveland Orchestra.

NAMES: Berg.

Tircuit, Heuwell. "At the Symphony: *Violin Concerto* About Concertos," *The San Francisco Chronicle* (09 May 1975) 46.

TYPE: review.

OTHER WORKS DISCUSSED: *Concerto for Violin and Orchestra, String Quartet No. 3.*

Webster, Daniel. "George Rochberg: American Music's Bellwether," *The Philadelphia Inquirer* (25 July 1982) 1-K, 13-K.

TYPE: article, interview.

PERFORMERS: Riccardo Muti, Philadelphia Orchestra.

OTHER WORKS DISCUSSED: *The Confidence Man, Phaedra.*

Webster, Daniel. "A *Symphony* Out of the Past: George Rochberg's Music Gets a Philadelphia Hearing," *The Philadelphia Inquirer* (10 March 1985) I, 11.

TYPE: article, interview, upcoming performance.

PERFORMERS: George Szell, Cleveland Orchestra.

NAMES: Richard Wernick.

OTHER WORKS DISCUSSED: *Symphony No. 1, Symphony No. 3, Symphony No. 5, Trio [No. 2] for Violin, Cello, and Piano, Variations on an Original Theme.*

Widder, Rose. "Cleveland," *Musical Courier* CLIX/4 (April 1959) 33.

TYPE: review.

PERFORMERS: George Szell, Cleveland Orchestra.

Symphony No. 3 for Vocal Soloists, Chamber Chorus, Double Chorus, and Large Orchestra

Breuer, Robert. "New York," *Schweizereische Musikzeitung* XI/4 (July–August 1971) 238-240.

TYPE: review.

NAMES: Bach, Beethoven, Berio, Ives, Mahler, Schütz, Stravinsky.

Brookhouser, Frank. "A Dead Son Lives on in Father's Music," *The Evening Bulletin [Philadelphia]* (05 November 1970).

TYPE: upcoming première.

PERFORMERS: Juilliard.

OTHER WORKS DISCUSSED: *Eleven Songs, Sacred Song of Reconciliation.*

Cox, Ainske. "The Juilliard Theater," *Music Journal* XXIX/2 (February 1971) 82-83.

TYPE: review.

PERFORMERS: Abraham Kaplan, Juilliard Theater Orchestra, Juilliard Chorus, Juilliard Collegiate Chorus.

NAMES: Bach, Beethoven, Berio, Foss, Hoffnung, Ives, Mahler, Peter Schickele [P.D.Q. Bach], Schütz.

Dixon, Joan DeVee. "George Rochberg's *Nach Bach, A Fantasy for Harpsichord or Piano,*" Unpublished (June 1988) 13pp.

TYPE: article, interviews with George Rochberg and Igor Kipnis.

OTHER WORKS DISCUSSED: *Chamber Symphony, Contra Mortem et Tempus, Music for the Magic Theater, Nach Bach, Partita Variations, Sonata-Fantasia.*

Felton, James. "At Lincoln Center: Passion of 20th Century," *The Evening Bulletin [Philadelphia]* (25 November 1970) 19.

TYPE: review.

PERFORMERS: Abraham Kaplan, Juilliard Orchestra, John Russell.

NAMES: Bach, Beethoven, Penderecki.

Felton, James. "Composers Are Sane But the World Isn't, Says Penn [University of Pennsylvania at Philadelphia] Rochberg," *The Sunday Bulletin [Philadelphia]* (13 February 1966) 11.

TYPE: interview.

OTHER WORKS DISCUSSED: *Contra Mortem et Tempus, Music for the Magic Theater, Night Music, String Quartet No. 2, Symphony No. 1, Symphony No. 2, Zodiac.*

Felton, James. "Concert Set March 17: *Fanfare for 144 Brass Horns,*" *The Philadelphia Inquirer* (03 March 1968).

TYPE: upcoming première, interview.

PERFORMERS: Juilliard.

NAMES: Mahler.

OTHER WORKS DISCUSSED: *Fanfare, Zodiac.*

Fogel, Henry. "George Rochberg: A Raproachment with the Past," *The Syracuse Guide* V (January 1976) 24-26, 42.

TYPE: article.

OTHER WORKS DISCUSSED: *Concerto for Violin and Orchestra, Phaedra, String Quartet No. 3.*

Freedman, Guy. "Metamorphosis of a 20th Century Composer," *Music Journal* XXXIV/3 (March 1976) 12, 13, 38.

TYPE: interview.

NAMES: J.S. Bach, Beethoven, Ives, Monteverdi, Schütz.

OTHER WORKS DISCUSSED: *Quintet for Piano and String Quartet.*

Hughes, Allen. "Juilliard Offers Rochberg's *No. 3*: Abraham Kaplan Conducts Première of *Symphony,*" *The New York Times* (26 November 1970) 58.

TYPE: review.

PERFORMERS: Abraham Kaplan, Joy Blackett, Joyce Mathis, John Russell, Robert Shiesley, Juilliard Theater Orchestra, Juilliard Chorale, Juilliard Collegiate Chorus.

NAMES: Bach, Mahler, Ives, Schütz.

Kolodin, Irving. "Music to my Ears," *Saturday Review* LIII/3 (12 December 1970) 46.

TYPE: review.

PERFORMERS: Juilliard personnel, Abraham Kaplan, two assistant conductors, Joyce Mathis, Joy Blackett, John Russell, Robert Shiesley.

NAMES: Beethoven, Berio, Mahler, Ives, Schütz.

Kozinski, David B. "Music Notes: Rochberg *Symphony No. 3* a Break-through," *The Evening Journal [Wilmington, DE]* (03 December 1970) 31.

TYPE: review.

PERFORMERS: Juilliard Orchestra, Juilliard Chorale, Juilliard Collegiate Chorale, Abraham Kaplan, Joy Blackett, Joyce Mathis, John Russell, Robert Shiesley, Robert Zimanski.

NAMES: Berio, Beethoven, Bach, Ives, Mahler, Schütz.

Miller, Karl F. "Rochberg: *Eleven Songs,*" *American Record Guide* XLVII/6 (July 1984) 66-67.

TYPE: record review.

OTHER WORKS DISCUSSED: *Eleven Songs, Symphony No. 2.*

n.a. "Musik in New York," *Neue Zuricher Zeitung [Zurich]* (07 January 1971).

TYPE: review.

PERFORMERS: Juilliard Orchestra, Juilliard Chorale, Abraham Kaplan.

NAMES: Bach, Beethoven, Berio, Ives, Schütz, Stravinsky.

n.a. "New York," *Schweizerische Musikzeitung* CXI/4 (July–August 1971) 239.

TYPE: review.

PERFORMERS: Juilliard Orchestra, Juilliard Chorale, Abraham Kaplan.

NAMES: Bach, Beethoven, Berio, Ives, Schütz, Stravinsky.

Putnam, Thomas. "Composer Hears *Magic Theater*: Played by Philharmonic with Melvin Conducting," *The Buffalo Courier Express* (26 January 1969).

TYPE: review, interview.

NAMES:

OTHER WORKS DISCUSSED: *Contra Mortem et Tempus, Music for the Magic Theater, Time-Span.*

de Rhen, Andrew. "Julliard: Rochberg Première," *High Fidelity/Musical America* XXI/3 (March 1971) MA-23, MA-24.

TYPE: review.

PERFORMERS: Juilliard, Abraham Kaplan.

NAMES: Beethoven, Ives.

Ringer, Alexander L. "Current Chronicle: New York, Jerusalem, and Urbana, Illinois," *Musical Quarterly* LVIII/1 (January 1972) 128-132.

TYPE: article, review.

PERFORMERS: Juilliard School.

NAMES: J.S. Bach, Beethoven, Ives, Mahler, Schütz.

OTHER WORKS DISCUSSED: *David, The Psalmist, Sacred Song of Reconciliation, Songs in Praise of Krishna.*

Scanlan, Roger. "Spotlight on Contemporary American Composers," *The NATS [National Association of Teachers of Singing] Bulletin* XXXIII/1 (October 1976) 48-49, 53-54.

TYPE: article.

OTHER WORKS DISCUSSED: *Blake Songs, David, The Psalmist, Eleven Songs, Four Songs of Solomon, Fantasies, Music for "The Alchemist", Phaedra, Sacred Song of Reconciliation, Songs in Praise of Krishna, String Quartet No. 2, Tableaux, Two Songs from "Tableaux".*

OTHER WORKS MENTIONED: many.

Webster, Daniel. "Impressive Musical Debut Offered the Chamber Groups," *The Philadelphia Inquirer* (19 February 1973) 9-A.

TYPE: review.

NAMES: Beethoven, Brahms.

OTHER WORKS DISCUSSED: *String Quartet No. 3.*

Webster, Daniel. "Rochberg's *Concerto* Sticks with Tradition," *The Philadephia Inquirer* (03 April 1975) 4C.

TYPE: review.

PERFORMERS: Juilliard School, Abraham Kaplan.

OTHER WORKS DISCUSSED:

Concerto for Violin and Orchestra.   Webster, Daniel. "Rochberg *Symphony* Is Premièred," *The Philadephia Inquirer* (25 November 1970).

TYPE: review.

PERFORMERS: Juilliard School, Abraham Kaplan.

NAMES: Bach, Beethoven, Ives, Schütz, Webern.

Webster, Daniel. "A *Symphony* Out of the Past: George Rochberg's Music Gets a Philadelphia Hearing," *The Philadelphia Inquirer* (10 March 1985) I, 11.

TYPE: article, interview, upcoming performance.

PERFORMERS: Juilliard School, Abraham Kaplan.

NAMES: Bach, Beethoven, Mahler.

OTHER WORKS DISCUSSED: *Symphony No. 1, Symphony No. 2, Symphony No. 5, Trio [No. 2] for Violin, Cello, and Piano, Variations on an Original Theme.*

Symphony No. 4 for Large Orchestra

Cambell, R. M. "Superb Reading of *Symphony*," *The Seattle Post-Intel-ligencer* (16 November 1976) D3.

TYPE: review.

PERFORMERS: Vilem Sokol, Seattle Youth Symphony.

Cera, Stephen. "Banks of the Wabash Echo to Modern Music," *The Sun [Baltimore]* (04 October 1981).

TYPE: review.

OTHER WORKS DISCUSSED: *Ricordanza, String Quartet No. 5.*

Henahan, Donal J. "Music: Rochberg Work by National Orchestra," *The New York Times* (17 April 1985) III, 18.

TYPE: review.

PERFORMERS: Alvaro Cassuto, National Orchestra of New York.

NAMES: Mahler, Stravinsky.

OTHER WORKS DISCUSSED: *String Quartet No. 3.*

Hoffman, W. L. "Arts and Entertainment: US [United States] Com-poser on Canberra Stint," *The Canberra Times [Australia]* (20 Oc-tober 1986).

TYPE: upcoming performances.

PERFORMERS: Chritopher Lyndon Gee, Queensland Symphony Orchestra [Brisbane, Queensland, Australia].

OTHER WORKS DISCUSSED: *Blake Songs, Octet, Quintet for Piano and String Quartet, Songs in Praise of Krishna, To the Dark Wood.*

OTHER WORKS MENTIONED: *Concerto for Violin and Orchestra, Sym-phony No. 5.*

Johnson, Galen. "Youth Symphony," *Argus [Seattle, WA]* (19 Novem-ber 1976).

TYPE: review.

PERFORMERS: Vilem Sokol, Seattle Youth Symphony.

NAMES: Brahms, Mahler, Schönberg.

Johnson, Wayne. "Old Styles in New *Symphony*," *The Seattle Times* (16 November 1976) A17.

TYPE: review.

PERFORMERS: Vilem Sokol, Seattle Youth Symphony.

NAMES: Beethoven, Brahms, Bruckner, Haydn, Mahler, Mozart, Ravel, Schubert, Strauss.

n.a. "Rochberg *Concerto* to be Unveiled," *The Evening Bulletin [Philadelphia]* (19 March 1975).

TYPE: upcoming première.

PERFORMERS: Vilem Sokol, Seattle Youth Symphony.
OTHER WORKS DISCUSSED: *Concerto for Violin and Orchestra.*

Watson, Emmett. "Puget Sound Fury," *The Seattle Post-Intelligencer* (15 November 1976) B-1.
TYPE: upcoming première.
PERFORMERS: Vilem Sokol, Seattle Youth Symphony.

Symphony No. 5 for Orchestra

n.a. "Composer Honored (Brandies Creative Arts Award," *Musical Opinion* CVIII/1294 (September 1985) 339.
TYPE: article, award.
OTHER WORKS DISCUSSED: *Trio [No. 2] for Violin, Cello, and Piano.*

Covell, Roger. "Lack of Scope Sees a Change in Style," *The Sydney Morning Herald [Australia]* (18 October 1986).
TYPE: review, interview.
NAMES: Tchaikovsky.
OTHER WORKS DISCUSSED: *Concerto for Violin and Orchestra, Ricordanza, String Quartet No. 3, To the Dark Wood.*

n.a. "1985-1986 Season Premières and Season Highlights: Illinois: Chicago Symphony Orchestra," *Symphony Magazine* XXXVI/5 (October–November 1985) 34.
TYPE: announcement of première.
PERFORMERS: Sir Georg Solti, Chicago Symphony Orchestra.

Marsh, Robert C. "CSO [Chicago Symphony Orchestra] Scores with Première of Rochberg," *The Chicago Sun-Times* (14 March 1986).
TYPE: review.
PERFORMERS: Sir Georg Solti, Chicago Symphony Orchestra.

von Rhein, John. "Pushing All the Right Buttons—Modern Music and the CSO [Chicago Symphony Orchestra]," *The Chicago Tribune* (21 July 1985) C12.
TYPE: review.
PERFORMERS: Sir Georg Solti, Chicago Symphony Orchestra.

von Rhein, John. "A Welcome but Disappointing Première," *The Chicago Tribune* (14 March 1986) C8.
TYPE: review.
PERFORMERS: Sir Georg Solti, Chicago Symphony Orchestra.
NAMES: Mahler.

Webster, Daniel. "Music: A New *Symphony* Created for Chicago," *The Philadelphia Inquirer* (18 March 1986) 5-D.

TYPE: review.

PERFORMERS: Sir Georg Solti, Chicago Symphony Orchestra.

NAMES: Mahler, Wagner.

Webster, Daniel. "A *Symphony* Out of the Past: George Rochberg's Music Gets a Philadelphia Hearing," *The Philadelphia Inquirer* (10 March 1985) I, 11.

TYPE: article, interview, upcoming performance.

PERFORMERS: Sir Georg Solti, Chicago Symphony Orchestra.

OTHER WORKS DISCUSSED: *Symphony No. 1, Symphony No. 2, Symphony No. 3, Trio [No. 2] for Violin, Cello, and Piano, Variations on an Original Theme.*

Symphony No. 6 for Orchestra

Apone, Carl. "'Incredible Energy': Symphony to Première George Rochberg Work," *The Pittsburgh Press* (15 October 1987) D-9.

TYPE: upcoming première.

PERFORMERS: Loren Maazel, Pittsburgh Symphony.

Apone, Carl. "New Works Add up to a Winner," *The Pittsburgh Press* (17 October 1987) B6.

TYPE: review.

PERFORMERS: Loren Maazel, Pittsburgh Symphony.

NAMES: Sibelius, Stravinsky.

Bustard, Clarke. "Somber *Symphony* Collects First Prize in the Freidheims," *The Times-Dispatch [Richmond, VA]* (31 October 1988) B9.

TYPE: review.

PERFORMERS: Robert Fitzpatrick, Curtis Institute of Music Symphony Orchestra.

NAMES: Bartók, Copland, Ives, Mahler, Shostakovich, Sousa.

Cr
oan, Robert. "On the Peace Front: Maazel Returns for Work's Première," *The Pittsburgh Post-Gazette* (16 October 1987) Weekend, 2.

TYPE: upcoming première.

PERFORMERS: Loren Maazel, Pittsburgh Symphony.

Croan, Robert. "Rochberg Première," *The Pittsburgh Post-Gazette* (17 October 1987) 12.

TYPE: review.

PERFORMERS: Loren Maazel, Pittsburgh Symphony.

NAMES: Ives.

Henry, Derrick. "ASO's [Atlanta Symphony Orchestra's] Third Place at Friedheim Awards," *The Atlanta Constitution* (31 October 1988) 1B, 5B.

TYPE: review.

PERFORMERS: Robert Fitzpatrick, Curtis Institute of Music Symphony Orchestra.

NAMES: Ives, Mahler, Stephen Sondheim.

Kanny, Mark. "Maazel Gives Powerful Performances," *The Jewish Chronicle of Pittsburgh* (22 October 1987).

TYPE: review.

PERFORMERS: Loren Maazel, Pittsburgh Symphony.

La Fave, Kenneth. "Music Scene: Composer George Rochberg: Melody Above the Storm," *The Chicago Tribune* (28 April 1988).

TYPE: article, interview.

PERFORMERS: Loren Maazel, Pittsburgh Symphony.

OTHER WORKS DISCUSSED: *Concerto for Violin and Orchestra, Night Music, String Quartet No. 4, String Quartet No. 5, String Quartet No. 6, Symphony No. 1.*

McLellan, Joseph. "On Center Stage: The Neoromantics," *The Washington Post [Washington, D.C.]* (30 October 1988).

TYPE: upcoming performance.

PERFORMERS: Robert Fitzpatrick, Curtis Institute of Music Symphony Orchestra.

n.a. "1987-1988 Premières and Season Highlights: Pennsylvania: Pittsburgh Symphony Orchestra," *Symphony Magazine* XXXVIII/5 (October–November 1987) 36.

TYPE: review.

PERFORMERS: Loren Maazel, Pittsburgh Symphony.

Sommers, Pamela. "Rouse Wins Friedheim: Baltimorean Tops in New Music Competition," *The Washington Post [Washington, D.C.]* (31 October 1988) D2.

TYPE: review.

PERFORMERS: Robert Fitzpatrick, Curtis Institute of Music Symphony Orchestra.

OTHER WORKS MENTIONED: *String Quartet No. 4.*

Valdes, Lesley. "Christopher Rouse *Symphony* Wins a $5,000 Prize," *The Philadelphia Inquirer* (01 November 1988).

TYPE: review.

PERFORMERS: Robert Fitzpatrick, Curtis Institute of Music Symphony Orchestra.

NAMES: Mahler.

Wigler, Stephen. "Composer Rouse of BSO [Baltimore Symphony Orchestra] Wins Friedhiem Contest," *The Morning Sun [Baltimore]* (31 October 1988) 1B, 4B.

TYPE: review.

PERFORMERS: Robert Fitzpatrick, Curtis Institute of Music Symphony Orchestra.

Wigler, Stephen. "Friedhiem Concert" *The Morning Sun [Baltimore]* (30 October 1988) 1B, 4B.

TYPE: review.

PERFORMERS: Robert Fitzpatrick, Curtis Institute of Music Symphony Orchestra.

Tableaux (Sound Pictures from the "Silver Talons of Piero Kostrov," by Paul Rochberg) for Soprano, Two Actors' Voices, Small Mens' Chorus, and Twelve Players

Henahan, Donal J. "Music: From Academe," *The New York Times* (29 April 1971) 47.

TYPE: review.

PERFORMERS: Robert Suderburg, University of Washington Contemporary Group.

NAMES: Blake, Paul Rochberg.

Hughes, Allen. "Concert: Philharmonic: Last 'Prospective Encounter' of the Season Has Pieces Based on Literature," *The New York Times* (16 May 1976) 53.

TYPE: review.

PERFORMERS: Pierre Boulez, Neva Pilgrim, members of the New York Philharmonic.

NAMES: Paul Rochberg.

Jenkins, Speight. "This Takes Some Brass," *The New York Post* (15 May 1976) 18.

TYPE: review.

PERFORMERS: Pierre Boulez, Neva Pilgrim, Paul Jacobs, members of the New York Philharmonic.

NAMES: George Crumb, Paul Rochberg.

Johnson, Wayne. "Rochberg Will Hear Rochberg this Friday," *The Seattle Times* (29 October 1969) 20.

TYPE: upcoming performance.

PERFORMERS: William O. Smith, Robert Suderburg, Elizabeth Suderberg, University of Washington Contemporary Group.

NAMES: Paul Rochberg.

OTHER WORKS DISCUSSED: *Contra Mortem et Tempus, Music for "The Alchemist", Music for the Magic Theater.*

Johnson, Wayne. "U.W. [University of Washington] Group Plays Great Concert," *The Seattle Times* (03 November 1969) 22.

TYPE: review.

PERFORMERS: William O. Smith, Robert Suderburg, Elizabeth Suderberg, University of Washington Contemporary Group, Philadelphia String Quartet, Soni Ventorum.

NAMES: Paul Rochberg.

OTHER WORKS DISCUSSED: *Contra Mortem et Tempus, Music for "The Alchemist", Music for the Magic Theater.*

Lowens, Irving. "Dorati Work Is Premièred," *The Washington Star* [Washington, D.C.] 10 November 1976) E5.

TYPE: review.

OTHER WORKS DISCUSSED: *Concerto for Violin and Orchestra.*

Reise, Jay. "Rochberg the Progressive," *Perspectives of New Music* XIX/1-2 (Fall-Winter 1980/ Spring-Summer 1981) 395-407.

TYPE: article, analysis.

NAMES: Steven Block.

OTHER WORKS DISCUSSED: *Contra Mortem et Tempus, String Quartet No. 3, Symphony No. 2.*

Rockwell, John. "Rochberg: *Tableaux,*" *High Fidelity/Music America* XXIII/11 (November 1973) 116.

TYPE: record review.

PERFORMERS: Richard Wernick, Jan DeGaetani, University of Pennsylvania Contemporary Players.

NAMES: George Crumb, Paul Rochberg.

Sable, Barbara Kinsey. "Disc Discussion," *The NATS [National Association of Teachers of Singing] Bulletin* XXXII/3 (February - March 1976) 54-57.

TYPE: record review.

PERFORMERS: Richard Wernick, Jan DeGaetani, University of Pennsylvania Contemporary Players.

NAMES: Paul Rochberg.

Salisbury, Wilma. "Half a Piano Recital Lifts Lid on Part Two of Oberlin Festival," *The Plain Dealer [Cleveland, OH]* (20 March 1970) 7C.

TYPE: review.

OTHER WORKS DISCUSSED: *Nach Bach, Prelude on "Happy Birthday"*.

Salzman, Eric. "Recording of Special Merit: Rochberg: *Tableaux*," *Stereo Review* XXXI/4 (October 1973) 147-152.

TYPE: record review.

PERFORMERS: Richard Wernick, Jan DeGaetani, University of Pennsylvania Contemporary Players.

NAMES: Paul Rochberg.

Scanlan, Roger. "Spotlight on Contemporary American Composers," *The NATS [National Association of Teachers of Singing] Bulletin* XXXIII/1 (October 1976) 48-49, 53-54.

TYPE: article.

OTHER WORKS DISCUSSED: *Blake Songs, David, The Psalmist, Eleven Songs, Four Songs of Solomon, Fantasies, Music for "The Alchemist", Phaedra, Sacred Song of Reconciliation, Songs in Praise of Krishna, String Quartet No. 2, Symphony No. 3, Two Songs from "Tableaux"*.

OTHER WORKS MENTIONED: many.

Stromberg, Rolf. "Two Young Musicians Gifted," *The Seattle Post-Intelligencer* (03 November 1969) S*45.

TYPE: review.

PERFORMERS: William O. Smith, Robert Suderberg, Elizabeth Suderberg, University of Washington Contemporary Group, Philadelphia String Quartet, Soni Ventorum.

NAMES: Paul Rochberg.

OTHER WORKS DISCUSSED: *Contra Mortem et Tempus, Music for "The Alchemist", Music for the Magic Theater*.

Thomas, John Patrick. "Vocal Music," *Notes: The Quarterly Journal of the Music Library Association* XXX/2 (December 1973) 365-366.

TYPE: score review.

NAMES: Paul Rochberg.

OTHER WORKS DISCUSSED: *Two Songs from "Tableaux"*.

Webster, Daniel. "Rochberg's *Tableaux* Show New Direction for Composer," *The Philadelphia Inquirer* (29 April 1971) 24.

TYPE: review.

PERFORMERS: Richard Wernick, Jan DeGaetani, University of Pennsylvania Contemporary Players.

NAMES: Paul Rochberg.

Wells, William B. "George Rochberg: *Tableaux*," *Notes: The Quarterly Journal of the Music Library Association* XXX/3 (March 1974) 616.

TYPE: score review, record review.

PERFORMERS: Richard Wernick, Jan DeGaetani, University of Pennsylvania Contemporary Players.

NAMES: David Bedford, George Crumb, Paul Rochberg.

Three Psalms for a cappella Mixed Chorus

Felton, James. "Suderburg's Choral Music Is Fresh Experience in Sound," *The Evening Bulletin [Philadelphia]* (31 March 1966) 39.

TYPE: review.

PERFORMERS: Robert Suderberg, The Philadelphia Musical Academy Choir.

Ringer, Alexander L. "Current Chronicle: United States: Cleveland," *Musical Quarterly* XLV/2 (April 1959) 230-234.

TYPE: article, review.

OTHER WORKS DISCUSSED: *Chamber Symphony, David, The Psalmist, Sonata-Fantasia, String Quartet No. 1, Symphony No. 1, Symphony No. 2, Twelve Bagatelles.*

BOOKS DISCUSSED: *The Hexachord and Its Relation to the Twelve-Tone Row.*

Ringer, Alexander L. "The Music of George Rochberg," *Musical Quarterly* LII/4 (October 1966) 409-430.

TYPE: article.

NAMES: Schönberg.

OTHER WORKS DISCUSSED: *Apocalyptica [I], Black Sounds, Blake Songs, La Bocca della Verità, Cantio Sacra, Capriccio for Two Pianos, Chamber Symphony, Cheltenham Concerto, Concert Piece for Two Pianos and Orchestra, Contra Mortem et Tempus, David, the Psalmist, Dialogues, Duo Concertante, Four Songs of Solomon, Music for the Magic Theater, Nach Bach, Night Music, Passions [According to the Twentieth Century], Serenata d'estate, Sonata-Fantasia, String Quartet No. 1, String Quartet No. 2, Symphony No. 1, Symphony No. 2, Time-Span, Trio for Clarinet, Horn, and Piano, Trio [No. 1] for Violin, Cello, and Piano, Twelve Bagatelles, Zodiac.*

OTHER WORKS MENTIONED: *Arioso, Bartokiana, Five Smooth Stones, Sonata No. 1 for Piano Solo, Sonata No. 2 for Piano Solo, Waltz Serenade.*

BOOKS DISCUSSED: *The Hexachord and Its Relation to the Twelve-Tone Row.*

Siebert, Mark. "Choral Music," *Notes: The Quarterly Journal of the Music Library Association* XIV/4 (September 1957) 618-619.

TYPE: score review.

Time-Span for Orchestra

Putnam, Thomas. "Composer Hears *Magic Theater*: Played by Philharmonic with Melvin Conducting," *The Buffalo Courier Express* (26 January 1969).

TYPE: review, interview.

PERFORMERS: Melvin Strauss, Buffalo Philharmonic Orchestra.

NAMES: Hermann Hesse, Ives, Mahler, Mozart.

OTHER WORKS DISCUSSED: *Contra Mortem et Tempus, Music for the Magic Theater, Symphony No. 3.*

Ringer, Alexander L. "Current Chronicle: St. Louis," *Musical Quarterly* LXVII/1 (January 1961) 101-103.

TYPE: review.

PERFORMERS: St. Louis Symphony Orchestra.

NAMES: Mozart, Webern.

OTHER WORKS DISCUSSED: *Symphony No. 2.*

Ringer, Alexander L. "The Music of George Rochberg," *Musical Quarterly* LII/4 (October 1966) 409-430.

TYPE: article.

PERFORMERS: St. Louis Symphony Orchestra, George Rochberg, Buffalo Philharmonic Orchestra.

OTHER WORKS DISCUSSED: *Apocalyptica [I], Black Sounds, Blake Songs, La Bocca della Verità, Cantio Sacra, Capriccio for Two Pianos, Chamber Symphony, Cheltenham Concerto, Concert Piece for Two Pianos and Orchestra, Contra Mortem et Tempus, David, the Psalmist, Dialogues, Duo Concertante, Four Songs of Solomon, Music for the Magic Theater, Nach Bach, Night Music, Passions [According to the Twentieth Century], Serenata d'estate, Sonata-Fantasia, String Quartet No. 1, String Quartet No. 2, Symphony No. 1, Symphony No. 2, Three Psalms, Trio for Clarinet, Horn, and Piano, Trio [No. 1] for Violin, Cello, and Piano, Twelve Bagatelles, Zodiac.*

OTHER WORKS MENTIONED: *Arioso, Bartokiana, Five Smooth Stones, Sonata No. 1 for Piano Solo, Sonata No. 2 for Piano Solo, Waltz Serenade.*

BOOKS DISCUSSED: *The Hexachord and Its Relation to the Twelve-Tone Row.*

Sherman, Thomas B. "Symphony in First Concert of Season," *The St. Louis Post-Dispatch* (23 October 1960) 13A.

TYPE: review.

PERFORMERS: Van Remoortel, St. Louis Symphony Orchestra.

To the Dark Wood, Music for Woodwind Quintet

Covell, Roger. "Lack of Scope Sees a Change in Style," *The Sydney Morning Herald [Australia]* (18 October 1986).

TYPE: review, interview.

PERFORMERS: Canberra Wind Soloists.

NAMES: Stravinsky.

OTHER WORKS DISCUSSED: *Concerto for Violin and Orchestra, Ricordanza, String Quartet No. 3, Symphony No. 5.*

Hoffman, W. L. "Arts and Entertainment: US [United States] Composer on Canberra Stint," *The Canberra Times [Australia]* (20 October 1986).

TYPE: upcoming performances.

PERFORMERS: Canberra Wind Soloists.

OTHER WORKS DISCUSSED: *Blake Songs, Octet, Quintet for Piano and String Quartet, Songs in Praise of Krishna, Symphony No. 4.*

OTHER WORKS MENTIONED: *Concerto for Violin and Orchestra, Symphony No. 5.*

Hoffman, W. L. "Music: Rochberg: Positive First Half," *The Canberra Times [Australia]* (22 October 1986) 29.

TYPE: review.

PERFORMERS: Canberra Wind Soloists.

OTHER WORKS DISCUSSED: *Blake Songs, Octet, Quintet for Piano and String Quartet.*

Tietze, Larry D. "To the Dark Wood," Notes: *The Quarterly Journal of the Music Library Association* XLIV/3 (March 1988) 589-590.

TYPE: score review.

NAMES: Barber, Stravinsky.

OTHER WORKS MENTIONED: *Duo for Oboe and Bassoon.*

Valdes, Lesley. "A Birthday Salute to Rochberg," *The Philadelphia Inquirer* (17 April 1988) 1-L, 10-L.

TYPE: upcoming performance, article, interview.

PERFORMERS: Curtis Institute of Music.

OTHER WORKS DISCUSSED: *Duo Concertante, Serenata d'estate, Slow Fires of Autumn, String Quartet No. 3, Trio [No. 2] for Violin, Cello, and Piano.*

OTHER WORKS MENTIONED: *Concerto for Violin and Orchestra, Sonata for Violin and Piano, Symphony No. 5, Symphony No. 6.*

Transcendental Variations for String Orchestra

Bargreen, Melinda. "Youth Triumphs in *Boheme*, Y.S.O. [Seattle Youth Symphony Orchestra],"*The Seattle Times* (16 May 1979) A-9.

TYPE: review.

PERFORMERS: Vilem Sokol, Seattle Youth Symphony Orchestra.

NAMES: Mahler.

Cambell, R. M. "Mahler's Funeral Songs Live On," *The Seattle Post-Intelligencer* (16 May 1979) E2.

TYPE: review.

PERFORMERS: Vilem Sokol, Seattle Youth Symphony Orchestra.

NAMES: Mahler.

OTHER WORKS DISCUSSED: *String Quartet No. 3.*

Trio for Clarinet, Horn, and Piano

Field, Corey. "George Rochberg: *Trio for B-flat Clarinet, F Horn, and Piano*," *Notes: The Quarterly Journal of the Music Library Association* XXXIX/1 (September 1982) 216-217.

TYPE: score review.

NAMES: Mozart.

Ganni, Kyle. "Rochberg," *Fanfare* X/6 (July–August 1987) 172.

TYPE: record review.

PERFORMERS: Larry Combs, Gail Williams, Mary Ann Covert.

NAMES: Riegger.

Gruenginer, Walter F. "Recorded Music in Review," *Consumers' Research Magazine* LXX/3 (March 1987) 43.

TYPE: record review.

PERFORMERS: Larry Combs, Gail Williams, Mary Ann Covert.

Hudson, Kevin. "Rochberg," *The New Records* (August 1986) 10.

TYPE: record review.

PERFORMERS: Larry Combs, Gail Williams, Mary Ann Covert.

Johnson, David. "Summer Chamber Festival," *The Washington Post* *[Washington, D.C.]* (15 June 1987) C7.

TYPE: review.

PERFORMERS: Anthony Cecere, Loren Kitt, Edmund Battersby.

NAMES: Hindemith, Mozart.

Loomis, James. "Larry Combs," *The Clarinet* XIV/2 (Winter 1987) 50.

TYPE: record review.

PERFORMERS: Larry Combs, Gail Williams, Mary Ann Covert.

Perna, Dana. "Record Reviews in Brief," *ClariNetwork* (Fall 1987) 7.

TYPE: record review.

PERFORMERS: Larry Combs, Gail Williams, Mary Ann Covert.

Ringer, Alexander L. "The Music of George Rochberg," *Musical Quarterly* LII/4 (October 1966) 409-430.

TYPE: article.

NAMES: Hindemith.

OTHER WORKS DISCUSSED: *Apocalyptica [I]*, *Black Sounds*, *Blake Songs*, *La Bocca della Veritá*, *Cantio Sacra*, *Capriccio for Two Pianos*, *Chamber Symphony*, *Cheltenham Concerto*, *Concert Piece for Two Pianos and Orchestra*, *Contra Mortem et Tempus*, *David, the Psalmist*, *Dialogues*, *Duo Concertante*, *Four Songs of Solomon*, *Music for the Magic Theater*, *Nach Bach*, *Night Music*, *Passions [According to the Twentieth Century]*, *Serenata d'estate*, *Sonata-Fantasia*, *String Quartet No. 1*, *String Quartet No. 2*, *Symphony No. 1*, *Symphony No. 2*, *Three Psalms*, *Time-Span*, *Trio [No. 1] for Violin, Cello, and Piano*, *Twelve Bagatelles*, *Zodiac*.

OTHER WORKS MENTIONED: *Arioso*, *Bartokiana*, *Five Smooth Stones*, *Sonata No. 1 for Piano Solo*, *Sonata No. 2 for Piano Solo*, *Waltz Serenade*.

BOOKS DISCUSSED: *The Hexachord and Its Relation to the Twelve-Tone Row*.

Watanabe, Ruth. "Music Received: Chamber Music II: Rochberg," *Notes: The Quarterly Journal of the Music Library Association* XXXVIII/4 (June 1982) 956.

TYPE: score review.

Wiser, John D. "The Input Emporium: A Little Chamber Music," *Fanfare* XI/3 (January–February 1988) 323.

TYPE: record review.

PERFORMERS: Larry Combs, Gail Williams, Mary Ann Covert.

Trio [No. 1] for Violin, Cello, and Piano

Danuser, Hermann. "Zur Kritik der musikalischen Postmoderne," *Neue Zeitschritft für Musik* CXLIX/12 (December 1988) 4-9.

TYPE: article.

OTHER WORKS DISCUSSED: *Contra Mortem et Tempus, Music for the Magic Theater, Quintet for Piano and String Quartet, String Quartet No. 2, String Quartet No. 3.*

BOOKS DISCUSSED: *The Aesthetics of Survival.*

Felton, James. "Rochberg's Chamber Music Is Aired at the Art Alliance," *The Evening Bulletin [Philadelphia]* (16 February 1966) 27.

TYPE: review.

NAMES: Webern.

OTHER WORKS DISCUSSED: *La Bocca della Verità, Contra Mortem et Tempus, Dialogues, Night Music, Symphony No. 1, Symphony No. 2.*

Gelles, George. "Bowdoin Festival: Accent on the New," *The Boston Globe* (15 August 1966) 15.

TYPE: review.

PERFORMERS: Aeolian Chamber Players.

OTHER WORKS DISCUSSED: *La Bocca della Verità, Contra Mortem et Tempus, Nach Bach.*

Hinson, Maurice. *The Piano in Chamber Ensemble: An Annotated Guide.* (Bloomington, IN: Indiana University Press, 1978) 336.

TYPE: review.

OTHER WORKS DISCUSSED: *Contra Mortem et Tempus, Dialogues, Ricordanza.*

Morgan, Robert P. "Rochberg: *Trio for Violin, Cello, and Piano,*" *High Fidelity/Musical America* XXIV/5 (May 1974) 84.

TYPE: record review.

PERFORMERS: Kees Kooper, Fred Sherry, Mary Louis Boehm.

Ringer, Alexander L. "The Music of George Rochberg," *Musical Quarterly* LII/4 (October 1966) 409-430.

TYPE: article.

PERFORMERS: Nieuw Amsterdam Trio.

NAMES: Schönberg.

OTHER WORKS DISCUSSED: *Apocalyptica [I], Black Sounds, Blake Songs, La Bocca della Verità, Cantio Sacra, Capriccio for Two Pianos, Chamber Symphony, Cheltenham Concerto, Concert Piece for Two Pianos and Orchestra, Contra Mortem et Tempus, David, the Psalmist, Dialogues, Duo Concertante, Four Songs of Solomon, Music for the*

Magic Theater, Nach Bach, Night Music, Passions [According to the Twentieth Century], Serenata d'estate, Sonata-Fantasia, String Quartet No. 1, String Quartet No. 2, Symphony No. 1, Symphony No. 2, Three Psalms, Time-Span, Trio for Clarinet, Horn, and Piano, Twelve Bagatelles, Zodiac.

OTHER WORKS MENTIONED: *Arioso, Bartokiana, Five Smooth Stones, Sonata No. 1 for Piano Solo, Sonata No. 2 for Piano Solo, Waltz Serenade.*

BOOKS DISCUSSED: *The Hexachord and Its Relation to the Twelve-Tone Row.*

Trotter, Herman. "Records: Classical: Rochberg Strikes a Happy Modern Medium," *The Buffalo News* (09 October 1981) 36.

TYPE: record review.

OTHER WORKS DISCUSSED: *Quintet for Piano and String Quartet, String Quartet No. 3, String Quartet No. 4.*

Webster, Daniel. "At the Art Alliance: Aeolian Players Shine Spotlight on Rochberg," *The Philadelphia Inquirer* (16 February 1966) 27.

TYPE: review.

PERFORMERS: Aeolian Chamber Players.

NAMES: Webern.

OTHER WORKS DISCUSSED: *La Bocca della Verità, Contra Mortem et Tempus, Dialogues.*

Trio [No. 2] for Violin, Cello, and Piano

n.a. "Composer Honored (Brandies Creative Arts Award," *Musical Opinion* CVIII/1294 (September 1985) 339.

TYPE: article, award.

OTHER WORKS DISCUSSED: *Trio [No. 2] for Violin, Cello, and Piano.*

Cope, David. "*Trio for Violin, Violoncello, and Piano*," *Notes: The Quarterly Journal of the Music Library Association* XLIV/3 (March 1988) 590.

TYPE: score review.

NAMES: Harrison, Hovhannes, Schubert.

Guether, Roy. "Beaux Arts Trio," *The Washington Post [Washington, D.C.]* (15 February 1988) D7.

TYPE: review.

PERFORMERS: Beaux Arts Trio.

Holland, Bernard. "Music: Beaux Arts Trio," *The New York Times* (29 October 1986) III, 24.

TYPE: review.

PERFORMERS: Beaux Arts Trio.

NAMES: Schubert.

Kozinn, Allan. "The Beaux Arts' New Boy," *The New York Times* (06 December 1987) II, 27.

TYPE: upcoming concert, interview with the Beaux Arts Trio.

PERFORMERS: Beaux Arts Trio.

Marsh, Robert C. "Beaux Arts Excels Quietly in Rochberg Debut," *The Chicago Sun-Times* (04 November 1986) 46.

TYPE: review.

PERFORMERS: Beaux Arts Trio.

n.a. "New York," *The Strad* XCVIII/1161 (January 1987) 7.

TYPE: review.

PERFORMERS: Beaux Arts Trio.

Payne, Anthony. "Beaux Arts Trio," *The Daily Telegraph [London]* (22 November 1986).

TYPE: review.

PERFORMERS: Beaux Arts Trio.

NAMES: Schönberg.

von Rhein, John. "Beaux Arts Refuses to Sound Too Familiar," *The Chicago Tribune* (04 November 1986) C9.

TYPE: review.

PERFORMERS: Beaux Arts Trio.

NAMES: Bartók, Beethoven, Brahms, Mahler, Szymanowski.

Tuck, Lon. "Beaux Arts' Romantic Rochberg," *The Washington Post [Washington, D.C.]* (28 February 1986).

TYPE: review.

PERFORMERS: Beaux Arts Trio.

Valdes, Lesley. "A Birthday Salute to Rochberg," *The Philadelphia Inquirer* (17 April 1988) 1-L, 10-L.

TYPE: upcoming performance, article, interview.

PERFORMERS: Beaux Arts Trio.

NAMES: Beethoven, Franck, Mozart.

OTHER WORKS DISCUSSED: *Duo Concertante, Serenata d'estate, Slow Fires of Autumn, String Quartet No. 3, To the Dark Wood.*

OTHER WORKS MENTIONED: *Concerto for Violin and Orchestra, Sonata for Violin and Piano, Symphony No. 5, Symphony No. 6.*

Valdes, Lesley. "New Member of the Beaux Arts Trio Makes His Debut," *The Philadelphia Inquirer* (08 December 1987).
TYPE: review.
PERFORMERS: Beaux Arts Trio.
NAMES: Franck, Persichetti, Ravel.

Webster, Daniel. "A *Symphony* Out of the Past: George Rochberg's Music Gets a Philadelphia Hearing," *The Philadelphia Inquirer* (10 March 1985) I, 11.
TYPE: article, interview, upcoming performance.
PERFORMERS: Beaux Arts Trio.
OTHER WORKS DISCUSSED: *Symphony No. 1, Symphony No. 2, Symphony No. 3, Variations on an Original Theme.*

Twelve Bagatelles for Piano Solo

Behrend, Jeannie. "George Rochberg: *Twelve Bagatelles,*" *Notes: The Quarterly Journal of the Music Library Association* XIII/1 (December 1955) 152.
TYPE: score review.
NAMES: Schönberg.

Burge, David. "Contemporary Piano: George Rochberg's *Twelve Bagatelles,*" *Keyboard* IX/5 (May 1983) 67, 80.
TYPE: score review, analysis.
NAMES: Dallapiccola.

Cohn, Arthur. "Gilt-Edged Aural Securities," *American Record Guide* XXXIII/5 (May 1976) 731, 732.
TYPE: record review.
PERFORMERS: David Burge.
NAMES: Dallapiccola.

Crump, Peter N. "Reviews of Music," *Music and Letters* XL/2 (April 1959) 200, 202.
TYPE: score review.
OTHER WORKS DISCUSSED: *Sonata-Fantasia.*

Gagne, Cole and Tracy Caras. *Soundpieces: Interviews with American Composers.* (Metuchen, NJ: Scarecrow Press, Inc., 1982).
TYPE: interview.
NAMES: Dallapiccola.

OTHER WORKS DISCUSSED: *Apocalyptica [I]*, *Black Sounds*, *Concerto for Violin and Orchestra*, *The Confidence Man*, *Contra Mortem et Tempus*, *Electrikaleidoscope*, *Music for the Magic Theater*, *Octet*, *Quintet for Piano and String Quartet*, *Ricordanza*, *Sonata No. 2 for Piano Solo*, *String Quartet No. 3*, *String Quartet No. 4*, *String Quartet No. 5*, *String Quartet No. 6*.

OTHER WORKS MENTIONED: many.

Gruen, John. "David Burge in Contemporary Piano Recital," *The New York Herald Tribune* (13 February 1961).

TYPE: review.

PERFORMERS: David Burge.

Hinson, Maurice. *Guide to the Pianist's Repertoire: An Annotated Guide*. (Bloomington, IN: Indiana University Press, 1973) 527.

TYPE: score review.

NAMES: Steven D. Jones.

OTHER WORKS DISCUSSED: *Arioso*, *Bartokiana*, *Nach Bach*, *Sonata-Fantasia*.

Hinson, Maurice. *Guide to the Pianist's Repertoire: An Annotated Guide, Supplement.* (Bloomington, IN: Indiana University Press, 1979) 275.

TYPE: score review.

OTHER WORKS DISCUSSED: *Arioso*, *Bartokiana*, *Carnival Music*, *Nach Bach*, *Partita Variations*, *Prelude on "Happy Birthday"*, *Sonata-Fantasia*.

Hinson, Maurice. *Guide to the Pianist's Repertoire: An Annotated Guide, Second, Revised, and Enlarged Edition.* (Bloomington, IN: Indiana University Press, 1987) 598-599.

TYPE: score review.

NAMES: David Burge.

OTHER WORKS DISCUSSED: *Arioso*, *Bartokiana*, *Carnival Music*, *Nach Bach*, *Partita Variations*, *Prelude on "Happy Birthday"*, *Sonata-Fantasia*, *Two Preludes and Fughettas from The Book of Contrapuntal Pieces*.

Horn, Daniel Paul. "*Carnival Music*: An Introduction to the Piano Music of George Rochberg," *Clavier* XXVII/9 (November 1988) 17-22.

TYPE: article.

OTHER WORKS DISCUSSED: *Arioso*, *Bartokiana*, *Book of Contrapuntal Pieces for Keyboard Instruments*, *Carnival Music*, *Four Short Sonatas*,

Nach Bach, Partita Variations, Prelude on "Happy Birthday", Sonata-Fantasia.
OTHER WORKS MENTIONED: *Sonata No. 1 for Piano Solo, Sonata No. 2 for Piano Solo.*

Hughes, Allen. "Program is Given by David Burge: Pianist Offers a Series of Twentieth-Century Works at Carnegie Recital Hall," *The New York Times* (13 February 1961) 24.
TYPE: review.
PERFORMERS: David Burge.

Kimball, George H. "Festival Pianist Excells in Heavy Modern Dose," *The Rochester Times-Union [Rochester, NY]* (10 May 1956).
TYPE: review.
PERFORMERS: David Burge.

n.a. "Recent Records," *Clavier* VI/4 (April 1967) 6.
TYPE: record review.
PERFORMERS: David Burge.

Ringer, Alexander L. "Current Chronicle: United States: Cleveland," *Musical Quarterly* XLV/2 (April 1959) 230-234.
TYPE: article, review.
NAMES: Schönberg, Webern.
OTHER WORKS DISCUSSED: *Chamber Symphony, David, The Psalmist, Sonata-Fantasia, String Quartet No. 1, Symphony No. 1, Symphony No. 2, Three Psalms.*
BOOKS DISCUSSED: *The Hexachord and Its Relation to the Twelve-Tone Row.*

Ringer, Alexander L. "The Music of George Rochberg," *Musical Quarterly* LII/4 (October 1966) 409-430.
TYPE: article.
PERFORMERS: Howard Lebow.
NAMES: Beethoven, Dallapiccola, Schönberg.
OTHER WORKS DISCUSSED: *Apocalyptica [I], Black Sounds, Blake Songs, La Bocca della Verità, Cantio Sacra, Capriccio for Two Pianos, Chamber Symphony, Cheltenham Concerto, Concert Piece for Two Pianos and Orchestra, Contra Mortem et Tempus, David, the Psalmist, Dialogues, Duo Concertante, Four Songs of Solomon, Music for the Magic Theater, Nach Bach, Night Music, Passions [According to the Twentieth Century], Serenata d'estate, Sonata-Fantasia, String Quartet No. 1, String Quartet No. 2, Symphony No. 1, Symphony No. 2, Three Psalms, Time-Span, Trio for Clarinet, Horn, and Piano, Trio [No. 1] for Violin, Cello, and Piano, Zodiac.*

OTHER WORKS MENTIONED: *Arioso, Bartokiana, Five Smooth Stones, Sonata No. 1 for Piano Solo, Sonata No. 2 for Piano Solo, Waltz Serenade.*

BOOKS DISCUSSED: *The Hexachord and Its Relation to the Twelve-Tone Row.*

Ringer, Alexander L. "Paul Harelson, in Piano Recital Introduces Kraft's *Partita* Here," *The New York Times* (04 December 1961) 50.

TYPE: review.

PERFORMERS: Paul Harelson.

Robby, Joseph. "Contemporary American Music: A World Competition," *RF [Rockefeller Foundation] Illustrated* III/4 (September 1977) 12.

TYPE: article.

Southgate, Harvey. "Pianist Excels in Taxing Music," *The Rochester Democrat and Chronicle [Rochester, NY]* (10 May 1956) 23.

TYPE: review.

PERFORMERS: David Burge.

Stewart, Paul. "The Piano Music of George Rochberg and the New Romanticism," *American Music Teacher* XXXVIII/3 (January 1989) 24-27, 62.

TYPE: article.

NAMES:

OTHER WORKS DISCUSSED: *Arioso, Bartokiana, Book of Contrapuntal Pieces for Keyboard Instruments, Carnival Music, Four Short Sonatas, Nach Bach, Partita Variations, Prelude on "Happy Birthday", Sonata-Fantasia, Two Preludes and Fughettas.*

Stronglin, Theodore. "Recordings: Advance with the Serialists and the Far-Out Avant-Garde," *The New York Times* (26 March 1967) II, 25.

TYPE: record review.

PERFORMERS: David Burge.

NAMES: Schönberg.

Susa, Conrad. "Debuts and Reappearances: Philadelphia Orchestra (Ormandy)," *High Fidelity/Musical America* XVIII/3 (March 1968) MA-14.

TYPE: review.

OTHER WORKS DISCUSSED: *Zodiac.*

W., E. "Young Pianist Featured in Ultra-Modern Recital," *The State Journal [Lansing, MI]* CVI/291 (14 February 1961) 15.

TYPE: review.

PERFORMERS: David Burge.

NAMES: Hindemith.

Two Preludes and Fughettas from The Book of Contrapuntal Pieces for Keyboard Instruments

Gowen, Bradford. "*Two Preludes and Fughettas* by George Rochberg," *Piano Quarterly* XXXI/122 (Summer 1983) 9-10.

TYPE: review, recording (exerpts).

Hinson, Maurice. *Guide to the Pianist's Repertoire: An Annotated Guide, Second, Revised, and Enlarged Edition.* (Bloomington, IN: Indiana University Press, 1987) 598-599.

TYPE: score review.

NAMES: Bach.

OTHER WORKS DISCUSSED: *Arioso, Bartokiana, Carnival Music, Nach Bach, Partita Variations, Prelude on "Happy Birthday", Sonata-Fantasia, Twelve Bagatelles.*

Stewart, Paul. "The Piano Music of George Rochberg and the New Romanticism," *American Music Teacher* XXXVIII/3 (January 1989) 24-27, 62.

TYPE: article.

NAMES: Beethoven.

OTHER WORKS DISCUSSED: *Arioso, Bartokiana, Book of Contrapuntal Pieces for Keyboard Instruments, Carnival Music, Four Short Sonatas, Nach Bach, Partita Variations, Prelude on "Happy Birthday", Sonata-Fantasia, Twelve Bagatelles.*

Two Songs from "Tableaux" [for Soprano and Piano]

Scanlan, Roger. "Spotlight on Contemporary American Composers," *The NATS [National Association of Teachers of Singing] Bulletin* XXXIII/1 (October 1976) 48-49, 53-54.

TYPE: article.

OTHER WORKS DISCUSSED: *Blake Songs, David, The Psalmist, Eleven Songs, Four Songs of Solomon, Fantasies, Music for "The Alchemist", Phaedra, Sacred Song of Reconciliation, Songs in Praise of Krishna, String Quartet No. 2, Symphony No. 3, Tableaux.*

OTHER WORKS MENTIONED: many.

Thomas, John Patrick. "Vocal Music," *Notes: The Quarterly Journal of the Music Library Association* XXX/2 (December 1973) 365-366.

TYPE: score review.

NAMES: Paul Rochberg.

OTHER WORKS DISCUSSED: *Tableaux.*

Ukiyo-e (Pictures of the Floating World) for Solo Harp

Allen, Susan. "Rochberg, George," *American Harp Journal* VIII/3 (Summer 1982) 48-49.

TYPE: score review.

NAMES: Marcella DeCray, Joseph Horowitz, Mahler.

Davis, Peter G. "Music: A Duo: Stallman and Allen Triumph in Flute-and-Harp Concert," *The New York Times* (03 October 1977) 39.

TYPE: review.

PERFORMERS: Susan Allen.

Donner, Jay M. "Rochberg: *Ukiyo-e,*" *The New Records* LI/7 (September 1983) 5.

TYPE: record review.

PERFORMERS: Marcella DeCray.

Fried, Alexander. "Intriguing Performance Opens Pillow Concerts," *The San Francisco Examiner* (29 April 1975) 22.

TYPE: review.

PERFORMERS: Marcella de Cray.

Horowitz, Joseph. "New Music: Susan Allen on the Harp," *The New York Times* (08 October 1979) III, 20.

TYPE: review.

PERFORMERS: Susan Allen.

NAMES: Mahler.

Kozinski, David B. "Harpist Costello's Recital Is a Bright Spot," (10 October 1977) *The Evening Journal [Wilmington, DE]* 27.

TYPE: review.

PERFORMERS: Marilyn Costello.

McCurdy, Charles C. "Music: Works of Rochberg and Schubel at Art Alliance," *The Philadelphia Inquirer* (20 February 1984) 6-C.

TYPE: review.

OTHER WORKS DISCUSSED: *Slow Fires of Autumn, Songs of Inanna and Dumuzi.*

Sachs, David. "Rochberg: *Ukiyo-e*," *Fanfare* VII/4 (March–April 1984).
TYPE: record review.
PERFORMERS: Marcella DeCray.
NAMES: Mahler.

Tucker, Marilyn K. "Modern Music that Can Communicate," *The San Francisco Chronicle* (30 April 1975) 46.
TYPE: review.
PERFORMER: Marcella de Cray.

Webster, Daniel. "Rochberg's Indian Love Songs Pulsing, Vital," *The Philadelphia Inquirer* (31 January 1978) 7-A.
TYPE: review.
PERFORMERS: Marilyn Costello.

Wierzbicki, James. "George Rochberg," *The St. Louis Globe-Democrat* (30 August 1980) 6B.
TYPE: record review.
OTHER WORKS DISCUSSED: *Concerto for Violin and Orchestra, Slow Fires of Autumn.*

Variations on an Original Theme for Piano Solo

Scher, Valerie. "Retrospective Concert Surveys Talents of Composer Rochberg," *The Philadelphia Inquirer* (26 March 1983).
TYPE: review.
PERFORMERS: Jerome Lowenthal.
NAMES: Stephen Foster.
OTHER WORKS DISCUSSED: *Nach Bach, Partita Variations, Sonata-Fantasia.*

Webster, Daniel. "A *Symphony* Out of the Past: George Rochberg's Music Gets a Philadelphia Hearing," *The Philadelphia Inquirer* (10 March 1985) I, 11.
TYPE: article, interview, upcoming performance.
OTHER WORKS DISCUSSED: *Symphony No. 1, Symphony No. 2, Symphony No. 3, Trio [No. 2] for Violin, Cello, and Piano.*

Waltzes for String Orchestra

Singer, Samuel L. "The National Scene: Philadelphia," *Musical Courier* CLV/2 (February 1957) 24.
TYPE: review.
PERFORMERS: Philadelphia Chamber Music Society, Herbert Fiss.
NAMES: Ravel, Shostakovich.

Waltz Serenade for Orchestra

Johnen, Louis John. "The National Scene: Cincinnati," *Musical Courier* CLVII/4 (April 1958) 37.

TYPE: review.

PERFORMERS: Thor Johnson, Cincinnati Symphony Orchestra.

NAMES: Ravel.

Zodiac for Orchestra

Felton, James. "Composers Are Sane But the World Isn't, Says Penn Rochberg," *The Sunday Bulletin [Philadelphia]* (13 February 1966) 11.

TYPE: interview.

PERFORMERS: Eugene Ormandy, Philadelphia Orchestra.

OTHER WORKS DISCUSSED: *Contra Mortem et Tempus, Music for the Magic Theater, Night Music, String Quartet No. 2, Symphony No. 1, Symphony No. 2, Symphony No. 3.*

Felton, James. "Concert Set March 17: *Fanfare for 144 Brass Horns,*" *The Philadelphia Inquirer* (03 March 1968).

TYPE: upcoming première, interview.

PERFORMERS: Settlement Music School, Sol Schoenbach.

NAMES: Mahler.

OTHER WORKS DISCUSSED: *Fanfare, Symphony No. 3.* @REVIEWER = Marsh, Robert C. "A Sense of Tradition: Cincinnati Report: Rockefeller Grant," *High Fidelity/Musical America* XV/8 (August 1965) 128, 131.

TYPE: review.

PERFORMERS: Max Rudolf, Cincinnati Symphony.

n.a. "New, Old Works at Academy," *The Philadelphia Inquirer* (10 December 1967).

TYPE: upcoming première.

PERFORMERS: Eugene Ormandy, Philadelphia Orchestra.

Pirie, Peter J. "Rochberg: *Zodiac,*" *Musical Times [Great Britain]* CXVII/1597 (March 1976) 241-242.

TYPE: score review.

Ringer, Alexander L. "The Music of George Rochberg," *Musical Quarterly* LII/4 (October 1966) 409-430.

TYPE: article.

PERFORMERS: Max Rudolf, Cinncinati Symphony Orchestra.

NAMES: Beethoven, Dallapiccola, Schönberg.

OTHER WORKS DISCUSSED: *Apocalyptica [I], Black Sounds, Blake Songs, La Bocca della Verità, Cantio Sacra, Capriccio for Two Pianos, Chamber Symphony, Cheltenham Concerto, Concert Piece for Two Pianos and Orchestra, Contra Mortem et Tempus, David, the Psalmist, Dialogues, Duo Concertante, Four Songs of Solomon, Music for the Magic Theater, Nach Bach, Night Music, Passions [According to the Twentieth Century], Serenata d'estate, Sonata-Fantasia, String Quartet No. 1, String Quartet No. 2, Symphony No. 1, Symphony No. 2, Three Psalms, Time-Span, Trio for Clarinet, Horn, and Piano, Trio [No. 1] for Violin, Cello, and Piano.*

OTHER WORKS MENTIONED: *Arioso, Bartokiana, Five Smooth Stones, Sonata No. 1 for Piano Solo, Sonata No. 2 for Piano Solo, Waltz Serenade.*

BOOKS DISCUSSED: *The Hexachord and Its Relation to the Twelve-Tone Row.*

Schonberg, Harold C. Music: Ormandy and the Philadelphia: Barenboim Is Soloist in Beethoven Work: Two Novelties Played at Philharmonic Hall," *The New York Times* (20 December 1967) 54.

TYPE: review.

PERFORMERS: Eugene Ormandy, Philadelphia Orchestra.

Susa, Conrad. "Debuts and Reappearances: Philadelphia Orchestra (Ormandy)," *High Fidelity/Musical America* XVIII/3 (March 1968) MA-14.

TYPE: review.

PERFORMERS: Eugene Ormandy, Philadelphia Orchestra.

NAMES: Max Rudolf.

OTHER WORKS DISCUSSED: Twleve Bagatelles.

Webster, Daniel. "The Lively Arts: Problems Assayed as Music Waits Coda," *The Philadelphia Inquirer* (26 May 1968).

TYPE: article.

IX. DISSERTATIONS AND THESIS

Angeletti, Richard Walter. "A Study of Various Textures Resulting from a Particular Use of the Twelve-Tone System in the *Sonata-Fantasia* by George Rochberg," Ph.D. Dissertation, Catholic University of America, 1971, 257 pp. [Although listed by UMI, this source does not exist.]

Buccheri, John Stephen. "An Approach to Twelve-Tone Music: Articulation of Serial Pitch Units in Piano Works of Schönberg, Webern, Krenek, Dallapiccola and Rochberg," Ph.D. Dissertation, University of Rochester, Eastman School of Music, 1975, 349 pp.

Casey, Robert Lowell. "Serial Composition in Works for the Wind Band," Ed. D. Dissertation, Washington University [St. Louis, MO], 1971, 209pp.

Coonrod, Michael. "Aspects of Form in Selected Quartets of the Twentieth Century," D.M.A. Dissertation, the Peabody Conservatory of Music of John Hopkins University, 1984.

Cordes, Joan Kunselman. "A New American Development in Music: Some Characteristic Features Extending from the Legacy of Charles Ives," Ph.D. Dissertation, Louisiana State University, 1976.

Engberg, Kristina L. "Linear Connections and Set Relations in George Rochberg's *Caprice Variations*," M.A. Thesis, University of Rochester, Eastman School of Music, 1982, 113 pp.

Glean, Elfreda Sewell. "A Selected, Graded List of Compositions for Unaccompanied Violin, with Preparatory Studies," D.A. Dissertation, Ball State University, 1979.

Groemer, Gerald H. "Paths to the New Romanticism: Aesthetic and Thought of the American Post-Avant-Garde as Exemplified in Selected Tonal Music," D.M.A. Dissertation, the Peabody Conservatory of Music of John Hopkins University, 1985.

Horn, Daniel Paul. "Change and Continuity in the Music of George Rochberg: A Study in Aesthetics and Style as Exemplified by

Selected Piano Solo and Chamber Music Compositions," D.M.A. Dissertation, Julliard School of Music, 1987, 168 pp.

Jennings, Vance Shelby. "Selected Twentieth Century Clarinet Solo Literature: A Study in Interpretation and Preformance," D.M.E. Dissertation, University of Oklahoma, 1972.

Johnson, June Durkin. "Analyses of Selcted Works for the Soprano Voice Written in Serial Technique by Living Composers," D.M.A. Dissertation, University of Illinois, 1967.

Jones, Steven D. "The *Twelve Bagatelles* of George Rochberg," Masters Thesis, Indiana University, 1974, 101 pp.

Lindorff, Joyce Zankel. "Contemporary Harpsichord Music: Issues for Composers and Performers," D.M.A. Document, The Juilliard School, 1982.

Puckett, Mark A. "*Twelve Bagatelles* by George Rochberg: Background, Structure, and Performance," Ph.D. Dissertation, University of Kansas, 1986.

Richards, Wendy Jo. "An Analysis of Three Works by Luening, Rochberg and Wolff as Representative of Unaccompanied Solo Violin Literature Composed 1970-1979," D.A. Dissertation, University of Northern Colorado, 215 pp.

Sams, Carol Lee. "Solo Vocal Writing in Selected Works of Berio, Crumb and Rochberg," D.M.A. Dissertation, University of Washington, 1975, 102 pp.

Satre, Paul James. "George Rochberg's Complete Works for Solo Piano: Their Style and the Culture They Reflect," D.M.A. Dissertation, American Conservatory of Music, 1985, 145 pp.

Scea, Susan. "Eclecticism and Contemporary Anerican Music: Rochberg, Druckman, and Del Tredici," Masters Thesis, University of Iowa, n.d.

Smith, Joan Templar. "The *String Quartets* of George Rochberg," Ph.D. Dissertation, University of Rochester, Eastman School of Music, 1976, 331 pp.

Walker, Mary Beth. "Selected Twentieth-Century String Quartets: An Approach to Understanding Style and Form, " D. Mus. Dissertation, University of Arizona, 1977.